CONVERGENCE IN SHAREHOLDER LAW

AF687951

On the one hand, it can be argued that the increasing economic and political interdependence of countries has led to the convergence of national legal systems. On the other hand, advocates of the counterhypothesis maintain that this development is both unrealistic and unnecessary.

Mathias Siems examines the company law of the UK, the USA, Germany, France, Japan and China to see how this issue affects shareholder law. The author subsequently analyses economic and political factors which may or may not lead to convergence, and assesses the extent of this development. Thus, *Convergence in Shareholder Law* not only provides a thorough comparative legal analysis but also shows how company law interconnects with political forces and economic development and helps in evaluating whether harmonisation and shareholder protection should be enhanced.

MATHIAS M. SIEMS is a Reader in Commercial Law at the University of Edinburgh and a Research Associate at the Centre for Business Research, University of Cambridge.

INTERNATIONAL CORPORATE LAW AND FINANCIAL MARKET REGULATION

Recent years have seen an upsurge of change and reform in corporate law and financial market regulation internationally as the corporate and institutional investor sector increasingly turns to the international financial markets. This follows large-scale institutional and regulatory reform after a series of international corporate governance and financial disclosure scandals exemplified by the collapse of Enron in the US. There is now a great demand for analysis in this area from the academic, practitioner, regulatory and policy sectors.

The *International Corporate Law and Financial Market Regulation* series will respond to that demand by creating a critical mass of titles which will address the need for information and high quality analysis in this fast developing area.

Series Editors
Professor Eilis Ferran, University of Cambridge
Proessor Niamh Moloney, University of Nottingham
Professor Howell Jackson, Harvard Law School

Editorial Board
Professor Marco Becht, Professor of Finance and Economics at Université Libre de Bruxelles and Executive Director of the European Corporate Governance Institute (ECGI).

Professor Brian Cheffins, S.J. Berwin Professor of Corporate Law at the Faculty of Law, University of Cambridge.

Professor Paul Davies, Cassel Professor of Commercial Law at the London School of Economics and Political Science.

Professor Luca Enriques, Professor of Business Law in the Faculty of Law at the University of Bologna.

Professor Guido Ferrarini, Professor of Law at the University of Genoa and Honorary Professor, Faculty of Law, University College London.

Professor Jennifer Hill, Professor of Corporate Law at Sydney Law School.

Professor Klaus J. Hopt, Director of the Max Planck Institute of Comparative and International Private Law, Hamburg, Germany.

Professor Hideki Kanda, Professor of Law at the University of Tokyo.

Professor Colin Mayer, Peter Moores Professor of Management Studies at the Saïd Business School and Director of the Oxford Financial Research Centre.

James Palmer, Partner of Herbert Smith, London.

Professor Michel Tison, Professor at the Financial Law Institute of the University of Ghent.

Andrew Whittaker, General Counsel to the Board at the UK Financial Services Authority.

Professor Eddy Wymeersch, Chairman of the Committee of European Securities Regulators (CESR), Co-Chair of the CESR-European Central Bank Working Group on Clearing and Settlement, and part time Professor of Commercial Law, University of Ghent, Belgium.

CONVERGENCE IN SHAREHOLDER LAW

MATHIAS M. SIEMS

CAMBRIDGE
UNIVERSITY PRESS

CAMBRIDGE UNIVERSITY PRESS
Cambridge, New York, Melbourne, Madrid, Cape Town,
Singapore, São Paulo, Delhi, Tokyo, Mexico City

Cambridge University Press
The Edinburgh Building, Cambridge CB2 8RU, UK

Published in the United States of America by Cambridge University Press, New York

www.cambridge.org
Information on this title: www.cambridge.org/9780521187916

© Mathias Siems 2008

This publication is in copyright. Subject to statutory exception
and to the provisions of relevant collective licensing agreements,
no reproduction of any part may take place without the written
permission of Cambridge University Press.

First published 2008
First paperback edition 2011

A catalogue record for this publication is available from the British Library

ISBN 978-0-521-87675-9 Hardback
ISBN 978-0-521-18791-6 Paperback

Cambridge University Press has no responsibility for the persistence or accuracy of URLs for external or third-party internet websites referred to in this publication, and does not guarantee that any content on such websites is, or will remain, accurate or appropriate.

CONTENTS

PREFACE AND ACKNOWLEDGMENTS

In the last fifteen years, the words 'globalization', 'internationalization' and 'Europeanization' have been seen and heard everywhere. The legal discussion has been no exception: on the one hand, it has sometimes been claimed that national legal systems are increasingly convergent. On the other hand, advocates of the counterhypothesis maintain that convergence of legal systems is neither realistic nor necessary. This book takes a look at how to approach this issue in relation to shareholder law. Although there are already some publications which deal with company law convergence, the reader is often left disappointed. With respect to similarities and differences between countries, the previous literature is dominated by broad statements about different corporate governance systems and anecdotal stories of convergence. A detailed legal analysis is, however, lacking. Similarly, with respect to convergence forces and hurdles, there has often been only a perfunctory analysis of particular topics, such as regulatory competition or shareholder ownership. But, again, a coherent and comprehensive account is missing. Thus, this book aims at filling that gap. Its structure is as follows. First, it compares the company laws of the United Kingdom, the USA, Germany, France, Japan and China. Secondly, it analyzes economic and political factors, which might (or might not) lead to convergence. Finally, it assesses this development.

I started writing the German version of this monograph in June 2001 when I was just finishing my LLM in Edinburgh. Since then I have worked and lived in Paris, Berlin, Hamburg, Florence, Cambridge (Massachusetts), Riga, Cambridge (England), and again Edinburgh. I thank everyone who encouraged my research. Specifically for the English edition, I would like to thank Iain Fraser (Florence), Chris Goddard (Riga) and Kim Hughes (Cambridge University Press) for their help and support, as well as Eilís Ferran, Niamh Moloney and Howell Jackson as the editors of the series on International Corporate Law and Financial Market Regulation.

ABBREVIATIONS

AC	UK Law Reports: Appeal Cases
AcP	*Archiv für die civilistische Praxis*
AG	*Aktiengesellschaft*
ALI-Principles	American Law Institute (ALI), *Principles of Corporate Governance*: Analysis and Recommendations, 1994
All ER	All England Law Reports
ALR	Australian Law Reports
Am. J. Comp. L.	*American Journal of Comparative Law*
Amer. Econ. Rev.	*American Economic Review*
Ariz. J. Int'l & Comp. L.	*Arizona Journal of International and Comparative Law*
BB	*Betriebs-Berater*
BCLC	Butterworths Company Law Cases
Bell J. Econ.	*Bell Journal of Economics and Management Science*
Berkeley Bus. L.J.	*Berkeley Business Law Journal*
Berkeley J. Int'l L.	*Berkeley Journal of International Law*
BGBl.	German Federal Law Gazette (Bundesgesetzblatt)
BGH	German Supreme Court (Bundesgerichtshof)
BGHZ	Decisions of the German Supreme Court (in private law matters)
BJIR	*British Journal of Industrial Relations*
Bond L. Rev.	*Bond Law Review*
Brook. J. Int'l L.	*Brooklyn Journal of International Law*
BT-Drucks.	Printed Matters of the German *Bundestag* (Bundestagsdrucksacke)

BU Int'l L.J.	*Boston University International Law Journal*
Bus. Hist.	*Business History*
Bus. Law.	*Business Lawyer*
BVerfG	German Constitutional Court (Bundesverfassungsgericht)
BVerfGE	Decisions of the German Constitutional Court
C. & SLJ	*Company and Securities Law Journal*
Cal. App.	California Appellate Reports
Cal. L. Rev.	*California Law Review*
Cal. Rptr.	California Reporter
CalGCL	California General Corporation Law
CalPERS	California Public Employees' Retirement System
Cardozo J. Int'l & Comp. L.	*Cardozo Journal of International and Comparative Law*
Cardozo L. Rev.	*Cardozo Law Review*
CEO	Chief Executive Officer
CFO	Chief Financial Officer
ch., chs., Ch., Chs.	Chapter, Chapters
Ch., ChD	UK Law Reports: Chancery Division
ChinArticles	Chinese Guide to Articles of Association of Companies Limited by Shares of 6 December 1997
ChinCA	Chinese Companies Act
ChinCG-Code	Code of Corporate Governance for Listed Companies of the China Securities Regulatory Commission (CSRC) (English translation available at www.csrc.gov.cn/en/homepage/index_en.jsp)
ChinMandProv	Chinese Mandatory Provisions in the Articles of Association for Companies Listed Overseas of 27 August 1994 (English translation available at *China Law and Practice*, Vol. 9 (1995), No. 4, p. 19)
ChinSA	Chinese Securities Act

CLJ	*Cambridge Law Journal*
Colum. Bus. L. Rev.	*Columbia Business Law Review*
Colum. J. Eur. L.	*Columbia Journal of European Law*
Colum. J. Transnat'l L.	*Columbia Journal of Transnational Law*
Colum. L. Rev.	*Columbia Law Review*
Comp. Law.	*Company Lawyer*
Comp. L. L. & Pol'y J.	*Comparative Labor Law and Policy Journal*
Conn. J. Int'l L.	*Connecticut Journal of International Law*
Cornell Int'l L.J.	*Cornell International Law Journal*
Cornell L. Rev.	*Cornell Law Review*
CSRC	China Securities Regulatory Commission
DB	*Der Betrieb*
DC Cir.	United States Court of Appeals for the District of Columbia
Del. Ch.	Delaware Court of Chancery
Del. J. Corp. L.	*Delaware Journal of Corporate Law*
Del. Supr.	Delaware Supreme Court
DelGCL	Delaware General Corporation Law
DStR	*Deutsches Steuerrecht*
DSW	Deutsche Schutzvereinigung für Wertpapierbesitz e.V.
EBLR	*European Business Law Review*
EBOR	*European Business Organization Law Review*
EC	European Community; Treaty establishing the European Community
ECFR	*European Company and Financial Law Review*
ECJ	European Court of Justice
ECR	European Court Reports
EEC	European Economic Community
ELJ	*European Law Journal*
E.L. Rev.	*European Law Review*
EU	European Union
Europ. Econ. Rev.	*European Economic Review*
Europ. J. Law & Econ.	*European Journal of Law and Economics*
EuZW	*Europäische Zeitschrift für Wirtschaftsrecht*

EWS	*Europäisches Wirtschafts- und Steuerrecht*
FASB	Financial Accounting Standards Board (USA)
Ford. Int. L.J.	*Fordham International Law Journal*
FrCCom	Code de Commerce (France)
FrCG-Principles	Principes de gouvernement d'entreprise résultant de la consolidation des rapports conjoints de l'AFEP et du MEDEF, 2003
FrCMon	Code monétaire et financier (France)
FrDécret	Décret No. 67-236 sur les sociétés commerciales (France)
FrRGAMF	Règlement général de l'Autorité des marchés financiers (AMF) (France)
FSA	Financial Services Authority
Ga. L. Rev.	*Georgia Law Review*
GATS	General Agreement on Trade in Services
Geo. L.J.	*Georgetown Law Journal*
GerAktG	German Law on Joint-Stock Companies (Aktiengesetz)
GerBGB	German Civil Code (Bürgerliches Gesetzbuch)
GerBörsG	German Stock Exchange Act (Börsengesetz)
GerBörsZulV	German Stock Exchange Admission Regulation (Börsenzulassungsverordnung)
GerCGK	German Corporate Governance Code (Deutscher Corporate Governance Kodex) (English version available at www.corporate-governance-code.de/index-e.html)
GerFGG	German Ex-Parte Jurisdiction Act (Gesetz über die freiwillige Gerichtsbarkeit)
GerGmbHG	German Law on Private Liability Companies (Gesetz betreffend die Gesellschaft mit beschränkter Haftung)
GerHGB	German Commercial Code (Handelsgesetzbuch)

GerStGB	German Criminal Code (Strafgesetzbuch)
GerUmwG	German Transformation Act (Umwandlungsgesetz)
GerWpHG	German Securities Trading Act (Wertpapierhandelsgesetz)
GerWpÜG	German Takeover Act (Wertpapiererwerbs- und Übernahmegesetz)
GerZPO	German Code of Civil Procedure (Zivilprozessordnung)
Harv. Bus. Rev.	*Harvard Business Review*
Harv. Int'l L.J.	*Harvard International Law Journal*
Harv. J. on Legis.	*Harvard Journal on Legislation*
Harv. L. Rev.	*Harvard Law Review*
IAS	International Accounting Standard
IASB	International Accounting Standards Board
IBL	*International Business Lawyer*
ICCLJ	*International and Comparative Corporate Law Journal*
ICCLR	*International Company and Commercial Law Review*
ICLQ	*International and Comparative Law Quarterly*
IFLR	*International Financial Law Review*
IFRS	International Financial Reporting Standards
Int. L.	*The International Lawyer*
IMF	International Monetary Fund
Int. J. Bus.	*International Journal of Business*
Int'l Rev. L. & Econ.	*International Review of Law and Economics*
IOSCO	International Organization of Securities Commissions
JapCA	Japanese Corporation Act (kaisha hô), Law No. 86/2005

JapCC	Japanese Commercial Code (Shôhô), Law No. 48/1899
JapCCExcA	Japanese law for special exceptions to the Commercial Code concerning audit, etc. of joint stock companies (Kabushiki gaisha no kans tô ni kansuru shôhô no tokurei ni kansuru hôritsu), Law No. 22/1974
JapCG-Principles	Tokyo Stock Exchange, Principles of Corporate Governance for Listed Companies 2004.
JapSEA	Japanese Securities and Exchange Act (Shôken torihikohô), Law No. 25/1948
JBL	*Journal of Business Law*
J. Corp. L.	*Journal of Corporation Law*
JCL	*Journal of Comparative Law*
JCLS	*Journal of Corporate Law Studies*
JCMS	*Journal of Common Market Studies*
JCP	*Juris Classeur Périodique*
J. Econ. Manage. Strategy	*Journal of Economics and Management Strategy*
J. Empirical Legal Stud.	*Journal of Empirical Legal Studies*
J. Finance	*Journal of Finance*
J. Finan. Econ.	*Journal of Financial Economics*
JJS	*Journal of Japanese Studies*
J. L. & Econ.	*Journal of Law and Economics*
J. L. Econ. & Org.	*Journal of Law, Economics and Organization*
J. Legal Stud.	*Journal of Legal Studies*
J. Polit. Economy	*Journal of Political Economy*
JZ	*Juristenzeitung*
Law & Pol'y Int'l Bus.	*Law and Policy in International Business*
Law & Soc. Inquiry	*Law and Social Inquiry*
Loy. LA Int'l & Comp. L.J.	*Loyola of Los Angeles International and Comparative Law Journal*
LQR	*Law Quarterly Review*
LSE	London Stock Exchange
MBCA	Model Business Corporation Act (USA)
Melbourne U. L. Rev.	*Melbourne University Law Review*

Mich. L. Rev.	*Michigan Law Review*
Minn. J. Global Trade	*Minnesota Journal of Global Trade*
MJ	*Maastricht Journal of European and Comparative Law*
MLR	*Modern Law Review*
NAFTA	North American Free Trade Agreement
NC J. Int'l & Com. Reg.	*North Carolina Journal of International Law and Commercial Regulation*
NJW	*Neue Juristische Wochenschrift*
No(s).	Number(s)
Nw. J. Int'l L. & Bus.	*Northwestern Journal of International Law and Business*
Nw. U. L. Rev.	*Northwestern University Law Review*
NYBCL	New York Business Corporation Law
NY Int'l L. Rev.	*New York International Law Review*
NYL Sch. J. Int'l & Comp. L.	*New York Law School Journal of International and Comparative Law*
NYSE	New York Stock Exchange
NYSE Manual	Listed Company Manual of the New York Stock Exchange
NYU L. Rev.	*New York University Law Review*
NZG	*Neue Zeitschrift für Gesellschaftsrecht*
OECD	Organization for Economic Co-operation and Development
OECD-Principles	OECD Principles of Corporate Governance (available at www.oecd.org/dataoecd/32/18/31557724.pdf)
OJLS	*Oxford Journal of Legal Studies*
Penn St Int'l L. Rev.	*Penn State International Law Review*
QJ Econ.	*Quarterly Journal of Economics*
RabelsZ	*Rabels Zeitschrift für ausländisches und internationales Privatrecht*
Rev.int.dr.comp.	*Revue internationale du droit comparé*
Rev. Int. Polit. Economy	*Review of International Political Economy*
Rev.soc.	*Revue des sociétés*
RG	Supreme Court of the German Reich (Reichsgericht)

RGZ	Decisions of the Supreme Court of the German Reich
RIW	*Recht der internationalen Wirtschaft*
s. (ss.)	section(s), sentence(s)
S. Cal. L. Rev.	*Southern California Law Review*
Sarbanes–Oxley Act 2002	Sarbanes–Oxley Act (Public Company Accounting Reform and Investor Protection Act) (USA) of 30 July 2002
SE	Societas Europaea (European Company)
SE-Reg	Council Regulation (EC) No. 2157/2001 of 8 October 2001 on the Statute for a European Company (SE)
SEC	Securities Exchange Commission (USA); Regulations and Rules of the SEC based on Securities Exchange Act of 1934; 17 CFR Parts 200–301
SI	Statutory Instrument
St John's J. Legal Comment.	*Saint John's Journal of Legal Commentary*
St Louis U. L.J.	*Saint Louis University Law Journal*
Stan. L. Rev.	*Stanford Law Review*
Transnat'l L. & Contemp. Probs.	*Transnational Law and Contemporary Problems*
Transnat'l Law.	*Transnational Lawyer*
Tul. L. Rev.	*Tulane Law Review*
U. Chi. L. Rev.	*University of Chicago Law Review*
U. Cin. L. Rev.	*University of Cincinnati Law Review*
UC Davis L. Rev.	*UC Davis Law Review*
UCLA Pac. Basin L.J.	*UCLA Pacific Basin Law Journal*
U. Pa. J. Int'l Econ. L.	*University of Pennsylvania Journal of International Economic Law*
U. Pa. L. Rev.	*University of Pennsylvania Law Review*
U. Pitt. L. Rev.	*University of Pittsburgh Law Review*
UK-CA	Companies Act 2006 (United Kingdom)
UK-City Code	City Code on Takeovers and Mergers of the Panel on Takeovers and Mergers (United Kingdom)
UK-Combined Code	Combined Code on Corporate Governance (United Kingdom)

UK-FSMA	Financial Services and Markets Act 2000 (United Kingdom)
UK-Listing Rules	UK Listing Rules
UK-Table A	Table A of the Companies (Table A to F) Regulations 1985 (United Kingdom)
US-GAAP	Generally Accepted Accounting Principles (USA)
US-SA	Securities Act of 1933 (USA), ch. 38, 48 Stat. 7, codified at 15 USC secs. 77a–77m
US-SEA	Securities Exchange Act of 1934 (USA), ch. 404, 48 Stat. 881, codified at 15 USC secs. 78a–78kk
US-UCC	Uniform Commercial Code (USA)
Va. J. Int'l L.	*Virginia Journal of International Law*
Va. L. Rev.	*Virginia Law Review*
Vill. L. Rev.	*Villanova Law Review*
Wash. ULQ	*Washington University Law Quarterly*
WLR	Weekly Law Reports
WM	*Wertpapier-Mitteilungen*
WTO	World Trade Organization
Yale J. Int'l L.	*Yale Journal of International Law*
Yale J. on Reg.	*Yale Journal on Regulation*
Yale L.J.	*Yale Law Journal*
ZEuP	*Zeitschrift für Europäisches Privatrecht*
ZfRV	*Zeitschrift für Rechtsvergleichung*
ZGR	*Zeitschrift für Unternehmens- und Gesellschaftsrecht*
ZHR	*Zeitschrift für das gesamte Handels- und Wirtschaftsrecht*
ZJapanR	*Zeitschrift für Japanisches Recht*
ZRP	*Zeitschrift für Rechtspolitik*
ZVglRWiss	*Zeitschrift für vergleichende Rechtswissenschaft*

TABLE OF CASES

European Union

United Kingdom

United States

Germany

Other countries

TABLE OF LEGISLATION

OECD

European Union

United Kingdom

United States

MBCA = Model Business Corporation Act

Germany

GerBörsZulV = German Stock-Exchange-Admission Regulation (Börsenzulassungsverordnung)

GerCGK = German Corporate Governance Code (Deutscher Corporate Governance Kodex)

GerFGG = German Ex-Parte Jurisdiction Act (Gesetz über die freiwillige Gerichtsbarkeit)

GerGmbHG = German Law on Private Liability Companies (Gesetz betreffend die Gesellschaft mit beschränkter Haftung)

GerHGB = German Commercial Code (Handelsgesetzbuch)

GerStGB = German Criminal Code (Strafgesetzbuch)

GerUmwG = German Transformation Act (Umwandlungsgesetz)

GerWpHG = German Securities Trading Act (Wertpapierhandelsgesetz)

GerWpÜG = German Takeover Act (Wertpapiererwerbs- und Übernahmegesetz)

GerZPO = German Code of Civil Procedure (Zivilprozessordnung)

France

FrCCom = Code de Commerce

Japan

JapCA = Japanese Corporation Act (kaisha hô), Law No. 86/2005

§ 306 111
§ 308 113, 114, 200
§ 309(1) 169, 170
§ 309(2) 158, 170
§ 311 106
§ 312 350
§ 314 122
§ 315(2) 111
§ 318 167
§ 320 104
§ 322 66
§§ 327, 328 72
§ 329 156
§ 331(3) 195
§ 332 157
§ 339 158
§ 341 158
§ 342 172
§ 348 153
§ 355 177, 193
§ 356 193
§ 361 159
§ 371 125
§ 390 156
§§ 390 *et seq.* 194
§§ 400 *et seq.* 195
§ 404(1) 156
§ 404(3) 160
§ 423 193
§ 426 155
§ 428 193
§§ 431 *et seq.* 127
§ 433 125
§ 437 100
§ 438 72
§ 444 133
§ 445(4) 73
§ 447 163
§ 450(2) 163
§ 454 72, 76, 77
§ 459 72
§ 466 162

JapCC = Japanese Commercial Code (Shôhô), Law No. 48/1899

China

INTRODUCTION

When social circumstances change, adjustments to law often occur too. It might therefore be concluded from advancing 'globalization' that national legal systems would come ever closer together. Yet both sides of this causal relationship can be attacked. On the one hand, on the factual side, one conceivable objection is that even today differing natural, economic, cultural and technical circumstances from country to country stand in the way of a uniform society. On the other hand, as regards the consequences, the effect of, for instance, path dependencies and differences in political systems might prevent a convergence of law. Whether internationalization and globalization trends will lead to a fundamental shift in legal systems is therefore an open question.

As regards the protection of shareholders in joint stock companies, current developments suggest further investigating the extent of 'convergence' and 'globalization'. For instance, the increasing cross-border movement of goods, services and capital and the use of the new media may also affect the shareholder's position and lead to a paradigm shift. The shareholder was even earlier often at the centre of the organizational structure of company law, but in the course of the twentieth century had to abandon that position in a number of legal systems, for one of more of a 'passive observer'. Now, however, the new media and the internationalization of shareholder circles might mean expectations of an internationally similar re-evaluation of shareholders' rights to participation, protection and information.

The basis and reference point for this study is the law on shareholder rights and duties of joint stock companies. However, to clarify the overall connections between law and reality, it will also look beyond the positive law. This interdisciplinary aspect accordingly brings an overlap with the debate on the future development of corporate governance. Opinion here ranges from success of the Anglo-American system via convergence on a hybrid system up to continuing divergence of the existing corporate governance systems.[1] This monograph will, however, make it clear that any such generalizations are problematic. Nor do the economic considerations that have found their way into the legal discussion through the corporate governance literature fully exhaust the interdisciplinary content of the present approach. Since convergence depends on the actions of political decision-makers, the findings of political science have also to be taken into account. Finally, the economic, political and social factors that might be decisive for any rapprochement have to be brought into the discussion of individual 'convergence forces'.

The analysis of this study will be divided into 'diagnosis', 'prognosis', and 'therapy'. Part I will specify the object of study, and Part II goes on to diagnose the present convergence in shareholder law. Here a principled ('typological') stance will be adopted, so as not to get stuck at the surface level of positive law. Moreover, economic and social connections will already be brought in at this point, so as not to study 'dead law' or misclassify the content of legal distinctions. In Part III, the main focus will shift. This prognostic part will ask how the convergence in shareholder law may develop in future, and for this purpose will in particular look closer into the political and social factors affecting convergence. The concluding Part IV returns to the law. In response to the two foregoing parts, it will assess whether, how and with what substantive orientation a convergence in shareholder law ought to develop.

Altogether, therefore, the questions explored will be how far convergence in shareholder law has already occurred *de lege lata* (Part II; Chs. 2–6; Theses 1–5), or is to be expected *de lege ferenda* (Part III; Chs. 7–11; Theses 6–10), or is desirable (Part IV; Ch. 12; Theses 11 and 12). The guideline throughout will be the following theses, to be further substantiated in the course of the study:[2]

1. For shareholder law in the UK, the US, Germany, France, Japan and China the division into different legal families is no longer a persuasive criterion of differentiation.
2. Present shareholder law is based, internationally largely concordantly, on a basic pattern of codifications of company and securities law, supplemented by case law, articles of association, shareholder agreements and corporate governance codes.
3. Although in Germany, France, Japan and China the reception of US law has increasingly expanded the investor aspect, all the legal systems

[1] For an overview see Van den Berghe (2002: 12 *et seq.*).
[2] See also the extended and footnoted version of these theses in Ch. 13.

studied here show a combination of the basic models of the shareholder as 'owner', 'parliamentarian' and 'investor'.

4. Similarly, all the legal systems studied here show a combination of the 'adjectival shareholder types' ('the profit-oriented, active, informed, anonymous, deciding, protected, litigating shareholder').
5. In detail, the provisions referring to the typical original shareholder rights (the 'shareholder as such') show a greater degree of convergence than the provisions on the 'shareholder in the power structure of the company'.
6. It follows from historical precedents, the findings of the public choice theory and studies on the influence of interest groups that changes in factual circumstances can exert decisive influence on future shareholder law and thus act as 'convergence forces'.
7. Although international and informal regulation will grow in importance, for the future development of convergence, it is still codified national law that will count most.
8. As the social, political and economic conditions that form the background to shareholder law come closer together internationally, the law itself will also grow more similar ('convergence through congruence').
9. In situations where individual interest groups press for an approximation of laws ('convergence through pressure'), 'regulatory competition for shareholders' will take on increasing importance compared with 'regulatory competition for company founders' and 'lobbying'.
10. It will be above all the internationalization of enterprises, the approximation of shareholder structures, the new media and shareholder pressure that will contribute to a convergence of law and of its implementation.
11. At legal-policy level, for a convergence in shareholder law the various modes of regulation must be coordinated and their procedures optimized.
12. For the converging law, the shareholder as 'empowered shareholder' should return to the centre of company law.

PART I

The object and course of the investigation

1

Dimensions of convergence in shareholder law

The delimitation of this book follows from the spatial, objective, temporal and legal methodological dimensions of convergence in shareholder law. The 'spatial dimension' (section I below) will include the legal bases of international organizations, the EU, the UK, the US, Germany, France, Japan and China. In the discussion on 'objective dimension' (section II below), it will be clarified what kind of companies and investors 'shareholder law' covers. In the discussion on 'temporal dimension' (section III below), the question of whether and how far the current process of convergence is to be regarded as a continuation or endpoint of the developments to date will be considered. Finally, the section on 'methodological dimension' (section IV below) will set out further steps of this monograph.

I. The spatial dimension: the legal systems covered

In selecting the legal systems to be studied, it is sensible to restrict their number, though without thereby narrowing the comprehensiveness of the study. Accordingly, I will consider the law of the US, the UK, Germany, France, Japan and China as well as international legal bases.

Further specification is needed for the EU, the US and China. At the European level, in addition to harmonization through directives, the European Company (Societas Europaea, SE) in particular now has to be taken into account. The focus here will be on the European law on the SE. This is not intended to give the impression that the SE is a uniform European legal form. Since the European rules are far from constituting a complete company law, there are instead, depending on the nationality of the state of establishment, various types of SE.[1] It has additionally to be borne in mind that, in the US, company law is also not uniform, since according to the US-Constitution legislative competence lies with the states.[2]

[1] Cf. Enriques (2004a); Siems (2005a).

[2] Cf. the interstate commerce clause in Art. I s. 8 of the US Constitution.

Federally, company law is regulated only insofar as securities law in part contains regulations with content that is to be classified as company law, and because the Model Business Corporation Act (MBCA)[3] of the American Bar Association and the Principles of Corporate Governance 1994 of the American Law Institute[4] set informal standards. The MBCA has contributed to a manifest convergence of states' company laws,[5] so that I will deal particularly also with the MBCA, as well as the Delaware General Corporation Law as the most important state act. Finally, some local differences also have to be taken into account for the People's Republic of China. While in principle the national Companies Act is decisive, older local provisions, especially those in Guangdong, Hainan, Shenzhen and Shanghai, continue to have validity as long as they are not in contradiction with national company law.[6]

The choice of these legal systems is based, first, on a search for countries of particular importance as business centres. The law of these legal systems serves as a model for other countries. Additionally, the choice of the larger legal systems offers the advantage of being able to consult large numbers of individual comparative legal studies. It is accordingly possible here to do without separate general country reports for the given shareholder law, and instead to differentiate between the various legal systems only within the individual subject areas.

Additionally, I refrained from taking only one country from each legal system, or comparing only two legal systems. A legal comparison of two or three countries is insufficient for the purposes of establishing an overall thesis of a convergence of legal systems. According to the usual subdivision, therefore, two countries each were taken from the common law (US, UK[7]), the civil law (Germany, France) and mixed Asian legal systems (Japan, China). This, however, makes it necessary, contrary to a widespread practice, to use primarily not the original company law technical terms but translations of them. This is not to ignore, for instance, that equating 'Gesellschaft', 'company', 'corporation' and 'société' can be problematic.[8] Since, however, with six legal systems the original words would tend rather to confuse, and the Chinese and Japanese terms are not

[3] Since the 1984 version the term RMBCA (Revised MBCA) is also used; the first version was produced in 1950.

[4] American Law Institute, *Principles of Corporate Governance: Analysis and Recommendations* (1994).

[5] See Carney (1998: 731 *et seq.*).

[6] Cf. Comberg (2000: 48 *et seq.*); Thümmel (1995: 15).

[7] Despite the devolution effected in the United Kingdom, the Scotland Act 1998, Schedule 5, para. C1, leaves competence for company law with the UK Parliament.

[8] Cf. Foster (2000: 578).

generally familiar anyway, 'multilingualism' is waived here for pragmatic reasons. It should accordingly be borne in mind that use of a common umbrella term like 'management' or 'company' is not intended to posit any legal identity.

Finally, the existing literature has not yet satisfactorily illuminated the convergence of shareholder law. Apart from studies confined to particular sub-areas of law,[9] more economics-oriented comparisons of corporate governance[10] and collections from groups of scholars,[11] this is true also of the much-cited research findings of Rafael La Porta, Florencio Lopez-de-Silanes, Andrei Shleifer and Robert Vishny.[12] La Porta *et al.* used a quantitative methodology in order to examine the differences in shareholder protection in forty-nine countries and its impact on financial development.[13] For this, eight variables were used as proxies for shareholder protection. These variables coded the law for 'one share one vote', 'proxy by mail allowed', 'shares not blocked before the meeting', 'cumulative voting', 'oppressed minorities mechanism', 'pre-emptive rights to new issues', 'share capital required to call an extraordinary shareholder meeting', and 'mandatory dividend'. In each case, a country was graded either '1' where shareholder protection was present or '0' where it was not. In recent years, many quantitative studies have used these La Porta *et al.* variables on shareholder protection.[14] Furthermore, the European Commission's impact assessment on the Draft Directive on Shareholders' Rights explicitly refers to La Porta *et al.*[15] The problem is, however, that the findings of La Porta *et al.* are inaccurate. Various studies have identified many coding errors,[16] and the limited number of La Porta *et al.*'s variables hardly provides a meaningful picture of the legal protection of shareholders.[17] Furthermore, a numerical comparative analysis has its intrinsic limits and only leads to a superficial understanding of different legal systems.[18] As in other academic fields, a quantitative approach does not therefore exclude a qualitative analysis, as it is pursued in this monograph.

[9] See e.g. Baums and Wymeersch (1999). [10] See e.g. Van den Berghe (2002).

[11] See e.g. Hansmann and Kraakman (2004); Hopt *et al.* (2005).

[12] See La Porta *et al.* (1998), (1999), (2000a), (2000b).

[13] On the 'law-matters thesis' see Ch. 7, section I. 1; Ch. 8, section IV. 1. a below.

[14] E.g. Dyck and Zingales (2004); Licht *et al.* (2005); Pagano and Volpin (2005).

[15] Impact assessment on the proposal for a directive on the exercise of shareholders' voting rights, SEC(2006)181, at pp. 7, 53; available at http://register.consilium.eu.int/pdf/en/06/st05/st05217-ad01.en06.pdf.

[16] Cools (2005); Braendle (2006); Spamann (2006).

[17] Lele and Siems (2007). [18] See Siems (2005e); Vagts (2002).

II. The objective dimension: the shareholder of a joint stock company

The shareholder of a joint stock company is to be distinguished above all from shareholders in 'small companies' and other types of investors.

1. Demarcation from shareholders in 'small companies'

At first sight, there is a distinction in many countries between joint stock companies and small companies. A closer look,[19] though, shows there are a number of national peculiarities, which are, however, coming closer together.

In Germany, the small company form 'GmbH' was created in 1892, without a historical model. The background was the interest of small, less capital-intensive firms in a flexible and simple legal form of association, which was nonetheless capable of excluding the personal liability of the shareholders. In the twentieth century, this idea was taken up by a number of countries. Comparable legal forms were accordingly adopted on the German model, in France in 1925 with the 'société à responsabilité limitée' (SARL), in Japan in 1938 with the 'yugen kaisha'[20] and in the People's Republic of China in 1993 with the 'you xian ze ren gong si'.[21] European law too contains a differentiation in the company law directives and the SE law between joint stock companies and private limited companies.[22]

The demarcation in detail varies, however. While internationally it is in principle uniformly the case that firms can freely choose the desired type of company, differences arise from the conditions for forming a joint stock company or a private limited company. For instance, in France and China – by contrast with Germany – no more than fifty shareholders may be involved in a private limited company (Art. L. 223-3 FrCCom; § 24 ChinCA). In China, on an international comparison, the conditions for setting up a joint stock company are set very high and the establishment procedure very costly, so that the Chinese joint stock company is decidedly a legal form exclusively for large firms.[23] By contrast, in Germany in 1994 a reform act deliberately opened up the law of joint stock companies

[19] From a comparative point of view see De Kluiver and Van Gerven (1995); Lutter (1998a).

[20] See Maruyama (1995: 284); Hayakawa (1996: 267); on the JapCA 2005 which repealed the 'yugen kaisha' see text accompanying note 39 below.

[21] See Tomasic and Fu (1999: 122 *et seq.*).

[22] Cf. Art. 1(1) of the Second Directive 77/91/EEC; SE-Reg, Annex I a.

[23] Cf. Comberg (2000: 51); Thümmel (1995: 46).

somewhat for smaller firms.[24] A further variant is offered by French law. There, a separate legal form, the SAS, was created, intended in its present form to cover the area between the big joint stock company (SA) and the small private company (SARL).[25]

The Anglo-American counter-model started originally from a unitary type of company.[26] The later distinctions between the 'closely held corporation' and the 'publicly held corporation' in the US, and between 'private' and 'public' companies in the UK, are therefore often today still seen as two different versions of a single company form.[27] This appears even in the terminology, since by contrast with the German term 'Aktionär', which refers only to joint stock companies, the term 'shareholder' is used comprehensively with all types of company.

One reason for the difference between the US and continental Europe has been seen by Roberta Romano in the fact that the European possibility of choice of legal form – a 'European genius of state competition' – is a functional equivalent to the American possibility of choosing the state of incorporation.[28] Since, however, there is no comparable choice in the UK, yet in principle only a single form of company existed, another reason is more plausible: in both the US and the UK, company law was permissive to a greater extent than in other countries.[29] Consequently, there was no comparable pressure from smaller firms for a new, less cumbersome legal form, since these firms too were content with the existing more flexible range of instruments.

However, the contrast between the two groups of countries is becoming increasingly diluted. There now exist in both the UK and the US strongly marked differentiations in company law. In the UK, since 1980, the distinction is made such that a company is in principle a private company (Ltd), unless specified in its articles of association as a public company (plc) and the tighter conditions of establishment (s. 4(2) UK-CA) complied with. No further barriers are set up. Thus, for private companies, by contrast with the previous situation, there is no limit on the number

[24] Gesetz für kleine Aktiengesellschaften und zur Deregulierung des Aktienrechts of 02.08.1994, BGBl. I 1961.

[25] See Ch. 2, section III. 1 below.

[26] For the US: Vagts (1998: 279–80, 288–9); for the UK: Lutter (1998a: para. 2-9); Cheffins (1997: 49).

[27] See Grantham (1998: 556–7); Goulding (1995: 57).

[28] Romano (1993: 138 *et seq.*); on regulatory competition see Ch. 9, section I. 1, VI. 1; Ch. 12, section II. 1.a below.

[29] See Ch. 2, section IV. 1. b below.

of shareholders allowed,[30] and there is now no longer any restriction on the transfer of shares.[31] For the substantive differences, the first decisive step came with the Companies Act 1989. Since EU directives in particular had over the course of time increased the mandatory requirements on (large) companies, more room was now left to private companies through special provisions. Secondly, the 2006 reform of British company law has extended the existing differentiation still further. For instance, with respect to resolutions at meetings, the more demanding rules now apply only to public or even only to quoted companies (ss. 336 *et seq.*, and ss. 341 *et seq.* UK-CA).

In the US, small firms can be established either as a close corporation or as a limited liability company (LLC). The success of state LLC laws[32] is based particularly on the fact that, while LLCs have the legal form of a company, for tax purposes they are treated as a partnership.[33] The regulations for close corporations are in some states contained in a close corporation supplement (e.g. §§ 341 *et seq.* DelGCL), while in other states exceptional provisions are integrated into the overall text.[34] These provisions are then applied where the shareholders deliberately so decide and the company does not, for instance, have more than fifty[35] shareholders. Additionally, in the US, a link is made with the distinction between public companies and other ones. For instance, the MBCA makes agreements departing from the Act impossible where shares are traded on a public capital market (§ 7.32(d) MBCA). Conversely, it is not just companies traded on the public capital markets which come under securities law. Instead, since 1964, special rules have also applied to all companies with more than 500 shareholders and total assets in excess of US$10 million.[36]

This overlap between company and securities law is not, however, a specifically American phenomenon. In other countries too, a stock exchange listing for the small company form (GmbH, Ltd, etc.) is disallowed.[37] By contrast, joint stock companies are potentially eligible for

[30] In the Companies Act 1907, the limit was fifty shareholders; see Cheffins (1997: 49).

[31] See Davies (2003: 37).

[32] See also National Conference of Commissioners on Uniform State Laws, Uniform Limited Liability Company Act (1995).

[33] See Goldman and Filliben (2000: 707); Cox and Hazen (2003: § 1.11).

[34] Cf. Cox and Hazen (2003: § 14.01); Lutter (1998a: para. 2-28).

[35] § 3(b) Model Statutory Close Corporation Supplement.

[36] For details see § 12(g) US-SEA. Similarly in Japan, see § 24(1) JapSEA; Hertig *et al.* (2004: 203).

[37] See e.g. for the UK: s. 755 UK-CA; Davies (2003: 628); for Germany: GerBörsG and GerBörsZulV which do not mention shares of a GmbH.

the capital market, so that the underlying model for them is the big public company. Moreover, company law differentiates according to the source of the company's capital. For instance, in France, since 1966, there have been two versions of the société anonyme (SA), namely, the public SA for companies whose securities are admitted to official exchange trading or the second marché of the stock exchange or are to be placed through the banks or stock exchange companies, and the ordinary SA (Arts. L. 225-4 and 225-2 FrCCom). Similarly, in Germany since 1994, the applicable law not only depends on the type of company (AG or GmbH) but also on the question of whether the company is listed.[38]

The most extensive change, however, occurred recently in Japanese company law. The 2005 reform of Japanese company law repealed the small type of company ('yugen kaisha'), so that now these companies automatically become joint stock companies.[39] At the same time, the law on joint stock companies has become more flexible for medium-sized and small companies. Furthermore, the reformed law provides a new distinction between restricted-share transfer companies and publicly held companies.[40] Finally, the reform establishes the new form of 'limited liability companies' ('gôdô kaisha'), modelled after the LLCs in the US, but without the advantage that they are taxed as partnerships.[41]

Consequently, despite the tendency to approximation in the distinction between the joint stock company and the 'small company', caution is still advisable. While in speaking of the 'shareholder law of joint stock companies' below I am in principle referring to large firms potentially eligible for the capital market, in many, though not all, legal systems the use of this legal form by small firms must also be borne in mind. This depends decisively on whether the legal form of the joint stock company already offers sufficient flexibility for smaller firms (as, for example, in the US) or else a flexible alternative to it exists (such as the GmbH in Germany). This circumstance is also reflected in the *de facto* differences in the utilization of the legal forms of the company.

The actual utilization of the legal forms of the joint stock company and the small company is very heterogeneous internationally. On the one hand, for instance in France, even small to medium-sized firms and family

[38] Gesetz für kleine Aktiengesellschaften und zur Deregulierung des Aktienrechts of 02.08.1994, BGBl. I 1961.

[39] See Saito (2004); Takahashi and Shimizu (2005).

[40] §§ 2(5), (6), 295–430 JapCA; for an overview see Ueda (2005: 424–5).

[41] Dernauer (2005: 129).

firms often have the joint stock form.[42] By contrast, in the second half of the twentieth century in Germany, both small and large firms often used the legal form of the GmbH, so that the number of joint stock companies was falling.[43] This trend has changed, however, since the 1990s, because small and medium-sized firms have been increasingly interested in the legal form of the joint stock company. The reasons advanced for this include the improvement in company and securities laws, as well as factual developments such as succession in many family firms, the increasing importance of private pension funds and the internationalization of the economy.[44]

In the UK, the number of 'plcs' lies between France and Germany.[45] In the UK – as in the US – stock exchange admissions for younger, smaller firms are more common than in other countries. Since this requires the legal form of the plc, less use tends to be made of the small-company form.

It follows from these country-specific preferences for the joint stock company that differing requirements are placed on company law. Where, as for instance in France, the joint stock form is relatively frequently used by small firms, the firms' expectations and the legislature's corresponding responses will lead to different laws than in countries where joint stock companies are mostly large public companies. Again, where the joint stock company is used by two completely different groups – namely, public companies and small firms – problems may arise in applying the law.[46] Finally, the relative use of company forms also has effects on the capital-market strength of a given legal system. However, the statement made about Germany, that the weakness of the capital market is connected with the frequent use of the GmbH,[47] cannot be generalized. Although, for example, in France, there are more joint stock companies than in the UK, in France the capital market is weaker. Yet a certain connection does exist, since the function of the capital market to attract outside investors is typically only of importance for joint stock companies. The capital market will accordingly remain weak so long as larger companies retain the legal form of the small company.

[42] See Merle (2005: para. 247); Hirte (2003: para. 1.59). The same used to be the case in Japan, see Kawamoto *et al.* (2001: para. 25).

[43] See report in AG 2001, R 315 *et seq.*

[44] Report in AG 2001, R 315, 318; for more details see Ch. 8, section IV. 2. b below.

[45] See Hulle (1994: 397); Edwards (1999: 12).

[46] See Hayakawa (1996: 270–1) for the old Japanese law.

[47] Escher-Weingart (2001: 31).

2. *Demarcation from other participants in the firm*

The demarcation of shareholders from the other participants in the firm at first seems clear. Only shareholders provide the firm with equity capital and receive in return, at the latest on the dissolution of the company, an entitlement to the yield remaining after deduction of contractual liabilities.[48] Additionally, classically shareholders as providers of equity capital share in the supervision of the company through their voting rights.[49]

However, this distinction between debt and equity can be questioned. For instance, Jennifer Hill states that it 'fails to accord with economic reality and looks artificial, arbitrary and increasingly passé'.[50] She first points out that *de facto* control of a company often lies with the creditors, and banks often have a dual position as creditors and shareholders. Additionally, because of new forms of financial contracts, the control and risk components are increasingly separated. Finally, the boundary between employee and shareholder is also sometimes blurred, when workers participate in controlling the firm through shareholdings, pension funds or more formal forms of worker participation.

A legal demarcation first becomes necessary where the *de facto* equity provider is not officially listed as the registered owner. This applies particularly to the cases where financial intermediaries, trustees or previous owners are entered *pro forma* as shareholders on the register of members. With the exception of France,[51] most legal systems, in the interests of legal security, treat the person registered and not the beneficial owner as the shareholder.[52] This does not rule out the granting of particular rights to the beneficial owner too.[53] The advantage of the formal focus on the register lies in, for instance, the possibility of trading in shares without having to amend the register. Record ownership also makes it possible for capital providers to remain anonymous.[54]

48 See e.g. Cheffins (1997: 54); Vagts (2000: para. 10-2); Hirte (2003: paras. 5.1 *et seq.*).

49 See Ch. 4, section II. 1 below.

50 Hill (2000a: 24), and, on what follows, also Hill (2000a: 21 *et seq.*); similarly Worthington (2001b: 311).

51 Cf. Guyon (1999: 107); Druey (1999: 375); ANSA (2003: 25).

52 See generally Weller and Zahn (2000: 179); for Germany: § 67(2)(s.1) GerAktG; for the UK: ss. 112, 126 UK-CA; Davies (2003: 638, 692); Davies (1999: 333); for the US: Gruson (2001: 215); Wunderlich and Labermeier (2000: 150–1, 165); but see also § 7.23 MBCA; for Japan: § 130(1) JapCA; Kawamoto *et al.* (2001: paras. 279, 337); for China: § 44(1) ChinArticles.

53 E.g. § 16.02(f) MBCA; ss. 146, 153 UK-CA; for the previous discussions see Company Law Reform (2005: 18–20, E1–2); Ferran (2003b: 512–13); Davies (1999: 345), (1997b: 596).

54 See Ch. 4, section IV below.

Moreover, hybrid forms of investment may call the concept of the shareholder into question. Hybrid investments can, on the one hand, arise because special rights enhance the position of bondholders. Examples of such mixed forms include convertibles, warrants and participation bonds.[55] On the other hand, it is also possible for the position of equity providers to be downgraded, because non-voting preference shares in particular functionally stand together with bonds, on a similar level.[56] Yet these more recent mixed forms, by which firms' financing needs and investors' interests are intended to be reconciled, are not evidence of a general retreat from the share as a form of investment. This concerns first the international acceptance of the basic principle of the joint stock company as such. For instance, in China, at the start of the economic modernization in the 1980s, initially only 'certificates' in state undertakings were issued. Since the immediate owner of the undertakings remained the state, these certificates were accordingly not shares in a narrow sense.[57] That changed with the second wave of modernization. Since the 1990s, joint stock companies with shareholders as equity providers have been politically and economically recognized. Secondly, on international financial markets too the share continues to be of enormous importance. Even though it may sometimes seem as if investors today are interested only in profit, and no longer in participation as members, this does not mean a levelling down between shares and bonds. Instead, one can see from the market valuation of non-voting preference shares that the rights attached to shareholdings continue to be relevant.[58]

However, in the following discussion it is to be borne in mind that for many investors there is a certain interchangeability between shares and other forms of investment. Thus, if, for instance, in one legal system these mixed forms are patterned unattractively in company, fiscal or accounting law, then enhanced interest in shares is to be expected (and *vice versa*). This interchangeability may also lead to a convergence of investors' positions. Thus, one might even propose to limit the rights of shareholders because

[55] For the UK: Davies (2003: 806–7); for France: Guyon (1995); for the US: Cox and Hazen (2003: § 18.15); for Germany: § 221 GerAktG; Siebel (1997: 661 *et seq.*); for Japan: §§ 288 *et seq.* JapCA; for China: Xi (2006: 255); for a comparative account: van Ryn (1990: paras. 5-167 *et seq.*).

[56] Cf. Hill (2000a: 23–4); see also Ch. 4, section II. 4. b below.

[57] See Comberg (2000: 75).

[58] Cf. Bezzenberger, in: GroßkommAktG (1999: § 139 para. 8); Modern Company Law for a Competitive Economy (1999: para. 4.11) ('It is now widely accepted that the right to vote a share has an economic value').

they mostly have a purely financial interest in their investment, not one as members.[59]

III. The temporal dimension

The term 'convergence' describes a development over time. The focal point of the discussion below will be more recent developments. Yet this does not mean that we should discount longer-term historical contexts, or that we have reached the 'end of history' of company law.

1. *'The End of History for Corporate Law'?*

Henry Hansmann and Reinier Kraakman, borrowing from Francis Fukuyama,[60] postulated, under the title 'The End of History for Corporate Law', that the historical differences in company law would fade in favour of approximation to the US model.[61] By contrast with existing views that stressed the institutional differences in management, shareholder structures, capital-market orientation and business culture, they saw path-dependent historical developments as of only minor interest for the law today.

That is, at the least, misleading.[62] Although Hansmann and Kraakman reveal a number of important developmental factors, their title in particular suggests a finality that is not accurate. The perception of convergence and globalization is not a new phenomenon. By the time of industrialization in the nineteenth century, it was already possible to speak of an accelerated approximation of the world's legal and social systems. This is conceded by Hansmann and Kraakman.[63] They state that, by the end of the nineteenth century, it was possible in every large trading nation to establish a joint stock company with a number of common features: full legal personality, limited liability for owners and managers, shared ownership by investors of capital, delegated management under a board structure, and transferable shares.[64] The reception of foreign law and legal convergence were thus already an accepted legal phenomenon early

[59] See Ch. 3, sections I. 3, II below.

[60] Fukuyama (1992). [61] Hansmann and Kraakman (2001).

[62] For further discussions of Hansmann and Kraakman see Ch. 5, section II. 1. a, Ch. 7, section I. 1, Ch. 8, section I. 2, Ch. 9, section I. 1. a. (2), III. 2, VI. 3. a, Ch. 10, section II. 2. a. (1) below.

[63] Hansmann and Kraakman (2001: 439–40).

[64] In the same way, Hansmann and Kraakman (2004: 5 *et seq.*).

on. And today's developments too thus fit in with the existing historical context and cannot be separated from it.

2. *Historical interconnectedness in Europe*

The interactions can be seen particularly clearly in Europe.[65] Connections existed right at the start of modern company law in the seventeenth century. The first European joint stock companies emerged with the colonial companies to exploit the newly opened-up colonies. The pioneers were the British and Dutch East India Companies in particular. In other countries too, though with some time-lag, a similar development came about (for example, in France, the Compagnie des Indes Orientales in 1664, and the Compagnie d'Occident in 1717). These companies were internationally typified by the charter system: a corporation with legal capacity arose only from a royal act of foundation and recognition, often at the same time conveying public-law rights of sovereignty. Since these companies thus primarily served the welfare of the state, at that time company law was still part of public law.[66]

Further developments occured on the continent with the establishment of the French 1807 Code de Commerce. This law for the first time regulated the institution of the joint stock company in abstract rules, so that, based on this model, the charter system was replaced by the concession system. By the end of the seventeenth century, the general meeting had been established as an organ of the participants, and shareholder law was thereby brought to a new stage of development. Following on from the ideas of the French Revolution and the Enlightenment, the equality of shareholders and the democratization of the general meeting were now taken as themes.[67] This development had effects in Germany, for instance in the Prussian Companies Act of 1843 and in the Allgemeines Deutsches Handelsgesetzbuch (General German Commercial Code) of 1861.

The concession system was turning joint stock companies increasingly into private-law entities. This development was enhanced by the free registration system, which, for instance in France since 1867 and in Germany since 1870, guaranteed founders a legal entitlement to an entry in the

[65] See e.g. Pistor *et al.* (2002: 798 *et seq.*); Frentrop (2002); Ducouloux-Favard (1992).

[66] See Assmann, in: GroßkommAktG (1992: Einl. para. 27); Hill (2000a: 18 *et seq.*). Elements of public-law origins can be seen in the mandatory provisions in some countries, see Ch. 2, section IV. 1 below.

[67] Frentrop (2002: 150). However, not until 1867 were there statutory provisions on the general meeting, see Horn (1979: 156).

commercial register. The economic and political backgrounds to these developments lay above all in the industrialization, capitalism and liberalism of the nineteenth century. Since with industrial development the capital needs of undertakings rose, it became necessary in all countries, for major economic projects such as railways, mining, insurance and industrial manufacturing, to make suitable financing mechanisms available. Along with this congruency came convergences from the communication of foreign laws. Accordingly, particularly in Germany with the reform projects of the nineteenth century (particularly those of 1861 and 1884), comprehensive comparative legal studies were undertaken.[68] Ultimately, here too, an approximation, caused by sharper international competition, was emerging. In the UK, under the Joint Stock Companies Registration, Incorporation and Regulation Act of 1844, the founding of a joint stock company no longer depended on governmental permission; thus French firms saw themselves as disadvantaged in competition, and their pressure led to the more liberal 1867 law.[69]

Otherwise, developments on the continent and in the UK in principle took differing courses. With the UK's entry into the European Community, however, continental legal traditions exerted a greater influence; for instance the principle of minimum capital may be noted. Earlier still, conversely, there was a reception of British law into Germany. For example, the Prussian Companies Act of 1843 took account of British developments.[70] Additionally, the British 1900 reform, on mandatory audits and the disclosure of annual reports, influenced German legislation.[71] Again, German accounting law, which was hither to influenced by Dutch and Italian law, was now marked by British influences.[72] Altogether, then, the German joint stock company has 'Dutch, French and British blood',[73] so that the current convergence is hardly a meeting of diametrically opposite poles.

3. *Receptions in the US, Japan and China*

By contrast with European developments, the reception of foreign law into the US, Japan and China was initially rather one-sided.

[68] See Assmann, in: GroßkommAktG (1992: Einl. paras. 63, 69, 70, 92, 105); Hopt (1980: 166).
[69] Cf. Pistor *et al.* (2002: 807).
[70] See Großfeld and Deilmann (1990: 256–7).
[71] Cf. Merkt (2001b: 76).
[72] Cf. Großfeld (1998: 2); Vagts (1972: para. 12A-2); see also Ch. 4, section III. 3 below.
[73] Großfeld (1998: 2).

a) USA

American corporate law is rooted in the traditions of the United Kingdom.[74] That is hardly surprising, since British colonial companies were also active in the American colonies, and thus formed the starting-point for company law there. All the same, initial developments after independence show some parallels with Europe. At the outset, in the US too the foundation of a joint stock company was still associated with an individual act of bestowal ('special incorporation') and was practised mainly by monopoly enterprises. It was only with growing industrialization that the need for capital rose considerably on both sides of the Atlantic. The foundation of a joint stock company by private persons was accordingly facilitated by the free registration system – for the US from around 1875, with the concept of 'general incorporation'.

At latest by the end of the nineteenth century, however, the separate developments in the US began to become clearer. From then on, in a number of US states, a manifest deregulation policy is perceptible, while in Europe – because of the absence of regulatory competition for founders[75] – there was no such deregulation. Nonetheless, communication with the UK and other European countries was maintained, as evident from, for instance, questions of financial disclosure:[76] the extension of disclosure in US securities law in 1933 and 1934 followed the British, and probably also the French and German, disclosure rules. But the influences were two-way: the publicity rules of the British Joint Stock Companies Act of 1844 had been cut back in the course of the nineteenth century, only to be expanded again under US influence in the second half of the twentieth. A corresponding influence of US publicity rules can also be seen after the Second World War in France and Germany.[77]

b) Japan

Japanese company law is marked by two phases of receptions of foreign law.[78] The first phase began with the general modernization of Japan and the reception of continental European law after the Meiji Restoration of

[74] For the history see e.g. Blair (2004); Cox and Hazen (2003: § 2); Klein and Coffee (2002: 115 *et seq.*).

[75] See Ch. 9, sections I. 1, VI. 1 below.

[76] See Merkt (2001b: 56, 74 *et seq.*, 106 *et seq.*, 114 *et seq.*, 117 *et seq.*); Licht (1998: 246 *et seq.*).

[77] See generally Ch. 4, section III.2 below.

[78] Cf. Rahn (1994: 3 *et seq.*); Kawamoto *et al.* (2001: paras. 88 *et seq.*); Hayakawa (1996: 268–9); generally also Schenck (1997).

1868. The codified company law of 1890 was dominated, alongside some French influence, by German influences, since the law was drafted mainly by Karl Friedrich Hermann Rösler, who was then working for the Japanese Ministry of Justice. This starting-point from legal history remained even with the recasting of company law in the 1899 Commercial Code, which – in harmony with the international trend[79] – replaced the concession system by the free registration system. In subsequent decades, in addition, continental theories were introduced. This changed, however, after the 1920s, which saw a gradual emancipation of Japanese law from its continental European origins and the first signs of US influence. But the great paradigm shift came only with the reception of US law after the Second World War. For company law, the 1933 Illinois Business Corporation Act was the essential model here. As with the model effect of German law fifty years earlier, this too depended decisively on a foreign adviser, since Lester Salwin, a lawyer from Illinois, had crucial influence here.[80] There was not, however, a wholesale copying of American company law. And, when it came recasting the Commercial Code, there was strong resistance by the Japanese business organization Keidanren to various elements of the US law.[81] Today, despite American influence, the new 2005 Corporation Act confirms the growing independence of Japanese company law as well as its hybrid features.[82]

The development of Japanese company law was examined in an interesting study by Mark West.[83] He compared the company-law provisions of Illinois and Japanese law in 1950 and 2000. His finding is that, during this period, there has been no (further) convergence but a divergence. This at first surprised him, because there were a number of similarities between the US and Japan, the countries were in extensive contact and the starting-point in company law after the Second World War was similar. He saw the decisive reason for the divergence in the fact that, in Japan, legislation tended to be changed only occasionally, after shocks, unlike in the US, where there is constant pressure to improve because of regulatory competition for founders. However, no general divergent development of Japanese company law should be deduced from this. The reception process of the last 120 years has on the whole meant that codified Japanese law is surprisingly familiar to Western observers. Additionally, in recent years, a tendency for the Japanese legislator to follow the US model

[79] See sections III.2 and 3. a above. [80] See Salwin (1962).

[81] See West (2001a: 538 *et seq.*); Matsudo (1959: 115).

[82] Dernauer (2005: 158). [83] West (2001a).

can be perceived.[84] Finally, West's methodology, and therefore also his finding of increased divergence, are subject to challenge. His comparison involves looking at each individual legal provision to test for convergence or divergence and then, for the overall result, adding the individual findings together. One objection to this procedure is that not every provision is equally important, so that, here too, 'numerical comparative law' has its limits.[85]

c) China

Chinese company law too bears the mark of various foreign legal influences.[86] Although, even in the nineteenth century, European trading companies were active in China and there was some reception of foreign law in the first half of the twentieth century, this prehistory is today largely superseded. With the nationalization of all companies after 1947, for thirty years pretty well all private economic activity was stopped. This changed gradually with the progressive economic opening-up after 1979. Initially, special forms were created for Chinese–foreign joint ventures and companies with foreign capital participation. At that stage, certificates in state undertakings, as a mixed form between bonds and shares, brought the first participation in firms, the first simple securities markets and, as from the mid-1980s, the first local companies acts. In 1992, the 'standardization views' led to the national regulation of company law by ministerial decree, which have an equivalent effect to statutes. In 1993, after ten years of drafting, the Chinese Companies Act, covering both the 'small company' and the joint stock company, was adopted. The models for the Chinese Companies Act were primarily the company laws of Taiwan, France, Germany and Japan. For language reasons, the Taiwanese law in particular was given close attention. Taiwan's company law is, however, itself a hybrid, since it was originally based on German and Japanese law and, after the Second World War, like the Japanese law, came under US influence.[87] Additionally, the 2005 reform of the Companies Act adopted some notions of US corporate law (for example, cumulative voting, derivate suits).[88] In line with earlier developments in other countries, this reform also abolished the concession procedure which was part of the 1993 Act.[89] Finally,

[84] See e.g. Ch. 2, section IV. 1. b; Ch. 4, sections I. 4, II. 4. b, III. 3. b below.
[85] See Ch. 1, section I above.
[86] For the history generally see e.g. Wei (2003: 83 *et seq.*); Comberg (2000: 19 *et seq.*).
[87] See Thümmel (1995: 10, 90). [88] See Ch. 5, sections I. 2. b, III. 1 below.
[89] §§ 8(2), 77 ChinCA 1993, but see now only § 6(2) ChinCA 2005.

reference can be made to Chinese securities law, which is in principle also based on Western law, in particular the US model.[90]

4. *Conclusion*

The reception of foreign law and convergence are nothing new. One ought not, therefore, to conceive of convergence in shareholder law as different legal systems simultaneously moving linearly towards each other from two opposite starting-points. Instead, there was already a certain congruency from the outset, followed by a sometimes diverging, sometimes converging, wave-like development.

IV. The methodological dimension

As with any comparative legal study, here too the question arises what legal and factual circumstances ought to be considered, and how legal distinctions ought consequently to be explained.

1. *Variants of convergence*

The concept of convergence was already being used in the second half of the twentieth century to raise the question of the possible approximation of capitalist and socialist industrial states.[91] By the same token, today there are discussions in political and social science of whether 'globalization' leads to a convergence of different economic systems.[92] Here, Colin Hay distinguishes between various causal chains within the framework of law-making, namely, among 'input', 'paradigm', 'policy', 'legimatory-rhetoric', 'outcome' and 'process' convergence.[93]

Similarly, the legal literature has recourse to various elements of law and its effects. In the US, in the context of the debate on the globalization of corporate governance trends, a distinction is drawn between formal, functional, contractual, hybrid, normative and institutional convergence. Ronald Gilson and John Coffee claim that functional convergence is more likely than formal convergence, since, while the underlying problems are similar, there are too many obstacles in the way of formal harmonization.[94] 'Functional' in this context accordingly means that a comparable result

[90] See Liu (2001: 2); for exceptions see Ch. 2, sections III. 1 below.

[91] See e.g. Krauss (1980).

[92] For references see Ch. 8, section I. 2 below.

[93] Hay (2004: 245 *et seq.*).

[94] See Gilson (2001: 337 *et seq.*); Coffee (1999b: 679); cf. also Rose (2001: 134).

is produced, with, say, bad managers being dismissed, but via different statutory paths. Alternatively, according to Gilson, there may be contractual convergence, where the formal differences may be functionally relevant, but equivalent effects can also be reached through contractual arrangements. Furthermore, the dualism between formal and functional convergence is supplemented by Paul Rose with the concept of hybrid convergence.[95] Hybrid convergence concerns the situation where a firm 'escapes' domestic law by shifting its registered seat to another country. Formally, the differences between the individual countries are thus maintained. Yet approximation comes about because firms of various countries are subject to the same rules ('convergence-by-the-backdoor'[96]).

Outside the legal sphere, one may, along with Curtis Milhaupt, raise the question of 'normative convergence'.[97] 'Normative' here means that the viewpoint of convergence is applied to extra-legal norms. Further, David Charny employs the term 'institutional convergence',[98] where *de facto* the structures in firms become more similar. This concerns, for instance, the question whether the shareholder ownership structure of firms changes, or whether firms are more frequently exposed to market influences such as the possibility of hostile takeovers. Finally, one might also choose a middle way between law and legal reality and focus on 'legal-cultural' convergence. This would link up with such theses as those generally raised by, for instance, Pierre Legrand.[99] He criticizes the concept of a convergence between civil law and common law on the ground that this approximation is only superficial, considering the deeper structures of legal culture.

Indeed, on the one hand, one cannot exclude the factual circumstances. Cultural-anthropological, sociological, economic and political facts may in comparative law explain differences, or reveal common features to be only superficial convergences.[100] On the other hand, in this book the law remains in the foreground, with extra-legal factors playing more of a supporting role. Borrowing from the methodology of the natural sciences, this can be explained by distinguishing between 'diagnosis', 'prognosis' and 'therapy'.

[95] Rose (2001: 134–5); Walker (2001: 448) calls this 'functional convergence'.

[96] Branson (2000: 691). [97] Milhaupt (2001). [98] Charny (1998: 165).

[99] Cf. Legrand (1996), (1997), (1999), (2006); see also Ch. 8, section II. 1 below.

[100] Similarly Branson (2001: 347); Großfeld (1996: 289).

2. *The division into 'diagnosis', 'prognosis' and 'therapy'*

After this introduction, Part II (Chs. 2–6) will make a 'diagnosis' of the current convergence in shareholder law. This part will focus on positive law. However, the legal rules of the different countries will not simply be enumerated. Instead, a more principled mode of observation will be adopted, so as not to focus too heavily on the surface of the positive law. Focusing on general principles ought thus to disclose common developments that would not emerge from a mere listing of details, which despite convergence will always vary in different legal systems. Notwithstanding this focus on law, however, even at this point economic and social connections will not be ignored, in order not to study 'dead law' or misclassify the content of legal differences. The focus will shift in Part III (Chs. 7–11). Since the question here is to forecast how convergence in shareholder law will develop further in future, looking behind the 'veil of law' is absolutely necessary. In the context of studying the convergence forces, accordingly, the economic, political and social factors that may be decisive for an approximation will be gone into. Moreover, the question whether the legislator will follow these factors, and accordingly to what extent accelerated convergence is to be expected, will be considered. The fourth and concluding part, Part IV (Ch. 12), will return to law. The assessment of convergence in shareholder law is here understood as a response to and 'therapy' for the circumstances and grievances emerging from the previous considerations. Thus it considers whether convergence is desirable, what drives it and what substantive direction it should take in relation to shareholder law.

As a result, to be able to make a comparison of real value, each part looks under the 'surface of the positive law' from a different point of view. The second part explains and investigates 'convergence' through principles, the third through facts and the fourth through evaluation.

3. *Shareholder law as the core of the study*

Recent inter-country studies in company and securities law have often been entitled 'comparative corporate governance'.[101] Shareholder law overlaps with this. Differences in shareholders' rights and obligations

[101] See e.g. Berrar (2001); Coffee (1999b); Cunningham (1999); Branson (2001); Gilson (2001); Wymeersch (2002).

have effects on corporate governance, just as, conversely, differences in corporate governance are of importance for the legal position of shareholders. Corporate governance topics will accordingly also be considered here. The prime focus is elsewhere, however. The primary interest is in the law that directly relates to the rights and obligations of shareholders. Other institutions that may have indirect effects for shareholders, such as monitoring of management by the supervisory board or independent directors, will by contrast not be covered to the same extent. But nor will they be left out of account, since such 'indirect shareholder provisions' present a functional equivalent to direct shareholder regulations and may thus explain differences between the individual countries.

When shareholder rights and obligations are discussed, common themes emerge, for example rights to information, disclosure, inspection, dividends, liquidity proceeds, equal treatment, and voting.[102] These themes can be classified, first, according to the range of persons entitled, thus distinguishing among shareholder rights, minority rights and general-meeting rights.[103] Secondly, studies often focus on the rights involved, differentiating between control rights, economic rights and special rights.[104] In this monograph, however, these distinctions will not be followed, nor will an individual listing of shareholder rights and duties be made. Instead, in accordance with the principled mode of observation (section IV.2 above), on the one hand basic concepts on the position of the shareholder, for instance the question of shareholder democracy and the shareholder's position as investor or owner, will be referred to. On the other hand, an adjectival description of the shareholder will be undertaken.[105] Such terms as 'active shareholder', 'modern shareholder' or 'empowered shareholder' will be used to clarify particular principles by which the shareholder's position is established.[106]

V. Summary

The investigation of convergence in shareholder law has various dimensions. First, the 'spatial dimension' will include the legal bases of

[102] E.g. for the US: Elsing and Van Alstine (1999: para. 610); for France: Bastian and Germain (1972: para. 38); for Finland: Poutianen (2001: 67).

[103] E.g. for Germany: Raiser (2001: § 12 paras. 10 *et seq.*); Mülbert, in: Großkomm-AktG (1999: vor § 118 para. 204 and note 361); for Japan: Kawamoto *et al.* (2001: para. 250); for China: Comberg (2000: 77); for Finland: Poutianen (2001: 67); see generally also van Ryn (1990: para. 5-137).

[104] Cf. the references in the previous note.

[105] See Ch. 3, section III.I below.

[106] See in particular Chs. 4, 5, 10, 12, section III, below.

international organizations, the EU, the US, the UK, Germany, France, Japan and China. Here, the decisive point was to draw a balance between a global perspective and an appropriate delimitation. Secondly, in its 'objective dimension', shareholder law of joint stock companies has to be demarcated against the law of shareholders in 'small companies' and that of other investors. Even if this is usually unproblematic, nonetheless imprecisions in this demarcation must be borne in mind, so as not to affect the comparative criterion. Similarly, and thirdly, in the 'time dimension' of convergence, no simple answer is possible. There have always been historical interactions and receptions of foreign law, so that it may very well be that the present convergence process involves 'only' an increase in the pace of convergence. Fourthly, there has to be differentiation according to 'what' will converge, thus distinguishing convergence of laws, legal rules, legal culture or legal reality. Below, this 'methodological dimension' will be approached by focusing first on the positive law ('diagnosis', Part II), then on the legal reality ('prognosis', Part III) and finally on legal policy ('therapy', Part IV).

PART II

The status quo of convergence

Classically, in many areas of law, a division is made into common law, civil law, and mixed legal systems. Although this distinction is today no longer undisputed,[1] for company law as well as for corporate governance systems this or a similar subdivision is often taken as a starting-point.[2] On one side, then, is the Anglo-Saxon common law model. This is seen as pursuing a market-based approach, where the shareholder's individual interests are to the fore. Moreover, in these countries, capital markets are seen as more developed, so that the interest in shares is broader and shareholder ownership is often dispersed. In other countries by contrast, especially Germany and France but also Japan and China, it is claimed, concentrated ownership structures mostly prevail in joint stock companies. Since management cooperates with the dominant shareholders, what counts is more relations within the company than control through the markets. This 'insider model' is to be explained by the fact that banks and employees hold a strong position. The firm is accordingly run not primarily in the interests of shareholders, but of all stakeholders in the undertaking. In these countries, too, state influence plays a big part, so that political views are brought inside the companies.

Insofar as this distinction refers to the economic and social environment it can, despite advancing convergence, still be justified today.[3] For shareholder law, however, a subdivision into different legal families is by now largely outdated. In Western countries, there has been not inconsiderable convergence. Additionally, for Japan and China too, the model effect of the company and securities law of the US and Europe has led to regulations in principle similar to that in the latter. Both the differentiation between common law, civil law and mixed legal systems and a division

[1] In favour of convergence see e.g. Gordley (1993); Markesinis (1994); for a critical stance see Legrand (1996), (1997), (1999), (2006); for a defence of the subdivision into legal families see Kötz (1998); for a new subdivision see Husa (2004); see also Siems (2007a).

[2] On what follows see e.g. Bratton and McCahery (1999: 218); Deakin (2001: 196–7); Doremus *et al.* (1998: 24 *et seq.*); Wymeersch (1995: 308); Cunningham (1999: 1136 *et seq.*, 1191); André (1998: 106); Chantayan (2002: 432) ('vast differences'); Licht (1998: 238) ('astonishing view of diversity'); McDonnell (2002); Mann (2003).

[3] See Part III, below.

into countries of the Commonwealth, Asia and Europe are thus no longer useful in the global context. Instead, most countries have a hybrid shareholder law, which from legal standpoints shows more in common than divides them. To substantiate this, I will first survey the regulatory bases on which shareholder law rests (Ch. 2). Secondly, the bases for a typology of shareholders will be discussed (Ch. 3). Then come the legal details of shareholder law (Chs. 4 and 5), followed by a concluding assessment of the status quo (Ch. 6).

2

Legal bases

The 'globalization' of the economy could encourage particular legal bases. It might intuitively be thought that, for complex global problems, international law (rather than regional law) and statute law (rather than case) law would be of importance (sections I and II below). Additionally, securities law (rather than company law) and self-regulation (rather than state regulation) might grow in weight (sections III and IV below), since globalization is driven above all by the capital markets and private actors (enterprises, lawyers, auditors, NGOs etc.). Looking at present-day law more closely, however, it is apparent that, while there is more mixing of legal bases, no substitution of one legal basis for another is coming about. Furthermore, similar basic patterns can be discerned in the individual countries. Yet, the remaining differences have also to be taken into account, since they may affect shareholder law in substance.

I. International and regional law

International and regional law are not diametrically opposed in shareholder law. Since international law prescribes no harmonization of shareholder law, it is instead left more to regional (or national) law to set mandatory standards.

1. International law

Although there are no uniformly binding regulations directly regulating the rights of shareholders internationally, international law is nonetheless not irrelevant to the legal position of shareholders. First, liberalizations of world trade and the international capital market may have effects for the future rights of shareholders.[1] Secondly, non-binding international standards contribute to a certain internationalization of law. This is

[1] See Ch. 8, sections III, V below.

particularly the case for the OECD Principles of Corporate Governance.[2] These principles were originally developed between 1996 and 1998 by the OECD's Business Sector Advisory Group on Corporate Governance, and were adopted in 1999 by the OECD Ministers. In 2004, an updated version was produced. In content, the OECD Principles deal in particular with general minimum standards on shareholder rights, the equal treatment of shareholders, and the relevance of stakeholder interests. The OECD also developed Guidelines for Multinational Enterprises.[3] These, like the 1982 UN Draft Code of Conduct on Transnational Corporations,[4] refer primarily to protection of the public interest of host countries of international enterprises and the principle of non-discrimination against foreign firms. The rights and obligations of shareholders are addressed only indirectly, since, for instance, disclosure of information pursuant to the OECD Guidelines also indirectly serves to protect shareholders. Much the same is true for the promotion of publicity by the International Organization of Securities Commissions (IOSCO) and the International Accounting Standards Board (IASB).[5] IOSCO, founded in 1974, is a private association of securities supervisors, formed to establish informal standards and to improve information exchange, the monitoring of securities transactions and cooperation among national supervisory bodies. To this end, IOSCO has proposed international objectives, which were recently consolidated in their Objectives and Principles of Securities Regulation. The IASB drafts uniform accounting standards. While these do not apply directly in individual legal systems, it has become increasingly the norm for companies to present their accounts in accordance with international accounting standards.[6]

2. *Regional law*

Supranational organizations like NAFTA and Mercosur were, as a rule, established only to expand free trade in those regions. Things are different with the European Union, since from the outset legal harmonization through directives was pushed furthest in the area of company law. In the 1970s in particular, matters of legal capital and the notification

[2] Available at http://www.oecd.org/dataoecd/32/18/31557724.pdf.

[3] Available at http://www.oecd.org/dataoecd/56/36/1922428.pdf (2000 version).

[4] Published in 23 International Legal Materials 626 (1984).

[5] See http://www.iosco.org and http://www.iasb.org.uk.

[6] Overview available at http://www.iasplus.com/country/useias.htm; see also Ch. 4, section III.3.b below.

of the annual accounts to shareholders were harmonized.[7] However, since this involved only piecemeal harmonizations, in a legal comparison with other countries it is necessary to look beyond these directives.[8] Moreover, in subsequent years the legal harmonization process in company law became bogged down. For instance, the Fifth Company Law Directive, which would have led to considerable uniformity for shareholders in Europe,[9] has failed, and will probably never be ressurected.

More recently, however, the Commission's Action Plan, based on a report by the High Level Group of Company Law Experts, has brought company law questions back onto the agenda.[10] Furthermore, the Transparency Directive now addresses, for instance, the possibility of exercising shareholder rights by proxy, and provides for information to be provided by public companies to shareholders in the run-up to a general meeting.[11] However, it can still be seen from the notion of minimum harmonization,[12] the subsidiarity principle (Art. 5 EC), the liberalization of the second Company Law Directive,[13] and the mere use of recommendations,[14] that a comprehensive harmonization of European company law is not to be expected.

A glance at company law in US states may lead to the conclusion that slow or no harmonization need not necessarily be harmful. Despite comparable discussions about uniform company law,[15] in the US there are in principle fifty independent company laws. The regulatory competition of these company law systems, and the model function of the DelGCL and the MBCA, have led, without formal harmonization, to an approximation of state company laws. It remains to be clarified whether the European

[7] See Second Directive 77/91/EEC; Fourth Directive 78/660/EEC.

[8] Otherwise, one gets the misleading impression that between the US and Europe there is increasing divergence (for this result see Carney (1997: 318 *et seq.*)).

[9] For the drafts see OJ C 240, 09.09.1983, p. 2; OJ C 321, 30.11.1991, p. 9.

[10] See Modernising Company Law and Enhancing Corporate Governance in the European Union – A Plan to Move Forward, Communication from the Commission, COM(2003) 284; High Level Group of Company Law Experts (2002); see also Directive 2003/58/EC amending the First Directive 68/151/EEC.

[11] See Art. 17 of the Transparency Directive 2004/109/EC; see also Directive 2007/36/EC for a critical comment see Siems (2005f).

[12] See e.g. Baum (2000: 107 *et seq.*); Drygala (2001: 299).

[13] Directive 2006/68/EC amending Directive 77/91/EEC.

[14] Commission Recommendation fostering an appropriate regime for the remuneration of directors of listed companies, 2004/913/EC; Commission Recommendation on the role of non-executive or supervisory directors of listed companies and on the committees of the (supervisory) board, 2005/162/EC.

[15] See Roe (2003b).

Union will undergo a similar development following the ECJ decisions in *Centros*, *Überseering* and *Inspire Art*, and how that development ought to be assessed.[16]

With respect to US law, it should also be borne in mind that the uniform federal securities law lays down certain minimum standards for the protection of shareholders of public companies. A comparable differentiation between company and securities law also seems to be developing in the EU. Until the late 1990s, European harmonization concerned only minimum standards for some aspects of securities law. However, following the 1998 Financial Services Action Plan (FSAP),[17] there now exists, a comprehensive and detailed web of various directives and regulations on European securities law. This has also led to the creation of the Committee of European Securities Regulators (CESR),[18] which is becoming increasingly influential, and might already be seen as a precursor to a European Securities Commission.

A halfway house to European uniformity are the projects for a uniform accounting law[19] and a uniform European Company (Societas Europaea, SE). The SE, intended in particular to establish a unitary legal form for companies wishing to merge or set up a joint holding company at the European level, is not actually a unitary legal form. Instead, the numerous references to national law create an opaque, legally uncertain hybrid mix of provisions. Therefore, it remains to be seen whether and to what extent the various types of SE will differ and the SE be adopted in practice.[20]

II. Statute law and case law

The general distinctions between civil law and common law legal systems are, first, that civil law is based more on statute and common law more on case law.[21] Secondly, civil law and common law also differ, according to the traditional view, in their style and application of statutory law.[22] In common law countries, legislation is usually very detailed in order to restrict the scope of statutory interpretation to the language of a statute, rejecting arguments based on its intent. Legislation tends accordingly, by

[16] See Ch. 9, sections I. 1, VI. 2; Ch. 12, section II. 1. a below.
[17] See http://ec.europa.eu/internal_market/finances/actionplan/index_en.htm.
[18] See http://www.cesr-eu.org. [19] See Ch. 4, section III.3.b below.
[20] Cf. Enriques (2004a); Siems (2005a).
[21] See e.g. Schulze-Osterloh (2001: 1438); Zweigert and Kötz (1998: 69–70).
[22] See e.g. Ogus (2002: 7); also Ogus (2002: 25) (no convergence); for a criticism see Gordley (2001: 63 *et seq.*); Vogenauer (2001).

contrast with civil law, to be piecemeal and to be neither too general nor too detailed.

For shareholder law, the distinction of 'codification versus case law' is largely superseded. In Europe, it was initially the directives of the EC (now the EU) and the case law of the ECJ that contributed to an approximation. But, more generally too, the codification idea – in continental Europe already realized in the nineteenth century – has in the meantime also made headway in the common law countries. In shareholder law, American and UK judges do not in general have greater room for manoeuvre through the shaping of case law. It has rightly been said about the US that their securities law 'is civilian in spirit' and that 'the American Law Institute has offered a code-like systemization of corporate law in the form of the Corporate Governance Project'.[23] Similarly, with respect to British company law, it has been suggest that, contrary to the cliché, UK judges have less discretion than those on the European continent, since the codification of company law no longer comes about only piecemeal.[24]

There are, however, still differences in legislative style. Company and securities laws in the US and the UK are more detailed than in Germany and France. Yet, on both sides of the Channel or the Atlantic, one nonetheless finds sometimes more detailed and sometimes more general provisions. On the one hand, in Germany and France too the regulatory density in company and securities law is continually on the increase, and the importance of general clauses declining. On the other hand, in the UK there is, for instance, the general-clause-like provision against unfair prejudice to shareholder interests (s. 994 UK-CA), which since it came into force in 1980 has been concretized in case law – using the traditional terminology – in a near continental style.[25] And it is in general not just the wording but increasingly also the purpose and intent of the regulation that are taken into account.[26] Again, despite the absence of binding precedent in civil law countries, case law is by no means (any longer) a purely common law phenomenon. For instance, the case law around the *Holzmüller* and *Gelatine* decisions of the German Federal Court of Justice (BGH) has similarities in style with common law, and in fact has correspondences in the US.[27] Since codified law is by its nature incomplete, an internationally

[23] Hansmann and Kraakman (2001: 459). [24] Davies (1997b: 8).

[25] See e.g. *Re a Company (No. 00709 of 1992)* [1999] 1 WLR 1092 (*O'Neill* v. *Phillips*) (House of Lords); Cheffins (1997: 318, 357–80).

[26] Cf. Cheffins (1997: 355); Kramer (2001: 34 *et seq.*); Vogenauer (2001: 963 *et seq.*).

[27] See Ch. 5, section I.1.d below.

concordant middle way between legally certain codification and room for the courts to manoeuvre has to be found.

Differences also exist within the common law family. The political appointment of judges in the US means that the law there is in general more boldly enlarged than in the UK.[28] Additionally, in the US itself the relationship between legislation and case law is not uniform.[29] The MBCA in particular contains very detailed provisions, in the interests of legal certainty. By contrast, in Delaware the DelGCL has remained more general. This is also connected with the fact that, in the context of regulatory competition, Delaware's attractiveness is decisively enhanced, apart from the legislation, by business-friendly case law.[30]

Globally, the important development is that in most countries Western-style companies legislation has been adopted. Furthermore, case law can also be relevant, as can be demonstrated, for instance, in the similarities between fiduciary duties in the US and Japan.[31] In detail, there is, however, no identity in the extent and pattern of the coexistence of legislation and case law. For instance, it is said of China and Japan that, in applying the law, legal construction takes second place to a more open balancing of interests.[32] Yet this does not mean that case law has a particularly strong position here – although neither is it entirely accurate to assume that there is a general dislike of litigation in Asain countries.[33] For China in particular, there is a common feature with civil law countries to the extent that laws are less detailed and there is no (true) precedent system.[34] The general language of the Chinese Companies Act is, however, only partly based on the reception of German or French law. In the continental legal systems too, today's company law is much more detailed than 'traditional civil law statutes', such as the Civil Codes. What is decisive instead is that in China the detailed rules are set out in the mandatory clauses for articles of association,[35] as well as the guidelines and directives of the Communist Party and the communications and views of government authorities.[36]

[28] See Großfeld (1996: 6); Coffee (1999a: 7).
[29] Cf. Dooley and Goldman (2001: 764 *et seq.*).
[30] See Romano (1993: 39–40); see also Ch. 9, section VI. 1. a below.
[31] See Aronson (2003b).
[32] For Japan, cf. Rahn (1994: 3 *et seq.*); for China, cf. Thümmel (1995: 62–3).
[33] See Ch. 5, section III.1, III.3 below; see also Kanda (2000: 74 *et seq.*).
[34] See Kun Luen Alex Lau (1999: 243); von Senger (1994: 180–1). Nevertheless, decisions of the higher courts may have a special authority; similarly in Japan, see Dean (2002: 135 *et seq.*); Oda (1999: 50 *et seq.*).
[35] See Ch. 2, section III.1 below.
[36] Cf. Comberg (2000: 48); von Senger (1994: 178–9).

As a result, from a formal points of view, the civil law concept of codified law as the primary legal source for shareholder rights has won the day internationally. Yet, convergence in this respect ought not to be overemphasized. First, the notion of a single company-law codification is 'threatened' because in most legal systems many other provisions outside company law affect the joint stock company. For shareholder law, accordingly, substitution phenomena arising particularly out of securities law will have to be included in the discussion below (section III). Secondly, the importance of statute law depends on whether and how far companies are allowed to shape the regulatory framework autonomously through their articles of association or other agreements. When, therefore, a statute deliberately leaves gaps or contains largely default provisions, private arrangements may play an important part at the expense of the statute law (section IV below). The difference between mandatory and default law also appears in connection with law enforcement. Mandatory law leads to *ex ante* monitoring, whereas when the parties have more extensive discretion *ex post* supervision through the courts is more relevant.[37]

III. Company and securities law

Securities law comes into play when a joint stock company participates in the capital market. However, according to some scholars the importance of this area of law differs between countries. In particular, it is said[38] that, in continental Europe and Japan, there are laxer securities laws than in the common law countries, and also that the capital market is thin, illiquid and volatile. By contrast, the US and UK have more developed capital markets and better protection of investors.

These country-specific differences are recognizable even today in reality.[39] Yet, with respect to the law, there is also some convergence. First, a statutory distinction is emerging between public and private companies, which is reflected in special stock exchange and/or securities laws, and also in differences in companies acts themselves.[40] Secondly, supervisory authorities play an important but internationally far from uniform role in monitoring the capital market.[41] Thirdly, non-governmental and

[37] See Ch. 5, section III.3 below.

[38] On the following see Bratton and McCahery (1999: 228); Vagts (2000: para. 10-1); Coffee (1999b: 663); Hill (2000b: 39, 58).

[39] See Ch. 8, section IV below.

[40] See Ch. 1, section II.1 above; Ch. 2, section III.1 below.

[41] See e.g. La Porta *et al.* (2006).

non-statutory regulations also differ according to the activity of the capital market. There may on the one hand be self-regulatory provisions, such as listings regulations or the UK City Code on Takeovers and Mergers. Here, however, the trend is more towards a weakening, since the existing self-regulation is often supplemented in the wake of scandals or perceived problems by a statutory framework. On the other hand, a differentiation comes about *praeter legem*, through capital-market-oriented corporate governance codes or best practice guidelines.[42] For instance, the OECD Principles of Corporate Governance are addressed basically only to publicly traded companies. Only in *ad hoc* cases are they also intended as a useful aid to improving management in other firms.[43] Additionally, for the effective implementation of such codes the pressure of the capital market is decisive.

1. *Comparative overview*

In the nineteenth and early twentieth centuries, the US trusted in the capacity of the stock exchanges for self-regulation.[44] But crisis conditions after the 1929 worldwide economic crash brought the trail-blazing regulation of securities law through the Securities Act 1933 and the Securities Exchange Act 1934. At the same time, a powerful federal authority charged with enforcing investor protection regulations was set up, in the Securities and Exchange Commission (SEC). The SEC is also competent to investigate breaches of law, to monitor stock exchange listing rules and to issue secondary rules. In substance, contrary to many trends in company law in US states, the federal securities law deliberately does not follow a *laissez-faire* approach. Instead, statutory protection of investors is afforded a prominent role, and protection against abuse of power by management is not left solely to the market. Securities law thus does not exclusively serve price efficiency, but is also intended, following the debates in the US on 'managerialism' and 'shareholder democracy movement',[45] to restrain management's power in the interests of investors.

US securities law has constituted a model for a number of other countries, and also for the European Union. In France, securities law is gradually taking shape as a legal discipline in its own right. The primary supervisory body was initially the Commission des Opérations de Bourse

[42] See Ch. 2, section IV.3 below. [43] Preamble OECD-Principles 2004.

[44] Cf. Vagts (2000: para. 10-4); on what follows see Becker (1997b); Cox and Hazen (2003: § 27).

[45] See Ch. 3, section I.2 below.

(COB), set up in 1967. The considerable powers of the COB, expanded further in 1983, 1985, 1989 and 1996, were modelled essentially on the American SEC.[46] Additionally, since 1996 there had been the Conseil des Marchés Financiers (CMF), responsible for drawing up provisions on the regulated market (especially the 'règlement général', Art. L. 622-7 FrCMon). In 2003, the COB, CMF and Conseil de Discipline de la Gestion Financière were brought together under a single authority, and this Autorité des Marchés Financiers (AMF) (cf. Arts. L. 621-1 *et seq.* FrCMon) was given further supervisory powers, notably over investment funds and rating agencies.[47] Beside securities law, in France company law too distinguishes between public companies and other joint stock companies. This applies, first, to the special rules for a joint stock company acting as a public company.[48] But, second, with the 'société par actions simplifiée' (SAS) the French legislature has also taken the opposite path. The SAS was created in 1994, initially for legal persons, as a special form of the joint stock company for holding companies and inter-company cooperations, specifically not allowed to publicly trade shares.[49] Since the 1999 extension, however, private persons too have been able to utilize this simplified form of company, with great freedom of pattern.[50]

UK stock-market law is older in origin than US securities law. The London Stock Exchange (LSE), founded in 1801, was the first stock exchange in the modern sense, organized as a self-regulated entity. Despite developments in the US, the UK long remained faithful to this trust in self-regulation. For instance, takeover law was from the outset regulated through private legislation, the City Code of Takeovers and Mergers. Statutory securities law initially remained underdeveloped as a separate area of law. That changed in 1986, when a package of reform measures (the 'Big Bang') in the Financial Services Act recognized investor protection as a governmental task. Statutory ties were also placed on the Listing Rules, so that the whole came to be seen as a 'self-regulatory regime within a statutory framework'.[51] Yet, at first, the lag behind US developments was great. The concept of self-regulation was only moderately toned down, and the Securities and Investment Board (SIB) not given a position comparable to that of the SEC. This led to 'co-regulation' – still

46 Cf. Vagts (2000: para. 10-7); Fanto (1998: 48); Sonnenberger (1991: para. III 27); Coffee (2001: 49 *et seq.*).

47 Loi n° 2003-706 du 1er août 2003 de sécurité financière.

48 See Ch. 1, section III.1 above. 49 See D. Schmidt (1998: 292–3); Guyon (1998: 302).

50 See Sonnenberger and Autexier (2000: 197); Hartmann (2000).

51 Cf. Cheffins (1997: 364 *et seq.*).

advocated today as a principle.[52] However, in 2000 the Financial Services and Markets Act (FSMA) brought a further reduction in self-regulation. Now, in the Financial Services Authority (FSA) there is a 'super-regulator', upon which responsibility for all financial products and financial-market segments devolves. Competence for listing requirements has been shifted from the LSE to the UK Listing Authority (UKLA), a component of the FSA. The general principle that the investor can protect himself through his own caution ('caveat emptor', 'let the buyer beware') has now been limited in favour of a differentiated approach to the relationship between the market and consumer protection (cf. ss. 2, 5 UK-FSMA).

In Germany too, the development of separate securities law began relatively late. For a long time, the law paid attention only to the joint stock company and the stock exchanges. Not until the 1970s did debate begin about whether 'the investor' and the functionality of the capital market as such should also be protected. Legislation followed only slowly at first. Today, however, the Bundesanstalt für Finanzdienstleistungsaufsicht (BaFin) is the overall financial supervisory body – by contrast with the still decentralized stock exchange supervision – and is (potentially) a very powerful federal authority.[53] BaFin's powers have also been extended to permit it to issue orders for compliance with securities law.[54] Furthermore, the Securities Trading Act (GerWpHG) and the Takeover Act (GerWpÜG) have brought a high level of protection, which has led to a reduction in the existing soft law on insider dealing and takeover law. Finally, a capital market orientation is today integral to the German Companies Act (GerAktG). By contrast with the original GerAktG of 1965, which followed the principle of equal treatment of all joint stock companies, since the 1994 amendment listed and unlisted companies are distinguished.[55] There are also calls for this distinction to be further extended,[56] and for statutory provisions that make no reference in their text to the capital market to be interpreted more onerously when applied to companies offering shares to the public.[57]

[52] See Modern Company Law: Final Report (2001: para. 3.60).

[53] Gesetz über die integrierte Finanzdienstleistungsaufsicht of 25.04.2002, BGBl. I 1310.

[54] Amendment of § 4 GerWpHG by the Gesetz zur Verbesserung des Anlegerschutzes (Anlegerschutzverbesserungsgesetz, AnSVG) of 29.10.2004, BGBl. I 2630.

[55] Gesetzes für kleine Aktiengesellschaften and zur Deregulierung des Aktienrechts of 10.8.1994, BGB1 I 1961; see now §§ 3(3), 20(8), 21(5), 58(2), 67(6), 110(3), 125(1)(s.3), 130(1)(s.2), 134(1), 171(2), 328(3) GerAktG.

[56] See Habersack (2001: 193).

[57] Hommelhoff (2000a: 769); cf. also Lutter (1998b: 376 *et seq.*).

Although stock exchanges were first established in Japan in the late nineteenth century, the actual development of Japanese securities law began under American influence after the Second World War.[58] In 1948, following the US model, the Japanese Securities Exchange Act (JapSEA) was enacted and a Japanese SEC set up. After the end of the American occupation, there was at first a counter-movement against this foreign system, which led in particular to the SEC being made a division of the Finance Ministry. After the mid-1980s, however, the trend began to reverse. Following a series of scandals, the JapSEA was reformed in the interests of investor protection and market efficiency, and an independent capital-market authority, the Securities and Exchange Surveillance Commission (SESC), set up. Today, this is a component of the Financial Services Agency (FSA) as the higher authority, so that there is a parallel here to the UK system. Additionally, the exchanges set certain standards, whereby, for instance, in 1999 the disclosure requirements on the Tokyo Stock Exchange were raised, to follow the example set by the US exchanges.[59]

The situation in China is unusual, in that Chinese law differentiates according to the person of the investor, the origin of the capital and the place a share is traded. This differentiation is, however, in general not made in the Chinese Companies Act (ChinCA) itself,[60] but in regulatory ordinances (cf. § 132 ChinCA) and model articles of association.

The first distinction is by nationality, so that there are different markets for A-shares (domestic investment shares, Renminbi shares) and B-shares (foreign investment shares). The main reason for this distinction is that the state wishes to maintain control over ownership structures in Chinese firms through different market segments with their own circulating capacity. Although, since December 2002, foreign shareholders are no longer barred from buying A-shares, the 2002 Qualified Foreign Institutional Investment (QFII) programme and the 2006 Provisions on Strategic Investment by Foreign Investors tie this to strict requirements. According to the QFII programme, foreign shareholders can only acquire 10 per cent of a firm, must invest the capital in China for one to three years, and can withdraw it thereafter only in stages. It is a further requirement that foreign investors manage at least US$10 billion in assets worldwide,

[58] On the following see Kelemen and Sibbitt (2002: 303 *et seq.*); Marutschke (1999: 226); Baum and Hayakawa (1994: 501, 572, 612); Baum (1997); Vagts (2000: para. 10-70); Kawamoto (1994: 216); Aoki (2001b: 102 *et seq.*); Pistor *et al.* (2002: 863–4).

[59] See Kelemen and Sibbitt (2002: 310–11).

[60] Exceptions: §§ 65, 130(2) ChinCA.

and promise to invest between US$50 and 800 million in China.[61] The 2006 Provisions on Strategic Investment only apply to investments in companies which have been approved by the Ministry of Commerce. The investment has to be at least 10 per cent of the shares and must be invested for at least three years. Apart from that, the requirements are less strict than for QFII schemes. Quotas do not exist, and it is only necessary that investors have at least US$500 million of assets under management.[62]

Secondly, there are H-shares, which can be traded only in Hong Kong. This is intended to embody the 'one country, two systems' principle laid down when Hong Kong was united with the People's Republic of China. Thirdly, A-shares are distinguished according to whether they are held by the state, legal persons or individuals. For example, until recently, there have been restrictions on trading in shares held by the state or by legal persons.[63] Fourthly, there are special rules for Chinese companies listed abroad, such as N-shares or L-shares for shares traded in New York or London respectively. Substantively, here for instance the minimum requirements of the so-called 'Mandatory Provisions in the Articles of Association for Companies Listed Overseas' (ChinMandProv) must be complied with, to encourage trust by foreign investors.

Apart from these unusual distinctions, there is a system of stock exchange and securities law familiar for the Western observer. A 1994 memorandum between China and the US provided that the American SEC would support the central Chinese supervisory body for securities matters (China Securities Regulatory Commission, CSRC) set up in 1992. Chinese personnel were accordingly granted internships at the SEC, and SEC experts organized courses in China and helped to draft new laws.[64] Thus the 1998 and now the 2005 Securities Act and a number of decrees in principle meet international standards.[65] Additionally, the Listing Rules, for instance the 2000 Shanghai Stock Exchange Listing Rules, are similarly oriented to the rules of Western stock exchanges.[66]

Yet there are also differences in the regulation and monitoring of the capital market. On the one hand, the Chinese Companies Act itself contains some provisions, which are closer to securities law than to companies law.[67] On the other hand, substantive and factual differences show a certain scepticism about capital markets. In particular, the listing

[61] See Pißler (2002c); Report in AG 2003, R 114. [62] See Guo (2006).
[63] See Huang (2005: 149–51) and Ch. 4, section I.3.b below.
[64] See Wang (2000: 4). [65] See Gebhardt (1999).
[66] See Liu (2001: 51); Kun Luen Alex Lau (1999).
[67] §§ 86 *et seq.* (on public offer), 121 *et seq.* (on listed companies), 139 (on trading) ChinCA.

requirements are very high, so that the official capital market is largely closed to smaller to medium-sized firms.[68] The exchanges are accordingly dominated by large companies, often still controlled by the state.[69] Moreover, it is questionable whether CSRC supervision is efficient. It is not uncommonly said that, for instance, in China there is no disciplining of management through the capital market, transparency is second-rate and sham accounts are overlooked by the CSRC.[70]

2. *Conclusions*

Increasingly, securities law is becoming a separate area of law distinct from company law. There also follows the widespread distinction between the 'investor' and the 'shareholder',[71] with the consequence for this monograph on 'shareholder law' that securities law could perhaps be left out of the discussion. Such a sharp distinction between these areas of law is not, however, be followed in this monograph. Particularly for comparative law, it cannot in principle matter whether a special law for public companies is formally located in company law or securities law. It would be different only if the capital-market reference had no place in company law and the latter concentrated exclusively on the internal structure of the company. But this is countered by the fact that the law of joint stock companies serves specifically to attract capital and is accordingly connected with basic ideas of securities law.[72] Shareholder protection within the company and on the capital market are therefore closely related.

All the same, it is important to differentiate between company law and securities law because company law, despite the overlaps, has a different focus in substance. It is often discussed whether the purpose of securities law lies solely in providing functional capital markets, or whether it is also to be seen as a protection for individual investors.[73] However, there is no reason why functional protection through the capital market should

[68] Cf. Wang (2000: 6); Leung *et al.* (2002: 5, 8 *et seq.*); for a brief comparative overview of listing requirements see Hertig *et al.* (2004: 209–10).

[69] Cf. Wang (2000: 2), and Ch. 8, section IV.2 below.

[70] See Handelsblatt, 07.08.2003, at 25; 19.09.2003, at 26; see also Heilmann (2001a: 30), (2001b: 6 *et seq.*).

[71] See Vagts (2000: para. 10-19).

[72] See Coffee (1999b: 669–70); Vagts (2000: para. 10-1); Licht (1998: 249).

[73] Cf. Merkt (2001b: 105, 296 *et seq.*); Hommelhoff (2000a: 771–2); Zimmer (1996: 40 *et seq.*); Escher-Weingart (2001: 179 *et seq.*); Heiser (2000: 66 *et seq.*); Mülbert (1996a: 112); Möllers (1997: 337, 340).

exclude protection for individual shareholders. Rather, a dual function suggests itself, because on the one hand the functionality of the market conditions investor protection, but on the other investors are induced by the legal protection to make investments, so that this protection is indispensable to an efficient market. Individual protection and institutional protection thus constitute a 'system of communicating tubes'.[74] Still, shareholder protections through company law and through securities law have differing orientations. Securities law serves to protect the assets of the investor, while company law by contrast has its focus sometimes on shareholder participation in the firm and sometimes on the share as an investment.[75] This distinction can also be evidenced by the different rules on conflicts of law, because in general in company law the place of the seat is decisive whereas in securities law in general the main focus is on the place of the relevant capital market.[76] In contrast, there is no clear differentiation brought by the temporal distinction that securities law would cover only purchase and sale of the share and company law only the time in between.[77] For securities law also covers the shareholder's decision deliberately *not* to sell his investment. Thus, securities law may also constitute cumulative or alternative protection to company law for the duration of the shareholding.

One likely major reason for the advance of securities law across countries is that legislatures, in the interests of the overall economy, wish to meet undertakings' need for capital. Economic studies indicate that the development of capital and financial markets promotes economic growth.[78] Additionally, at international level the model effect, or the pressure, of particular countries (notably the US) has been decisive. However, in view of the differences that nonetheless persist, it will still be necessary to clarify whether and to what extent convergence forces will lead to a further approximation of laws.[79] Much the same applies to the factual area, since despite the internationally increasing popularity of investment in shares, such matters as the influence of supervisory authorities, the

[74] Hopt (1975: 52) ('System kommunizierender Röhren'); see also Licht (1998: 264) ('in a healthy and functioning legal system they must be balanced and coherent with each other').

[75] See also Ch. 3, section I below.

[76] On conflict of laws see Ch. 8, section III.4. c; Ch. 9, section I.1.a below.

[77] But cf. Vagts (2000: para. 10-19).

[78] See Ruffner (2000: 144 *et seq.*, 397 *et seq.*); Walker (2001: 445).

[79] See Ch. 7, section III.2 below.

actual enforcement of law,[80] and the importance of the capital market in general are far from uniform.[81]

The acceptance of securities law has led to a double or even a triple subdivision of law connected with joint stock companies.[82] For listed companies or those otherwise selling shares to the public, by contrast with other companies, other legal bases in addition to the companies acts are applicable. Alongside securities laws, these are the exchanges' admission rules, which are today, however, mostly not based on free competition among exchanges as self-regulators, but are rather embedded in statutory law.[83] Additionally, the question whether participants themselves ought to be permitted to regulate independently their own interests may be answered differently for these different types of joint stock companies.

IV. Self-regulation and state regulation

The division between self- and state regulation is not uniform internationally. For example, accounting in the US and takeover law in the UK are delegated to private organizations (the FASB and the Takeover Panel, respectively), whereas in other countries these regulatory areas are reserved to statutory law. Across the board, it is the articles of association (subsection 1 below), shareholder agreements (subsection 2 below) and corporate governance codes (subsection 3 below) that come into consideration. Here too, however, the extent of self-regulation depends on how far the state allows room for this. Yet, despite national differences, overriding trends can be discerned.

1. Articles of association

Since different types of companies need different corporate governance structures, regulation in the articles of association is in principle possible, and a distinction is often made between mandatory and default statutory law. Yet differences exist. This subsection will look at the theoretical arguments in favour of regulation primarily by statute but also through

[80] See e.g. on the differences between the US and Japan: Kelemen and Sibbitt (2002: 312) (personnel); West (1999: 783) (enforcement); Henderson (1995: 906) (divergence between law in books and law in practice in Japan).

[81] Cf. generally Vagts (2000: para. 10-3); see also Ch. 8, section IV below.

[82] See also Vagts (2000: para. 10-1); High Level Group of Company Law Experts (2002: 35) (distinction between listed companies, open companies and close companies).

[83] For a critical view see Mahoney (1997).

articles of association, as this reveals some general insights on regulatory approaches in company law.

a) The academic debate

Contractual theories today see a basis for the joint stock company primarily in the articles of association. Although contractual theories were around even earlier,[84] it was only in the second half of the twentieth century, with the neo-classical theory of the Chicago School and the economic analysis of law, that they were elevated into an unambiguous demand for deregulation. According to this theory, the company is nothing but a 'nexus-of-contracts',[85] so that statutory provisions are desirable only as default rules. This can reduce transaction costs and thus suit the hypothetical will of the parties, which is all that counts.

The main focus of this theory is not, however, on classifying the legal bases of the joint stock company, but rather on its function as a market theory, trusting in principle to the market's ability to resolve problems. Market forces, together with the ability to draft the articles to suit the circumstances, are said to lead, even without statutory control, to a highly efficient and at the same time flexible solution, since securities prices ideally reflect immediately and completely all (publicly) available information (the 'efficient capital market hypothesis').[86] Nor does this lead to an unfair privileging of management at the expense of shareholders (the 'principal–agent problem').[87] Even without internal restraints, abuse is prevented because management is monitored by external markets – in particular the capital market, the takeover market, the market for incorporations and the market in managers.

Yet, on the prevailing view, this does not imply complete *laissez faire.* On the one hand, state intervention is necessary if a market is inefficient, since only efficient markets would be subject to no regulation (the so-called 'nirvana fallacy').[88] On the other hand, utilitarian concepts are often taken to imply that the primacy of contract and the market applies

[84] See e.g. Foster (2000: 596 *et seq.*); Grantham (1998: 582 note 175).

[85] See e.g. Easterbrook and Fischel (1991); Jensen and Mecking (1976); Fama (1980); Fama and Jensen (1983); Coase (1937); cf. also Ferran (1999: 10 *et seq.*, 133); Cheffins (1997: 31 *et seq.*, 264 *et seq.*).

[86] See e.g. Klein and Coffee (2002: 398 *et seq.*); Cheffins (1997: 55 *et seq.*); Vagts (2000: para. 10-4); on the distinction between strong, semi-strong and weak forms of efficiency see Fama (1970).

[87] Jensen and Meckling (1976); Fama (1980); Fama and Jensen (1983); see also e.g. Hansmann and Kraakman (2004: 21 *et seq.*).

[88] See Ruffner (2000: 350).

only where no participant is worse off than before, and at least one better off. Statutory regulation is accordingly necessary particularly in cases of asymmetric distribution of information, since here one party cannot evaluate the disadvantageous effects of the contract.[89] The 'strict contract theory', however, sees this as unwarranted paternalistic interference with contractual freedom. An efficient market can, it is claimed, evaluate articles of association, including possible subsequent amendments thereby adjusting the share price. Even if market deficiencies were to arise here, this would not justify any restriction on the freedom to contract. A less drastic recourse would be, for example, to prevent abuse through qualified majorities or appraisal rights.

Counter-views start first by attacking the theoretical foundations of the contractual theory. The concept of contract is said not to apply to public companies, since here the components of the contract are not negotiated, but as a rule the investor rather regards the share as a fixed product.[90] It may accordingly be preferable to use other theories to stress the special, statutorily fixed nature of the joint stock company. It is, for instance, said that the company is an institution, fiction or real person,[91] and the articles too constitute not a simple contract but (at least also) an objective rule.[92] Moreover, a company is more than just the combination of its several components, so the importance of hierarchical organization[93] or of the enterprise ('as such')[94] is not adequately grasped by contractual theories.

Secondly, the (strictly) market-oriented view that a functioning capital market needs no mandatory legal rules is disputed. Mandatory provisions of company law lead to a standardization of the share, so that time-consuming and costly negotiation of contractual elements becomes unnecessary and trade in shares is promoted.[95] The same is true of mandatory securities law, if it ensures that investors can rely on common sets of disclosure provisions.[96] Mandatory provisions thus both protect the

[89] Cf. Romano (1993: 86 *et seq.*, 110–11); Simmonds (2001: 514).

[90] Cf. Grantham (1998: 579 *et seq.*); Foster (2000: 585).

[91] Cf. generally e.g. Foster (2000: 581 *et seq.*, 601 *et seq.*), (2006: 300–1); Worthington (2001b: 263, 308); Ferran (1999: 9 *et seq.*); Merle (2005: para. 75).

[92] See e.g. Noack (1994: 106–7); Escher-Weingart (2001: 210).

[93] Eisenberg (1999) ('dual nature'). [94] See Ch. 5, section II.1.a below.

[95] See Schäfer and Ott (2000: 609).

[96] Coffee (1999b: 694) ('As issuers conform to common disclosure, accounting and listing standards, investors gain the ability to compare securities in a common language and scoring system').

market against unfair competition from low-price offerings and also promote investor trust at a psychological level.

Thirdly, according to the counter-view, the principal–agent problem argues against purely default rules. Linking up with the views of Adolf Berle and Gardiner Means, shareholders in public companies with dispersed ownership structures are said to be largely powerless.[97] Since management does not need to fear controlling shareholders, they may hoard more cash than necessary in order to increase their independence from capital markets.[98] Furthermore, management may act to enhance their personal prosperity or satisfy their personal ambition, so that they may, for instance, seek expansion at the expense of profitability.[99] This cannot be prevented through market forces alone, since share prices are not totally rational and direct constraints on conduct might in any case be more efficient.[100] Mandatory law is therefore said to be necessary in order to prevent abuses of power. The same applies in the case of a company whose ownership is not dispersed so that the separation of ownership and control is not the main problem. Since majority shareholders can then control both the general meeting and the management, there is no efficient division of powers within the company, so that the position of minority shareholders is endangered.

Fourthly and finally, it is objected that, with a contractual conception and a pure play of market forces, general public interests, such as social justice, may suffer.[101] Additionally, the interests of other stakeholders in firms, such as employees or creditors, might necessitate mandatory regulations.[102]

b) Comparative overview

Although theoretical stances are rare in legislation,[103] in individual countries the preferences for one of the two concepts can be discerned. Yet one should beware of any schematic subdivision of legal families. This can be seen even from an historical perspective. Previously, in both common law and civil law countries the pattern of the law of joint stock companies was left exclusively or at least mainly to their articles of association.[104] Not

[97] Berle and Means (1932). [98] On the 'free-cash-flow problem' see Jensen (1986).
[99] On the 'empire-building problem' see Roe (2003a: 9); Klein and Coffee (2002: 174); Ruffner (2000: 218, 222–3, 233).
[100] See Assmann (2003: 10–1). [101] See e.g. Grantham (1998: 579 *et seq.*).
[102] Cf. e.g. Escher-Weingart (2001: 64, 105); Spindler (1998: 71 *et seq.*).
[103] But for Australia see Hill (2000b: 56); Ellett (2000: 174).
[104] Cf. Horn (1979: 138); see also Ch. 1, section III.2, above.

until the mid-nineteenth century was there a growth of statutory law, in which, however, differences arose that can still be seen today.

German law takes the starting-point that the law of joint stock companies is mandatory (§ 23(5) GerAktG). Exceptions to this principle of restrictive freedom to contract out of statutory company law ('Satzungsstrenge') can only be done by an explicit provision to that effect in statutory law. The room for manoeuvre in German law ought not, however, to be underestimated. Thus, one commentator from the US notes with surprise that German company law is astonishingly flexible as regards shareholder influence.[105] And the long-dominant regulatory trend in Germany has in recent times been exposed to a notable counter-tendency.[106] Additionally, certain tendencies to relax the rules can be found in the case law.[107] In the literature, moreover, *de lege lata* a broader interpretation of § 23(5) GerAktG is advocated,[108] and *de lege ferenda* a continuation of deregulation called for. It should, however, be noted that these calls, as well as current trends in legislation, relate mainly only to small companies and company law provisions on the use of new media and corporate finance.[109] There is therefore no general reduction in mandatory regulations in company law.

The starting-point for the law on the Societas Europaea is based on the German model of restrictive freedom to contract out of statutory company law. Art. 9(1)(b) of the SE Regulation allows provision through the articles only where the Regulation explicitly allows this. Nonetheless, in contrast to German law, for the SE a choice is available between a monistic and a dualistic structure (Art. 38 SE-Reg). Moreover, the SE provisions allow national legislatures relatively broad discretion. Thus, by virtue of the provisions (particularly Arts. 9(1)(c), 53 SE-Reg) referring to national law, it is possible for Member States to refrain from mandatory introducing any provisions beyond those established in the SE Regulation.

[105] Gordon (1999: 233 *et seq.*).

[106] Gesetz für kleine Aktiengesellschaften und zur Deregulierung des Aktienrechts of 02.08.1994, BGBl. I 1961; Gesetz zur Namensaktie und zur Erleichterung der Stimmrechtsausübung (NaStraG) of 18.01.2001, BGBl. I 123; Transparenz- und Publizitätsgesetz (TransPuG) of 19.07.2002, BGBl. I 2681; Gesetz zur Kontrolle und Transparenz im Unternehmensbereich (KonTraG) of 27.04.1998, BGBl. I 786.

[107] E.g. BGH, BGHZ 136, 133 (*Siemens/Nold*); see also Ch. 5, section II.2.b below.

[108] See Hirte (1998), (2000: 289); Hopt (1998a: 144).

[109] On small companies see e.g. Spindler (1998); Group of German Experts on Corporate Law (2002: 6); on the new media see e.g. Spindler (2000: 445); Fleischhauer (2001); on corporate finance see Ch. 4, section I.4, II.4.a; Ch. 5, section I.1.d, II.2.b below.

In France, the legal bases for the joint stock company address both its institutional and its contractual aspects (Art. 1832 Code Civil ('instituée'; 'contrat'); Art. L. 235-1 FrCCom ('contrat')). There is no explicit general statement in French company law on mandatory or default law. However, it is assumed that statutory company law, in order to protect both shareholders and third parties, constitutes an in principle comprehensive regulation, leaving scarcely any room for contractual freedom.[110] As in Germany, however, in France too it is possible to discern a countermovement, relating in particular to small companies and the use of new media. To be sure, the reform programmes in France (Rapport Marini; Rapports Viénot; Rapport Bouton)[111] also go beyond this. The Marini Report, for instance, says that the role of company law is not so much to forbid as to enable.[112] There is, therefore, in France a renewed reflection on the contractual roots of the joint stock company.[113]

In US states too, the first companies acts consisted predominantly of mandatory rules, because joint stock companies came close to public organizations in exercising quasi-governmental functions.[114] That changed at the end of the nineteenth century when, *inter alia* with the regulatory competition for founders,[115] a clear deregulation trend became apparent in a number of states. However, here too the outcome was a differentiated legal position. First, not all states prefer deregulated legislation for shareholder law. For instance, one major jurisdiction, California, has deliberately decided against participating in the 'deregulation race'. Secondly, no state has adopted the wholly *laissez-faire* approach of 'anything goes', and even in Delaware there are mandatory rules and a debate on whether the predominant aspect of company law is its mandatoriness.[116] Thirdly, in some states mandatory 'blue-sky laws' lay down substantive requirements to protect investors.[117] Although these acts mostly involve securities regulations, such as the admissibility of issues, or trade in securities, nevertheless they sometimes also contain company-law provisions, such as voting rules, 'by the back door'. Fourthly, mandatory federal law,

110 Cf. Bastian and Germain (1972: para. 30.10.4); D. Schmidt (1998: 291 *et seq.*); Guyon (1998: 297 *et seq.*).

111 Cf. e.g. Merle (2005: para. 248); Omar (2001); Guyon (1998: 299).

112 Rapport Marini (1996: 8) ('Son rôle est moins d'interdire que de permettre').

113 M. Ulmer (1998: 128 *et seq.*).

114 Cf. Cox and Hazen (2003: § 12.04), and Ch. 1, section III.3.a above.

115 See Ch. 9, section I.1, VI.1.a below.

116 Cf. Eisenberg (1989: 1481–2).

117 Cf. Romano (1993: 108 *et seq.*); Cox and Hazen (2003: §§ 27.02 *et seq.*); Hertig *et al.* (2004: 207–8) (also discussing 'merit regulation' in other countries).

particularly federal securities laws and penal sanctions,[118] play an important role. There are, for instance, provisions on disclosure, insider dealing and takeover bids which limit the freedom of manoeuvre of listed companies. But federal securities law does not stop there. Particular rules also apply to other companies, in which more than 500 shareholders participate.[119] Similarly, securities law goes beyond its general technical area of application: for instance, SEC Rule 14a, with its exhaustive provisions on voting by proxy, mandatorily settles matters which in other legal systems, being provisions on convoking the general meeting, would belong to company law.[120] Much the same applies to the 2002 Sarbanes–Oxley Act and the new listing requirements of the NYSE, which, despite being regulations of securities and stock exchange law, contain many rules for the corporate governance of public companies, with the result that they considerably restrict the freedom to contract out of statutory law and establish a very high regulatory level. On the whole, therefore, for the US too, commentators have spoken of a 'differentiating opinion', a 'motley collection', and a 'mixed system'.[121] And similar to other countries, public companies are allowed less room for manoeuvre than private companies.

Likewise, in the United Kingdom, companies originally had relatively great freedom in the regulation of their own affairs. This can be seen in, for instance, the fact that the powers of the general meeting, on the continent usually laid down by law,[122] used to be contained only in the articles of association. However, since 1948, a general trend towards increasingly mandatory law can be noted.[123] This was further enhanced by the influence of EU directives, which lay down a basic standard of mandatory law. By way of a counter-movement, however, as in Germany and France, less onerous rules are becoming increasingly common for private companies.[124]

Japanese company law, following its German model, originally consisted predominantly of mandatory provisions.[125] Since the Second World War, however, the proportion of default rules has been increasing,[126] so that here too there is a mixed legal position. In recent years, this has led, as in other countries, to a liberalization of the company law provisions

[118] See Romano (1993: 112 *et seq.*). [119] For details see § 12(g) US-SEA.
[120] See Ch. 4, section II.3.c below.
[121] Hopt (1998a: 125); Vagts (1998: 289–90); Gordon (1989: 1554).
[122] See Ch. 5, section I.1.a below.
[123] Cf. Davies (1999: 344); Cheffins (1997: 252 with note 176).
[124] In particular the Companies Acts 1989 and 2006. [125] See Shishido (1997: 160).
[126] Cf. West (2001a: 596); Ködderitzsch (2001b: 143); Oda (2002: 8 *et seq.*).

on corporate finance.[127] Additionally, companies now have the option to choose either the existing 'European' management system for a company or a new 'American' one,[128] and may establish classes of shares at will through definitions in the articles of association.[129] The JapCA 2005 confirmed these changes. The Act's approach is, on the one hand, highly regulatory, containing almost 1,000 provisions. On the other hand, the Act distinguishes between small and large companies, and between restricted-share-transfer and publicly-held companies (§ 2(5), (6) JapCA), and grants the former types of companies more freedom.

In China, the law is rather restrictive by international comparison. First, the provisions of company law are predominantly mandatory, in order to standardize the organization and activities of companies (§ 1 ChinCA). Secondly, there are detailed mandatory specimen articles of association for listed companies. For companies listed on a domestic exchange, the Guide to Articles of Association of Companies Limited by Shares (ChinArticles) apply. For companies listed abroad, the provisions of the Mandatory Provisions in the Articles of Association for Companies Listed Overseas (ChinMandProv) must be complied with. Thirdly, the Chinese Corporate Governance Code contributes to a further restriction of drafting freedom. By contrast with most other countries' codes, in China some provisions are obligatory preconditions for a domestic stock exchange listing.[130] However, there are also a number of indicators of a certain flexibility in Chinese company law. The ChinCA is often not particularly exhaustive, and application of its provisions is often unclear, failing practice, so that mandatory provisions are blunted. Moreover, a certain pragmatism in applying the law can be discerned. For instance, the courts can waive the nullity of a particular act if this is appropriate for economic development and the development of the socialist market economy or for the maintenance of proper economic order.[131]

c) Conclusions

The legal systems dealt with here do not clearly follow either of the two theories mentioned above. Instead, despite some differences, there is a common mixture of articles of association and mandatory and default

[127] See Ch. 4, section I.4, II.4.a; Ch. 5, section I.1.d, II.2.b below.

[128] See Janssen *et al.* (2002: 267); Hashimoto (2002: 10 *et seq.*); see also Ch. 5, section II.1.b below.

[129] See Ch. 3, section II below.

[130] See Pißler (2002b: 11); for codes from other countries see Ch. 2, section IV.3 below.

[131] Cf. Thümmel (1995: 62–3); on legal culture see also Ch. 8, section II below.

rules, such that it is not possible to speak of major differences in legal culture, rooted deep in the legal system or in modes of thought.[132] Mandatory statutory law guarantees the maintenance of a certain level of protection, within which adjustment of the articles of association is allowed. This is true for the US too, despite, for instance, the closeness of Delaware company law to the contract theory.[133] It has therefore rightly been said that elaborate economic theories have had no direct influence here, and that the present law is instead explicable historically.[134]

Similarities can also be seen in the fact that, by contrast with public companies, small companies have more freedom in drafting their articles of association. This is not a matter of course. While shareholders in public companies have more possibility of negotiating for their own benefit, they nonetheless lack a secondary market on which they can sell their shares without further ado, so that many areas of minority protection are concerned specifically with such companies. Moreover, it is not possible to draw the conclusion from the various deregulation trends that deregulation of company law, along with regulation of securities law, is coming about.[135] In spite of increasing regulation of the capital market, a general trend towards deregulation can be seen only in specific areas of company law.

Irrespective of these similarities, there are differences in the extent of the mandatoriness of the law. Several influencing factors are decisive here. First, regulatory competition in the US strongly enhances the flexibility of states' company laws. This is not refuted by the fact that for large companies Delaware today holds an almost monopolistic position, so that no real competition may in practice exist.[136] As the example of New Jersey's company law around 1910 shows,[137] a previously desirable – for its flexibility – jurisdiction may very well lose its importance because of a shift to restrictive regulations. Secondly, the relative differences in shareholder structures in the US and the UK on the one hand and continental Europe on the other should be noted.[138] In continental Europe the concentrated shareholdings make the majorities necessary for amendments of the articles of association easier to attain than with the fragmented ownership structures in the US and UK. The greater degree of mandatoriness of the law, as well as the higher majority thresholds,[139] on the continent can

[132] Contra M. Ulmer (1998: 127–8). [133] Roe (1996b: 245).
[134] Meier-Schatz (1991: 72–3). [135] Contra Escher-Weingart (2001: 174, 186–7).
[136] Contra West (2001a: 597). [137] Cf. Papmehl (2002: 215–16); Gelter (2004: 174).
[138] See Ch. 8, section IV below. [139] See Ch. 5, section I.2.a below.

accordingly be seen as compensation for the greater freedom to contract out of statutory company law in other legal systems, so that here too the conduct of business remains in the hands of management. Thus, legal *ex ante* protection can be less where, as in the US, more value is placed on protection *ex post*.[140] And the *de facto* greater importance of the capital market in the US, and the UK may be a surrogate for mandatory law, if the clauses of the company's articles are thereby subjected to the price and testing mechanisms of the capital market or shareholders have a greater ability to sell their shares.[141] Finally, legal-cultural considerations may play a part. Thus, stricter law, as in Japan or China, may well look different in legal reality, if enforcement is less strict than in other countries.[142]

2. *Shareholder agreements*

Even where mandatory law forbids a particular provision in the articles of association, in many countries an agreement among shareholders purely under the law of contract remains possible. The relevance of such shareholder agreements is less debated than that of articles of association. This may be connected with the fact that the effects of shareholder agreements start to bite only once legal disputes over their enforcement develop. It is therefore not surprising that, in Japan and China, the depth of discussion of shareholder agreements is less, since in those countries legal disputes are, at least traditionally, less common than in other legal systems.[143]

Shareholder agreements are addressed only sporadically in EU law, and also often not codified in Member States, but rather are left to practice and dogmatics.[144] For instance, the Transparency Directive merely mentions agreements about voting rights.[145] One cannot, however, deduce from this the implicit admissibility of such agreements, since it merely links the transparency of major shareholders with factual circumstances without approving these Europe-wide.

However, in most European countries shareholder agreements are permitted. This is true particularly where, as for instance in Germany and the UK, it is stressed that only general contractual rules apply to

[140] See Ch. 5, section II.2.c, III below.
[141] Cf. Ruffner (2000: 158); Romano (1993: 45 *et seq.*).
[142] See also e.g. Ch. 2, section III.1 above; Ch. 4, section II.2; Ch. 6, section III below.
[143] See Ch. 5, section III below; for Japan see West (2001a: 550) (voting agreements possible).
[144] Werlauff (2003b: 207 *et seq.*). [145] Art. 10 of Directive 2004/109/EC.

shareholder agreements.[146] This has, to be sure, been criticized,[147] and is not consistently followed. For instance, according to UK case law, a unanimous informal agreement of all shareholders can legally be equated with a resolution of the general meeting.[148] For unanimous shareholder agreements, there may also be an obligation to make them public by forwarding them to the registrar of companies (ss. 29(1)(b), (c), 30 UK-CA). In both Germany and the UK, agreements on shareholder voting rights are in principle possible.[149] A fundamental cultural difference – whereby in the UK the right to cast a vote is allegedly a freely alienable property right, whereas in continental Europe the emphasis is more on protecting the interests of the company and the general body of shareholders[150] – can accordingly not be discerned.

In France by contrast, the reference to contractual freedom is not regarded as decisive. It is instead said that agreements outside the articles would interfere with the 'ordre public' of company law.[151] Here too, though, a trend can be noted increasingly to accept such agreements, which are playing a growing role in practice.[152] Thus, agreements among shareholders on purchase options are in principle permissible.[153] Agreements on voting rights were originally largely prohibited, so that after debate at the general meeting the shareholder could opt freely for a position.[154] More recently, however, a relaxation of this position has become evident, and according to the case law voting agreements are, under particular conditions (notably, temporal and substantive limitations), valid.[155] A general definitive statement on the legality of shareholder agreements is, however, not yet possible for France.

In the US, by contrast, agreements among shareholders are largely permissible. This is true, first, for voting agreements, which are valid, and in most states are subject to no restrictions (e.g. § 7.31 MBCA; § 218

146 See Stedman and Jones (1998: 57, 63); Xuereb (1989: 26 *et seq.*); for Germany cf. Noack (1994: 63).

147 Noack (1994).

148 Stedman and Jones (1998: 59 *et seq.*). Similarly, in Germany it is possible that an agreement by all shareholders can be of consequence for the company: see BGH, NJW 1983, 1910; Noack (1994: 162 *et seq.*).

149 For Germany see RG, RGZ 133, 90; 158, 248; BGH, BGHZ 48, 163; Rodemann (1998: 24 *et seq.*); for the UK: Xuereb (1989: 101–2); Rodemann (1998: 327 *et seq.*).

150 Xuereb (1989: 101), (1989); on limits on voting rights see Ch. 5, section II.2.a below.

151 See D. Schmidt (1998: 293 *et seq.*); Guyon (1998: 305 *et seq.*).

152 See Merle (2005: para. 58).

153 See Merle (2005: para. 326); Dalloz (2005: Art. L. 228-23 paras. 18 *et seq.*).

154 Cf. Rodemann (1998: 180 *et seq.*); Sonnenberger and Autexier (2000: 190).

155 See Guyon (1998: 306–7).

DelGCL). Only in a few states is there, for instance, a requirement that – in accordance with the provisions on voting trusts – agreements are valid for only ten years and must be deposited at the seat of the company.[156] For private companies, moreover, agreements among the shareholders which modify statutory provisions are also permissible (e.g. § 7.32 MBCA). These may, for instance, govern the exercise of corporate powers, the management of the business of the corporation, or the relationship among shareholders, directors and the corporation, unless it is contrary to public policy (§ 7.32(a)(8) MBCA).

Summarizing, then, at an individual level shareholders can in principle conclude agreements. Since by now the largely private utility of the joint stock company is acknowledged,[157] it is consistent for shareholders to be able freely to decide whether and how far they wish to exercise their rights. This is of importance particularly to shareholders in unlisted companies. Since for them selling the shares may be difficult for legal or practical reasons,[158] it may be necessary to ensure for oneself further protection through the articles of association or contractual agreements.

3. *Corporate governance codes*

Although the development of 'best practice guidelines', 'codes of conduct', 'corporate governance principles' and 'corporate governance codes' is not a new phenomenon,[159] it seems recently to have been growing in dynamism. This is true, first, of the guidelines from international organizations, particularly in the present connection the OECD Principles of Corporate Governance.[160] Secondly, a variety of other interest groups, working groups and companies themselves draw up principles that *praeter legem* guarantee compliance with particular standards of conduct.

In Europe, corporate governance codes began to make headway initially in the UK. After scandals in the early 1990s, historical tradition led to a decision to adopt self-regulation. This was also in the interest of the business community, as it gave them a say in the content of the codes. Subsequently, the Cadbury, Greenbury and Hampel Committees drafted various documents,[161] which were finally amalgamated into the

[156] See Cox and Hazen (2003: §§ 14.03 *et seq.*). [157] See Ch. 1, section III.2, 3 above.
[158] See Ch. 4, section I.3.c, d below. [159] See Kolk (1999).
[160] See Ch. 2, section I.1 above.
[161] Committee on the Financial Aspects of Corporate Governance, *Report of the Committee on the Financial Aspects of Corporate Governance*, 1992 (Cadbury Report); Study Group on Directors' Remuneration, *Directors' Remuneration: Report of a Study Group Chaired by Sir Richard Greenbury*, 1995 (Greenbury Report); Committee on Corporate Governance, *Report of the Committee on Corporate Governance*, 1997 (Hampel Report).

Combined Code of Best Practice. Today, this Combined Code is being further developed by the Financial Reporting Council (FRC), a private institution, which can however act without competitive pressure.[162] It is of importance particularly for listed companies. While the Combined Code is not a requirement or a formal component of the Listing Rules – but is, in principle, to be assessed by shareholders themselves[163] – it is attached to the Listing Rules as an annex and therefore obliges companies listed on the London Stock Exchange to make a statement in their financial reports, stating whether, or to what extent, they comply with it ('comply or explain'). Moreover, since institutional investors frequently insist on compliance with the Combined Code,[164] there is considerable pressure not only to give such a statement but to follow it *in toto*.

There are now corporate governance codes also in France, Belgium, Spain, the Netherlands, Italy, Germany, the US, South Africa, Canada, Japan, China and Hong Kong, among others. For the European Union, a study has shown that the various codes display a notably high degree of commonality.[165] But there are also differences in pattern, importance, enforcement and language. Since these differentiations are beyond the scope of this study and there are good summaries available electronically,[166] I will here[167] merely consider the US and Germany by way of example.

In the US, by contrast with the UK, there is no uniform nationally recognized corporate governance code. Such codes are instead mostly drawn up by the companies themselves[168] and by institutional investors. However, the principles of influential institutional investors like the California Public Employees' Retirement System (CalPERS), investor associations like the Council of Institutional Investors, or the Business Roundtable, an association of American CEOs, have the power to affect business practice in the US generally.[169] Moreover, the NYSE's rules now require every company listed on the NYSE to publish a code of business conduct and

162 For criticism see Ferran (2001: 390 *et seq.*).

163 Preamble point 4, UK Combined Code.

164 Davies (2001: 278–9); see also Cheffins (1997: 645); for criticism, see MacNeil and Li (2006).

165 See Modernising Company Law and Enhancing Corporate Governance in the European Union – A Plan to Move Forward, Communication from the Commission, COM(2003) 284, at 11, 17.

166 E.g. http://www.icgn.org; http://www.ecgi.org; http://europa.eu.int/comm/internal_market/company/docs/corpgov/corp-gov-codes-rpt-part1_en.pdf.

167 But see also Ch. 7, section III.3; Ch. 12, section II.3 below.

168 E.g. http://www.gm.com/company/investor_information/corp_gov/ guidelines.html.

169 Cf. http://www.ecgi.org/codes/all_codes.php#USA; http://www.businessroundtable.org.

ethics and corporate governance guidelines on its website (§§ 303A.09-10 NYSE Manual). As with the UK's Combined Code, the company must make it clear whether it follows a code or – if this is not the case – give an explanation of why this is not the case (§ 406 Sarbanes–Oxley Act 2002).

Developments in Germany began relatively late. Towards the late 1990s, various initiative groups[170] and individual firms began to draw up corporate governance principles. A German Corporate Governance Code was established in 2002, which like the UK's Combined Code brings together some basic recommendations for good corporate governance. Listed companies must state publicly whether and to what extent they comply with the code.[171] Empirical research has found a high level of Code conformity.[172]

This transnational trend in corporate governance codes might at first seem surprising. It has in fact been stated in the literature that corporate governance codes are typical of laxer company law regimes in common law countries, since firms there are given greater discretion in structuring their management and governance.[173] The apparent success of these codes could accordingly be explained by a trend towards deregulation in the civil law countries, were the law there too is beginning to develop in the direction of Anglo-American *laissez-faire*. This notion, however, clashes with the facts that no general deregulation trend exists, and that the differences in the strictness of the law are not as unambiguous as they might seem.[174] The reason for the current trend is thus to be seen primarily in the internationalization of capital markets and of investors.[175] International investors active on the capital market expect foreign firms to furnish reliable information concerning what principles determine the management and governance of the company. Moreover, through this pressure they also influence the content of codes, so that there ought also to be convergence of the codes themselves.

Yet it should not be overlooked that this picture may change. For instance, in most countries self-regulation of stock exchanges has over time given way to a statutory framework. In the US too, following the

[170] See e.g. the Corporate-Governance-Grundsätze of the 'Grundsatzkommission Corporate Governance' (Frankfurter Initiativkreis) AG 2000, 109 *et seq.*; German Code of Corporate Governance of the 'Berliner Initiativkreis' DB 2000, 1573 *et seq.*

[171] § 161 GerAktG; §§ 285, 314(1)(no.8) GerHGB, § 325 GerAktG.

[172] Werder *et al.* (2005).

[173] Schulze-Osterloh (2001: 1436); see also Erhardt and Nowak (2002: 342).

[174] See Ch. 2, section IV.1.b above. [175] See Ch. 8, section III, IV below.

Enron scandal, there has been an intensification of governmental supervision. It is accordingly also conceivable in relation to corporate governance codes that the legislator may decide in the event of further scandals and abuses to anchor some of these rules in statute, in order to enable more effective governmental enforcement.

V. Conclusion

International and European law tends to have piecemeal effects for shareholder law, so that even today it is primarily national sources of law which are the focus. In the context of national law, continental European, Anglo-American and Asian company and securities laws display similar legal bases in their fundamental patterns. Theoretical views that only or mainly rely on a single source of law have not become reality in the present law. Nor have market forces alone brought purely *de facto* control in any country. Instead, in all the legal systems discussed here, codifications of company and securities law, supplemented by case law, are to be found. Moreover, there are common differentiations within companies as a class, providing in particular for special laws for public companies. Finally, statutory provisions are supplemented by articles of association, shareholder agreements and corporate governance codes. Nonetheless, it is possible to discern a number of differences, which also affect the substantive pattern of shareholder law. For instance, in countries whose law is oriented towards listed companies, there is more information publicly available,[176] and it seems likely that less mandatory law is balanced out by enhanced legal *ex post* protection.[177]

[176] See Ch. 4, section III.1, 2 below.

[177] See Ch. 5, section III below.

3

Bases for a shareholder typology

It is not possible to consider all the details of the shareholder law of the various legal systems under review. Accordingly, proceeding in principled fashion, I will start with a consideration of what 'type' of shareholder the law focuses on. Using this methodology, I will then determine how the typical features of the shareholder's position have been reflected in the laws of the UK, the US, Germany, France, Japan and China (Chs. 5, 6).

I. The shareholder in the theoretical debate

Many approaches to classifying the shareholder into types can be found in the literature. One particularly exhaustive subdivision comes from Jennifer Hill, who distinguishes the shareholder as 'owner/principal', as 'beneficiary', as 'bystander', as 'participant in a political entity', as 'investor', as 'cerberus' and as 'managerial partner'.[1] Whether all these divisions can be applied to all countries could be doubted. In Bernhard Großfeld's words, the risk might be that we are looking at a foreign system through the spectacles of our own experience of the world, our language and our linguistic understanding.[2] The subdivision below makes it clear, however, that in the present context there are internationally similar models for explaining the shareholder's position.

1. The shareholder as 'owner' or 'quasi-partner'

In olden times particularly, but still today too, the terminology of the shareholder as owner of the company was and is widely used. There are

[1] Hill (2000b: 42 *et seq.*).

[2] Großfeld (1996: 106) ('daß wir die fremde Ordnung durch die Brille unserer Welterfahrung, unserer Sprache, unseres Sprachverständnisses vernehmen').

many examples of this in the literature,[3] in court decisions,[4] in best-practice guidelines,[5] and in legislative materials.[6]

This 'ownership analogy' does not, however, require that property-law principles are to be applied to the position of the shareholder. Since such principles are not appropriate, the point is rather the notion that economic ownership of the joint stock company is used to describe or promote certain rights genuinely given to shareholders. Thus, the analogy entails, for example, that shareholders as owners are entitled on dissolution of the company to the assets remaining after deduction of other outstanding liabilities. The ownership position also means that on the one hand the shareholders as a totality can in principle freely do with the company what they like and thus in principle need not tolerate any restrictions imposed by the state or other participants in the enterprise. Furthermore, the legal position of each individual shareholder is also protected, so that interference by fellow shareholders the rights of the former is unlawful. Finally, the share is, on this view, not just something that encapsulates particular rights. Instead, its legal nature is to convey a portion of the total property in the company.[7] Through his participation, the shareholder is thus the owner not just of the share, but also of the enterprise itself.

This intensive rights-and-duties position of the shareholder fits in with a quasi-partner conception of the shareholder.[8] On this concept, the principle of the legal person[9] does not rule out the assumption of direct legal relations between individual shareholders and between shareholders and management. If these relations are given a trusteeship pattern, one can accordingly justify the protection of shareholders against abuse of power by majority shareholders or by management.[10]

[3] See for Germany: Lutter (1991: 16); for China: Comberg (2000: 75–6); for the UK: Grantham (1998: 554–5); MacNeil (2005: 256); for the US: Donald (2005).

[4] *Gambotto* v. *WCP Ltd.* (1995) 127 ALR 417 (High Court of Australia); on this decision see also Davies (2003: 489–90); Hill (2000b: 42 *et seq.*, 64 *et seq.*).

[5] See Cadbury Report (1992: para. 6.1); No. 1 ChinCG-Code; Appendix JapCG-Principles; Ministry of Economy, Trade and Industry (METI) and Ministry of Justice (MOJ), *Guidelines Regarding Takeover Defense for the Purposes of Protection and Enhancement of Corporate Value and Shareholder's Common Interests*, 2005 (English version in (2006) 21 *ZJapanR* 143), Purpose 2(i).

[6] Begründung zum Regierungsentwurf GerAktG 1965, printed in Kropff (1965: 13); Modernising Company Law (2002: para. 2.38).

[7] See Grantham (1998: 562 *et seq.*); Davies (2003: 615); Henn (2002: para. 1591).

[8] Cf. Hill (2000a: 21); Worthington (2001b: 261–2, 264); Guntz (1997: 36, 51).

[9] See Ch. 4, section I.1 below. [10] See Ch. 5, section III below.

2. *The shareholder as 'member of an association' or 'parliamentarian'*

The association-membership view[11] is marked by the notion that in any association individuals come together in order jointly to pursue an objective that would be precluded to each of them individually. Here, the legal relations among shareholders, as well as between shareholder or management and the association, play a decisive part. Membership as a special legal relation thus gives the shareholder rights *vis-à-vis* the company. Moreover, the association, rendered autonomous *vis-à-vis* its members, counts, so that its purpose and functionality may set bounds to the exercise of shareholder rights.

The importance of the overall organization, with its emphasis on the position of the shareholder, is also stressed by the democratic or political model of the company. Furthermore, the notion that the company is a political entity implies a certain separation and limitation of powers.[12] The analogy with democracy, debated for instance in the US, Japan and Germany,[13] highlights, however, that essential control over the company is to remain with the shareholders. In this respect, the shareholders are mostly seen not as the 'citizens'[14] but as the 'parliamentarians' of the company, so that the general meeting is to be regarded as the parliament of the company[15] and thus as its 'highest body'.[16]

In detail, however, there are differences in the justification and shape of the democratic model. First of all, it may be a metaphor for the political nature of decision-making and thus in particular a theoretical justification for voting rights[17] and the powers of the general meeting. The competence of the general meeting is not, however, all-embracing on this view. A certain delegation of power to management as the 'government' of the company and a residual competence of the general meeting for questions of principle may very well fit the political model.[18] Equally, however,

[11] See generally Lutter (1980); Habersack (2001: 194–5); cf. also Habersack (1996); Mülbert, in: GroßkommAktG (1999: vor § 118 paras. 188, 196 *et seq.*); similarly, Ireland (1999: 32 *et seq.*, 47 *et seq.*).

[12] Cf. Parkinson (1993: 21 *et seq.*); Hill (2000a: 20); Comberg (2000: 88–9); K. Schmidt (2002: 866).

[13] See generally Großfeld (1971: para. 4-194); for the US: Cheffins (1997: 152); *Hoschett* v. *TSI International Software Ltd.*, 683 A 2d 43, 45–6 (Del. Ch., 1996); for Japan: Inaniwa and Brondics (1987: 17); Taniguchi (1988: 195); for Germany: K. Schmidt (2002: 837); Becker (2001: 1).

[14] But see Lutter (1973: 35 *et seq.*); Donald (2005: 308).

[15] Davies (1997b: 15).

[16] See Ch. 5, section I.1.a below.

[17] See Ch. 3, section II.1 below.

[18] Cf. Hill (2000b: 52–3); Werlauff (1993: 212); Licht *et al.* (2001: 47 note 76).

in this case efficient monitoring of the company management by the shareholders, and its responsibility for its conduct, must be guaranteed,[19] since it would not be democratic if management could act autocratically and 'monarchically' according solely to its own ideas.

The parliamentary model must not, however, be confined to this level of delegation. Based on the political element of shareholder democracy, it is possible in addition to extend the shareholders' sphere of influence beyond mere control of management. It is therefore argued that at least institutional shareholders can be actively engaged partners of management.[20] This fact can also be strengthened on the ground of general public interest, if it is considered politically desirable to regard shareholders as more than mere suppliers of capital.[21] Finally, the political model is of importance not just for the position of shareholders. For the democratic legitimation of corporate governance, it may also be concluded that all those whose interests are affected ought to be involved in the company.[22] Alongside the shareholders, who are already involved because of their financial risk, this may include, for instance, employees and other stakeholders.[23]

3. *The shareholder as 'investor' or 'bystander'*

The shareholder's active position contradicts the view that today the shareholder is above all an investor. The US version of contractual theory[24] in particular stresses that shareholders, like bondholders or other creditors, merely bring capital into the company and as a corollary obtain only this investment opportunity. In the UK, the focus is also often on the interests of the shareholder as an investor, and it is for instance said that the large company, where the participation of shareholders is restricted to their investment, is the archetype of company law.[25] A similar position is discussed in Japan.[26] Some academics advocate here that, for example, the company is to be regarded as a foundation, making the shareholders not members, but mere beneficiaries, receiving only pecuniary benefits.[27] In Germany, there is an intensive debate on the nature of shareholdership. In general, it is emphasized that, by contrast with the members of a small company (GmbH), the shareholders of a joint stock company are more capital-providers than co-entrepreneurs, so that the company is to be

[19] See Hill (2000b: 60); Parkinson (1993: 159). [20] Cf. J. Pound (1995), (1993).
[21] Lutter (1973: 44). [22] See Hill (2000b: 52–3); Bachmann (2001: 639–40).
[23] See Ch. 5, section II.1.a below. [24] See Ch. 2, section IV.1.a above.
[25] Grantham (1998: 557); similar Worthington (2001b: 260, 310–11).
[26] See Taniguchi (1988: 199). [27] Cf. Kliesow (2001: 65).

regarded as a pool for capital.[28] More specifically, in the nineteenth century Otto von Gierke already saw the joint stock company as a pure asset cooperative, in which participatory rights are only auxiliary to the purpose of guaranteeing the assets.[29] Günther H. Roth also questions whether joint stock companies are still associations, or not rather institutions that should be treated like investment funds.[30] Finally, Peter Mülbert points out that capital-market-oriented features can be identified in the German Companies Act 1965 (GerAktG). He therefore sees the shareholder in a hybrid dual role as association member as well as investor, which has also to be taken into account in interpreting the GerAktG.[31]

At the level of the persons acting for the company, the 'shareholder as investor' is more of a bystander, with management instead constituting the 'most important body'.[32] The investor-oriented view is thus explicitly directed against the concept of shareholder democracy.[33] A specialized and centralized management is seen as suiting the essence of the joint stock company.[34] This is also regarded as most effective, since most shareholders lack the interest or ability themselves to guide the enterprise's destiny.[35] By selling his shares the shareholder can correct his investment decisions at low cost and with little trouble. Finally, the democracy analogy is criticised, because in the joint stock company the shareholder counts not as a member with equal rights, but as a capital-provider. For instance, in the joint stock company it is not the principle 'one shareholder one vote' but the principle 'one share one vote' that applies.[36] Whereas in a democracy a parliamentarian can always have only one vote, a shareholder can by controlling more shares gain more voting rights and consequently more influence.

II. Real types of shareholder

A distinction is often drawn between short-, medium- and long-term investors. Further, it can be distinguished according to the person of the

[28] See e.g. Lutter (1991: 16–17); Kübler (1998: 8–9); Mülbert (1996a: 63).

[29] O. von Gierke (1868/1954: 533 *et seq.*); see also Mestmäcker (1958: 346).

[30] Roth (1972).

[31] Mülbert (1996a: 94 *et seq.*); Mülbert in: GroßkommAktG (1999: vor § 118 paras. 199 *et seq.*).

[32] See Buxbaum and Hopt (1988: 181–2); Hirte (2003: para. 3.218).

[33] E.g. Wiethölter (1961: 49 *et seq.*, 77 *et seq.*, 135); Roth (1972: 209–10); Wiedemann (1980: 352–3); Bachmann (2001: 639–40); Licht *et al.* (2001: 47).

[34] See also Ch. 5, section I.1.b below. [35] See also Ch. 4, section II.1.b below.

[36] See Ch. 3, section II; Ch. 4 II.4.b below.

investor and the fraction of the company he or she owns. The result is that there are different types of investor, such as small private shareholders, holders of employee shares, major investors, and institutional investors, who all pursue different investment strategies. This is also reflected in their expectations of the law. For dissatisfied small investors in particular, the simplest option is often to sell their shares. By contrast, for institutional investors, co-administration rights are of greater importance. This is true even where they are investing more in the market than in a specific firm, since the sale of a particular firm's shares would mean sacrificing their risk-efficient portfolio. Moreover, for a typology of shareholders, the various real types of company have to be taken into account. The main types here are the company with widely dispersed shareholdings, the company with one or several blockholders, the company with one majority shareholder and the company incorporated as a subsidiary in a group of companies.

Legally, the question arises which type of shareholder is or ought to be favoured in the given regulations. Here it is by no means a matter of course for the legislator to use the real types as the basis for his legislation. For instance, in Germany, the drafters of the 1937 GerAktG explicitly rejected a differentiation of long-term and speculative shareholders, since the shareholder's legal position could not depend on his intentions.[37] Chinese law, in distinguishing according to the person of the investor, constitutes a rare exception internationally.[38]

Moreover, different types of shareholder may also be brought about through provisions in the articles of association. Here the question arises not just what position articles of association have in general in the country in question,[39] but also whether within the individual company a distinction may be made according to the different types of shareholder.

As a general starting-point, it can be taken that in most countries all shareholders have the same rights, a principle frequently accompanied by the equal-treatment principle in company law[40] and the 'one share one vote' principle.[41] Yet it is possible to depart from this basic principle to a greater or lesser degree and to set up various shareholder types defined in the articles.[42] The shareholders then mostly enjoy some protection of

[37] See Mülbert (1996a: 61); Brändel, in: GroßkommAktG (1992: § 12 para. 20).

[38] See Ch. 2, section III.1 above. [39] See Ch. 2, section IV.1 above.

[40] See Ch. 5, section II.2.b below. [41] See Ch. 4, section II.4.b below.

[42] In the UK this is also possible outside the articles; cf. generally van Ryn (1990: para. 5-156); for Germany: §§ 11, 26(1) GerAktG; for the US: O'Kelley and Thompson (1996: 196–7).

their vested rights, since their assent is required, at least for a change in their type.[43]

In detail, in the US, the UK and the Japan, there is considerable discretion in the issuing of different types of share.[44] In Germany, France and other countries of continental Europe, special provisions commonly lay down the admissibility and form of transfer-limited shares, preference shares, multiple voting rights, voting caps etc.[45] An exception to this general picture is China. Here, § 132 ChinCA empowers only the government to make special provisions on the issue of new types of share, so that at present it is doubtful whether and to what extent departures from the principle of the uniform share are possible.[46]

Finally, a distinction has to be made between different types of companies. Usually, for private companies there is more flexibility in structuring different types of shares than for public companies. The reason for this is, first, that, for a stock exchange listing, departures from the uniform share are often impermissible.[47] Secondly, corporate governance codes may stipulate the 'one share one vote' principle,[48] so that pressure is exercised against particular modes of differentiation. Thirdly, market forces are not to be underestimated. Since unusual share types may hamper trading on the exchange, the market's need for standardization brings an (even internationally) convergent homogeneity of the share.[49] This convergence will, however, not be absolute. While in the political debate the uniform share is often called for, nevertheless in the OECD consultations and in the new European Takeover Directive, for instance, no agreement on the 'one share one vote' principle could be reached.[50]

III. Conclusions

A typology of shareholders is possible from various standpoints. From theoretical viewpoints, the models of the shareholder as owner,

[43] Cf. van Ryn (1990: para. 5-157); § 10.04 MBCA; § 242(b)(2) DelGCL; Art. 60(1) SE-Reg; Art. 25(3) of the Second Directive 77/91/EEC; Art. L. 225–99 FrCCom; s. 630 UK-CA; § 322 JapCA; §§ 138, 141(3), 179(3) GerAktG.

[44] §§ 6.01(a), 8.04 MBCA; s. 630 UK-CA; Art. 46 Draft Model Articles of Association for Public Companies (June 2006) (old Arts. 2 and 3 of UK-Table A); §§ 107, 108 JapCA.

[45] See Ch. 4, section I.3.c, II.4.b below.

[46] See Ch. 4, section I.3.c below.

[47] Cf. Coffee (1999b: 683 *et seq.*) and Ch. 4, section II.4.b below.

[48] No. 2.1.2 GerCGK; Euroshareholders Corporate Governance Guidelines (2000: No. II).

[49] For empirical data see Deminor (2005).

[50] See annotation to No. III.A.1 OECD-Principles 2004 ('The Principles do not take a position on the concept of "one share one vote". However, many institutional investors and shareholder associations support this concept'); on the EU Takeover Directive see Ch. 5, section II.1.a below.

quasi-partner, association member, parliamentarian, investor and bystander can be distinguished (section I above). Since reality does not exactly reflect these models, further indications have been given of various real types of shareholder, where differentiation may for instance be made according to duration of investment, extent of involvement or the person of the investor. This also includes the possibility of addressing different types of shareholder through the articles of association (section II above).

Consequently, there is no uniform model of shareholdership. Jennifer Hill has already correctly stated that 'it is not surprising, that a one-dimensional model of the past, such as the "shareholder as owner" is inadequate today and can result in a disjunction between law and reality. An examination of the variety of possible roles for shareholders in the corporate enterprise is justified.'[51] Across the various countries under study, there are indeed both shareholders with an exclusively financial interest and those involved entrepreneurially. Any theoretical schematization is thus in tension with reality, where 'the shareholder' with necessarily determined behaviour patterns and primary interests does not exist.

The following investigation of the *status quo* approaches each statutory type of shareholder, first, through an 'adjectival' characterization of various features of shareholders. These terms, such as 'the informed shareholder' or 'the protected shareholder', are to be understood here neither absolutely nor conclusively. Instead, the question asked is whether this type is a reality in shareholder law in the individual countries. Secondly, the types of shareholder addressed in this part will be used to analyze whether there has been convergence in shareholder law. As details will always differ in different legal systems, this principled approach[52] is used to determine how the typical features of the shareholder's position have been reflected in UK, US, German, French, Japanese and Chinese company law.

[51] Hill (2000b: 78). [52] See also Ch. 1, section IV.2 above.

4

The 'shareholder as such'

The term 'shareholder as such' refers to those elements in the shareholder's position that relate to his typical original rights.[1] These involve, first, the expectation that his investment will pay off at some time in the future, through selling his shares or receiving dividends (section I below: 'the profit-oriented shareholder'). Secondly, shareholders, by contrast with creditors, typically have a legal entitlement to become active through their vote (section II below: 'the active shareholder'). Both options are enhanced by the information the shareholders receive, or must furnish about themselves (sections III and IV: 'the informed shareholder'; 'the anonymous shareholder'). For, if a shareholder had no information about, say, the company's situation or other shareholders, he would have difficulty deciding when to become active or to realize his profit. In contradistinction to these aspects, when it comes to the 'shareholder's position in the power structure of the company' (Ch. 5), the focus shifts to the shareholder's relationship to other people or institutions of the company ('the deciding shareholder', 'the protected shareholder', 'the litigating shareholder').

I. The profit-oriented shareholder

The profit-oriented shareholder is interested, first, in avoiding claims being made on him for the company's expenditure (subsection 1 below). Secondly, he wants his investment to bring a profit in the short, medium or long term (subsections 2 and 3 below) – although he is not certain of this profit expectation, since investment in a firm's equity is closely tied to the firm's fate and not limited to the credit risk.

From a theoretical viewpoint,[2] various focuses could be taken. The 'shareholder as owner' is in principle unrestricted in his conduct. Since his personal interests are relatively closely bound up with the company's, he can dispose of his own enterprise's money by selling his share of ownership

[1] See also Ch. 1, section II.1 above. [2] See Ch. 3, section I above.

or drawing value from the undertaking through dividends. The 'shareholder as investor', too, values these possibilities. Although he is similarly interested in a regular dividend, here he is primarily interested in buying and selling the shares. For, if the investor is dissatisfied with company policy, including its failure to distribute profits, he will not intervene in the company's business policy, but instead sell his shares. This is different with the 'democratic model of the company'. Since here the primary responsibility lies with the shareholders, the general meeting has to decide on the distribution of profits. However – as with the sale of shares – it is also the interest of the overall organization that counts. It may therefore be that statutory restraints should prevent short-term speculation or excessive distribution of profits.

1. Limited liability

The shareholders must bear the costs arising from their becoming shareholders. These costs may arise because of initial capital costs or through the buying price. Payments made in connection with the founding of a company[3] are typical in particular of the model of the shareholder as owner, since founder members are often closely associated with the company. The purchase – and also the sale (see further subsection 3 below) – of shares is, by contrast, an expression of an investor-oriented mode of becoming a shareholder.

Furthermore, a person who has become a shareholder may subsequently, apart from falls in the value of the shares, incur financial losses by, exceptionally, being called on directly to meet demands on the company. This is not, however, the usual case, since the principle of limitation of liability is there to promote investors' investment-readiness and thus promote the company's ability to attract capital.[4] The background here is the concept of the joint stock company as a legal person[5] or separate legal entity,[6] which is today by and large universally accepted. Historically, however, this has not always been the case. For instance, in the UK

[3] E.g. § 54 GerAktG; § 34 JapCA; § 3 ChinCA; for a comparative overview see van Ryn (1990: paras. 5-122 *et seq.*).

[4] See generally van Ryn (1990: para. 5-134), and e.g. § 54(1) GerAktG, Art. L. 225-1 FrCCom.

[5] Cf. on Germany: § 1(1) GerAktG; on Japan: Bottomley (1999: 45); on China: Tomasic and Fu (1999: 149); Wei (1998: 368); but as with the French concept of the 'personne morale' (Merle (2005: para. 74)), Chinese law also regards partnerships as 'legal persons', cf. Sharma (1999: 370).

[6] On the UK: Davies (2003: 27), Griffin (2000: 6); on the US: Hamilton (1992: 196).

it was not untill the fundamental *Salomon* v. *Salomon* judgment that the concept of a separate legal entity came to be accepted.[7] And, for a long time, many legal systems were inconsistent about the separation of company and shareholder, since the one-person company was denied recognition. Today, however, in most countries, one-person companies are permitted.[8]

Regarding the question of shareholders' liability, in most countries there are two situations where limitation of liability does not operate. First, founders can be liable where the legal or statutory capital is not paid-up.[9] Secondly, according to the case law in the US,[10] the UK,[11] Germany,[12] France[13] and Japan,[14] in exceptional cases 'lifting the corporate veil' is possible.[15] Although the attempts are made to establish general requirements and legal consequences, ultimately it amounts to a form of abuse control in the individual case. The differences that exist between these jurisdictions are thus not based on differing conceptual approaches. Instead, the importance of direct liability depends on, for instance, whether special provisions for groups of companies operate, or whether the requirement for a minimum level of capital makes undercapitalization of new firms less likely.

[7] *Salomon* v. *Salomon & Co.* [1897] AC 22 (House of Lords); cf. also *Lee* v. *Lee's Air Farming Ltd* [1961] AC 12 (Privy Council); Grantham (1998: 557 *et seq.*); Ireland (1999: 42 *et seq.*).

[8] See e.g. § 2 GerAktG; § 25 JapCA; § 2.01 MBCA; s. 7 UK-CA; Art L. 223-4 FrCCom (for the 'entreprise unipersonelle à responsibilité limitée') and Art. L. 227-1 FrCCom (for the 'SAS unipersonelle'); § 24 ChinCA (for the Ltd; for a plc two persons are required, § 79 ChinCA); for the EU see also the Twelfth Directive, 89/667/EEC, and Art. 5 of the Second Directive, 77/91/EEC.

[9] E.g. § 65 GerAktG; Art L. 228-28 FrCCom; § 52 JapCA.

[10] See e.g. *Walkovszky* v. *Carlton*, 276 NYS 2d 585 (2nd Cir. 1966); *Laya* v. *Erin Homes Inc.*, 352 SE 2d 93 (West Virginia 1986); *Baatz* v. *Arrow Bar*, 426 NW 2d 298 (South Dakota 1990); *Sea-Land Services* v. *Pepper Source*, 941 F 2d 519 (7th Cir. 1991); *Kinney Shoe Corp.* v. *Polan*, 939 F 2d 209 (4th Cir. 1991).

[11] See e.g. *DHN Food Distributors Ltd* v. *Tower Hamlets LBC* [1976] 1 WLR 852 (Court of Appeal); *Adams* v. *Cape Industries plc* [1990] Ch 433 (Court of Appeal); *Creasey* v. *Breachwood Motors Ltd* [1993] BCLC 480 (Queen's Bench); *Yukong Line Ltd* v. *Rendsburg Investment Corporation* [1998] 1 WLR 294 (Queen's Bench).

[12] BGH, BGHZ 20, 4; 54, 222; 68, 312; 122, 123; ZIP 1994, 867. The German Constitutional Court has confirmed its constitutionality (BVerfG, BVerfGE 13, 331).

[13] See Hertig and Kanda (2004: 93–4) (also on the 'de facto director').

[14] See Takahashi and Sakamoto (2005: 253–5) (on a decision by the Fukuoka District Court); Kawamoto *et al.* (2001: paras. 233 *et seq.*); Kliesow (2001: 72 *et seq.*); Bottomley (1999: 45); Hayakawa (1996: 271); Kawamoto (1994: 78–9).

[15] This is being discussed for Chinese law too: see Schipani and Liu (2002: 62).

2. *Profit realization while remaining in the company*

The parallels to limited liability do not extend to the question of how the shareholder remaining in the company can realize his profit. Yet, here too, one can discern some convergence.

a) Legal bases for profit distribution

In early times, joint stock companies were as a rule established for a particular project, so that shareholders were entitled to a profit payout only after the project came to an end. This changed, however, after the eighteenth century, whereafter the duration of the company was as a rule no longer limited. Given the advantages of a supra-individual and permanent legal existence, it became common to distribute profits in the course of active business. Yet, in none of the countries studied here is there a mandatory right to a dividend.[16] Although in Germany, say, the right to a dividend has a statutory basis (§§ 58(4), 60, 174(1) GerAktG), this is merely an entitlement to a decision on profit utilization. Only after this decision has been made is there a claim to a distribution of dividend.[17]

A resolution to distribute the annual dividend[18] presupposes the adoption of the annual accounts. While in Germany the general meeting was until 1937 competent for both decisions, nowadays the general meeting is usually only responsible for the decision on the use of the operating profits (§§ 119(1)(no.2), 174(1) GerAktG). Adoption of the annual accounts is as a rule done by the supervisory board (§ 172 GerAktG), unless the supervisory board does not approve the accounts or the executive and supervisory boards resolve to leave adoption to the general meeting (§ 173 GerAktG). The general meeting's powers of decision-making are broader in France and China. Here, the general meeting decides on both the approval of the annual accounts and on the distribution of profits.[19] In France, this is partly because smaller firms too have traditionally been run as joint stock companies.[20] Since these firms are mostly not listed, making sale of their shares harder, it is more important for shareholders to be able to take profits through dividends. Moreover, shareholders in small firms are closer to business operations, so that they may be better able to decide on the annual accounts. In China, by contrast, while it is usually the case that

[16] Sweden is different: see Milman (1999: 8).
[17] Cf. generally van Ryn (1990: para. 5-138).
[18] On interim dividends see Ch. 4, section I.2.d below.
[19] Arts. L. 232-11, 232-12 FrCCom; §§ 100, 38(nos. 5, 6) ChinCA.
[20] See Ch. 1, section II.1 above.

only larger firms are run as companies, the general meeting's power here is in line with the usual full powers of Chinese general meetings, which permits the state, as the major shareholder, to secure its influence.[21] A mixed form of competences can be found in Japan. In principle both the adoption of the annual accounts and the decision on profit utilization are for the general meeting (§§ 438, 454 JapCA). This has, however, gradually been relaxed, first for companies with more than 1,000 shareholders (§ 16(1) JapCCExcA) and then for the monist model of corporate governance (§ 21-31 JapCCExcA). According to the current law, the board of directors decides on the distribution of profits if this is provided for in the articles and if the company has an 'accounting auditor'[22] (§ 459 JapCA). This moves Japanese law closer to US law. Under the US approach, the board of directors decides generally, independently of the general meeting, on the amount of the dividend.[23] It is not yet clear whether shareholders can require profit distribution to be decided on by the general meeting. Entitlement to a decision on distribution exists only in cases of abuse, something rarely presumed in public companies.[24] A primary competence of the management would also be possible in the UK by means of a provision in the articles of association.[25] The model articles, however, provide for adoption of the dividend by the general meeting.[26]

Altogether, then, shareholders in the continental European countries and China seem more easily able to draw profits from the company through their own actions. This assessment, however, changes if the provisions on the amount of the dividend and actual practice are taken into consideration.

b) Provisions on the amount of dividend

In the legal systems with minimum legal capital requirements, dividends can usually be distributed only out of net profits. Moreover, the general meeting may be obliged to put a particular proportion of profit into the

[21] See also Ch. 5, section I.1.b below.

[22] All companies with committees (in contrast to a board of auditors) and all large companies (§ 2(6) JapCA) must have an accounting auditor (§§ 327(5), 328 JapCA).

[23] E.g. § 6.40 MBCA; § 170 DelGCL.

[24] See *Sinclair Oil Corp.* v. *Levien*, 280 A 2d 717 (Del. 1971); *Eshleman* v. *Keenan*, 22 Del. Ch. 82, 194 A 40 (1937), aff'd, 23 Del. Ch. 234, 2 A 2d 904 (1938); *Treves* v. *Menzies*, 37 Del. Ch. 330, 142 A 2d 520 (1958).

[25] See *Re Weller (Sam) & Sons Ltd* [1990] BCLC 80 (Chancery Division); Farrar *et al.* (1998: 205); Xuereb (1989: 48 *et seq.*).

[26] Currently Art. 102 UK-Table A; see also Art. 71 Draft Model Articles for Public Companies (June 2006).

company's statutory reserves. Under Chinese law, 10 per cent of the profits have to be paid into the statutory common reserve fund until such time as total reserves have reached 50 per cent of the registered capital (§ 167(1) ChinCA). In Germany and France, 5 per cent of the profits have to be paid into reserves until they reach 10 per cent of the registered capital (§ 150 GerAktG; Art. L. 230-10 FrCCom). In Japan, it used to be 10 per cent of the profits up to 25 per cent of the registered capital (§ 288 JapCC); now, however, the figure is 10 per cent of an amount determined by secondary legislation (§ 445(4) JapCA).

In Germany and France, the general meeting's room for manoeuvre is also restricted by accounting law. Under accounting law, less profit is distributable in continental European countries than in the Anglo-American countries, since for instance unrealized profits are in principle left out of account.[27] This is related particularly to the concept of minimum capital.

To the extent that room for manoeuvre exists, the general meeting in Germany has as a rule no significant influence on the amount of the dividend.[28] Until 1965, management could set the amount of net profit through reserves and thus bring about 'forced saving', since shareholders were not trusted to take a responsible decision on the distribution of profits. The 1965 GerAktG by contrast contains a compromise solution. In order to satisfy the interests of both the shareholders and the company, the legislation provided that management could at most pay half the annual surplus into reserves (now: § 58(2)(s.1) GerAktG). This 'halving rule' has, however, since been weakened, as § 58(2)(s.2) GerAktG now permits alternative provision to be made in the articles of association.[29] On the whole, thus, both the general meeting and management have some room for manoeuvre. The general meeting's decision here must be in the company's interest.[30] As regards management discretion, it is disputed whether misuse can give rise to damages.[31] This is, however, mostly not decisive, since management has considerable room for manoeuvre through the

[27] Cf. van Ommeslaghe (1990: paras. 5-49, 5-54), and Ch. 3, section III.4.a below.

[28] See Roth (2003: 370); Mülbert (1996a: 159, 207 *et seq.*); Lutter (1991: 25 *et seq.*): Großfeld and Deilmann (1990: 258).

[29] Initially through the Gesetz zur Kontrolle and Transparenz im Unternehmensbereich (KonTraG) of 27.04.1998, BGBl. I 786; subsequently through the Transparenz- and Publizitätsgesetz (TransPuG) of 19.07.2002, BGBl. I 2681.

[30] Similarly in France, see Rock *et al.* (2004: 149); van Ryn (1990: para. 5-138); Großfeld (1971: para. 4-68); cf. also Arts. L. 232-10, 232-12(2) FrCCom.

[31] Cf. Henze, in: GroßkommAktG (2000: § 58 para. 45).

accounting provisions on ascertainment of profits.[32] It can, for instance influence the amount of the dividend through valuation rights.[33]

For France and Japan, the residual discretion permitted to the general meeting is often regarded as insignificant. It is said that, because of its greater technical expertise, the amount of dividend is *de facto* set by management.[34] For Japan, this is further confirmed by the fact that in practice (traditionally) the amount of the dividend is unrelated to actual profit. Since as a rule the same amount is always distributed,[35] it appears to be possible for management to pursue their dividend policy regardless of the company's economic success.

In the US,[36] management has great autonomy in most states in paying out dividends. It can take its decision in accordance with considerations of business policy, and benefits thereby from the business judgement rule. An absolute limit is set in some states only by the company's insolvency. In other states, limits may be set based on the operating surplus and earnings. In part, distribution is here permitted only out of earned surpluses, but sometimes distributions are also permitted from the capital stock or the net profit from the current and previous business years. Furthermore, it should be noted that, as an alternative creditor-protection mechanism, financial covenants in credit contracts may act to prevent insolvency.

In the UK, the articles of association often provide that management may make expedient reserve provision, and dividends may not exceed a set figure.[37] This is monitored only as to whether in the individual case a failure to distribute a dividend is an unfair disadvantage within the meaning of s. 994 UK-CA.[38] Additionally, profit (s. 830 UK-CA) distributed by the general meeting may not be greater than that proposed by management.

Irrespective of national differences, thus, shareholders seem to lose out. However, boosting the reserves may also help shareholders. Reserves raise the undertaking's value and thus – at least in a rational market – the share price, so that shareholders can realize a profit through selling their shares. Moreover, market forces may intervene, to the shareholders' advantage. If

[32] §§ 252–256, 279–283 GerHGB.

[33] Lutter, in: Kölner Kommentar AktG (1988: § 58 para. 9); Roth (2003: 371); see also Ch. 3, section III.4 below.

[34] For Japan: Inaniwa and Brodics (1987: 17); for France: Großfeld (1971: para. 4-68); see also Art. L. 232-12 FrCCom.

[35] Cf. Milhaupt and West (2003a: 309).

[36] Cf. § 6.40 MBCA; Dooley and Goldman (2001: 740 *et seq.*); Cunningham (1999: 1180); LaChance (2001: 282); van Ryn (1990: para. 5-138); van Ommeslaghe (1990: para. 5-53).

[37] Pennington (1994: para. 90.10.132); cf. also van Ryn (1990: para. 5-138).

[38] Cf. *Re Weller (Sam) & Sons Ltd* [1990] BCLC 80, 88 (Chancery Division).

distributable profits are available, management can actually be forced to distribute by shareholder pressure. If instead the firm's economic position would be impaired by paying dividends, management may through 'open dialogue'[39] seek agreement to a low dividend. Whether it will be successful here is, however, doubtful. In weak periods, profit realization by selling shares is unattractive to shareholders. In such times, therefore, relatively high dividends are often distributed, because investors favour solid firms and would like at least to have regular earnings.[40]

c) Dividend practice

Dividend practice is not uniform internationally. But there is a trend towards convergence. It is traditionally said that in common law countries companies pay higher dividends, and more often, than in civil law countries.[41] Yet, in common law countries, there is also no 'dividend absolutism'. For instance, management conduct is criticized for tending rather to reinvest than to distribute dividend.[42] Moreover, the 'shareholder value approach' discourages over-generous dividends, because what counts is growth in the firm's value and in the share price, taking account of dividends paid out.[43] For continental Europe and Asia, despite the general meeting's comprehensive powers, it is said to be typical for continual but smaller payouts to be made.[44] This statement is broadly true. For instance, the linkage between the commercial and fiscal accounts means that, in many continental European countries, for tax reasons companies are interested in setting low values.[45] A further decisive factor is that, in these countries, more often than in the US and the UK, shareholders have concentrated or cross-shareholdings.[46] In such cases, shareholders are less interested in dividends. Additionally, it may happen that firms that could distribute profit use it instead for mutual participations. The stricter laws in continental Europe and Asia thus also constitute a functional equivalent to the greater influence of market forces in the US and the UK.

[39] Regierungsentwurf TransPuG, BT-Drucks. 14/1869, at 21.

[40] See also Handelsblatt, 31.03.2003, at 29; 11.06.2003, at 29; 15.06.2003, at 27.

[41] For the US: Cunningham (1999: 1181); for the UK: Cheffins (1997: 55); see also Cheffins (2006: 1306 *et seq.*).

[42] Cf. Merkt (1991: para. 54).

[43] Cf. Rappaport (1986).

[44] Cf. Bratton and McCahery (1999: 227); Escher-Weingart (2001: 25); for Japan: Kawamoto (1994: 92); Kawamoto *et al.* (2001: para. 47); Kliesow (2001: 88); for China: Handelsblatt, 03.09.2003, at 30.

[45] Cf. Großfeld (1996: para. 721).

[46] See Ch. 8, section IV below.

However, one should be wary of monolithic contrasts. Even the traditional oppositions are not as dyed-in-the-wool as might seem. First, in early twentieth-century Japan for instance, very high dividends were distributed.[47] Investors took out loans in order to buy shares, and needed the money to pay the loans back. This changed only when in the 1940s the government deliberately kept dividends low through a special law, and in the 1960s cross-shareholdings increased. Secondly, until recently, notwithstanding the generally high dividend levels in the US, it was common among firms in the IT sector not to pay dividends. This seems to be changing only with the latest tax reform in the US. Thirdly, internationalization trends in dividend payouts have recently been emerging. Practice is, however, far from uniform worldwide, since the size of dividends depends also on, for instance, factors such as a country's economic strength, the ranking of shareholder interests, the rule-of-law principle, and the efficiency of the legal system.[48] Nevertheless, enhanced pressure from the increasingly strong international capital markets means that, at least for firms aiming at a global range of investors, the dividend rate gradually levels out.[49]

Approximations are, finally, also to be seen in the possibilities of shaping profit distribution in the articles of association. In addition to the admissibility in principle of preference shares[50] and dividends in kind,[51] tracking stocks and interim dividends are also worth noting. Tracking stocks are shares with dividend rights extending to only part of the whole company, so as to reach investors interested specifically in these. This form of investment originated in the US. Recently, the use of, or at least the debate about, tracking stocks has extended to other countries too, such as France, Germany and Japan.[52] Interim dividends are dividends distributed irrespective of the date of the annual general meeting. Interim dividends are already admissible in many countries. Moreover, their importance is

[47] On what follows see Hayakawa (1997: 239 *et seq.*); Takahashi (2003: 125).

[48] Lombardo and Pagano (2000); see also Ch. 5, section II.1.a below on the 'shareholder-stakeholder discussion'.

[49] For Japan: Kliesow (2001: 89); Milhaupt and West (2003a: 320); for the US and Europe: Handelsblatt, 15.06.2003, at 27; more critical for Japan: Dore (2000: 120 *et seq.*) (just rhetoric).

[50] Cf. van Ryn (1990: para. 5-151); on non-voting preference shares see Ch. 4, section II.4.b below.

[51] At least in the US, the UK (Davies (2003: 284)), Germany (§ 58(5) GerAktG) and Japan (§ 454(4) JapCA; for the different old law see Osugi (2002: 29, 37)).

[52] For France: Jacobs and Macours (2001); for Japan: Aoki (2001a: 110); Hashimoto (2002: 7); Osugi (2002: 29); for Germany: Tonner (2002); Friedl (2002).

set to grow, since interim dividends naturally follow from the increasingly common use of interim reports,[53] and the capital market is also demanding more than merely annual profits.[54]

d) Conclusion

On the whole, from the viewpoint of the model categories,[55] a mixed picture emerges. In favour of the ownership and democracy analogy is the fact that, in several countries, the general meeting is competent to set profits and in part also for adopting the annual accounts. Country-specific upper and lower bounds on the amount of dividend can also be justified using these concepts: too little dividend would contradict the ownership model, since the shareholder as owner is due at least a considerable share in the profits. Too much dividend would conflict with the notion of shareholder democracy, since 'parliamentarians' ought to act specifically as representatives of the overall organization (state/company), thus ruling out *de facto* liquidation. But including details of profit calculation and practice in dividend distribution brings these legal systems closer to the investor model for public companies. In general, dividend distribution depends essentially on management decisions, economic developments and capital-market pressures.

3. *Profit realization by selling shares*

Leaving the company is – apart from appraisal rights against the company[56] – possible mainly by selling shares to third parties. Yet the permissibility in principle of trading in shares has not always been as apparent as it is today (subsection a below). Even today, though, it is conceivable for statutory provisions (subsection b below), private sales restrictions (subsection c below) or practical problems (subsection d below) to hamper profit realization by selling shares.

a) Permissibility of trading in shares

Free trade in shares used to be problematic for the US version of contractual theory.[57] Since according to this doctrine there was a contractual relationship among the shareholders, the assumption of free

[53] See Ch. 4, section III.3 below.

[54] On interim dividends generally see Ommeslaghe (1990: para. 5-51); for Japan: § 454(5) JapCA; for the EU: Art. 2 of the Second Directive 77/91/EEC.

[55] See Ch. 3, section I above. [56] See Ch. 5, section II.2.c below.

[57] Cf. Merkt (2000: 78–9) and also Ch. 2, section IV.1.a above.

transferability without the assent of all the other shareholders (now § 8-105 US-UCC) was not plausibly justifiable. On the typological models too there were differences in the meaning of share trading. For the investor theory, trading is the *prima ratio*, whereas for the shareholder as owner or as member of an association it is instead the *ultima ratio*, after vain attempts to change company policy.[58]

Nowadays, the general acceptability of share trading has increasingly won through. The possibility of selling shares is necessary because an investment in shares is in principle not time-limited. The shareholder is therefore interested in being able to terminate his business relationship with minimal complication by selling the shares. Today, it is also accepted in principle that it is sensible for the economy as a whole because share trading facilitates capital flows to those companies which can use it most efficiently. However, the very ease of share trading can also lead to speculation, and in late nineteenth-century Germany even led to calls to ban the joint stock company.[59] Easy transferability encourages abuse, because shareholders' personal profit interests do not always coincide with the long-term interests of the company.[60] Moreover, a developed capital market may promote short-termism by management[61] and thus run counter to long-term economic development. John Maynard Keynes put this as follows: 'Short-term trading leads us to focus on what the stock market is doing rather on what companies are doing.'[62] Consequently, even today, potential restraints on share trading remain topical.[63]

b) The influence of statutory provisions

Various areas of law affect the possibility of selling shares. Company law regulates in general how shares can be transferred. However, it is sometimes assumed that it also sets up obstacles to trade in shares. Continental European company law in particular is sometimes accused of blocking trade in shares through the obligation to deposit them by a certain time before the start of the general meeting.[64] This is not, however, accurate, at least for Germany and France. Instead, in Germany, until 2005, a deposit obligation in the articles of association only excluded the exercise of

[58] See also Ch. 3, section I above. [59] Cf. Hommelhoff (1985: 57 *et seq.*).
[60] Cf. Horn (1979: 179).
[61] On the 'myopia hypothesis' see e.g. Cheffins (1997: 51 *et seq.*).
[62] Keynes, in Moggridge (1993: 103–4).
[63] See also Ch. 8, section I.2, III.1 below on the 'anti-globalization movement'.
[64] E.g. La Porta *et al.* (1998: 1127); cf. also Regierungsentwurf TransPuG, BT-Drucks. 14/1869, at 40 and Druey (1999: 369–70).

voting rights by anyone who had not deposited their shares. Furthermore, this provision is now entirely replaced by a mere notice.[65] In France, until 2002, there was a bar on selling, since during a particular period prior to the general meeting no trading on the stock exchange was permitted. The reform of 2002, however, explicitly removed this restriction.[66]

With respect to other formalities for trade, traditionally a distinction had to be drawn between bearer shares and registered shares.[67] More recently, however, there has been convergence between the different types of shares. Neither the link to paper with the bearer share nor the need to change the name in the register with the registered share fit the need for fungibility of shares in today's financial world. There has accordingly in most countries been an immobilization and dematerialization, which have replaced the classical forms of transfer (e.g. by delivery or endorsement). Moreover, the notion that registered shares are less negotiable and the range of shareholders more stable is now out of date. Various factors have contributed to this.[68] First, trade is facilitated because of collective custody of shares by for instance Euroclear and Clearstream in Europe and DTCC in the US. Secondly, trade is simplified since often nominee shareholders – brokers or banks – are entered in the register of members.[69] Thus, when the economic owners sell 'their shares', the central register does not have to be updated. Thirdly, trade in shares is speeded up by electronic systems, because changes to the register of members can be processed faster and more cheaply.

Securities law supplements company law with a regulatory environment that facilitates share trading for shareholders in public companies. This can be explained by the concept of ordo-liberalism that effective freedom can be achieved only through legal rules.[70] Furthermore, in terms of the economic analysis of law, securities law can reduce transaction costs and thus contribute to an efficient capital market.

But there are also restrictions. For example, in the US and China, for a period of twelve months after an IPO, shares not bought in the IPO

[65] § 123(2), (3) GerAktG as amended by Gesetz zur Unternehmensintegrität und Modernisierung des Anfechtungsrechts (UMAG) of 22.09.2005, BGBl. I 2802.

[66] Art. 136(2) FrDécret, as amended by Décret No. 2002-803 du 3 mai 2002.

[67] See also Ch. 4, section IV.1, 2 below.

[68] For France: Weller and Zahn (2000: 190–1); for Germany: Gruson (2001: 227 *et seq.*); Grumann and Soehlke (2001: 580); for Japan: Kawamoto (1994: 106); for the US: Gruson (2001: 222, 231); for the UK: Davies (2003: 682, 698 *et seq.*); generally Vagts (2000: paras. 10-3, 10-22).

[69] See also Ch. 4, section IV.3 below.

[70] See Siems (2002a), (2004b) with further references.

must not be traded.[71] In countries where there are no such regulations, a comparable legal situation may be brought about through private-law agreements. For instance, in Germany, a lock-up clause is possible for the period after a listing.[72] The reason for these restrictions is the protection of recently listed companies and capital-market liquidity. If, for instance, founders could sell their blocks of shares immediately after a listing, there would be the risk of a massive fall in the share price. This would harm the general willingness to invest in shares, and thus weaken share trading on the capital market.

More general limitations used to exist in Chinese law. Until recently, shares held by the state or by legal persons were untradable, so that only one-third of all shares of listed companies could be freely traded.[73] But the CSRC then announced that all listed companies' shares would be tradable, though at the discretion of the company.[74] Moreover, recently, the provision barring individuals from owning more than 0.5 per cent of the shares in a company was repealed, and the market in A-shares opened up to foreigners.[75] Thus in China too, there is a trend towards the gradual liberalization of the trade in shares.

c) Agreed selling restrictions

In principle, shares can be freely sold.[76] For bearer shares, the articles of association cannot alter this principle. It would not be sensible to reverse the (traditionally) higher fungibility of bearer shares by means of provisions in the articles of association. Legal certainty is also served, since a selling restriction on bearer shares would be hard to enforce.[77] For registered shares, by contrast, restrictions in the articles of association are often possible. This is particularly true of companies which do not offer shares to the public. For them, shareholders are typically more closely connected with the company, and a sale is therefore harder to bring about

[71] SEC Rule 144(d)(1); § 142(1) ChinCA. According to the pre-2005 Chinese law the period was three years. This was criticized as 'overkill': see Liu (2001: 42).

[72] Cf. Schlitt (2003: 61); Bericht des Finanzausschusses zum 4. Finanzmarktförderungsgesetz, BT-Drucks. 14/8601, at 15. The EU Prospectus Regulation (EC) No. 809/2004, Annex III 7.3 and V 27.14 requires only disclosure.

[73] See Huang (2005: 151–3); Schipani and Liu (2002: 63); Leung *et al.* (2002: 11); Pißler (2002b: 7); Wang (2000: 6–7); see also Ch. 2, section III.1 above.

[74] See Dam (2006: 29); Xi (2006: 256).

[75] See Ch. 2, section III.1 above.

[76] E.g. Art. L. 228-10 FrCCom; § 127 JapCA; s. 544 UK-CA; for Germany see BGH, WM 1987, 174, 175.

[77] See van Ryn (1990: para. 5-116).

than with public companies. Shareholders may also have an interest in not permitting an unknown third party to 'force their way in' to the company. For a public company, this interest exists only where a majority shareholder wishes to secure his position. Otherwise, transfer restrictions would principally help management to ward off a hostile takeover. But securities law, for instance in Europe and Japan, makes it in principle impossible to restrict the transferability of shares in listed companies.[78] And, in countries where there is no such regulation, market forces may lead to a similar result. Purely contractual agreements are, however, in general possible alternatives.[79]

In company law, of the countries considered here, only China makes all transfer restrictions impermissible. Since there is no rule in the ChinCA, according to the People's National Congress guidelines the articles of association may regulate only the details of transfer.[80] It may at first be surprising that China, of all places, gives priority to free transferability, having to that extent a more liberal law than other countries. This situation can, however, be explained by the fact that in China there is in general also less flexibility in drafting individual articles of association.[81] In the UK also, there are also no statutory provisions. Since it is possible in the UK to contract out of the statutory company law,[82] the sale of shares can here however be restricted.[83] If selling is linked to assent by management, management must exercise its discretion in good faith and in the interests of the company.[84] Such consent clauses are also possible in most other countries.[85] Comparably with the UK, in Germany the management board's decision must take appropriate account of the interests of the company and the shareholders.[86] While in France there is only a bar on abuse of law, according to the prevailing view, a sale of shares to fellow shareholders may not be linked to management assent.[87] In other respects too, a block by management is not permitted. Instead, it must

[78] Cf. for Europe: Art. 46(1) of Directive 2001/34/EC (but also Art. 46(3): exception possible if the clause does not disturb the market); for Japan: Kawamoto *et al.* (2001: para. 312); Kozuka (2003: 140).

[79] See Wymeersch (2001c: para. 84); van Ryn (1990: para. 5-121).

[80] See Thümmel (1995: 55).

[81] See Ch. 2, section IV.1.b above.

[82] See Ch. 2, section IV.1.b above.

[83] Cf. Davies (2003: 37–8); Xuereb (1989: 130 *et seq.*); Green (2001: 7).

[84] See, more generally, Ch. 5, section II.1 below.

[85] E.g. §§ 68(2)(ss.1, 2), 180(2) GerAktG; Arts. L. 228-23 *et seq.* FrCCom; § 6.27(d)(3) MBCA; § 202(c)(3) DelGCL; §§ 107(1), 136 JapCA.

[86] See Baums and Möller (2000: 76); Hüffer (2006: § 68 para. 15).

[87] Cf. Dalloz (2005: Art. L. 228-24 para. 16); Merle (2005: paras. 321, 324 note 7); Schindler (1999: 230 *et seq.*).

name an alternative buyer, or acquire the shares itself (Art. L. 228-24(3) FrCCom). The same has also been true since 1966 in Japan.[88] Moreover, in most countries, clauses allowing only particular persons as purchasers or giving them a right of first refusal are permissible.[89] Matters are different in Germany, since mandatory rules of company law[90] would stand in the way of such a rule. General limits can be found in the US: any restriction on selling must be reasonably in the company's interest, and it is necessary for the share certificate to contain a reference to the restrictions (§ 8-204 US-UCC) or for the purchaser to know of them.[91]

On the whole, except for the UK and China, there is a mixed picture, where legal systems seek to balance the interests of small-company shareholders. For public companies, however, sale is in general possible. The interests of the shareholder as investor thus seem in principle guaranteed.

d) Practical difficulties

In practice, the sale of shares often depends on whether a liquid and efficient share market exists in the first place. Since public share trading is still more common in the US and the UK than in France, Germany or Japan, price determination on the exchanges is more reliable here, and exit more readily available.[92] For China, there is the further problem that the state itself buys and sells shares to stabilize prices, thus influencing the market.[93] Finally, there is the danger that alternative trading systems or 'internalization' may set prices for a growing number of shares outside the exchanges. The prices determined on the exchanges may thus become less reliable unless, as provided for instance in the EU,[94] transparency standards compel the financial institutions to open their trading books to competitors when processing securities orders internally.

Secondly, clearing and settlement of securities transactions in cross-border trade may raise problems. These obstacles and possible solutions are being looked into by a number of European and international initiatives. At the international level, in 2001, IOSCO and the Committee on Payment and Settlement Systems (CPSS) of the Bank for International

[88] § 140 JapCA; previously § 204-2(1) JapCC; see generally Kawamoto *et al.* (2001: paras. 99 *et seq.*) (from 1950 to 1966 mandatory possibility of sale).

[89] See van Ryn (1990: para. 5-117); Schindler (1999: 232); Merle (2005: para. 325).

[90] §§ 54, 55, 68(3) with 23(5) GerAktG.

[91] See Cox and Hazen (2003: § 14.10); van Ryn (1990: paras. 5-116 *et seq.*).

[92] For Japan and Germany: Fu (2001: 498, 508); for France: Mojuyé (2000: 101).

[93] See Heilmann (2001a: 27 *et seq.*).

[94] Arts. 27–8 of Directive 2004/39/EC.

Settlements (BIS) made nineteen recommendations proposing various minimum standards for securities settlement systems.[95] In 2003, these recommendations were taken up in Europe by the Committee of European Securities Regulators (CESR) and the European System of Central Banks (ESCB), which submitted detailed proposals for Standards for Securities Clearing and Settlement Systems.[96] Additionally, the Giovannini Group set up by the European Commission has submitted two reports on EU cross-border clearing and settlement arrangements. The 2001 report found fifteen barriers here.[97] For instance, fragmented infrastructure, with different processing techniques in individual Member States or national restrictions on cross-border clearing and settlement service providers, increases the costs of cross-border trade. The 2003 report therefore proposed creating a single legal regime for registering securities in the European Union. There should also be an adequate monitoring structure to guarantee all market participants the advantages of free movement in cross-border clearing and settlement.[98] The European Commission has recently taken up these reports and combined them in a Communication.[99] It is accordingly to be expected that a draft framework directive will soon be presented.

Thirdly, the question arises whether 'exit' from the company is the most important option for the shareholder, or whether voting rights ('voice') is just as important.[100] Although the shareholder can in principle most easily, painlessly and effectively express dissatisfaction by selling his shares, he cannot rely on the exit option alone. In view of the bounded rationality of the capital markets, protection through the price mechanism[101] does not work in all situations. If the shareholder wants to escape a planned change in business policy by selling, it is possible that the market will already have valued this planning negatively, so that the sale will not effectively protect him. For a shareholder with diversified investments,

[95] Available at http://www.bis.org/publ/cpss46.htm.

[96] Available at http://www.ecb.int/ecb/cons/previous/html/escbcesr-standards.en.html.

[97] Giovannini Group, Cross-Border Clearing and Settlement Arrangements in the European Union (2001), available at http://ec.europa.eu/economy_finance/giovannini/clearing_settlement_en.htm.

[98] Giovannini Group, Second Report on EU Clearing and Settlement Arrangements (2003), available at http://ec.europa.eu/economy_finance/giovannini/clearing_settlement_en.htm.

[99] Clearing and Settlement in the European Union – The Way Forward, Communication from the Commission, COM(2004)312 final.

[100] For the distinction between 'exit' and 'voice', see in particular Hirschman (1974: 39, on shareholders); on voting rights see Ch. 4, section II.1 below.

[101] On the 'efficient capital market hypothesis' see Ch. 2, section IV.1.a above.

moreover, every sale represents a risk because he thus changes his balanced portfolio and is dependent on whether a suitable alternative investment opening is available to him. Finally, the sale option fails to lead to adequate protection if all shareholders sell at the same time, or a block shareholder has just sold his share, since in these situations too the price of the shares falls.

Fourthly, the term 'exit' implies the exertion of pressure on the firm, which may be misleading. Selling shares is different from, say, a customer no longer buying a firm's products. In the latter case, a reduced profit brings a direct disadvantage for the firm. A sale of the firm's shares is different. It will often be a matter of indifference to the firm whether Mr A or Mr B is its shareholder.[102] This is true at least as long as only slight changes in everyday business are involved, and the issuer is not dependent on additional capital. With bigger falls in share prices, a sale may by contrast act as a signal that corporate management is inadequate.[103] Additionally, in this case a hostile takeover of the firm will become easier, and pressure on the firm from the remaining shareholders will increase, so that the sale may constitute a surrogate for influence through the general meeting.

e) Conclusion

There is international harmonization of the principle that the shareholder can realize his profit by selling his shares. At the statutory level, securities law seeks to promote share trading whereas company law is largely neutral towards trade in shares. The legal systems studied here allow the articles of association to restrict the transferability of shares to differing extents. This is by no means unusual for private companies. For shareholders in public companies too, selling shares may in practice be difficult or unsatisfactory if, for instance, the capital market is too inefficient or no pressure can thereby be exercised to change the management's course.

4. *Share buybacks*

For the shareholder, the case where the company back buys its own share constitutes a hybrid between sale and a dividend. On the one hand, the shareholder sells his shares. On the other, this situation resembles a

[102] Lowenstein (1999: 7–8); see also Cheffins (1997: 54); Hirschman (1974: 104).
[103] See Kalss (2001: 371); Worthington (2001b: 262 note 39).

dividend because surplus money is given out by the company to the shareholder.

The law of most countries used to be negative towards share buybacks. Since the early twentieth century, however, it has been possible in the US in company law, with only slight restrictions, and increasingly also without assent from the general meeting.[104] Certain limitations are imposed to prevent, for instance, share buybacks in cases of insolvency. According to general rules,[105] moreover, there must be no infringement of the duty of care and loyalty, although here too the business judgement rule guarantees management some room for manoeuvre. Securities law further requires, for instance, the grounds for the buyback, the source of the funds, and the volume and the price of the buyback to be disclosed (§ 13(e) US-SEA).

By contrast, in the EU, share buybacks used to be tied to narrower requirements in company law. The basic reason for the provisions in the Second Company Law Directive permitting the choice of either prohibiting the acquisition of a company's own shares or permitting them under strict conditions[106] lies in the European concept of minimum capital.[107] Although this concept has in principle remained untouched, liberalization tendencies can nonetheless be discerned. Thus, a recent amendment to the Second Directive has, *inter alia*, led to an extension of the period of management authorization from eighteen months to five years and an increase in the amount which may be purchased from the current limit of 10 per cent of assets to the whole of the distributable assets.[108] Furthermore, buybacks in Europe are now also regulated by securities law, because a regulation implementing the EU Market Abuse Directive stipulates in what circumstances trading in own shares does not constitute insider dealing or market manipulation.[109]

With respect to company law, in Germany, France, the UK and China moreover, restrictions on share buybacks have lately also been eased.[110] In Japan in 1994 and 1997, the ban on share buybacks was first gradually

[104] E.g. § 160(a) DelGCL; § 6.31(a) MBCA. [105] See Ch. 5, section II.1.b below.

[106] Arts. 19 *et seq.* of the Second Directive 77/91/EEC.

[107] For further reasons see e.g. van Ommeslaghe (1990: para. 5-55); Hirte (2003: para. 5.95); Drygala (2001: 295 *et seq.*).

[108] Art. 19(1) of the Second Directive 77/91/EEC, as amended by Directive 2006/68/EC.

[109] Art. 9 of the Market Abuse Directive 2003/6/EC; Council Regulation (EC) No. 2273/2003.

[110] § 71 GerAktG as amended by the Gesetz zur Kontrolle und Transparenz im Unternehmensbereich (KonTraG) of 27.04.1998, BGBl. I 786; Arts. L. 225-206 *et seq.* FrCCom; ss. 658 *et seq.* UK-CA; Companies (Acquisition of Own Shares) (Treasury Shares) Regulations 2003; § 143 ChinCA 2005 which extends the exceptions of § 149 ChinCA 1993.

relaxed and in 2001, on the US model, almost entirely removed.[111] Additionally, Japanese law, following US and UK law, contains a provision allowing the issue of redeemable shares.[112]

In the upshot, these relaxations point to a move away from the concept of minimum capital. It also demonstrates that the interest in flexible corporate financing, for which a company's own shares can be used, can induce the legislator to deregulate.[113] This need not be associated with deregulation in other areas of company law,[114] since here other policy considerations may also play a part.

5. *Conclusions*

Despite some remaining differences, the law's profit orientation is comparable internationally. The countries studied here are to that extent tending today to follow an investor-oriented model. The shareholder need not in principle fear any personal liability, and can in return realize his profit by way of a dividend or by selling his shares. Additionally, profit distribution through company share buybacks is increasingly possible. That does not, however, mean that the shareholder's financial investment will also actually pay off. That depends, first, on purely factual circumstances. Thus, besides micro- and macroeconomic developments, the specific investment strategy is decisive. This often leads to a 'multiplication' of the shareholder's position. Since many investors have only limited resources for observing the market, they would run a high risk of loss from an investment in only one company. Help comes from diversification or investment in funds.[115] Secondly, the prospects of making a profit depend on a number of other legal aspects that may indirectly affect the level of profit. Alongside external factors (such as fiscal incentives), good disclosure and effective shareholder protection can increase the value of shares coming under a particular legal system, or increase the dividends being paid out by those companies.[116] Yet it is questionable whether such increased

[111] §§ 155 *et seq.* JapCA; see also Takahashi and Rudo (1998); West (2001a: 581–2); Ködderitzsch (2001b: 139–40); Janssen *et al.* (2002: 256); Hashimoto (2002: 2 *et seq.*); Takahashi and Kirchwehm (2003: 757).

[112] §§ 108(1)(no.7), 171 JapCA; s. 684 UK-CA; cf. generally van Ryn (1990: para. 5-152); Art. 39 of the Second Directive 77/91/EEC (redeemable shares possible).

[113] See also Ch. 4, section II.4.a; Ch. 5, section I.1.d, II.2.b below.

[114] Contra Escher-Weingart (2001).

[115] See Markowitz (1971); Luck (2001: 306); Cheffins (1997: 58).

[116] For the connection between shareholder protection and dividends see La Porta *et al.* (2000a).

protection for profits would be sufficient. Some studies have demonstrated that increased shareholder activity affects the value of a share positively.[117] Following on from what Albert O. Hirschman found for associations generally,[118] for joint stock companies a combination of 'voice' and 'exit' accordingly suggests itself.

II. The active shareholder

By contrast with bondholders and other creditors, the typical shareholder can actively involve himself in the fate of the company through his vote. It is, however, not self-evident why the legislator should take an 'active shareholder' as a basis (subsection 1 below). And it is also a complex question whether there actually are legal rules which encourage active involvement (subsections 2–4 below).

1. The purpose of shareholder participation

From an historical viewpoint, it is not a matter of course that every shareholder has the right to cast a vote. Although the general meeting had by the early nineteenth century become established as a body,[119] often only major shareholders could take part in it.[120] And, in Germany in 1929, Rudolf Müller-Erzbach was still calling for the joint stock company to be recast as a 'core company of responsible major shareholder', since small shareholders did not guarantee the shareholder's interest would coincide with the firm's.[121]

a) The different types of shareholder

Today, most notions of shareholdership[122] allow shareholders to vote. Under the ownership model, the voting right is called 'the prime right of the shareholder',[123] the essential characteristic of equity,[124] the most important administrative right of members[125] or one of the shareholder's

[117] See Tuerks (2000: 122); for a different view see Romano (2002: 507 *et seq.*).
[118] Hirschman (1974: 103); see also Kalss (2001: 341–2).
[119] See Ch. 1, section III.2 above.
[120] Cf. Zöllner (1963: 125–6); Hopt (1980: 151); Horn (1979: 159); von Rechenberg (1986: 17–18) (also for France).
[121] Müller-Erzbach (1929).
[122] See generally Ch. 3, section I above.
[123] Cf. Mülbert (1996a: 56, 58, 143) on the GerAktG 1884 ('Das vorzüglichste Recht des Aktionärs').
[124] Shleifer and Vishny (1997: 751).
[125] BGH, BGHZ 70, 122.

essential participatory and creative rights as co-owner of the company.[126] The background here is, first, that shareholders indirectly bear the costs and benefits of the economic development of the company and there is therefore an incentive to grant and to exercise joint administrative rights. Secondly, shareholders typically cannot protect themselves through contract, so that by way of compensation voting rights are granted.

For the shareholder-as-parliamentarian model, shareholder participation provides 'checks and balances', thus helping with monitoring management and with management responsibility. This is not only in the interest of the shareholders, but also serves the efficiency of the company as a whole, the legitimacy of power structures within the company and good corporate governance in general.[127]

The investor-oriented view may both support and reject the voting right. On the one hand, voting monitors the shareholder's original investment decision. For the investor, thus, the vote has primarily an economic 'emergency-brake function', setting bounds on excessive risk-taking or risk-averseness of management. That makes participation at general meetings rational, thus helping to avoid ill-informed individual investment decisions.[128] Additionally, the market for corporate control[129] shows that the vote can be of interest to investors. Takeovers are of decisive importance especially for the investor-oriented view that relies on market forces. The market for corporate control, however, presupposes not just the saleability of shares but also the right to vote, since otherwise taking over control of a company would not be possible.

On the other hand, however, a contrary view may be advanced that the investor has swapped control of the company for marketability of the shares. With a transparent, open and efficient market, the value of shares will correspond to the real worth of the involvement.[130] The possibility of selling shares can therefore adequately guarantee the shareholder's interests. Even if this is exceptionally not the case, a voting right could be neither necessary nor reasonable.[131] The value of the share, which is all that concerns the investor, could be guaranteed by, say, an appraisal right or the possibility of suing management. Moreover, some studies have

126 DSW-Europastudie (1999: 85).

127 Cf. Simmonds (2001: 510, 512); Ferran (1999: 259); Davis (1999: 384); Grantham (1998: 575).

128 See Easterbrook and Fischel (1991: 66 *et seq.*); Ferran (1999: 245–6).

129 See Ch. 5, section II.1.a below.

130 On the 'efficient capital market hypothesis' see Ch. 2, section IV.1.a above.

131 Roth (1972: 206 *et seq.*); Wiedemann (1980: 353); cf. also Hill (2000b: 39, 58–9), (2000a: 20).

shown that no significant relationship can be established between shareholder activism and a firm's performance.[132] Voting rights might even be harmful, since managers know better what measures should be taken, whereas with shareholder votes at general meetings there is a danger of inconsistent, erratic and short-sighted decision-making.[133]

b) The 'rational apathy' of shareholders

Additionally, a sceptical view may be put forward that in practice the 'rational apathy' of shareholders prevents a lively shareholder democracy. This is by no means a new phenomenon. Adam Smith described the practice as follows:

> The trade of a joint stock company is always managed by a court of directors. This court, indeed, is frequently subject, in many respects, to the control of a general court of proprietors. But the greater part of those proprietors seldom pretend to understand anything of the business of the company; and when the spirit of faction happens not to prevail among them, give themselves no trouble about it, but receive contentedly such half-yearly or yearly dividend as the directors think proper to make to them.[134]

Rational apathy is present where the costs to shareholders of activism exceed its benefits. Typical cases concern companies with dispersed shareholdings whose shares are traded on a developed capital market.[135] Here, institutional investors (and also individuals) can if dissatisfied simply sell their shares and invest in other shares. A greater level of activism would not only be more costly, but would also boost one's own interest only to a small extent. Since in these companies every shareholder has only a small share, he would primarily be helping other shareholders. This 'free-rider effect' leads to the classic dilemma of collective action:[136] while it would be better for all shareholders if all took an informed decision, it is rational for the individual shareholder to keep the costs of exercising the voting right as low as possible and not get actively involved.

Passivity is not, however, confined to this sort of share structure. Where one or more shareholders in a company have large blocks of shares, active exercise of voting rights by the other shareholders is mostly pointless. And even the blockholders themselves do not necessarily exert their influence through participation in the general meeting. Instead, they may often act

[132] B. Black (1997: 459, 462–3) with further references.

[133] See Gordon (1991: 359–60) ('social choice' and 'cycling' as problems); Lipton and Rosenblum (2003: 78) (investors 'self-interested' and 'short-sighted').

[134] Smith (1776: 741). [135] Berle and Means (1932). [136] See generally Olson (1965).

on management through informal channels, thus influencing the firm's course.[137]

On the whole, it is thus not surprising that in all the countries – both those with mainly concentrated, and dispersed, shareholder ownership – there is talk of the inefficiency of the general meeting:[138] in the US and the UK, one major cause of inefficiency is that the exercise of voting rights is often pre-empted by voting proxies in favour of management.[139] At the general meeting, accordingly, there is hardly any communication or discussion between management and shareholders. While things may be different in Germany, because many shareholders make active use of their right to information, inefficiency then lies in misuses of the right to question and the low attendance at general meetings.[140] A combination of these problems is to be found in Japan. It is said that, in Japan, interlocking shareholdings and the system of written voting, with assent from large shareholders mostly secured beforehand, lead to 'skeletonization' ('keigaka') of the general meeting into a mere ceremony.[141] On the other hand, in Japan there are also the 'sokaiya', shareholders who deliberately disrupt the general meeting by their behaviour.[142] For the position in China, the decisive point is that, in many companies, the state has predominant influence. General meetings are then either short, meagre in content or even not held at all.[143] Similarly, for France, it is said that, for small joint stock companies, the general meeting is often pointless (since in practice all decisions will be made outside of the meeting), whereas for public companies it is problematic that shareholders are often uninformed or unmotivated.[144]

Nonetheless, the passivity of shareholders and the inefficiency of the general meeting should not be regarded as insuperable. Rather, it depends on the legal rules to determine how shareholder participation rights can be made more attractive and effective, and the general meeting made into a genuine decision-making body of the company.[145]

[137] See also Ch. 4, section II.4.c below.

[138] See generally Großfeld (1971: paras. 4-244 *et seq.*); for the US: Wohlwend (2001: 77–8); for the UK: Davies (1999: 332), (2003: 327); for Japan: Menden (1999: 53); for Germany: Kessler (1998: 608); for France: Merle (2005: para. 456); for China: Schipani and Liu (2002: 36).

[139] See Ch. 4, section II.3.c below.

[140] See the data in Zetzsche (2004: Appendix C) and Spindler (2006: 32).

[141] See Taniguchi (1988: 201, 230–1); Kawamoto *et al.* (2001: para. 452); Marutschke (1999: 233); Learmount (2002: 134 *et seq.*).

[142] See Ch. 4, section II.4.a below.

[143] See Schipani and Liu (2002: 26).

[144] Cf. Merle (2005: para. 456).

[145] Großfeld (1971: para. 4-194); for the UK cf. Davies (2003: 327); for France: Mojuyé (2000: 77 note 12, 100).

2. *Modes of shareholder voting*

In general, shareholder voting happens at ordinary or extraordinary general meetings.[146] Other forms of shareholder voting are less widespread.

Particularly in the US, it may, however, be possible for a measure to be adopted by a written consent procedure without calling a general meeting. In most US states all shareholders have to agree.[147] For public companies with a large number of shareholders, the consent procedure is thus impossible in practice. Delaware is different, because consent by the majority that would be needed to pass such a measure in the general meeting is sufficient (§ 228(a)–(c) DelGCL). This provision does not, however, apply to the election of directors. Moreover, in practice the majority rule is mostly excluded by agreement.[148]

Written procedures in other countries are provided for smaller companies. In France and Germany, the general meeting can be foregone only in the case of private companies (GmbH, srl) and with consent of all members.[149] Unanimity was also required in the pre-2006 law in the UK (s. 381A UK-CA 1985). Now, however, the law provides that private companies can use the written consent procedure, without requiring any particular majority.[150] In Japan, it is not unusual with small close companies that the general meeting is actually not held. Since general-meeting documents are checked only for completeness, it is in practice possible through fictitious minutes, for which computer programs are available, to do without a general meeting entirely.[151]

Although these exceptions are at present not widespread, the 'classical model' whereby shareholders act through the general meeting as the 'company's parliament' may change.[152] However, since at present the classical general meeting with attendance is still predominant, the issue will be analyzed in the next two subsections of whether its procedures encourage or hinder shareholder activity.

[146] For ordinary general meetings see e.g. §§ 120(1)(s.1), 175(1)(s.2) GerAktG; Art. L. 225-100 FrCCom; s. 336 UK-CA; Art. 54(1) SE-Reg; § 101 ChinCA; § 43(s.2) ChinMandProv; § 52(s.2) ChinArticles; § 296(1) JapCA; for extraordinary meetings see generally DSW-Europastudie (1999: 9, 80) and e.g. §§ 7.01, 7.02 MBCA.

[147] See § 7.04(a) MBCA; Cox and Hazen (2003: § 13.12).

[148] See Dooley and Goldman (2001: 759).

[149] § 48(2) GerGmbHG; Art. L. 223-27(1)(s.2) FrCCom.

[150] See ss. 288 *et seq.* UK-CA and also Company Law Reform (2005: 31–2, D7); Modernising Company Law (2002: paras. 2.13, 2.27, 2.31 *et seq.*).

[151] Cf. Rodatz (1995: 251); Hayakawa (1996: 271); Marutschke (1999: 234–5). However, a claim for nullification of the decision of the general meeting would be possible: see Kliesow (2001: 61, 123).

[152] See Ch. 10, section I.2.d below.

3. *Shareholder involvement prior to the general meeting*

Shareholder activity depends decisively on the legal provisions which protect their interests prior to the general meeting. If shareholders had no influence on the date and agenda of the general meeting (subsection a below), and were not informed about it in good time and transparently (b below), and were not able to appoint representatives to look after their interests (subsection c below), then shareholder activity would become practically impossible.

a) Shareholder influence on convocation and agenda

Intuitively, it might be thought that convoking the general meeting and setting its agenda ought to be incumbent on the shareholders themselves, since it is 'their' body. But this is not the case. Instead, competence lies in principle with management. Only in exceptional cases are shareholders able to influence these matters. This approach cannot be fitted uniformly into the theoretical models of the shareholder.[153] On the ownership model, active conduct by shareholders, and not just management, could be expected in matters of convocation. The situation is more compatible with the parliamentary model of separation of powers. Since management as the executive body has the best picture of the opportunities and risks of business practices, it seems sensible to give it primacy in presenting these points to the general meeting and administratively preparing the latter. This is also in line with investors' interests. Since investors are interested primarily in their financial gain, they would probably find the business of convocation and agenda-setting too much trouble.

(1) Competences. Calling the general meeting is in general incumbent on management (board).[154] An exception is made in some countries, where the ordinary general meeting is not called in a given year. In this case, the courts or government may impose convocation.[155] It is potentially more controversial if shareholders call, independently of the annual recurrence, for convocation of a general meeting. No internationally uniform threshold for how many shareholders are required to impose this

[153] See Ch. 3, section I above.

[154] E.g. § 121(2)(s.1) GerAktG; § 102 ChinCA; § 296 JapCA; Art. L. 225-103(1) FrCCom; s. 302 UK-CA (in contrast to the previous law where this was only based on the articles: see Ferran (1999)).

[155] § 7.03(a)(1) MBCA; § 211(c) DelGCL. In the UK s. 367 UK-CA 1985 was repealed by the 2006 reform.

exists. Most frequently, the figure is 5 per cent[156] or 10 per cent[157] of registered voting capital. More rarely, there is a 3 per cent threshold (§ 297 JapCA) or a requirement for shareholders to have held their shares for a given period.[158] It is, moreover, exceptional that some US states have no statutory regulation in this matter, so that this minority right can be granted only in the articles of association.[159]

Differences also exist in the details of convocation rights. In Germany and Japan, the minority can be authorized by a court to call the general meeting.[160] In France, convocation may be done by petition through a court agent (Art L. 225-103(2)(no.2) FrCCom) and, in the US, on the model of § 7.03(a)(2) MBCA, sometimes by the court itself. By contrast, UK law provides that the minority can without any court involvement call the general meeting (s. 305 UK-CA). What model China will choose is not yet clear. It is a matter of debate in China whether a court procedure is necessary, or whether exceptionally convocation may also be done by the shareholder minority itself.[161]

Where the courts are involved, they are sometimes (though not in Germany)[162] given some discretion. In France, it is within the court's discretion whether to call a general meeting in the 'intérêt social'.[163] In Japan, the court may refuse to convoke where the issue is not within the general meeting's competence or the demand for convocation constitutes an abuse of law, is pointless or is contrary to the company's interests.[164] In the UK, the minority shareholders may convoke a general meeting, and the courts have a discretion where, for instance, it is impracticable to conduct the meeting in the manner prescribed by the articles or the Companies Act (s. 306 UK-CA).

(2) The agenda. Competence to set the agenda basically for the general meeting arises out of the rules for convocation. Here too, the initiative

156 E.g. § 122(1), (2) GerAktG; Art. L. 225-103(2)(no.2) FrCCom.

157 E.g. s. 303(3) UK-CA, § 7.02(a)(2) MBCA, § 101(no.3) ChinCA; see also Art. 55 SE-Reg (at least 10 per cent of the subscribed capital).

158 §§ 122(1)(s.3) with 147(1)(ss.2, 3) GerAktG: three months; § 297 JapCA: six months.

159 Cf. Cox and Hazen (2003: § 13.13).

160 §§ 121, 122(1), (3) GerAktG; § 297(4) JapCA.

161 See Comberg (2000: 104–5); For listed companies self-enforcement is possible: see Notice of the CSRC on Promulgating the Rules for the General Meetings of Shareholders of Listed Companies 2006, Art. 9.

162 See Wiedemann, in: GroßkommAktG (1993: § 122 para. 59).

163 Cf. Guyon (1999: 97); Dalloz (2005: Art. 225-103 paras. 4 *et seq.*).

164 See Taniguchi (1988: 206).

lies in principle with management, and only in exceptional cases is it given to shareholders. This is not surprising, since putting an item on the agenda can be likened to a second convocation of the general meeting and its linkage with the original convocation. Nonetheless, there exist divergences, because the right to set an agenda item often has less strict requirements. This can be explained by the practical argument that convocation of a new meeting is costlier than merely setting an agenda item, so that stricter requirements should naturally be placed on the right to convoke.

The number of shareholders required to set an agenda item for the general meeting is usually 5 per cent of the registered capital.[165] Lower thresholds are found for instance in Japan at 1 per cent (§ 303(2) JapCA), in China at 3 per cent (§ 103(2) ChinCA), in France with a graduated threshold which for large companies may be 0.5 per cent (Art. 128 FrDécret), and in the US at 1 per cent, or even only one share (discussed further below). Again, an absolute figure (i.e. regardless of the number of shares owned) is sometimes used, for instance support from 300 shareholders (§ 303(2) JapCA), shareholders with nominal holdings of €500,000 (§ 122(2) GerAktG), or a market value of US$2,000 (SEC Rule 14a-8(b)(1)), or support from holders of not less than 100 shares on which there has been paid up an average sum of not less than £100 (s. 314(2)(b) UK-CA).

Further details of the exercise of this minority right also demonstrates differences. Securities regulation in the US, associated with the system of proxy voting, lay down particular requirements.[166] Here, two possibilities are to be distinguished. First, under the shareholder communication rule (SEC Rule 14a-7), any shareholder may collect proxies for matters relating to the general meeting. To enable contact with fellow shareholders, management may at its discretion either send the shareholder a list of other shareholders or pass on his communication to the other shareholders. The problem is, however, that in either case the shareholder must bear the costs. Since the companies to which the proxy-voting provisions apply[167] are usually public companies, the costs are usually out of proportion to the benefit the shareholder may gain. Accordingly, and secondly, shareholders who have held 1 per cent of shares for at least one year may

[165] E.g. § 122(2) GerAktG; Art. L. 225-105 FrCCom; ss. 314(2)(a), 338(3)(a) UK-CA; Art. 6(2) of Directive 2007/36/EC (not more than 5 per cent); for China see also: § 57 ChinMandProv; § 54 ChinArticles.

[166] SEC Regulation 14a; § 14(a) US-SEA; on what follows see e.g. Cox and Hazen (2003: §§ 13.29 *et seq.*); B. Black (1997: 459–60); Tuerks (2000: 87 *et seq.*); Merkt (1991: paras. 633 *et seq.*); Wunderlich and Labermeier (2000: 153 *et seq.*) and Ch. 4, section 3.c below.

[167] See Ch. 1, section II.1 above.

require proxy documents to be included, at the company's expense, with the general voting documentation (SEC Rule 14a-8). Particular areas are, however, excluded. These notably include proposals that relate to an election for membership to the company's board of directors, and proposals that directly conflict with one of the company's own proposals to be submitted to shareholders at the same meeting.[168] In these cases, only the cumbersome path via SEC Rule 14a-7 is possible.

By contrast, most other countries use company law rather than securities law to govern voting proxies. Nor is there a distinction between two variants, in only one of which the company bears the cost. But there are differentiations here too. German law provides for a distinction between the general right to motions, the right to counter-motions and the right of proposal for elections (§§ 122(2), 126, 127 GerAktG). It is only for the general right to motions that a minimum number of shares is required, whereas to avoid abuses the right to counter-motions, here open to every individual shareholder, is subject to a number of restrictions (§ 126(2) GerAktG). Since in France and Japan a threshold always has to be passed (see above), there are no such comprehensive provisions for exceptional situations in those countries. French, German and Japanese law all provide no differentiation as regards the expense of communication. Here, by contrast with the US, the company must bear the costs of communications in every case, since the need for court involvement (see above) reduces the risk of needless costs. A comprehensive catalogue of abuses has accordingly not had to be established.[169] Similarly, there are only minor substantive restraints in the UK (cf. s. 317 UK-CA). As justification for this one may point to the higher thresholds in the UK by comparison with the US.[170] Furthermore, it used to be the case that the shareholder minority had to bear the costs itself (ss. 376(1), 377(1)(b) UK-CA 1985). However, the 2006 reform included a provision to the effect that the costs need not be borne by the shareholders if the proposals were received before the end of the financial year preceding the general meeting (ss. 316, 340 UK-CA).

(3) Conclusion. There are two competing interests. On the one hand, shareholder involvement prior to a general meeting is to be made effective.

[168] SEC Rule 14a-8(i)(8), (9); see also the proposal Directors Nominations, Exchange Act Release No. 34-48626 of 14.10.2003 (available at http://www.sec.gov/rules/proposed/34-48626.htm).

[169] § 304 JapCA excludes a proposal if the proposed solution would violate any law (including the articles), or was unsuccessful not more than three years ago.

[170] Davies (1999: 348–9); see also Ferran (1999: 265 note 146).

On the other, too great an involvement may damage the overall interests of the company, and of shareholders who do not wish to become active. In some countries, there is accordingly a requirement for a 'qualified membership'. The qualification may lie in formal thresholds, such as minimum number of shares or a minimum period they have been held for, or in material limits, such as the exceptions to the right to (counter-) motions in the US and Germany.

Country-specific differences are hardly surprising given these opposing interests and different legislative means. Yet a certain approximation can be discerned. For instance, in 1983 in the US the provision giving every shareholder a right of proposal for proxy-voting documents was restricted in favour of a 1 per cent threshold by SEC Rule 14a-8. The same threshold also exists in current Japanese law. Approximation came from another starting-point, however, in 1981, since previously there was no general provision for a minority right to an agenda item. This tendency towards shareholder activism is also confirmed in the debates in Germany and the UK. Here too, less strict requirements are being called for.[171] This happened only recently in France, where now only 5 per cent (reduced from 10 per cent) of registered capital suffices. For the UK, additionally, the threshold for the right to place an item on the agenda was lowered in the nineteenth and twentieth centuries, from 20 per cent to 10 per cent and then 5 per cent.

b) Timely information on the general meeting

An effective exercise of shareholder rights before and during the general meeting is not possible without timely information. Thus, early information about the general meeting is indispensable in order to permit shareholders to take an active part in the meeting.

(1) Form. The mode of communication is traditionally connected with the preference for registered or bearer shares in the individual countries. Since with registered shares the identity of the shareholder should in principle be known, these shareholders are to be informed personally.[172]

171 See Bachmann (2001: 635, 636); Regierungskommission Corporate Governance (2001: para. 101) (also on the UK).

172 E.g. § 125(2)(no.3) GerAktG, Art. 125 FrDécret, § 229(1) JapCA; s. 310 UK-CA. In China the legal position is not yet clear: cf. Comberg (2000: 98 *et seq.*). Additionally, according to §§ 20, 22 ChinMandProv and § 53 ChinArticles, two invitations might be necessary, see Wang (2000: 11).

Furthermore, in the UK no public notice is necessary.[173] The same is true in France for the case where a company has only registered shareholders (Art. 124(2) FrDécret), whereas in Germany the possibility of dispensing with public notice depends on there being a provision in the articles of association (§ 121(4)(s.1) GerAktG). For bearer shares by contrast, the emphasis is on the public notice, which may be published in, for instance, the electronic Federal Gazette, the Bulletin des Annonces Légales Obligatoires or daily newspapers.[174] Furthermore, financial intermediaries who have custody of shares can be obliged to forward information to bearer shareholders (§ 128(1) GerAktG).

This distinction in the form of information is, however, losing its importace with the convergence of registered and bearer shares.[175] Also, where it is, or is becoming, the practice that trustees or financial intermediaries are entered in the register of members, those substantively entitled can no longer be directly reached in the case of registered shares. The solution need not, however, lie in public notification only. Instead, to improve communication, those substantively entitled may also have the information on the general meeting supplied to them individually, being forwarded by the registered shareholders. For the future too, at least for public companies, having detailed information published on the firm's website in the run-up to the general meeting may be considered.[176]

(2) Time-limit. The time-limits for calling the general meeting vary between one month and ten days.[177] The pattern depends in particular on how minority rights are exercised (see subsection a above). In France, for instance, public companies must make the agenda publicly available thirty days before the general meeting. Then, shareholders have ten days for amendment and extension proposals. After a further five days, finally, comes the official invitation (including proxy documents), which will now take account of the shareholders' motions (Arts. 126, 130 FrDécret). By contrast, in Germany, official notice of the meeting must be given one month before the date of the general meeting (§ 123(1) GerAktG). Minority rights are met by notifying shareholders of further agenda items

[173] See Pennington (1994: para. 90.10.110).

[174] See §§ 25, 121 GerAktG; Art. 124 FrDécret.

[175] See also Ch. 4, section IV below. [176] See Ch. 10, section I.2.c below.

[177] See § 123(1) GerAktG (one month); § 103(1) ChinCA for bearer shares (thirty days); Art. 5 of Directive 2007/36/EC (at least twenty-one days); s. 307(2)(a) UK-CA (twenty-one days for annual general meeting); § 103(1) ChinCA (twenty days); § 229(1) JapCA (two weeks); § 7.05(a) MBCA and § 222(b) DelGCL (ten days).

at least ten days before convocation (§ 124(1)(s.2) GerAktG) and by making countermotions or election proposals accessible (§§ 126(1), 127 GerAktG). In the US, the convocation provisions are again connected with the provisions on proxy voting. While here too company law provides for a notice period of, for instance, ten days before the date for the general meeting,[178] for companies to which the proxy rules apply[179] a special procedure requires the taking of motions under SEC Rule 14a-8 into account in good time. This procedure starts very early, since for ordinary general meetings proposals must as a rule have been submitted 120 days before proxy statements are sent out. This is also necessary because the further procedure of examination, forwarding and voting instructions is highly time-consuming, and is regulated in detailed fashion.

All in all, no uniform practice can be found. It is also hard to discern any trends. It has been suggested on the one hand that notice periods are tending to lengthen.[180] The explanation offered for this is the growing size of companies, since that makes the questions increasingly complex and thus also calls for longer preparation time. This may also be because the shareholdership is becoming more international, and thus information channels are being extended. This development need not be based only on greater spatial distances. Additionally, information may pass more slowly because especially with international investors information frequently flows through various levels of financial intermediaries. In practice, accordingly, it has been reported that meetings have been held before some foreign shareholders have received notice of it.[181]

On the other hand, in the UK, the suggestion has been made to shorten the notice period from twenty-one to fourteen days.[182] This corresponds to the need to be able to react flexibly to current events through the general-meeting. Moreover, the new media enable faster and simpler communication. Internationalization and intermediarization may thus not really be a problem, since for electronic communications spatial distances and the interposition of third parties need not be a problem.

(3) Content.[183] The documents accompanying the convocation should inform shareholders about the forthcoming meeting and enable them

178 E.g. § 7.05 MBCA; § 222(b) DelGCL. 179 See Ch. 1, section II.1 above.

180 Druey (1999: 368). 181 See DSW-Europastudie (1999: 95).

182 See Company Law Reform (2005: D 25); Modernising Company Law (2002: para. 2.17). Yet, the new law itself kept the twenty-one days requirement for the annual general meeting of public companies: s. 307 UK-CA.

183 For disclosure in general see Ch. 4, section III below.

to plan accordingly. The shareholder must therefore receive at least an agenda.[184] How detailed this has to be depends on various factors. Thus, distinctions are often drawn between an ordinary and extraordinary meeting, private and public companies, and provisions defining proxies and other regulations.

Since it is mostly known what ordinary general meetings will be about (namely, dividends and elections), the agenda is of more interest with regard to extraordinary general meetings. In Delaware, for example, an agenda has to be attached only for cases of extraordinary general meetings (§ 222(a) DelGCL). Other countries' laws are more moderate in this respect. In the UK, the agenda for ordinary general meetings need in general contain only the essential content of proposals for resolutions, while, for general meetings where 'special' resolutions are to be dealt with, the 'entire substance' of the proposal must be given.[185] The same is true in China for companies listed on stock exchanges abroad. For these, a description of the object of the resolution, for which a special majority is required, is necessary (§ 56 ChinMandProv). Otherwise, the company's articles of association is determinative (§ 82(no.12) ChinCA). In Germany, by contrast, proposals for resolutions must appear in the agenda on every topic the general meeting has to decide (§ 124 GerAktG).[186] Differentiations can be found here too, however, since in special cases, such as amendments to the articles of association (§ 124(2)(s.2) GerAktG), exclusion of pre-emption rights (§ 186(4) GerAktG)[187] and basic or structural measures,[188] the precise content of resolutions, or a special report thereon, must be communicated to the shareholders. The provisions of the pre-2005 Japanese Commercial Code were similar,[189] whereas now details on information in the run-up of the general meeting are delegated to secondary legislation (§ 298(1)(no.5) JapCA).

[184] E.g. § 124 GerAktG; §§ 299(4) with 298(1)(no.2) JapCA; § 103(1) ChinCA; Art. 123 FrDécret.

[185] See Davies (1997b: 573–4), (2003: 357–8); Modern Company Law for a Competitive Economy (1999: para. 4.45); see also *Normandy* v. *Ind Coope & Co.* [1908] 1 Ch 84 (Chancery Division) (for requirements which may follow from a provision in the articles).

[186] This is as a rule different in France (Art. 123(2) FrDécret) unless there are proxies (Art. 133 FrDécret). Moreover, the shareholder can get the proposals himself (Arts. 135, 138, 139, 141 FrDécret).

[187] This is based on Art. 29(4)(s.3) of the Second Directive 77/91/EEC.

[188] §§ 293 a, 319(4) GerAktG; §§ 8, 63, 127, 192 GerUmwG.

[189] §§ 245(2), 342, 275(2), 408(2) JapCC.

For the ordinary annual general meeting, shareholders must be informed about which board members are seeking election[190] and about the annual accounts. In Japan, and essentially also in the UK and the US, the annual accounts are sent out along with the notice of the meeting.[191] In Germany and France by contrast, the annual accounts are in principle only available at the company's head office.[192] On request, however, here too shareholders can obtain a copy of the annual accounts. While the effectiveness of this right might be doubted, since small shareholders in particular would first have to overcome their 'rational apathy' towards such a request, in the upshot this difference, and thus the distinction between a 'pull' and a 'push' system, is hardly decisive. Small shareholders will as a general rule in any case be unable to grasp the content of the annual accounts. Instead, the evaluation is done by third parties, such as analysts and banks, which then, in the ideal case, pass their analysis on to shareholders.

For larger companies, there are often further requirements in company or securities law.[193] Securities-law provisions are especially important in the US, as compensation for their liberal company law. Under the provisions on proxies, here – and similarly in Japan – proxy documents must contain considerable information,[194] since, by using a proxy, shareholders must vote in advance based on the information they have to hand. By contrast, the shareholder who attends the general meeting can in principle fill any information gap whilst there. However, since the 1960s the link to the capital market and to proxies has been loosened. Apart from the applicability of state securities law to other large companies (§ 12(g) US-SEA), even where no management authorization is sought, an information statement (SEC Rule 14c-2) is required.

By contrast, the UK, France and Germany have no provisions regarding detailed information necessary for proxies.[195] In Germany, only proxies to credit institutions and shareholders' associations are specifically

[190] E.g. §§ 124(1)(s.3), 125(1)(s.3) GerAktG; Art. 135(no.5) FrDécret; Art. 22(3) Draft Model Articles of Association for Public Companies (June 2006) (old Art. 77 UK-Table A); Notice of the CSRC on Promulgating the Rules for the General Meetings of Shareholders of Listed Companies 2006, Art. 17.

[191] § 437 JapCA; § 16.20 MBCA; SEC Rule 14a-3(b); ss. 423 *et seq.* UK-CA (with the option to provide a summary financial statement only).

[192] § 175(2) GerAktG; Art. 135(no.6a) FrDécret.

[193] See e.g. Art. 130 FrDécret; § 56 ChinArticles; ch. 13 UK-Listing Rules.

[194] For the US see Ch. 4, section II.3.a above; for Japan: Smith (1996: 167).

[195] For France see Art. 133 FrDécret; for the UK see Ch. 4, section II.3.c below.

regulated (§§ 125(1), 128, 135 GerAktG). Otherwise, there are no specific rules regarding the conferment of a voting proxy. This absence of regulation follows, first, from the fact that, because of the fairly comprehensive agenda, supplementary information for proxies is less important. Secondly, the legal position is connected with the person of the proxy. By contrast with other countries, in Germany a proxy to management was traditionally uncommon, and according to commentators even inadmissible.[196] There was thus, by comparison with the US, less danger of management's being able to misuse its information advantage in combination with the management vote to control the course of the general meeting. This has changed, however. Since 2001, proxies to management have been explicitly admissible.[197] However, even now the German legislature has refrained from further regulation for the time being, so as to allow time to test out this form of proxy.[198]

All in all, across the countries studied here, shareholders have information available that could enable active participation. However, there are limits to this. In principle, it is quite justified for the information to be confined to essential aspects of the planned general meeting. If all even tangentially relevant information had to be provided, that would mean not only a disproportionate cost for management, but also a needless flood of information for the shareholders. Again, too much information could be harmful for the general meeting as an institution. For it might create a presumption that only these aspects and arguments would be dealt with at the general meeting,[199] thus imposing inflexibility on the meeting.

c) Voting in advance

If a shareholder cannot or does not wish to attend the general meeting, he may vote in advance. On the one hand, some countries enable shareholders to vote on their own behalf before the general meeting through a postal vote. On the other, there are possibilities in all countries of authorizing others to vote for you.

[196] Cf. e.g. Tuerks (2000: 227 *et seq.*); Hanloser (2001: 356); Noack (2001b: 61–2), (2000b: 1475 *et seq.*); Hüther (2001: 71).

[197] Gesetz zur Namensaktie and zur Erleichterung der Stimmrechtsausübung (NaStraG) of 18.01.2001, BGBl. I 123.

[198] See Ch. 4, section II.3.c below.

[199] For Germany see: § 124(4) GerAktG; for the UK: Davies (2003: 344–5) ('alters the substance of the resolution as set out in the notice').

(1) The different types of shareholder.[200] Advanced voting is most suited to the investor-related model. For investors it makes sense to participate actively only if that is economically efficient. However, despite the customary 'dividend in kind' at general meetings in the form of food and drink, personal attendance would not be efficient.

With respect to the shareholder-as-owner model, the admissibility of representation depends on whether exercising the voting right is seen by the shareholder as a highly personal decision. This will not be the case where the shareholder is interested only in the profits to be made from his shareholding, but will be much more likely where the shareholder is personally involved in the company, where monitoring and supervision are much more important, and, which might be voided if third parties or even management itself were given a proxy. Since – as in constitutional law – there is a dialectic between utility to self and others in ownership,[201] this model thus does not provide an unambiguous solution.

A similar result follows from the democratic model. In its traditional version, the general meeting acts as the 'company parliament' for discussion and decision-making by 'its shareholders'. From a parliamentary viewpoint, a voting proxy is thus not possible, since the vote – as with a real parliament – is strictly personal and cannot be delegated. While this inadmissible delegation does not occur with postal voting, it is also incompatible with this parliamentary analogy. Were all shareholders to vote by post, the general meeting as an institution would become obsolete, since all that would be needed would be to count the votes. Moreover, if a sizeable number of shareholders voted in this way, the dynamic and communication element of the general meeting as a 'parliament' would be lost. Additionally, with postal voting – as also with proxies giving detailed instructions – there would be a risk that the anticipated exercise of the voting right would come to nought in the event of unforeseen circumstances.[202]

However, the democratic model need not necessarily be reduced to the concept of a parliamentary analogy. A conception can also be democratic that merely on the whole seeks to ensure as high, as effective and as intensive a participation as possible. This may be the case specifically with proxy or postal voting, since they enable uninformed shareholders to exercise their participation rights at all and informed ones to do so

[200] See Ch. 3, section I above.

[201] At least, according to the European perception: see Dine (2006: 345 *et seq.*).

[202] This case is explicitly addressed in French law: see Art. 131-4(no.3) FrDécret; Art. L. 225-107(2)(s.2) FrCCom.

efficiently. Yet the danger is that unregulated proxy voting may constitute an open invitation to management irresponsibility.[203] Accordingly, a proper form for voting proxies in detail matters.

(2) **The US model.** Proxy voting is very important in the US today. That was not always the case. Here, as in the UK,[204] in the nineteenth century the common law accepted that the vote was a matter of personal trust and therefore could not be delegated.[205] By contrast, today proxies are in principle admissible in voting.[206] In the case of public companies, they are so intensively used that the notion of personal attendance at general meetings is regarded as a myth.[207]

This may be surprising because quantity of regulation can actually get in the way: The voting documents have to be submitted to the SEC, which if it finds irregularities can temporarily prevent the general meeting from being held. Voting proxies apply to a single general meeting, and can give the proxy discretion only if this is explicitly stated in bold letters. And the voting documents cannot simply be sent to 'the shareholders', because they must also reach the beneficial owners. This may be done either through direct communication with those actually entitled or through forwarding by the registered owners.

However, the decisive factor in the popularity of voting proxies in the US is the fact that managements can deploy them in their own interest. Even if 'proxy fights' are now, after a decline since the late 1960s, again happening more often because of the growing influence of institutional investors,[208] there are a number of reasons why recourse to them is infrequent. First, as a general rule only management can use company resources in favour of its position, whereas opposing shareholders will themselves have to bear the considerable costs for proxy voting.[209] Secondly, there is, once again, the free-rider problem,[210] since the outcome of a successful proxy fight ultimately benefits all shareholders. Thirdly, management knows the composition and identity of its shareholders better than do the

[203] Cf. Großfeld (1971: para. 4-216) (citing Louis Loss).

[204] See Davies (2003: 360 *et seq.*).

[205] See Großfeld (1971: para. 3-217).

[206] E.g. § 7.22 MBCA, § 212(b)–(e) DelGCL; also § 402.00 NYSE Manual and the SEC rules, subsection b above.

[207] *Stoud* v. *Grace*, 606 A 2d 75, 86 (Del. Supr. 1992) ('Realities in modern corporate life have all but gutted the myth that shareholders in large publicly held companies personally attend their annual meetings').

[208] See Romano (1993: 74–5); Tuerks (2000: 120); on institutional investors see also Ch. 4, section II.4.c below.

[209] See Ch. 4, section II.3.a above.

[210] See Ch. 4, section II.1.a above.

minority shareholders, who may have to seek access to the shareholder register through the courts.[211] Fourthly, the 'Wall Street rule' operates at the expense of opposition shareholders. Many dissatisfied shareholders will often simply sell their shares, so that the remaining shareholders will tend to have a more positive attitude to the management.

In Japan, the law is similar to that in the US. After the Second World War, particularly in securities law – in company law there is only a rudimentary regulation in § 320 JapCA – a corresponding regulatory system was introduced.[212] The details, such as canvassing for votes, are, as in the US, regulated in secondary rules (cf. § 194 JapSEA). On the whole, then, here too in public companies managements are usually given proxies by shareholders.[213] This concentration of power is furthered by two specifically Japanese circumstances. First, in Japan the general meetings of most companies are held on the same day of the year.[214] For shareholders with diversified investments, personal attendance at several general meetings is thus practically excluded. Secondly, in Japan shares are often held in reciprocal holdings with other undertakings.[215] In view of the close connections between management and shareholders, supervision through the general meeting is accordingly often unnecessary.

(3) Counter-models. There is less regulation in the UK. The rules of company law, the model articles of association and securities law are relatively brief.[216] With respect to company law, the 2006 reform can be seen as an improvement. There are now, for instance, provisions on company-sponsored invitations (s. 326 UK-CA) and the rights which a proxy has, for instance, to vote and to speak at the meeting, to be elected its chairman, or to demand a poll.[217] In securities law, voting proxies must allow an alternative vote (§ 9.3.6(2) UK-Listing Rules). However, as in other countries, management controls the voting-rights mechanism.[218] It has

[211] See Ch. 4, section IV.1.b below.

[212] See Inaniwa and Brondics (1987: 16); Kawamoto *et al.* (2001: para. 474); Kawamoto (1994: 87); for differences see Smith (1996: 163 *et seq.*).

[213] See Menden (1999: 8); Inaniwa and Brodics (1987: 19); Smith (1996: 174); Oda (1999: 238); on requirements in the articles of association see Kawamoto *et al.* (2001: para. 473); Kliesow (2001: 91).

[214] See Ch. 4, section II.4.a below.

[215] See Ch. 8, section IV.2 below (also for recent changes).

[216] See ss. 324–331 UK-CA; Arts. 42, 43 Draft Model Articles for Public Companies (June 2006) (old Art. 60 UK-Table A); §§ 9.26, 13.28, 13.29 UK-Listing Rules.

[217] See ss. 324, 328, 329 UK-CA. The old law was different: see s. 372(1), (2)(c) UK-CA 1985.

[218] Cf. Davies (1997b: 360); Strätling (2003: 75).

the tactical advantage of being able first to inform the shareholders about controversial topics from its viewpoint. Additionally, in the UK, the developed market for corporate control constitutes a functional equivalent to contests over proxies which are rare in the UK.[219]

The regulation of voting proxies in China is equally meagre. § 107 ChinCA merely provides for the admissibility and written nature of voting proxies. Special regulations for public companies, local provisions and the Code of Corporate Governance further provide that proxies need not themselves necessarily be shareholders.[220] Any consolidated development is, however, yet to come about. Neither the possibility of a proxy to management nor one to banks is specifically regulated or encouraged. However, the fact that shares are mostly held at state-controlled deposit offices, rather than by banks, militates against the use of proxies.

German law displays ambivalence between these forms of proxy. The starting-point is that § 134(3) GerAktG makes a voting proxy possible, without setting limits on its duration or the person of the proxy. However, because of the traditional use of bearer shares in Germany and their depositing with banks, as well as the generally strong position of the banking sector,[221] special attention is paid to the exercise of the vote by banks on behalf of shareholders. For example, reference must be made to the possibility of revocation (§ 135(2) GerAktG), and in various provisions the potential conflict of interests of banks has been addressed.[222] Additionally, *de facto* the depository vote has lost its importance due to the trend to registered shares,[223] the increasing influence of direct banks and the internationalization of investor structures. Furthermore, the introduction of the management proxy in German law was argued for, *inter alia* on the ground that it could reduce the banks' influence.[224] Since the 2001 reform, it is explicitly admissible for a proxy to be given to the management.[225] The German legislator has not, however, set out detailed legislation of the management proxy during an initial trial. Protective measures as in the US, with special provisions on shareholder information, shareholder notification and monitoring by a federal authority, thus do

[219] See Davies (1999: 336 *et seq.*); but see also Ch. 4, section II.4.c below.

[220] § 48(no.3) ChinMandProv; § 59(s.1) ChinArticles; Nos. 9–10 ChinCG-Code; cf. also Comberg (2000: 113); Pißler (2002d: para. 3).

[221] See also Ch. 8, section IV.2.a below.

[222] § 135(1)(s.3), (5) GerAktG; § 128(2)(s.2) GerAktG; see also § 34 a GerWpHG.

[223] See Ch. 4, section IV.1.a below. [224] See Hanloser (2001: 355).

[225] § 134(3)(s.3) GerAktG as amended by Gesetz zur Namensaktie und zur Erleichterung der Stimmrechtsausübung (NaStraG) of 18.01.2001, BGBl. I 123; see also No. 2.3.3 GerCGK and note 196 above.

not exist. However, the *opinio juris* is that, by analogy with § 135(1)(s.2) GerAktG, a management proxy can be used only if accompanied by binding instructions.[226]

In France, only another shareholder or a spouse can be given a proxy (Art. L. 225-106(1) FrCCom). Further provisions relating to proxy conferment can be found in Arts. 132 to 134 FrDécret, but without setting out detailed rules, as in the US. Furthermore, the possibility exists of giving 'carte blanche' (Art. 133(no.6) FrDécret). This proxy in blank is a 'spurious' management proxy, exercised by the chair of the general meeting in favour of the board's proposed resolutions (Art. L. 225-106(6) FrCCom). Finally, in France, a postal vote is possible, which may include use of fax or e-mail (Art. L. 225-107 FrCCom; Arts. 131-1, 134 FrDécret).

Internationally, this postal vote is fairly unusual. A postal vote is also explicitly allowed in Japan. It was introduced in 1981, first for large companies,[227] and in 2001 other companies too.[228] In the other countries studied here, explicit provisions are lacking, so that, in line with the basic concepts on optionality in company law,[229] in Germany and China postal voting may be presumed to be inadmissible, and in the US and the UK, with an appropriate provision in the articles of association, postal voting may be presumed to be admissible.[230] In practice, however, the differences are not all that great. For, if a proxy is given clear instructions, this means in effect that any decision which needs to be taken at the general meeting will have been already taken before the general meeting.

(4) Conclusion. A number of striking differences appear from the analysis. The differences ought not, however, to be over-emphasized. For instance, it would be going too far to imagine that the different proxy rules make the decisive time the period prior to the general meeting in the US, and the general meeting itself in Germany.[231] While it is true that in the US, for public companies, the proxy provisions of US securities law shift a considerable part of the decision-making process into the period prior to the general meeting, it is also often the case with German public

[226] Habersack (2001: 187–8); Noack (2001b: 62), (2002c: 625); for a different view see Riegger (2001: 214).

[227] § 21-3(1) JapCCExcA; see also Taniguchi (1988: 202); Schneider (1990: 322).

[228] § 239-2(1) JapCC; now: §§ 298(1)(no.3), 311 JapCA.

[229] See Ch. 2, section IV.1.b above.

[230] For the UK: Becker (2001: 58); for China: Sharma (1999: 388) (implication from § 107 ChinCA). Art. 12 of Directive 2007/36/EC will however lead to a change of the German law.

[231] Contra Hüther (2002: 329 *et seq.*, 341).

companies that the outcome is known before the start of the general meeting. Additionally, the proxy rules do not apply to close companies, so that in such cases, in both Germany and the US, the general meeting itself can play an important part.

Moreover, common trends are discernible. Voting proxies are now in principle possible, so that the 'narrow ownership or democracy models'[232] are not followed. Additionally, a certain convergence in the person of the proxy can be noted. The singular system of the depository vote, long prevalent in Germany, is on the decline. Instead, the genuine – or, as in France, spurious – management proxy is increasingly recognized. Since management can rely on a proficient organizational apparatus, and has an information advantage and often also a cost advantage, however, this is associated with the danger of bringing a concentration of power in the hands of management and a loss of power by shareholders.[233] Nor does it necessarily matter here how strictly the exercise of the management proxy is regulated. For the proxy rules in the US, which by contrast with Germany and the UK do not rely on *laissez-faire*, are said to put the proxy 'machinery' basically in management hands, thus pre-empting the general meeting in favour of the board.[234] Consequently, while the management proxy leads to higher vote participation at the general meeting, this may be only a pseudo-democratic situation, since management also controls the general meeting through a 'dictatorship of the board'.[235] From a theoretical viewpoint, this would be justified only if the 'shareholder as investor' were to be merely a spectator, with no active involvement in the firm. It is better, however, to grant even the 'shareholder as investor' certain participatory rights, so as to ensure the value of his shares and the quality of the conduct of business.[236]

d) Conclusion

Both the common features and the differences make it clear that for the provisions governing the run-up to the general meeting a strict separation into legal families makes little sense. Instead, a number of special features, such as the capital-market focus in the US, the postal vote in France, the depository vote in Germany, the uncertainties regarding minority rights

[232] See subsection (1) above.

[233] For the US and UK: Großfeld (1971: paras. 4-240 *et seq.*); for the UK: Davies (2003: 360); for France: Sonnenberger (1991: para. III 169); for Germany: Hüther (2001: 72–3); Noack (2001b: 62).

[234] Cf. Cox and Hazen (2003: § 13.33); Merkt (1991: para. 628).

[235] Davies (2003: 360).

[236] See Ch. 4, section II.1.a above, and Ch. 12, section III below.

in China and the calling of a meeting by the shareholders without court involvement in the UK are specific to the country concerned, without any generalization about legal families being possible. Convergence can be seen both on individual points, such as limits on the right to propose, or rules on proxy voting. Furthermore, the basic conflict between active shareholder participation on the one hand and the possibilities for abuse and inefficiency on the other are taken account of in all countries. This can be seen, for instance, in the quantitative, temporal and substantive limits on shareholder minority rights. The law is thus a compromise in all the countries studied, so that an easy allocation into the theoretical models[237] is not possible. However, one can with caution point to the (moderate) investor-oriented model as being the most appropriate. This is based less on rules on convocation, agenda-setting and information provision (subsections a and b above), since, although management is primarily active here, shareholders can in principle exercise influence. In most countries, however, the proxy rules (subsection c above) give management a *de facto* advantage over shareholders.

4. *Participation in the general meeting*

The participation of shareholders or shareholder representatives in the general meeting includes attendance and voting. As with the invitation, however, here too management is not uninvolved. Moreover, the participation right, in principle equal, may be statutorily limited or may be modified in the articles of association (subsections a and b below). A strictly democratic model whereby shareholders with fully equal rights take decisions at the general meeting is at any rate to that extent not followed. Further, a distinction has to be made according to whether the provisions on participation in the general meeting tend more to encourage or inhibit shareholder activism, in particular with respect to institutional investors (c below).

a) The right to attend and to speak

The 'shareholder as parliamentarian' and the 'shareholder as owner'[238] will at any rate demand to be allowed to attend the general meeting and to speak there. The purpose of the general meeting can accordingly not be reduced to a vote. Instead, the meeting acts as a 'forum for rendering

[237] See Ch. 4, section II.1.a above. [238] See Ch. 3, section I above.

account',[239] forcing management to face criticism and questions from shareholders and enabling participants to state their positions. By contrast, on the narrow investor-based position,[240] not only may the investor waive personal participation, it may also suit him very well for the law to prevent other shareholders from using and abusing, for personal or political reasons, their right to attend and speak. This can be effected by preventing particular shareholders from attending. Alternatively, abuse may be checked in individual cases by withdrawing the right to speak, or by means of other penalties.

(1) General restrictions on attendance. The principle applying today is that all shareholders and their representatives can, with adequate legitimation, attend the general meeting. Even if this principle is not necessarily provided for by statute, it is at least presumed,[241] and also follows from the nature of the general meeting as the 'shareholders' voice'. The right to attend usually extends also to holders of non-voting preference shares.[242] Their participation may, however, in some countries be restricted or excluded by the articles of association.[243]

However, in China until recently, attendance was in practice allowed only to those holding more than a minimum number of shares.[244] Since accumulation of votes was possible, the general meeting became more of a shareholder representatives' meeting than a shareholders' one. Today, the prevailing opinion regards the exclusion of the attendance right as inadmissible because of the equal-treatment principle. Moreover, the mandatory articles,[245] as well as a number of local provisions, explicitly provide for an attendance right for all shareholders. A comparable development can also be pointed to in France. Here, it was previously admissible for a provision in the articles to link attendance at the general meeting to possession of a minimum number of shares not more than ten (Art. L. 225-112 FrCCom). In 2001, however, this provision was repealed,[246] so that here too there is a comprehensive right to attend.

239 Flume (1960: 26) ('Forum der Rechenschaftslegung').
240 See Ch. 4, section II.1.a above.
241 Cf. §§ 118(1), (2), 131(2)(s.2) GerAktG; No. 2.2.3 GerCGK; Art. 136(1) FrDécret.
242 For the UK: Druey (1999: 372); for Germany: Noack (2002c: 624).
243 See DSW-Europastudie (1999: 41); German law is different: see Bezzenberger, in: GroßkommAktG (1999: § 140 para. 6).
244 On what follows see Comberg (2000: 109 *et seq.*); Thümmel (1995: 47–8).
245 §§ 45(2) ChinArticles, 35(2) ChinMandProv; Notice of the CSRC on Promulgating the Rules for the General Meetings of Shareholders of Listed Companies 2006, Art. 23.
246 Loi no. 2001-420 du 15 mai 2001 relative aux nouvelles régulations économiques.

(2) Checks on abuses. Alongside the right of attendance, shareholders – and in many countries also their proxies[247] – typically have the possibility of addressing the general meeting, so as to influence the opinions of other shareholders. Legally, however, a right to speak is mostly not explicitly laid down by statute.[248] Instead, it results more from an interpretation of the overall complex of general meeting,[249] soft law,[250] and, indirectly, provisions affecting the shareholders' right to ask questions.[251]

This reluctant recognition of a right to speak is on the one hand a consequence of the partial anticipation of the general meeting by the convocation and proxy authorization procedure. For since in the run-up to the general meeting a range of information is transmitted, and the shareholder can decide on this basis to remain passive or to give a proxy to a third party, a right to speak that calls everything into question again would be in contradiction with this. On the other hand, a comprehensively patterned right to speak might also encourage abuse, and thus on the whole have negative consequences for the effectiveness of the general meeting.

The possibility of abuse by 'disruptive shareholders' can be seen particularly plainly in the Japanese phenomenon of the 'sokaiya'.[252] The sokaiya appear in two different varieties. First, their conduct may be directed against minority shareholders, in the interest of the board and paid for by the board. This happens through their deliberately disrupting other shareholders and thus ensuring a speedy course for the general meeting. Secondly, management may instead be the victim. Here, the sokaiya threaten to exercise their right to speak and to ask questions with the aim of asking unwelcome questions or breaking up the meeting. They therefore ask for money for not engaging in disruption, so as – in this version too – to ensure the smooth running of the general meeting.

The chair of the general meeting might deal with this conduct by calling on the sokaiya to leave the meeting in the event of a disruption, pursuant

[247] For Germany: Mülbert, in: GroßkommAktG (1999: vor §§ 118–147 para. 166); for China: § 59(no.1) ChinArticles; for the UK s. 324 UK-CA (the old law was different).

[248] The Netherlands are different: see van Ryn (1990: para. 5-141).

[249] Siepelt (1992: 3 *et seq.*).

[250] See s. D.2 UK-Combined Code. Furthermore, common law principles apply; *Wall* v. *London & Northern Assets Corporation Ltd* [1898] 2 Ch 469 (Court of Appeal).

[251] Cf. Taniguchi (1988: 216) (for Japan).

[252] On what follows see Kliesow (2001: 74 *et seq.*); Inaniwa and Brodics (1987: 19); Aoki (2001a: 100); Kawamoto (1994: 85, 219–20); Taniguchi (1988: 201–2, 217 *et seq.*); Hayakawa (1997: 245); West (2001a: 576, 583); Marutschke (1999: 233–4); Menden (1999: 11 *et seq.*); Takahashi and Rudo (2000: 72–3).

to § 315(2) JapCA. Nonetheless, management often succumbs to sokaiya pressure. Why this is so is not, however, entirely clear. First, factual circumstances may be decisive. On the one hand, it is speculated that this response is based on the traditional Japanese need for harmony, since peace and quiet are thereby restored to the general meeting – in the interest also of the effect on the public.[253] On the other hand, it is stressed that the sokaiya are paid off principally because management presumes it is acting in the company's interests, and therefore has no awareness of wrong.[254] Secondly, however, legal aspects may also be decisive. It is pointed out that in Japan the level of information is lower than, for instance, in the US. Management is therefore particularly interested in short general meetings, at which no (negative) information on the conduct of business becomes known, so that there is a greater potential for blackmail than in other countries.[255] Thirdly, the two variants of sokaiya activity should be focused on. If the point were only for particular shareholders to blackmail management, it would be hard to see why management so frequently succumbs. But the decisive point is that management can, in the first version, use the sokaiya as helpers, to its benefit. There is therefore a certain dependence, making it hard for management to detach itself from the sokaiya without further ado.

However, some measures have been taken in order to check the sokaiya. Legally, a remedy was sought mainly through a provision prohibiting companies from granting anyone pecuniary advantage in connection with the exercise of shareholder rights (§ 120 JapCA). This prohibition is accompanied by penalties (§ 970 JapCA), which in 1997 and 2005 were increased still further. Indirectly, since 1981 new minority rights and improved information have been supposed to promote more intensive debate with minority shareholders and thus reduce the potential for blackmail by sokaiya.[256] Yet, in practice, increased shareholder activism is stifled by two measures through which managements sought to protect themselves against the sokaiya. First, employee shareholders were introduced to intimidate the sokaiya (and also other shareholders) at general meetings. Secondly, since the mid-1980s, the duration of general meetings and therefore the potential for disruption have been reduced by having almost all general meetings of Japanese companies held on the same date.

[253] Cf. Taniguchi (1988: 201 note 48); similarly Aoki (2001a: 103–4).

[254] Hayakawa (1997: 245).

[255] West (2001a: 564), (1999: 767); Takahashi and Rudo (2000: 100).

[256] Additionally, according to § 306(1) JapCA the company can apply to the court to appoint an inspector in order to secure the objective fairness of the meeting procedure.

Shareholders with shares in several companies thus cannot personally attend several general meetings, and therefore it was also made impossible for one sokaiya to disrupt more than one company's meeting.

From a comparative perspective, 'disruptive shareholders' and thus the conflict between activism and efficiency are a general problem.[257] In most countries, however, it is enough for the chair of the meeting, usually a board member,[258] to exercise his power over the meeting and, for instance, set limits on speaking time or expel people from the room. Blackmail potential like that in Japan more frequently arises with respect to legal actions. Here, too, there may be the problem that the basically positive activism of minority shareholders is employed as a means of pressure.[259]

(3) Conclusion. In general, shareholders can attend the general meeting and also speak. Restrictions are being considered particularly in China and Japan. Yet, current developments point towards change. In China, restricting the attendance right of small shareholders is probably no longer admissible. In Japan, the practice of having employees influence the course of the general meeting by occupying the front seats has been found invalid by the courts.[260] Also, a lengthening of the duration of general meetings can be seen, with a gradual reduction in the number of general meetings all held on the same date.[261] However, across all the countries, general meetings are seldom conducive to a lively 'parliamentary forum'. With institutional investors, however, there are also indications of increasing activism to be noted.[262]

b) The voting right

What a democratic form of voting right ought to look like is not clear. While a strictly democratic model is not ruled out, since, given a vote cap of one share, each shareholder would have one vote, it seems more apposite to cast the shareholder democracy in the mould of a 'capital democracy'[263] or 'plutocracy'.[264] The risk a shareholder takes corresponds to the number

[257] For the UK: Davies (1999: 344); for Germany: Lehmann (1990: 51 *et seq.*).

[258] E.g. Art. 146 FrDécret; § 110(1) ChinCA; § 7.08 MBCA; Art. 11 Draft Model Articles of Association for Public Companies (June 2006) (old Art. 42 UK-Table A). In Germany, it depends on the articles: see Mülbert, in: GroßkommAktG (1999: vor § 118 paras. 75 *et seq.*); for criticism on the UK law see Cheffins (1997: 240).

[259] See Ch. 5, section III below.

[260] Cf. Milhaupt and West (2003a: 320).

[261] Cf. Igarashi (2001: 72 *et seq.*); Milhaupt and West (2003a: 320).

[262] See Ch. 4, section II.4.c below.

[263] Wiethölter (1961: 131) ('Kapitaldemokratie').

[264] Dunlavy (1998: 5 *et seq.*).

of shares he owns. What matters is the nominal amounts of shares, so that the principle applying is not 'one shareholder one vote', but 'one share one vote'.[265]

The law in the UK has a different starting-point.[266] The vote is in principle by show of hands, so that each shareholder has only one vote, and voting proxies are not taken into account. It is only upon a motion that a formal vote based on capital holdings ('poll') is taken. The finer details are left to the articles of association.[267] A poll must be taken if five members or members together having more than 10 per cent of all votes or of the registered capital so request (s. 321 UK-CA). Additionally, the chair of the meeting is also obliged to take a poll when a difference between the vote by show of hands and one by capital shares seems likely.[268] Thus, here too as a general rule a count by shares and not by shareholders will be taken on controversial issues.[269]

For Japan, companies can under the latest reforms provide in their articles of association that for shareholder rights what counts is not the individual share, but a grouping of shares into a 'unit'.[270] The principle then applying to shareholders will be 'one unit one vote'. The pre-2005 law provided that the maximum size of a unit must be no more than 1,000 shares or 0.5 per cent of the registered capital. The new JapCA does not provide a fixed percentage but secondary legislation may prescribe it (§ 188(2) JapCA).

Apart from these peculiarities, in most other countries it is also possible for the articles of association to modify the legal position of shareholders.[271] The most important are voting caps, multiple voting rights, and non-voting preference shares.

(1) Vote capping and multiple voting rights. From a theoretical viewpoint,[272] restricting voting rights by voting caps seems to fit the investor

265 E.g. §§ 12(1), 134(1)(s.1) GerAktG; § 104(s.1) ChinCA; § 7.21(a) MBCA; § 212(a) DelGCL; see also Pistor *et al.* (2001: 23); Dunlavy (1998).

266 On what follows see Davies (2003: 363 *et seq.*): Modern Company Law for a Competitive Economy (1999: para. 4.46); Poutianen (2001: 71–2); Chinese law is similar but less restrictive: see Comberg (2000: 121); § 66 ChinArticles.

267 Cf. also Arts. 38–41 Draft Model Articles of Associations for Public Companies (June 2006) (old Arts. 46–52 UK-Table A).

268 See Ferran (1999: 267).

269 See Davies (1997b: 364).

270 §§ 188, 308 JapCA; previously §§ 241(1), 221(1) JapCC; see also Oda (2002: 14); Janssen *et al.* (2002: 260); Kawamoto *et al.* (2001: paras. 289 *et seq.*).

271 See also Ch. 2, section IV.1; Ch. 3, section II above.

272 See generally Ch. 3, section I above.

model. It can prevent over-large blocks of influence from arising, and investors from risking unfair advantage being taken by blockholders. The power gain for management associated with this dispersed ownership structure could be tolerated by the shareholder as investor, since the possibility of selling his shares makes him in any case more likely to reverse his investment decision than to get actively involved. The position is opposite with multiple voting rights. They enable a deliberately active stance by one or more particular shareholders. These shareholders may thus, even in a company without blockholders, obtain stronger control over the company and act like an owner. The fact that the market evaluation of a multiple voting right can be difficult does not trouble these shareholders, since they are anyway not primarily oriented towards a quick-sale option. As well as shareholder-democracy considerations, however, another disadvantage of vote capping and multiple voting rights is the fact that they hinder the market for corporate control. Voting caps may make it impossible for a third party to buy into the company. Similarly, multiple voting rights can counteract excessive outside influence, since the old shareholders will retain their influence even though their shareholding has been diluted.

Nonetheless, the law regarding voting caps and multiple voting rights is often not uniform. Likewise, a classification into legal families is hard. For instance, voting caps are admissible in France (Art. L. 225-125 FrCCom) and the UK,[273] but not in Japan and for listed companies in Germany and the US.[274] Multiple voting rights are prohibited in Germany (§ 12(2) GerAktG), Japan (§ 308(1) JapCA) and in principle also in France. French law, however, allows holders of registered shares to be given a double voting right in the articles of association, if the shares have been held for two years by the same owner (Art. L. 225-123 FrCCom). In the UK[275] and often also in the US, multiple voting rights are admissible (cf. §§ 151(a), 212(a) DelGCL). The attempt by the American SEC to provide for a ban on multiple voting was invalidated by the Court of Appeals for the District of Columbia Circuit.[276] According to NYSE rules, however, the use of multiple voting rights is in principle not possible (§ 313.00 NYSE Manual). In China, there are no provisions allowing a departure

[273] Cf. Pennington (1994: para. 90.10.120).

[274] For Japan: § 308(1) JapCA; Kliesow (2001: 90); Kozuka (2003: 140); for Germany: § 134(1)(s.2) GerAktG; for the US: *Providence & Worcester Co.* v. *Baker*, 378 A 2d 121 (Del. 1977) (according to corporate law possible), but § 313.00 NYSE Manual for listed companies.

[275] Cf. *Bushell* v. *Faith* [1970] AC 1099 (House of Lords); van Ryn (1990: para. 5-155); Davies (2003: 620–1); Green (2001: 4).

[276] *The Business Roundtable v. SEC*, 905 F 2d 406 (DC Cir. 1990).

from the 'one share one vote' principle (§ 104(s.1) ChinCA).[277] However, it is at least debatable whether voting caps and multiple voting rights are not to some extent already admissible. This state of uncertainty in the law may be explained by the fact that the legality of such provisions has not to date become a major issue, for factual reasons. The state in any case has a controlling influence in many companies, so that there is typically no need for vote capping or multiple voting rights.[278]

As a result, once again[279] it becomes clear that in the UK and the US there is more room for manoeuvre in the articles of association than in other countries. In these countries too, however, departures from the mandatory one-vote rule are widely permissible. What seems decisive in determining whether vote capping and multiple voting rights are permissible is the market for corporate control – and its political ramifications[280] – and on whether the market accepts them, or places value on standardization. Although a single uniform share structure generally facilitates trade on the exchange, the market can nonetheless accept a special form of share with well-defined rights. This is also the case in some countries for non-voting preference shares.

(2) **Non-voting shares.** The purpose of non-voting preference shares is to attract more capital, since these shares are aimed at investors who, as pure investors, agree to have no voting right, but instead a preferential right to dividend. A certain differentiation may therefore suit the market, so that from this point of view the trend towards the admissibility and (at times) growing popularity of non-voting preference shares makes sense.

However, non-voting shares may also be problematic for the capital market. Their purpose of allowing hitherto closed companies access to the capital market without fear of being swamped from outside and taken over conflicts with a concept of the capital market that sees its decisive advantage in the free play of market forces. Accordingly, while in the UK and the US there have since the nineteenth century been no or only slight restrictions in company law on them,[281] and while non-voting ordinary shares are also admissible,[282] NYSE rules make them difficult to list, and

[277] § 127 ChinCA and § 80(no.1) ChinArticles mention classes of shares but do not enable them, because a decision of the State Council would be necessary (§ 132 ChinCA).

[278] See generally Comberg (2000: 115–16); Thümmel (1995: 89); but see also § 80(no.1) ChinArticles ('class of shares which have equal or greater voting rights').

[279] See Ch. 2, section IV.1.b above. [280] See Ch. 5, section II.1.a below.

[281] For the UK: Davies (2003: 620–1); for the US: Pistor *et al.* (2001: 28).

[282] For the US: Cox and Hazen (2003: §§ 13.34); for the UK: Davies (2003: 624–5); but see also van Ryn (1990: para. 5-146) for fundamental decisions.

the UK Listing Rules provide that the voting right revives if no dividend has been paid for six months.[283]

Other countries restrict the use of non-voting shares even in company law. Their very basis, equity without voting rights, is seen as contradicting the principle of shareholder control and the shareholder's 'ownership position'. And it is also often said that this 'unhealthy hybrid' between shares and bonds brings the further danger of exploitation of ordinary shareholders.[284] In many legal systems, accordingly, non-voting ordinary shares are inadmissible, and non-voting preference shares subjected to restrictions in company law. Thus, while in Germany after 1937, on the Anglo-American model, the mandatory link between the position of the shareholder and the vote was broken, the maximum number of non-voting preference shares was initially restricted to one-third of the registered capital, raised in 1965 to one-half. As to content, there is a requirement that the shares have a preference on the distribution of profits (§§ 139(1), 12(1)(s.2) GerAktG). In this case, the voting right may in principle be excluded (§ 140(1) GerAktG). This 'sleeping vote' is revived if the preference has not been granted for two years in succession (§ 140(2) GerAktG). This German provision was a model for France's and Japan's laws.[285] The latter two limited the proportion of non-voting preference shares originally to one-quarter of the registered capital. In 2004, however, the French rules on 'actions à dividende prioritaire sans droit de vote' were replaced by the general provisions on 'actions de préférence' (Arts. L. 228-11 *et seq.* FrCCom). According to this new law, up to one-quarter of the shares for public companies and up to one-half of shares for private companies can be preference shares without voting rights (Art. L. 228-11(3) FrCCom). In Japan in 1990, the proportion was increased to one-third, and in 2001 to one-half (§ 115 JapCA).[286] Additionally, in Japan since 2001, following the Anglo-American model, non-voting ordinary shares have also been admissible (now § 105(2) JapCA). In China, by contrast, there has been no consolidated development as yet. The law merely authorizes the government to enact specific provisions on the issuing of types of share (§ 132 ChinCA). This has not been made use of yet,

283 For the US: § 313.00(C) NYSE Manual; for the UK: Davies (2003: 622, 624–5); Cheffins (1997: 475).

284 Cf. Pellens and Hillebrandt (2001: 57 *et seq.*); Davies (2003: 620).

285 For France: Siebel (1997: 641); Sonnenberger (1991: para. III 149); for Japan: Inaniwa and Brodics (1987: 16); Pistor *et al.* (2002: 852).

286 Previously §§ 222(1), (6), 242(1), (3) JapCC.

so that the extent to which non-voting preference shares can be used is debatable.[287]

In summary, the different rules on non-voting preference shares reflect the general differences between company-law and securities-law predominance and between differences in the freedom to contract out of statutory company law. However, there is also some convergence. This again confirms the insight that, in questions of corporate finance, legal imitation is particularly likely.[288]

c) Participation of institutional investors

For institutional investors, in general the same problems arise with activism as for other shareholders. However, some see an active stance by institutional inverstors as the decisive factor for orderly, efficient corporate governance.[289] Whether this will happen and really does have positive effects is, however, uncertain.

One impulse to involvement might come from the institutional investor's contract with clients. However, this type of obligation is uncommon, nor can it, at least in principle, be derived from some unwritten subsidiary obligation.[290] By law, however, in the US particular institutional investors – the details depend on the relevant authority – are obliged to exercise their voting right. This is not the case in most other countries, and is also rejected by the European Commission.[291] While there is a statutory provision in France, it enters into force only when a corresponding decree is enacted.[292] In Germany and the UK, an obligation to vote is being discussed,[293] and in the UK the Combined Code suggests that institutional investors should vote.[294]

Although, thus, no compulsion is widely imposed, institutional investor activism is possible at least where, like banks traditionally in

[287] Cf. Comberg (2000: 54 *et seq.*); Thümmel (1995: 55); cf. also § 11 ChinArticles.

[288] For other examples see Ch. 4, section I.4 above, and Ch. 5, section I.1.d, II.2.b below.

[289] See e.g. Miles (2000: 142); McCormack (1998: 131 *et seq.*); Davies (1997a); Coffee (1991); B. Black (1990a); Fraune (1996).

[290] See Davies (1999: 338) (for the UK).

[291] Modernising Company Law and Enhancing Corporate Governance in the European Union – A Plan to Move Forward, Communication from the Commission, COM(2003) 284, at 13.

[292] Cf. Guyon (1999: 105).

[293] For Germany: Regierungskommission Corporate Governance (2001: para. 126); Wohlwend (2001: 107); for the UK: Cadbury Report (1992: para. 6.16); Myners (2001); Davies (2004: 204).

[294] See s. E.3 UK-Combined Code; for depository votes in Germany see § 135(10) GerAktG.

many civil law countries, they have large shareholdings.[295] Furthermore, in some countries, increasing activism by institutional investors at general meetings is apparent.[296] In particular, the involvement of foreign institutional investors[297] may help to make the general meeting more productive. For instance, in Japan investments by Anglo-American institutional investors have been leading to longer and more argumentative general meetings.[298] This is not necessarily an inevitable pattern, however. It is also conceivable for foreign shareholders to see attendance (or even just a proxy) as too troublesome, and therefore prefer the sale option.

Attending the general meeting is also not necessarily the typical form of active involvement by institutional investors. Institutional investors often exert their influence indirectly through the vote, but through 'secret backroom lobbying' and 'behind-the-scenes actions'.[299] Even so, their voting power is not unimportant. The intensity and effectiveness of their action depends decisively on what pressure they can bring to bear. But such action is questionable from the viewpoint of 'shareholder democracy'. It leads not just to a disempowerment of the general meeting, but also to the exclusion of other shareholders and thus to conflicts with the principle of equal treatment.[300] It is, furthermore, debatable whether active institutional investors in general benefit the interests of other shareholders. On the one hand, institutional investors are typically more informed and experienced than private investors, so that the latter may benefit from the former's greater knowledge. Again, in connection with the 'problem of collective choice', it is emphasized that the shareholders in a company are the group with the most homogeneous interests, so that by contrast with other voting processes with many participants the likelihood of inconsistent and illogical decisions is (relatively) small.[301] On the other hand, institutional investors are regarded as more risk-averse and conservative than other shareholders,[302] and in practice the interests of block and small shareholders are often not identical.[303] Moreover, with institutional

295 See Ch. 8, section IV.2.a below.

296 Cf. Farrar *et al.* (1998: 10); Cheffins (1997: 64); Davies (2003: 338); Hamermesh (1998: 411); Romano (2002: 509); Hill (2000b: 74).

297 See Ch. 8, section III.4.b below.

298 See Marutschke (1999: 234); Hayakawa (1997: 242–3).

299 On what follows see Davies (2003: 338); Cheffins (1997: 243); B. Black (1997: 460, 464); Ferran (1999: 259); Menden (1999: 12, 53–4); Kawamoto (1994: 219–20); Tuerks (2000: 153, 408).

300 For this principle see Ch. 5, section II.2.b below.

301 Ruffner (2000: 174, 358).

302 Cf. Oquendo (2001: 985); Merkt (1991: paras. 82–3).

303 Cf. Smith (1996: 159–60); Romano (2002: 507 *et seq.*); Ruffner (2000: 184–5).

investors there may be conflicts of interest if as well as their investment they also have other business relations with the company.[304]

5. *Conclusion*

On the whole, the picture is a mixed one. In part the concept of shareholder democracy applies, since the basic legal structures (convocation, agenda, discussion, vote) resemble a parliamentary procedure. Further, the shareholder has in part the possibility of influencing the time, content and outcome of the general meeting, and is thus able to affect 'his company' as 'owner'. Again, a shareholder with a purely financial interest as investor has the possibility of, say, giving a proxy and thus reducing both his personal involvement and the costs of his activism.

One can accordingly speak of an 'active shareholder' insofar as in principle minority rights are due him in the run-up to the general meeting, and an attendance and voting right at it. 'Exit' and 'voice' are not to be seen legally as alternatives, since in principle both options are open to the shareholder. Only *de facto* will on the one hand shareholders with small holdings have more recourse to the 'exit' option, since sale is easier but active participation harder. Shareholders with larger holdings may on the other hand be less ready to give up their investment, and active involvement will be more effective. This does not however yet mean that these blockholders use their vote actively. Since they also have other possibilities of influencing the company, it may remain the case that there will be a lack of productive and efficient general meetings.

As to the legal details, no clear distinctions are revealed in the legal systems studied here. However, there are a number of differences in detail that even today may make the cross-border exercise of voting rights something of an adventure.[305] The future of shareholder activism, however, does not depend solely on the regulatory complex just studied. Instead, what matters is, first, whether the general meeting has important matters to decide freely at all.[306] Secondly, the effectiveness of the voting right (and also of the sale of shares) depends on whether shareholders are adequately informed about the company and the identity of their fellow shareholders (sections III and IV below), since otherwise 'hidden actions' by management would be possible.[307]

304 Cf. also No. II.F OECD-Principles 2004.

305 Cf. Noack (2002d).

306 See Ch. 5, section I.1 below.

307 On the principal–agent problem see Ch. 2, section IV.1.a above, and Ch. 5, section II.1.a below.

III. The informed shareholder

In the US and the UK, it is often stressed that company and securities laws in those countries guarantee the best level of information. Thus, allegedly the reporting and disclosure system in the US is better than in all other countries, since there the principle of full and fair disclosure is most clearly realized.[308] Here, and in the UK, publicity is the underlying principle of shareholder and investor protection.[309]

The background to this disclosure philosophy is the notion of a (semi-) efficient capital market.[310] If the capital market properly assesses the quality of the conduct of business, shareholders can be protected simply through the possibility of buying or selling shares. The prevailing view assumes that, to prevent the asymmetrical distribution of knowledge and to ensure the accuracy of share prices, mandatory disclosure is necessary.[311] The market cannot achieve this alone. While, if information is available, markets can efficiently evaluate it through prices, for the disclosure of information it is not enough to rely simply on the financing needs of companies. Information is not traded like an ordinary good. There is therefore a risk of market failure, since information, by contrast with other products, is not consumed, and the purchaser can at no great cost make it generally known as a public good. Only mandatory law could therefore ensure that shares are priced correctly and shareholders protected.

From this starting-point, the argument suggests itself that the supposedly high level of information available in the US and the UK in particular has led to relatively wide use of the share as a form of investment and hence to shareholder structures with dispersed holdings. Countering this argument, however, is the fact that these shareholder structures were present even before disclosure requirements were imposed.[312] It is therefore also conceivable that the law was decisively marked by the *de facto* structures.[313] Moreover, blockholders have less need of statutory disclosure rules, since with no separation of ownership and control they are less powerless *vis-à-vis* management, so that the informational asymmetry is less.[314] Again, here the market for corporate control plays a smaller role, another reason

308 Lowenstein (1999: 31).

309 Hodgson *et al.* (1995: para. 70); Davies (2003: 533); Goddard (2003: 408–9).

310 See also Ch. 2, section IV.1.a above.

311 On what follows see Hertig *et al.* (2004: 204 *et seq.*); Kraakman (2004: 96 *et seq.*); Romano (1993: 91 *et seq.*); Cheffins (1997: 127 *et seq.*).

312 See Ch. 8, section IV.1.a below.

313 See also Ch. 7, section I.1 below.

314 Cf. Bratton and McCahery (1999: 223, 226); Cunningham (1999: 1140); for Japan: Aoki (2001a: 104); Milhaupt (2001: 2103); Baum (1998: 761).

why less information is typically demanded. The concentrated shareholding structures typical for continental Europe, Japan and China thus, on this argument, mean that statutory and *de facto* disclosure is less in those countries. Instead, abuses of power are prevented by mandatory rules and a supervisory structure within the company such as a more powerful general meeting or a supervisory board. Moreover, the cross-holdings in these countries allegedly mean that, because information is exchanged among the companies, public transparency is unnecessary, and undesired by those involved.

It is, however, questionable whether these statements accurately reflect the present law. In particular, the distinction has to be drawn among two forms of information. First, a shareholder may be due individual rights *vis-à-vis* the company, so that he can call for particular information (subsection 1 below). Secondly, information may be published in other ways. This information need not necessarily be based on a corresponding right of the shareholder, since it is also possible for a third party, such as a supervisory authority or auditor, to guarantee their effectiveness (subsections 2 and 3 below).

1. *Individual information rights*

Information may be made available to shareholders individually in various ways. They may have documents for the general meeting sent to them individually,[315] or they become active themselves and proactively seek information (subsection a below) or inspection (subsection b below). These rights are also often connected with the general meeting.

a) The right to demand information

The reference to the general meeting is clear in the case of the right to demand information, to which shareholders in Germany, and following it Japan and China, are entitled.

The greatest importance attaches to this right in Germany (§ 131 GerAktG). Subject to some exceptions, shareholders have the right for the management board to answer its questions at the general meeting. The exact object of the rule is, however, controversial. It is well established that this right exists to support the exercise of shareholder rights at the general meeting, as a corollary of membership.[316] Since this principally concerns

[315] See Ch. 4, section II.3.b above.

[316] Decher, in: GroßkommAktG (2001: § 131 paras. 5 *et seq.*); Merkt (2001b: 257 *et seq.*).

the effectiveness of the right to vote, the right to demand information is in accord with the ownership and shareholder democracy analogies.[317] Beyond this, however, it is argued that § 131 GerAktG is additionally aimed at protecting the shareholder as investor.[318] With respect to enforcement, the management's right to refuse disclosure has since 1965 been fully subject to judicial review. This allows an action to void resolutions of the general meeting with which the (wrongly refused) information was concerned. A problem with this, however, is that actions can block entry in the commercial register, bringing the danger of abuse of law. This problem has, however, now been restricted by decisions of the German Supreme Court[319] as well as recent legislative reform.[320] Additionally, according to this reform, management may reject disclosure if the information is available on its website.[321]

A provision with a comparable starting-point to the German law is found in China, since here too shareholders are entitled to put questions at the general meeting (§ 98 ChinCA). However, the Chinese law confines itself to this statement, so that, for instance, refusal of disclosure is probably possible only in an individual case.[322] It is not yet clear what legal consequences may derive from infringement of the disclosure right. While it is presumably possible for shareholders to file suit against a resolution taken in breach of the information right (§ 22 ChinCA),[323] it remains open whether the right to demand information may also be pursued through the courts.

In Japan, an action for disclosure is not possible. While in 1981 shareholder democracy was meant to be promoted through the right to disclosure (now § 314 JapCA), for fear of abuse by the sokaiya[324] it was deliberately couched not as a shareholder right but as a duty on management.[325] Moreover, disclosure can be refused if there is justifiable reason. Otherwise, refusal may make management punishable (§ 919(1)(no.9)

[317] See Ch. 3, section I above.

[318] Mülbert, in: GroßkommAktG (1999: vor § 118 para. 203); Mülbert (1996a: 80, 160 note 27); for criticism see Wilhelm (1998: paras. 1026 *et seq.*).

[319] BGH, BGHZ 146, 179 (*MEZ*); BGH, NJW 2001, 1428 (*Aqua-Butzke*); see also Ch. 5, section III.2 below.

[320] § 243(4)(s.2) GerAktG as amended by Gesetz zur Unternehmensintegrität und Modernisierung des Anfechtungsrechts (UMAG) of 22.09.2005, BGBl. I 2802.

[321] § 131(3)(no.7), (6) GerAktG as amended by UMAG (see previous note).

[322] Cf. Comberg (2000: 114).

[323] See Ch. 4, section II.4.a below.

[324] See Ch. 4, section II.4.a above.

[325] Cf. Inaniwa and Brodics (1987: 17); Taniguchi (1988: 214); Kawamoto *et al.* (2001: para. 480).

JapCA) and lead to a voiding of the resolution concerned (§ 831(1)(no.1) JapCA).

French law takes a different approach. There is no statutory right of spontaneous questioning at the general meeting. However, shareholders can send questions to management before the general meeting, to be answered at it (Art. L. 225-108(3) FrCCom). Moreover, shareholders with at least 5 per cent of the registered capital can put questions to management twice a year, which must then be answered outside the general meeting (Art. L. 225-232 FrCCom; Art. 195-1 FrDécret). Finally, prior to the engagement of a special auditor, it is possible for shareholders holding at least 5 per cent of the registered capital to question the board in writing about the measure at issue (Art. L. 225-231 FrCCom).

By contrast, UK and US law contain no explicit right to demand information. It is, however, usually possible for shareholders to put questions. In the UK, for instance, general question-and-answer sessions at general meetings are common, but an explicit statutory provision to this effect was recently rejected; instead, the conduct of the general meeting is to be left to 'best practice'.[326] The 2006 reform only introduced a minority right of shareholders of quoted companies to require website publication of audit matters (s. 527 UK-CA) without imposing a duty of directors or auditors to reply.

In summary, then, the right to demand information is weaker in the US and the UK than in the other countries studied here. This finding need not necessarily be a drawback for public companies of these countries. For instance, in Germany there is problem of abuse arising from overuse of the right to question. The opposite is the case in Japan, since there even the right to question has not been widely used in general meetings.[327] Furthermore, it is doubtful whether these information rights can lead to an equality of information for all shareholders. In practice it is hard to prevent large shareholders from engaging in more intensive information exchange with management outside the general meeting.[328] Finally, the right to demand information, at least for the shareholder as investor,[329] is not of primary importance, because more general disclosure may be more practicable and may better guarantee the equal treatment of all shareholders.

[326] See Ferran (1999: 266); Davies (1997b: 583), (1999: 351). However, Art. 9 of Directive 2007/36/EC will change this.

[327] See generally Ch. 4, section II.1.b, 4.a above.

[328] See also Ch. 4, section II.4.c above.

[329] See Ch. 3, section I.3 above.

b) Rights of inspection

In French law, the right of inspection is relatively comprehensively patterned. When the concession system was abolished in the nineteenth century,[330] the right of inspection was seen as a way to enable shareholders to monitor management. Independently of the date of the general meeting, shareholders are entitled to a 'droit de communication permanent'. They have, for instance, the possibility of seeing and copying the last three years' documents on the inventory, the annual accounts, management and auditors' reports, management remuneration and the list of shareholders (Arts. L. 225-115, 225-117 FrCCom; Arts. 142, 152 FrDécret). To prepare for the general meeting, shareholders or a proxy have the further right ('droit de communication temporaire') to inspection or to have background information sent out on the motions for resolutions, the candidates etc. (Arts. 135, 138 FrDécret).

In Germany and the UK, by contrast, there are no comprehensive rights of inspection. In Germany, particular documents may be seen, or obtained, before the general meeting (e.g. §§ 175(2), 179a(2) GerAktG), but there is no general right to inspect company books or documents. The same is true in essence in the UK. Here, however, shareholders may, in accordance with certain special provisions, inspect the directors' contracts and the resolutions and minutes of the general meeting (ss. 162(3), 229, 238, 358 UK-CA). These differences to French law can be explained on the ground that in France many small businesses are carried on as joint stock companies.[331] For these, it is likelier for company members to exercise supervision through rights of inspection.

With this explanation, however, US law initially presents difficulties. Although joint stock companies are typically larger than in France, here shareholders can inspect business documents. This right is based, by contrast with the UK, on the one hand on a right of inspection of records and books in common law, as long as the shareholder can demonstrate a legitimate purpose.[332] On the other hand, state laws contain rights of inspection, although sometimes shareholders need to demonstrate a good reason for seeking the information.[333] To explain these far-reaching rights, it should be noted that it has only very recently become possible to grant the statutory inspection right to every shareholder. Where, as earlier, only

330 See Ch. 1, section III.2 above. 331 See Ch. 1, section II.1 above.

332 See *State ex rel. Cochran* v. *Penn-Beaver Oil Co.*, 34 Del. 81, 143 A 257 (1926); *State ex rel. Healy* v. *Superior Oil Corp.*, 40 Del. 460, 13 A 2d 453 (1940); Cox and Hazen (2003: §§ 13.02–3).

333 § 16.02 MBCA; cf. also § 220(c) DelGCL.

shareholders holding 5 per cent of the registered capital or who have been shareholders for six months are entitled, it was relevant mainly only for close corporations. Secondly, the right of inspection is connected with the relatively far-reaching US legal remedies.[334] This can be clearly seen in § 16.03 MBCA, which also grants a shareholder's lawyer a right of inspection. Thirdly, by contrast with Europe and Japan, in the US there is no commercial register.[335] Functionally, therefore, inspection may act as a surrogate.

Japanese law too has been influenced by the US trend to ease the right of inspection. Since 1993, the threshold for the right to inspect the accounting books has been lowered from 10 per cent to 3 per cent (now § 433(1) JapCA). Furthermore, even a single shareholder has a right to inspect the minutes of the board of directors (§ 371(2) JapCA) and to request documents relating to reorganizations, mergers and divisions.[336] There are, however, limits to these rights. In the first and second case, information rights are excluded, from fear of the sokaiya, where there is a risk of abuse (§§ 371(6), 433(2) JapCA). The second right usually requires permission from the court (§ 371(3) JapCA). And, with respect to the third right, the shareholder has to pay a fee for inspecting the documents.[337]

By contrast, Chinese law is less comprehensive. No quorum is required. The right of inspection (§ 98 ChinCA), however, refers only to the company's financial accounting reports, so that substantively a narrower framework is taken.

c) Conclusion

With respect to individual information rights, German law focuses on information at the general meeting, French law on information outside the general meeting, US law on rights of inspection, UK law on *laissez-faire* and Japanese and Chinese law on the reception of Western law. However, one should not be too ready to doubt legal convergence. It is to be expected that, for public companies, the new media will have positive effects on the right of inspection and negative effects on the right to question. Personal inspection of particular documents at the company or proactively seeking particular information presupposes initiative on the shareholder's part that is likely to occur only with the (ideal) 'owner' or

334 See Ch. 5, section III.1 below.

335 For Europe: First Directive 68/151/EEC, as amended by Directive 2003/58/EC; for Japan: Yanaga (2001: 152); West (2001a: 545 note 72).

336 §§ 775(3), 782(2), 791(3), 794(3), 803(3), 811(3), 815(3) JapCA.

337 See the provisions cited in the previous footnote.

'parliamentarian'. For the investor, who has to overcome rational apathy,[338] inspection becomes more attractive only when the information can be accessed by logging on to the information database on the company's website. By contrast, an 'investor-oriented' form of the right to question is probably not practicable. If it is permissible to take part in the general meeting online, it may also in principle be possible to put questions in electronic form. Since, however, in public companies questions from thousands of shareholders cannot be answered while a general meeting is taking place, the 'French system' where questions can be submitted beforehand is most achievable in practice.[339]

2. *Securities law*

By contrast with individual modes of information, disclosure in securities law is of a general nature. It is important here because the rationale of disclosure in secondary markets is not confined to the public interest, but also concerns the protection of shareholders.[340]

a) Convergence in law

The focus in securities law is on market transparency. It is therefore not surprising that the advance of securities law across countries[341] has been associated with convergence in content too. The starting-point for the development of this kind of public disclosure is frequently seen as lying in the US Securities Act of 1933 and the Securities Exchange Act of 1934.[342] This is however to ignore the fact that earlier, for instance in the UK and in France, disclosure provisions existed, by which the US legislator was very likely influenced.[343] To be sure, US securities law today has a model effect that justifies talk of not so much approximation of various legal systems as alignment on American standards from the 1933 and 1934 Acts, the SEC Rules and the NYSE Manual.

Disclosure on the US secondary market covers, first, continuing reporting requirements through annual and quarterly reports, and more recently also a disclosure of the corporate governance rules.[344] Secondly, in

[338] See Ch. 4, section II.1.b above. [339] See also Ch. 10, section I.2.c below.

[340] See Ch. 4, section III, preamble above. Disclosure in primary markets will not be addressed here (for a comparative overview see Hertig *et al.* (2004: 197 *et seq.*)).

[341] See Ch. 2, section III above.

[342] E.g. Hopt (1976: 203 *et seq.*); Großfeld (1995: 120 *et seq.*); Becker (1997a: 11).

[343] See Ch. 1, section II.3.a above.

[344] See § 13(a)(2) US-SEA with SEC Forms 10K and 10Q; on corporate governance codes see also Ch. 2, section IV.3 above.

particular situations major business developments have to be made transparent, for instance, in the case of tender offers.[345] This corresponds today in principle with the law of other countries. For instance, it is said that transparency and disclosure with the ultimate aim of a 'glass company' is the focus of European company law,[346] and that German law too is developing from 'institutional to informational' investor protection.[347] In detail, this can be seen first of all in the fact that, across the countries, annual and interim reports must be published.[348] Although in many countries the interim report is usually a half-yearly one,[349] in both Europe and Asia a trend – not least due to US pressure – to quarterly reports can be discerned. As well as corporate governance codes and listing requirements,[350] the new EU Transparency Directive prescribes interim management statements,[351] the extent of which is, however, lower than in the US-mandated reports. Similarly, across the countries new and material information is generally to be made public 'ad hoc',[352] the purchase of large holdings in a company to be disclosed[353] and special information obligations to be complied with in cases of public takeover bids.[354] Finally, according to a new directive companies have to make their corporate governance rules and principles transparent.[355]

All in all, one might – at a somewhat casual glance – therefore assume that now or before long a good public information system would exist

[345] See § 13(a)(1) US-SEA with SEC Form 8K; 1968 Williams Act which led to § 14(d)-(f) US-SEA and SEC Schedule 14 D-1.

[346] Klauer (1998: 178–9); see also High Level Group of Company Law Experts (2002: 34); Merkt (2004c).

[347] Hommelhoff (2000b: 101); similar Merkt (2004a: 6).

[348] For annual reports see Art. 4 of the Transparency Directive 2004/109/EC; §§ 289, 325 GerHGB; ss. 423 *et seq.* UK-CA; § 65 ChinSA; §§ 431 *et seq.* JapCA.

[349] Cf. Art. 5 of the Transparency Directive 2004/109/EC; § 9.9 UK-Listing Rules; § 40 GerBörsG with §§ 53 *et seq.* GerBörsZulV; § 146 ChinCA; § 65 ChinSA.

[350] Eurosharehoiders Corporate Governance Guidelines (2000: No. IV); on the requirements for the German 'Prime Standard' see § 63 of the regulation of the Frankfurt Stock Exchange.

[351] Art. 6 of the Transparency Directive 2004/109/EC.

[352] Cf. e.g. Art. 6 of the Market Abuse Directive 2003/6/EC; § 67 ChinSA; Merkt (2001b: 142 *et seq.*, 174); Davies (2003: 591–2).

[353] See Ch. 4, section IV.4 below.

[354] Cf. Arts. 6, 10 of the Takeover Directive 2004/25/EC; General Principle 2 and Rules 2.5, 24.1 *et seq.* UK City Code; §§ 3(2), 10, 11, 14, 23 GerWpÜG; §§ 27-2 *et seq.* JapSEA; § 87 ChinSA; Arts. 231-16, 231-17 FrRGAMF.

[355] Art. 46a of the Directive 78/660/EEC as introduced by Directive 2006/46/EC; see also High Level Group of Company Law Experts (2002: 45 *et seq.*).

everywhere, and shareholders in public companies would be adequately informed internationally.

b) Reservations

First, despite convergence on the principle, the law displays differences in detail. For instance, there is US criticism that in some foreign countries reports are too few and too late. This applies on the one hand to the time that may elapse till completion of the reports. On the other, it relates to the sometimes absent quarterly reports. The difference between half-yearly and quarterly reports is important not just for the costs entailed for the firm: the information cycle also affects the conduct of those involved significantly. The more frequent the reports, the shorter the term management acts in, and the more the shareholders' focus is on the hold-or-sell option (rather than on exercising voting rights).

Secondly, it matters not only that information is disclosed, but also whether and how it can be utilized. In an international context this may be a problem for non-English-speaking countries. Since English is more widespread in business life than, say, Japanese, Japanese companies have to bear extra costs for translating their reports, or else investors will invest elsewhere. Moreover, the published information must also be substantively usable by the shareholder. That entails, on the one hand, exhaustive reporting. On the other, however, there may also be a danger of a flood of fairly irrelevant *ad hoc* information purely for publicity purposes, to encourage the share price upwards.[356] A further problem is that most small shareholders lack the practice, the understanding or the interest to interpret information based on securities law requirements. It is thus decisive whether or not, for instance, investment advisers, rating agencies, the financial press or institutional investors bring information closer to the broader public and thus be able to exert pressure on managements.

Thirdly, information made available must also actually be used by those involved. This is by no means a matter of course. In Japan, capital-market information is not regarded as particularly important. Instead, information exchange through private networks fits in with the close contacts and cross-holdings between management and shareholders.[357] Thus, it may also be decisive how shareholder structures and legal culture will change.[358]

[356] This point is addressed by Art. 2(1)(s.3) of Directive 2003/124/EC implementing the Market Abuse Directive 2003/6/EC.

[357] Cf. Aoki (2001a: 104); Baum (1998: 761); Poe *et al.* (2002: 93).

[358] See Ch. 8, sections II, IV below.

Fourthly, disclosure requirements must be effectively enforceable and enforcement must also actually happen. This can be done by different mechanisms, such as market forces, civil or criminal liability, private gatekeepers (auditors, lawyers etc.), or supervisory authorities. Here too there are differences, since for instance the SEC is seen as having greater enforcement capacity than its Chinese or German counterparts.[359] This is based partly on legal provisions giving the SEC powers the supervisory authorities in other countries do not have. Furthermore, purely factual factors like ample financial resources and qualified staff play an important part.

Fifthly, transparency serves above all to determine the correct price of shares.[360] Market manipulation must accordingly be ruled out. Here too a convergence of law can be seen, since in most legal systems a basically similar prohibition exists.[361] However, this has also to be actually enforced, something which is, for instance, said to be more likely to happen in the US than in China.[362] Additionally, a correct share price also presupposes a market with a sufficient number of participants. Large stock exchanges thus have an advantage over smaller exchanges, where fluctuations are likelier and the risk for investors correspondingly higher.

c) Conclusion

In principle, today in all countries surveyed here securities laws are in place in order adequately to inform shareholders of public companies. This is not, however, necessarily reflected in the *de facto* level of information available. In line with the traditional view, the capital markets in the US and the UK are probably still more efficient than in the other countries studied here. The 'exit' option is thus more important here, so that the shareholder is approached more *qua* investor. By contrast, for the 'shareholder as owner' and thus the 'voice' option, the high level of individual information rights in France and Germany are more important.[363]

However, the role of capital-market-oriented disclosure should also not be over-estimated. Shareholder protection through disclosure does not operate for all companies in the same way. For close companies, different issues arise, and other forms of protection are accordingly necessary.

359 For China: Fu (2001: 520, 522); for Germany: Decher, in: GroßkommAktG (2001: § 131 para. 2).

360 See Ch. 4, section III, preamble above.

361 Cf. SEC Rule 10b-5; Art. 5 of the Market Abuse Directive 2003/6/EC; for Japan: Baum and Hayakawa (1994: 616 *et seq.*); Milhaupt (2001: 2103).

362 For China: Walker (2001: 441 note 43); Wang (2000: 7).

363 On this typology see generally Ch. 3, section I above.

Moreover, even among public companies, one has to distinguish between listed, regulated and free markets, so that the maximum level of disclosure is not justified for every public company. Finally, apart from disclosure, it may be necessary to protect shareholder interests through structural or direct regulations. Even if, in the US for example, the disclosure philosophy acts as a functional equivalent to substantive company-law protection, additional protective mechanisms may still be necessary, as the 2002 Sarbanes–Oxley Act shows.[364]

3. *Financial reporting*

Financial reporting in general and transparency of annual reports in particular have their origin in the nineteenth century. Since the concession system was dropped and companies opened up to a broader public, there has been a need for regular public accounting to counteract possible shortcomings in financial matters. Here, the annual report as a medium of information stands between individual and capital-market-oriented disclosure. On the one hand, it enables shareholders to monitor their investment and determine profits. They are therefore individually informed of the annual report, irrespective of whether the general meeting is competent for adopting the annual report and for the distribution of the dividend.[365] On the other, the annual report is always directed, at least in the EU, at the general public.[366] While there are no corresponding provisions in the laws of US states, it follows there from securities law that public companies must make their annual report public.[367] Similarly, in other countries, there are distinctions linking the ways of publication, as well as other questions of financial reporting, with the size of the company or its exchange listing.[368]

a) Regulatory philosophies

Despite common roots, a distinction is usually made between two accounting philosophies. On the one hand, is the model traditionally prevalent in civil law countries, whereby the aim and object of accounting

[364] Which, of course, has been criticized: see Romano (2005).
[365] See Ch. 4, section I.2.a, II.3.b above.
[366] See Fourth Directive 78/660/EEC; for Japan see Hayakawa and Raidl-Marcure (1992: 289).
[367] Cf. Hertig and Kanda (2004: 79 *et seq.*); Merkt (2001b: 184).
[368] For Germany: §§ 264, 267, 325 GerHGB; for the UK: ss. 380 *et seq.* UK-CA; for Japan: Kawamoto *et al.* (2001: paras. 593 *et seq.*); Förster (2002: 101–2).

lies primarily in protecting creditors and taxation, but only indirectly in protecting shareholders.[369] This is historically explicable since by contrast with the position in the US and the UK, in nineteenth-century Germany, say, financing through banks was more important than capital-market financing.[370] Again, traditionally the interests of other stakeholders play a larger part in continental Europe than in Anglo-American law.[371] A feature of this model is, for instance, the principle of cautious evaluation, whereby it is more important that losses are taken into account than profits. Again, assets are basically valued at acquisition cost, so that hidden reserves can be formed. Finally, there are often options whereby the firm may, say, through contingency funds make the firm 'look poorer', because this does not impair creditor protection.

The UK and US counter-model instead focuses primarily on investor protection through disclosure.[372] This is aided by valuation at market values ('mark to market') and by the pre-eminent importance given to the accuracy of the accounting ('true and fair view' in the UK; 'fair presentation' in the US). By comparison with civil law countries, there is therefore a more frequent appearance of profits, and hidden reserves are rare. But there is room for manoeuvre in this system too, since accounting law is marked, by comparison with continental Europe, more by a practice-oriented consideration of individual cases than by abstract and general rules. Moreover, the US-GAAP (General Accepted Accounting Principles) in particular are very comprehensive and therefore sometimes offer various ways of covering positions in the accounts. More principled in style are the IAS (International Accounting Standards) or – in the new terminology – IFRS (International Financial Reporting Standards), drawn up by the International Accounting Standards Board (IASB), a private association of professional organizations. Substantively, however, these rules follow the Anglo-American principle of fair market evaluation.

b) Convergence

In the EU, the accounting directives have brought a level of harmonization. The British system has prevailed here, to the extent that the principle of the 'true and fair view' was adopted,[373] although considerable discretion

[369] Cf. Merkt (2001b: 255); Schruff (1996: 166–7); Schulze-Osterloh (2003: 95 *et seq.*); Romano (1993: 101).

[370] See also Ch. 10, section IV.2.a below.

[371] See Ch. 5, section II.1.a below.

[372] On what follows see Großfeld (1998: paras. 729–30); Davies (2003: 540 *et seq.*); Ekkenga (1998: 109 *et seq.*).

[373] Art. 2(3) of the Fourth Directive 78/660/EEC.

exists for the Member States, and for instance in Germany the principle of the 'true and fair view' was hitherto only laxly applied.[374] The EU directives have now been reworked in accordance with the IAS/IFRS rules. For instance, in 2001, the Fair Value Directive was adopted whereby particular financial instruments could, in a departure from the realization principle, be assessed at market value.[375] In 2003, there followed the Accounting Modernization Directive, allowing Member States, in harmony with IAS/IFRS, to permit or prescribe valuation at the current value.[376]

Going still further, new laws on consolidated accounts have been established, based on the fact that consolidated accounts usually have a purely informational function, even in continental Europe. Some Member States have opened up the possibility of drawing up group accounts according to an international standard (US-GAAP or IAS/IFRS).[377] This also made it easier for groups to prepare accounts, which must for a listing in the US be in accordance with US-GAAP. Since accounting in accordance with IAS/IFRS or European standards is not in general accepted in the US, firms wishing to draw on the US capital market have no option but to draw up their accounts in accordance with US-GAAP, or at least accompany them with a US-GAAP reconciliation.

The European legislator also brought the law on consolidated accounts closer to international standards. Companies whose securities are admitted to trading on a regulated market must as from 2005 prepare their consolidated accounts in accordance with IAS/IFRS.[378] Additionally, national legislators are given the possibility of permitting or prescribing IAS/IFRS also for annual accounts and other companies.[379] While on the one hand the new law promotes internationalization, on the other hand, use of IAS/IFRS may be problematic for companies listed in the US and drawing up accounts in accordance with US-GAAP. It will therefore decisively matter whether IAS/IFRS is also recognized in the US, thus bringing truly global accounting rules for groups of companies. An approximation of

[374] Cf. Hommelhoff (2000a: 758–9); Möllers (1997: 341); but see also *Waltraud Tomberger v. Gebrüder von der Wettern GmbH*, C-234/94 [1996] ECR I-3133.

[375] Directive 2001/65/EC. [376] Directive 2003/51/EC.

[377] See overview at http://ec.europa.eu/internal_market/accounting/docs/studies/1998-seventh-dir_en.pdf.

[378] Art. 4 of Regulation (EC) No. 1606/2002 on the application of international accounting standards; see also http://ec.europa.eu/internal_market/accounting/docs/ias/ias-adoption-process_en.pdf on the adopted standards.

[379] Art. 5 of Regulation (EC) No. 1606/2002 on the application of international accounting standards; see also http://ec.europa.eu/internal_market/accounting/docs/ias/ias-use-of-options_en.pdf.

IAS/IFRS and US-GAAP seems, despite their inherent contradictions, not out of the question, as can be seen, for instance from them convergence agreement between the FASB and the IASB.[380]

An approximation to IAS/IFRS and US-GAAP is also taking place in Japan and China. In Japan,[381] there used to be no obligation to draw up consolidated accounts, so that it was possible to shift profits or losses into the accounts of subsidiaries. Moreover, preparing accounts was burdensome because commercial, fiscal and securities law each followed different accounting conceptions. For commercial-law valuation, following the tradition of German law, in principle the original cost was decisive. Since 1999, however, groups of companies have had to produce consolidated accounts (now § 444 JapCA), focusing since 2001 on the market value of assets. Additionally, accounting requirements under commercial and securities law are in general being harmonized. For future developments, the influential enterprise association Keidanren, for instance, has come out in favour of the development of global accounting standards.[382]

Finally, Chinese accounting standards are in principle based on the pattern of foreign legal systems.[383] Before 2007, it used to be possible for companies with B-shares to prepare their accounts according to international or foreign standards.[384] All public companies are now required to meet international accounting standards.[385]

c) Prospects

Irrespective of the tendencies to convergence, one might doubt their persistence. Sometimes convergence in an international context is regarded as unnecessary, it being instead sufficient for the various standards to be set out openly and then 'translated' by experts for the investor.[386] There might also be alternative information available through other sources such as business reports or press conferences. Were that not possible, parallel accounting would in any case be a more appropriate method than simply imposing foreign law. Each accounting system being based on

[380] http://www.fasb.org/intl/convergence_iasb.shtml; see also Hellwig (2005: 372–3).

[381] On what follows see Yanaga (2003); Kishida (1999: 570 *et seq.*); Milhaupt and West (2003a: 305, 314); Poe *et al.* (2002: 90); Aoki (2001b: 114); Narusawa *et al.* (2001: 9); Hashimoto (2002: 2); Kawamoto *et al.* (2001: paras. 64–5).

[382] Keidanren (2001); similarly the companies mentioned by Learmount (2002: 52).

[383] Cf. Thümmel (1995: 76 *et seq.*); Wang (2000: 12–13).

[384] Cf. Wang (2000: 9–10); on the different types of shares see Ch. 2, section III.1.

[385] See *International Herald Tribune*, 16.08.2006, at 14.

[386] Cf. Thompson (1999: 1245–6, 1350); Easterbrook in Schruff (1996: 176).

cultural concepts, an expression of Western rationality, say, might not be automatically exportable to Asia.

An argument against 'translated' accounting, however, is the point that, even where experts are available, the risk of 'translation errors' remains, so that standardized accounting offers a better comparison. This is also confirmed by the fact that stock exchanges like the NYSE or exchange segments like the German 'Prime Standard' expect certain rules to be complied with, and do not want their market made dependent on an interpretation of foreign rules. And both 'translated' and parallel accounting create additional costs. Moreover, an argument against parallel accounting is the fact that two different accounts may confuse the markets. Separate accounts should therefore be drawn up only for the purpose of the calculation of distribution volume or taxable profit.[387] In respect of information to shareholders and the capital market, however, international uniformity does make most sense. Nor do differences in legal culture really stand in the way of this.[388] For instance, recent developments in Japan and China suggest that these countries are not reluctant to adopt an accounting system focused on the interests of the capital market and of shareholders.

The real problem, however, is often the existence of an effective infrastructure. It is not enough that auditing for annual accounts is usually required for public companies in all the countries studied here. It is instead problematic that, for example, Japan and China may lack an adequate number of independent, qualified auditors.[389] But there are also problems and a need for reform in the Western countries. A new European directive calls for the setting up of audit committees on the Anglo-American model and for the assurance of auditors' independence.[390] In the United Kingdom, a recent law stipulates extending the powers of the Financial Reporting Review Panel (FRRP) and allowing checks on firms' accounts even without specific suspicion of abuse.[391] Finally, the US accounting scandals of 2002 (Enron, Worldcom etc.) have shown that because of, for instance, considerable conflicts of interests regarding auditors there was

387 See Kleindiek (2003: 132 *et seq.*); Ebke (2000: 124).

388 On legal culture and convergence see Ch. 8, section II below.

389 For Japan: Keidanren (2001); Learmount (2002: 131 *et seq.*); for China: Thümmel (1995: 76 *et seq.*); Wang (2000: 11 *et seq.*).

390 Arts. 22–24 of Directive 2006/43/EC on statutory audits; see also Commission Recommendation on the role of non-executive or supervisory directors of listed companies and on the committees of the (supervisory) board, 2005/162/EC.

391 Companies (Audit, Investigations and Community Enterprise) Act 2004 (Ch. 27), ss. 14–15, 21–24.

a need for action.[392] What was also shown is that the trend to privatization in accounting is not irreversible. In the US, auditors' self-regulation has now been supplemented by a powerful Public Company Accountability Oversight Board (PCAOB).[393] Similarly, the European Union initially investigated whether a European oversight body for auditors ought to be set up as a counterpart to the US body. The present directive[394] suggests that a network of Member States' systems of oversight is sufficient. Auditors from third countries are offered a special licensing and registration procedure by national authorities. Exemption is conceivable where this is also possible for European auditors in the third country.

For the US, the Enron case also shows that even substantive accounting rules which, like the US-GAAP, put the protection of investors to the fore can operate to their disadvantage. This is on the one hand specific to a system where uncertain profits or losses are assessed according to value, since this brings the danger that companies may want to use accounting wiggle-room to 'look rich'. For instance, there are reports that in 2002 in the US the profits of the largest 500 firms were on average overstated by one-fifth.[395] On the other hand, there is the general problem that accountancy is not an exact science.[396] Despite the differences in regulatory style between US-GAAP, IAS/IFRS, GerHGB etc., the danger of incorrect accounts is not a problem specific to one legal system, but possible with any accounting system. Although considerable convergence has or will come in regulations on the content of the annual report, that will not mean an 'end of history'[397] in the form of an optimum system.

4. *Conclusion*

The OECD Principles of Corporate Governance state, first, that shareholders should, within reasonable limits, be able to demand information from management.[398] Secondly, they stress that timely and regular disclosure of important information about the firm is among the basic rights of shareholders.[399] This fits in with the above findings that individual and general information to shareholders is supposed to facilitate the

[392] See now §§ 201, 401A of the Sarbanes–Oxley Act 2002, SEC Release No. 33-8154 ('Strengthening the Commission's Requirements Regarding Auditor Independence').

[393] Title 1 of the Sarbanes–Oxley Act 2002.

[394] Arts. 44 *et seq.* of Directive 2006/43/EC on statutory audits.

[395] See *Zeit*, 04.04.2002, at 26.

[396] Davies (2003: 285).

[397] See Ch. 1, section III.1 above.

[398] No. II.C.no.2 OECD-Principles 2004.

[399] No. II.A.3 OECD-Principles 2004.

exercise of their rights ('voice' or 'exit'). Here, no trend to deregulate the law on the 'informed shareholder' can be discerned, so that it is not left to market forces alone to ensure an optimum level of information. Nonetheless, there are sometimes other legal focuses, as for instance the stronger capital-market orientation in the US and the UK shows. These differences do not, however, mean that in those countries only the 'shareholder as investor' and in other countries only the 'shareholder as owner'[400] are covered. US company law also provides for individual information rights. And in other countries too shareholder protection through disclosure by securities and accounting law is on the increase. Therefore, today, no entirely unique conceptions exist in the law on information, disclosure and transparency. Instead, it is primarily questions of enforcement of law, of infrastructure and of economic efficiency that determine the differences in the actual level of information available.

IV. The anonymous shareholder

A typical characteristic of shareholders is that, by contrast with members of a partnership, their own person disappears behind the joint stock company, as a 'reservoir of capital'. This is particularly evident in the French term 'société anonyme'. The term does not, however, mean that the shareholders can in general remain anonymous. Instead, it refers to the fact that an objective firm name is permissible, so that, at any rate at first sight, the shareholders are not recognizable. In other respects too, it is plausible, at least for the 'shareholder as investor',[401] to indicate that as a mere provider of capital he wishes to remain anonymously in the background. However, various reasons may be adduced for making exceptions to this principle. First, the assertion of shareholder rights may presuppose the shareholder's disclosing his identity. Secondly, management may want to address shareholders in order, for the purpose of investor relations, to give them information going beyond the statutory requirement. This also, thirdly, increases management responsibility to shareholders, since, for instance, anonymous shareholders would otherwise be regarded as less important to it than employees in-house. Fourthly, disclosure of identity may also benefit fellow-shareholders, enabling them together to overcome legal hurdles in the run-up to the general meeting[402] and effectively to assert their interests. Fifthly, it is of interest to both management and

[400] On the shareholder typology see generally Ch. 3, section I above.
[401] See Ch. 3, section I.3 above. [402] See Ch. 4, section II.3.a above.

shareholders and the capital market to be able to react in a timely manner to threatened hostile takeovers. Sixthly, and finally, with registered shareholdings it may be necessary in the case of purchase or sale of shares to make the change of owner clear on the register of members.

Despite these manifold reasons, however, the sacrifice of anonymity in favour of a concept of the 'glass shareholder' is not justified in every case. Instead, a distinction should be drawn according to whether bearer or registered shares, 'spurious' shareholders or influential shareholders, are involved.

1. Anonymity of the registered shareholder

Classically, there are two types of shares. The first links up with the ownership of the share in property law ('bearer share'). The second focuses on entry of the name in a register of members ('registered share').[403] Developments here are not favourable to the bearer share (subsection a below), so that management and, in certain circumstances, fellow shareholders too (subsection b below) can in principle establish the identity of any registered shareholder from a glance at the register of members.

a) Reasons for the success of the registered share

In earlier times, bearer shares were sometimes forbidden because of scepticism about rapid, easy transfer in property law. In the UK in the nineteenth century, the use of bearer shares was initially not possible, and after 1867 was possible only under strict conditions. This has meant that, until now, bearer shares are still not widespread there. Much the same is true of the US. Bearer shares are mentioned in § 8-105 US-UCC, but, in company law (cf. § 16.01(c) MBCA) and listing requirements, they are often not possible. This is to be explained historically since trading in shares did not fit the conception of contractual relations in the joint stock company.[404] Now, though, with bearer shares the danger is readily apparent that big shareholders may conceal their controlling holdings, and illegal actions like tax evasion or money laundering may be encouraged.

Across the countries, active trading in shares is as a rule no longer regarded negatively.[405] Neither the paper basis of bearer shares nor the need to change the name on the register with registered shares any longer

[403] Even in case of registered shares there may, however, be a certificate: see van Ryn (1990: paras. 5-108 *et seq.*) and e.g. s. 768 UK-CA; § 178 DelGCL; § 214 JapCA.

[404] See also Ch. 2, section IV.1.a; Ch. 4, section I.3.a above.

[405] See Ch. 4, section I.3.a above.

suit the desired fungibility of shares. Accordingly, in most countries, an immobilization and dematerialization of shares has come about, overtaking the classic forms of share transfer.[406] This has been consistently pushed in France, where shares are now in general dematerialized, with transfer by merely changing the entry in a register. For registered shares, this change is handled by the company itself. By contrast, for bearer shares (admissible since 1981 only for listed companies),[407] financial intermediaries necessarily keep track of ownership. Despite technical approximation, thus, the distinction between bearer and registered shares is maintained, since with bearer shares the company does not learn the identity of its shareholders (at any rate not automatically).

In Germany,[408] it is not possible to speak of a full dematerialization of the share. Yet here too the renaissance of the registered share since the late 1990s was greatly helped by easier processing through the inclusion of the registered share in a global depository and the development of electronic registers. A peculiarity to be noted, though, is that with the industrial revolution the bearer share initially drove out the previously dominant registered share. The rapid, uncomplicated trading associated with the bearer share was here – by contrast with other countries – unrestricted, so that even today companies can choose between bearer and registered shares. For international firms, however, the choice is increasingly often in favour of the registered share. For, in the case of bearer shares, listing on US exchanges is possible only indirectly through American Depositary Receipts, whereas direct listing of registered shares enables for instance their use for acquisitions.

The law in Japan and China was influenced at the outset by German law, since here too bearer or registered shares were both permitted. On the US model, however, after 1990 in Japan only registered shares could be issued.[409] In China, the admissibility of bearer shares is excluded for all shares held by legal persons.[410]

Overall, thus, the bearer share is losing its importance in favour of the registered share. At first sight, this is paradoxical in the age of global trade, since the anonymous bearer share was earlier 'suspect' for its easy

[406] See also Expert Group on Cross-Border Voting in Europe, Final Report (2002: 14–15); J. Winter (2003: 396 *et seq.*); Noack and Zetzsche (2002); Company Law Reform (2005: 36–7).

[407] See Merle (2005: para. 286); van Ryn (1990: para. 5-113).

[408] On what follows see e.g. Merkt (2000: 81, 83 *et seq.*); Noack (2000a: 291); Siems (2000: 628–9); Schmitz (2002: 6 *et seq.*).

[409] Cf. Marutschke (1999: 249); Hayakawa and Raidl-Marcure (1992: 286).

[410] See §§ 130, 131 ChinCA and Comberg (2000: 66, 98–9).

transferability, whereas the individualized registered share could more easily be related to the quasi-partnership concept of the joint stock company.[411] But these ideas are largely outdated today, since even with registered shares the shareholder can buy and sell quickly and easily. However, a shareholder might still not like registered shares, since he has to make his identity known through the register of members kept by management.[412] Yet this can be readily circumvented in most countries by not entering the economic owner in the register.[413] In this case, both ease of share trading and the shareholder's anonymity are guaranteed even with the registered share, so that what earlier precisely typified the bearer share may now be accomplished with registered shares.

b) Anonymity *vis-à-vis* fellow shareholders

Knowing who your fellow shareholders are is intended to enable shareholders to agree among themselves and thus to effectively assert their rights. Since with registered shares management knows the identity of all registered shareholders, informational asymmetry between management and shareholders is also avoided.

Various situations are to be distinguished in the details. Particular importance attaches to communication in the run-up to the general meeting. This is true especially where the use of voting proxies mean that much of the decision-making process has already taken place before the general meeting. For this situation, then, in the words of the OECD Principles, effective participation in general meetings 'can be enhanced by developing secure electronic means of communication and allowing shareholders to communicate with each other'.[414] Where specific proposals and countermotions are involved, however, these are in many countries forwarded or made accessible to other shareholders through management. Disclosure of identity and direct contact between shareholders as a rule do not happen.

However, shareholders in some countries can access the register of members and thus obtain the names and addresses of fellow shareholders. But this right of inspection is not uniform in its pattern. In the UK, it is open to all and hence also to any third party, with shareholders having the sole advantage of not having to pay for it (s. 116 UK-CA). The provisions

411 On this concept see Ch. 3, section I.1 above.

412 Cf. e.g. § 67(1), (2) GerAktG; § 131(no.1) ChinCA; § 16.01(c) MBCA; s. 113 UK-CA.

413 See Ch. 4, section IV.3 below.

414 OECD-Principles 1999, note to No. 1.C.3; see now also No. II.G OECD-Principles 2004; similar for the UK Modern Company Law for a Competitive Economy (1999: para. 4.60).

in the US are based on the general rules for access. Both in common law and in state corporate law,[415] accordingly, a proper purpose is required, but not (any longer) a quorum.[416] In France, there is a time limitation, with the right of access confined to the period immediately before the general meeting.[417] In Japan, all shareholders have the right to inspection but there are exceptions, for instance, on the basis of the common interest of the shareholders or where the demand is for the purpose of informing a third party for profit (§ 125 JapCA).

By contrast, German law has recently developed in a different direction. Since 2001, shareholders in listed companies can no longer obtain information on fellow shareholders from the register of members.[418] The same applies to unlisted companies, unless a provision in the articles of association stipulates otherwise. In justification it is pointed out in particular that the provisions on disclosure by major shareholders[419] already ensure adequate transparency of participation structures.[420] From a comparative point of view this justification is not convincing, since in other countries that sort of disclosure obligation coexists with a right of access. It seems more plausible to point to the particularly pronounced right of privacy in the German private-law context[421] because the right to informational self-determination and data protection was also debated in connection with the 2001 reform.[422]

However, the shareholder who attends the general meeting becomes in any case recognizable to fellow members. In most countries, shareholders therefore also have the right to inspect the record of attendance at the general meeting.[423] But restrictions apply here too. In Germany, since 2001, registered shareholders may be represented anonymously at the general meeting (§§ 129(2), 135(4) GerAktG). Particularly in the US, moreover, the fact that the economic owner often differs from the registered shareholder[424] leads to *de facto* anonymity of shareholders.

[415] Cf. §§ 16.01(c), 16.02(b)(3), (c) MBCA; § 220(b) DelGCL.
[416] See Ch. 4, section III.1.b above.
[417] Art. L. 225-116 FrCCom; Art. 140 FrDécret.
[418] § 67(6) GerAktG as amended by Gesetz zur Namensaktie und zur Erleichterung der Stimmrechtsausübung (NaStraG) of 18.01.2001, BGBl. I 123.
[419] See Ch. 4, section IV.4 below.
[420] Regierungsentwurf NaStraG, BR-Drucks. 308/00, at 19.
[421] See generally Zweigert and Kötz (1998: 688 *et seq.*).
[422] See e.g. Wiebe (2002: 199).
[423] E.g. § 7.20 MBCA; § 219 DelGCL; §§ 98, 108 ChinCA; § 129(1)(s.2), (4)(s.2) GerAktG; Arts. L. 225-114, 225-117 FrCCom; Art. 142 FrDécret; for France see also Art. L. 225-116 FrCCom and Art. 140 FrDécret on the possibility of inspecting the list before the general meeting.
[424] See Ch. 4, section IV.3 below.

This factual aspect is of importance not just for the record of attendance. Instead, the separation of the legal and economic ownerships may lead to *de facto* devaluation of the relatively far-reaching rights of access in the US and the UK. Investors wishing to remain anonymous thus basically have available a functional equivalent to the restrictive German law. The next question is then whether and how far this form of circumvention is permitted, or whether the anonymity of the economic owner is to be lifted.[425]

For the future, communication through the register system must in any event be rethought, given the new electronic technologies. This need not mean that the identity of shareholders is to be disclosed online. Instead, for instance, information on companies' website, forums or e-mail services may facilitate communication where this is desired by the shareholders.[426] This range of choice would also make sense in terms of the model categories of shareholder:[427] an active shareholder as 'owner' or 'parliamentarian' will be more likely to disclose his identity, while the 'investor' may decide to remain in the background.

2. *Anonymity of the bearer shareholder*

Because of the lesser importance of bearer shares in many countries, exhaustive provisions are to be found only in Germany and France. As there is no register at the outset, the identity of shareholders is known to neither management nor fellow shareholders. In France, however, the articles of association may provide that bearer anonymity must be given up (Art. L. 228-2 FrCCom). Additionally, the articles may provide for advantages to registered shareholders who have held their shares for over two years (Art. L. 232-14 FrCCom) and thus offer an incentive to convert bearer into registered shares. Both in Germany and in France, the basic anonymity is, naturally, also given up if the shareholder personally attends the general meeting. The same applies as a rule also to cases where he has himself represented or – in France – votes by post or e-mail, since the shareholder's name is given in the voting list.[428] In Germany, it is, however, possible here too to remain anonymous, by exercising the vote covertly. This is also true *vis-à-vis* management, unless it is itself proxied by the shareholder.[429]

425 See Ch. 4, section IV.3 below.

426 See Ch. 10, section I.2.c below.

427 See Ch. 3, section I above.

428 § 129(1) GerAktG; Art. 145(nos. 2–4) FrDécret.

429 See Wiebe (2002: 188).

For other shareholders, the problem arises of how to communicate with bearer shareholders in the run-up to the general meeting. Here it is a help that because of the immobilization and – in France – dematerialization even bearer shareholders cannot hide behind individual share certificates. Thus, the lists of bearer shareholders kept by banks can be used to pass information on to them.

As a result, there has been convergence between registered and bearer shares in simple transferability,[430] communication with other shareholders, possibilities of anonymous voting (in Germany) and prevention of anonymity by provisions in the articles of association (in France). In other respects, however, the holder of a bearer share continues to enjoy a greater degree of anonymity. However, it cannot be concluded that in countries where bearer shares are inadmissible or uncommon it will therefore be easier to discover who is participating in the company with their own capital. This is where a functional equivalent may be for investors to participate economically in a company without being entered in the register of members.

3. *Anonymity of the 'spurious' shareholder*

The separation of registered ownership from economic ownership of the share is widespread particularly in the US, but also in the UK.[431] The economic owner is often hidden behind several layers of depositories, banks and brokers. A principal advantage of this system is to make trade in shares easier and cheaper, since the name of the legal owner seldom changes. Again, the economic owner can remain anonymous, and the owner of record can retain the share as security against him.

Similarly, it is usual in the case of cross-border investments, as the Expert Group on Cross-Border Voting in Europe has noted, for shares to be held not by the foreign investors, but by financial intermediaries.[432] Here again, on the one hand, trade in shares is made easier, since 'real transactions' often become superfluous. On the other, the economic owners of the share are, because of the spatial and legal distance from their investment, particularly endangered. For, according to most countries'

[430] See also Ch. 4, section I.3.b above.

[431] For the US: Cox and Hazen (2003: § 13.10 and 2004 Supplement § 28); J. Winter (2003: 419); for the UK: Stapledon and Bates (2002: 568, 570 *et seq.*); Goergen and Renneboog (2001: 261).

[432] Expert Group on Cross-Border Voting (2002: 14 *et seq.*); see also High Level Group of Company Law Experts (2002: 53 *et seq.*); J. Winter (2003: 397 *et seq.*).

laws, in the interests of legal certainty it is the owner of record and not the beneficial owner who counts as shareholder of the company.[433]

Management and 'other' shareholders, however, have a comparable interest in learning the identity of the beneficial owner. The 'spurious' shareholder's contractual agreement with the financial intermediary makes him resemble a 'genuine' shareholder. He decides on the purchase and sale of shares, receives the dividends and sometimes participates in the general meeting. Moreover, the 'spurious shareholder' sometimes has definite rights in law too.[434] In Europe, these rights are, according to the ideas of the Expert Group on Cross-Border Voting, to be unified: the 'ultimate accountholder' is mandatorily to have particular monitoring rights (the 'primary rule'). Additionally, it should be possible for him to entrust the exercise of shareholder rights to his clients (the 'supplementary rule').

Nonetheless, full disclosure of the identity of all investors is not the rule. In the US, communication is in principle enabled by requiring the financial intermediary to convey the information to the beneficial owner.[435] However, a company can ask the financial intermediary to ask the beneficial owner if he agrees to the forwarding of his data to the company. If he does not object, he is entered in a NOBO ('Non Objected Beneficial Owner') list, so that management can send him particular documents (e.g. the annual report) directly. The NOBO list can also be inspected by 'other' shareholders.[436]

UK law used to deal only with the owner of record, so that the beneficial owner had no rights as a 'spurious' shareholder.[437] However, the 2006 reform provides that the owner of record can nominate the beneficial owner to enjoy information rights (s. 146 UK-CA). And, some minority rights can also be asserted by a group of at least 100 beneficial owners (s. 153 UK-CA). Finally, even before the 2006 reform, management or shareholders holding 10 per cent of the registered capital could demand disclosure of the beneficial owner's identity (ss. 793, 795 UK-CA). If the owner of record refuses without a valid reason, this may have the consequence of his being barred from, for instance, selling his shares or exercising his voting rights (s. 797 UK-CA).

433 See Ch. 1, section II.2 above. 434 E.g. § 16.02(f) MBCA; s. 153 UK-CA.

435 On what follows see e.g. Cox and Hazen (2003: § 13.10); J. Winter (2003: 420).

436 See SEC Rule 14b-1(c); *Shamrock Assocs.* v. *Texas Am. Energy Corp.*, 517 A 2d 658 (Del. Ch. 1986) (shareholders soliciting proxies are also entitled to inspect the NOBO list).

437 See Company Law Reform (2005: 18–20, E1–2); Modernising Company Law (2002: para. 2.40); Davies (1997b: 596); Ferran (2003b: 512–13).

Although French law has an a-typical basis that the beneficial owner and not the financial intermediary is the shareholder,[438] it has nonetheless been influenced by the UK provisions. Since the 2001 reform, it has been permissible for financial intermediaries to be entered as 'intermédiaire inscrit' in the register of members (Arts. L. 228-1(3), (4), 228-3 FrCCom). Management may, however, call on financial or (other) registered shareholders it suspects of not being the beneficial owners of the shares to disclose to it and in the interest of the other shareholders the identity of the (real) shareholder (Arts. L. 228-3, 228-3-1 FrCCom). The suspension of voting and dividend rights may be imposed as a penalty for failure to comply (Art. L. 228-3–3 FrCCom). Additionally, for foreign financial intermediaries the voting right depends on the disclosure of the identity of the (real) shareholder (Arts. 151-1 *et seq.* FrDécret).

The Expert Group on Cross-Border Voting in Europe has come out against following the French disclosure obligations.[439] Provisions restricting the anonymity of beneficial owners are also absent in Germany, Japan and China. This may be explained principally by factual circumstances. Since in these countries shares are traditionally held directly by banks, other firms and the state, the problem of fiduciary shareholding arises less often. Again, in Germany, China and earlier in Japan, the alternative exists of using bearer shares.

It is also by no means a matter of course for statutory provisions to grant rights to beneficial owners (as in the US, the UK and France) or to 'lift' their anonymity (as in the UK and France). First, this brings the problem that alongside the registered shareholder an additional person is regarded as a 'quasi-shareholder'. This contradicts the principles of legal certainty, precisely what the register of members is supposed to ensure. Secondly, it is questionable whether mandatory provisions are necessary. Since capital markets are becoming increasingly open and more liquid, the potential for pressure by investors is growing. 'Spurious' shareholders interested in voting rights could thus contractually ensure through their influence that they could become active as shareholders. The fact that this is not happening can be explained because many (small) shareholders are interested mainly in the financial gain from their investment, not in voting rights.[440] Moreover, the new media might also help. They enable intermediaries registered as shareholders to take instructions from the

438 Cf. Guyon (1999: 107); ANSA (2003: 24); see also Ch. 1, section II.2 above.

439 Expert Group on Cross-Border Voting (2002: 33).

440 See Ch. 4, section II.1.b above on 'rational apathy'.

economic owners, pass these on to management and pass the results back to the economic owners at no great cost. Thirdly, the need for a special legal basis for disclosure of the identity of beneficial owners is debatable. For they too are mostly covered by the general provision that capital providers with high proportions of shares cannot remain anonymous.

4. *Anonymity of the influential shareholder*

Regulations governing shareholders who have a substantial holding in one company mean that capital providers whose proportion of the vote approaches or exceeds a particular threshold must inform management, the other shareholders and the public accordingly. This serves, first, to increase the transparency and functionality of the capital market generally. Disclosure of influential shareholders makes it clear who controls the company or aspires to secure control, so that potential investors can make a better-informed judgment on whether to invest. Were that not so, insiders might exploit this information unilaterally and investor trust in the capital market would be adversely affected. Furthermore, it is in the interest of management and current shareholders to discover whether anyone is starting to buy their way into the company. Especially for management, disclosure thus has a warning function, since management is thereby enabled to take measures against an impending takeover. This is important particularly in countries with dispersed shareholding structures, where the market in hostile takeovers generally plays an important part. By contrast, with concentrated participation structures it is of interest particularly to minority shareholders and potential investors to be informed of potential dangers from new blockholders.

Initial disclosure of participation is most often associated with a 5 per cent proportion of the votes.[441] This is now also the minimum threshold of the EU Transparency Directive.[442] Yet in the UK it is just 3 per cent,[443] and in France there is the further possibility for the articles of association to set an additional 0.5 per cent threshold (Art. L. 233-11 FrCCom). For the level of participation it is not just the proportion of the voting shares the shareholder has that is decisive but the indirect influence. Beneficial

[441] E.g. § 13(d) US-SEA; § 21 GerWpHG; Art. L. 233-6 FrCCom; § 86 ChinSA; §§ 27-23 *et seq.* JapSEA.

[442] Art. 9 of the Transparency Directive 2004/109/EC.

[443] Disclosure Rules and Transparency Rules sourcebook, s. 5.1.2, introduced by the Transparency Obligations Directive (Disclosure and Transparency Rules) Instrument 2006 (FSA, 2006).

owners too, or coalitions, may thus also in principle be covered.[444] The practical problem consists, however, of how to determine whether there is a fiduciary holding or a coalition. This is particularly difficult where foreign firms hold shares, since here information may be restricted.

Where the shareholder crosses the first participation threshold or subsequent ones, in either direction, he must in a timely manner supply certain information as to his person, and where appropriate also the background to the purchase.[445] This information is then disclosed publicly,[446] so that not only management and current shareholders but also potential investors are informed. These kinds of disclosure rules are therefore conceived only for listed or other public companies. Yet sometimes there are also obligations on other companies to disclose sizeable shareholdings (e.g. §§ 20, 21 GerAktG), something that is, however, to be seen as justified in the law on groups of companies,[447] because of the danger of impending dependency.

In consequence, one can, despite the differences in detail that have only been touched on here, note the trend to make influential shareholders disclose their voting power. The enforceability of this provision is, however, put into question by the fact that the register of members provides no assistance in respect of bearer shares or fiduciary holdings, so that management may not know who might really have a powerful position. The question accordingly arises whether protection against concealed influence ought not to be made more effective through 'preventive disclosure' by all registered and beneficial owners.

5. *Conclusions*

The overall picture is a mixed one. Convergence – but no more than that – can be seen for instance in the increasing dominance of registered shares, communication by nominee owners to the ultimate investors and disclosure of holdings of influential shareholders. And, while it should in most countries be legally possible for management and fellow shareholders to learn the identity of share owners, bearer shares or the separation

[444] See Art. 10 of the Transparency Directive 2004/109/EC; § 22 GerWpHG; Arts. L. 233-7, 233-9 FrCCom; § 13(d)(1) US-SEA; SEC Rules 13d-3, 13d-5(b); §§ 27-23(3), (4) JapSEA.

[445] See e.g. Arts. 9, 12(1) of the Transparency Directive 2004/109/EC; § 86 ChinSA; SEC Schedule 13 D.

[446] See e.g. Arts. 12(6), 21–22 of the Transparency Directive 2004/109/EC; Art. L. 225-240 FrCCom; §§ 285(no.11), 286(1), (2), 313(2)(no.4) GerHGB.

[447] Which only exists in a few countries; see Hopt (2000: 124 *et seq.*); Immenga (1985: paras. 7-66 *et seq.*).

of economic and legal ownership often mean that no probative register of members is available. Fitting these findings into the shareholder models,[448] the result is that there is no general principle of the 'anonymous' or 'known' shareholder. Instead, a distinction has to be made between the shareholder as 'active parliamentarian' and 'influential owner' on the one hand and as investor on the other. Only for the former is anonymity justifiable. It is otherwise with the mere investor, with no great holdings and who does not seek actively to shape the firm's course.

The recommendations of the Expert Group on Cross-Border Voting in Europe would make little change to the problem of the 'anonymous shareholder'. While it is proposed that the 'ultimate accountholder' be given rights, from the viewpoint of anonymity no clear position is taken: four different options are offered for transposition, with quite different effects for the disclosure of identity.[449] The Expert Group follows neither the specifically German right to informational self-determination nor the specifically French duty of disclosure on all concerned, even if these provisions were not forbidden by the proposed law.

In my view, the starting-point is the principle of the anonymity of the shareholder. For communication and transaction matters, disclosure of identity is not absolutely necessary. For the shareholder who sees himself as a mere investor and neither has large holdings nor wishes actively to shape the firm's course, it is not necessary that he discloses his identity. It is different for influential shareholders, where at least *ex post* disclosure is justified. If that cannot be effectively enforced, *ex ante* measures may nonetheless be contemplated, which would naturally affect all registered and beneficial shareholders.

V. Conclusions to this chapter

The common features and the differences noted above have shown that, as regards provisions on the 'shareholder as such', a division into different legal families is not meaningful. Instead, a number of trends can be discerned, which, especially if considered from a principled point of view, allow one to conclude that there is increasing convergence. Therfore, the shareholder may in law be described by the adjectives 'profit-oriented', 'active' and 'informed'. There is no one-sided fixation on 'voice' or 'exit', so that shareholders in principle benefit from 'double safeguarding'. This

[448] See Ch. 3, section I above.
[449] See Expert Group on Cross-Border Voting (2002: Recommendation 4).

combination can be explained particularly on the ground that the law thereby wishes to suit both the more active shareholder as 'owner' or 'parliamentarian' and the more passive shareholder as 'investor'.[450] The common law countries thus do not confine themselves to the 'investor'. Since there too there are closed and other small companies with block-holdings, the law also has to have provisions available for the other model types.[451] Conversely, in the other countries, many shareholders see themselves as investors and put a value solely on their financial interests. In these countries, accordingly, in recent years specifically investor-related provisions have been enacted.[452] Yet, even today, there are still differences. It was shown above that, in the US, securities law plays a larger part than in other countries.[453] This is, however, not necessarily associated with better protection for shareholders, since in other areas, conversely, US law provides weaker protection.[454]

Based on the laws studied so far, it is apparent that legal-cultural obstacles and path dependencies[455] in principle do not stop convergence. The frequency of reception of foreign law in provisions on the 'shareholder as such' may be connected with the fact that they do not relate primarily to relations with other participants in the firm (Ch. 5 below). However, one should not overlook that even differences in detail may hamper the exercise of shareholder rights in foreign companies. The question accordingly arises for the future (Part 3) whether, for instance, the law on notice periods for convocation, multiple voting rights and voting caps, inspection rights, and the anonymity of shareholders will continue to differ. Another point to be explored is that, despite convergence in the law, so far, country-specific differences in legal reality continue to exist.[456]

[450] For this typology see Ch. 3, section I above.
[451] See e.g. Ch. 4, sections II.3.a, III.1 above.
[452] See e.g. Ch. 4, sections II.4.c, III.2, 3.b above.
[453] See e.g. Ch. 2, section III.1; Ch. 4, section III.2 above.
[454] See e.g. Ch. 4, sections I.2.a, II.3.a, III.1.a above.
[455] See Ch. 8, sections I, V.2; Ch. 9, section VI.3.b below.
[456] See e.g. Ch. 4, sections I.2.c, II.3.c, III.1.a, 2.b, 3.c, IV.3 above.

5

The shareholder in the power structure of the company

The shareholder's position in the power structure of the company highlights the shareholder's relationship with other persons or bodies. This includes the powers of the general meeting (section I below), the protection of shareholders (section II below) and the possibility of enforcing these rights (section III below). Dangers threaten here from two sides. First, management might abuse its position of power. This can be resolved by limiting management's power (section I.1 below), and giving shareholders additional substantive legal protection (section II.1 below) that is also enforceable through the courts (III.1 below). Secondly, the interests of the minority shareholder may be disregarded by the majority. In this case, the minority is to be protected through majority threshold requirements (section I.2 below) or substantive legal rules for a resolution of the general meeting (section II.2 below). These rights must also be enforceable (section III.2 below).

Altogether, then, we have the following matrix:

The shareholder in the power structure of the company (Ch. 5)	*The deciding shareholder (Ch. 5, section I)*	*The protected shareholder (Ch. 5, section II)*	*The litigating shareholder (Ch. 5, section III)*
Protection against management (subsection 1 in each case)	Powers of the general meeting	Substantive legal protection	Actions against management conduct
Protection against majority shareholders (section 2 in each case)	The necessary majority	Substantive legal protection	Actions against decisions of the general meeting

I. The deciding shareholder

The totality of shareholders decides as a rule through the general meeting.[1] For the shareholder's decision-making power, then, what matters is what competences the general meeting has in contradistinction to management (subsection 1 below) and what quantitative preconditions have to be set for passing a resolution of the general meeting in order for it in principle to be binding on all shareholders (subsection 2 below).

1. The powers of the general meeting

The shareholder has a right to vote at the general meeting.[2] This statement, however, leaves it open which decisions this right relates to (subsections b–e below) and on what legal basis these powers rest (subsection a below).

Looking at the shareholder models,[3] a shareholder who considers himself merely to be an investor may wish that the general meeting only has powers in exceptional cases. Since technical expertise lies with management, and since extensive powers for the general meeting are costly and time-consuming, investors might be interested in participation only were the fundamental conditions underlying their investment decision to change. By contrast, the conception of shareholder democracy implies a more powerful position for the general meeting as the 'highest body' of the company. Since, however, the analogy with the political model further implies a separation of powers, management as the executive body is also entitled to certain competences. The general meeting's function then becomes a supervisory one, so that on the whole the separation of ownership and control can be overcome. This also fits the model of the shareholder as owner. The position of the shareholder is, however, even further developed on this model: the general meeting basically has the general power to decide who is in charge ('Kompetenzkompetenz'). It delegates this, in specific areas only, to management, which as its 'representative' has to uphold its interests and is responsible to it.

a) Legal bases

By contrast with the 'ownership model' and the law until the mid-nineteenth century, in most countries today the basic division of powers between management and the general meeting is regulated in the national companies acts.

[1] See Ch. 4, section II.2 above. [2] See Ch. 4, section II.1.a, 4 b above.
[3] See Ch. 3, section I above.

This is particularly marked in Germany. Even if § 119(1) GerAktG says that the general meeting is competent in the cases defined by law and in the articles, the latter variant is largely obsolete. Since the statutory division of powers is mostly mandatory,[4] the general meeting may be left with for instance only the setting up of additional bodies with no organic role. It has thus since 1937 lacked the general power to decide on competences within the company, so that the prevailing opinion no longer regards the general meeting as the 'highest body'.[5] Yet the mandatory regulatory role also has the advantage for the general meeting that some essential powers cannot be taken away from it.

Although in France, Japan and China the 'highest body' terminology is quite common,[6] there too most decisions are statutorily allotted to either the general meeting or management. Only to a limited extent is there room for the articles of association. § 295 JapCA and §§ 100, 38(no.11) ChinCA to that extent follow the tenor of § 119(1) GerAktG. Moreover, in Japan, as in France, there are some provisos permitting arrangements to be made through provisions in the articles of association.

In some US states (especially Delaware) and, at least traditionally, in the UK, company law is restrained about mandatory competences.[7] For a number of basic decisions, however, there are mandatory provisions in these legal systems too,[8] and for listed companies the UK-Listing Rules also contain certain rules.[9] Furthermore, in practice it would be hard to enforce the exclusion of the usual general-meeting powers for public companies. The converse is, however, also true. For over-rigorous restrictions on management would not, in the case of large companies, guarantee the necessary flexibility of action.

[4] See Ch. 2, section IV.1.b above.

[5] Kübler (1998: 167, 194–5); Mülbert, in: GroßkommAktG (1999: vor § 118 para. 3); Assmann, in: GroßkommAktG (1992: Einl. para. 164); also Wiethölter (1961: 92) (was never highest body); for a different view see Henn (1994: 21), (2002: para. 685); cf. also von Rechenberg (1986).

[6] For France: Arlt (2005: 472); Borgmann (1996: 95); Bastian and Germain (1972: para. 30.10.100); for Japan: Kawamoto *et al.* (2001: para. 451); for China: Shumo and Yingxia (2001: 455); Schipani and Liu (2002: 34–5); Comberg (2000: 88); Ranft (1999: para. 61); Liu (2001: 41); see also for Europe: Werlauff (1993: 212) ('Also in states whose basic approach to the division of competence between the company organs is characterised by checks and balances, it is correct to describe the general meeting as the company's highest organ'); for the UK: Davies (2003: 300) ('supreme organ' in the nineteenth century).

[7] See generally Ch. 2, section IV.1.b above; for the UK see also Griffin (2000: 289 *et seq.*); Farrar *et al.* (1998: 305, 363 *et seq.*); McCormack (1998: 136 *et seq.*).

[8] See Ch. 5, section I.1.b-f below. [9] Chs. 10 and 11 UK-Listing Rules.

As a result, at least for public companies variations through unusual provisions in the articles of association remain within limits. For close companies, however, this need not be so, since an individual arrangement tying the general meeting more closely into the regular processes of business may make sense in these cases. However, this decision need not necessarily come in the form of the joint stock company, if and to the extent that the legal form of the 'small company'[10] offers a satisfactory model.

b) Decisions on conduct of business

There is another aspect where the ownership analogy no longer fits, because ordinary business decisions are today essentially in the hands of management (directors, managers and officers).

(1) Competences of management. In earlier times, the general meeting could often intervene in the normal running of the business. Today, for the most part this is no longer possible. Thus, in Germany until 1937, it was, unless otherwise provided in the articles, permissible for the general meeting to give individual instructions on matters relating to the conduct of business.[11] On this model, the same applied in Japan, until the comprehensive reform of company law in 1950 restricted the centrality of the general meeting.[12] In the UK and Commonwealth countries, the change came early in the twentieth century. Until then, the basis here too was that management was under full control by the general meeting.[13] Usually, however, shareholders delegate most of their competences to management.[14] If this is done, the shareholders must respect this separation of powers, so that – as also already in the US – the shareholders are as a rule excluded from the day-to-day operations of the company.[15]

[10] See Ch. 1, section II.1 above.

[11] See Mülbert, in: GroßkommAktG (1999: § 119 para. 1).

[12] Cf. Kawamoto (1994: 70); Hayakawa (1997: 238). § 295 JapCA now makes an exception for restricted share-transfer companies which do not have a board of directors.

[13] See *Isle of Wight Railway* v. *Tahourdin* (1883) 25 ChD 320 (Court of Appeal); Grantham (1998: 556).

[14] See also Art. 2 Draft Model Articles of Association for Public Companies (June 2006) (old Art. 70 Table A).

[15] *Howard Smith Ltd* v. *Ampol Petroleum Ltd.* [1974] AC 821, 837 (Privy Council); Davies (1997b: 183 *et seq.*); Lord Wedderburn (1985: 27); for the US: Großfeld (1971: para. 4-63); Abeltshauser (1998: 26) (may be feasible for close corporations).

A residual competence of the general meeting still appears in cases where the articles are incomplete or management is unable to act.[16]

These developments came about because the conducting of business by the general meeting was regarded as inefficient and also not (any longer) desired by the shareholders.[17] The efficiency of the division of powers in the sense of a political model[18] presupposes that for business decisions a rapid, informed and expert response can be made. Since shareholders as a general rule cannot do this, everyday matters relating to the running of the business rely on the firm's specialized, expert management. This division of competences also fits at least the basic idea of those shareholders who see themselves primarily as investors. Shareholders in large public companies with dispersed ownership basically want to supply only capital, not personal commitment, since they lack the interest or the ability themselves to act as managers. Additionally, shareholders can as a rule safeguard their interests by selling their shares on the capital market.

In most countries, it is accordingly taken as a basic tenet that the conduct of business is incumbent on the board of directors and other members of the management.[19] It is said, for instance, that today in Germany the management board is the most important body[20] and in France the 'conseil d'administration' has not derivative but original rights.[21] These statements seem to contradict the common view in Japan that the general meeting is the supreme body of the company[22] or the view in the US of a principal–agent relationship between the general meeting and management.[23] But it should be borne in mind that the model categories can be used at different levels of abstraction. On the one hand, it may be said that even today the general meeting is the 'highest body' because in electing the board and in competence for basic decisions[24] the general meeting does take central decisions. On the other hand, however, reference may also be made to the legal separation of powers and the *de facto* power position of

[16] Cf. Davies (2003: 304–5); similar in China, see Sharma (1999: 372).

[17] See Grantham (1998: 564 *et seq.*); Whincop (2001: 420–1); Fanto (1998: 50); Großfeld (1971: paras. 4-58, 187); Mülbert (1996a: 60); Mülbert, in: GroßkommAktG (1999: § 119 para. 7); Tuerks (2000: 174).

[18] See Ch. 3, section I.2 above.

[19] § 141(a) DelGCL; § 8.01(b) MBCA; Art. L. 225-35 FrCCom; § 76 GerAktG; § 348(1) JapCA; Arts. 39(1)(s.1), 43(1) SE-Reg.

[20] See Hirte (2003: para. 3.218); Ulmer (2002: 153).

[21] See Merle (2005: para. 395); Großfeld (1971: para. 4-61).

[22] Cf. Taniguchi (1988: 200) and Ch. 5, section I.1.a above.

[23] See Ch. 2, section IV.1.a above, and Ch. 5, section II.1.a below.

[24] See Ch. 5, section I.1.c, d below.

management. The same applies to the agency theory. In a metaphorical sense, it is quite right to call management a (quasi-) agent, since management is obliged to uphold the interests of the shareholders.[25] For positive law, however, it is not appropriate to assume a direct contractual mandate from shareholders, since that would go beyond the competence granted by statute or in the articles of association.

(2) The 'mixture of competences' in China. By contrast with this internationally predominant legal position, in China the general meeting shares responsibility for the conduct of business. Yet here too the general meeting has no general power to decide who is in charge, as there are explicit lists of competences (§ 100 with § 38, § 109(4) with § 47 ChinCA). Again, when § 99 ChinCA states that the general meeting is the company's 'authoritative organ' and the literature adds the term 'supreme organ'[26] this is concordant with the position in many other legal systems.

What is, however, extraordinary in China is the general meeting's competence for 'the company's operational policies and investment plans' (§§ 100, 38(no.1) ChinCA). Management is by contrast 'competent for the company's business plan and investment proposals' (§§ 109(4), 47(no.3) ChinCA). This is demarcated in the prevailing view to make the general meeting responsible for general guidelines and management responsible for specific business decisions.[27] For even in China it is often stressed that in the company ownership and control are to be separate.[28] This separation is, however, hindered not only by §§ 100, 38(no.1) ChinCA but also by the share structure of Chinese companies. Since many companies still serve to restructure state enterprises, the Chinese government is, despite formal privatization, often still the undertaking's largest shareholder.[29] This also explains the far-reaching statutory powers of the general meeting. They are an attempt to ensure the state's influence even where new capital is procured through a sale of minority shareholdings in the company.

There ensue dangers for the effective control of companies ('governance vacuum',[30] 'absent owner'[31]). First, a true division of powers is missing, since both management and the majority shareholders are part of the same

[25] See Ch. 5, section II.1.a below.

[26] Cf. Shumo and Yingxia (2001: 455); Schipani and Liu (2002: 34–5); Comberg (2000: 88); Ranft (1999: para. 61); Liu (2001: 41).

[27] See Comberg (2000: 90).

[28] See Tan (2000: 91).

[29] See Ch. 8, section IV.2 below.

[30] Wei (2003: 199).

[31] Or 'suoyouzhe quewei'; see Clarke *et al.* (2006: 49); Huang (2005: 162–3).

system. While it is generally said that with blockholdings management can be better monitored than with dispersed shareholder ownership,[32] blockholdings are only effective where the blockholder does not form a power block with management. Secondly, there is a danger threatening minority shareholders. The concept that institutional investors should actively guarantee the interests of all shareholders as 'managerial partners'[33] does not work where there is dominant government participation. Questions of overall economic development and social concerns are of prime interest to the state, but not to minority shareholders. Thirdly, it is to be doubted whether state officials can effectively control a multiplicity of (formally) privatized enterprises. If that is not so, then despite comprehensive powers for the general meeting shareholder interests will not be adequately protected.[34]

c) Regular decisions

In spite of management's monopoly of the conduct of business (except in China), particular regular decisions are incumbent on the ordinary general meeting. This is intended to ensure that management acts in the shareholders' interests and is subject to regular monitoring.

(1) Profit distribution and discharge. The rules differ as to whether the shareholders decide the establishment of the annual accounts and the distribution of profit[35] and give a discharge to the board.[36] Even where this is so, competence for these questions should not be overestimated. Management often has broad room for manoeuvre in drawing up the annual accounts, and with profit distribution it is usual for the general meeting to follow the board's proposals.[37] Finally, the possibility of regular discharge serves merely to indicate the collective opinion of the shareholders' meeting – it is not a waiver of claims.[38] Waiver of claims is instead – where at all permissible[39] – often bound up with special requirements[40] and in any case cannot as a rule be presumed.

[32] See Ch. 5, section II.1.b below. [33] Cf. Hill (2000a: 30–1), (2000b: 61 *et seq.*).

[34] Cf. Wei (1998: 365), (2002: 228–9); Comberg (2000: 132–3); Shumo and Yingxia (2001: 456).

[35] See Ch. 4, section I.2.a above.

[36] Usually, this is not expressly provided; but see §§ 119(1)(no.3), 120 GerAktG.

[37] See Ch. 4, section I. 2. b, c above.

[38] For a comparison between German and US law see André (1998: 91).

[39] For France see Art. L. 225-253(2) FrCCom.

[40] E.g. §§ 93(4)(s.3), 116 GerAktG; §§ 8.50 *et seq.* MBCA; § 426 JapCA; Davies (2003: 437 *et seq.*) (for the UK).

(2) Appointments. The powers to appoint the official bodies are more important. As well as the choice of auditors,[41] this particularly concerns influencing the composition of the board(s). The possibility of electing or ejecting directors is not, however, unreservedly available in all the countries under review here. In Germany, shareholders have only indirect influence upon the appointment of management board members. The management board in Germany has since 1937 been mandatorily appointed by the supervisory board, not the general meeting (§ 84(1)(s.1) GerAktG). This differs not only from the one-tier systems where the general meeting decides the composition of the sole board.[42] Even in a two-tier systems it is conceivable for both boards to be appointed by the general meeting.[43] Additionally, in Germany, the influence of the shareholders is limited, since the supervisory board is made up not only of shareholder representatives but also of employee representatives. And the shareholder representatives are in practice preselected by the supervisory board in office and the management board.

But the general meeting's powers in other countries ought also not to be over-estimated. That can be seen particularly in the US. US shareholders are on the one hand disadvantaged by having, by contrast with the current board, themselves to bear the costs of an opposing candidacy.[44] In practice, in public companies, therefore, the election amounts to not much more than approving a single list of candidates drawn up by a nomination committee[45] and proposed by the current board. On the other hand, one may criticize the fact that only the board of directors is elected, so that other important management positions are filled without shareholder involvement. This problem is connected with the fact that in one-tier countries a trend has lately been emerging to separate conduct of business and supervision, and thus to develop an approximation to the two-tier system. For if, as widely called for, the board primarily contains

[41] § 119(1)(no.4) GerAktG; § 318 GerHGB; Art. L. 225-228 FrCCom; s. 489(3) UK-CA; § 329(1) JapCA; § 155 ChinArticles, § 50(no.11) ChinMandProv; but see the power of the audit committee under § 301(2) Sarbanes–Oxley Act 2002; see also Art. 37 Directive 2006/43/EC on statutory audits, which leaves this question to the discretion of the Member States.

[42] E.g. § 329(1) JapCA; Art. L. 225-18(1) FrCCom; Arts. 19, 20 Draft Model Articles of Association for Public Companies (June 2006) (old Art. 78 UK Table A); §§ 8.03(c) MBCA; but according to § 223(a)(1) DelGCL in some cases vacancies may be filled by the directors then in office.

[43] As in §§ 100, 38(no.2) ChinCA; § 329(1) JapCA for the board of auditors (§ 390 JapCA); but differently Art. 39(2) SE-Reg; Art. L. 225-59 FrCCom.

[44] See Ch. 4, section II.3.a above.

[45] Cf. § 8.25 MBCA; also § 404(1) JapCA.

independent members but not for instance the CEO, then that body will be limited to monitoring activities similar to a supervisory board's. The actual conduct of business would then be handled by managers who, like the management board in Germany, are appointed not by the general meeting but by the supervisory body. In summary, a 'contractual convergence'[46] is emerging where a representative system with a monitoring body replaces direct control by the general meeting.

(3) **Duration of appointment.** A member leaves the board when his term expires or he is dismissed. For the securing of shareholder interests, both events are of decisive importance. If board members are 'untouchable' because of long terms and a lack of power of dismissal, the danger exists that the management can without risk pursue the interests of other stakeholders or its own, at its own discretion. Moreover, it is protected from hostile takeovers, since its position would be legally guaranteed even were control purchased by another firm.

In detail, the strong position of management in Germany is strengthened still further by the fact that the management board and the supervisory board can be appointed for terms of up to five years.[47] In most other countries, by contrast, a maximum period of one to three years is usual.[48] This is being called for by US institutional investors for Germany, too,[49] and the German Corporate Governance Code similarly recommends that for initial appointment a term of five years ought not to be the rule.[50]

In Germany, it is also relatively hard for the general meeting to bring about a change during the term of appointment, since there is often a requirement for an important reason as justification, a large majority or the involvement of some other body: the management board can be dismissed by the supervisory board only in the event of sufficiently grave circumstances, which is presumed if the general meeting withdraws its confidence in the board (§ 84(3) GerAktG). Dismissal of supervisory board members is, unless otherwise provided in the articles of association, possible only by three-quarters of the votes cast, unless there is overriding justification (§ 103(1), (3) GerAktG).

[46] See Ch. 1, section IV.1 above. [47] §§ 84(1)(s.1), 102(1) GerAktG.

[48] §§ 8.03(c), 8.06 MBCA; §§ 211(b), 141(d) DelGCL; Art. 21 Draft Model Articles of Association for Public Companies (June 2006) (old Art. 73 UK Table A); s. A.7.1 UK Combined Code; §§ 256(1), 332(1) JapCA; §§ 109(3), 46, 118(4), 53 ChinCA; but differently: Art. L. 225-18 FrCCom: maximum six years.

[49] See André (1998: 156–7); Wymeersch (2001c: para. 34).

[50] No. 5.1.2 GerCGK; similarly No. 12 FrCG-Principles (not more than four years).

By contrast,[51] in the other countries studied here, dismissal is usually possible without needing to meet any particular threshold requirements,[52] and in France the dismissal need not even be on the agenda. Yet studies have shown that job security and risk are fairly similar across the developed countries.[53] As one reason it can be pointed out that management can sometimes control the run-up to the general meeting.[54] Its influence on voting proxies may thus in practice counteract the possibility of dismissal. Moreover, in Delaware shareholders can themselves call a general meeting to vote out board members only if there is a provision in the articles of incorporation or the by-laws to that effect (§ 211(d) DelGCL). Furthermore, problems may arise where dismissing a board member entails financial compensation to be paid to him. In Japanese law dismissal without sufficient justification will by statute bring a compensation claim (§ 339(2) JapCA). Additionally, there is often a contractual entitlement to compensation for dismissal. For instance, in UK law, an agreement whereby the (ex-) director receives compensation is permissible (s. 168(5)(a) UK-CA). Moreover, members of the board may often agree a separate service contract[55] with long notice periods, so that they have to be compensated in the event of early dismissal.

However, this indirect erosion of the power to dismiss sometimes has statutory limits placed on it. In the UK, a contract with a term of more than two years (previously five years) can be concluded only with the consent of the general meeting (s. 188 UK-CA). Additionally, in the UK and Germany, consultancy contracts with non-executive directors or supervisory board members, respectively, on matters already covered by their monitoring task are without effect.[56] In order to prevent circumvention of the law, moreover, in Germany a contract going beyond the period of appointment to the body is not possible.[57] In France, separate contracts have to relate to actual employment (Art. L. 225-22(1) FrCCom) in order

[51] Cf. Großfeld (1971: paras. 4-56, 57); Pistor *et al.* (2001: 25); for Japan contrast §§ 257, 280, 343 JapCC to the new § 309(2)(no.7) JapCA (qualified majority only for directors appointed by cumulative voting).

[52] § 8.08 MBCA; § 141(k) DelGCL; Arts. L. 225-18(3), 225-105(3) FrCCom; s. 168 UK-CA; §§ 339, 341 JapCA; §§ 100, 38(no.2) ChinCA.

[53] Roe (1997: 176–7); Pistor *et al.* (2001: 24); Cheffins (2003b: 10–11).

[54] See Ch. 4, section II.3 above.

[55] For the UK: Davies (1997b: 190 *et seq.*), (2003: 311 *et seq.*); for China: Comberg (2000: 145–6); for Germany: Grunewald (2002: para. 2 C 49).

[56] For the UK: Davies (1997b: 194–5); for Germany: BGH, BGHZ 114, 127.

[57] BGH, BGHZ 3, 90, 93; 8, 348, 360; 10, 187, 194–5.

to prevent the power of dismissal – which in France is possible at any time – being circumvented.[58]

Irrespective of these restrictions, the retreat to contractual agreements leads here too to a certain 'contractual convergence'. This can be seen particularly from the legal comparison between Germany and other countries. The legal restrictions guaranteeing the board member's position in Germany may find a counterpart in other countries through the deterrent effect of contractual compensations.

(4) **Remuneration.** In order to prevent self-enrichment by directors, the idea suggests itself of having their compensation set by the general meeting or by the supervisory board. This division of competences is clearly apparent in Germany. The normal remuneration of supervisory board members is set in the articles of association or by the general meeting (§ 113(1) GerAktG). Where exceptionally an additional consultancy contract is concluded with a supervisory board member, its effectiveness, including the remuneration components, is dependent on assent by the whole supervisory board (§ 114(1), (2) GerAktG). The supervisory board also sets the remuneration of management board members (§ 87(1) GerAktG). In France, Japan and China, by law the general meeting has competence for the remuneration of the board.[59] Japanese law further provides that the remuneration may also be laid down in the articles of association directly, or they may delegate it to the board if the methods of calculation are specified.[60] In the UK, there is no statutory provision. However, here too it is taken that the normal remuneration of board members is to be decided by a general-meeting resolution or in the articles.[61] This fits with the rule that formerly, as common law, applied in the US. Today, however, the statutory provision is that in principle the board of directors sets its own compensation.[62] Since this creates a danger of abuse, the shareholders have the possibility of challenging the level of compensation through a derivative suit. This should test whether the compensation is appropriate and fair.[63]

[58] See Merle (2005: paras. 389 *et seq.*).

[59] Art L. 225-45 FrCCom; Art. 93(1) FrDécret (but the board distributes the overall amount among its members (Art. 93 FrDécret) and sets the remuneration of the 'président directeur général' (Art. L. 225-47 FrCCom)); § 361(1) JapCA; §§ 100, 38(no.2) ChinCA.

[60] § 361(1) JapCA; see also Takahashi and Sakamoto (2004: 244).

[61] See Davies (2003: 402).

[62] E.g. § 8.11 MBCA; § 141(h) DelGCL.

[63] Cf. Cox and Hazen (2003: §§ 11.04–5); Cheffins (2003b: 15); the law is different for 'officers', see Cheffins (2001b: 527).

On the whole, there are some differences regarding the traditional components of remuneration. Nor is the actual total income of board members uniform, since especially in the US the board members earn more than their counterparts in other countries.[64] The decisive reason for this is seen as partly that in the US the higher payments compensate for greater job insecurity ('supermodel syndrome').[65] More recent studies have not, however, confirmed this relationship.[66] It is instead likely that, in the US, boards can relatively easily increase its compensation because public companies lack influential major shareholders. Additionally, the incentive-based components of compensation are an important reason for their overall higher remuneration.

However, in other countries too board members increasingly receive incentive-based additional remuneration, and the statutory provisions on the issue of shares have accordingly been adapted to allow stock options.[67] To avoid abuse, there has also been a tightening of disclosure obligations and a clarification of competences. While in countries with mandatory minimum capital the general meeting is in principle already competent, if only because basically it alone can increase the company's capital and exclude pre-emption rights,[68] there are also often special requirements in company or securities law.[69] And for the more detailed pattern, following US ideas, the competence of compensation committees with a mostly independent membership is increasingly being provided for or called for.[70]

d) Fundamental changes

(1) Background. Fundamental changes to the company were often not possible at all in the nineteenth century. The joint stock company was regarded as a binding and time-limited contract for those involved, so that, in the absence of provisions in the articles of association, the shares

[64] See Cheffins (2003b: 9–10). [65] Cf. Hill (2000a: 32).

[66] Roe (1997: 176–7); Pistor *et al.* (2001: 240; Cheffins (2003b: 10–11).

[67] See Ch. 5, section II.1.a below. [68] See Ch. 5, section I.1.d below.

[69] See Art. L. 225-177 FrCCom; §§ 192(1), (2)(no.3), 193(2) GerAktG; § 9.4.1 UK-Listing Rules (for new long-term incentive schemes); s. 439 UK-CA (for quoted companies); s. B.2.4 UK-Combined Code; §§ 312.03(a), 303A.08 NYSE Manual; see also No. II.C.3 OECD-Principles 2004.

[70] For a comparison among the EU Member States see Ferrarini and Moloney (2004: 332 *et seq.*); see also High Level Group of Company Law Experts (2002: 66); Commission Recommendation fostering an appropriate regime for the remuneration of directors of listed companies, 2004/913/EC; Cheffins (2001b: 528 *et seq.*); for the US: § 3A.05 ALI-Principles; for Japan: § 404(3) JapCA; Appendix JapCG-Principles.

could not be sold[71] nor the fundamentals altered.[72] Shareholders therefore had a vested right that the company's nature remained the same.[73]

This view shifted with the growing autonomy of the joint stock company as a legal entity.[74] Additionally, economic reasons made it necessary, with ever-larger companies, for adjustments to changed conditions or ideas to be possible. This meant not just that the articles of association could be amended at all. Today, there is also no longer a binding effect for previous rules. Special rights or particular components of the articles that cannot be amended at all, or only unanimously, are today mostly no longer recognized. Protection for shareholders is instead guaranteed by other means.[75] Furthermore, if the company's fundamentals are to be altered, the general meeting must often give its consent. Various justifications may be adduced here. First, competence follows from the potential harm that could be done to the value of shareholders' participation. With fundamental changes, the interests of management and of shareholders often differ considerably, and for shareholders there is an incentive to become active. Secondly, the shareholders' reliance interest has to be protected. Shareholders join the company on certain terms, by which they leave the conduct of business to management. Before fundamental changes are made, they must accordingly again consent, since otherwise they would be participating in a company they had not agreed to join. Thirdly, while it is possible on the ownership model for business operations to be delegated to management,[76] if the company is fundamentally changed the power of decision remains with the shareholders as owners. Fourthly, shareholder involvement accords with principles of shareholder democracy, since it is in line with the parliamentary concept for at least all the essential decisions to be taken by the general meeting.[77] Fifthly, this possibility of a check by shareholders is also in the interest of the general public. In this way, the public interest in fairly and efficiently conducted businesses can be met, compensating for the previously common state concession.[78]

All in all, the competence of the general meeting for amendments and fundamental changes meets various purposes. While this does not mean

[71] See Ch. 4, section I.3.a above.
[72] Cf. Conard (1969: para. 6-7); Mestmäcker (1958: 7).
[73] See Cox and Hazen (2003: § 25.04); Siegel (1995: 86).
[74] See Ch. 4, section I.1 above. [75] See Ch. 5, section II below.
[76] See Ch. 3, section I.1; Ch. 5, section I.1, preamble above.
[77] See also Ch. 3, section I.2 above. [78] See Ch. 1, section III.2, 3 above.

the specific historical legislator may not have had a particular intention,[79] from a comparative point of view it becomes clear that legislators have at least in part decided subjectively what provisions the articles of association are to contain and what measures necessitate involvement of the general meeting. However, some convergence can also be noted.

(2) **Amendments to the articles of association.** In most of the countries studied here, only the general meeting can amend the articles of association.[80] US law differs here in two respects. First, amendments mostly also require the consent of the board of directors.[81] Since however in other countries the articles of association are also in almost all cases not amended against the will of the board, a second peculiarity of US law is of greater importance. In the US, as also in the UK, two types of articles of association may be distinguished. This distinction goes back to the origins of the joint stock company. At that time, the 'charter' (or: 'memorandum', 'articles of incorporation', 'certificate of incorporation') was granted by government concession and only the 'by-laws' (or 'articles') were adopted by the company itself. Since in the meantime the concession system has ceased to exist, in the pre-2006 UK company law a substantive approximation of the two parts came about, because both could be amended by the general meeting (ss. 9, 17 UK-CA 1985). The Company Law Review Steering Group even suggested removing this differentiation as such.[82] However, the new law retains the memorandum but restricts its content to the names of the founders and first shareholders (s. 8 UK-CA). The rules on the internal workings of the company are therefore to be set out only in the (alterable) articles (ss. 18, 21 UK-CA). In the US, it is only for an amendment to the articles of incorporation that the general meeting has mandatorily to be involved.[83] The by-laws can mostly be amended both by the general meeting and by the board.[84] It is disputed whether and to what extent the articles of incorporation can shape or restrict this dualism, and whether the board can reverse a decision of the general meeting.[85] The question of the place of the by-laws is of topical interest particularly in takeovers. Shareholders seek to use by-laws to limit management's room

[79] For Germany see Mülbert (1996a: 161 *et seq.*).

[80] §§ 119(1)(no.5), 179 GerAktG; Art. L. 225-96 FrCCom; § 466 JapCA; § 100, 38(no.10) ChinCA; No. II.B.1 OECD-Principles 2004.

[81] § 10.03(b) MBCA; § 242(b)(1) DelGCL; for a critique see Bebchuk (2006).

[82] Modern Company Law: Final Report (2001: para. 9.4).

[83] § 10.03 MBCA; § 242 DelGCL. [84] Cf. § 10.20 MBCA; § 109(a) DelGCL.

[85] Cf. Hamermesh (1998: 413 *et seq.*).

for manoeuvre. How far this is permissible has not yet been conclusively clarified.[86]

(3) **Capital measures.** US law, and following it also Japanese law, takes a particular position also on the question whether the general meeting must take decisions about capital measures. In these two countries, primary competence lies with the board, so that as a rule it decides on its own responsibility about the issue of new shares or buybacks of shares. The general meeting becomes involved, however, where the upper limit to shares set in the articles of incorporation is reached, since amendment to the articles would then be required.[87] Additionally, companies listed at the NYSE must obtain the general meeting's consent for certain capital measures according to § 312.03 NYSE Manual.

In the other legal systems, it is in principle the general meeting that is competent for capital increases, capital reductions or share buybacks.[88] However, it is increasingly possible to empower the board to take capital measures. This applies particularly to the authorized share capital, which for a certain period – mostly five years – allows the distribution of new shares by the board.[89] A similar five-year rule can also be found in UK law (s. 551 UK-CA). Technically, this rule is, however, not about 'authorized legal capital' but about authorizing the directors to allot shares. If directors use this authorization and allot new shares, this automatically leads to an increase in share capital (s. 617(2)(a) UK-CA).

It can thus be seen that the board increasingly can decide on capital measures. As with other deregulation trends,[90] this delegation points to flexibility of company law in the area of corporate finance. Competitive pressures cause firms to seek to use flexible financing instruments. The involvement of shareholders in such measures is then reduced at least to a time-limited general-meeting empowerment or an amendment of the articles of association with no time limit.

[86] See Hamermesh (1998: 414–15); Cox and Hazen (2003: § 3.12).

[87] E.g. §§ 6.01 *et seq.* MBCA; §§ 152, 154, 161 DelGCL; §§ 201, 240, 447, 450(2) JapCA.

[88] For the EU: Arts. 19(1)(lit. a), (3), 25 *et seq.*, 30 *et seq.* of the Second Directive 77/91/EEC; van Ommeslaghe (1990: para. 5-66); Werlauff (1993: 212 *et seq.*); for China: §§ 100, 38(no.7), 134 ChinCA; see also No. II.B.2 OECD-Principles 2004; Euroshareholders Corporate Governance Guidelines (2000: No. II).

[89] Arts. L. 225-129 *et seq.* FrCCom; §§ 182, 237 GerAktG; cf. also Art. 25(2) of the Second Directive 77/91/EEC; Ommeslaghe (1990) paras. 5-3, 35 *et seq.*; Werlauff (1993: 212 *et seq.*); Wymeersch (2001c: paras. 6, 9). The law in China is probably still different: see Liu (2001: 38–9).

[90] See Ch. 4, sections I.4, II.4.a above, and Ch. 5, section II.2.b below.

(4) Mergers, divisions, etc. In most Western countries since the late nineteenth century, alongside growth of the firm itself external growth through mergers and acquisitions has also been recognized. A 'horror of bigness' thus in principle no longer exists.[91] This is now also the case for China, because the 2005 reform abolished the requirement that mergers and divisions of companies needed government approval.[92] Additionally, as is common in other countries, the consent of the general meeting is as a rule required for measures which, like mergers, divisions, changes of form and voluntary dissolution of the company, affect both the fundamental legal and the *de facto* structure of the company.[93]

It is not an exception to this that in the US a change from close to public company does not need the consent of the general meeting. In the US, the distinction between 'small companies' and joint stock companies is less marked than in other countries,[94] so that this is more of a modification in content than a change in form. Moreover, in other countries, the listing or delisting of a company mostly does not require the consent of the general meeting. This is plausible at any rate for listing, since, for companies that can in theory be listed, this can be expected in order to raise capital.[95] By contrast, with delisting there is a risk of taking the exit option through the capital market away from shareholders, so that here the heightened need to protect shareholders can be covered by giving competence to the general meeting.[96]

One exception to consent by the general meeting is sometimes provided for where on a merger the acquiring company already has considerable influence over the acquired company. Since in these 'short-form' or 'small-scale' mergers the necessary majority of the general meeting of the acquired company would be easy to obtain, in the US and Japan the general meeting often need not give its consent.[97] In other countries and in other US states, those involved may by contrast only be exempted from

[91] Cf. Conard (1969: para. 6-72 *et seq.*); Pistor *et al.* (2002: 813).

[92] See § 173 ChinCA 2005 in contrast to § 183 ChinCA 1993.

[93] See generally Rock *et al.* (2004: 131 *et seq.*); for the EU: Art. 7 of the Third Directive 78/855/EEC, Art. 5 of the Sixth Directive 82/891/EEC; Pistor *et al.* (2002: 812 *et seq.*); for the other countries: §§ 251, 275 DelGCL; §§ 100, 38(no.9) ChinCA; § 71(no.3) ChinArticles; §§ 471(1)(no.3), 776(1), 783(1), 795(1), 804(1) JapCA.

[94] See Ch. 1, section II.1 above.

[95] However, approval might be necessary due to an increase in the statutory capital.

[96] This is e.g. the case in Germany: see BGH, BGHZ 153, 57 (*Macrotron*).

[97] § 11.05 MBCA; §§ 251(f), 253 DelGCL; §§ 784(1), 796(1), 468 JapCA.

a resolution of the acquiring company's general meeting.[98] The reason for this exemption is that from the viewpoint of this company the transaction is not an extraordinary one. It is, however, questionable whether this exception should – as is partly the case in the US (§ 11.04(g)(1) MBCA) and is being called for in Europe too by the High Level Group of Company Law Experts[99] – be extended to all mergers by absorption and divisions by fusion. In support of this view is the point that even with a hostile takeover the general meeting of the bidder as a rule does not need to consent.[100] While against this view it is pointed out that mergers and takeovers are equivalent only in the case of an own-share offer,[101] in the case of a capital measure at least authorization by the general meeting is in any case often necessary.[102]

(5) **De facto changes.** As a rule, changes relating not to the company itself but only to its physical or other assets do not require the consent of the general meeting. It is often different where a *de facto* measure operates so radically as to be tantamount to a change in the legal bases. In most countries and according to No. II.B.3 of the OECD-Principles of Corporate Governance, it is therefore provided that in the event of the transfer of the whole or substantial company assets the general meeting must consent.

In detail, however, there are considerable differences, cutting across the division into civil law and common law countries. According to the UK Listing Rules, as from 25 per cent of total assets the involvement of the general meeting is required for listed companies.[103] Since 2005 Chinese law has been similar. Here too there is a special provision only for listed companies, which requires approval by the general meeting in the case of any sale of assets in an amount in excess of 30 per cent of the total assets (§ 122 ChinCA). For Japan, the transfer of an important part of the company's business requires consent by the general meeting (§ 467(1)(no.2) JapCA). Previous case law had assumed it as from

[98] Arts. 8, 24 *et seq.* of the Third Directive 78/855/EEC and e.g. § 62 GerUmwG; s. 916 UK-CA; also §§ 784(3), 796(3), 805 JapCA.
[99] High Level Group of Company Law Experts (2002: 107).
[100] Renner (2002). Japanese law is, however, different: see § 467(1)(no.3) JapCA; Kawamoto *et al.* (2001: para. 680).
[101] Group of German Experts on Corporate Law (2002: 28).
[102] See subsection (3) above.
[103] For details see chapter 10 of the UK-Listing Rules.

10 per cent of the whole firm,[104] whereas the 2005 law explicitly excludes cases where the value of the assets does not exceed 20 per cent.

The situation in France, Germany and the US is more generous to directors. Since in France there is no explicit provision on the sale of major parts of the company's assets, it is debated, first, whether a *de facto* measure constitutes a change in the object of business, for which the general meeting is competent. Secondly, it is argued that the major assets can be equated with the whole assets within the meaning of Art. L. 237-8(no.4) FrCCom.[105] Although German law contains a similar provision in § 179a GerAktG, the case law uses § 119(2) GerAktG as a starting-point. According to this provision, the management board should in general be obliged to refer questions of conduct of business to the general meeting if a serious interference with shareholders' rights and interests is likely.[106] This is presumed particularly on the spinning off of an operation constituting the most valuable part of the company's assets to a subsidiary. Statutory clarification was rejected by the governmental Commission on Corporate Governance, because 'as in US law' further clarification was to be left to the literature and the case law.[107] Yet differences remain. In the US, for instance, there are more detailed specifications in the MBCA, whereby for instance the disposal of 75 per cent of the total assets requires consent by the general meeting (§ 12.02 MBCA). Delaware law is more like a general clause, because it talks only about 'substantially all of its property and assets' (§ 271(a) DelGCL). Here too, though, the case law similarly clarifies the law, so that for ordinary parts of operations disposal of around 75 per cent of the assets requires consent.[108] In Germany by contrast, according to some of the literature even 20–25 per cent requires the involvement of the general meeting.[109] This has, however, recently been rejected by the German Supreme Court: in order not to needlessly disrupt the balanced relationship of the company's bodies, the involvement of the general meeting on the ground of a major impairment of the unwritten participatory rights of shareholders would come into question only in exceptional cases. The 'threshold of seriousness' would

104 See Osugi (2002: 36).

105 See Schindler (1999: 320); Wymeersch (2001c: para. 7); Fanto (1998: 66 and note 186); Regierungskommission Corporate Governance (2001: para. 80).

106 BGH, BGHZ 83, 122 (*Holzmüller*).

107 Regierungskommission Corporate Governance (2001: para. 82).

108 See Dooley and Goldman (2001: 752 *et seq.*); but see also *Gimbal* v. *Signal Companies*, 316 A 2d 599 (Del. Ch.) affirmed in part, 316 A 2d 619 (Del. 1974) (no specific qualifying percentage but qualitative and quantitative characteristics of the transaction at issue).

109 See the references in Abeltshauser (1998: 211–12); Raiser (2001: § 16 para. 14).

accordingly as a rule be reached only if a sale accounted for some 80 per cent of company assets.[110]

The various provisions thus do not display typical differences according to particular models, but have the nature of a compromise. On the one hand is the interest in legal certainty and the flexible conduct of business. This is satisfied if management is free in purely factual measures, or the general meeting has only occasional and clearly defined participatory rights in this area. On the other hand, there is the danger of the participatory rights of shareholders being circumvented by *de facto* measures if there are no or very limited powers of the general meeting.

e) Special situations

In a number of other situations, the general meeting can be responsible for supervising management. Among these are, for instance, the appointment of experts and special auditors,[111] approval of transactions between directors and the company,[112] or collaboration on defensive measures against hostile takeovers.[113] Generalizations are difficult, since there is often a connection with other protective mechanisms. Alongside supervision by a public authority, derivative suits[114] may, for example, be an alternative to special audits. In the case of transactions by directors, legal systems may also limit the risks by entirely prohibiting such transactions or requiring consent from a committee, a supervisory board or the whole board.[115] Finally, involvement in defence against hostile takeovers depends first of all on whether such measures are at all permissible.[116]

f) Conclusions

On an overall comparison of competences of the general meeting, it is striking that in China the general meeting is competent for many decisions that in the US are in the hands of management. The other countries display an intermediate legal position, with some special rules in German law which restrict shareholder influence.

[110] BGH, BGHZ 159, 30 (*Gelatine*).

[111] Cf. §§ 119(1)(no.7), 142, 258 *et seq.* GerAktG; Art. L. 225-231 FrCCom; § 318 JapCA; Modernising Company Law and Enhancing Corporate Governance in the European Union – A Plan to Move Forward, Communication from the Commission, COM(2003) 284, at 16.

[112] See e.g. Art. L. 225-40 FrCCom; s. 190 UK-CA; § 11.1.7(3) UK-Listing Rules; for Germany: Mülbert, in: GroßkommAktG (1999: § 119 para. 8).

[113] See Ch. 5, section II.1.a below.

[114] See Ch. 5, section III.1 below.

[115] See Ch. 5, section II.1.b below.

[116] See Ch. 5, section II.1.a below.

These differences can be explained, first, on the ground that only in China, for political reasons, is the collaboration of the (often government-dominated) general meeting in the conduct of business desired. Secondly, the restricted possibilities in Germany of influencing the appointment and dismissal of management can be explained by additional protection through the supervisory board system and comprehensive substantive powers for the general meeting. These substantive powers enable the supervision of conduct and can thus be seen as a substitute for the limited 'personal supervision'. Thirdly, in the US the lesser competences of the general meeting are connected to other protective mechanisms. In the US, suits against management are more common. Additionally, shareholders of public companies are more substantially protected by securities law and capital-market forces.

Yet, there are also a number of congruencies and convergences, so there are no unbridgeable legal-cultural contrasts.[117] The decisive common aspect is the specialization of areas of competence and the division of powers between the general meeting and management. Management conducts the firm's business, whereas the general meeting is responsible for monitoring the board and deciding on fundamental changes. This means that management is primarily competent in business questions and not subject to any power of instruction by the general meeting. However, according to the legal model, the shareholders retain ultimate control.[118] On the one hand, the general meeting, through the power to amend the articles of association and decide the fundamentals of the company, has the 'rule-making' function.[119] There are exceptions where quick action is necessary, as for instance the increasing admissibility of authorized capital shows. On the other hand, the general meeting as a rule decides on the composition of the board. From these viewpoints, accordingly, the (earlier) greater importance of the general meeting is still apparent today, and it is possible to speak of a hierarchy between general meeting and management.[120]

[117] Contra M. Ulmer (1998: 118).

[118] Yet, in practice this might be different due to the 'rational apathy' of shareholders (Ch. 4, section II.1.b above), cross-shareholding (Ch. 8, section IV below), management proxies (Ch. 4, section II.3.c above), and the influence of institutional investors outside the general meeting (Ch. 4, section II.4.c above).

[119] McCormack (1998: 137).

[120] See Ch. 5, section I.1.a above.

2. *The necessary majority of shareholders*

As with the governing bodies of political organizations or other associations, for the general meeting the question arises of what majority justifies attributing the decision to the whole organization. The room for manoeuvre here ranges from a requirement for unanimity to a relative majority of shares entitled to vote.

a) Relative, absolute and qualified majorities

Although the unanimity requirement was still common in the nineteenth century, today unanimity is no longer required, or is only fairly rare.[121] Particularly with public companies, unanimity would be a bar to change and would reduce the necessary flexibility.[122] Here there is also a major difference between shareholders and other capital providers. For the latter, the contractual terms cannot in principle be altered by a majority decision of all the creditors. However, for shareholders, quorums or qualified majorities sometimes constitute a compromise between the more cumbersome unanimity principle and the principle of the simple majority.

First, there is the question of how to take account of abstentions. In most legal systems, only participating shareholders count, so that abstention by not turning up is ignored.[123] An exception is Delaware law, which for certain basic decisions focuses on the 'outstanding stock of the corporation'.[124] It is more controversial whether abstentions at the general meeting are to be simply ignored or treated as dissenting votes. Predominantly, the focus is on the relative (simple) majority and does not take abstentions into account.[125] Things are different for instance in France, Japan and (with the exception of elections) Delaware, so that abstentions act as dissenting votes (absolute majority).[126]

Secondly, however, there is sometimes a requirement for a minimum proportion of all shareholders with voting rights in order for a resolution

[121] Cf. Pistor *et al.* (2001: 26–7); Fanto (1998: 67).

[122] *Inhabitants of Waldoborough* v. *Knox and Lincoln R. R.*, 24 A 942, 942–3 (Maine 1892) ('When there are differences in opinion, aggregate bodies of men must act by majorities, or they cannot act at all'); see also Ch. 5, section I.1.d above.

[123] E.g. § 133(1) GerAktG; Art. L. 225-98 FrCCom; § 104(s.2) ChinCA; § 309(1) JapCA; § 206 DelGCL.

[124] §§ 242(b)(1), 251(c), 271(a), 275(b) DelGCL.

[125] E.g. § 133(1) GerAktG; § 104(s.2) ChinCA; §§ 7.25(c), 7.26(a) MBCA.

[126] See Dalloz (2005: Art. L. 225-37 para. 11, Art. L. 225-98 para. 7); § 309(1) JapCA; § 216(2), (3) DelGCL; for a comparison between DelGCL and MBCA see Dooley and Goldman (2001: 759–60).

to be valid. The trend is, however, against such quorums. In Germany and China, they would have to be brought in by a provision in the articles of association. The same applies in principle in the UK, even if there the statutory quorum requires two shareholders to be present (s. 318 UK-CA). While Japanese law provides for a quorum of 50 per cent of the voting rights (§ 309(1) JapCA), it is nonetheless – except for elections – permissible and usual for the articles of association to depart from this.[127] The same is not possible for the quorum in France. Here, however, the 25 per cent quorum does not apply to an adjourned general meeting, so that it is usual for public companies immediately to convoke the second session too as a precautionary measure. Finally, the law is special in the US. Alongside provisions for optionality in the certificate of incorporation or by-laws (e.g. § 216(1) DelGCL), the MBCA provides for a 'quorum consisting of at least a majority of the votes entitled to be cast' for particular basic decisions.[128]

Thirdly, in most legal systems, supermajorities are required for particular decisions. In substance, there are often similar lists: amendments to the articles of association, mergers, and voluntary liquidations,[129] as well as capital measures[130] and sales of major parts of the company.[131] Most countries require a two-thirds majority here.[132] Also common, however, is a three-quarters majority of the – mostly present – capital.[133] US law is different, since today often a simple majority suffices.[134] As a surrogate here, however, is the fact that for instance Delaware focuses on all shares for basic decisions, while the MBCA calls for a quorum to be complied with (see the two previous paragraphs above).

The differences in all of these provisions are of more than just formal significance. Quorums and qualified majorities are supposed to operate

[127] See Kawamoto *et al.* (2001: para. 466); Kawamoto (1994: 90).

[128] §§ 10.03(e), 11.04(e), 12.02(e), 14.02(e) MBCA. Furthermore, the majority shareholder who engages in a conflict of interest transaction may seek approval of the disinterested shareholders (i.e. the majority of the minority) because in this case fairness of the transaction is presumed (*Kahn* v. *Lynch Communication Sys., Inc.*, 638 A 2d 1110 (Del. 1994); 669 A 2d 79 (Del. 1995)).

[129] §§ 269(2)(s.1), 263(1)(no.2) GerAktG, § 65(1) GerUmwG; Arts. L. 225-96, 225-246, 236-9 FrCCom; § 104(s.3) ChinCA; § 309(2)(nos.11, 12) JapCA.

[130] §§ 182(1)(s.1), 193(1)(s.1), 222 GerAktG; § 104(s.3) ChinCA; § 309(2)(nos.1–6, 9) JapCA.

[131] § 309(2)(no.11) with § 467(1) JapCA.

[132] Art. L. 225-96(3) FrCCom; §§ 106(2), 104(s.3) ChinCA; § 309(2) JapCA; cf. generally DSW-Europastudie (1999: 88–9); Art. 7 of the Third Directive 78/855/EEC (at least two-thirds).

[133] § 179 GerAktG; s. 283 UK-CA.

[134] Previously, there was a two-thirds requirement, see Pistor *et al.* (2001: 29).

in the interest of 'shareholder democracy', ensuring that all or at least major decisions are supported by a clear majority of shareholders, so that decision-making is enhanced and random majorities avoided. It is, however, problematic that, in public companies with dispersed holdings, quorums and qualified majorities are hard to obtain, so that a necessary change might be prevented. Furthermore, those who abstain cannot later object to a vote cast by active shareholders. As an objection to qualified majorities, finally, it may be pointed out that in public companies the capital market often ensures adequate protection through the sale option. Where that is not the case, moreover, compensation can offer sufficient protection for the shareholder who perceives himself primarily as an investor.

The legal differences can accordingly be explained by the fact that, particularly in the US, the sale of shares and appraisal rights[135] are of greater importance than active participation, so that protection by qualified majorities may be foregone. Additionally, differing shareholding structures have an effect. The concentrated shareholdings in continental Europe, Japan and China make larger majorities easier to obtain than with the dispersed holdings in public companies in the US and the UK.[136] The tighter majority requirements on the Continent can thus be seen as functionally equivalent to the fact that here too the conduct of business remains in the hands of management.

For shareholders in small companies or blockholders, it may be more appropriate to ensure protection through quorums or majority thresholds in the articles of association. The active shareholder is here more closely connected with the firm, because he lacks the ready possibility of selling his shares on the capital market. The articles of association can accordingly often provide for a tightening of majority requirements and the introduction of quorums.[137] A farther-reaching freedom exists, as in other respects too, in the UK,[138] and to some extent also in Germany.[139] French law is restrictive, with the majority rules not alterable by the articles of association.[140]

135 See Ch. 4, section I.3.d above, and Ch. 5, section II.2.c below.

136 On different shareholding structures see Ch. 8, section IV below.

137 See §§ 7.27(a) MBCA; § 102(b)(4) DelGCL; for China: Comberg (2000: 124).

138 See Davies (2003: 483, 505 *et seq.*).

139 § 179(2)(s.2) GerAktG (in general higher or lower thresholds possible; but for amendment of the purpose of the enterprise lower thresholds are excluded).

140 Cf. Sonnenberger (1991: para. III 167); Michalsky (1991: 1568).

b) Cumulative voting rights

Since elections have to be held regularly, quorums or qualified majorities do not help to further protect the minority. As an alternative, in the US, the system of the cumulative vote was developed, so that minority shareholders too are represented on the board. Every shareholder thus has as many votes as there are seats on the board to be filled, so that he can bundle them together behind one candidate.[141]

For various reasons, however, the cumulative vote has not been taken up in other countries, and is also on the retreat in the US. First, disproportionate minority influence may arise where the minority uses its cumulative vote effectively, but the majority does not come to an internal agreement. Secondly, the functionality of the board may be hampered. While it may be argued theoretically that with a plural membership structure the members monitor each other, so that there is effective control over management,[142] in practice the danger exists that a body with a mixed composition may be dominated by unproductive clashes among several hostile parties, to the detriment of the good of the company. Thirdly, the minority protection sought by cumulative voting rights may not necessarily be achievable. By reducing the size of the board or by using a 'staggered board',[143] minorities may be prevented from actually being represented.

In US law, accordingly, there are no compulsory cumulative voting rights but either 'opt out' (e.g. § 301.5(a) CalGCL)[144] or 'opt in' provisions (e.g. § 214 DelGCL). In Japan, under US influence following the Second World War, cumulative voting rights were introduced, bindingly enforceable by shareholders holding 25 per cent of the registered capital. Since 1974, however, it has been possible to exclude them through the articles of association (now § 342 JapCA), and this is in practice often done.[145] France and Germany have no statutory provisions on cumulative voting rights. Yet, in France, it can be provided in the articles of association.[146] In Germany, this is controversial, and not yet clarified by the courts.[147] Finally, the Chinese situation may be surprising, because the 2005 reform introduced an 'opt-in' system into the new Companies

[141] See Gordon (1994).

[142] Glanzmann (2002: 419 *et seq.*); cf. also Cox and Hazen (2003: § 13.22).

[143] See e.g. § 141(k) DelGCL; for this question in Germany see BGH, BGHZ 99, 211, 215; Krause (2002: 141–2).

[144] The law is different for close companies: see § 708(a) CalGCL.

[145] Cf. Kawamoto (1994: 213); West (2001a: 558, 571–2).

[146] See Cools (2005: 23).

[147] Cf. Lutter (1973: 38); Hüffer (2006: § 133 para. 33).

Act (§ 106 ChinCA).[148] This is probably the consequence of foreign legal advice which – against the trend in other countries – recommends that emerging markets introduce cumulative voting as part of 'good corporate governance'.[149]

c) Conclusion

The quasi-political requirements on quorums, qualified majorities and cumulative votes make it clear that the decision-making rules for the general meeting ought to take account of the minority's interests. Considering them in isolation would not, however, suffice. First, mandatory regulations may as a stricter measure bar the general meeting from making particular decisions in substance (*ex ante* control).[150] Secondly, the principle that the majority decides may be maintained, and *ex post* checks done. Among the possibilities for these are leaving the company with compensation, or review of the content of the general meeting's measures. As will be shown below,[151] these control mechanisms tend to be extended in such a way as to explain thereby the trend to cut back on quorums, qualified majorities, and cumulative voting rights. Also in favour of this idea is the fact that provisions on the necessary majority protect the minority only schematically, since the remaining minority continues to be exposed to the risk of exploitation.

3. Conclusion

The 'parliamentary model'[152] is a good starting-point for the shareholder's relationship to management and fellow shareholders in connection with questions of competences and majorities. Moreover, there is a discernible trend away from the ownership analogy to the model of the shareholder as investor. The individual shareholder's interest must in questions of competences increasingly take second place to the company's ability to act and function rapidly and flexibly. Thus, the conduct of business is basically and primarily for management, and general-meeting resolutions by majority decision are possible. Again, many deregulation trends, such as with capital measures or cumulative voting, show that, particularly

[148] See also Xi (2006: 292). Cumulative voting was already recommended in No. 31 ChinCG-Code.

[149] Jordan (2005: 1016–24) describes this phenomenon.

[150] See Ch. 2, section IV.1 above.

[151] See Ch. 5, section II.2 below.

[152] On the shareholder typology see generally Ch. 3, section I above.

with public companies, shareholder protection through decision-making powers is being replaced by other forms of protection.

II. The protected shareholder

Many provisions of company and securities law are aimed at shareholder protection.[153] This section will consider the legal means intended to protect the shareholder directly against the conduct of (other) decision-makers. For shareholders of public companies with dispersed holdings, it is particularly the danger from management (subsection 1 below) that is important, since they are here 'outsiders' and able to act independently of an influential shareholder. With other companies, by contrast, management (board) members are often linked with shareholders as 'insiders', so that minority shareholders must be protected primarily against abuse of power by the majority of shareholders (subsection 2 below). It is therefore unsurprising that in the individual countries the forms of protection are connected with the *de facto* structures of participation. Nonetheless, one must not too readily conclude that in the US and the UK dispersed holdings have led to better protection against management, and in the other countries concentrated holdings have brought better protection against the shareholder majority. For, despite country-specific differences, in most countries 'outsider' and 'insider' companies exist, so that 'twofold protection' is necessary.[154]

1. *Protection against management*

There are various ways of preventing the board from pursuing primarily its own interests or those of third parties, at the expense of shareholders. The simplest solution is for the legislature to forbid or prescribe particular conduct. It is also possible to create an institutional framework in private law intended to prevent dishonest conduct through supervisory boards, committees or independent directors, or in public law through supervisory authorities or the courts. Additionally, the forces of capital markets may also, indirectly, help. Finally, it is conceivable for corporate governance codes, the press or cultural constraints to prevent abuse of management power to the detriment of shareholders.

[153] For example, 'exit' (Ch. 4, section I.3 above), 'voice' (Ch. 4, section II above), information (Ch. 4, section III above) and powers (Ch. 5, section I above).

[154] Similarly Cook and Deakin (1999: 30).

I will not go into all the facets of these issues below. Instead, I will first consider the basic question of whether management is primarily bound in its actions by the welfare of shareholders (subsection a below). Secondly, on the basis of some provisions aimed at oversight of management I will look at the question of convergence or divergence of protective concepts (subsection b below).

a) The ranking of shareholder interests

The institution of the joint stock company serves, according to its historical origins, at least partly to uphold public interests.[155] From this point of view, it is plausible that management has to consider, alongside shareholder interests, also those of other persons. Since the nineteenth century, of course, the dominant conception of the company has been as a private organization.[156] However, even today it is the case that large and international firms are meant to take into account not just the interests of shareholders, but also those of other stakeholders.[157]

These two basic concepts reappear in the context of the principal–agent model. Here, it is controversial whether management acts as agent for the shareholders or for the entire company. Shareholder primacy fits the models of the shareholder as owner or investor, where individual interests – with differing tendencies – are more importance.[158] The democracy model by contrast focuses more on the overall organization, so that it seems appropriate to assume duties of loyalty to a broader range of stakeholders or to the firm itself.[159] Finally, a clear answer does not emerge from the contractual theory.[160] On the one hand, primary importance is often attached to the interests of shareholders:[161] since it is hardly possible for shareholders to assert their interests through individually negotiated agreements, the 'investment contract' has to be interpreted in such a way as to protect them. On the other hand, it may also be argued that for the concept of a comprehensive web of contracts it should be the interests of all those associated with the firm that should be taken into account.[162]

155 See Ch. 1, section III.2 above.

156 See Großfeld (1971: para. 4-133) and Ch. 1, section III.2 above; on the utilitarian background see Hill (2000a: 20).

157 Cf. Wheeler (2002); Teubner (1978: 157); Hopt (1992: 119) ('In modern society the company cannot, in the long run, afford to neglect the interests of its workforce or to act against public welfare'); see also Ch. 9, sections IV, VI; Ch. 10, section II.2.a below.

158 See Ch. 3, section I.1, 3 above.

159 See Ch. 3, section I.2 above.

160 See Ch. 2, section IV.1.a above.

161 Cf. Hill (2000b: 48); Romano (1993: 2–3).

162 Cf. Cook and Deakin (1999: 10).

(1) Comparative starting-points. On the traditional view, this contrast is also reflected in the difference between common law and civil law countries. It is said that, in the US and the UK, shareholder interests take legal primacy.[163] The sole or at least primary object of the company is seen as lying in achieving a rise in the share price and high dividends. By contrast, in continental Europe, Japan and China, a pluralist, stakeholder approach is seen as prevailing, the law being understood less individualistically, since it also (or even primarily) takes account of the social and financial interests of employees, consumers and creditors.[164]

As a starting-point, this distinction is plausible. In the UK, the commonly accepted principle is that the board must pursue the interests of the company as a whole,[165] and this is usually understood to refer to the interests of the shareholders.[166] Much the same applies to the US: here too the traditional view puts the maximization of shareholders' profit in prime position, so as to safeguard their investment and to attract capital.[167]

By contrast, the prevailing view in Germany stresses that it is not only shareholder interests that are to be taken into account.[168] Until the 1965 reform, this position was explicitly codified in a general-welfare clause (old § 76 GerAktG). But, according to the prevailing opinion, even the repeal of this clause did not intend to make any material change here, since according to the tenor of the ministerial draft it was in any event accepted that the management had to take account of the interests of shareholders, employees and the general public. A similar finding comes from focusing – as some advocate – on the enterprise interest or the 'firm as such'.[169] Thus, questions of the conduct of business ought not to be determined solely by reference to maximizing shareholders' profit. Furthermore, the supervisory board can be seen as a guardian of the interests of the company as a whole, including, through co-determination, the employees' interests.

[163] See e.g. Mace (2000: 56); Yavasi (2001: 47); Wymeersch (2001a: 128); Hansmann and Kraakman (2001: 467); Cook and Deakin (1999: 3); Dore (2000: 5, 9 *et seq.*); for differences between the US and the UK see Armour *et al.* (2003); Williams and Conley (2005).

[164] See e.g. Cook and Deakin (1999: 8); Cunningham (1999: 1134); Mitnick (2001: 713); Ferrarini (2003: 229 *et seq.*); see also preamble to Part II, above.

[165] Cf. Smith (1998: 285); for a critical account see Parkinson (1993: 76–7).

[166] See e.g. *Alexander* v. *Automatic Telephone Co.* [1990] 2 Ch 56 (Court of Appeal); Ferran (1999: 125 *et seq.*); Davies (2003: 491–2).

[167] Cf. Cox and Hazen (2003: § 4.10); Hansmann and Kraakman (2001: 442); see also Milton Friedman, *New York Times Magazine*, 13 September 1970, at 4 ('the social responsibility of business is to increase its profits').

[168] See Ulmer (2002: 153); Mülbert (1997: 144 *et seq.*).

[169] Cf. Krämer (2002: 27 *et seq.*); Mülbert (1997: 142–3); Großfeld (1971: para. 4-134); Zöllner (1963: 67 *et seq.*), (1994: 337).

The French view of the company as an institution corresponds to the German view.[170] This notion too implies that the company serves social ends, and that it is the overall organization with its manifold interests which matters most.[171] Moreover, the Code de Commerce now explicitly provides that the board must set out in its annual report how its business activities affect the environment and the employees' situation (Art. L. 225-102-1 FrCCom). The same applies in other European countries by virtue of the Accounting Modernization Directive.[172]

Statutory provisions used to mark Chinese company law still more prominently. The old Companies Act obliged companies to promote socialist aims, protect employees, support collective negotiations by trade unions, consult with union representatives, and apply a proportion of profit to a fund for the collective welfare of labour (§§ 14–16, 121, 122, 177, 180 ChinCA 1993). The 2005 version has reduced this list. But the law still requires companies to observe social morals and business ethics (§ 5 ChinCA) and to consult trade unions and provide them with the conditions necessary for carrying out their activities (§ 18 ChinCA).[173] This law is to be explained historically by the fact that many of today's companies were previously state enterprises and therefore as such responsible for all the social concerns of the employees as well as for the public interest. In practice, management is also sometimes limited in its autonomy because government bodies continue to exercise political influence over companies.[174]

Japanese law states only that directors shall perform their duties faithfully for the benefit of the company (§ 355 JapCA). There are no specific provisions on the 'shareholder–stakeholder' issue. The question of whose interests management has to consider is instead chiefly determined by social factors. Here, to date, it has usually been said that the company is less the property of the shareholders than of its employees. The firm's survival and the durability of its jobs should accordingly take priority even over the maximization of shareholder profit.[175] The background is that

[170] Art. 1832 Code Civil; see also Foster (2000: 596 *et seq.*).

[171] Cf. Mojuyé (2000: 98–9); Oquendo (2001: 1026); Fanto (1998: 47); Großfeld (1971: para. 4-137).

[172] Directive 2003/51/EC which led to an amended Art. 46(1) of the Fourth Directive 78/660/EEC.

[173] Stakeholder responsibility is also mentioned in No. 81 ChinCG-Code; § 116(no.1) Chin-Articles.

[174] Cf. Schipani and Liu (2002: 30).

[175] Takahashi and Rudo (1998: 620); Marutschke (1999: 232); Takahashi (1997: 235); Menden (1999: 1).

most directors are promoted employees. Accordingly, they see themselves primarily as representatives of the firm as a whole and not of shareholders, and see the firm as a community of fate and survival.[176]

(2) Convergences. Recently it has sometimes been assumed that the model of shareholder supremacy has now emerged victorious, whereas the (old) American manager-oriented, European employee-oriented, Franco-Japanese state-oriented and international stakeholder models have in the past failed.[177] This is, however, too sweeping a statement. There are a number of legal and factual arguments in favour of convergence, which cannot be unambiguously assigned to one model.

First, it is indeed increasingly being urged in the (traditional) 'stakeholder countries' that the interests of shareholders are to be given priority. Thus, the Marini report in France criticized the concept of the company interest, since it brought the danger of having management act primarily for their own benefit.[178] While the Japanese Corporate Governance Principles on the one hand suggest that a balance of various interests must be drawn, they stress on the other hand that the providers of the capital lie at the core of corporate governance.[179] In Germany too, current legal developments are seen as showing a trend towards the 'shareholder value idea'.[180] Also in line with this is the fact that the creditor-oriented accounting in continental Europe is increasingly having investor-specific valuations superimposed on it.[181]

Secondly, in the 'shareholder countries', maximizing shareholder profit does not always take primacy. In the UK, the view is sometimes taken that the interests of the company as a separate entity may outweigh shareholders' interests.[182] And the courts rarely practise strict shareholder supremacy, but are instead increasingly recognizing the entitlements of other interests.[183] Additionally, since 1980, some statutory provisions have explicitly protected employee interests,[184] and, when insolvency threatens, the interests of creditors must – as in principle in other countries

[176] Cf. Taniguchi (1988: 229–30 note 242); Menden (1999: 20); Henderson (1995: 908 *et seq.*); Baum (1996: 399 *et seq.*).

[177] Hansmann and Kraakman (2001: 443 *et seq.*).

[178] Marini Report (1996: 8–9).

[179] See ss. 1, 3 JapCG-Principles; similarly, the Chinese Corporate Governance-Code is regarded as a 'synthesis', Pißler (2002d: para. 32).

[180] Cf. e.g. Ulmer (2002: 158–9); Henle (1999).

[181] See Ch. 4, section III.3.b above.

[182] E.g. Leader (1995: 85); Farrar *et al.* (1998: 14); for a different view see *Brady* v. *Brady* [1988] BCLC 20, 40 (Court of Appeal); Davies (2003: 372 note 5).

[183] Cf. Grantham (1998: 567, 569 *et seq.*).

[184] Now s. 172(1)(b) UK-CA; see also Insolvency Act 1986, s. 187.

too[185] – be taken into account.[186] In summary, it is possible to speak of an 'enlightened shareholder model', which reform commissions saw no fundamental need to alter.[187] Quoted companies must also demonstrate in their directors' report how far they take stakeholder interests into account.[188] Moreover, at a political level, the UK Prime Minister has stressed that firms are not just instruments of the capital market, but ought to constitute a community in which employees and others also have a stake.[189]

In the US debate, it is, similarly, controversial whether and to what extent other interests ought also to be taken into account alongside shareholder interests. Peter Dodd already maintained, in his famous debate with Adolf Berle, that managers and directors were trustees of all those involved in the firm, not just the shareholders.[190] Later, the positions of the 'corporate social responsibility movement' and the 'communitarians' brought further social considerations into the debate about management conduct.[191] And these ideas also persist in the view that company law is about the general 'team production problem' and not just shareholders and directors.[192] The case law too sometimes acknowledges the interests of stakeholders.[193] As in the UK, donations to social organizations are often permissible. Here the focus today is mostly not just on whether the firm's interests are directly promoted ('direct benefit test'). Instead, it is sufficient for a non-economically oriented decision to be indirectly connected with the company's profit-maximization objective and/or improve the long-term prospects for businesses through model behaviour ('corporate good citizenship concept').[194] Additionally, where decisions rhetorically focus on 'shareholder supremacy', it is doubted whether they truly ensure a link with shareholder welfare.[195] In company-law legislation, finally,

[185] See Hertig and Kanda (2004: 88 *et seq.*).

[186] See *West Mercia Safetywear Ltd* v. *Dodd* [1988] BCLC 250 (Court of Appeal); *Brady* v. *Brady* [1988] BCLC 20 (Court of Appeal); Cheffins (1997: 538); Modern Company Law: Final Report (2001: para. 3.17); Goddard (2003: 416–17).

[187] See Company Law Reform (2005: 6, 20, and B3); Modern Company Law for a Competitive Economy (1999); Miles (2003: 57 *et seq.*); Goddard (2003: 404 *et seq.*).

[188] See s. 417(5)(b) UK-CA. The background is the Accounting Modernization Directive: see note 172 above.

[189] Cf. Hicks (2000: 92). [190] Dodd (1932); Berle (1932).

[191] Cf. e.g. Lord Wedderburn (1985: 10 *et seq.*); Hill (2000b: 55); Licht (2004b); Stiglitz (2006: 190, 198, 203).

[192] Blair and Stout (1999).

[193] See *A. P. Smith Mfg Co.* v. *Barlow*, 98 A 2d 581 (New Jersey 1953).

[194] Cf. Lord Wedderburn (1985: 11–12, 22–3); Teubner (1978: 152–3); Großfeld (1971: para. 4-135).

[195] Smith (1998) on *Dodge* v. *Ford Motor Co.*, 170 NW 668 (Michigan 1919).

anti-takeover acts often permit a balancing with stakeholder interests,[196] so that all in all the picture is rather a 'mixed bag'.[197]

Consequently, contrary to the 'basic cliché', primacy for shareholder interests is by no means absolute, even in the US and the UK. This also becomes clear from the fact that the US and the UK have, if not permitted, then at least not prevented, the OECD Principles upholding the interests of all stakeholders.[198]

Thirdly, the degree of contrast between systems is lessened by the fact that the interests of shareholders and stakeholders often actually overlap. If management takes suitable account of stakeholder interests, this often has good effects on the business climate and the firm's acceptance by the public, leading to positive developments for the enterprise. Indirectly, therefore, this may also lead to a rising share price and to profits for shareholders. Conversely, it can similarly be argued that a company that offers shareholders good profit opportunities is also good for other stakeholders. If a firm can successfully attract capital, other participants in the firm also benefit. This is particularly true if the question whether shareholder interests are to mean short-term or long-term interests, or those of only the present shareholders or also of future shareholders[199] is answered in each case with the latter alternative. In that case, the doctrine of the primacy of shareholder interests comes close to the stakeholder solution, since long-term interests are served particularly where the firm cultivates a good relationship with other stakeholders.

Fourthly, the difference between the shareholder and stakeholder models is lessened by the fact that the protection of third parties is in any case mostly regulated outside of company law. This suggests itself, if only because, say, questions of employee, consumer or competition protection are independent of legal form.[200] The most important differences between a pure market economy and a welfare state are accordingly rooted not primarily in company law, but in other areas of law.

Fifthly, management is entitled to discretion in its upholding of the various interests, so that what matters is not the crude outcome but compliance with its procedural duty of conduct. In the stakeholder countries,

[196] See subsection (3) below.

[197] Coffee (1999b: 655); similarly Cunningham (1999: 1171).

[198] No. IV.A OECD-Principles 2004.

[199] See Siems (2002d: 152) on the inconsistent case law in the UK; for the US see Strine (2006: 1769) (for Delaware case law).

[200] Likewise Siems (2002d: 159); Werlauff (1993: 106 *et seq.*); Hansmann and Kraakman (2001: 442).

management therefore often *de facto* has the freedom to pursue the interests of shareholders. The converse is true in the shareholder countries. Here, management can *de facto*, because of the business judgement rule,[201] depart from the primacy of shareholder interests. The danger often feared about 'stakeholder countries' – that management may turn its freedom to balance interests in favour of its own preferences[202] – cannot therefore be dismissed out of hand for the 'shareholder countries' either.

Sixthly, in practice the two systems are coming together. On the one hand, increasingly global competition for investors and reception of the US shareholder-value idea means that shareholder interests are taking on emphatic importance in (traditional) stakeholder countries too. Thus, in France, since the late 1990s, the argument that 'valeur actionnariale' is also to be taken into account has been omnipresent.[203] For Germany, there are indications that today value is not (any longer) placed primarily on products and employees but on high profits for shareholders.[204] For Japan, the view that shareholders are disadvantaged is even regarded as a fairytale, since there too managements are dismissed for the poor performance of the firm.[205] Moreover, it is becoming clear that such typically Japanese circumstances as the principle of lifelong employment or the emphasis on employee and consumer interests are losing importance, and themes of corporate governance and shareholder value are gaining ground.[206]

On the other hand, in 'shareholder countries' the interests of (other) stakeholders are *de facto* taken into account. As a substitute, in the US, for instance social share indices, ethical investments and 'public policy committees' in companies are more common than in other countries. Moreover, there is a *de facto* partial overlap between the interests of shareholders and of other stakeholders, since because of the more dispersed shareholder ownership[207] employees and consumers are more often also shareholders. Additionally, studies of the US have generally shown that management considers the interests not just of shareholders, but also of

[201] See Ch. 5, section II.1.b below.

[202] Cf. Grier (1998: 650); Parkinson (1993: 370); Großfeld (1971: paras. 4-138, 141); Easterbrook and Fischel (1991: 38) ('A manager told to serve two masters (a little for equity holders, a little for the community) has been freezed for both and is answerable to neither').

[203] Rebérioux (2002: 120). [204] André (1998: 110); Cheffins (2001b: 505).

[205] Baum (1998: 751 *et seq.*); Shishido (1997: 162 *et seq.*); Takahashi (1997: 235–6); Kanda (1997: 185); cf. also Learmount (2002: 145).

[206] See e.g. Poe *et al.* (2002: 75); Narusawa *et al.* (2001: 11); Dore (2000: 71 *et seq.*).

[207] See Ch. 8, section IV below.

the firm as a whole and of stakeholders.[208] This is, finally, confirmed by corporate governance codes and demands from institutional investors referring to responsibility towards consumers, employees, suppliers and the community.[209]

All in all, thus, the classical distinction between shareholder and stakeholder systems is indeed out of date. It has been rightly said that 'in short, US practice more nearly resembles German practice than it resembles US rhetoric and German practice more nearly resembles American practice than it does German rhetoric'.[210] Nonetheless, differences remain, based for instance on legal culture, ownership structures, the importance of the capital market[211] or legal provisions not referring directly to the shareholder–stakeholder issue.[212] To gain a still more exact picture, the following will consider two specific situations that put the shareholder–stakeholder dichotomy to the test.

(3) Defences against hostile takeovers. If a hostile takeover looms, the conflict between the interests of shareholders, management and other stakeholders emerges particularly clearly. A successful takeover may mean a reduction in jobs, a change in management and – in the cross-border context – a weakening of the domestic economy. For shareholders, there is, therefore, the justified fear of their interests not being properly considered.

In 1969, it was stressed that 'outside the English-speaking countries, jurists have very little to say about sale of control'.[213] Today, though, the topic of 'takeovers' is discussed worldwide, so that, for instance, the OECD Principles too contain a brief statement.[214] Since at international level competition is increasing, it is unsurprising for firms to seek to enhance their positions and optimize their business operations through takeovers and mergers.[215] Furthermore, factors that earlier stood in the way of hostile takeovers in many countries are today on the decline, since, for

[208] See Smith (1998: 290–1); Farrar *et al.* (1998: 563); Cunningham (1999: 1155–6).

[209] See e.g. General Motors (http://www.gm.com/company/investor_information/ corp_gov/ guidelines.html); CalPERS (http://www.ecgi.org/codes/documents/calpers.pdf).

[210] Cunningham (1999: 1163).

[211] On these aspects see Ch. 8 below.

[212] For instance, the law on dividends (Ch. 4, section I.2 above), voting proxies (Ch. 4, section II.3.c above), and accounting (Ch. 4, section II.4 above).

[213] Conard (1969: para. 6-66).

[214] No. II.E.2 OECD-Principles 2004 (anti-takeover devices should not be used to shield management and the board from accountability).

[215] See also Ch. 8, section III.1, 4 below.

instance, capital-market orientation and transparency are increasing and cross-holdings declining.[216]

Various reasons can be advanced as to why one should favour neutral conduct by the management of the target company. First, it is in the interests of shareholders and of the more competitive bidder. Secondly, this fits in with the fact that management, as the administrator of the assets of others, may not use those assets against the interests of their owners. Thirdly, the principle of free transferability of shares[217] makes the decision on the composition of the shareholder body a matter for the old and new shareholders alone. Fourthly, the market for corporate control can ensure that managers run the company in the shareholders' interests. The principal–agent problem can thus be minimized and macroeconomic performance as a whole optimized.[218]

This positive conception of hostile takeovers is most clearly realized in the UK. The legal basis is the comprehensive City Code on Takeovers and Mergers, which stands out as an instrument of self-regulation[219] for flexibility, informality and practice-orientation. It is also pointed out that, by contrast with the statutory provisions in other countries, the Panel on Takeovers and Mergers feels particularly committed to the interests of investors.[220] Substantively, management may accordingly, from the time there is reason to believe a takeover is imminent, not take any action which could effectively result in any *bona fide* offer being frustrated or in the shareholders being denied an opportunity to decide on its merits.[221] For instance, it usually must not sell any sizeable company assets, buy back shares, pay extraordinary dividends or issue authorized capital without a resolution of the general meeting. Alongside measures in the run-up to the takeover,[222] thus, the board essentially only has the possibility of looking for a 'white knight' to ward off the takeover. Only indirectly does the need for a mandatory bid[223] prevent takeovers or make them more costly, something that can be seen as a functional counterweight to the neutrality precept.

216 See Ch. 2, section III, Ch. 4, section III.3 above, and Ch. 7, section IV.2.b below.
217 See Ch. 4, section I.3 above.
218 See generally Manne (1965); Bebchuk (2002); B. Black and Kraakman (2002).
219 Although now part of a regulatory framework: see s. 943 UK-CA.
220 See Armour and Skeel (2007); Hansmann and Kraakman (2004: 53); Davies and Hopt (2004: 173, 190–1).
221 General Principle 3 and Rule 21 UK City Code.
222 Unless companies opt into a 'breakthrough' of these defences: s. 968 UK-CA.
223 See Ch. 5, section II.2.c below.

US law clearly differs on this. Despite the principle of shareholder supremacy, management here mostly has greater room for manoeuvre. In detail, however, there are considerable differences among the states, since federal securities law on tender offers is essentially confined to information duties and procedural regulations.[224] Some states have, however, adopted anti-takeover acts, in order to prevent corporate raids, induce companies to incorporate in their state and protect employees of firms domiciled in it.[225] While takeover bids cannot require permission,[226] it is possible, for example, for management to take stakeholder interests into account and to take defensive measures without the consent of the general meeting. In other states, such as Delaware, the law is friendlier to takeovers, and in particular marked by the case-law treatment of the business judgement rule (especially, reversal of the burden of proof).[227] Regarding possible defensive measures, it is for instance debated whether 'shark repellent amendments', 'poison pills', 'dual class common stock' and 'golden parachutes' may be used to hamper hostile takeovers in advance.[228]

The continental European rules are influenced by UK and US law. However, there are a number of specific features that have also prevented a high-level European harmonization that was to have been oriented to the strict UK duty of neutrality. The EU Takeover Directive[229] lays down a duty of neutrality in Art. 9. Furthermore, according to Art. 11, restrictions on the transfer of securities and restrictions on voting rights have no effect in the case of takeover bids (the so-called 'breakthrough'). However, by Art. 12(1) Member States may exclude these provisions and thus retain the existing defensive possibilities. This option model does not facilitate unification of the law. Instead, the Takeover Directive relies on shareholder responsibility, since by Art. 12(2) it must at any rate be possible for the general meeting to rule out the use of protective measures in its company. Whether this may lead to convergent practice thus depends, after transposition of the directive, particularly on the future influence of shareholders.[230]

[224] 1968 Williams Act which led to §§ 14(d)–(f) US-SEA.

[225] See Cox and Hazen (2003: § 14.10); Bebchuk and Ferrell (2001); Bebchuk *et al.* (2002); Miller (1998: 68–9).

[226] *Edgar v. MITE*, 487 US 624 (1982) (US Supreme Court).

[227] For differences in detail see *Unocal Corp.* v. *Mesa Petroleum, Co.*, 493 A 2d 946 (Del. Supr. 1985); *Revlon, Inc.* v. *MacAndrews & Forbes Holdings, Inc.*, 506 A 2d 173 (Del. Supr. 1986); *Paramount Communications, Inc. v. QVC Network, Inc.*, 637 A 2d 34 (Del. Ch. 1994).

[228] See e.g. Klein and Coffee (2002: 187 *et seq.*); Romano (1993: 70 *et seq.*); Harbarth (2001: 291 *et seq.*).

[229] Directive 2004/25/EC.

[230] See Ch. 9, section III below.

In France, defence comes about mostly preventively, since dual voting rights, vote caps, pre-emption rights and until recently also 'golden shares'[231] could considerably reduce the chance of a successful hostile takeover in the run-up to it. After the takeover bid there used to be a limited neutrality duty:[232] the target company had to ensure that its actions, statements and decisions did not harm the company interest or the principle of equal treatment of shareholders. However, there was only one specific provision in the Code de Commerce which barred management from any further use of an authorization for a capital increase after the start of the takeover bid (Art. L. 225-129-3 FrCCom (old)). The implementation of the Takeover Directive has now led to a general duty of neutrality (Art. L. 233-32 FrCCom). Yet, French law opted out of the breakthrough of most pre-bid defences. Thus, these defences remain possible unless a company opts into them (Arts. L. 233-34 to 233-39 FrCCom).

The German takeover law provides that, after the filing of a takeover bid, management must take the interests of the target company into account (§ 3(3) GerWpÜG). The legislative materials see this 'interest of the firm' as equivalent to a stakeholder position, embracing *inter alia* the interests of shareholders and of employees.[233] In other respects, the GerWpÜG, by contrast with the rapporteur's draft, takes no position binding management strictly to a duty of neutrality. Instead, the management board is not bound by the bar on measures to obstruct a takeover (§ 33(1)(s.1) GerWpÜG) where it has been given authorization by the supervisory board or the general meeting, or where what is involved is everyday conduct of business or the search for a competing bid (§ 33(1)(s.2), (2) GerWpÜG). This has in part been interpreted as 'Fortress Germany' and as a 'blow against the capital market'.[234] However, authorization is not used very often in practice.[235] Furthermore, the highly restrictive freedom to contract out of statutory company law (§ 23(5) GerAktG) gives management only limited room for manoeuvre in questions going beyond

[231] On golden shares see *Commission* v. *Belgium*, C-503/99 [2002] ECR I-4809; *Commission* v. *French Republic*, C-483/99 [2002] ECR I-4781; *Commission* v. *Portugal*, C-367/98 [2002] ECR I-4731.

[232] See Faugérolas (2003: 330 *et seq.*); Wallace (2002: 4 *et seq.*); Grundmann and Möslein (2003: 328–9); Merle (2005: para. 651).

[233] Regierungsentwurf zum GerWpÜG, BT-Drucks. 14/7034 35, at 52.

[234] Cf. *Financial Times Germany*, 5 March 2002, at 29; *Handelsblatt*, 14 January 2003, at 20; similarly Schaefer and Eichner (2003: 155).

[235] Cf. Fabritius (2004: 70).

normal conduct of business.[236] And, since 2006, it is also possible for German companies to opt into a strict duty of neutrality (§ 33a GerWpÜG).

In Japan and China, takeover law used to be less developed. While in Japan defensive measures were basically possible and were barely limited by the case law, in reality there were two factors which hindered the occurrence of hostile takeovers:[237] first, the common cross-holdings prevented hostile takeovers arising at all. Secondly, there was a social norm against hostile takeovers, as indicated by the term 'nottori' applied to them, which also means 'hijacking'. But both factors are in the process of change. Interlocking holdings are – as in other countries too[238] – diminishing, and the social norm weakening.[239] There are accordingly more and more attempts at hostile takeovers.[240] In parallel, legal takeover protection is gaining importance. For instance, the increasing flexibility of Japanese company law regarding classes of shares, buybacks, stock options and share issues without pre-emption rights is helping management to ward off takeovers by these means.[241] In general, it is for example possible to issue shares which grant veto rights (§ 108(1)(nos.4, 8) JapCA) or to provide that the company can acquire rights to subscribe for new shares conditional upon occurrence of a takeover attempt (§ 236(7) JapCA). The defensive issuance of shares has recently also led to a more extensive case law. In these cases, the question whether the issuance of new shares in order to prevent a takeover was substantially unfair was considered (§ 210 JapCA). It was held that these and other defensive measures are justified in cases where a company is being exploited. However, if this is not the case, the primary purpose of the issuance must not be to dilute the share of a certain shareholder and maintain the control of the incumbent management.[242] Finally, there are now non-binding guidelines jointly issued by the Ministry of Economy, Trade and Industry and the Ministry of Justice.[243] These guidelines provide safe harbours in using defensive

[236] See Ch. 2, section IV.1.b above.

[237] Cf. Milhaupt and West (2003a: 297, 304, 307); Baum and Hayakawa (1994: 624); Henderson (1995); Crabb (1987).

[238] See Ch. 8, section IV.2.b below.

[239] See Milhaupt (2001: 2112 *et seq.*); McDonnell (2002: 365 note 117).

[240] See Igarashi (2001: 94): Milhaupt (2001: 2112 *et seq.*); Milhaupt (2005).

[241] On classes of shares see Ch. 3, section II above; on own shares see Ch. 4, section I.4 above; on stock options see subsection (4) below; and on pre-emption rights see section II.2.b, below.

[242] See Kozuka (2006); Takahashi and Sakamoto (2006).

[243] Ministry of Economy, Trade and Industry (METI) and Ministry of Justice (MOJ), *Guidelines Regarding Takeover Defense for the Purposes of Protection and Enhancement of Corporate Value and Shareholder's Common Interests* (2005), English version in (2006) 21 ZJapanR 143.

measures. And, they are also interesting more generally because they clearly focus on shareholder interests (Principle 1), and address the interests of stakeholders only briefly in stating that respect for employees, suppliers and customers can enhance the company's corporate value and ultimately shareholder interests (Purpose 1).

In China, takeovers are in principle possible, and this is addressed not only in §§ 85–101 ChinSA but also in the 2006 CSRC Takeover Measures. This Code states that the directors and managers of the target company shall not damage the interests of the company and its shareholders, and that particular measures require the approval of the general meeting.[244] Yet, public takeovers are rare in practice, since the state shareholdings mean that there are few companies with dispersed shareholder ownership. Sometimes, however, there are takeovers of listed companies by unlisted ones, because this allows the company taking over automatically to secure a listing, which is otherwise allowed only restrictively by the CSRC.

In summary, one is first struck by the legal differences, which however cut across the distinction between common law and civil law countries. However, even so, convergence may nevertheless be possible. Even today, in all the countries studied here, disclosure obligations and the equal-treatment principle should allow shareholders to make a rational, autonomous decision in the event of takeover bids.[245] Moreover, it is also possible to conclude that the legal systems are, from differing starting-points, gradually coming together: in the US a 'market for corporate control' already exists, so that in recent decades restrictions have been brought in, whereas in continental Europe the law has only recently set about creating such a market.[246] Finally, it might be pointed out that takeovers do not stop at borders, and the debate on the shareholder's position in the event of a hostile takeover is today taking place in all countries.

These trends ought not to be over-estimated, however. Far-reaching legal convergence is unlikely in the short term. First, the phenomenon of hostile takeovers is primarily of a non-legal nature, so that legal provisions on the objects of management action are often of only secondary importance.[247] Secondly, the likelihood of hostile takeovers depends on numerous other provisions. For example, the difficulty of replacing management

[244] Arts. 8 and 33 of the Measures for the Administration of the Takeover of Listed Companies (Decree No. 35 of the CSRC of 31 July 2006).

[245] See §§ 14(d)–(f) US-SEA and Schedule 14 D-1; General Principles 2-5 and Rule 2.5 UK City Code; Arts. 6, 10 of the EU Takeover Directive 2004/25/EC; §§ 3(2), 10, 11, 14, 23 GerWpÜG; Arts. 231-16, 231-17 FrRGAMF; §§ 27-2 *et seq.* JapSEA; § 89 ChinSA; on the principle of equal treatment see Davies and Hopt (2004: 176 *et seq.*).

[246] Hertig (2004: 343). [247] Similarly Roe (2002: 18).

may considerably hamper a takeover of control. Again, prior decisions, such as the introduction of multiple voting rights or voting caps, transfer restrictions, authorizations for capital measures or high majority thresholds may make hostile takeovers impossible or very difficult. Thirdly, the principal–agent problem cannot be reduced to takeover regulations. If management is not subject to any restrictions in the event of hostile takeovers, this may be simply because the use of other legal and extra-legal norms result in the replacement of unqualified managers.

(4) Stock options. Stock options for members of the management are intended to ensure that a firm will be managed in the shareholders' interests simply out of self-interest. While earlier, under the influence of a partnership conception of the company, most legal systems required that board members be simultaneously shareholders,[248] today's stock options by contrast constitute a new type of model. They offer the advantage that management does not share in a loss, so that an attractive means of securing qualified staff to head the firm is created. Moreover, the proportion of shares subject to options in relation to all the firm's shares ought to be insignificant, in order not to endanger the separation of ownership and control.

This notion of outside directors fits with the fact that stock options were first used in the US. Moreover, tax considerations, the liquid capital market and the potential deficit in oversight because of dispersed shareholdings in the US promote the use of stock options.[249] Internationally, however, a similar trend can also be noted. Stock options have become an internationally acknowledged element of remuneration. First, this can be seen from legislative reforms which have since 1970, first in France and then in Germany, Japan and China, facilitated the issuing of stock options.[250] Secondly, stock options are increasingly being called for by practice and by corporate governance guidelines[251] and also made use of.[252] This is true particularly for firms operating internationally, since

[248] This is still the case in France: see Arts. L. 225-25, 225-72 FrCCom; generally see Wymeersch (2001c: para. 34); Großfeld (1971: para. 4-23); Pistor *et al.* (2001: 21); Davies (2003: 308) (for the UK); Smith (1998: 300) (for the US).

[249] Cheffins (2003b: 12, 17).

[250] For China, this was only the case in 2005: see §§ 142(2), 143(1)(no.3) ChinCA; for the old law see Liu (2001: 44); Shumo and Yingxia (2001: 457).

[251] See s. B.1 UK-Combined Code; No. 4.2.3 GerCGK; No. 77 ChinCG-Code; Preface JapCG-Principles.

[252] For Germany: Ulmer (2002: 145); for Japan: Milhaupt and West (2003a: 313–14); for China: Schipani and Liu (2002: 52).

here managers and US institutional investors often place value on performance-based remuneration.[253]

There is, however, a danger that managers with stock options may seek primarily to raise their own earnings. As with institutional investors,[254] here too the problem accordingly arises that the interests of various types of shareholder need not necessarily coincide, so that promoting the interests of one group of shareholders may be at the expense of the shareholder as a whole. Contrary to the notion of a positive incentive structure, there is an intensification of the principal–agent problem, since management can, for instance through its disclosure policy and the time it chooses to exercise the option, pursue interests of its own.[255] This can lead to management short-termism, risk aversion contrary to the shareholders' interests, and 'windfall gains' based not special abilities but on general market developments.

These dangers of abuse are supposed to be remedied, not just by benchmarking[256] and the involvement of the general meeting and compensation committees,[257] but by comprehensive disclosure and proper accounting. Here a distinction is traditionally drawn between the US and the UK on the one hand and continental Europe on the other. The former require publication of the remuneration for each member of the board.[258] By contrast, on the Continent, usually only the total amount of payments to management is disclosed.[259] However, most recently there have been changes in France and Germany,[260] and the EU Commission has also called for more transparency.[261] Movement is also happening as regards the question of properly accounting for stock options. If they are not taken into account on the balance sheet, there is a danger that they may be used to 'beautify' the balance figures and damage shareholders through a dilution of the

[253] Cf. Cunningham (1999: 1175); West (2001a: 582–3); Cheffins (2001b: 506–7, 510).

[254] See Ch. 4, section II. 4. c above.

[255] Cf. Bebchuk and Fried (2004).

[256] See e.g. Cheffins (2001b: 521 *et seq.*); No. 4.2.3 GerCGK.

[257] See Ch. 5, section I. 1. c above.

[258] See Hertig and Kanda (2004: 103–4); Wymeersch (2001c: para. 38); Cheffins (2001b: 533 *et seq.*); Van den Berghe (2002: 81–2).

[259] See Wymeersch (2001c: para. 38); Milhaupt and West (2003a: 309); Cheffins (2003b: 16).

[260] For France: Arts. L. 225-102-1, 225-184 FrCCom; Merle (2005: paras. 535, 544); Storp (2002: 415–16); for Germany: Nos. 4.2.4, 5.4.5 GerCGK; Gesetz zur Offenlegung der Vorstandsvergütung (VorstOG), 03.08.2005, BGBl. I 2267.

[261] Commission Recommendation fostering an appropriate regime for the remuneration of directors of listed companies, 2004/913/EC; Modernising Company Law and Enhancing Corporate Governance in the European Union – A Plan to Move Forward, Communication from the Commission, COM(2003) 284, at 16.

stock price. The booking of stock options as costs is therefore increasingly being provided or called for.[262]

Altogether, though, stock options have nonetheless so far not led to a strengthening of protection for shareholders at the expense of stakeholders. Instead, it is not uncommonly the case that management enriches itself through them. It is accordingly decisive for stock options to be properly used, disclosed and accounted for. The same must also apply to other performance-based forms of remuneration. Here, a further change has recently been discernible. Since institutional investors are increasingly critical of stock options because of the dangers of abuse, since the accounting advantages of stock options have disappeared with new accounting rules, and since managers have sometimes not been able to profit from their options because of negative stock-market development, alternatives to stock options are (again) becoming more popular. Because of this dependency on factual circumstances, it is apparent here too that the law has only a limited capacity to bring about a parallel course for the interests of management and of shareholders.

(5) Conclusion. The dialectical subdivision into shareholder and stakeholder countries can be seen to be a largely incorrect abbreviation of the 'first part' of the principal–agent theory. While, for instance, creditor interests play a larger part in EU countries' company law than in the US, there has not been a clear primacy or subordination of shareholder interests in the individual countries or legal families, either on issues of whether there is a general tie to shareholder welfare or on the more specific problem areas of hostile takeovers and stock options. Most legal systems thus lie between a model of shareholder democracy and one of company democracy,[263] since on the one hand shareholders have a prominent position and on the other the interests of others involved in the firm are not left out of account.

b) Oversight of management

One basic problem for companies is how misconduct by management can be prevented. As Adam Smith said: 'The directors of such companies, however, being the manager rather of other people's money than of their own, it cannot well be expected, that they should watch over it with the same anxious vigilance with which the partners in a private copartnery

[262] Cf. http://www.fasb.org/news/nr033104.shtml (on US-GAAP); http://www.iasplus.com/standard/ifrs02.htm (on IAS/IFRS); High Level Group of Company Law Experts (2002: 66); Cheffins (2001b: 538), (2003b: 18–19); Crook (2004); Keidanren (2001).

[263] Cf. Lord Wedderburn (1985: 32 *et seq.*) on 'industrial democracy'.

frequently watch over their own.'[264] For the modern conception of the company, this problem has taken on still more importance. Since in the twentieth century the principle that management and not the shareholders conduct business has become still stronger,[265] it is especially problematic today how best to ensure that management acts responsibly and honestly.

(1) Duties of care, loyalty and good faith. It is often said that shareholders in the UK and the US are better protected than in civil law countries. By contrast with the common law countries, there are said to be no fiduciary duties in civil law countries to which management has to abide,[266] so that shareholders with little influence are not exploited.[267]

This statement is, however, accurate only in its starting-point. In common law countries, it is traditionally stressed that management acts as an agent or trustee for the shareholders as principal or beneficiary.[268] In detail, this embraces the duty of care and skill, the duty to act in good faith, the duty of loyalty, the duty to deal fairly, as well as the duty not to exploit corporate opportunities for its own benefit.[269]

On the one hand, however, this protection is not unlimited in common law countries. First, shareholders can often ratify breaches of duty by management.[270] Secondly, in some two-thirds of US states directors' liability for damages for breach of the duty of care can be excluded in the articles of incorporation.[271] Thirdly, legislators are increasingly adopting, not strict prohibitions, but milder regulatory mechanisms. For protection against 'self-dealing', it is today primarily participatory powers of the general meeting, disclosure obligations or a fairness test in the individual case which provide oversight of management.[272] This also points, fourthly, to

264 Smith (1776: 741). 265 See Ch. 5, section I.1.b above.

266 Coffee (1999b: 698–9); Romano (1993: 134); Lord Wedderburn (1985: 24–5).

267 Coffee (1999b: 681); Johnson *et al.* (2000).

268 See Hill (2000b: 44 *et seq.*); on the principal–agent problem see Ch. 2, section IV.1.a, Ch. 5, section II.1.a above.

269 E.g. §§ 8.30 *et seq.*; 8.60 *et seq.* MBCA; Parts IV, V ALI-Principles; ss. 170 *et seq.* UK-CA; see also Cox and Hazen (2003: § 10); Coffee (1996); Allen (1998); Davies (2003: 370 *et seq.*).

270 See s. 239 UK-CA; Worthington (2000: 638 *et seq.*); Davies (2003: 437 *et seq.*, 672 *et seq.*).

271 E.g. § 102(b)(7) DelGCL; § 2.02(b)(4) MBCA; reaction to *Smith* v. *Van Gorkum*, 488 A 2d 858 (Del. Supr. 1985). UK law is different: s. 232(1) UK-CA but indemnification is possible (ss. 234 *et seq.* UK-CA).

272 See generally Wymeersch (2001c: paras. 40 *et seq.*); Goshen (2003: 17 *et seq.*); Hertig and Kanda (2004: 101 *et seq.*); for the US § 144 DelGCL; §§ 8.60 *et seq.* MBCA; but also § 402 Sarbanes–Oxley Act 2002 (prohibition of certain insider loans); for the UK ss. 177, 182, 190 UK-CA (disclosure; shareholder approval for substantial property transactions).

the fact that management duties are being increasingly codified.[273] Such regulations thus also change the traditional case-based fiduciary conceptions. Fifthly, in the US the business judgement rule gives management some latitude.[274] Something similar is being considered in the UK, even if recent developments suggest more of an objectivization and intensification of liability.[275] As a functional equivalent, however, for the UK one may point to the fact that derivative suits are still less developed than in the US.[276] Moreover, the courts can relieve managers from their liability if the breach of duty can in the circumstances be excused (s. 1157 UK-CA).

On the other hand, in Germany, France, Japan and China, management is subject to similar duties as in the US and the UK. While these cannot be subsumed under a single fiduciary duty towards shareholders, there nonetheless are terminological parallels. Already in 1873 the Higher Commercial Court of the German Reich referred to the general meeting as the 'principal of all administrative organs',[277] and in the literature too the members of the administrative bodies are termed 'mandataries' or 'fiduciary administrators of the company members' assets'.[278] Substantively, the French and German law in part go even beyond the duties in the US and the UK. In Germany (to date) the comprehensive liability for negligence and partial reversal of the burden of proof in § 93 GerAktG is particularly strict.[279] For France, it is said that a breach of duties of care (Art. L. 225-251 FrCCom) is at least as grave as in the US.[280] Exemption from the liability is – in harmony with the predominantly mandatory nature of company law – possible in only very restricted circumstances in Germany and France.[281] Furthermore, there are provisions on how to

[273] Cf. §§ 8.30 *et seq.*, 8.60 *et seq.* MBCA; ss. 170 *et seq.*, 994 UK-CA; for the preceding discussion see Modern Company Law Final Report (2001: paras. 3.5 *et seq.*); Worthington (2001a: 439 *et seq.*).

[274] See e.g. § 4.01 ALI-Principles; *Aronson* v. *Lewis*, 473 A 2d 805, 812 (Del. 1984); *Sinclair Oil Corp.* v. *Levien*, 280 A 2d 717, 720 (Del. 1971).

[275] See Davies (2003: 432 *et seq.*); for signs of a convergence to the 'business judgment rule' see e.g. *Re City Equitable Fire Insurance Co.* [1925] 1 Ch 407, 427 (Court of Appeal); *Re Smith & Fawcett Ltd* [1942] Ch 304, 306 (Court of Appeal); *Howard Smith Ltd* v. *Ampol Petroleum Ltd* [1974] AC 821, 832 (Privy Council).

[276] See Ch. 5, section III.1 below.

[277] ROHG, ROHG XI, 118, 125 ('Principalin aller Verwaltungsorgane').

[278] Horn (1979: 140, 157) ('Beauftragte'); Hopt, in: GroßkommAktG (1999: § 93 para. 12) ('treuhänderische Verwalter des Vermögens der Gesellschafter').

[279] See Hopt, in: GroßkommAktG (1999: § 93 para. 10); Ulmer (2002: 164).

[280] Fanto (1998: 56–7).

[281] § 93(4)(s.3) GerAktG; Art. L. 225-253 FrCCom.

prevent conflicts of interest in management.[282] Chinese and Japanese laws also provide measures against abuse of power by management. In China, it used to be controversial whether there was a general duty of loyalty and care.[283] Since the 2005 reform, however, the Companies Act states explicitly that directors and managers 'owe duties of loyalty and diligence to the company' (§ 148(1) ChinCA). Furthermore, a number of provisions, which for listed companies derive not just from the ChinCA but also from the mandatory articles of association, ban various types of abuse and also contain rules on liability.[284] Japanese law has lately been in the throes of change. Here too there are provisions aimed at guaranteeing loyalty to law and the company's interest, as well as avoiding conflicts of interest.[285] On the US model, the liability of directors can, however, be limited by the articles of association or by a resolution of the general meeting (§§ 425–427 JapCA).

This general overview makes it clear that duties aimed at preventing abuse of power by management are not a specifically common law phenomenon. Instead – as parallels to the business judgement rule in other countries[286] also show – in all the legal systems studied here ways are being sought to bring about a balance between shareholder protection and entrepreneurial discretion in decision-making. Moreover, obligations in private law are not the only factor which governs management behaviour, because other structural and institutional mechanisms may lead to a functionally comparable effect.

(2) Functional equivalents to private-law duties. Relatively extensive penal provisions for breaches of company law are to be found in France, Germany and China.[287] Although this is associated with high deterrent

282 See generally Hopt (2004: 53 *et seq.*); Fleischer (2004: 384 *et seq.*); Enriques (2000); Hopt (1985: 287 *et seq.*); Hertig and Kanda (2004: 116); for France: Arts. L. 225-38 *et seq.* FrCCom; for Germany: §§ 88(1), 93(1)(s.2), 404 GerAktG; No. 4.3 GerCGK.

283 See Wei (1998: 373); Tan (2000: 90); Liu (2001: 45); Clarke (2006b).

284 §§ 149, 150, 113(3) ChinCA; §§ 80, 81 ChinMandProv; §§ 114 *et seq.* ChinArticles; No. 19 ChinCG-Code; cf. also Comberg (2000: 156 *et seq.*).

285 §§ 120(4), 355, 356, 423, 428 JapCA; on the changes by the JapCA 2005 see Takahashi and Shimizu (2005: 54–6).

286 For Germany: BGH, BGHZ 135, 244, 253–4 (*ARAG/Garmenbeck*); § 93(1)(s.2) GerAktG as inserted by the Gesetz zur Unternehmensintegrität und Modernisierung des Anfechtungsrechts (UMAG) of 22.09.2005, BGBl. I 2802; for Japan: Kawamoto *et al.* (2001: para. 568); Shishido (1997: 150); Hayakawa (1996: 900); Utsumi (2001); Kanda (2004: 30).

287 Arts. L. 242-6 *et seq.* FrCCom; §§ 399 *et seq.* GerAktG; § 264a GerStGB; § 361 GerHGB; §§ 199 *et seq.* ChinCA.

potential, the penal law is in general rather on the retreat.[288] Penal sanctions for directors are in a certain tension with the concept of the legal person. The effectiveness of penal sanctions is also questionable, since offenders as a rule do not expect to be caught, and the percentage of undetected crime is high in business-crime law. However, penal sanctions may be appropriate where the public interest in particular conduct exceeds the interest of individuals or where there is no identifiable victim. In the context of a graded system of penalties, the penal law may thus be necessary in particularly severe cases, as is also clear from the latest enhancements of penal sanctions in securities law in the US.[289]

'Internal-corporate governance' solutions are of more general importance. Their advantage lies particularly in being able to prevent abuses through a kind of self-regulation within the company, without the need for recourse (invariably) to the courts to enforce obligations and prohibitions. And, despite some presumptions to the contrary,[290] the reforms in recent times suggest that institutional solutions will be extended and refined.

Frequently, the civil law countries are seen as having the advantage in these protective mechanisms. In those countries, the general meeting usually has more extensive powers than in common law countries.[291] This is further strengthened by the structural distribution of shareholdings, since the blockholdings more common there[292] mean that the general meeting can *de facto* control management better. Moreover, in some civil law systems, there is a separate monitoring body. This is true particularly of Germany. Here, since 1870, the supervisory board has acted as a substitute for comprehensive governmental oversight, monitoring the conduct of business and representing the firm against the management board in the event of conflicts of interest (§§ 89, 111 *et seq.* GerAktG). The Chinese supervisory board (§§ 118 *et seq.* ChinCA) and the Japanese statutory (corporate, internal) auditor (§§ 390 *et seq.* JapCA) have lesser powers. Additionally, since the latest reforms in Japan – as also in France and for the Societas Europaea – a separate supervisory body is no longer mandatory.[293]

288 For France: Storp (2002: 420); Merle (2005: paras. 248, 414); Fanto (1998: 84–5); for the UK: Worthington (2001a: 458).

289 § 906 lit. c Sarbanes–Oxley Act 2002.

290 Hopt (2002a: 1024); Assmann, in: GroßkommAktG (1992: Einl. para. 244).

291 See also Ch. 5, section I.1 above.

292 See Ch. 8, section IV.2.a below.

293 For France: Art. L. 225-57 FrCCom and e.g. Merle (2005: paras. 371 *et seq.*); for Japan: Janssen *et al.* (2002: 267); Hashimoto (2002: 10 *et seq.*); Takahashi and Shimizu (2005: 43);

It is, however, doubtful whether these internal control mechanisms really do establish a superiority of civil law over common law countries. While dispersed shareholder ownership may raise particular problems of motivation and control as regards oversight by the general meeting,[294] there is the danger with concentrated holding structures that influential shareholders and management may form a strategic alliance, so that here too 'checks and balances' will be lacking. Again, the increasing activism of institutional investors in the US and the UK and the largely similar provisions on the 'active' and 'deciding' shareholder argue against monolithic contrasts.[295] Furthermore, while there are no special supervisory bodies in one-tier systems, here too there is often a separation between management and supervision. In the US and the UK, special committees are supposed to guarantee the soundness of the conduct of business. As an argument for their effectiveness, often the majority of these committee members – and of boards in general – must be independent, thus setting up a requirement that supervisory board systems usually do not make.[296] To be sure, the establishing of committees with predominantly independent members is increasingly being called for outside the Anglo-American countries too,[297] so that – as the discussion of the election of directors have already shown[298] – the contrast between the one-tier and two-tier models does not seem insuperable.

Finally, alongside legal provisions and shareholder structures other factual elements may be of considerable importance for protecting shareholders. While legal provisions may avert abuse of power, they are not very good at regulating the effectiveness of management performance and, for instance, preventing management from 'empire building' at the

for the EU: Siems (2005a: 441) (on the SE); Modernising Company Law and Enhancing Corporate Governance in the European Union – A Plan to Move Forward, Communication from the Commission, COM(2003) 284, at 15.

294 See Ch. 4, section II.1.b; Ch. 5, section II pr. above.

295 See Ch. 4, section II; Ch. 5, section I above.

296 For the US: § 301 Sarbanes–Oxley Act 2002; § 303A.01 NYSE Manual; Cox and Hazen (2003) § 9.02 and (2004 Supplement) § 9.02A; for the UK: Higgs-Report (2003), available at http://www.dti.gov.uk/bbf/corp-governance/higgs-tyson/page23342.html; UK-Combined Code, at 59 *et seq.*; Farrar *et al.* (1998: 332 *et seq.*).

297 Commission Recommendation on the role of non-executive or supervisory directors of listed companies and on the committees of the (supervisory) board, 2005/162/EC; Modernising Company Law and Enhancing Corporate Governance in the European Union – A Plan to Move Forward, Communication from the Commission, COM(2003) 284, at 15; No. 5.3 GerCGK; No. 8.2 FrCG-Principles; §§ 331(3), 400 *et seq.* JapCA; § 123 ChinCA; Clarke (2006a) (for China).

298 See Ch. 5, section I.1.c above.

expense of profitability. For comprehensive oversight, accordingly, a decisive part is also played by, for instance, the financial press, informal internal control mechanisms, business ethics, and competition for products. Additionally, for public companies, 'external-corporate governance' protection through the capital market is often more important. In order to achieve this, however, a statutory framework must – at least on the prevailing view[299] – be set up, through supervisory authorities as well as provisions on information and abuse.

(3) Protective mechanisms under securities law. Details on securities law are beyond the scope of this book. However, at least on a general level some convergence can be seen. For example, share trading by insiders was first forbidden in 1934 in the US.[300] Following separate laws in France, the UK and Germany,[301] in 1989 the European Community addressed insider dealing in a first directive, which is now part of the EU Market Abuse Directive.[302] After the Second World War, Japan adopted a provision similar to the US one, which although watered down in the interim has recently been tightened up again.[303] Similarly, in Chinese law, there have since 1997 been provisions against insider dealing.[304] Yet there are differences in detail and in actual enforcement. But enforcement of insider-trading provisions is not a particularly continental European and Asian problem, because of greater personal interaction and less transparency in those countries as compared to the more effective enforcement in the US.[305] Instead, with insider dealing it is hard to measure abuse, so that in the US too it is likely that there is substantial undetected insider trading.[306]

Securities law may be enforced by various means. Among direct methods are civil law liability, criminal law sanctions, and oversight by a supervisory authority. Indirectly, disclosure provisions, threatened takeovers and shareholders' 'exit option' through the market may affect the conduct of management. The sale of shares in principle here constitutes the easiest way of protecting investors. But this option is of little use if, say,

[299] See Ch. 4, section I.3.b, III, preamble above.
[300] §§ 10, 16 US-SEA; SEC Rule 10b-5.
[301] Cf. generally Großfeld (1971: paras. 4-163 *et seq.*); Vagts (2000: para. 10-20); see also e.g. Arts. 621-1 *et seq.* FrRGAMF; s. 109 UK-FSMA; §§ 12 *et seq.* GerWpHG.
[302] Arts. 2–4 Market Abuse Directive 2003/6/EC; originally: Directive 89/592/EEC.
[303] Cf. § 167 JapSEA; Baum and Hayakawa (1994: 613, 618 *et seq.*); Kawamoto *et al.* (2001: paras. 351 *et seq.*); Kawamoto (1994: 216–17); Vagts (2000: para. 10-20).
[304] See §§ 73 *et seq.* ChinSA; for a recent reform see Xi (2006: 289–91).
[305] Contra Steinberg (2003).
[306] Cf. Romano (1993: 102); Hertig and Kanda (2004: 113).

absent or false information affects the share price.[307] In view of current instances of abuse, accordingly, across the countries measures are being taken to make management responsibility more effective in such cases. For example, in the US, the 2002 Sarbanes–Oxley Act has brought far-reaching changes. Among other things, the certification of reports by the principal executive and the financial officers has been prescribed, civil and criminal liability enhanced, auditor independence and auditor supervision strengthened, and reimbursement of any incentive or equity-based compensation in case of misconduct ordered.

Regardless of the pioneering position of the US, however, in other countries the need to promote efficient enforcement of securities law is also acknowledged as an important concern. This can be seen, first, in an expansion of the position of supervisory authorities.[308] Secondly, liability provisions are being tightened, or more frequently enforced. For instance, there have been the first civil and criminal proceedings against directors and managers in China.[309] Although in France the system of penal sanctions is dominant, the courts are now also extending civil liability.[310] In Germany recently, liability for breach of the duty to keep the public informed about matters affecting the company ('*ad hoc* publicity') was codified (§§ 37 b, c GerWpHG). Furthermore, according to a decision of the German Supreme Court, personal liability of managers is now also conceivable.[311]

(4) Conclusion. The special origins of Anglo-American shareholder protection can still be seen in the more general scope of management's duty of loyalty and in the law's greater capital-market orientation. However, for all the differences in protective mechanisms, at least functionally similar elements exist. Across the countries, the law provides, through both company and securities law, for management to be restricted by for instance prohibitions, institutional measures and market forces. Yet, management also enjoys a certain autonomy, since without entrepreneurial freedom skilled managers would be paralyzed, the decision process slowed and economic innovation impaired. The point is thus to create not a maximum but an optimum of oversight and self-regulation. In detail, one can for instance see convergence in the instrumental oversight of management, and the expansion of securities law. Moreover, good corporate

[307] See also Ch. 4, section I.3.d above. [308] See Ch. 2, section III above.
[309] See Pißler (2001), (2002a). [310] See Fleischer and Jänig (2002: 735–6).
[311] BGH, BGHZ 160, 149 (*Infomatec*); Siems (2005c) (also on US law).

governance is also based on purely factual circumstances. The approximation of economic infrastructures[312] may thus also bring an approximation of shareholder protection.

c) Conclusions

It was found, first, that protection of shareholders from management did not show a clear contrast between different legal families. Such crude categorizations as 'shareholder supremacy' v. 'stakeholder model', or 'external corporate governance' v. 'internal corporate governance', are of only limited value for today's legal world. Across the countries, instead, mixed provisions aim neither one-sidedly at an interest group, nor at one form of protection. This is also confirmed by the fact that the debate on 'good corporate governance' today cuts across frontiers and embraces the regulations and the experience of other countries. Secondly, it may nonetheless seem surprising that not only in details, but also in basic protective concepts, differences continue to exist. They are to be explained, as regards the position of shareholder interests, by the fact that here the outcome – primacy, equality or subordination of shareholder or stakeholder interests – is controversial. In the search for a balance, different solutions are accordingly arrived at. By contrast, it is basically undisputed that abuse of power by management against shareholders is to be prevented. Since it is however not clear which oversight means guarantee best shareholder protection, in this area legislative solutions also differ. Thirdly, the classification under model categories of shareholder[313] also leads to mixed results. As with the 'ownership analogy', shareholder interests have particular value and managers and directors are subject to particular duties of care and loyalty to shareholders. By analogy with the 'parliamentary model', however, structural measures such as oversight by a supervisory board or outside directors are also employed. Moreover, the advance of securities regulations in many countries with hitherto weak capital markets points to the fact that investor-related protective mechanisms are becoming more important.

2. Protection against the shareholder majority

With dispersed shareholder ownership, a majority decision by the general meeting is upheld by various interests, so that as a rule one may presume a balanced outcome. By contrast, with concentrated shareholdings the structural hazard arises that the shareholder minority may be taken unfair

[312] See Ch. 8, sections III, IV below. [313] See Ch. 3, section I above.

advantage of by the majority. Since in continental Europe (as well as in Asia) dispersed shareholder ownership is traditionally rare, it should, according to some commentators, be particularly likely here for a majority to engage in self-enrichment.[314] Sometimes, however, it is also suggested that in continental Europe there is better minority protection, because in the US and the UK the law sees shareholders purely as investors, for whom the sale option alone is decisive, and sufficient.[315]

Both statements are, however, too broad, because one must look at individual protective means. First, special voting rules may procedurally prevent majority shareholders from deciding in their own case (subsection a below). Secondly, the decisions of the general meeting may be tied to substantive requirements and the minority thus protected (subsection b below). Thirdly, it is conceivable for disadvantaged minority shareholders to have the right to leave the company, for fair and full compensation, so that at least their financial interests are guaranteed (subsection c below).

a) Voting in case of special interests

In principle, it is legitimate for a shareholder to pursue his own interests in a vote. The position might be different if a particular topic affects his interests not only as a shareholder but also as, say, a business partner in the firm or board member. However, on the shareholder models,[316] it is not beyond doubt whether in such cases of conflicts of interests the relevant shareholder's vote should be excluded. On the one hand, because of this special interest it is not functionally guaranteed that management will be effectively monitored by the general meeting, in the sense of 'shareholder democracy'. On the other hand, according to the 'ownership model' shareholders are not subject to any restrictions on their voting right, since how the company is to act is in their hands. An inadmissible bias may also seem unlikely for the 'shareholder as investor', since for him the legal relations with the company are exhausted primarily with the contribution of capital so that no special duty exists.

In the UK and the US, the law, with few exceptions, follows the view that voting is not subject to any formal restrictions.[317] By contrast, most other countries consider it conceivable to exclude voting right because of

[314] Bratton and McCahery (1999: 220); similarly Johnson *et al.* (2000).

[315] Cheffins (2000: 41); similar Windbichler (2000: 624); Wymeersch (1995: 312); Dine (2006: 356).

[316] See Ch. 3, section I above.

[317] For the UK: *Carruth* v. *Imperial Chemical Industries Ltd* [1937] AC 707 (House of Lords); Cheffins (1997: 238), (2001c: 99); Grantham (1998: 573); Ferran (1999: 258); but see also § 11.1.7(4) UK-Listing Rules; for the US: van Ryn (1990: para. 5-135); for an exception see § 8.63(b) MBCA.

bias. They focus either on specifically designated subjects or in general on the presence of a conflict of interests.[318] What position German law takes here has not yet been clarified. Apart from individual provisions,[319] it is disputed whether for joint stock companies the voting right is excluded, by analogy with the law on partnerships and small companies.[320]

The contrast between the Anglo-American and other countries is, however, lessened by other considerations. First, in common internationally, voting is not possible for the company's own shares,[321] since otherwise management could dominate the general meeting. Secondly, a similar danger threatens with reciprocal shareholdings. Here too, accordingly, the voting right is often excluded above a certain level of participation.[322] Furthermore, sometimes there are provisions whereby any sizeable reciprocal holding is even inadmissible.[323] Thirdly, as a milder recourse, there are often disclosure provisions. Particularly in the US and Japan, securities and accounting laws require large transactions with block shareholders to be made transparent.[324] Furthermore, in common internationally, the identity of influential shareholders must be disclosed.[325] If, therefore, the potential dominance of blockholders is known, the danger of possible special interests becomes clear to the minority. Fourthly, special resolutions by the possibly aggrieved shareholders may constitute an equivalent protection. For instance, in the US disinterested shareholder approval leads to the presumption that a conflict-of-interest transaction is fair.[326] And in China there is the rule that the majority of the holders of the tradable shares (which are usually the minority shareholders!)[327] has to approve various transactions in order to prevent self-dealing by the majority.[328]

[318] See generally Wymeersch (2001c: para. 25); Hertig and Kanda (2004: 111); for France: Becker (2001: 126); for Japan: § 831(1)(no.3) JapCA; Kliesow (2001: 95); for China: § 72 ChinMandProv; Comberg (2000: 116); Schipani and Liu (2002: 39).

[319] §§ 136, 142(1), (2), 243(2)(s.1) GerAktG.

[320] § 34 GerBGB; § 47(4)(s.2) GerGmbHG.

[321] See e.g. Art. 22(1) of the Second Directive 77/91/EEC; § 71 b GerAktG; § 308(2) JapCA; generally van Ommeslaghe (1990: para. 5-59); Wymeersch (2001c: para. 11).

[322] See e.g. Art. 24a of the Second Directive 77/91/EEC; §§ 71 b, d, 136(3), 328 GerAktG; generally Wymeersch (2001c: para. 83). US law is more liberal, see Immenga (1985: para. 7-36); van Ommeslaghe (1990: para. 5-61); but also § 7.21(b) MBCA (from 50 per cent).

[323] Art. L. 233-29 FrCCom; s. 136 UK-CA; § 135 JapCA.

[324] For a comparative overview see Hertig and Kanda (2004: 119 *et seq.*); see now also Art. 43(7b) of the Fourth Directive 78/660/EEC as amended by Directive 2006/46/EC.

[325] See Ch. 4, section IV.2 above.

[326] *Fleigler* v. *Lawrence*, 361 A 2d 218 (Del. 1976); see also Hertig and Kanda (2004: 122); for Japan: Oda (2002: 18–19).

[327] See Ch. 4, section I.3.b above.

[328] See Xi (2006: 254, 258) for changes in 2002 and 2004.

Fifthly, such procedural and typified measures need not necessarily be relied upon. In contrast to exclusions from voting or special resolutions, which seek to counter beforehand the danger that the interests of minority shareholders may be injured, they may also be protected directly through substantive requirements on the outcome of a decision of the general meeting.

b) Substantive control of decisions

The starting-point is that majority decisions of the general meeting must be accepted by the outvoted minority ('majority rule').[329] This is basically in the shareholders' interest, since in this way the general meeting remains functional, and the financial interests of the minority shareholders can be protected otherwise. The majority rule also fits the shareholder democracy model, whereby not company law but the general meeting should determine what is right and what wrong.

Nonetheless, it may become necessary to check or test the decisions of the general meeting using substantive criteria. According to the 'quasi-partnership model', shareholders are also obliged to take account of the interests of their fellow shareholders.[330] Moreover, checks on decisions may raise the attractiveness and thus the price of the share, since fairness within the company is enhanced and the possibilities of 'plunder' by the majority reduced. Finally, a parallel may also be drawn with the obligations of management. If a shareholder holds a position of power enabling him to exercise considerable influence on the company's destiny, it may be – as is also the case for management – justified to attribute to him as 'trustee' a corresponding responsibility.

Across the countries studied here, the law thus does not allow any absolute majority dominance, often setting limits to the general meeting's power through general limits on abuse or duties of loyalty and fairness. Additionally, in the minority's interest particular shareholder rights may be laid down. This is, for instance, true of the pre-emption right, which is intended to protect old shareholders' pecuniary and control rights against dilution.

The law in the US is marked particularly by general limits. The obligation to take account of shareholder interests[331] applies just as much to

[329] For the UK: Davies (2003: 481, 483 *et seq.*); for the US: Cox and Hazen (2003: § 9.01); for France: Borgmann (1996: 127–8); for the old German law: RG, RGZ 68, 235, 245–6 *(Hibernia)*, cf. also Mülbert (1996a: 150).

[330] See Ch. 3, section I above. [331] See Ch. 5, section II.1.a above.

the interests of the shareholder minority,[332] and is today overlain particularly by the doctrine of minority oppression.[333] Over and above that, it is presumed that dominant shareholders have a duty of care or of fairness towards the minority, since they hold *de facto* controlling power over the company.[334] The pre-emption right was in nineteenth-century common law still mandatory. Today, some states have 'opt-out' and some 'opt-in' statutes.[335] However, with close companies the general duty of loyalty may also mean in the individual case that the pre-emption right cannot be excluded.[336]

UK law is only partly similar, particularly since the common law rules are here couched more narrowly. A duty of loyalty by the majority is in principle not assumed, and also the statement that action should be 'bona fide for the benefit of the company as a whole' is mostly not regarded as a significant limitation on majority power.[337] To be sure, there is a general limit on 'fraud on the minority', which may operate for example in the event of amendments to the articles of association or the ratification of management misconduct.[338] Beyond this, today statutory provisions play an important part. First, there are the rules against unfair impairment of shareholder interests.[339] Secondly, since the EU Capital Directive,[340] UK law contains a pre-emption right in the event of cash capital increases, which by contrast with the US was not provided for in UK common law.[341]

For the other countries studied here, it is, first, typical that mandatory provisions are used more frequently than in the US and the UK to exclude

332 See Hansmann and Kraakman (2001: 442).

333 See Smith (1998: 305 *et seq.*); Licht *et al.* (2001: 28); Romano (1993: 127); Hertig and Kanda (2004: 126).

334 *Allied Chem. & Dye Corp.* v. *Steel & Tube Co. of Am.*, 14 Del. Ch. 1, 120 A 486 (1923) (stockholders have a fiduciary duty to other stockholders); *Hartford Accident & Indem. Co.* v. *W. S. Dickey Clay Mfg Co.*, 26 Del. Ch. 16, 21 A 2d 178 (1941), aff'd, 26 Del. Ch. 411, 24 A 2d 315 (1942) (right to amend must be exercised fairly and impartially), but also *Weinberger* v. *UOP, Inc.*, 457 A 2d 701 (Del. 1983) (no business purpose test); generally Cox and Hazen (2003: § 11.11).

335 For the latter see e.g. § 6.30(a) MBCA; § 102(b)(3) DelGCL.

336 See MacNeil (2002: 90 *et seq.*).

337 Cf. MacNeil (2002: 93 *et seq.*), (2005: 260–1); Cheffins (1997: 325–6); Modern Company Law: Final Report (2001: paras. 7.52 *et seq.*).

338 *Ebrahimi* v. *Westbourne Galleries Ltd* [1972] 2 All ER 492, 500 (Chancery Division); Davies (2003: 438 *et seq.*, 673, 709 *et seq.*, 716–17); Dine (1995: 116–17); Grantham (1998: 573); Worthington (2000: 648–9); MacNeil (2005: 262).

339 See s. 994 UK-CA; s. 122(1)(g) Insolvency Act 1986.

340 Art. 29 of the Second Directive 77/91/EEC.

341 See s. 561 UK-CA and Myners (2005: 13 *et seq.*).

abuse of the minority *a priori*.[342] Yet, here too there are often some flexible limits to majority rule. The principle of equal treatment ought to prevent a redistribution among various shareholders or shareholder groups.[343] Furthermore, in France the concept of abuse of majority control prevents the taking of a decision against the company's overall interest or in order to favour the majority over the minority.[344] While no objective control over exclusion of the pre-emption right follows, this is partly compensated for by formal requirements such as voting-right exclusions, high majority thresholds, and special requirements on public offerings.[345] Furthermore, the additional protection provided by the comprehensive powers of the French auditor, extending for instance also to verification of the offer price, have to be taken into account in the exclusion of the pre-emption right.[346]

In Japan, it is disputed in the literature whether there is a duty of loyalty among shareholders.[347] A statutory pre-emption right existed in only a few cases under the pre-2005 law (§§ 280-2 *et seq.* JapCC). The new law has further reduced its relevance because it is now for the board and/or the general meeting to decide whether to allot shares to the existing shareholders (§§ 199 *et seq.* JapCA). However, the issue of new shares may be suspended if it is substantially unfair (§ 210 JapCA). Similarly, in China a duty of loyalty or a statutory pre-emption right was lacking under the Companies Act 1993. In respect of the former, the 2005 reform has, however, led to a major change. There is now, first, the provision that shareholders shall not abuse their rights to injure the interests of the company and other shareholders (§ 20 ChinCA). Secondly, for majority shareholders the standard is probably even stricter because they shall not take advantage of their influence in an attempt to harm the company's interest (§§ 21, 217(2) ChinCA).

The case law in Germany goes further than in France, Japan and China, by requiring a general-meeting decision as a rule to be justified to

342 See Ch. 2, section IV.1.b above.

343 See e.g. Art. 42 of the Second Directive 77/91/EEC; Art. 17 of the Transparency Directive 2004/109/EC; Art. 4 of Directive 2007/36/EC; § 109(1) JapCA; in the US, equal treatment concerns only shares of the same class, see § 6.01(a) MBCA; Branson (2001: 330 note 41); similarly s. 2 JapCG-Principles; see also No. III.A OECD-Principles 2004.

344 Cour de Cassation, Chambre commerciale et financière of 18.04.1961, JCP 1961 II, 69087 (*Piquard*).

345 See Bagel (1999: 164 *et seq.*, 190, 248).

346 Schindler (1999: 325–6); see also Art. L. 225-135(s.2) FrCCom; Arts. 155 *et seq.* FrDécret.

347 See Kliesow (2001: 72).

shareholders by some objective reason,[348] and for the shareholders' duty of loyalty within the company not to be infringed.[349] However, according to recent decisions, resolutions passed by a qualified majority are often self-justifying,[350] and the courts do also not examine the reasonableness of delisting resolutions.[351] There has recently also been a liberalization in relation to the statutory pre-emption right. On the one hand, the case law loosens the requirements on exclusion of the pre-emption right on authorized capital, since the authorization need describe the reasons for the exclusion only abstractly.[352] On the other hand, exclusion of the pre-emption right for capital increases of listed companies has been facilitated by the legislator (§ 186(3)(s.4) GerAktG), since here the participation quota can also be assured through purchase on the exchange.

This differentiation in pre-emption right between listed and other companies can also be seen, for instance, in France. For listed companies, on the one hand exclusion of pre-emption right is easier.[353] On the other hand, the shareholder must, through appropriate terms of issue, have the possibility of buying further shares on the market. As with other company law provisions on corporate finance,[354] there is therefore a trend to liberalize the pre-emption right for public companies. Even if in principle a pre-emption right is granted, its exclusion must be possible. Otherwise the function of the joint stock company to attract capital would be impaired, although in public companies old shareholders need not in general be protected by a pre-emption right.[355] By contrast, a pre-emption right may be justified for shareholders with large holdings or participations in close companies. Finally, there is international convergence to the extent that, especially for small companies, case law and/or, statute law brings a certain check on abuse or unfairness. The remaining differences may be justified particularly by other protective mechanisms.

[348] See BGH, BGHZ 71, 40; BGH, BGHZ 83, 319.

[349] See BGH, BGHZ 103, 184, 194–5 (*Linotype*); BGH, BGHZ 129, 136, 148 (*Girmes*); BGH, NJW 1999, 3197.

[350] See BGH, BGHZ 76, 352; 103, 184; Mülbert (1996a: 353 *et seq.*).

[351] BGH, BGHZ 153, 57 (*Macrotron*).

[352] BGH, BGHZ 125, 239 (*Deutsche Bank*); BGH, BGHZ 136, 133 (*Siemens/Nold*). However, *ex post* control is possible: see BGH, ZIP 2005, 2207 (*Mangusta/Commerzbank II*).

[353] Arts. L. 225-136, 225-137 FrCCom as amended by Loi No. 2003-706 du 1er août 2004 and Ordonnance No. 2004-604 du 24 juin 2004 portant réforme du régime des valeurs mobilières émises par les sociétés commerciales.

[354] See Ch. 4, sections I.4, II.4.a; Ch. 5, sections I.1.d, II.2.b above.

[355] But see also Ferran (2003a: 115 *et seq.*) (institutional investors continue to value pre-emption rights); similarly Myners (2005).

c) Leaving the company

For cases where a shareholder leaves the company or the majority wishes to exclude him against his will, the same questions arise: whether this is possible, and if so how the shareholder can be adequately compensated financially. Here, however, a number of distinctions have to be drawn.

(1) **Mandatory bid and appraisal rights.** In the general case, the shareholder's position is terminated not by his leaving the company, but by sale to third parties. In this way the individual shareholder can in principle avoid adverse harm caused by decisions of the shareholder majority.[356] This is however not necessarily so, especially where extraordinary legal or factual circumstances, such as an imminent merger or takeover, mean that simple sale does not adequately guarantee the shareholder's financial interests.

It is accordingly conceivable to protect him by imposing a purchase obligation on a third party seeking to take over the company. This mandatory bid at an appropriate level of compensation – on the UK model, mostly arising on purchase of 30 per cent or one-third of the shares – must be made to shareholders in listed companies in the UK, France, Germany, China and Japan.[357] The new EU Takeover Directive also provides for a mandatory bid.[358] In other respects, the duty on third parties to purchase shares is regulated in various different ways in these countries. In Germany, § 305 GerAktG provides merely for a statutory duty to purchase on conclusion of a control or profit transfer agreement. Furthermore, in the event of delisting, recent case law requires that (as well as the company) a major shareholder too may be obliged to buy the shares.[359] The public withdrawal procedure in France, whereby a minority shareholder can sell his shares to the majority shareholder, is farther-reaching. This, like the sell-out right in UK law and under the new EU Takeover Directive, links, first, with the squeeze-out right.[360] If a majority shareholder with 90 per cent (UK) or 95 per cent (France) can exclude the other shareholders, it also makes sense to allow him a withdrawal right.[361] Secondly, in France,

356 See Ch. 4, section I.3 above.

357 Rule 9.1 UK City Code; §§ 35(1), 29(2) GerWpÜG; Art. 234-2 FrRGAMF; §§ 88, 96 ChinSA; § 27-2(1) JapSEA (although not for all outstanding shares; but see Oda (2005: 266–7) on the forthcoming reform).

358 Art. 5 of the Takeover Directive 2004/25/EC.

359 BGH, BGHZ 153, 57 (*Macrotron*).

360 See subsection (2) below.

361 Art. 236-1 FrRGAMF; s. 983 UK-CA; similarly, Art. 16 of the Takeover Directive 2004/25/EC.

a public withdrawal procedure may operate where there are fundamental changes, such as changes of corporate form, mergers or divisions (Arts. 236-5, 236-6 FrRGAMF). It is, however, disputed whether in the event of conflict the majority shareholder is really affected by a legal duty to take over the shares, or alternatively whether only a duty to notify the change to the regulatory authority.[362]

By contrast with these duties to purchase, in most US states there are no comparable provisions, and fiduciary duties in case of a sale of corporate control are recognized only to a limited extent.[363] The reason given for this is that takeovers would otherwise be made more costly and the market for corporate control diminished.[364] However, this is not very convincing from a comparative point of view, since in the UK a takeover-friendly law[365] and mandatory bids do coexist.

However, for the US and Japan 'appraisal rights' in the event of fundamental decisions open up the possibility for the shareholder to leave the company. Since this does not involve a sale to a third party, the shareholder receives appropriate compensation for his shares from the company itself. This procedure may be advantageous for both him and the company, since in this way he can realize his financial interests without a particular measure being prevented or delayed by formal or substantive barriers to decision-making.

In the US, appraisal rights were introduced as long ago as 1859 as *quid pro quo* for the fact that for fundamental changes a unanimous decision of the general meeting was no longer required.[366] Shareholders have this right today mostly in the event of mergers, and partly also for amendments to the articles of incorporation and sales of major company assets.[367] To determine the value of the shares, there are detailed provisions, the procedural implementation of which is facilitated since lawyers' and experts' costs can be charged to the company.[368] Similar provisions to those in the

[362] See Cools (2005: 33); Rock *et al.* (2004: 142); Schindler (1999: 346–7).

[363] See Cox and Hazen (2003: §§ 12.01, 12.02). In Delaware, the courts have repeatedly emphasized that controlling shareholders may obtain a premium for their shares which they need not share with other shareholders; see *In re Sea-Land Corp. S'holders Litig.*, No. 8453, 1987 WL 11283 (Del. Ch. 1987); *Harris* v. *Carter*, 582 A 2d 222, 234 (Del. Ch. 1990); *Thorpe v. CERBCO, Inc.*, 676 A 2d 436, 442 (Del. 1996).

[364] Cf. Bebchuk (1994: 967); Fanto (1998: 76–7); Mitnick (2001: 709 *et seq.*); Davies and Hopt (2004: 180).

[365] See Ch. 5, section II.1.a above.

[366] See Siegel (1995: 86 *et seq.*); Fanto (1998: 67).

[367] See § 13.02 MBCA; § 262 DelGCL; Siegel (1995: 81); on the controversial 'de facto merger' see Cox and Hazen (2003: § 22.07).

[368] E.g. § 13.31 MBCA; § 262(j) DelGCL.

US can be found in Japan. Appraisal rights were initially introduced in 1950, first for mergers and the sale of major shareholdings. Later these rights were extended to most fundamental transactions.[369] Despite the reception of US law in Japan, there is practically no case law on it, because the costs to be borne by the shareholder are extremely high.[370]

By contrast, in the other countries studied here, there are in general no comparable duties for the company to purchase its own shares. Such duties do not exist at all in China.[371] In France, a shareholder can compel an exit only in the case of a transfer restriction on shares (Art. L. 228-24 FrCCom). In UK law, s. 996(2)(e) UK-CA provides that unfair prejudice may give rise to an obligation to purchase its own shares. Additionally, if a purchase offer has previously been made, it may be harder to show unfair prejudice.[372] In German law, it is on the one hand debated whether the shareholder can leave the company for a substantial reason. This is, contrary to the formerly prevailing opinion, assumed by the more recent literature under strict preconditions,[373] though without the right yet having acquired any practically important significance. On the other hand, provisions on change of corporate form provide for rights of exit and compensation.[374] Their sphere of application cannot, on the hitherto prevailing opinion, be generalized.[375] However, the most recent case law requires that, on delisting, every shareholder should have the right to leave the company, for the full value of the shares.[376] In order to determine the appropriate value, a special shareholders' compensation procedure is carried out, which was hitherto very time-consuming, and was therefore recently reformed.[377]

These differences from the US and Japan can be explained on the one hand by the European principle of minimum capital. Since an appraisal right constitutes an own-share purchase, the company assets are potentially endangered. On the other hand, outside the US and Japan other

[369] §§ 116, 469, 777, 785, 797, 806, 808 JapCA.

[370] See Ködderitzsch (2001a: 81); Bälz (2002: 165).

[371] For China, see Comberg (2000: 82); Thümmel (1995: 89).

[372] *Re a Company (No. 00709 of 1992)* [1999] 1 WLR 1092, 1107 (*O'Neill* v. *Phillips*) (House of Lords).

[373] Grunewald (1997: 111 *et seq.*); Schindler (1999: 36 *et seq.*); Hirte (2003: paras. 4.83, 6.15 *et seq.*).

[374] §§ 29, 125(s.1), 207 GerUmwG. This is enabled by Art. 28 of the Third Directive 78/855/EEC.

[375] See Grunewald (1997: 106–7); for a different view see Schindler (1999: 205 *et seq.*).

[376] BGH, BGHZ 153, 57 (*Macrotron*).

[377] Spruchverfahrensgesetz (SpruchG) of 17.07.2003, BGBl. I 838.

means of protection may operate. It should, however, be noted that the sphere of application and the *ratio legis* of appraisal rights is controversial. Traditionally, their purpose was seen *ex post* in the protection of shareholders: the shareholder having joined the company on certain terms, when those terms change he must have the possibility of leaving the company with compensation for their fair value. If this cannot be provided through sale – whence the 'market-out exception' in some US states[378] – the company itself ought then to buy the shares at a fair price. However, a more recent view stresses that appraisal rights are in the first place supposed to work not *ex post* for shareholders of close companies, but rather *ex ante* for all companies.[379] Appraisal rights will increase the costs of a fundamental change. However, this ought not to be seen as a drawback, since a majority decision might not otherwise be attainable.[380] Instead, it is economically efficient to prevent inefficient restructuring of firms *ex ante*.

This *ex ante/ex post* dialectic also appears in alternative protective mechanisms in other countries. By contrast with the US, in for example France and Germany shareholder minorities are protected *ex ante* by majority thresholds, mandatory provisions, voting prohibitions in cases of special interests and mandatory bids.[381] The same is true of majority qualifications and mandatory provisions in China, and of mandatory bids in the UK.[382] *Ex post*, finally, the protection is supplemented by the fact that, alongside the possibilities of substantive checks on decisions in Germany, the interests of shareholders are protected even if they choose to remain in the firm, through the law on groups of companies.[383]

(2) Squeeze-out. By contrast with sale or voluntary departure from the company, it is in principle not possible to exclude a shareholder against his will. In a number of countries, an exception is made to this and a squeeze-out permitted. In 1969, it was still being stated that: 'An original feature in the English law of takeover is a provision which permits the acquirer of over 90 percent of a company's shares to requisition the rest.'[384] Today, however, in almost all EU countries as well as in the new EU Takeover

[378] § 13.02(b)(1)(i) MBCA; § 262(b)(1) DelGCL.

[379] See Ruffner (2000: 195 *et seq.*); Schindler (1999: 370); Bälz (2002: 170) (for Japanese law).

[380] Contra Conard (1969: para. 6-25); Schindler (1999: 328).

[381] See Ch. 5, section I.2.a; Ch. 2, section IV.1.b; Ch. 5, section II.2.a-c above.

[382] See Ch. 2, section IV.1.b; Ch. 5, section II.2.c above.

[383] §§ 291 *et seq.* GerAktG; for a comparative overview see Hopt (2000: 124 *et seq.*); Immenga (1985: paras. 7-66 *et seq.*).

[384] Conard (1969: para. 6-68).

Directive, there are comparable provisions for listed companies, triggered mostly at a participation of 90 per cent or 95 per cent.[385] In Germany, the law covers even unlisted companies. Moreover, as in France, there is no requirement for there to be a public takeover bid. The US and Japanese laws go farther still. Although there are no special squeeze-out provisions, in a merger by absorption where shareholders in the target company are paid in cash, exclusion is in principle possible even with smaller majorities.[386] However, here too there will often in practice be clear majorities, since the need to pay off large minorities can, as with appraisal rights, have a deterrent effect.

A parallel can similarly be seen in the fact that, with both appraisal rights and the squeeze-out, only the financial position of shareholders is taken into account. It follows that, in both cases, a full and fair valuation is essential for the minority, but may also often in practice be problematic. Moreover, in support of the squeeze-out it may be noted that the minority shareholders are in any case already powerless in this situation, so that only their purely financial interest is affected.[387] The notion that in this situation the shareholder's ownership rights run counter to a squeeze-out[388] is thus today mostly no longer accepted.[389] Instead, in the interest of the shareholder majority the considerable costs of ultra-small shareholdings can be saved. One can also thus eliminate the danger of preventing management from forcing financial concessions and thus indirectly also the danger of hampering the efficiency of the market for corporate control.

d) Conclusion

The simplistic statements about the differences in minority protection between common law and civil law countries have not been confirmed. Despite the strong emphasis on a capital market with dispersed shareholdings in companies, in the US and the UK there are also close companies in which the majority is restricted in its freedom of action. Similarly, the

[385] See Art. 15 of the Takeover Directive 2004/25/EC; Arts. 237-1 *et seq.* FrRGAMF; §§ 327a *et seq.* GerAktG; §§ 39a *et seq.* GerWpÜG; s. 979 UK-CA.

[386] For the US, see § 11.02(c)(3) MBCA; Gilson and Gordon (2003: 796 *et seq.*); for Japan: §§ 749(1)(no.2), 751(1)(no.3) JapCA; Bälz (2002: 28–9).

[387] See Grantham (1998: 583); Mülbert (2003: 450).

[388] This was the opinion of the High Court of Australia in *Gambotto* v. *WCP Ltd.* (1995) 127 ALR 417. Subsequently, however, Australian law was changed: see Hill (2000b: 66 note 196).

[389] Cf. Wirth and Arnold (2002: 503); Fleischer (2002: 763–4); similarly BVerfG, BVerfGE 100, 289, 302–3; BVerfG, NJW 2001 279 (*Moto Meter*); Cour de Cassation, Rev.soc. 1998, 337.

other countries studied here have not capitulated to the possibilities of abuse by the shareholder majority, but have provided various types of protective mechanism. Among these minority protection mechanisms, mandatory regulations, qualified majority rules, voting rules in cases of special interest, substantive checks on decisions and exit rights can be found. The differences in legal patterns here on the one hand confirm the method generally favoured in the given legal system, since, for instance, German law uses procedure-oriented measures and US law focuses primarily on protecting financial interests. On the other hand, a number of nuances are also evident, which make convergences (e.g. on limits on majority rule, or the squeeze-out) clear.

3. *Conclusions*

The complex phenomenon of shareholder protection can be summarized in negative statements. First, no clear subdivision into common law, civil law and Asian law can be discerned. Secondly, it cannot be stated about any of the legal systems concerned that legal system clearly offers more or less protection. Instead, there is a mixed picture, with the focus sometimes on one version of protection and sometimes on another. Thirdly, the law does not follow the simple slogan 'as much shareholder protection as possible', since other interests are also recognized, and the possibly oppressive nature of over-strong restraints has to be considered. Fourthly, it cannot be said that any one system's solution is generally superior. Since the question of shareholder protection also depends on real factors and alternative protection through market forces, there can be no universal solutions. Fifthly, the countries studied do not follow any unambiguous shareholder model.[390] In all the countries, there are provisions lying both procedurally in the tradition of the democratic model, substantively in that of the ownership model and financially in that of the investor model. There is therefore no general convergence. However, a number of provisions show that receptions of foreign law are desired and can be rational. Whether this partial convergence will lead further, to a legally enhanced degree of uniformity, remains to be discussed.[391]

III. The litigating shareholder

It is sometimes assumed that, in company law, judicial proceedings are more accessible in common law countries than in continental Europe

[390] On these models see Ch. 3, section I above.

[391] See Ch. 10, section II.2 below.

and Asia.[392] This fits with the widespread notion of a 'general cultural orientation towards judicial dispute resolution'[393] in common law. By contrast, in civil law countries mandatory law and therefore *ex ante* control traditionally played a bigger part.[394] For the Asian countries, it is further stressed that the individualistic system of shareholder litigation ill accords with the unwritten collectivist traditions.[395] Most recently, however, the law of the 'litigating shareholder' has been adjusted in many countries. Furthermore, one has to dinstinguish between legal actions which are asserting one's own or someone else's rights.

For shareholders asserting their own rights, recourse to the law is as a general rule open.[396] It therefore matters which substantive rights are owed to shareholders. Often they play a part in participatory and information rights. In many countries, minority rights like convoking the general meeting or appointing special auditors are also covered, since to enforce them necessarily requires judicial proceedings.[397] Moreover, shareholders can also attack general-meeting decisions (subsection 2 below).

By contrast, it is more controversial whether and to what extent actions by shareholders on behalf of the company against misconduct by management (subsection 1 below) should be advocated. In favour of such actions is, in particular, alongside the trusteeship and parliamentary analogy,[398] the shareholder's role as 'watchdog', because they may guarantee effective oversight of the company.[399] However, legal proceedings do not necessarily constitute an effective means of discipline. First, they may disrupt the company's business and therefore be regarded from the shareholder majority's point of view as undesirable and from the public's as inefficient. Secondly, for effective oversight it is insufficient merely to regulate the admissibility of these suits. For instance, it matters also whether or not shareholders have access to the necessary information for an action, procedural and cost provisions have deterrent effects, and legal-cultural factors stand in the way of taking action. Thirdly, review of business decisions is subject to the objection that it is not the courts' job to replace entrepreneurial discretion by their own 'second-guess corporate decision-making'.[400] It might instead be more efficient for clear,

392 Hertig (2000: 279 *et seq.*).

393 Cunningham (1999: 1186).

394 See Ch. 2, section IV.1.b above.

395 See Ch. 5, section III.1; Ch. 8, section II.2.b below.

396 See generally No. III preamble OECD-Principles 2004; Großfeld (1971: para. 4-255); for the UK: Modern Company Law: Final Report (2002: paras. 7.34 *et seq.*); for the US: Cox and Hazen (2003: § 15.03); for France: Art. L. 225-252 FrCCom; for China: § 153 ChinCA.

397 See Ch. 4, section II.3.a; Ch. 5, section I.1.e above.

398 See Ch. 3, section I. 2 above.

399 See Hill (2000b: 59) ('The Shareholder as Cerberus').

400 Cheffins (1997: 314).

mandatory law, internal monitoring mechanisms, supervisory measures and capital-market forces to make litigation unnecessary.

1. Actions against management conduct

In the US, it is in principle possible for a shareholder to assert claims on behalf of the company against management by way of derivative suit.[401] Frequent use is made of this, particularly because lawyers promote these suits and shareholders run hardly any risk: in the US, lawyers can agree on contingency fees and thus expect considerable gains if successful. This incentive is further enhanced by the possibility of a class action, since in this case the amount sued for and therefore also the potential profits increase still more. Moreover, in other respects too the cost provisions for the litigating shareholder are favourable to the shareholder. The starting-point is the 'American rule', according to which each party pays their own lawyers' costs irrespective of the outcome of the trial. If the shareholder wins the suit, this would of course mean being burdened with his own costs. Yet often a claim for reimbursement against his own company is possible. According to the 'common fund theory', it was permissible for the shareholder's costs to be reimbursed from the compensation that the company had secured through the suit. Today, it is additionally provided that, in the event of lawsuits substantially benefiting the company, the (successful) shareholder's costs are borne by the company (e.g. § 7.46(1) MBCA). If he loses, under the American rule the shareholder does not have to pay the winner's legal costs. In rare cases, costs may be payable where the action was commenced or maintained without reasonable cause or for an improper purpose (e.g. § 7.46(2) MBCA). Moreover, a shareholder who has agreed contingency fees with his lawyer runs no risk, to the extent that in the event of failure at any rate no lawyers' fees arise for him.

In view of these factors that favour litigation, the danger of abusive lawsuits presents itself. This danger is today countered by a number of measures that have led to a decline in the number of derivative actions.[402] On the one hand, this is furthered by the preconditions for derivative actions.[403] It is necessary for the shareholder to have been a shareholder continuously since the date the damage was incurred, for possible

[401] For details see e.g. Cox and Hazen (2003: § 15); Klein and Coffee (2002: 199 et *seq.*).

[402] See Rosenthal, in: Brancanto and Price (2002: 62 *et seq.*).

[403] On what follows see §§ 7.40 *et seq.* MBCA; Rule 23.1 Federal Rules of Civil Procedure, and similarly Rule 23.1 of the Court of Chancery of the State Delaware; Cox and Hazen (2003: § 15.20).

remedies within the company to have been exhausted,[404] and in some states, if he holds less than 5 per cent of the shares, to have posted a bond. On the other hand, there are special remedies against 'strike suits'. Settlements and voluntary discontinuances of actions often require the court's consent (§ 7.45 MBCA). Furthermore, duties of loyalty on shareholders and the possibilities of release from liability or of D&O (directors and officers) insurances are aimed at countering the success of extortion attempts.

Although the US derivative suit has its origin in the English equity case law of the nineteenth century, UK law used to differ considerably. Following the fundamental House of Lords judgment in *Foss* v. *Harbottle*, it was in principle not possible for a shareholder to bring an action on behalf of the company.[405] However, this has changed. First, since 1980 shareholders can with court authorization sue on behalf of the company for compensation for damages to enforce the ban on unfair conduct.[406] Secondly, the 2006 reform has introduced the possibility of derivative claims.[407] What role they will play, however, remains to be seen. The courts probably have a significant discretion to channel them. Shareholders have to apply to court for permission to 'continue' a derivative claim. In its decision, the court can, for instance, take into account whether the claim will harm the interests of the company, whether the claimant is acting in good faith, and whether the company has decided not to pursue the claim.[408]

For the cost question, in the UK – as in most of the other countries studied here[409] – the loser has to pay the winner's costs ('English rule'). By contrast with the US, thus, what is particularly problematic is the risk the shareholder runs by losing the suit. In this case, alongside his own costs and the high UK court fees, he also has to bear the opponent's lawyers' fees. However, recently there has been some easing. First, the ban on

404 In particular, with respect to special litigation committees see *Auerbach* v. *Bennett*, 47 NY 2d 619, 393 NW 2d 994, 419 N. Y. S.2d 920 (1979) (NY Court of Appeals); cf. *Zapata Corp.* v. *Maldonado*, 430 A 2d 779 (Del. 1981) (the court will use its own business judgement), but also *Aronson* v. *Lewis*, 473 A 2d 805 (Del. 1984) (*Zapato* only applicable for demand-unnecessary cases).

405 *Foss* v. *Harbottle* (1843) 2 Hare 461 (House of Lords); for exceptions see Boyle (2003); see also Davies (2003: 467) ('primitive state of our version of derivative actions and the appalling cost of litigation').

406 See ss. 994, 996(2)(c) UK-CA.

407 See ss. 260 *et seq*. UK-CA; for the discussions see Company Law Reform (2005: 34–5); Modern Company Law: Final Report (2001: paras. 7.46 *et seq.*); Davies (2003: 464 *et seq.*).

408 For details see s. 263 UK-CA.

409 See Oquendo (2001: 1014–15).

contingency fees is gradually being loosened.[410] Secondly, following the Court of Appeal's ruling in *Wallersteiner* v. *Moir (No. 2)* and rule 19.9(7) of the Civil Procedure Rules 1998, it may be possible for the shareholder to be due a claim for reimbursement against the company if the action was *ex ante* to be regarded as reasonable.[411]

Since the mid-nineteenth century, French law has allowed a derivative suit (today, Art. L. 225-252 FrCCom). Both the simplified representation provisions for an action by several shareholders (as a rule 5 per cent: Art. 200 FrDécret) and the subsidiarity in relation to an action by the whole board[412] make it clear that in France it is the oversight function, not the entitlement of members to sue, that is important. From a factual viewpoint, the derivative suit has to date played little role. This is partly because of questions of the burden of proof, but also and especially because of cost issues. It is particularly the legal costs that are problematic, since the winner in the commercial courts is not able to recover his costs from the loser. As the shareholder who loses a suit also has no claim for reimbursement against the company, he is left burdened with his own legal fees. This risk might have been reduced by contingency fees. However, after they failed to be endorsed by the Marini Report,[413] contingency fees continue to be impermissible in France. In practice, therefore, a more favourable alternative is for shareholders to assert a claim for compensation for damages against members of the board through a so-called 'action civile' in connection with criminal proceedings.[414] However, the importance of penal provisions in company law was recently reduced and instead a preventive procedure enabling a temporary order against an action by management was established (Art. L. 238-1 FrCCom). Additionally, the possibility for shareholder associations to combine shareholder votes and bring actions as representatives was facilitated.[415] Whether this quasi-class action will acquire any practical importance is, however, doubtful. The issue of costs will militate against this, since the shareholder association must itself bear the costs of organizing the shareholders.

410 For a discussion see Reisberg (2006).

411 See *Wallersteiner* v. *Moir* (*No. 2*) [1975] 1 All ER 849 (Court of Appeal); Davies (2003: 454–5).

412 See Planck (1995: 37 *et seq.*, 46 *et seq.*); Merle (2005: para. 409).

413 Marini Report (1996: 96).

414 See Arts. 2 *et seq.* Code de Procedure Penale; Planck (1995: 77 *et seq.*); Merle (2005: para. 416).

415 Art. 126 of Loi No. 2003-706 du 1er août 2003 de sécurité financière which led to an amendment to Art. L. 452-1 FrCMon; cf. also Arts. L. 225-120, 225-252 FrCCom.

German law differs from the legal systems just addressed particularly because of the supervisory board, which is intended to enforce claims against the management board.[416] Only a few provisions in the law on groups of companies have to date allowed a shareholder to sue directly.[417] Moreover, in 1884 a shareholder minority was given the possibility of enforcing an internal compulsion procedure to bring an action against members of management (§ 147(1), (3) (old) GerAktG). Since the mid-1990s, however, proper derivative actions, reduction in quorums, improvement in cost provisions and the introduction of class actions have frequently been called for.[418] The legislature responded initially only to a limited extent. A reform in 1998[419] supplemented the provision that shareholders with 10 per cent of the registered capital can enforce claims (§ 147(1) GerAktG) with a provision that even 5 per cent of the registered capital may suffice if facts suggest the possibility of a gross breach of duty (§ 147(3) (old) GerAktG). The 2005 reform,[420] however, brought a more fundamental change. While by § 147(1) GerAktG a general-meeting resolution can still for instance compel the supervisory board to assert a claim against the management board, additionally a shareholder minority with a 1 per cent share of the registered capital or a stock exchange value of 100,000 has the possibility of bringing an action in its own name (§ 147a GerAktG). To prevent abusive exercise of the right, however, preliminary judicial proceedings are provided for. The court is to admit an action only if the minority has previously called on the company to file suit, damage appears to have arisen from dishonesty or gross breach of law and there are no overriding reasons of company welfare not to do so. If the application for admission is unsuccessful, the shareholder minority must bear the costs. If instead the action is admitted but then dismissed, the shareholder minority is in principle entitled to a claim for reimbursement of costs (§ 147a(6) GerAktG).

Japanese company law, which earlier followed the (old) German model, has since 1950 contained a derivative action on the US model: shareholders who have held shares for at least six months can, after a request to the company and if necessary lodging security, assert company damage claims

[416] Cf. § 112 GerAktG and BGH, BGHZ 135, 244, 253–4 (*ARAG/Garmenbeck*).

[417] §§ 309(4), 310(4), 317(4), 318(4) GerAktG.

[418] See Joussen (2000: 255 *et seq.*); Ulmer (1999a: 290 *et seq.*).

[419] Gesetz zur Kontrolle und Transparenz im Unternehmensbereich (KonTraG) of 27.04.1998, BGBl. I 786.

[420] Gesetz zur Unternehmensintegrität und Modernisierung des Anfechtungsrechts (UMAG) of 22.09.2005, BGBl. I 2802; for a critical comment see Siems (2005d).

themselves (now § 847 JapCA). Despite the basic similarity to US law,[421] the number of suits in Japan was initially low. The reason often adduced was legal-cultural, sociological and economic aspects: the Japanese mentality was said often to attach more importance to social harmony than to a sense of rights.[422] Additionally, actions were said to be undesirable in the business sphere, since the dominance of the banks and of groups of firms made oversight through derivative suits institutionally incompatible with the concepts of Japanese economic life.[423]

These explanations, however, are less convincing in the light of recent developments. Since court fees were reduced and a regulation on reimbursement of lawyers' fees (now § 852 JapCA) was introduced in 1993, the number of derivative suits has risen sharply.[424] However, one should still be wary of seeing a simplistic cause–effect relationship here. Apart from this amendment, the economic crisis, scandals and the increasing importance of foreign investors have led to a *de facto* approximation to the US system.[425] As in the US, from the management standpoint, the problem of abuse of the derivative action is now increasingly becoming apparent. Under pressure from the business association Keidanren, there has therefore in 2001 been an extension of the dispute resolution procedure within the firm from thirty to sixty days (now § 847 JapCA) and an easing of settlements in the course of proceedings (now § 850 JapCA). Additionally, the increase in derivative suits in particular was used to argue that liability limits ought to be set for directors.[426] A similar tendency can also be seen in some parts of the 2005 reform, because, for instance, it excludes a claim if it is unfair or would damage the company's interests (§ 847(no.1) JapCA) or if the shareholder has not first demanded that the management board file a lawsuit (§ 847(no.4) JapCA). However, there is also an important provision which aims at enhancing of shareholder rights: in contrast

[421] There are, for instance, differences regarding class actions (see West (2001b: 353)); pre-trial discovery (see Shishido (1997: 161)); costs and fees (see Takahashi and Rudo (2000: 71, 101); West (2001b: 355)); and pre-examination by an independent body (see Kawamoto (1999: 538)); for a general comparison see Utsumi (2001).

[422] E.g. LaChance (2001: 296); Kawamoto (1994: 215–16); for a different view see already Haley (1978): 'The Myth of the Reluctant Litigant'; cf. also Wollschläger (1997: 89 *et seq.*); Dean (2002: 3 *et seq.*, 356).

[423] Cf. Hayakawa (1997: 247); Aoki (2001a: 99); Takahashi and Rudo (2000: 71, 75).

[424] Cf. Rodatz (2002: 301–2); West (2001a: 579–80); Aoki (2001a: 103); Igarashi (2001: 93); Nottage (2001: 275); Kawamoto (1999: 529); Kliesow (2001: 172 *et seq.*); Aronson (2003a and 2003b).

[425] See Kawamoto (1999: 530); Kawamoto *et al.* (2001: para. 590); West (2001b: 357 *et seq.*).

[426] See Ch. 5, section II.1.b above.

to recent case law,[427] it has been clarified that shareholders do not lose the standing to sue if due to mergers or other reorganizations they become shareholders of another company (§ 851 JapCA).

The practical application of the law enacted in China is still largely yet to be established. The sphere of the old provision (§ 111 ChinCA 1993) was disputed,[428] and thus it was characterized merely as 'a cryptic and potentially powerful way to protect shareholders'.[429] The 2005 reform has clarified that shareholders who hold at least 1 per cent of the shares can file a derivative action against directors and managers (§ 152 ChinCA). As in the US, it is, however, required that the shareholder has been uninterrupted owner of the share and has exhausted the possible internal remedies within the company. Furthermore, there needs to be an irreparable loss if legal proceedings are not initiated immediately. Given these limits, one may doubt whether this derivative action will become important in China. Furthermore, it is sometimes emphasized that Chinese legal culture is not based on individual rights and their implementation, and that Chinese courts do not work properly.[430] However, this situation is now changing. At the level of securities law there have already been suits by deceived shareholders,[431] and legal culture is also beginning to change,[432] so that for China it is likely that the importance of derivative suits will continue to grow.

On the whole, thus, a legal convergence emerges, to the extent that on the one hand in the countries where shareholders hitherto could not, or only restrictedly, pursue management misconduct through the courts (e.g. the UK and Germany) this has increasingly been made available, while on the other hand countries that allowed derivative suits more generously have had to recognize that 'disruptive shareholders' may abuse this right. Regarding the legal options to remedy this (e.g. provision of security, internal proceedings, quorum), however, there are different solutions. The same is true of provisions on lawyers' fees and on the apportionment of costs. It is therefore unsurprising that the practical importance of derivative suits is still very varied. One should not, however, be over-hasty to conclude that there is a deficit of protection in those countries where

[427] See Takahashi and Shimizu (2005: 58–9); Takahashi and Sakamoto (2005: 248–2).

[428] See Comberg (2000: 84 *et seq.*); Tomasic and Fu (1999: 166, 170 *et seq.*); Deng (2005: 356–7).

[429] Liu (2001: 11). Additionally, in 2003 the High Courts of Shanghai and Jiangsu promulgated rules according to which derivative actions were possible.

[430] See Tan (2000: 92).

[431] See Pißler (2001), (2002d); Deng (2005: 365 *et seq.*).

[432] See Ch. 8, section II.2.b.

there is less frequent recourse to litigation. Alongside the other conceivable enforcement mechanisms it should be borne in mind that the value of derivative suits to shareholders is not beyond doubt. Studies from the US found that derivative suits especially benefit the lawyers involved, but are in the end less important for shareholders.[433] Similarly, in Japan there is the view that the now rising number of actions cannot be justified by good profit prospects for shareholders.[434]

2. *Actions against resolutions of the general meeting*

Protection against abuse by the shareholder majority becomes acute particularly where resolutions of the general meeting threaten to injure the interests of the minority. All the legal systems studied here accordingly provide that individual shareholders can defend themselves against unlawful resolutions of the general meeting.

According to German law, the unlawfulness of a general-meeting resolution leads as a general rule only to voidability (§ 243 GerAktG). This means that, on the one hand, any shareholder opposed to the resolution can bring about a check on the decision, but, on the other hand, in the interests of legal certainty and of the shareholder majority, that the resolution cannot be challenged after the one-month time limit for appeal has expired (§ 246(1) GerAktG). Exceptionally, though, in particularly severe cases, a resolution is void by law (§ 241 GerAktG). Here too, however, an action for nullity with effect *inter omnes* is possible (§§ 249(1)(s.1), 248(1) GerAktG). Moreover, the resolution is deemed valid if no action for nullity has been lodged within three years of the resolution's entry in the commercial register (§ 242(2) GerAktG). The costs are in principle borne by the losing party (cf. § 91 GerZPO). However, the shareholder may, apart from a split of the amount at issue by § 247 GerAktG, minimize the risks of losing the case by reaching a settlement with the company. As extra pressure on the company, the shareholder was able to block entry of the resolution into the commercial register, since registry judges usually made use of the possibility of postponing its entry until a final decision had been made on the question of voidness (§ 127 GerFGG). This has led to abusive actions brought purely with the intention of having the 'nuisance value' paid off.[435] Where this intention can be demonstrated,

[433] See Romano (1993: 22); West (2001b: 358–9, 366).

[434] See West (2001b: 357 *et seq.*).

[435] See e.g. Schindler and Witzel (2001: 577 *et seq.*); Baums (2000: Ch. F 144 *et seq.*); Guntz (1997: 269 *et seq.*).

the claim will be dismissed.[436] By contrast, the requirement for provision of security was dropped in 1965. Calls to introduce a quorum or a minimum period of ownership, to require proof of an infringement of individual rights or to subject settlements to the obligation of judicial consent[437] have not been taken up by the legislature. However, a special shareholders' compensation procedure has gradually been extended[438] and made more effective,[439] with the aim of preventing obstructive actions. If the appropriateness of the compensation is separately tested, the threat to have the general-meeting decision wholly suspended or rescinded on those grounds alone may be dropped.[440] Moreover, the 2005 reform[441] has introduced a general release procedure, because courts can order that despite a pending claim against a decision by the general meeting it can be entered in the commercial register (§ 246a GerAktG).

Japanese law differentiates, on the German model, between actions to quash a resolution (i.e. actions for avoidance) and actions for declaration of the nullity of resolution (§§ 828–831 JapCA). The time limit for avoidance here is three months (§ 831(1) JapCA). Moreover, by contrast with the German model, the court may require the provision of security (§ 836(1) JapCA).

In China, since the 2005 reform, there has been an explicit provision which deals with unlawful decisions of the general meeting. An action for avoidance is necessary in case of violations of the articles and procedural provisions (e.g. regarding the convening of the general meeting) (§ 22(2) ChinCA). It has to be filed within sixty days, and the court may order the shareholder to provide security (§ 22(3) ChinCA). In contrast to this, all other resolutions passed contrary to laws and administrative rules are null and void (§ 22(1) ChinCA). Although it is not clearly stated, a claim to declare this nullity is probably admissible.[442]

436 BGH, BGHZ 107, 296; BGH, NJW 1992, 569.

437 See Hüffer, in: MünchKommAktG (2001: § 243 para. 15); Zöllner (1994: 339), (2000: 147); Decher, in: GroßkommAktG (2001: § 131 para. 54).

438 § 327a(1)(s.1) GerAktG (for squeeze-out); BVerfG, NJW 2001, 279 (*Moto Meter*) (for devolving liquidation); BGH, BGHZ 146, 179 (for violation of information rights in case of change of corporate form); BGH, BGHZ 153, 57 (*Macrotron*) (for delisting).

439 Spruchverfahrensgesetz (SpruchG) of 17.07.2003, BGBl. I 838.

440 BGH, BGHZ 146, 179 (*MEZ*); BGH, NJW 2001, 1428 (*Aqua-Butzke*); § 243(4)(s.2) GerAktG as amended by Gesetz zur Unternehmensintegrität und Modernisierung des Anfechtungsrechts (UMAG) of 22.09.2005, BGBl. I 2802.

441 Gesetz zur Unternehmensintegrität und Modernisierung des Anfechtungsrechts (UMAG) of 22.09.2005, BGBl. I 2802.

442 For the old law see Comberg (2000: 126 *et seq.*); Ranft (1999: para. 70); Thümmel (1995: 52).

At first sight French law a contains provisions only on the nullity of resolutions of the general meeting (Arts. L. 235-1 *et seq.* FrCCom). However, there is a distinction here, comparable in approach, between relative and absolute nullity.[443] With relative nullity, only the rights of particular persons are affected, and it is only through the judicial decision that the resolution of the general meeting is annulled. By contrast, if general principles are infringed, bringing absolute nullity, the finding is merely declaratory. Moreover, French law provides for one further distinction: by contrast with comprehensive review of legality for ordinary decisions, Art. L. 235-1(1) FrCCom puts amendments to the articles of association on a par with acts of foundation, so that in principle nullity is to be presumed only on the grounds explicitly mentioned in the Commercial Code. Finally, French courts can amend the general meeting's decision, so that – similar to the compensation procedure in Germany – a whole decision need not be rescinded because of a slight error.

In the UK and the US, there are no detailed statutory provisions, but the law results primarily from case law. And actions against general-meeting decisions, though admissible in principle,[444] tend to be of minor importance. By way of explanation for this, one could cite the higher proportion of companies in the US and the UK with dispersed shareholder ownership, since in such companies there is less danger of the general meeting's ignoring the interests of minority shareholders and therefore more likelihood of a general-meeting resolution being accepted by all. However, against this argument is the fact that in France too, despite a lower proportion of these kinds of companies, actions against general-meeting resolutions do not play any great part.[445] Conversely, for smaller companies in the US and the UK the possibility of action might indeed be interesting. However, there are substantive and procedural legal grounds in the way. Substantively, the 'majority rule' is more developed in the US and the UK,[446] so that, for instance, procedural errors are often irrelevant. Moreover, the appraisal rights which are particularly strong in the US,[447] may constitute a functional equivalent. Although these rights do not focus on the unlawfulness of a decision, they can make it unattractive or even impossible for a shareholder to take the more circuitous route of an action against a resolution of the general meeting. From a procedural viewpoint, it is first

443 Cf. Planck (1995: 168); Merle (2005: para. 487).

444 For the US see Cox and Hazen (2003: §§ 22.23, 23.02); for elections see also § 225(b) DelGCL; for the UK: *Edwards* v. *Halliwell* [1950] 2 All ER 1064, 1067 (Court of Appeal).

445 See Planck (1995: 178) (reference to burden of proof and costs).

446 See Ch. 5, section II.3.b above.

447 See Ch. 5, section II.2.c above.

decisive that, in the US and the UK no pure voidability of decisions is provided for. In the tradition of the *ultra vires* theory, now largely abandoned in relation to management actions, unlawful decisions are null even if not proceeded against in good time. It follows that shareholders are not under any pressure to challenge decisions as quickly and as often as possible. Secondly, preventive judicial measures are, at any rate in the US, usual and permissible, so that through a temporary order a shareholder may object even prior to a decision being made.

In summary, while in all countries studied here taking legal action against general-meeting resolutions is possible, reasons of legal certainty and majority protection often mean that mere voidability, time-limits for action or limited relevance for procedural errors are provided for. For the future, furthermore, it is doubtful whether such suits ought to be the primary means of protecting minority shareholders against the majority. On an investor-oriented view,[448] what suggests itself is mainly offering financial compensation – through liability provisions or appraisal rights. Moreover, one might also focus more strongly on shareholder-democracy considerations[449] and guarantee the propriety and validity of the outcome of the general meeting by activating it.

3. *Conclusions*

US law can be seen as the most developed with respect to both the legal admissibility of derivative suits and their practical importance. Usually this is explained by the following reasons.[450] First, judicial *ex post* protection in the US is seen as *a quid pro quo* for the greater permissiveness of state company law when compared to the company law of other countries, and for the deficits in the proxy rules of US securities law. Secondly, the greater importance of the capital market and disclosure obligations may be pointed to. Suits are typical specifically for informed shareholders in public companies with dispersed holdings. Otherwise, management errors may either not be sufficiently transparent or may already be sanctioned informally through the influence of blockholders. Thirdly, a US legal-cultural preference for litigation is frequently adduced, since here, by contrast with other countries, informal protection plays a smaller part ('order without law' v. 'order with law').

448 See Ch. 3, section I.3 above. 449 See Ch. 3, section I.2 above.

450 See Großfeld (2001: 32), (1971: paras. 4-256, 4-298, 4-331 *et seq.*); Cunningham (1999: 1183).

Although these explanations point to truths about the US, they are however more doubtful if the situation in other countries is brought into consideration. Thus, these causes basically also apply to the UK, without the derivative suit being as developed here as in the US. The converse is true for France. Although, on the traditional view, the arguments would be against derivative suits, the French provisions are favourable to them. Finally, developments in Japan argue against the traditional grounds of differentiation, since there one decisive factor was the mere reduction of costs.

This procedural influence can also be generalized. The different conditions to which adjudication is subject in the countries studied here are of considerable importance for the differences regarding the 'litigating shareholder'. For instance, this is true of the differences in cost provisions (e.g. the question of contingency fees or reimbursing the opponent's legal costs), the selection and qualification of judges (e.g. a selected jury v. professional judges),[451] the possibility of pre-trial discovery, the extent of judges' freedom of manoeuvre and the existence of a specialized legal profession.

All the same, the combination of substantive and procedural protective rights does display some convergence. On the one hand, even in the countries focused according to the traditional view more on *ex ante* control like Germany, France, Japan and China, recourse to the courts is open to shareholders on certain conditions. On the other hand, the disciplinary function of *ex post* control in the other countries is not absolute. Although a multiplicity of cases helps to make the case law certain, there is also an awareness, especially in the US, that too many suits may lead to considerable intimidation of management and thus be a brake on firms' growth.

IV. Conclusions to this chapter

As we saw with the 'person of the shareholder as such' (Ch. 4 above), the 'shareholder's position in the power structure of the company' is marked by cumulative characteristics: their own powers of decision, substantive protective provisions and possibilities of action are all intertwined, so that shareholders can, according to the legislators' intention, take precautionary measures or defend themselves against abuses by management or

[451] On the relevance of judges to the quality of company law, see also Enriques (2002: 775 *et seq.*).

majority shareholders. In detail, despite this basic agreement, differences may be noted, which often however cut across the subdivision into civil law, common law and Asian law countries. Instead, there are peculiarities in each of the legal systems studied here. These are, for instance, the minor qualified-majority limits and developed derivative suits in the US,[452] the strict neutrality duty on management in the event of hostile takeovers in the UK,[453] the particularly easy ways of dismissing management in France,[454] the law on groups of companies in Germany,[455] the extensive appraisal rights in Japan[456] and the general meeting's powers in relation to measures of conduct of business in China.[457] These differences are in part to be explained by the fact that particular regulatory variants can functionally replace each other, so that despite differing forms of shareholder protection there is no pressure to adapt. Moreover, convergence meets with obstacles particularly where, as for instance with the 'shareholder–stakeholder' issues or the 'litigating shareholder',[458] evaluations or legal rules lying outside of shareholder law have an influence.

452 See Ch. 5, sections I.2.a, III.1 above.

453 See Ch. 5, section II.1.a above.

454 See Ch. 5, section 1.c above.

455 See Ch. 5, section II.2.c above.

456 See Ch. 5, section II.2.c above.

457 See Ch. 5, section I.1.b above.

458 See Ch. 5, sections II.1.a, III.3 above.

6

Conclusions to Part II

The study so far has shown that, from a number of viewpoints, a convergence of the legal systems can even now be seen. This finding must, however, be further refined, so as also to bring out the connection with future development trends and development patterns (Part III below). Following a survey of indications of divergence and convergence (section I below), I will accordingly consider whether there is true convergence or merely a one-sided reception of US rules (section II below), or whether continuing factual differences mean there is merely artificial convergence (section III below).

I. Divergence and convergence

There are divergent developments to the extent that the traditional subdivision into different legal families in current shareholder law is no longer a convincing criterion of differentiation. For instance, there are clear differences between UK and US company and securities law. While the two countries have common roots and show basic similarities in the development of capital markets and in shareholding structures, for instance, the powers of their regulatory authorities, the federal structures, the extent of mandatory law, the availability of appraisal rights and the rules on derivative suits clearly differ. The same is true between France and Germany, for instance on questions of shareholder anonymity, of substantive review of decisions and of derivative suits. For Japan and China, apart from many differences in detail (for instance, on the powers of the general meeting and provisions on the distribution of profits), it is generally to be noted that China is in a transitional stage, whereas Japan has in the last 100 years established Western-influenced law.[1]

All the same, in the countries studied here convergence in shareholder law has come about. This can be seen, first, in the relevant legal bases (Ch. 2 above). While international and European law affect national company

[1] Ginsburg (2001: 34).

and securities law, this tends to be on a piecemeal basis, so that for shareholder law what continues to matter is national sources of law. But, for all the legal systems discussed here, there are similar basic patterns, with codifications of company and securities law being supplemented by case law, articles of association, shareholder agreements and corporate governance codes. Moreover, market forces play an important part, without a legal system necessarily on that account giving up statutory control mechanisms. Secondly, for the provisions on the 'shareholder as such' a subdivision into different legal families no longer makes sense (Ch. 4 above). Instead, the shareholder may, concordantly, be described by the adjectives 'profit-oriented', 'active' and 'informed'. There is no one-sided fixation on 'voice' or 'exit', so that shareholders in principle receive 'double safeguards'. Nonetheless, even the remaining detail differences may hamper the exercise of shareholder rights in foreign companies. The question accordingly arises whether, for instance, the provisions on minimum notice of convocation, voting proxies, multiple voting rights, voting caps, and rights of inspection may continue to differ in future. Thirdly, the 'shareholder's position in the power structure of the company' (Ch. 5 above) is also typified in all the countries studied here by cumulative characteristics, since the shareholder's own powers of decision, substantive protective provisions and possibilities to sue (the 'deciding', 'protected' and 'litigating' shareholder) interpenetrate. All the same, the legal specificities are more marked in this area, since functionally various alternatives often exist, and values or legal rules lying outside shareholder law play a greater role.

If this law is classified into the models of a typology of shareholders (Ch. 3 above), a varied picture emerges. In favour of the 'ownership analogy', for instance, is the fact that shareholders can in principle freely sell their shares, and are entitled to special rights. In the sense of the 'democratic model', however, there are also mechanisms intended to enable the company to have a self-governing organization. This also fits in with the fact that, alongside the powers of the general meeting, the interests of the overall organization and a division of powers and checks on power within the company are to be noted. In view of the company's ability to attract capital, finally, the 'shareholder as investor' also enters into the picture, because finance- or disclosure-related provisions of company and securities law are aimed primarily at them. Although legal systems often lay emphasis on one model type of shareholder, because for instance they provide for highly developed general-meeting powers or extensive disclosure rules, the overall legal situation is nonetheless a hybrid one.

This may seem surprising, since the *de facto* participation structures do still display the distinction between dispersed shareholder ownership and blockholder systems.[2] Contrary to the statements 'no one size fits all' and 'there is no single right form of organizational structure',[3] it is therefore possible for a legal system simultaneously to embrace different shareholder types. This can be explained by the fact that, despite the factual differences, there are even in common law countries closed and small companies with blockholdings, and in most other countries companies with dispersed holdings, so that everywhere regulatory forms have to be found for both types of company. This also means that the cumulative characteristics are not some incompatible syncretism, but constitute an appropriate synthesis.

De lege lata a 'combination principle' derives from this. Neither the model categories (owner, parliamentarian, investor) nor the adjectival types of shareholder (profit-oriented, active, informed, anonymous, deciding, protected, litigating) should be used to 'play off' one conception against another. Instead, it follows both from the historical development of company and securities law and from the pragmatic approach of the modern law-maker that, for instance, various mechanisms of good corporate governance interpenetrate.

II. Globalization and Americanization

The term 'convergence' means that changes in various legal systems lead to an approximation – but not to identity. That is to be distinguished from the situation where the law of one country is one-sidedly copied by other countries. This reception of foreign law is often seen in company and securities law as an increasing 'Americanization'.[4] What is true in this is that, most recently, continental Europe and Asia have copied a number of provisions from US law, without there being a converse feedback to US law. As the examples of corporate finance, proxy voting rules and securities regulation show,[5] these chiefly involve investor-related provisions. Law-makers in other countries thus wish to improve the ability of their companies to attract capital, because of intensified international

[2] See Ch. 8, section IV below. [3] Wymeersch (2001b: 294, 304–5); Hill (2000a: 41).

[4] Cf. Wiegand (2000); Hertig (2000: 270 *et seq.*); Noack (2000b: 1480); Assmann (2003); for Japan: Ködderitzsch (2001b: 143); Osugi (2002: 29); for transition economies: Coffee (2001: 12–13); generally see also Higgott and Reich (1998: 8); J. Wiener (1999: 197).

[5] See Ch. 4, sections I.4, II.4.a; Ch. 5, sections I.1.d, II.2.b, above; Ch. 4, section II.3.c above; Ch. 2, section III.1; Ch. 4, section III.2, Ch. 5, section II.1.b above.

competition. US law is particularly influential here because large foreign companies are often listed on US markets, US institutional investors have particular weight, and the US as a world power can exert political pressure.[6]

However, one may also adduce factors arguing against one-sided Americanization in shareholder law. One indication here comes from the OECD Corporate Governance Principles. While it has been said that they have an underlying Anglo-American tendency, so that their influence is less beneficial for other legal cultures,[7] against this is the fact that, for instance, German company law too largely corresponds to these principles.[8] In some provisions, moreover, it can be seen that – as the taking of the interests of all stakeholders into account shows[9] – the OECD Principles very much show a compromise nature. Secondly, US company, accounting and securities law has come under criticism after the recent crises. Such abuses as cronyism, lack of transparency and poor conduct of business, of which foreign legal systems were hitherto often accused in the US, are now occurring there too.[10] Moreover, a slow 'end of US hegemony' could be coming about in business life, since, for example, in the last twenty years the US share of world trade has fallen,[11] whereas Asia has become the world's fastest-growing region ('easternization'[12]). Thirdly, in the past it was not exclusively US concepts that were 'imported'. Experience in the Asian countries instead makes it clear that there has been a sort of 'cherry-picking', with elements of various legal systems being adopted.[13] For Europe, additionally, aspects of Americanization have been overlain by a Europeanization of commercial law, to that extent weakening the influence of (English) common law ('La civilisation de la common law'[14]). Fourthly, historical, political and cultural differences, regulatory competition and the more common dispersed shareholdings in the US may argue against a farther-reaching reception of US law.[15] However, it is equally conceivable for approximations to the US model to come about even given these circumstances (see Part III below).

[6] See generally Hertig (2000: 270 *et seq.*); see also Part III below.

[7] McCormack (2000: 58).

[8] Seibert (1999: 339); Claussen and Bröcker (2000: 486); Regierungskommission Corporate Governance (2001: para. 5).

[9] No. IV.A OECD-Principles 2004.

[10] On Enron see e.g. Coffee (2003).

[11] See Jacoby (2000: 28–9).

[12] Cf. Glenn (2004: 51, 338).

[13] See e.g. for Japan Ch. 4, sections I.2.a, II.3.a, c, 4.b, III.1.a, 3.b, IV.1.a; Ch. 5, sections I.1.b, d, 2.b, II.2.c, III.1, 2 above.

[14] Glenn (1993).

[15] See Hertig (2000: 272 *et seq.*).

III. Convergence and artificial convergence

So far, I have focused on 'formal', 'functional' and 'contractual' convergences.[16] In part, the positive law has been 'formally' approximated, by copying foreign law.[17] In other respects, despite varying regulatory concepts in the individual legal systems, 'functionally' comparable outcomes have sometimes been arrived at.[18] Moreover, in some cases contractual agreements are helping to uphold particular interests just as with statutory provisions.[19]

The question of *de facto* convergence has, by contrast, so far only been addressed piecemeal.[20] It is, however, necessary to look more comprehensively at the 'law in action'. On the one hand, the reasons underlying the convergence of law and perhaps its future continuance ('convergence forces') need to be elaborated. On the other hand, a restriction on the positive law would involve the risk that this might be only 'artificial convergence'. Even with similar legal provisions, it is not infrequent in the shareholder law of different countries for the practical consequences to be widely divergent.[21] This divergence between legal and *de facto* convergence appears particularly where company and securities law are comprehensively recast or newly introduced. In such cases, the competent courts and authorities, and also the managers and shareholders involved, may lack the practical experience of how to apply this law. Additionally, effective implementation also means that economic institutions, such as specialized auditors, lawyers and consultants, must also actually accept and make use of the new law. Finally, shortcomings in the rule of law must not be allowed to lead to mistrust in the share as an investment form. Apart from defects in judicial procedures, examples here are, above all, corruption, lack of legal consciousness, and political influence. For the future, accordingly, the question arises whether there will also be a 'convergence of law and reality'. If that happens,[22] it is likely that the law will similarly come closer together internationally.

16 On the term 'convergence' see also Ch. 1, section IV.1 above.

17 See e.g. the examples on Japan, note 13, above.

18 See e.g. Ch. 4, section I.2 (possibilities for management to determine amount of dividends) and Ch. 5, section II (ways of protecting shareholders).

19 See e.g. Ch. 4, section IV.3 (possibility of shareholders to remain anonymous) and Ch. 5, section I. c (appointment and removal of board members).

20 See e.g. Ch. 4, sections I.2.c, 3.d, II. b, 4.c; Ch. 5, sections II.1.a, III.3 above.

21 E.g.: for Japan: Milhaupt (1996: 14 *et seq.*), (2001: 2127); Kliesow (2001); Rodatz (1995: 247); Hayakawa (1996: 270); for China: Clarke (2006b); Tan (2000: 94); Thümmel (1995: 70 *et seq.*): for Germany: Lutter (1973: 26).

22 See Ch. 11, section III below.

PART III

Developmental trends and patterns

In the social sciences there have often been attempts to establish that historical development is oriented towards a particular goal and is thus moving inexorably in one direction. This 'historicism' and 'determinism', attributed to, for instance, Plato, Hegel and Marx,[1] were rightly attacked by Sir Karl Popper,[2] who denied that the course of world history is borne by absolute laws. Since we cannot today know what knowledge we shall have tomorrow (otherwise we should already have it), it is impossible to predict the future course of history with certainty. Individual knowledge can accordingly not be extended into a universal statement ('problem of induction'[3]). Additionally, the conduct of individuals acting on their own responsibility is subject to errors, so that for this reason too history is open and not subject to any automatism.

Yet this does not mean that an agnostic position is justified. Even if there are no stringent regularities, there may nonetheless be historical forces that allow developmental trends to be perceived and forecasts to be made. The findings of Part II have already made clear how far the convergent development in shareholder law can be seen at present. These considerations will be extended below. To this end, it is first of all necessary to study the way law-making functions, and the regulatory levels decisive for convergence (Ch. 7 below). There follows an examination of some convergence forces (Chs. 8 and 9 below). Finally, I will enquire into possible consequential effects on shareholder law (Ch. 10 below).

The wider purpose of this part is, on the one hand, to analyze the context of legal change in shareholder law in order to provide a general understanding of the forces which shape legal development in commercial law. On the other hand, this analysis has a political dimension. If, for instance, it were found that convergence does not require formal harmonization, advocates of uniform rules would not need to press the EU

[1] More recently, the names P. Kennedy (1987), Chandler (1990), Fukuyama (1992) and Kissinger (1994) could be added.

[2] Popper (1944/1987), (1958/1992).

[3] See Popper (1934/1994).

or other organizations for further harmonizations. And, if, for instance, it were found that convergence leads to a 'race to the bottom', advocates of stakeholder interests would be encouraged to demand a restriction or channelling of the convergence forces. Thus, Part III is also linked to Part IV, which will discuss whether convergence should be seen as a model for the future.

7

Bases

This introductory chapter addresses two important preliminary points for the future convergence of shareholder law. The first section analyzes how law-making functions and to what extent factual and political factors mark shareholder law (section I below). Secondly, it is clarified who exactly the decisive law-making institutions are. Thus, it is discussed whether in the future national acts of parliament or rather international and informal regulations will be of primary interest (sections II and III below).

I. The dependency of shareholder law

It appears to be likely that actual development and the influence of interest groups are reflected in the law. This causal relationship is not, however, a matter of course. It might also be that, conversely, law primarily influences reality, and political decision-makers feel committed to the common weal and not to private interests. Thus, it has to be clarified in which direction causality goes (subsection 1 below), why law-making institutions act in a particular way (subsection 2 below), and what role interest groups play (subsection 3 below).

1. The causality problem

There are differing views on the interaction between law and reality in company and securities law. One view stresses the importance of law (the 'law matters' thesis). First, the institutional advantages of the joint stock company as a legal form are highlighted. When in the nineteenth century restrictions on the establishment of joint stock companies were removed, waves of foundations followed, since it then became possible to pursue capital-intensive projects in a permanent, differentiated organizational form.[1] Secondly, it is asserted that for actual developments the extent of

[1] Cf. Horn (1979: 176–7).

legal protection for shareholders is decisive.[2] Depending on the pattern of shareholder protection, there are differing finance and participation structures: With a low level of protection, concentrated shareholdings are said to dominate, since the demand for shares is small and a shareholder needs many shares in order actually to be able to protect himself. By contrast, good shareholder protection motivates more investors to invest in shares and thus leads to a broader distribution.

Sometimes, however, the causality relationship is also presented as being that actual developments precede the legal development (the 'history matters' thesis,[3] the 'law follows' thesis[4]). The joint stock company is seen as a 'cultural product' and a 'legal form for industrialization', so that company law is a 'mirror of economic developments'.[5] Only if strong markets exist and shareholders become powerful groups does legislation react and protects shareholder interests.[6] By contrast, it is scarcely possible for legislation to proactively anticipate problems it has not yet seen. Receptions of foreign law are accordingly mostly not effective.[7] Instead, the reforms of company law are seen as reflecting a seismographic picture of changes in society and its economic policy programmes.[8] This connection is also underpinned using the history of company and securities law in the US and the UK. In the US, in the nineteenth century, no effective legal protection of shareholders was guaranteed. Yet industrialization increased the number of investors and the importance of the capital market. Initially, checks by investment banks, and later also stock exchange regulations, operated as protective mechanisms.[9] It was only in the twentieth century that in securities law statutory regulations arrived, since it emerged that self-regulation was not always effective and shareholders could now emerge as a strong lobby.[10] The development in the UK was comparable: until the end of the nineteenth century, the law displayed no substantive protection for minority shareholders. Only thereafter was there a gradual enhancement of protection through accounting, stock exchange and securities law, and it was, for instance, only in 1980

[2] La Porta *et al.* (1998); see also Ch. 1, section I above, and Ch. 8, section IV.1.a below.
[3] Heine and Kerber (2002: 53).
[4] Hansmann and Kraakman (2001: 454–5); see also Vagts (2000: para. 10-23).
[5] Citations by Großfeld (2002: 8); Wilhelm (1998: para. 11); Horn (1979: 174).
[6] Coffee (2001: 80).
[7] Berkowitz *et al.* (2003a and 2003b); Coffee (2002a: 86).
[8] Assmann, in: GroßkommAktG (1992: Einl. para. 183; also para. 236).
[9] See Coffee (2002a: 94 *et seq.*).
[10] Coffee (2002a: 85, 91–2, 104); Cheffins (2003a: 7 *et seq.*).

that insider dealing was criminalized, and overall shareholder protection strengthened.[11]

It might, however, also be deduced from this that on the whole the importance of legal rules by comparison with other factors is secondary (the 'triviality thesis' or 'irrelevance thesis').[12] According to these, actual and economic development often run independently of the development of company and securities law. In the national context, a causal relationship is opposed by the fact that natural resources, the education system, monetary policy, product competition and cultural and demographic factors are of more decisive importance for economic development.[13] And, from a legal viewpoint, banking and fiscal law and the rule of law[14] in particular are more important than details of shareholder law. Internationally, moreover, it is more the economic strength of a country than its law that attracts investors.[15] In practical terms, this can be confirmed for the US, which despite improved shareholder protection in the twentieth century saw the concentration of shareholdings increase slightly.[16] And, on the one hand, in the nineteenth century in France, a technically good company law (for the time) did not particularly promote industrial development, on an international comparison.[17] On the other hand, for instance, in China, even before adoption of the ChinCA 1993, strong economic growth came about without any legally sophisticated corporate governance.[18]

On the whole, the various examples make it clear that the causal relation between legal and economic development cannot simply be answered in one direction or the other. Instead of a monocausal interpretation, the point is to follow the interactions between law and facts. Since the object of this study is, however, shareholder law, this appears not on the factual side but on that of consequences. The point below will accordingly be which (convergence) forces the legislator takes as a guide. In this respect, looking at the public choice theory can be of particular use.

[11] See Cheffins (2001c: 88 *et seq.*), (2001a: 459 *et seq.*), (2003a: 12 *et seq.*); Coffee (2002a: 100 *et seq.*), (2001: 42–3).

[12] B. Black (1990b); Easterbrook and Fischel (1991); for a different view see West (2001a: 530–1); see also Roe (2003a: 7) ('the mechanical rules and institutions could be the same, but if politics sharply differs, so might the corporate results').

[13] See Branson (2001: 329–30); McDonnell (2002: 380).

[14] See Pistor *et al.* (2000) (for developing countries).

[15] Branson (2001: 329). [16] See Roe (2002: 250 note 24); Rock (1995: 294).

[17] Horn (1979: 177). [18] Liu (2001: 34).

2. *The public choice theory*

The public choice theory lies in the interdisciplinary field between political and economic science. Its explanation for political happenings may however, very well, be of interest to legal research too.[19] The main argument of the public choice theory is that, by contrast with the public interest theory, the content and direction of regulation are determined by the self-interested conduct of voters, parties, politicians and bureaucrats.[20] Since efficiency and the common weal mean different things to different individuals and groups, politics does not follow an objectively definable efficiency or common weal of the whole people.[21] Instead, the law constitutes a response to (quasi-) market forces, so that the modern apparatus of economic theory can be applied to the analysis of politics.

a) Voters, parties and politicians

Voters decide as 'homines oeconomici' for the political party promising them the highest net utility.[22] For instance, the economic situation and the unemployment rate have great influence on voter behaviour. Private interests may also be promoted by sending one's own representatives to parliaments and supporting particular politicians. The limits to rationalizability, however, lie in the fact that on many political questions voters cannot determine the relative benefit, so that, for instance, questions of competence are ordinarily not determined by the voters' will. There may also be 'rational apathy' among voters where they are of the opinion that their vote is in any case not decisive, so that the effort to inform themselves and vote is not worth it.[23]

Following Anthony Downs,[24] the prevailing view of the public choice theory holds that political parties want primarily to gain votes and therefore influence. This opportunism does not, however, mean a complete abandonment of ideologies. Instead, party programmes are intended to lower information costs, since over-differentiated opinions are not transparent to voters, and would therefore not offer the parties a better chance of success. The objectives of political parties thus lead to a crude guidance of policy, which however still needs fine-tuning for the parties elected.

[19] See also Cheffins (1997: 19 *et seq.*).
[20] Downs (1968: 27); Franke (1996: 11, 17); Behrends (2001: 7–8).
[21] Stigler (1971); Peltzman (1976); Schumpeter (1987: 397 *et seq.*); see also Licht (1998: 265–6); Hantke-Domas (2003).
[22] On what follows see Frey (1980: 660 *et seq.*).
[23] See Downs (1968: 240), and Ch. 4, section II.1.b above (on shareholders).
[24] Downs (1968); see also Schumpeter (1987).

This relates to the behaviour of politicians.[25] Politicians too do not primarily act to attain the best for the citizen. Instead, the public choice theory replaces the 'benevolent dictator' by the 'selfish democrat'. Government and parliamentary majority have neither the possibility nor the incentive to pursue a policy that maximizes social welfare. Instead, on the one hand, private interests like the search for power, income and prestige, and the need for re-election, are decisive. On the other hand, political decision-makers, like the government and also, for instance, the central bank, are endogenous components of the overall social system. Laws are thus enacted in a ramified process between internal and external decision-makers, where along with the bureaucracy and interest groups (subsection 3 below), with involvement of the public and academics, a package of objectives able to secure consensus has to be found.

b) Problems of application

The public choice theory is an important aid in questions of convergence in shareholder law. Since in commercial law often only purely financial interests are present, it is particularly likely that those producing regulations will primarily act pragmatically. And the convergence perceptible in the present law (Part II above) has already made clear that in shareholder law legislators, in harmony with the public choice theory, do not (necessarily) follow clear ideologies or traditional legal cultures, but are influenced by social forces.

Nonetheless, for the present study special features are to be borne in mind, on the side of both voters and decision-makers, as follows.

For voter behaviour, this applies particularly to the law of China. The public choice theory normally relates to democratic societies, so that considerations of the personal interests of voters and various parties cannot to that extent be used here. However, this fact need not necessarily be reflected in differences in shareholder law. For Western democracies too, the efficiency of political competition is doubted, since by comparison with competition over goods it involves not a thing but a package of ideas with only a small number of suppliers.[26] Additionally, shareholder law is scarcely an electoral issue, and is thus mostly not 'political law'. One exception is the debate on the accountability of multinational enterprises.[27] Another is where in cases of hostile takeovers or severe cases of abuse (e.g. Enron in the US) questions of corporate governance affect a

[25] On what follows see Frey (1980: 666); Franke (1996: 68 *et seq.*).

[26] Pappenheim (2001: 49 *et seq.*). [27] See Ch. 7, section II.1 below.

broader range of persons so that more intensive exchange with the public comes about.[28]

For the conduct of decision-makers it is, for instance, problematic that in the countries studied here the parliaments have different compositions. Apart from the number of parties represented in the parliament, this also concerns the professional and social background of politicians. Additionally, the political decision-making process differs in the individual countries, as therefore also does, for instance, openness to influence from private interest groups.[29] Finally, the public choice theory usually analyzes the behaviour of the national legislator. But shareholder law is not confined to this, because international and soft law have some importance as well (sections II and III below).

3. *The influence of interest groups*

Business associations, trade unions, other interest groups and individual companies have an interest in seeing their views taken into account by political decision-makers. Accordingly, national legislators as well as the executive branch and international and supranational organizations are acted on by various interest groups. This behaviour and its effects on the political decision-making process are studied by meso-economics, (general) political science, the public choice theory and constitutional legal theory.

The background to meso-economics is that micro- and macro-economics are basically confined to firms and the overall economy respectively, thus not adequately embracing the behaviour of groups and associations. In the area in between ('meso') macro- and micro-economics, accordingly, meso-economics, developed by Hans-Rudolf Peters, studies the interaction of organized interest groups and structural-policy decision-makers.[30] Intensive use is, however, made of findings of the neighbouring sciences, so that for the present overview no detailed presentation is necessary.

(General) political science considers mainly the methods used by interest groups and associations to influence policies. These are, for example, according to Klaus von Beyme, corruption and bribery, persuasion, friendly contacts, threats, coercion, violence, non-violent resistance and alternative strategies, and according to Peter Bernholz market power,

[28] For hostile takeovers see also Ch. 9, section VI.2.b; Ch. 10, section II.2.a below.

[29] See Ch. 7, section I.3.; Ch. 9, section VI.2.b below.

[30] Peters (1981).

information gathering, information superiority, financial support to politics, social disruptive potential and influences on appointments.[31] A special form of influence is present where interest groups are 'incorporated' into policy development. This sort of corporatism existed in the former class society in which public order was conveyed to social organizations. Today's 'neo-corporatism' is to be distinguished from the action of a pure pressure group, where interest groups 'merely' exert influence through discourse-oriented communication and argument. For it to be incorporated into new forms of governance, it is necessary for networks of politicians and interest groups to emerge through mutual negotiation and bargaining. Interest groups may thus directly participate in the political opinion-forming and decision-making process, and become high-ranking or even equal partners of politics.[32] In this respect, a further distinction is made between macro- and meso-corporatism. In macro-corporatism, the interaction of state, unions and business associations to solve pan-social problems is of primary importance. Meso-corporatism (or sectoral corporatism) covers the relationship between associations and the state in specific policy areas, containing as further sub-areas collective self-regulation and collective involvement in law-making.

In political assessment, it could be advanced in favour of influence or participation by interest groups that the state can thus come to terms with the holders of social power, unburden its own resources and enable stable control closer to the problem.[33] However, lobbying and neo-corporatism are often perceived critically. Reference is made particularly to the findings of the public choice theory. The public choice theory starts from the position that not all groups in society can be equally well organized. Collective action in a common interest group may lower transaction costs and thus make influence more effective. Then, however, it has to be distinguished: smaller groups possess a comparative advantage in relation to large groups.[34] Small groups are more stable and less exposed to the danger of the free-rider effect,[35] since here the individual members' interest in the collective good is greater, and those involved are easier to press into joining. Furthermore, groups differ in their opportunity to influence because economically strong groups can put more pressure on

[31] Von Beyme (1980); Bernholz (1969); similarly Frey (1980: 661–2); Pappenheim (2001: 68 *et seq.*).

[32] Franke (1996: 34); similarly Leggewie (2003: 158 *et seq.*); see also Behrends (2001: 131 *et seq.*, 153–4, 210, 214 *et seq.*).

[33] See von Alemann (2000).

[34] Olson (1965).

[35] See also Ch. 4, section II.1.b above.

the state by refusing their services and are thus more 'conflict-capable'.[36] Since interest mediation is thus distorted, an overall asymmetrical distribution of power arises. Additionally, the influence and participation of interest groups may operate at the expense of an economic policy favouring competition. If particular interest groups were able directly or indirectly to secure policy advantages, the danger would threaten that this rent-seeking behaviour would replace profit seeking and render market forces ineffective.

These reservations build a bridge to the considerations of constitutional legal theory. Here, on the one hand the limits and problems of influence by interest groups are explored. The participation of private persons brings the danger of an occupation of the state by non-representative group interests. Were the special interests of individuals brought to the fore, the view for the common weal as a whole would be lost, detrimentally to the democratic principle.[37] On the other hand, Armin von Bogdandy emphasizes that the co-operation of interest groups may be justified through the postulate of the state's real power of control ('Postulat realer Steuerungsmacht des Staates'). The participation of private interest groups may guarantee proper and effective law-making. Co-operation also serves preventive protection of worthy interests. Additionally, on a controversial view, the democratic principle may be adduced in justification, since private organizations are better able than political parties to bring the will of population groups into the political process.[38] All in all, accordingly, such terms as co-operation principle, private–public partnership, co-regulation, and enforced self-regulation[39] denote the ambivalent attitude of legal academia towards the influence of private interest groups on the political process.

4. *Conclusion*

The development of company law does not follow deterministically solely from factual factors. Nonetheless, shareholder law is 'dependent' in at least three respects. First, examples from history show that legal development

[36] See Behrends (2001: 59).

[37] See von Arnim (1977: 130 *et seq.*, 163 *et seq.*); Reicherzer (2005); similarly the 'new republicans' in the US, see e.g. Michelman (1988); Sunstein (1985).

[38] See von Bogdandy (2000: 64, 68–9, 70 *et seq.*, 74 *et seq.*); Ladeur (2003: 20).

[39] For the first see von Bogdandy (2000: 79): for the second see Leggewie (2003: 27); for the last two see J. Black (1996: 26); Ogus (2000: 596); on co-regulation see also European Governance – A White Paper, COM(2001) 428, at 27–8.

is at least also a reflection of economic circumstances (subsection 1 above). Secondly, this finding can be confirmed by the public choice theory, which also says that external influence from third parties and the decision-makers' own interests come into the law-making process (subsection 2 above). Thirdly, interest groups play a part that should not be under-estimated (subsection 3 above). Where the influence of interest groups becomes similar internationally or they become active across various countries, their power may influence the law in similar ways, thus leading to convergence.

II. Regulatory levels of shareholder law

The dependency of shareholder law and thus any possible convergence forces may be reflected at various regulatory levels. One must accordingly investigate whether in a globalized economy national laws can be evaded and thus in practice devalued (subsection 1 below), and how the mixture of international, regional and national legal bases[40] will develop further (subsections 2 and 3 below).

1. Multinational firms and national law

It is often said that for multinational firms the importance of the national legislator is reduced with globalization.[41] These firms are allegedly more powerful than many states, and are often not subject to the state's laws, but can pursue their strategies largely autonomously. Multinational firms can, for instance, by shifting production or transferring their profits to subsidiaries, escape the grip of a particular national legal system. Additionally, they may even become 'stateless firms',[42] because government action is territorially delimited so that a 'negative conflict of jurisdiction' may come about in which no national law is applicable or enforceable. Accordingly, in future national law will allegedly not matter so much. What will instead be more important is how, through the law of international organizations, international arbitration and international trade usages, a regulatory structure for multinational firms can be developed.

40 See Ch. 2 above.

41 On what follows cf. Higgott and Reich (1998: 2); Großfeld (1995: 5 *et seq.*, 331); Herdegen (2002: § 2 para. 35, § 3 para. 37); similarly Dahrendorf (2002).

42 Grant (2000: 3).

This 'hyper-globalist view' is denied by the 'realists', 'internationalists', 'regionalists' or 'relativists'.[43] They presume that decisive influence remains with the nation states. Each undertaking is founded in accordance with a national legal system, so that for that reason the national legislator is of decisive importance even for multinational undertakings. Additionally, at the global level, there is no effective enforcement of law, and in other respects too the international commercial law is full of gaps. Nor is any comprehensive global standard to be expected for the future, in view of the consensus nature essential to international conventions. International or regional law may thus supplement national law, but there is no global law as an autonomous legal system, so that a link back to national law does not become superfluous.

In my view, it has to be differentiated according to individual areas of law. Globalization is more important for some areas of law (e.g. securities law) and less so for others (e.g. real-estate law). Company law is an ambivalent case. On the one hand, even transnational enterprises have no international legal capacity,[44] but are, apart from a few exceptions (e.g. the Societas Europaea), national entities, for which reason alone national law remains of decisive importance. On the other hand, for investors and perhaps also for founders of companies the possibility remains of 'fleeing' abroad.[45] These possibilities of avoidance thus mean that the national legislator may very well lose autonomy. Additionally, distinctions have to be drawn according to whether international and regional regulations affect shareholder law directly or indirectly.

2. *Internationalization*

The employment of direct, mandatory international regulation is rather unlikely in shareholder law. While worldwide company-law standards might be regarded as desirable, since global markets call for global framework regulations,[46] harmonization by direct, mandatory law, still less a supranational global legal form of the joint stock company, is not to be expected, given political resistance. Nonetheless, even now a number of international regulations indirectly affect company and securities law. This is true particularly of the liberalization of the movement of goods, services and capital promoted by international organizations (IMF, World

[43] Cf. Gessner and Budak (1998: 3 *et seq.*); Neyer (1998: 404 *et seq.*); Doremus *et al.* (1998: 3); Higgott and Reich (1998: 2).

[44] Großfeld (1995: 38 and 325) (for a different view).

[45] See Ch. 9, section I.1, III.1 below.

[46] See e.g. Farrar (1998: 751); Stober (1999: 1176); Stiglitz (2006: 21).

Bank, WTO, OECD). It might follow from this that the structure of companies will become more similar internationally, with shareholders being able to exert pressure on their national legislator through the possibility of moving abroad, thus bringing convergence in the law.[47]

Additionally, international soft law may constitute an alternative to mandatory law. Where there are agreements among states below the threshold of law, their sovereignty is protected. Entirely private rule-making mechanisms, as is even today the case in the areas of accounting and arbitration, are conceivable in commercial law in general. For shareholder law, one might point here particularly to the importance of the OECD Principles of Corporate Governance. First, for the legislatures of developing countries, they constitute a matrix for balanced good corporate governance.[48] Secondly, the OECD Principles are also a standard whereby the IMF and World Bank decide to make loans.[49] Thirdly, investors take the OECD Principles into account. This is also fostered by the fact that rating agencies use the OECD Principles in order to rank companies' quality of corporate governance.[50] Fourthly, the reasons that in the UK led to the comprehensive Combined Code also exist in comparable fashion at international level. In the UK, these reasons were notable scandals in the economy, privatizations of national enterprises, an active financial press, the growing interest in shares, pressure from non-governmental organizations and institutional investors, and the threat of a recession. Comparable factors can be discerned internationally too. This background is also mentioned in the foreword to the OECD Principles of 2004:

> The Principles have now been thoroughly reviewed to take account of recent developments and experiences [. . .] Policy makers are now more aware of the contribution good corporate governance makes to financial market stability, investment and economic growth. Companies better understand how good corporate governance contributes to their competitiveness [. . .] As companies play a pivotal role in our economies and we rely increasingly on private sector institutions to manage personal savings and secure retirement incomes, good corporate governance is important to broad and growing segments of the population.

[47] See Ch. 8, section III, IV; Ch. 9, section III, VI.3 below.

[48] See Ch. 2, section I.1 above; Pißler (2002d: para. 1) (for the influence on China); Kim (2001: 34) (for the influence on South Korea).

[49] Reports on the Observance of Standards and Codes (ROSCs) of the IMF, available at http://www.imf.org/external/np/rosc/rosc.asp; see also OECD-Principles 2004, at 9.

[50] See Sherman (2004: 7).

Nonetheless, the importance of the OECD Principles should not be either over-estimated or under-estimated. It is, for instance, over-sceptical to state that there can be no globally uniform corporate governance principles because each country has developed a model of its own on the basis of differing cultural, social and legal conditions.[51] By contrast with the traditional view, this study has found no fundamentally differing systems of present shareholder law, and an approximation might come about in factual respects too.[52] However, the OECD Principles also have limits. They are not supposed to be a uniform code but offer different possibilities as to what good corporate governance may look like. They also do not act globally, but only internationally. This means that, while they contribute to the emergence of international approximations, they do not constitute a sufficiently detailed quasi-legal regime for worldwide shareholder law.

3. *Regionalization*

As well as international organizations, supranational regions may also gain importance. While this may be associated with a danger of regional compartmentalization strategies leading to a fragmentation of the world economy and renewed bloc formation,[53] this is not a necessary outcome. Regional agreements may also be seen as 'small-scale internationalization', whereby particular rules around which global consensus has not yet been found is first anticipatorily applied to a particular region. Since its meaning and purpose would then lie in promotion of the regions but not in discriminating against third countries, this sort of 'open regionalism', as attributed for instance to the EU,[54] could promote globalization and convergence more than hinder them.

Specifically for shareholder law, though, it is by no means clear whether advancing European harmonization will come about. Against it is, first, that specific shareholder-law provisions have scarcely been harmonized yet. The failure of the Fifth Company Law Directive and the deliberate gaps in the regulation of the Societas Europaea and in the Takeover Directive can accordingly be seen as indications of considerable resistance to harmonization in this area.[55] Although harmonizing of some rules on

[51] Schneider (2000: 2415). [52] See Part II above, and Ch. 8 below.
[53] Herdegen (2002: § 9 para. 7); Luttermann (1999: 773–4).
[54] Grant (2000: 7–8). [55] See Ch. 2, section I.2 above.

shareholder law for public companies is now under way,[56] this will not lead to the end of 'national company law'. It follows in particular from the principle of minimum harmonization and the subsidiarity principle (Art. 5 EC) that comprehensive harmonization of European company law is not to be expected. Additionally, the effects of the ECJ decisions in the *Centros*, *Überseering* and *Inspire Art* cases are to be taken into account.[57] These decisions have facilitated the foundation and mobility of companies within the EU. It is accordingly conceivable that in regulatory competition some Member States will seek to attract investors by deregulated company law and thus block further harmonization by directives.[58] Also in favour of this is the call sometimes made in the literature for harmonization in the EU to pay less attention than hitherto to substantive law than to conflict of laws.[59]

These limits make it clear that convergence through harmonization is likely to look rather spotty, both in the supranational context and in content. In line with this, the report of the Commission's Action Plan constitutes a response to current debates and to abuses in the area of corporate governance, more than an internally cohesive reform concept.[60] Similarly, for securities law it is said that a European Securities Commission is not to be expected, or only if there is some great scandal.[61]

One conceptual alternative to formal law for the EU too might be soft law. Among the possibilities being discussed here are the introduction of European corporate governance codes and model statutes.[62] One argument for self-regulation at this level might be that this would, by contrast with global regulations, avoid cultural and legal friction.[63] This argument can, however, be attacked from two sides. On the one hand, Europe-wide soft law could be regarded as too far-reaching: a European corporate governance code would be premature since in view of the differences in national law joint statements on the management of all public companies are allegedly scarcely possible.[64] The same argument applies against model statutes. The US example of the MBCA can allegedly not be

[56] See Art. 17 of the Transparency Directive 2004/109/EC; Directive 2007/35/EC; Modernising Company Law and Enhancing Corporate Governance in the European Union – A Plan to Move Forward, Communication from the Commission, COM(2003) 284, at 13–14; for a critical comment see Siems (2005f).

[57] See Ch. 9, section I.1.a below.

[58] See also Ch. 9, section VI.1.b below.

[59] Wymeersch (2001a).

[60] See Ch. 2, section I.2 above.

[61] Coffee (2001: 23).

[62] Ebke (1999a: 661), (1999b: 212 *et seq.*).

[63] Cf. Seibert (1999: 339).

[64] High Level Group of Company Law Experts (2002: 72); Modernising Company Law and Enhancing Corporate Governance in the European Union – A Plan to Move Forward, Communication from the Commission, COM(2003) 284, at 11–12.

transferred to the European company-law landscape, based on different concepts, both in legal systematics and sociologically. At best, for voting proxies, say, model rules might be conceivable by way of informal and organic convergence.[65] On the other hand, going on from what was said in Part II of this book, it should be pointed out that in shareholder law there has already been considerable convergence between common law and civil law countries. Nor does Asian law constitute a special legal family here, since in broad areas it is a mixture of US and European influences. Additionally, globally operating institutions (international organizations, financial institutions, investors etc.) will value compliance with minimum standards not just in particular regions but worldwide. On the whole, thus, a stage model seems likely: some basic standards might be set up through worldwide soft law; other more detailed provisions are conceivable only at regional or – if enough consensus cannot be found – at national level.

4. Conclusion

It is not to be expected that in shareholder law national law will become obsolete through possibilities of avoidance or international and regional law. Even if in individual cases multinational enterprises may be able to avoid legal constraints, and internationalization and regionalization is likely to advance, no fundamental paradigm shift is to be expected here: a company is in principle established according to national company law and is therefore tied to it.

III. Regulatory forms at the national level

At the national level, the focus on shareholder law will be primarily on codifications of company and securities law. To be sure, other sources of law should also be brought into consideration. How the mixture in contemporary law[66] will develop is, however, far from certain.

1. Statute and case law

The influence of the quality of adjudication is not to be under-estimated. If the courts are hesitant over enforcing the law, it may be that despite high-grade statutes the law remains inefficient, whereas by contrast active

[65] High Level Group of Company Law Experts (2002: 32). [66] See Ch. 2, section II above.

judges may be able to supplement lacunae in the positive law through case law. For instance, it is stressed for the US that Delaware's case law has been a decisive factor for its success in regulatory competition:[67] the volume of judicial decisions and the expertise of the courts made Delaware particularly attractive since its well-developed case law provides predictability for structuring transactions, and is also more flexible and dynamic than statutory law only.[68]

Nonetheless, for convergence of shareholder law statutes are more important than courts. The codification ideal has in principle won the day.[69] In an area like company law, structural problems cannot be tackled, nor legal certainty adequately ensured, through case law alone. Additionally, statutes are easier to transplant than case law. For instance, for the US it has been said that, because of the difficulty of copying judge-made law, Delaware's competitive advantage today can no longer be equalled.[70] Additionally, reception of foreign law generally starts from codified law. To the extent that in the (Anglo-)American common law area case law still shapes the law, no Americanization[71] can be expected. The German Association for Technical Co-operation (GTZ), which *inter alia* promotes the spread of German law in China, has accordingly stated:

> In principle the Anglo-Saxon concept of law is ill-suited to adaptation for countries in transformation, for lack of a mature tradition of adjudication. This can also be seen in the fact that many former British colonies have recognized British higher courts as the last instance long after independence. For a sovereign transformation country like China, this is excluded. Accordingly, the Continental legal tradition is better suited.[72]

2. *Company and securities law*

Since shareholder law can be shaped through both company and securities law,[73] distinctions have to be drawn for the development of convergence in that respect too. There are indications that for securities law the convergence might be more marked. A developed capital market enables large firms to meet their capital needs, innovative enterprises to be financed and free financial resources to be efficiently allocated. This also requires good company law. Yet, as the US example shows, differences

[67] On regulatory competition in the US see Ch. 9, section I.1, VI.1.a below.
[68] See Romano (1993: 33, 37 *et seq.*).
[69] See Ch. 2, section II above.
[70] Kamar (1998).
[71] See also Ch. 6, section II above.
[72] Own translation; original text available on request.
[73] See Ch. 2, section III above.

in company law can very well be 'lived with', whereas with securities law largely uniform provisions may be necessary.[74] Also in favour of convergence is the fact that an increasing number of companies are listed on several stock exchanges.[75] Since in this case in principle the same stock exchange and securities law applies to companies from various countries, the law has also to take account of peculiarities of foreign companies.[76] Otherwise, problems would arise for firms with shares listed on various exchanges, because they would have to comply with contradictory provisions, thus endangering the tradability of their shares. Also in favour of convergence is the point that in securities law, alongside parliaments, law-making by exchanges and supervisory authorities plays an important part. These institutions are often more open to business influences, so that the interest of firms and investors in internationally similar regulations can be reflected here.[77] Finally, securities law can balance out the diversification between small and large firms and take account of their specific interests. For smaller firms the need for flexibility is greater, and the need for protection of the public less. By contrast, different criteria have to be applied to global players, and legislation cannot afford to overlook them. It is also to be expected that in future, alongside the distinction between joint stock companies and private limited companies,[78] the question whether a company offers shares to the public will be decisive. Since such companies approach a broad range of addressees, their more fragmented and more international shareholder structure requires, for instance, specific forms of communication, information and protection. Additionally, this link will avoid frictions that may arise from national differences in the frequency of utilization of small-company legal forms.[79]

The advance of securities law also ought to (further)[80] enhance the flexibility of company law. If, internationally, capital markets become more efficient, company law can allow more room for private contracting. Additionally, an internationalized capital market exerts a disciplining function on the national legislator, so that, for reasons of competitiveness, pressure for change may be exerted on over-regulated company law. Much the same is true of other areas of market-led control. The increasingly stronger markets for company founders, corporate control, investors, managers and products thus produce some pressure for deregulation.

[74] See Coffee (1999b: 652). [75] See Ch. 8, section III.4.c below.

[76] See also MacNeil and Lau (2001: 810) (listing rules as 'mechanism for the creation and enforcement of hybrid systems of corporate regulation'); for particular provisions on foreign companies see also Ch. 8, section III.4.c below.

[77] See Licht (1998: 279 *et seq.*). [78] See Ch. 1, section II.1 above.

[79] See Ch. 1, section III above. [80] See Ch. 2, section IV.1 above.

Yet it would be too simple to say that the possibility of private contracting in the case of private companies and market forces for public companies will now make convergence of the articles of association in general of primary interest. The dialectic whereby regulation of the capital market is accompanied by deregulation of company law[81] is true for the US. Worldwide, however, the fact that many regulatory complexes (e.g. voting proxies) may be covered by both areas of law runs counter to this. Additionally, the danger of market failure sets a limit to deregulation, so that also in company law particular mechanisms of incentives and controls may be necessary. Moreover, even if a solution through the market were possible, no deregulation may come about. Since the findings of the public choice theory show that legislators do not seek the most efficient solution independently of other interests,[82] it may be that pressure by individual interest groups will mean that the law remains over-regulated in particular areas.

3. *Corporate governance codes*

In many countries there is a trend to enact corporate governance codes.[83] This development will continue with a sort of snowball effect. Investors familiar with such codes in their home countries will also demand them abroad. Additionally, enterprises will ask for the same thing in order to attract investors from those countries. Since corporate governance codes relate primarily to public companies, the growing importance of the capital market is also leading to a demand for corresponding codes. Finally, the reasons in favour of corporate governance codes at international level[84] also apply *mutatis mutandis* at national level.

Yet this trend does not answer the question whether and how far codes can be effective and in the long term shape shareholder law. The decisive point is who enacts the codes and how they are to be enforced. Both a 'too legal' and a 'too market-oriented' approach might be problematic here.

A more legal approach is evident when, for instance, at the level of the regulator, a commission set up or influenced by the government (as e.g. in Germany or the UK) adopts the code.[85] Regarding enforcement, on a legal approach it is conceivable that (as e.g. in Belgium) the courts will use the code in order to elaborate the principles of proper corporate governance

[81] Escher-Weingart (2001: 174, 186–7).

[82] See Ch. 7, section I.2.a above.

[83] See Ch. 2, section IV.3 above.

[84] See Ch. 7, section II.1 above.

[85] See Ch. 2, section IV.3 above.

or (as is being discussed in Germany) regard it as a commercial usage.[86] One might also consider making compliance with a code a condition for stock exchange listing (as in China[87]). These juridifications would have the advantage that there would be a uniform code, which could also be effectively enforced. The counter-argument, however, is that an over-legalistic approach might negate the advantages of a code (i.e. its flexibility, practice orientation etc.).[88]

By contrast, with a market-oriented approach no direct political influence is present. Here (as to date in the US)[89] it is companies themselves or institutional investors that draw up codes. Their implementation is achieved through market forces alone. It is, however, problematic here whether such an approach can be effective. In countries with no tradition of self-regulation and a relatively weak capital market, a voluntary code is often not acceptable.[90] A code may then be only 'tactical disinformation'.[91] Finally, self-regulation is often only a transitional solution. For example, in Germany the private codes on insider dealing and takeover law were in the course of time subsumed into a statutory framework.[92] It is accordingly conceivable as regards corporate governance codes that the legislator will also intervene and transform rules it regards as essential into statutory law.

4. *Conclusion*

While it may be said that codified company law is open to attack from various quarters, no 'decodification' in favour of case law, or 'end of company law' in favour of securities law, or 'privatization of law' in favour of corporate governance codes will occur. Instead, codified shareholder law will continue to be the decisive starting-point for studying the convergence of legal systems.

IV. Conclusions to this chapter

Regarding possible 'convergence forces', it was, first, important to note that the development of shareholder law depends on factual circumstances

[86] See Wymeersch (2001b: 315); Berg and Stöcker (2002); Seidel (2004); for a general overview see Wymeersch (2005), (2006).

[87] See Pißler (2002b: 11).

[88] See also Ch. 12, section II.3 below.

[89] See Ch. 2, section IV.3 above.

[90] See Rossi (2003: 493 *et seq.*) (effects of corporate governance codes are part of a 'new mythology of corporate law').

[91] Henderson (1995: 906).

[92] See Erhardt and Nowak (2002: 343 *et seq.*).

and pressure from interest groups. For the way this dependency relation works, reference can also be made to the public choice theory (section I above). Secondly, it was found that shareholder law will continue primarily to depend on national acts of parliament. Although international and informal provisions are gaining importance, the convergence of positive national law is the most important effect that may be brought about by possible convergence forces (sections II and III above).

For future development trends and development patterns, thus, it is not unification through international or regional law but a 'legal unification from below', 'spontaneous harmonization', 'evolutionary convergence' and 'bottom-up approximation'[93] that will be most important. This may occur in either of two ways. When considering possible convergence forces, the debate has so far been mostly on factors exerting pressure on national legislators ('convergence through pressure', Ch. 9 below). The causes of convergence are not, however, confined to this. Instead, as a 'milder variant', it is also conceivable for a convergence of other circumstances to lead to a convergence of law ('convergence through congruence', Ch. 8 below).

In both cases, factual and legal developments will be examined that can work as 'convergence forces'. For instance, the enhanced use of modern forms of communication, approximations in economic policy, in company and shareholder structures, increasing cross-border investment and mergers, as well as the liberalization of international capital markets and reforms in pension provisions may all be reflected in shareholder law. Additionally, weakening 'brakes on convergence' may be seen as convergence forces. Often, such factors as political and legal-cultural path dependencies are adduced only as arguments against convergence,[94] but, since convergence denotes merely approximation but not identity, the withering of existing path dependencies can also be a reason for convergence in shareholder law.

[93] For these terms see e.g. Dreher (1999: 110); Van den Bergh (2000: 444); Merkt (2001a: 334); Berger (2001: 4–5); Hopt and Wymeersch (2003: VI).

[94] Roe (1997); Bebchuk and Roe (1999: 168–9); Jacoby (2000: 18 *et seq.*); Branson (2000); Jayme (2003: 213–14).

8

Convergence through congruence

It follows from the dependency of company and securities law and the findings of the public choice theory that the overall socio-political system and the institutional environment decisively influence shareholder law.[1] When these influencing factors come closer together internationally, convergence of law is also possible.[2] Convergence forces are accordingly to be found in general cultural and economic-policy approximations (section I below), the internationalization of the economy (section III below) and approximations of legal culture and shareholder structures (sections II and IV below). These convergence forces are to be seen as part of an overall complex, since they may mutually enhance each other. For instance, economic-policy approximations may encourage the internationalization of business, just as, conversely, economic policy depends on internationalization trends in the economy. Yet, in the future too, no identity of law is to be expected. Even if one may basically presume convergence, path dependencies may continue to account for differences (section V below).

I. General cultural and economic-policy approximation

Differences in the cultural, political, social and economic environment will continue to exist in the future. However, there is already some approximation, and this is likely to continue further.

1. 'Clash' or 'convergence' of cultures

Samuel Huntington has claimed that a 'clash' of civilizations is to be expected. There will not be a monistic universal culture, but rather modernization without cultural convergence. Cultural paths will continue to exist, and even intensify, since differences will in future be marked not

[1] See Ch. 7, section I above.

[2] This may also be called 'natural convergence': see Merryman (1999: 30 *et seq.*); de Cruz (1999: 491).

primarily ideologically, politically or economically, but culturally.[3] On the one hand, allegedly, nation states will lose importance, since what matters are eight cultural regions ('Western, Eastern Orthodox, Chinese, Japanese, Muslim, Hindu, Latin American, African'). On the other hand, it will not be possible to speak of a global society. Instead, the effects of globalization will be confined to a small portion of the world population, for whom – as for the participants in the World Economic Forum in Davos – tightening networks are in fact to be seen (the 'Davos culture').[4]

This latter aspect brings out a basic weakness in Huntington's line of reasoning: since for globalized population groups membership in a 'civilization' does not matter, the general statement of a conflict between various culturally determined regions comes into doubt. It seems better instead to focus on the differences between modern and conservative population groups which may exist even within a country or a region.[5] The worldwide transformation of traditional into modern societies is producing diversification of social memberships, with many differing identities and interests. Thus, across borders, there may be a differentiation between a local and a global sphere, and for the global social strata there may very well be a convergence of cultures.

The question is what this may mean for shareholder law. According to Amir Licht *et al.*, culture, as the 'mother of all path dependencies', is the decisive reason for the multiplicity of corporate governance systems.[6] Licht *et al.* proceed by studying culture-specific behaviour of schoolteachers and IBM workers in individual countries according to seven psychological criteria.[7] They go on to correlate these cultural factors with the strength of shareholder protection in the various countries – referring to La Porta *et al.*[8] It follows that good legal shareholder protection chiefly requires positive findings in the areas of 'individualism' and 'masculinity' and negative ones in those of 'harmony' and 'uncertainty avoidance'.[9] This is allegedly to be seen in the fact that the distinctive high shareholder protection in the US and the UK correlates with their distinctive culture,[10] whereas in East Asia in view of a greater need for harmony the

[3] Huntington (1993), (1996), (1999).

[4] Huntington (1999: 2–3); similarly Higgott and Reich (1998: 10–11).

[5] Senghaas (1998); similarly Leggewie (2003: 49); Zehou (1999: 38).

[6] Licht (2001a); Licht *et al.* (2001), (2005); similarly Salacuse (2003); Stout (2003: 54 *et seq.*).

[7] Following Hofstede (1980/2003), these are: embeddedness/autonomy, hierarchy/egalitarianism; mastery/harmony; uncertainty avoidance; power distance; individualism/collectivism; masculinity/femininity; cf. Licht *et al.* (2001: 8).

[8] For criticism see Ch. 1, section I above.

[9] Licht *et al.* (2001: 28, 31).

[10] Licht *et al.* (2001: 20).

positive law plays a smaller role for shareholders.[11] The possibility that globalization may make the different systems develop in the direction of an international culture of corporate governance is recognized, but it is ultimately emphasized that even for 'global players' the national cultures are stronger and more stable than any possible global culture.[12]

It rightly becomes clear from these statements that cultural factors mark the content and importance of the law and may hamper change. It is also true that for the future no ethical universalism can be expected, and cultures may draw boundaries that other systems, like the economy, ignore or tear down. Cultural differences may accordingly continue to limit the effectiveness of reforms and stand in the way of full legal convergence.

Following up the criticisms of Huntington, however, it is doubtful whether the emphasis on the uniqueness of all cultures[13] and the division into cultural families[14] are helpful. The same applies, for instance, to the statements that in China and France trust is limited to the family and close friends, so that the culture opposes large enterprises,[15] or that Japanese culture is guided by flexible and pragmatic action, not by principles of economic rationality.[16] The globalization process is not confined to the economy, but leads, for instance, through the media, also to the beginnings of cultural 'hybridization' and 'creolization'.[17] This can be seen not just in the Western world. Instead, we hear from China, say, that the culture does not necessarily oppose changes, because 'people are not celestial spirits, but physical beings who want to maintain their life and hope for a better one in this world'.[18] This is particularly true of economic life.[19] 'Ego-culture' and public-spiritedness are universally in a relation of tension, and 'merely' have different weightings in different cultures. For the question of convergence in shareholder law, moreover, the point is not the whole world population – or schoolteachers and IBM workers as with Licht *et al.* – but the groups of people for whom the operation of undertakings in the legal form of the joint stock company is relevant. Here the focus must primarily be on cultural convergence in metropolitan cities. Since these are the places where the cultural values decisive for company and securities law are formed, at least in this respect one can speak of loss of tradition and approximation to an individualistic, consumption-oriented

[11] Licht *et al.* (2001: 22–3, 27).

[12] Licht (2001a: 199 *et seq.*). [13] Licht *et al.* (2001: 7). [14] Licht *et al.* (2001: 32).

[15] Cf. Huntington (1999: 6). [16] Cf. Baum (1998: 739, 759); similarly Dore (2000: 38).

[17] Leggewie (2003: 17–18, 21); similarly Seita (1997: 491). [18] Zehou (1999: 38).

[19] Cf. also Baum (1998: 759) ('When large amounts of money are at stake competitive markets know no history').

and cosmopolitan culture.[20] This decline in local differences with simultaneous diversification of social memberships is further enhanced by the fact that international banks, firms and interest groups will make cross-border demands, and modern communication media like the Internet and e-mail make it easier to overcome spatial boundaries.[21] Accordingly, it is at least to be expected that for the circumstances underlying company and securities law cultural differences will lose importance.

2. *'TINA' or 'THEMBA'*

A dialectic similar to the question of convergence of cultures arises with issues of the unity or diversity of economic systems. In the political debate, the view that today the West's free market economy has prevailed and there is no alternative to it is often referred to in Margaret Thatcher's famous phrase, 'There is no alternative' (TINA).[22] Historically, this absence of an alternative can be underpinned by the fact that the collapse of Communism in Eastern Europe has left the market economy as the victor of the Cold War, so that, in Francis Fukuyama's words, we have arrived at an 'end of history'.[23] Against this universalism of an unrestricted market economy, critics of globalization reply with the slogans 'Another world is possible' or 'There must be an alternative' (THEMBA).[24] Resistance, they say, is not just necessary in the interest of social justice, but also to be expected given the shortcomings of a market fundamentalism[25] so that what we can expect is an end of the globalization empire,[26] not an end of history in the sense of a pure market economy.

These debates are also being taken up by economic, political and legal science. In economics the view presented is commonly that the increasingly global markets will exercise pressure on the social forms of the market economy and thus lead to convergence towards a pure market economy.[27] This is often denied particularly in political science.[28] Despite

[20] Similarly Reimann (2002). [21] See Ch. 8, section III. 2 below.

[22] In particular, the 'anti-globalization movement': see e.g. http://www.converge.org.nz/pma/rob00397.htm; http://www.findarticles.com/p/articles/mi_m0JQV/is_3_31/ai_84558658/; http://en.wikipedia.org/wiki/TINA/.

[23] Fukuyama (1992); see also Ch. 1, section III. 1 above.

[24] Furthermore, 'themba' means 'hope' in Zulu: see http://www.mediachannel.org/views/dissector/survivor.shtml.

[25] Cf. Soros (1998); Stiglitz (2006). [26] Hardt and Negri (2000).

[27] See the references in Hay (2004: 232 *et seq.*); but see also Bhagwati (2004: 99–101, 122–34) who emphasizes that institutions prevent a 'race to the bottom'.

[28] See Hay (2004: 235 *et seq.*).

globalization, different forms of capitalism continue to exist.[29] Differences in political preferences and decision-making processes are seen as leading to a divergence of economic systems, a convergence on two models ('liberal market economies' and 'coordinated market economies') or a non-uniform development. Comparably with this debate, the corporate governance literature talks on the one hand about employee- and state-oriented models having failed in favour of the capitalist model of 'shareholder supremacy' in reality.[30] On the other hand, here too the absence of an alternative to Western economic policy is questioned, and economic-policy differences are seen as a decisive reason for a continued divergence of law. Nor do these authors expect anything to change here in the future. Since for many countries capitalism on the US model is said to be unacceptable, there will be movements against Westernization, and in other countries more social variants of the market economy will remain.[31]

With all this, one should bear in mind that forecasts of future development not uncommonly also reflect one's own preferences.[32] There is, however, no denying the fact that in recent decades in more and more countries a free market economy has come to prevail. Even the resistances to globalization of the economy on a Western pattern make it clear that this process does exist. Peculiarities in general political or cultural areas do not necessarily stand in the way of this. As the Chinese example shows, even in countries where, for instance, there are basic differences in constitutional or family law, it is not impossible that there is a liberalization of the economic system. This is also associated with change in the legal infrastructure. For instance, a free market economy presupposes private property, contractual freedom and effective legal protection.[33] Nor is it any longer a Western peculiarity for joint stock companies to be permissible, so that in this way 'private greed' is to serve the public benefit.[34]

Nonetheless, despite this increasing consensus on some features of the market economy, there is not just one possible shape for economic policy. Even if, for instance, a number of European countries are showing a loosening of social networks, this does not, contrary to 'TINA', mean that

[29] See also Albert (1991); Whitley (1999); Hall and Soskice (2001); Lynch Fannon (2003); Higgott and Reich (1998: 16 *et seq.*).

[30] Hansmann and Kraakman (2001: 443 *et seq.*); see also Ch. 1, section III.1.

[31] Branson (2001: 332 *et seq.*, 349 *et seq.*), (2000: 685); for France see also Foster (2000: 613); Fanto (1998: 43).

[32] Popper (1947/1987). [33] Eucken (1990: 254 *et seq.*).

[34] Cf. generally Lutter (1991: 16, 28); for China: Comberg (2000: 13–14, 42).

enhanced competition can lead only to a radical liberal model. Instead, the economic-policy strategies of individual countries may differ, and at any rate in democracies social interests too will continue to remain important in view of voter desires. Additionally, a number of detailed factors such as historical experience, the political decision-making process, national resources or the economic influence of a country may mean that different economic systems converge 'only' in basic structures.

II. The convergence of legal cultures

The debate around the convergence or divergence of cultures is continuing for legal culture. While it is often stressed that different legal cultures run counter to a successful reception of foreign law (subsection 1 below), current developments in shareholder law point to the very opposite: approximations in legal culture will also be reflected in a convergence of the positive law (subsection 2 below).

1. The importance of legal culture

Legal culture means those elements in law that go beyond the mere content of statutory or case law. For instance, the concept of legal culture covers the historical background to a legal system, the emergence of sources of law, the systematization of legal systems, the style of argument and codification, and the ranking of law in a country's social order.[35] The importance of these factors should not be underestimated in comparative law. Even if it is sometimes usual for the law of individual countries to be systematized and compared according to the content of the positive law, at any rate a limitation to these aspects is not satisfactory.

It is, however, questionable what conclusions are to be drawn from this. In particular, Pierre Legrand in the debate on harmonization of private law in the European Union has criticized the fact that convergence of law is only superficial.[36] Taking into account deeper structures and especially the legal culture, he sees major differences continuing to exist. For instance, civil law and common law are even today marked by such oppositions as deductive v. inductive, logical and systematic v. pragmatic, rule-bound v. fact-bound, future-oriented v. past-oriented, etc. For comparative law,

[35] See generally e.g. Nelken (1997); Friedman (1990); Van Hoecke and Warrington (1998); Scholler (2000).

[36] Legrand (1996), (1997).

accordingly, legal norms should be treated not as value-free rules but as fitting into the differing mentalities of the legal systems. From this there follows in particular the impossibility of 'legal transplants'. Even formally identical rules are interpreted and applied differently in different legal systems, not surviving the journey from one legal system to another unchanged. Additionally, there is a threat of a rejection effect where a new rule cannot be integrated into the existing law.[37] Altogether, therefore, in view of the singularity of legal cultures and the tensions arising when they clash, at international and regional level one can neither note convergence nor advocate harmonization.

This sceptical view, however, ascribes a blocking function to legal culture that in reality is not entirely true.

2. Changes in legal cultures

Like positive law, legal cultures are subject to change. The subdivision of legal cultures into separate legal families seems – just as with the classification of positive law[38] – no longer to be very useful for shareholder law. The cause of this development is, first, the circumstances which – like general cultural and economic-policy approximations or the internationalization of the economy – are presented here as separate convergence forces. Additionally, a number of specific reasons can be adduced for showing that legal cultures will come closer in the present context, both between civil and common law and between Western and Asian law.

a) Civil and common law

On the traditional view, civil and common law are distinguished and their combination as 'Western Law' rejected.[39] Things are seen differently – from a Japanese perspective – by Tsuyoshi Kinoshita: the political and social influence of Judeo-Christian morality and liberalism and capitalism have led to similar ideologies, mentalities and a convergence in the legal culture of civil and common law. It is accordingly justified to speak of a comprehensive Western legal culture ('droit occidental').[40]

Similarly, for shareholder law, this study has already stressed that the codification trend in common law countries means that the distinguishing

[37] See also Berkowitz *et al.* (2003a: 167), (2003b: 163); cf. Watson (1974/1993); Kahn-Freund (1974: 9): 'Industrialisation, urbanisation, and the development of communications have greatly reduced the environmental obstacles to legal transplantation'.

[38] See Part II above.

[39] Großfeld and Deilmann (1990: 271).

[40] Kinoshita (2001: 32).

criterion of 'statute law in civil law' and 'case law in common law' has only a minor weight today.[41] Similarly, for instance, differences and similarities in enforcement of shareholder law cannot be explained from the subdivision into common law and civil law, since there are also, for instance, clear differences between the US and UK on the one hand and between Germany and France on the other.[42] Finally, the study of the *status quo* has shown that in company and securities law there have been many legal transplants without in principle rejection reactions.[43] The decisive factor here was that it was not just the text of a specific provision that was copied. Instead, approximations in theory and in practice suggest that today, at least in shareholder law, the legal culture tends rather to encourage than to obstruct the reception of foreign law.

To elaborate, first, there is the transnational debate on optimized corporate governance, referring not just to the positive law but also to theoretical, economic and legal-cultural factors. The assumption that a foreign culture cannot be understood[44] and that language barriers are as effective as 'Chinese walls'[45] is not confirmed here. For instance, Germany and France have been influenced by Anglo-American legal thinking, which can, for example, be seen in the adoption of a number of technical terms (e.g. due diligence, asset deal, share deal, tracking stocks, stock options, stakeholder, corporate governance, takeover, mergers and acquisitions, initial public offering).[46] Additionally, theories like the economic analysis of law are being similarly debated today in continental Europe. Even if the reception of economic theory is not uncommonly critical,[47] its discussion here is nonetheless of particular hermeneutical importance, since in company and securities law economic arguments are inherently reflected.

Secondly, changes in practice are bringing legal cultures closer together. Together with easier global communications and the internationalization of national economies,[48] it is in particular the increasing number of international law firms which is encouraging this phenomenon. Candidates applying to continental European law firms with global operations are often required also to have studied at English-speaking universities. Again, their international clients and colleagues frequently make it necessary to

[41] See Ch. 2, section II above. [42] See Ch. 6, section I above.

[43] See Part II above. [44] Legrand (1996: 78). [45] Tunc (1991: 203).

[46] For Germany: Schulze-Osterloh (2001: 1433); for France: Merle (2005: paras. 248 ('corporate governance'), 535 ('stock option'), 539 ('leverage management buy out'), 651–2 ('squeeze out'), 654 ('due diligence')).

[47] For Germany cf. Tuerks (2000: 166 *et seq.*); for France cf. Foster (2000: 576, 618).

[48] See Ch. 8, section III below.

communicate with lawyers and firms from various countries and to take international rules and customs into account in drawing up contracts. By contrast, for purely national law firms and courts, international aspects mostly play a small part, even today.[49] Here, then, at least the speed of convergence may be markedly reduced.

What emerges from what has been said so far is chiefly an approximation of civil law countries to Anglo-American legal culture. But, despite this trend, the legal-cultural development is by no means a one-way street. In the 1990s, in the US, the German and Japanese models of corporate governance were intensively debated.[50] Since civil law traditions predominate in the EU, the UK is further influenced by continental European styles of codification and argument through EU directives and regulations.[51]

b) Western and Asian law

Even if the positive Japanese and Chinese company and securities laws are based largely on Western models, it is more questionable whether legal-cultural reasons could hinder effective convergence.

(1) Japan's legal culture. For a successful reception of foreign law, the functioning of foreign regulations must be recognized, alternatives taken into account and the solution harmonized with the local environment. When in Japan after the Second World War under US pressure elements of American law were adopted, this was often not the case. It is accordingly not surprising that subsequently the law has in part since been amended and in part *de facto* not accepted.[52]

Nonetheless, for Japanese company and securities law, the reception of foreign law is generally regarded as successful.[53] A certain divergence between the transplanted law and the original foreign law is in any case to be expected, since any reception of foreign law happens only at a particular point in time, whereafter each will develop separately.[54] Additionally, in Japan before the current reform projects began, as had already been the case before reception of the German Commercial Code in the late

[49] See also, more emphatically, Tunc (1991: 221) ('Most practicing lawyers are still very far from the legal cultures of Germany, England, Italy or the Netherlands. Some, of course, are excellent international lawyers, but most of the others are very parochial and completely ignore what is going on outside the Hexagon.').

[50] Cf. Bratton and McCahery (1999: 235 *et seq.*); Licht (1998: 241–2); Rock (1995: 291 *et seq.*).

[51] See also Ch. 6, section II above. [52] See Osugi (2002: 30).

[53] Kanda (2000: 74). [54] Großfeld and Deilmann (1990: 273).

nineteenth century, comprehensive comparative legal studies had been carried out.[55] Thus, these receptions were as a rule voluntary decisions[56] whereby the Japanese legislator wished to take account of changed economic, political and legal-cultural circumstances.

However, it is also not uncommonly pointed out that the foreign law which was transplanted to Japan has in practice, for legal-cultural reasons, made only qualified headway.[57] This is connected in general with the fact that in Japan the law plays a smaller part because the social system is not marked by a 'struggle for law'[58] with winners and losers, but disputes are resolved by consensus. The interests of harmony have therefore primarily made extra-legal values decisive, so that the principle of the rule of law, individual rights and formal legalistic reasoning are regarded as alien to Japanese legal thinking.[59] For company law too, it is said that the law in books and in practice diverges widely.[60] This view regards any change as unlikely. The legal culture is held – possibly even for genetic reasons[61] – to show a particularly strong path dependency.[62] By contrast with Germany's approximation to the US model, accordingly, convergence of the Japanese with Western economic models is not to be expected.[63] At best, there can, internationally, be a 'regime of constrained pluralism', in which consensus can be achieved only on a few principles such as the bar on exploiting minority shareholders. A principle such as 'shareholder supremacy' will, however, not develop in Japan.[64]

This sceptical view takes its reservations too far, however. It is underlain by 'orientalism', i.e. a stereotyped view of Asian countries which at least today should no longer be followed.[65] The current increase in derivative suits and hostile takeovers[66] shows that here too the law is not 'naturally' secondary, and individualism and rivalry can very well push aside the need for harmony and informal resolution mechanisms. This is also contributed to by other convergence forces. Cultural and economic convergence and the internationalization of the economy are leading to a gradual shift in mentality. One example for the interplay of convergence forces here is the internationalization of the legal profession. The

[55] Cf. e.g. Ködderitzsch (2001a: 66); West (2001a: 557, 563–4, 566).
[56] But see also Ch. 9, section V below on the SII Agreement.
[57] Kinoshita (2001: 7); Milhaupt (2001: 2126). [58] In the sense of von Jhering (1915).
[59] Kinoshita (2001: 23 *et seq.*); Fu (2001: 511); Maslen (1998).
[60] Rodatz (1995: 247); Hayakawa (1996: 270); Milhaupt (1996: 14 *et seq.*), (2001: 2127); Kliesow (2001).
[61] Kinoshita (2001: 10). [62] Cf. Milhaupt (2001: 2126–7); Baum (1998: 775, 779).
[63] Dore (2000: 222). [64] Milhaupt (2001: 2127–8).
[65] Similarly Anderson (2001: 37–8). [66] See Ch. 5, sections II.1.a, III.1 above.

increasing trade between Japan and the US and the increased need for international legal advice that this creates has led, first in 1987 and then in 1995, to the establishment of foreign lawyers in Japan,[67] and in 2003 the setting up of partnerships between Japanese and foreign lawyers was eased.[68] Additionally, the international capital market demands legally certain and effective law, thus exerting pressure on a (presumably) rather anti-legal culture. This can also be seen in, for instance, the fact that, since the end of the 1980s, in Japan too there has been talk of corporate governance ('koporeto gabanansu'), and similar solutions to those in the US and Europe discussed for its optimization.[69] Finally, a study has shown that in Japan not just the positive commercial law but also the behaviour and perceptions of economic circles are gradually changing. For instance, even now managers of firms estimate that in future shareholder interests will play a more important part than those of consumers and employees.[70]

On the whole, thus, a further reduction in Japan's legal-cultural peculiarities is to be expected. Here again, though, this does not mean identity with the West. Existing differences, even if not insuperable, such as the still comparatively small number of judges and lawyers or the shareholder ombudsman,[71] will accordingly lead to a synthesis of Japanese and Western elements.

(2) China's legal culture. The debate over the importance of legal culture in China displays similarities with that in Japan. However, this should not lead us to conclude that there is a common Asian legal culture. Further, the question whether there is an approximation to the West leads to different considerations in Japan and China.

On China, the literature stresses that legal awareness and law enforcement through the courts is weak, with personal relations ('guanxi') being more important.[72] There are accordingly deficits in the area of the rule of law. The reliability of law is not always guaranteed because judges act as bureaucrats[73] and sometimes do not take unlawful conduct into

67 See Haley (1988); Fukushima (1988); Oda (1999: 98 *et seq.*).

68 See Schimmann and Janssen (2004: 197–8); Ishikawa (2005); for empirical data see Chan (2005).

69 See Takahashi (2003: 121); Baum (1998: 741–2); Hayakawa (2002: 32–3); Kliesow (2001: 54–5); Learmount (2002: 18 *et seq.*).

70 Igarashi (2001: 89 *et seq.*).

71 See Kawamoto (1999: 534); Kawamoto *et al.* (2001: para. 70).

72 See Png (1996: 202); Walker (2001: 437 *et seq.*); Branson (2001: 343 *et seq.*).

73 Dam (2006: 16).

account if that would be unacceptable for economic growth, the development of the socialist market economy or the maintenance of an orderly economic system.[74] Additionally, insider dealing and other forms of personal enrichment at the expense of shareholders occur, and decisions are often not taken objectively.[75] By contrast, corporate governance rhetoric is seen as remote from Chinese law,[76] and in particular the US model as incompatible with the anti-individualistic Chinese legal culture.[77]

Here again, though, these doubts about convergence overstep the mark. Confucian and socialist habits in China are currently being 'shaken up',[78] so that hitherto accepted statements about the Chinese understanding of law have to be rethought. In Chinese academia, Western conceptions of legal theory and legal philosophy are debated, and are being adopted to a substantial extent.[79] And the opening of legal culture to Western influences can also be seen in the facts that the codification and reception process is supported through consultancy by the West,[80] and that a variety of legal systems[81] – and for company law also corporate governance theories[82] and the new institutional economics[83] – are being taken into account. Again, the enhanced importance of private law points to a certain retreat of politics in favour of personal responsibility of individuals. Thus, in China too, a gradual separation of state and society is coming about, with increasing acceptance of a pluralism of interests.[84]

Finally, the principles of the rule of law and private property are today explicitly rooted in Art. 13 of the Chinese Constitution (as amended in 2004). Since, in the modern differentiated Chinese society, morals and custom are increasingly failing to ensure a stable order, the need for legal rules is increasing, and there is a growing emphasis on law in chinese society.[85] Furthermore, in the last twenty years, the number of lawyers has mushroomed.[86] And, according to the ideas of the Chinese leadership, a market economy and the rule of law are also compatible not only with capitalism and democracy but also with socialism of the Chinese type.[87] Measures by the China Securities Regulatory Commission and civil and

[74] Thümmel (1995: 62–3).
[75] See Comberg (2000: 42); Walker (2001: 438); for Asia in general see Campbell (1999: 11–12).
[76] Tan (2000: 91). [77] Branson (2001: 343 *et seq.*). [78] Cf. Blumental (1998: 261).
[79] See the references in Chen (1999: 125 *et seq.*, 138 *et seq.*); Wei (2003: 35–6, 48, 111, 119).
[80] See Schulte-Kulkmann (2003). [81] See Ch. 1, section III.3.c above.
[82] Wei (2002: 227 *et seq.*), Wei (2003) for the ChinCA. [83] Chen (1999: 139).
[84] See Chen (1999: 139 *et seq.*, 142). [85] Dam (2006: 12–13).
[86] Clarke *et al.* (2006: 7) (8,600 lawyers in 1983; well over 100,000 in 2005).
[87] See Chen (1999: 136).

penal proceedings against managers here suggest that this approach ought also to be imposed in the interest of the capital market and of China's competitiveness. And, although, according to the Transparency International Corruption Index, China still displays a very high level of corruption on an international comparison,[88] a survey among German firms trading in China shows that corruption has become less of a problem.[89] One further step to strengthen the rule of law in China is that, since 2002, special qualifications have been necessary for becoming a judge.[90] Additionally, WTO regulations require judges to be independent and impartial.[91] For the legal profession, enhanced Anglo-American influence can be noted. In addition to lawyers who have studied abroad or who bring British customs in from Hong Kong, this involves the increasing number of foreign lawyers now present in China. While the establishment of a single law firm with Chinese and foreign lawyers is not allowed, a foreign law firm can have an agency in China, and form an informal cooperation with a Chinese law firm. Additionally, WTO accession has brought a liberalization of the admission requirements, since now, for instance, foreign law firms are no longer limited to particular regions.[92]

c) Conclusion

Since legal culture reflects the particular historical, sociological and anthropological features of a country, there will not internationally be any monism of legal cultures.[93] In particular, it cannot be said that, say, Asian countries are only 'pre-modern' so that in future there will inevitably be an approximation to the Western legal consciousness.[94] Yet, in the countries studied here, specifically for shareholder law a convergence of law, legal culture and reality is to be expected. As with other social circumstances, the legal culture of a country can also change. Although resistance to change is conceivable, legal culture is not an insuperable barrier to convergence or to the reception of foreign law. In the area of commercial law, instead, resistance is relatively light. Here, convergence of legal cultures may on the one hand be a response to changes in law. On the other hand, it is possible that the legal culture of different countries converges and thus also forces changes in the law. This 'convergence through congruence' is

[88] Index available at http://www.transparency.org.
[89] *Handelsblatt*, 29 August 2003, at 7. [90] Cf. Knieper (2002: 230–1).
[91] See Zinser (2002: 212). [92] See Wong and Cox (2002).
[93] Similarly Schemann (1998: 577); but see also Luhmann (1997: 162): 'emerging global legal culture' ('sich anbahndende weltgesellschaftliche Rechtskultur').
[94] Cf. Rahn (1994: 13–14).

particularly likely here, since the social circumstances that condition legal culture in commercial law can change more easily and faster than the law as such.

III. Internationalization of the economy

The breaking down of national barriers to trade and investment and the use of new media (subsections 1 and 2 below) have made markets grow together and have reduced the importance of spatial boundaries. It follows that such private institutions as analysts or auditors, as well as undertakings themselves, are increasingly internationalizing (subsections 3 and 4 below). These developments will also be reflected as a convergence in law (subsection V below). Additionally, the opening of markets may enhance the potential for pressure by particular groups (especially investors), so that 'convergence through pressure' will also arise (Ch. 9 below).

1. *International economic law*

Regional, international and bilateral arrangements are increasingly opening up national economies and globalizing economic relations. At regional level, for instance, the EU, NAFTA and MERCOSUR remove barriers to the movement of goods, services and capital. In parallel, international organizations (WTO, IMF, World Bank, OECD) encourage the opening up of markets. Thus, the WTO's international economic law provides for the elimination of tariffs and price fixing, a ban on discrimination, and the most-favoured-nation principle. Additionally, the IMF and the World Bank insist when making loans that debtor countries set up a free market economy, in particular privatizing state enterprises and allowing investments by international undertakings. Finally, trade and services are increasingly also being liberalized through bilateral agreements.

The background to this breaking down of borders is the theory of comparative advantage going back to David Ricardo.[95] According to the theory, foreign trade enables a division of labour at the international level,

[95] Ricardo (1817/1973); see also Adam Smith (1776/1976: Vol. I, Book IV, Ch. II 422) ('It is the maxim of every prudent master of a family, never to attempt to make at home what it will cost him more to make than to buy . . . What is prudence in the conduct of every private family, can scarce be folly in that of a great kingdom. If a foreign country can supply us with a commodity cheaper than we ourselves can make it, better buy it off them with some part of the produce of our own industry, employed in a way in which we have some advantage').

thus contributing to a general rise in prosperity. This idea that economic liberalization not only lowers territorial transaction costs but ultimately benefits all countries ('positive-sum game') is taken up today by advocates of globalization. They point to current studies showing that only countries that have opened up to the international markets in goods, services and capital have increased their prosperity.[96]

However, the limits to and resistance to current developments should not be overlooked. Each country seeks to procure individual advantages despite internationalization. If, then, an influential country like the US or an influential region like the EU pursues unilateralism or takes to protectionist measures, this may well lead to a spiral of protectionism, bringing a halt to globalization.[97] Additionally, the failure of the WTO's Doha Development Round shows that there remain particular conflicts between developed and developing countries.[98] Both sides place different expectations on a global system of rights and allocations. The developed countries would on the one hand like developing countries' markets to be open to their enterprises and investors, while on the other hand protecting sensitive national economic sectors like agriculture and education from competition. By contrast, the developing countries expect that free trade will enable them to sell their goods to wealthy consumers in developed countries, but will still assist them with credits and protect their more sensitive economic sectors.

In practice, the limits to liberalization are reflected on the one hand in the exceptions to international economic law. For instance, China's accession to the WTO has not removed protectionism, despite the trend to liberalization. The opening up of the financial sector and the possibility of foreign investments are subject to a series of limitations based partly on the general provisions of the GATS (General Agreement on Trade in Services) and TRIMs (Trade Related Investment Measures) and partly on special agreements for China.[99] One basic reason for this is that the Chinese currency, the renminbi, is not yet freely convertible, so that complete liberalization might lead to a collapse of the Chinese financial system.

On the other hand, the attempt to reach international agreements has partly failed. One example here is the OECD's Multilateral Agreement on Investment (MAI).[100] This Agreement was intended to promote

[96] See e.g. Larsson (2001); Norberg (2003); Wolf (2004); Bhagwati (2004).
[97] Cf. James (2002) ('the end of globalization').
[98] See Stiglitz (2006: 76 *et seq.*); Yuan (2001: 201). [99] See Peerenboom (2002).
[100] On what follows see Lang (1998); Geiger (1998); Canner (1998); Kurtz (2003).

competition and economic efficiency by granting investors access to foreign financial markets and effectively protecting them against expropriation and discrimination. In particular, a formal arbitration procedure was provided, so as to avoid the weaknesses of earlier OECD efforts. Additionally, a comprehensive liberalization of the capital market had not yet been reached by WTO law, which primarily concerns trade and only indirectly cross-border investments too. Nonetheless, the project for a multilateral investment agreement failed in late 1998 because of conflicts of interest. Exceptions in the areas of culture, labour and the environment were particularly controversial. Additionally, in view of its economic strength, the US regarded a multilateral approach as unnecessary, since it could maintain its economic independence and effectively assert its interests through bilateral agreements. Similarly, a renewed attempt by the WTO to create an international framework for investments as one of the so-called 'Singapore themes' has so far been unsuccessful, since now the developing countries perceive themselves as being taken unfair advantage of by the developed countries.[101]

There are criticisms from other quarters of the economic globalization process in general. It is, for instance, said that the opening up of domestic markets is unnecessary for economic growth. For example, in the late twentieth century China was very successful, despite its protectionism.[102] Additionally, the liberalization of the international economy is regarded as harmful by the critics of globalization. This kind of 'monoeconomics' is said to disadvantage particularly the developing countries.[103] By contrast with developed countries that can protect themselves by protectionist measures, developing countries are fully exposed to liberalization and are thus exploited by transnational enterprises. Out of solidarity with economically weaker countries it is accordingly reasonable to let developing countries protect their economies by subsidies, tariffs etc. Otherwise, there might also be a deregulation race at the expense of non-economic interests, since for instance social or environmental factors play no part in the yield on capital.[104] Finally, risks are said to arise from the instability of a global financial market that is too liquid. As was seen in the 'Asian crisis' in the late 1990s, short-term financial transactions may set off a panic on the exchanges and thus cause considerable economic damage. To prevent such forms of market failure, accordingly, market regulation,

[101] See Berrisch (2004: 70). [102] See Stiglitz (2006: 10, 39, 40).
[103] Weisbrot (1998: 634); also Stiglitz (2006).
[104] Weisbrot (1998: 631 *et seq.*); Stiglitz (2006: 190, 196).

rather than further deregulation of the international economy, is allegedly necessary.[105]

On the whole, however, developments in recent decades show that one can speak of a liberalization trend. Even if a complete opening up of all markets is not realistic, this trend is an important factor influencing national commercial law in general, and shareholder law in particular. While the criticisms from opponents of globalization are to be taken seriously, it is unlikely that their influence will lead to, say, a global tax on currency transactions ('Tobin tax') or a change of direction in international economic policy.

2. *Internationalization through 'new media'*

Alongside liberalization of the law, factual changes are also contributing to the internationalization of the economy. In the nineteenth and twentieth centuries, the invention of railways, cars and planes accelerated the interpenetration of national economies, primarily by facilitating the transport of goods. Today, there are further possibilities brought about by the new media. Their essential feature is the acceleration and simplification of communications and information exchange. This extends to almost all areas of economic life. For instance, firms can more easily contact customers throughout the world and thus expand into new markets. It is also conceivable that the Internet and e-mail make it easier for a firm to communicate with registration or supervisory authorities. Securing permits and publishing statutorily required information is thereby made simpler and cheaper. Moreover, interaction within the company can be improved. Companies with multiple sites may, for instance, discuss and act through online conferences independently of geographical distance. Additionally, the new media facilitate communications between a firm and its shareholders, so that, for instance, shareholders' rights to information and participation can be optimized. Finally, trade in shares becomes faster and less complicated. The direct and discount broking sector lowers costs for securities transactions and enables rapid trading in shares.

For these (and other) reasons, the new media may accordingly exert considerable influence on commercial law. Since these new technical

[105] Weisbrot (1998: 645 *et seq.*); Rodrik (1999: 85 *et seq.*); see also Bhagwati (2004: 199 *et seq.*); Nunnenkamp (2006).

possibilities are a worldwide phenomenon, the same legal challenges arise across borders, making similar solutions seem conceivable.[106]

3. *The internationalization of private institutions*

For company law and securities law, private institutions that support or act on management or investors play an important part. Although there are differences internationally, an approximation in economic infrastructures can be discerned, and might also be reflected in shareholder law. Thus, it may in general be noted that large business consultants (McKinsey, BCG etc.), audit firms (KPMG, PwC etc.), law firms (Baker & McKenzie, Freshfields etc.), investment banks (Goldman Sachs, Morgan Stanley etc.) and rating agencies (Standard & Poor's, Moody's etc.) are today active in most developed countries. Since these private institutions are often of US origin, it is primarily Europe that has been (and will continue to be) influenced by US economic culture. For Japan and China by contrast, the 'Americanization' of economic infrastructure is a more recent phenomenon. For instance, in Japan there were until the 1990s no business consultants, and far fewer external auditors than in other developed countries.[107] Recently, however, the number of consultants and external auditors in Japan has been increasing.[108]

These trends are set to continue with the internationalization of the economy (subsection 2 above) and of undertakings (subsection 4 below). For instance, the GATS facilitates market access for financial undertakings, and increases the competitive pressure on banks hitherto active only domestically.[109] This is today true also for Japan. For a long time, Japanese banking was strictly regimented and protected against foreign competition. By the end of the 1990s, however, partly through US pressure, the barriers to foreign financial undertakings were gradually removed.[110] Something similar is under way for China. To date, the four large state banks predominate in China. With WTO accession, however, the Chinese banking sector is opening up to foreign competition.[111] Additionally, at the

[106] See also Ch. 10, section I.2.c, d below.

[107] See Milhaupt and West (2003a: 310); Milhaupt (2001: 2103).

[108] See Milhaupt and West (2003a: 319).

[109] See generally Hall (2001: 60 *et seq.*); on cross-border mergers see Norton and Olive (2001: 591 *et seq.*).

[110] See Menden (1999: 36–7); Kawamoto *et al.* (2001: para. 57); Kelemen and Sibbitt (2002: 308).

[111] See Schick (2002); *Handelsblatt*, 10 January 2003, at 21; 20 January 2003, at 19.

international level the new capital accord 'Basel II'[112] will speed the interpenetration of economic infrastructures. Apart from banking, this concerns particularly the rating system, because for banks the soundness of an enterprise depends basically on an internal or external rating. Finally, the increasing internationalization of undertakings is also promoting, across the countries, the internationalization of private institutions that advise, assess and support them. This influence equally goes in the other direction, since these private institutions contribute through consultancy in cases of mergers and takeovers to the internationalization of enterprises. There is accordingly an interaction whereby each group of institutions profits from the internationalization trends in all the others groups.

4. *The internationalization of undertakings*

The internationalization of undertakings may be distinguished according to various degrees of intensity. Internationalization through cross-border mergers has the strongest effects (subsection a below). In this case, international undertakings in the narrower sense arise, since as a rule they extend both spatially (production plants, sales markets etc.), and in personnel terms (shareholders, employees etc.) to various countries. There is accordingly less internationalization if the national frontiers are overcome in only one sub-aspect. This covers particularly the cases where the involvement of foreign shareholders contributes to a certain internationalization of undertakings (subsections b and c below). Finally, as in other cultural spheres, the enterprise culture of national undertakings may also become more similar (subsection d below).

a) International mergers

Even though at the start of the twenty-first century, for economic reasons, the overall figure for the number of mergers and acquisitions has been falling, it is nonetheless to be presumed that the growing proportion of cross-border consolidations of enterprises will continue in the future. Undertakings have an interest in being present in as many countries as possible, in opening up new markets, in acquiring new technology and skills and optimizing production capacities. For the consequences of this development, we hear on the one hand that 'cross-border alliances . . . are leading to the articulation of a new global governance template that uses existing tools to build a new corporate world

[112] See http://www.bis.org/publ/bcbsca.htm.

order'.[113] On the other hand, there are some doubts as to whether such firms are truly 'global', or act globally. Global mergers are seen as not having fundamentally changed national legal systems.[114] And such mergers tend more to extinguish one culture than to lead to convergence. Multinational undertakings are accordingly only superficially similar, but at bottom remain national undertakings, so that the concept of a global company is regarded simply as a myth.[115]

This scepticism about convergence is right in saying that multinational firms are not just global but also nationally typified through their head office. However, in such undertakings, national differences are reduced. Where, for instance, sceptics say of Germany that the role of the banks, cross-holdings and the absence of a market for hostile takeovers are cultural features that cannot simply be suppressed, all this is being weakened by current developments.[116] The competitiveness of enterprises and the drive to grow globally are leading to some convergence of enterprises, as can already be seen in, for instance, questions of the best systems for remuneration and monitoring.[117]

Objections can, however, also be raised from a legal perspective. By contrast with joint ventures, a direct merger of companies is difficult to achieve in many countries when a foreign firm is involved.[118] Furthermore, there are specific problems such as, for instance, approval and verification procedures in China,[119] and restrictions on the use of cross-border mergers executed through stock swaps in Japan.[120] And, even in the European Union, it took decades before the law on the European Company (Societas Europaea) and the Directive on Cross-Border Mergers were adopted.[121] However, the increasingly internationalized private institutions (subsection 3 above) have in practice also been finding alternative means to make cross-border mergers possible. A unitary undertaking may, thus, emerge by the purchase of either all the shares in the target company ('share deal')

[113] Cunningham (1999: 1194). [114] Bratton and McCahery (1999: 239).

[115] Branson (2001: 339 *et seq.*), (2002: 123 *et seq.*); Doremus *et al.* (1998: 3 *et seq.*); Rugman (2001).

[116] See Ch. 8, section IV.2.b below. [117] See Ch. 5, section II.1.a, b above.

[118] See generally Cornette de Saint-Cyr (2002); Siems (2004c); for joint ventures in China see Ch. 8, section III.4.b below.

[119] See Fu-Tomlinson (2005).

[120] See Benes (2005) and Ueda (2005: 427) (for the new law); Osugi (2002: 37–8); Hayakawa (2003: 61–2).

[121] Regulation (EC) No. 2157/2001 on the Statute for a European Company (SE); Directive 2005/56/EC on cross-border mergers of companies with shares; on the history see Siems (2004c); see now also the decision *SEVIC Systems AG*, C-411/03, [2005] ECR I-10805 with a comment in Siems (2007b).

or all the firm's individual economic assets ('asset deal').[122] Additionally, for instance with the Daimler/Chrysler merger, a pattern has been set for a more complex form of combination. Here, initially, a new parent company, DaimlerChrysler AG, acquired the shares of Daimler and Chrysler in exchange for its own shares. Thereafter, Daimler-Benz AG was merged into DaimlerChrysler AG, and thus a unitary company emerged.[123]

b) Foreign investors

The sceptics also do not see the increase in foreign investors as an indication of a globalization process.[124] They are right in that cross-border investments are strongly regionalized and unequally distributed globally, being concentrated essentially, for instance, on the OECD or G7/G8 countries, with investments mostly disproportionately in the home country.[125] Nonetheless, these facts do not deny the trend to internationalization by foreign investors. The proportion of foreign shareholders in domestic companies has been steadily increasing in recent decades.[126] And these shareholders influence the firms themselves, as can be seen particularly in the financial power of and calls for good corporate governance by US institutional investors.[127]

The reasons for this increase in foreign investors suggest that this trend will continue. The basic economic advantage is that a worldwide spread of their investments can minimize economic and legal risks. Additionally, for the EU the introduction of the euro, and in the global context the liberalization of international economic law, have made investments simpler and safer. Even though the OECD's multilateral investment agreement has failed,[128] most countries want inflows of foreign capital for the domestic economy and do not subject them to significant barriers. This is also true today for Japan.[129] Until Japan's accession to the OECD in 1964, the purchase of Japanese shares by foreigners and foreign shares by the Japanese was possible only in very restricted circumstances. Japan has

[122] See e.g. Trendelenburg (2002); Siems (2004c).
[123] See Baums (1999); Gruson (2001); Johnson (2002: 81 *et seq.*).
[124] Branson (2001: 339 *et seq.*); Doremus *et al.* (1998: 143).
[125] See Cornelius and Kogut (2003: 4); Doremus *et al.* (1998: 143); Baum (2000: 83).
[126] See generally Van der Elst (2003: 28–9); Van den Berghe (2002: 46 *et seq.*); for Japan: West (2001a: 593–4); Komiyama and Masaoka (2002: 2–3); for Germany: Zetzsche (2004: Appendix F); for France: ANSA (2003: 2); for China: Comberg (2000: 40–1); for the UK: Strätling (2003: 76).
[127] See Ch. 9, section III.2 below.
[128] See Ch. 8, section III.1 above.
[129] See Baum (1996: 403); Baum and Hayakawa (1994: 501 *et seq.*, 505–6); Menden (1999: 36–7); Kawamoto *et al.* (2001: para. 57).

since gradually liberalized its law, and in the 1998 'Big Bang' removed the remaining barriers.

China was long a special case. Since it joined the WTO, however, Chinese firms have been able to obtain foreign currency more easily and therefore to invest abroad. Additionally, the Qualified Domestic Institutional Investor programme (QDII) has enabled Chinese institutional investors to trade in shares on foreign exchanges.[130] Conversely, subject to government permission,[131] foreigners can also acquire shares in Chinese firms. The possibilities for this have been steadily expanding in recent years. Foreigners are now able to buy state shares and the shares of legal persons on certain conditions.[132] Since the adoption of the Qualified Foreign Institutional Investor programme (QFII) and the Strategic Investment Provisions, they can buy not just B-shares but also A-shares.[133] Since buying A-shares is, however, bound up with considerable burdens and the capital market for B-shares is relatively thin, in practice direct, one-off investments prevail. For this, the Chinese legislator has created different forms of participation – Equity Joint Venture (EJV), Contractual Joint Venture (CJV), Foreign Invested Investment Company (FIIC), Wholly Foreign-Owned Enterprise (WFOE), Foreign Investment Companies Limited by Shares (FICLBS, or FICLS) – and subjected them to various regulations.[134] The most recent company form, FICLBS, in particular has been described as a 'giant step forward',[135] since their shares can be freely traded inside and outside China.

c) Exchange listings abroad

Companies may in principle be listed either only domestically or only abroad, or both. Listing only abroad is used, for instance, by some Israeli companies, listed only on the American Nasdaq, since in Israel there is no exchange for venture capital.[136] More commonly, however, listing abroad is part of a dual or multiple listing. The number of firms listed on foreign exchanges (especially the NYSE and the LSE) has clearly increased in recent decades.[137] Yet the economic troubles in the early twenty-first century and the high costs entailed by the 2002 Sarbanes–Oxley Act for a

[130] See *Handelsblatt*, 20 August 2003, at 26; 9 September 2003, at 38.
[131] See Neumann (2003).
[132] See Pißler (2002c: 2). [133] See Ch. 2, section III.2 above.
[134] See Yuan (2001: 195, 202 *et seq.*); Zhang and Lowe (2001: 409 *et seq.*).
[135] Zhang and Lowe (2001: 433).
[136] See Luck (2001: 310); Licht (2001b) (on the effort to lure companies back home).
[137] See e.g. Baum (2000: 81); Comberg (2000: 40–1); Coffee (2002b: 1771).

listing in the US have meant that the number of new listings has decreased in recent years. And recently some firms have given up multiple listings.[138] However, since delisting is usually done on the exchange least liquid for the firm, this development ought not to be over-estimated. Moreover, large firms will usually be unwilling to delist, because doing so may create the impression that the firm is in financial or other difficulties. Finally, particularly in the US, delisting may not be sufficient, since disclosure obligations continue to apply if more than 300 shares are held by US citizens.[139]

(1) Causes. Four reasons can be adduced for listing abroad.[140] First, the aim may be to address a broader range of investors. Although investors today may in principle buy shares anywhere, market segmentations may stand in the way of purchasing shares listed abroad. For instance, taxation or internal rules may lead institutional investors to favour shares listed domestically. Additionally, a listing abroad may enhance a firm's name recognition and prestige, thus overcoming the foreign investor's information deficits. As a result, expansion of the range of investors is aimed at promoting the demand for the firm's shares, so that liquidity improves, the share price rises and capital costs fall.

Secondly, it is also conceivable that the better law on a particular market will increase the value of the shares. A company may through a listing abroad voluntarily bind itself to tighter disclosure and minority-protection provisions, so that its shares receive a smaller risk premium and their price rises. 'Good legal systems' are thus rewarded. If this 'bonding effect' is the main reason for a listing abroad, then one may expect an international 'race to the top'.[141]

Thirdly, a firm's growth following multiple listing may result not just from improved liquidity but also because a listing on a foreign exchange makes it easier to acquire foreign firms. National legal systems sometimes do not allow hostile takeovers to be financed by foreign shares.[142] Additionally, market forces may lead to a similar result, where shareholders of

[138] See e.g. *Financial Times*, 21 June 2006, at 26 (concerning DaimlerChrysler).

[139] SEC Rule 12h-3. However, SEC Release No. 34-55540 of 27 March 2007, available at www.sec.gov/rules/final/2007/34-55540.pdf, has modified this rule, because an approach based on the trading volume standard can now also be used.

[140] See e.g. Coffee (2002b: 1779 *et seq.*), (1999b: 673, 676 *et seq.*, 682, 691–2); MacNeil and Lau (2001: 789–90); MacNeil (2000: 13 *et seq.*); Pagano (2002).

[141] For the 'race to the bottom'–'race to the top' discussion see also Ch. 9, sections I.1, VI.1 below.

[142] See Gruson (2001: 190–1); for Germany see §§ 31(2), 2(7) GerWpÜG.

the target company prefer domestic shares and thus make the success of a takeover dependent on a listing abroad.

Fourthly, personal considerations by directors also play a part in listings abroad. A multiple listing enhances their prestige, because the firm can grow further and acquire an increasingly global image. These grounds alone may justify salary increases for directors. Additionally, a listing in a country where stock options are more common than domestically may also lead to higher earnings. Finally, management's position may become safer. As a rule, more shareholders mean a wider spread of shareholdings. The absence of influential shareholders will thus make it less likely for a majority of shareholders to turn against them.

(2) **Problems.** In weighing up these considerations, however, the problems of an exchange listing abroad ought also not to be overlooked. Each of the reasons stated above also entails potential drawbacks. An expansion of the range of investors through more international investors (the first reason mentioned above) may hamper communication with shareholders and make shareholder behaviour less reliable. Although, based on the 'bonding thesis' (the second reason mentioned above), an improvement in legal conditions may occur, the tighter disclosure requirements etc. may also entail considerable costs. And there might be problems if the new foreign rules are not be entirely compatible with the existing corporate governance culture.[143] Furthermore, the possible facilitation of hostile takeovers (the third reason mentioned above) may have disadvantageous effects because it also, conversely, makes the firm more susceptible to hostile takeovers. Finally, management's improved image (the fourth reason mentioned above) may have its dangers, since the public has higher expectations of global firms.

In addition, a listing of foreign companies may entail contradictions between foreign and domestic law. This may be caused either by differences in securities laws, or by differences between securities and company law. It may thus happen that shares in the same firm are, depending on the location of the exchange, subject to different regulations on, for instance, insider dealing or financial disclosure. Additionally, it is conceivable that – as is commonly the case in the US – the securities law also contains regulations on voting proxies or committees,[144] thus coming into conflict with foreign company laws.

[143] See Licht (2004a). [144] See Ch. 4, section II.3.c; Ch. 5, section II.1.b above.

National legislators, securities supervisors and stock exchanges may respond to these regulatory contradictions either uncooperatively or cooperatively.[145] An uncooperative and unilateral system insists on its own law having extraterritorial effect. A country is seen as having an interest in subjecting foreign companies listed in that country to its regulations. This can be justified, since these foreign companies have listed themselves there voluntarily and aim to profit from the consequent advantages. By contrast, a cooperative model seeks to reduce conflicts. This may come about directly through the harmonization of substantive securities law, so that a uniform international capital-market system develops. However, a purely indirect process is also conceivable, whereby the domestic system of companies listed abroad is recognized at bilateral, regional or multilateral levels. So the barriers to entry to a foreign capital market are lowered, and (in contrast to the harmonization solution) regulatory competition promoted.

The US and the UK in principle act unilaterally towards foreign companies listed on their exchanges, so that their securities laws in part have extraterritorial effect. For instance, foreign companies in the US must comply with the regulations on tender offers, delisting, disclosure obligations by influential shareholders and the utilization of the SEC's electronic data system (EDGAR) for forms and reports.[146] Additionally and especially, the 2002 Sarbanes–Oxley Act obliges compliance with securities law provisions, such as tightening of management obligations and the setting up of audit committees, which are objectively more of a company-law nature.[147] Yet, some unilateral concessions are made to foreign companies. Thus, in the US and the UK, the disclosure requirements for foreign companies are reduced, so that, for instance, the exhaustive US proxy regulations and the strict UK regulations on influential shareholders apply only restrictedly.[148] However, in this case too, there may be pressure on firms not to accept any exemption from the foreign law. Institutional investors sometimes require their domestic law to be complied with in its entirety.[149] For the UK, however, EU law also has to be taken into account. In the EU, decisions of the supervisory authorities of other Member States

[145] See Baum (2000: 88 *et seq.*); MacNeil (2000: 8 *et seq.*).

[146] See e.g. Coffee (1999b: 683 *et seq.*); Großfeld (1995: 121 *et seq.*); Vagts (2000: para. 10-22); Nahr (2003: 115 *et seq.*).

[147] For its applicability to foreign companies see e.g. Perino (2003); Cardilli (2004).

[148] For the US: Baum (2000: 85–6); Coffee (1999b: 706); for the UK: MacNeil and Lau (2001: 798 *et seq.*); MacNeil (2000: 13 *et seq.*).

[149] See Leube (2003: 98–9).

are in principle recognized, so that, for instance, a prospectus authorized in one Member State will be authorized in the whole European Union.[150] This does not mean that the EU is thereby following the concept of regulatory competition. For national legislators are not running any great risk by recognizing the law of other Member States, since the EU securities law has already created high European standards.

This ambivalence in approach to the possible contradictions between foreign and domestic law is also reflected in the ranking of the reasons and the forecasts for multiple listings. On the one hand, a listing abroad is associated with costs and risks. There may also be legal problems either caused by the extraterritorial effect of foreign law, or if the company is exempted from foreign law, the desired 'bonding effect' may fail to occur. On the other hand, however, it is to be expected that the number of double or multiple listings will increase further. For countries where foreign shares are listed, it is an advantage that the demand for domestic investment services, lawyers, auditors etc. will increase, thus helping the country's economy. Similarly, as present trends show, in principle a listing abroad may also be an advantage for firms.

(3) **Effects on the convergence debate.** If domestic law is also applied to foreign companies, John Coffee speaks of functional convergence.[151] This means that (at least initially) no formal convergence comes about through the foreign listing, since domestic law does not change. However, the results become functionally similar between companies from various countries, since – subject to certain exemptions – they come under the same securities law.

This functional convergence may also affect the positive law of the legal system in which the company was founded. It is conceivable for this legal system to adapt its securities law to the foreign law.[152] This will have the consequence that the 'bonding effect' also works in favour of the domestic legal system, so that fewer companies emigrate and foreign companies may possibly immigrate. This behaviour is not, however, automatic. For smaller exchanges in particular, it is not worth entering into competition with 'global players' like the NYSE or LSE. Here, it may therefore be the better strategy to specialize and address a particular market segment.[153]

[150] Prospectus Directive 2003/71/EC; Commission Regulation (EC) No. 809/2004; see also Ferran (2004: 147 *et seq.*).

[151] See Ch. 1, section IV.1 above, and Coffee (1999b: 650, 681).

[152] See Hellwig (2001: 580); Coffee (2002b: 1766).

[153] See Coffee (2002b: 1811 *et seq.*).

Irrespective of this question, an increasing number of firms listing abroad acts as a convergence force for shareholder law. As with the increase in cross-border mergers and foreign investors (subsections a and b above), this circumstance too means that the range of shareholders and therefore the firms themselves become internationalized.

d) Enterprise culture

Management is not uniform internationally. For instance, even between European countries top managers are trained differently.[154] And, even with firms operating on the international market, boards still largely consist of executives from one country, or at least one language area. Moreover, it can be seen from special training programmes aimed at sensitizing managers from one country to the enterprise culture of another[155] that despite globalization no cultural conformity exists. However, it is to be expected that the macro-economic changes will also be reflected at micro-economic level. For instance, cross-border mergers and participation by foreign shareholders (subsections a to c above) and the breaking up of interlocking participation structures (section IV.2 below) contribute to the approximation of enterprise cultures. One might also, as in other cultural areas,[156] point to a number of other factors such as the internationalization of education and future executives studying abroad.

It follows that global enterprises will come closer together than local firms. Additionally, pan-social differences between cultures may stand in the way of a convergence of enterprise culture. However, it would be going too far to say, for instance, that on the question of individualism Japan and the US are diametric opposites, so that in the US they do not understand Japanese enterprises.[157] The discussion on the 'shareholder–stakeholder' dichotomy have, for instance, already made it clear that the differences between the countries are not as profound as traditionally presented.[158] Moreover, a study by PricewaterhouseCoopers shows, for example, that in Japanese firms there is also a trend away from a collective, company-oriented pattern to an individualistic orientation.[159] Here, once again, one can therefore expect growing convergence (though not identity).

[154] For the UK, Germany and France see Whittington and Mayer (2000: 110 *et seq.*).

[155] See e.g. http://www.sietar.org.; http://www.berlitz.co.uk/front_content.php?idcat = 1058.

[156] See Ch. 8, sections I, II above.

[157] *Contra* Henderson (1995: 898).

[158] See Ch. 5, section II.1.a above.

[159] See *Süddeutsche Zeitung*, 13 February 2002, at 22; more cautiously Igarashi (2001: 72 *et seq.*); Dore (2000: 104 *et seq.*).

IV. Approximation of shareholder structures

The question of shareholder structure is sometimes seen as a central point of the corporate governance debate, since on it depends how a firm is financed and who controls it. One decisive point in particular is whether primarily one or more large shareholders control a firm ('blockholder systems') or (whether or also) dispersed shareholdings are more common, so that management has considerable room for manoeuvre ('dispersed ownership systems'). It is usually emphasized that in the US and the UK dispersed shareholdings prevail, and in other countries blockholdings prevail.[160] However, it is questionable how these differences are to be explained (subsection 1 below). Again, shareholder structures are currently going through changes (subsections 2 and 3 below).

1. *Explanatory models*

From a theoretical point of view, the ownership structure of joint stock companies can be explained in different ways. Additionally, in practice, developmental lines in various countries do not show a uniform picture.

a) The role of law and politics

La Porta *et al.* assume that, depending on the pattern of shareholder protection, there will be different shareholder structures.[161] With a low level of protection, concentrated shareholdings will dominate, since the demand for shares will be small and a shareholder will need many shares to be able actually to protect himself. By contrast, good minority protection in company and securities law[162] induces more investors to invest in shares and thus initially leads to more dispersed shareholder ownership in a few companies. In further developments, the more competitive companies with dispersed holdings will increasingly make headway. What is seen as particularly decisive here is that given one or a few blockholders the other shareholders may be disadvantaged, and management selected according to the blockholders' desires rather than quality. Companies with dispersed holdings are by contrast more efficient, so that countries

[160] See e.g. Coffee (1999b: 641); Cheffins (2001c: 88 *et seq.*); Berndt (2002: 5 *et seq.*); Whittington and Mayer (2000: 90 *et seq.*); Barca and Becht (2001); Van den Berghe (2002: 34 *et seq.*).

[161] La Porta *et al.* (1998); see also Ch. 1, section I; Ch. 7, section I.1 above.

[162] La Porta *et al.* (1998) analyze company law only. However, they have also extended their approach to securities law: see La Porta *et al.* (2006), and for a critical account see Siems (2005b).

with good shareholder protection will, at least in the large-firm sector, see companies with blockholders slowly 'dying out' ('Darwinian struggle').

However, the debate in the literature has shown that this supplies at most a partial explanation for different shareholder structures. Shareholder protection may be a necessary but not a sufficient precondition for the separation of ownership and control through dispersed holdings.[163] Good positive law is not enough, since enforcement must be possible, and corruption must be excluded by rule-of-law structures. Additionally, the law can help only against, say, abuse of power by management, but not against a flawed business policies. To induce a multiplicity of investors to invest in shares, accordingly, the economic, social and political environment must also be favourable. Finally, shareholder protection may even be irrelevant for shareholder structure. It seems from the history of company and securities law in the US and the UK that it is only once strong markets exist and shareholders become powerful groups that more developed legal regulations are established to protect shareholder interests.[164] Additionally, in the US, despite improved shareholder protection in the twentieth century, the concentration of shareholdings even slightly increased.[165] Finally, as already noted, methodological arguments oppose the findings by La Porta *et al.*[166]

A counter-concept taking other legal criteria into account was developed by Mark Roe.[167] Roe denies the 'Darwinism thesis' whereby in the US dispersed shareholder ownership came to prevail in large firms for reasons of economic efficiency. Instead, it was specifically not the market but limited market freedom for banks that contributed to it. Since the nineteenth century the US has seen a regional fragmentation of banking. Additionally, to prevent concentrated financial power, the 1933 Glass–Steagall Act required investment and commercial banks to be separated. Because of the weak position of banks it was not possible for firms to sell large share packages to them or to finance themselves primarily through bank loans. According to Roe, in the US financing through the capital markets and therefore relatively widespread dispersed shareholdings came about as a substitute for large nationwide banks. In continental Europe by contrast, banks were not hampered in their growth. The lesser importance of capital markets is thus partly to be explained by the fact that the demand for shares was smaller here. Roe goes on to point to

[163] Roe (2002: 233 *et seq.*). [164] See Ch. 7, section I.1 above.

[165] See Roe (2002: 250 note 24); Rock (1995: 294).

[166] See Ch. 1, section I above. [167] Roe (1991), (1994), (1996b), (1997), (2003a).

further factors:[168] strong capital markets are incompatible with social-democratic ideas such as dominated continental Europe and Japan in the second half of the twentieth century. In particular, employee influence here meant that the 'shareholder supremacy' principle did not apply.[169] Additionally, further economic and social circumstances would have to join in to produce a capital market with more dispersed ownership. For instance, intensive product competition, incentive-based remuneration and hostile takeovers would promote the financial need of firms and trust by potential investors. Finally, account has to be taken of whether institutional investors are powerful financial providers because, say, private pension funds predominate in a country.[170]

However, Roe's argument too has been criticized. Among counter-examples to the banking background in the US are, first, the position in the UK.[171] Although here no such law as the Glass–Steagall Act was adopted, many UK public companies have also developed dispersed holdings. Even without legal requirements, banks in the UK too deliberately act conservatively and do not hold blocks of shares, since that is too risky for them and would reduce their liquidity. Secondly, Japan can be pointed to as a counter-example. Here, on the US model, until the 1990s a separation between investment banks and commercial banks was prescribed. Nonetheless, interlocking shareholdings dominate in Japan, and the influence of banks is (so far) considerable.[172] Moreover, in the US since the early 1990s the banking landscape has changed. There has been a turning away from the regional principle and an increasing number of mergers among banks. Furthermore, the Gramm–Leach–Bliley Financial Modernization Act of 1999 repealed the Glass–Steagall Act. This has not, however, meant that in the US banks have now set themselves up as blockholders. Finally, the alleged influence of basic policy attitudes is also not beyond doubt. In the twentieth century, in Western democracies, political majorities have changed several times without this automatically being tied up with changes in the composition of companies.[173] For instance, the US during the New Deal period in the 1930s and the UK before the Thatcher government can be termed social democratic.[174] But changes in shareholder structure did not follow. Even if it is sometimes assumed for the UK that

168 Roe (2003a), (2002b: 263 *et seq.*).

169 For criticism see Ch. 5, section II.1.a above.

170 Roe (2000: 585) (but not primarily); see also Branson (2001: 329–30); McDonnell (2002: 380).

171 See e.g. Cheffins (2002: 153 *et seq.*); Coffee (2002a: 105); Romano (1993: 146).

172 See Ch. 8, section IV.2.a below.

173 Pistor *et al.* (2001: 56 *et seq.*).

174 Coffee (2002a: 93); Cheffins (2002: 160–1).

in the late 1970s dispersed holdings came to prevail, reasons other than the change of government from Callaghan to Thatcher were decisive.[175]

b) The role of private law-making and individualism

The criterion of 'social democracy' was already employed by Mark Roe to denote the 'intensity' of the market economy as a criterion of differentiation. Here his view overlaps with those of John Coffee, Brian Cheffins and Curtis Milhaupt.[176] Yet Coffee sees the cause of differing shareholder structures as already rooted in the older distinction between common law and civil law.

Common law countries, according to Coffee, are distinguished by positive attitudes to individualism and private initiatives. As can be seen *inter alia* from the traditionally absent codifications, there are fewer interventionist operations by the state, so that the economy and society take to forms of self-regulation and private contracting. For instance, in the US in the nineteenth century, it was investment banks and stock exchanges in particular that ensured an active capital market. Investment banks were represented on the boards of directors of many companies and protected minority shareholders against hostile takeovers. The exchanges, especially the NYSE, pursued a restrictive listing practice, so that only sound firms came onto the exchange, minimizing investor risk.[177] In the UK, development was somewhat slower.[178] Besides occasional statutory provisions, here it was not until after the First World War that protection by the LSE was enhanced. Finally, for both the UK and the US, the early importance of professionalized private institutions should be noted.

By contrast with this development, which left it to market forces to develop the capital market, the civil law countries are seen as traditionally marked by state control over the economy and the paternalism of those involved, so that no separation between market and politics came about.[179] Coffee points particularly to Germany and France. Industrialization in nineteenth-century Germany was financed mainly by the big banks and not through the capital market. This instrumentalization of the banks was deliberately encouraged by the government. Examples of this were the central bank's policy, the fiscal burdens on shares and the restrictive Stock Exchange Act 1896.[180] In France, the Paris Stock Exchange was long a private monopoly under close state control. Exchange listing came about

[175] Cheffins (2002: 153 *et seq.*); for a different view see Roe (2003a: 98 *et seq.*).

[176] Coffee (2001: 49 *et seq.*, 78–9); Cheffins (2003a), (2003c); Milhaupt (1998: 1145, 1166).

[177] See Coffee (2002a: 94 *et seq.*).

[178] See Coffee (2002a: 100 *et seq.*), (2001: 42–3).

[179] See Coffee (2001: 62, 64); see also Roe (1996b: 257), (2003a: 65 *et seq.*).

[180] See Coffee (2001: 51 *et seq.*).

through the Finance Ministry. And the brokers on the exchange were civil servants permitted to act only on commission. Once the shadow market that emerged was banned, the government retained a strong influence and was not interested in improving the quality of trading on the exchange.[181] An active capital market with dispersed holdings thus developed in neither Germany nor France.

But this explanation for the differences in shareholder structure is not convincing. The division into legal families is in the present context no longer relevant to the current law and legal culture.[182] Moreover, even if Coffee is correct in relating the division into legal families more to the historical development of commercial law than to today's law, the contrast between civil and common law is nevertheless not so marked as in classical private law (contract, tort, etc.).[183] Since the initial stages of the development of company and securities law, there has been an intensive exchange between the two cultures.[184] Additionally, in commercial law, on the European continent private arrangements have always played an important part ('lex mercatoria'), nor was interventionism by the state in cases of abuse foreign to common law countries (e.g. the UK Bubble Act of 1720). Finally, the division into legal families is contradicted by the fact that widespread shareholding did not develop in the UK until the twentieth century, and that even today concentrated shareholdings prevail in Canada, Australia and New Zealand.[185]

c) Conclusion

There is no single model to explain shareholder structures in all countries. With any model it may be the case that there is at least one country where a particular circumstance has not reflected either a theoretical conception or an historical pattern. Thus, the following will look at specific examples in order to determine whether there is convergence in shareholder structures (subsection 2 below). Because of their important role, institutional investors will be addressed separately (subsection 3 below).

2. The decline in concentrated shareholder structures

The distinction between dispersed shareholdings in the US and the UK and concentrated shareholdings in Germany, France, China and Japan should not be over-emphasized. Just as in the US and the UK there are

[181] See Coffee (2001: 45 *et seq.*).
[182] See Part II and Ch. 8, section II above. [183] Similarly Vagts (2002: 598).
[184] See Ch. 1, section III above. [185] See Cheffins (2002: 152 *et seq.*).

companies without dispersed holdings, so conversely there are also ones with dispersed holdings in the other countries studied here.[186] Nor will anything change as such in this co-existence, since the composition of companies in the individual case depends on, for instance, their size, age and risk structure. It is, however, to be expected that, in Germany, France, China and Japan, the trend towards a decline in concentrated shareholder structures will continue.

a) Features to date

In Germany, France, Japan and China, companies have so far mostly been controlled by one or a few influential shareholders – for instance, banks, the state or other firms.

The German position is typified particularly by ring shareholdings and cross-holdings by firms ('Deutschland AG' or 'Germany Inc.'). This hinders control of managements by outside shareholders, and in practice removes the risk of hostile takeovers.[187] The financing of companies is done through the German universal banks. This means that the banks have, as shareholders and creditors, considerable influence on companies. In addition to their function as capital providers, they can also control companies by means of the deposit vote and by their involvement on the supervisory board and thus influence the firm's strategy.[188] Because companies were financed through the banks, the capital market have long remained thin. In addition to the historical and legal reasons,[189] this was also furthered by the fact that after the Second World War the demand for shares was small. The bulk of the German population did not have the free capital to invest in shares, and was more interested in secure savings and in buying their own home. Since old-age provision was guaranteed by the state, there was also no need to put money into pension or investment funds.

While in France in 1913 stock market capitalization to GDP was higher than in the UK or the US,[190] after the Second World War the importance of the capital market declined. Various factors were decisive in this.[191] First, in France there is a disproportionately large number of small joint

[186] See e.g. Hansmann and Kraakman (2001: 443); Cheffins (2001c: 89), (2003a: 8); La Porta *et al.* (1998: 1146); La Porta *et al.* (1999: 471).

[187] See e.g. Adams (1994: 148); Wymeersch (1995: 302); Doremus *et al.* (1998: 37).

[188] See André (1998: 127 *et seq.*).

[189] See Ch. 8, section IV.1.b above.

[190] See Roe (2003a: 69); Rajan and Zingales (2003).

[191] On what follows see O'Sullivan (2001: 4 *et seq.*); Whittington and Mayer (2000: 95–6, 101–2, 104, 108–9); Pastre (1998: 81–2); Mojuyé (2000: 74 *et seq.*); Fanto (1998: 39–40); Wallace (2002: 25); Korch (2002: 13–14).

stock companies[192] not dependent on financing through the capital market. Secondly, despite the restrictions on interlocking shareholdings,[193] many firms are still interwoven with each other. Thirdly, families keep a considerable proportion of companies continuously in their own hands, so that their shares have little liquidity. Fourthly, strong state influence reduces the relative importance of the capital market. After 1945, a number of firms were nationalized or the state bought their shares, and often there were 'golden shares' ('action privilégiée') with special rights. Fifthly, firms were therefore decisively dependent on financing through bank loans. And, sixthly, this was enhanced by the fact that individuals did not have to invest their money in pension funds, nor invest directly in shares.

State influence is still stronger for Chinese companies. When, in the economic reforms in the 1980s, companies were once again permitted to be established,[194] only a formal privatization of enterprises was intended. Shares in the newly created companies remained in the hands of the state ('corporatization not privatization') and were administered by state-owned holding companies.[195] Even though a limited proportion of shares has since gone to private persons, this has not led to liquid trading in shares or widespread shareholding. The state still holds a controlling influence in many companies. Moreover, firms in close contact with the issuing firm often acquire the shares, so that group structures emerge.[196] Finally, China has to date been dominated by financing through bank loans, since 90 per cent of the capital for firms is provided by banks and only 10 per cent is provided through the exchanges.[197]

The Japanese position is typified mainly by the close relations between firms, including the banks. The historical starting-point was the 'zaibatsu', in which until 1945 groups of companies were held together under a holding company dominated by a single family and maintaining close contacts with politics.[198] After the Second World War, under US pressure, an anti-monopoly act brought in a regulation banning holding companies and therefore leading to the dissolution of the zaibatsu.[199] However, since this

[192] See Ch. 1, section II.1 above.

[193] See Ch. 5, section II.2.a above.

[194] See Ch. 1, section III.3.c above.

[195] See e.g. Wei (2003: 78); Pißler (2002b: 6 *et seq.*); Leung *et al.* (2002: 15); Heilmann (2001b: 4 *et seq.*); Comberg (2000: 14).

[196] See Liu (2001: 48–9); Wei (2003: 57 *et seq.*); Howson (2005: 242).

[197] *Handelsblatt*, 25 February 2003, at 13; see also Leung *et al.* (2002: 6).

[198] See Eisele (2004a: 3 *et seq.*); Menden (1999: 25); Takahashi (1997: 227); Kawamoto *et al.* (2001: para. 42).

[199] Art. 9 of the Law concerning the Prohibition of Private Monopoly and Maintenance of Fair Trade (Shiteki dokusen no kinishi oyobi kôsei torihiki no kakuhô ni kansuru hôritsu), Law No. 54/1947; recently amended by Law No. 35/2005.

law did not ban other forms of interlocking, Japanese firms quickly combined their interests again, thus bringing groups of firms ('keiretsu') again into being. The six largest keiretsu, each comprising around 200 firms, partly coincide with the former zaibatsu. Additionally, further horizontal and vertical keiretsus were formed. In a horizontal keiretsu (like the 'Big Six'), no firm is superior, and mostly only one firm from each sector is involved. By contrast, a vertical keiretsu consists of a dominant firm and several subordinate firms which are often its suppliers and distributors.[200]

One method for keeping these groups of firms together is capital participation in other group members.[201] While these holdings are mostly only small, so that one can regard even Japan as having a dispersed shareholder structure,[202] so far some 70 per cent of all shares are held by other companies, and therefore the capital interpenetration overall leads to a stabilization of the groups of companies. Additionally, the keiretsu's informal linkage is promoted, for instance, through intensive information, informal meetings or exchanges of employees.[203] All this gives the firms involved the advantage of being able to strengthen their position on the market. Furthermore, the influence of independent shareholders is reduced, smooth and efficient general meetings ensured and the risk of hostile takeovers minimized.[204]

The cohesion of a group of firms is, finally, enhanced by its main bank. The Japanese banks, despite legal restrictions, have great influence on companies.[205] Financing has to date come mainly from loans, and thus the importance of the capital market is slight.[206] The main bank is also linked with the firms through informal relations, such as the exchange of management personnel, and since the 1980s additionally through equity capital.[207] Again, banks actively intervene in crises and – as far as possible – bring about rehabilitation and reorganization of the firm concerned.

[200] See Eisele (2004a: 70–1); Menden (1999: 27 *et seq.*); Takahashi (1997: 231); Kawamoto *et al.* (2001: paras. 32–3); Baum (1996: 401).

[201] See e.g. Igarashi (2001: 76 *et seq.*); Menden (1999: 27 *et seq.*); Oda (1999: 236–7); Milhaupt and West (2003a: 310); Learmount (2002: 56 *et seq.*).

[202] Shishido (2000: 279); see also Miwa and Ramseyer (2002a), (2005b: 548–58), who regard the keiretsu as a 'fable'; against this view see Milhaupt (2002).

[203] See Eisele (2004b: 119 *et seq.*); Rodatz (1995: 258); Igarashi (2001: 70–1); Menden (1999: 27 *et seq.*); Learmount (2002: 68 *et seq.*).

[204] See Baum (1998: 746 *et seq.*); Menden (1999: 27 *et seq.*); Igarashi (2001: 70–1); Takahashi (1997: 228, 231–2); Baum and Hayakawa (1994: 502).

[205] See e.g. Roe (1996a: 320), (2003a: 91); Bottomley (1999: 59–60); Milhaupt (2001: 2103); Doremus *et al.* (1998: 43).

[206] See Kawamoto (1994: 109); Kawamoto *et al.* (2001: para. 360).

[207] See Igarashi (2001: 72 *et seq.*); Menden (1999: 39 *et seq.*); Oda (1999: 256); Baum (1998: 747–8); Milhaupt (2001: 2087–8); but see also Miwa and Ramseyer (2002b), (2005a),

b) Current developments

Recently, in Germany, France, China and Japan, the depth of the capital market has been increasing, and the network orientation of the economy and the concentration of shareholding declining.

First, in Germany and Japan, cross-holdings are reducing, so that more shares are traded on the capital market. For Germany, a decisive initiator of change was the tax reform of 2002. Since then, capital gains made by companies have been tax-free.[208] Large firms are therefore dissolving their reciprocal participations, thereby optimizing participation structures and employing the redistributed capital more productively. This dismantling of 'Germany Inc.' therefore means a loosening of the 'power fabric' of business, politics and social groups.

In Japan, since the early 1990s, there has been a slow decline in reciprocal shareholdings, without this also leading to a dissolution of the keiretsu.[209] One reason for this development is that firms wanted to improve their liquidity on the collapse of the 'bubble economy' by downsizing participations. Changes in the law are also contributing to this: tax relief was provided for the case where reciprocal shares were transferred to pension funds;[210] the acquisition of a company's own shares was liberalized, so that firms could disentangle themselves from each other;[211] Japanese accounting has recently been focusing on the market value of assets,[212] so that large shareholdings bring the further risk of considerable fluctuations in their accounts;[213] and, finally, the restructuring of groups of companies has been eased. As well as tax facilitations and the law on mergers and divisions,[214] this chiefly concerns the removal of the ban on holding companies.[215] According to the legislative idea, this should enhance the competitiveness of firms and their attractiveness for the capital market, since the restructuring of inefficient conglomerates ought to lead to stronger units.[216] Admittedly, it is also feared that permitting

(2005b: 553–61) who regard the notion of the main bank as a 'myth'; against this view see Milhaupt (2002).

208 § 8b KStG (Körperschaftssteuergesetz); Erlass des Bundesfinanzministeriums, BMF IV A 2 – S 2750a – 7/03.

209 Cf. Nottage (2001: 268–9); Milhaupt and West (2003a: 318); Igarashi (2001: 69, 76 *et seq.*); Kawamoto *et al.* (2001: paras. 44, 361); Moerke (2003: 150).

210 See Dore (2000: 94).

211 See Takahashi and Kirchwehm (2003: 759); see also Ch. 4, section I.4 above.

212 See Ch. 4, section III.3.b above.

213 See Poe *et al.* (2002: 74, 77); Narusawa *et al.* (2001: 9).

214 See Eisele (2001); Lebrun (2001); Bälz (2005).

215 See e.g. Kawamoto *et al.* (2001: paras. 118, 696 *et seq.*).

216 Cf. Takahashi and Rudo (1998: 617–18); Milhaupt and West (2003a: 313).

holding companies may lead to a further concentration and a return to the zaibatsu.[217] Whether that is realistic, however, is doubtful. As can be seen from the increase in mergers and acquisitions,[218] in Japan too the trend seems to be not towards a system with groups of companies resisting change, but towards a more mobile enterprise landscape.[219]

Secondly, in Germany and Japan, the power of the banks too is on the decline, so that financing through the capital market becomes more important. In Germany, deposit voting has lost its importance through management voting proxy, the trend to registered shares, the growing influence of direct banks and the internationalization of investor structures.[220] Additionally, banks are increasingly selling their shares and not taking supervisory board posts.[221] This creates a trend towards a concentration on their core business, which is also reflected in a certain *de facto* approximation to the separate banking system.[222] The idea that banks as rent-seekers would resist a loss of power to the capital market thus cannot be confirmed.[223]

In Japan, banks are also increasingly selling their holdings. The background here lies first in increasing competition among the banks. Both the opening up of the financial sector to foreign competition[224] and – with a corresponding increase in monitoring – deregulation in the national sphere have made it necessary for the banks to loosen their close relations with companies.[225] While firms still want the banks to meet sudden financing needs,[226] the banks have been more cautious recently in making loans, and are even occasionally willing to let their clients become insolvent.[227]

Thirdly, in France and China too, changes in hitherto dominant structures are discernible. The 'nouveau capitalisme français'[228] is typified, first, by changes in shareholder structures. Firms are concentrating on

[217] See Takahashi and Rudo (1998: 617).
[218] Cf. Milhaupt and West (2003a: 301, 303, 315 *et seq.*); Hashimoto (2002: 2).
[219] Eisele (2004a: 315 *et seq.*).
[220] See Ch. 4, section II.3.c above. [221] See Ulmer (2002: 145).
[222] See Tuerks (2000: 134) ('konvergierende evolutionäre Entwicklung').
[223] Similarly McDonnell (2002: 378) ('Banks and capital markets need not to be incompatible alternatives. Indeed, in important ways, banks can benefit from access to sophisticated capital market, and capital markets in turn work better with active, sophisticated banks serving as monitors and financial intermediaries').
[224] See Ch. 8, section III.3 above.
[225] See Tanabe (2000: 60); Ueda (2000: 179, 184); Baum (1998: 769 *et seq.*).
[226] See Igarashi (2001: 69, 73 *et seq.*). [227] See Nottage (2001: 278).
[228] On what follows see Fanto (1998: 41 *et seq.*); Pastre (1998: 87); O'Sullivan (2001: 5 *et seq.*); Berrar (2001: 115–16); Korch (2002: 13–14); Rebérioux (2002: 121–2).

their core activities, so that reciprocal holdings are in decline. Additionally, the proportion of firms controlled by families or the state is falling. While for the relative importance of the capital market it is emphasized that many firms use it more to restructure than to attract new capital,[229] there are also various pointers towards more fundamental changes. The importance of loans in corporate finance is clearly falling. The legislature itself has – with the Nouveau Marché and current reforms of securities law on the supplier side, as well as through the 'plan d'épargne action' (PEA), which fiscally favours the purchase of shares or mutual funds by individuals, on the demand side – contributed to invigorating the capital market.

In China, state influence on companies is still considerable. Nonetheless, changes can be seen here too. A sector comprised of small and medium-sized firms, including completely private companies, is gradually emerging. Additionally, in various branches of industry – except politically sensitive sectors – government shares are being sold to private investors. After WTO accession, the special position of former state enterprises was reduced even further. Statements from politicians suggest that substantive privatization with a diversity of holdings will begin.[230] One reason for this is that, in view of the growing deficit in the national pension fund, the state budget can thereby be improved.[231] This will also help to reduce the current problems of companies. The existing high level of government sharesholdings means that there is often no substantive division of powers within the company, thus limiting the supervision of management.[232] On the whole, therefore, there is a transitional phase in which state influence on companies is gradually declining and private influence increasing.

Fourthly, in the 1990s, the increase in public offerings led to a deepening of capital markets in Germany, France, Japan and China.[233] While at the beginning of the twenty-first century the numbers decreased, now the number of initial public offerings is again increasing.[234] Additionally, the scope of this development is not countered by the fact that after a listing concentrated participatory structures may initially prevail.[235] The very

[229] O'Sullivan (2001: 36).

[230] See Liu (2001: 32 note 79); Schipani and Liu (2002: 59); Wang (2000: 15).

[231] See Leung *et al.* (2002: 20). [232] See Ch. 5, section I.1.b above.

[233] See Coffee (2001: 17 *et seq.*), (2002a: 88 *et seq.*), (1999b: 660–1); Van den Berghe (2002: 30 *et seq.*).

[234] Cf. *Handelsblatt*, 8 July 2004, at 25.

[235] Coffee (2001: 5–6); Davies (1999: 353 note 1).

increase in public offerings makes clear the paradigm shift that firms are no longer exclusively dependent on financing through banks or large investors, but are relying on financing through the capital market.

Fifthly, new investors are participating in companies because other enterprises, banks or the state are no longer available, and more shares than previously are traded on the exchanges. These new investors may have been gained since changes in company and securities law led to greater investment willingness in (hitherto) 'blockholder countries'.[236] For instance, in 1994 in Germany, there were calls for an improvement in the transparency of large shareholdings, enhancement of the right to sue, transparency of management remuneration, removal of voting caps and multiple voting rights, and limits on deposit proxies.[237] Part II his study has shown that despite differences there has been convergence on these and other legal issues. Additionally, for instance in Germany, the late twentieth century saw a growing shareholding culture being established.[238] Among the reasons for this were the increasing interest in companies on the share market, banks' consulting practices, the rising importance of the financial media, the growing value of legacies and the need for personal asset and retirement planning. Of course, the economic downturn in the early twenty-first century led to a decline in share investments in favour of other forms of investment. Yet, this was an internationally uniform phenomenon. Furthermore, in 2003, the number of private shareholders was still twice as high as in 1997,[239] and the number of institutional investors is also rising.

3. *The influence of institutional investors*

In recent decades in the UK – and to a lesser extent in the US – the proportion of shares held by private persons has decreased. Instead, shareholdings by institutional investors, particularly investment funds, pension funds and insurance companies, have been steadily increasing.[240] However, the institutional investors usually concentrate their financial resources not on a few firms, to exert influence over managements, but instead in various small holdings, in order thereby – partly in accordance

[236] But see Ch. 7, section I.1; Ch. 8, section IV.1.a for the causality question.
[237] Adams (1994: 153 *et seq.*).
[238] See also Gordon (2003: 214 *et seq.*), (2004: 166 *et seq.*).
[239] See *Handelsblatt*, 23 September 2003, at 31.
[240] For the UK: Poutianen (2001: 70); Davies (2003: 279 *et seq.*); for the US: B. Black (1990a: 567 *et seq.*); Narusawa *et al.* (2001: 8).

with statutory provisions – through diversification to minimize the risk to their clients.[241] Since institutional investors taken together invest more than private investors, the concentration of shareholding has somewhat increased in the US and the UK.[242] Additionally, in recent years, the institutional investors have become more active, monitoring the behaviour of enterprises and seeking to prevent abuses.[243] Accordingly, here too one may see a small approximation to the system (hitherto) of active blockholders in other countries.

For Germany, France, Japan and China, the number and importance of institutional investors is increasing. Previously, investment and pension funds played a minor role in these countries. The internationalization of investments[244] is, however, changing this, if only because Anglo-American institutional investors are acquiring shares here too. But at national level the number of investment funds is also rising.[245] One reason is that in general the supply and demand of shares is increasing (subsection 2 above). Additionally, diversified investment funds allow investors to minimize their risk, lowering the threshold for investment particularly for private persons. Finally, in continental Europe and Japan, pension funds are now gaining importance. The starting-point for this development is that rising expectation of life and falling birth rates are causing problems for state pension systems. Yet, it does not necessarily follow that there has to be a move away from state pension systems, because the demographic problem is in principle independent of the form of pension financing.[246] For instance, it makes little difference for the current burden on the younger population whether, on the one hand, alongside a basic state pension private forms are promoted or even prescribed, or whether, on the other hand, the contributions for state pensions are raised. However, the trend shows that the contributory pension system whereby the young pay for the old ('pay-as–you-go') is growing weaker, in the direction of the predominantly private Anglo-American model of capital-covered pension provision.[247] While substitution is unlikely because in economic crises

241 For legal requirements see Doremus *et al.* (1998: 28 *et seq.*); B. Black (1990a: 551 *et seq.*); Cheffins (2001c: 116 note 184).

242 See Wymeersch (1995: 308); Rock (1995: 294).

243 See Ch. 4, section II.4.c above. 244 See Ch. 8, section III.4.b, c above.

245 See generally Gerke *et al.* (2003: 363); for Germany: Escher-Weingart (2001: 187 *et seq.*); for France: ANSA (2003: 2); Becker (2001: 149); for Japan: Kanda (2000: 70); *Handelsblatt*, 30 June 2003, at 15; for China: Xi (2006); Gebhardt (1999); Liu (2001: 340); Leung *et al.* (2002: 12).

246 Dore (2000: 6 *et seq.*).

247 Cf. Clark (2002); Coffee (1999b: 671); Jacoby (2000: 15); Escher-Weingart (2001: 177).

a purely private system may be risky, in continental Europe and Japan private pension funds are increasingly being advocated to supplement the state pension.[248] Furthermore, the Pension Funds Directive in the EU has brought a first step towards enabling an internal market for pension funds.[249] It permits a fund to hold up to 70 per cent of the assets in shares.[250] Even if in economically weak periods a shift to bonds may take place, it is nonetheless on the whole to be expected that in these countries too in coming decades there will be increasing investment by pension funds in shares as well.

4. *Conclusion*

The real structure of joint stock companies cannot be defined 'historicistically' to make dispersed or blockholdings form automatically under strictly defined conditions. However, one may deduce from a number of factors the direction in which the ownership structure in companies will develop. The general trends here are privatization, internationalization and institutionalization, calling chiefly the established participation structures in Germany, France, Japan and China into question and making an increase in dispersed shareholder ownership likely.

V. Legislative responses

Since social, political and economic circumstances will become more similar, one can basically expect 'convergence through congruence' in shareholder law (subsection 1 below). Nevertheless, path dependencies may obstruct the speed and content of convergence (subsection 2 below).

1. *Reform and reception*

It follows from the dependency of company and securities law that legislators adapt to changes of the overall socio-political system and the institutional environment.[251] Since the latter factors will be constantly

[248] In Europe, for instance, the 'Riester-Rente' in Germany, and the 'plan d'épargne retraite populaire' (PERP) in France; for Japan: Conrad (2003: 199 *et seq.*); Janssen (2001: 249 *et seq.*); Poe *et al.* (2002: 94); Horioka (2001: 99 *et seq.*); Dore (2000: 125 *et seq.*).

[249] Directive 2003/41/EC on the activities and supervision of institutions for occupational retirement provision. However, no comprehensive harmonization has been achieved by this Directive.

[250] For details, see Art. 18(5)(a), (7)(a) of Directive 2003/41/EC.

[251] See Ch. 7, section I above.

evolving, there will accordingly be continual reforms in shareholder law.

How future shareholder law may develop will be explained in some detail in Chapter 10. Yet, even here, some examples shall be given of how the influencing factors studied above will operate on the positive law: shareholder law is dependent on cultural and economic-policy circumstances (section I above). This is true particularly of the shareholder's position in the power structure of the company,[252] since, for instance, with a social-democratic policy the interests of stakeholders, and with an individualistic culture the relative value of subjective rights, will be attributed major significance. The influence of the legal culture (section II above) may for example appear in the fact that, where the relative importance of law in a country's social order increases, the legislator will seek to counter abuses of power at the expense of shareholders through legal measures.[253] Manifold effects may result from the internationalization of the economy (section III above). For instance, legislatures are already reacting to the fact that the new media are improving communication and disclosure. The professionalization of private institutions and the growth in their importance may mean that, on the one hand, a legal regime is created for these institutions and, on the other hand, state monitoring and regulation of companies themselves are reduced. The internationalization of companies makes it necessary for the law to respond, by for instance facilitating the cross-border voting and information provision for such firms.[254] For changes in shareholder structures (IV above) it may, finally, be of importance on the one hand that institutional investors gain influence. Since they act professionally, and according to recent trends their activity is increasing,[255] the legislator might, for instance, make voting and information rights more effective.[256] On the other hand, it is apparent that alongside concentrated shareholder structures there will also, across the countries, be companies with more dispersed shareholdings. It may follow, for instance, that it becomes easier to contract out of the statutory company law so as thereby to be able to agree on a corporate

[252] For the present law see Ch. 5 above; for the future see Ch. 10, section II below.

[253] For instance, by means of shareholder suits; for the present law see Ch. 5, section III above; for the future see Ch. 10, section II.3 below.

[254] For the present law see Ch. 4, sections II, III above; for the future see Ch. 10, section I below.

[255] See Ch. 4, section II.4.c above.

[256] For the present law see Ch. 4, sections II, III above; for future development see Ch. 10, section I below.

governance style specifically suited to the respective type of companies.[257] Additionally, increasingly dispersed shareholder ownership suggests new protective measures. Since here the danger to shareholders lies particularly in the fact that management is subject to no checks, shareholder protection could be increased on this point. For instance, investor-related elements of protection such as the sale of shares or appraisal rights might become more important, since with dispersed shareholdings the individual shareholder's position is often confined to his financial interests.[258]

Nevertheless, it is to be expected not only that legislators will change their law, but that in content too, these reforms ought to contribute to convergence. To be sure, the notion that legislatures in similar circumstances come up with similar organizational patterns[259] is open to the objection that this sort of 'praesumptio similitudinis'[260] is an unsubstantiated assumption.[261] When forecasting future developments, it is nonetheless to be assumed that, where influencing factors and thus problems become more similar internationally, the legislative response will also become more similar than with a less uniform factual situation. What is decisive here is chiefly medium- and long-term developments, since reforms may initially very well take divergent courses. In theoretical arguments, this may be justified either by the 'dialectical triad' (Fichte) or by the 'trial-and-error method' (Popper).[262] On the dialectic, what is decisive is that the contradiction – i.e. the antithesis – to a thesis should be the driving force for a solution in a synthesis. In relation to law, resistances or counter-arguments thus lead to a legislative conception that may then prevail. By contrast, the concept of trial and error focuses on the fact that the author of an initial attempt learns from the results and can then make a further attempt. This leads to a gradual correction of errors, so that for legal developments here too a long-term trend can be seen.

Additionally, communication with other countries and the reception of foreign law contributes to legislators providing not just 'randomly' functional, but also deliberately formally similar legal regulations. There have already been many receptions of foreign company and securities

[257] For the present law see Ch. 2, section IV; Ch. 3, section II above; for the future see Ch. 10, sections I.2.d, II.1 below.

[258] For the present law see Ch. 5, section II.2.c above; for the future see Ch. 10, section II.2.b below.

[259] See e.g. Großfeld (2001: 57).

[260] See e.g. Zweigert and Kötz (1998: 40); de Cruz (1999: 232–3).

[261] For a polemic against the 'praesumptio similitudinis' see Legrand (2005).

[262] See Popper (1973).

law.[263] This reflects the fact that conceptual or cultural barriers here are lower than in most other areas of law, making rules easier to copy.[264] This can be done by either an 'export' or an 'import' of law.[265] Export is based on the influence of foreign advisers and is often practised by Western countries.[266] With import, the initiative starts from the copying country. Since this spares one's own resources, it is usual in company and securities law in most countries to look at foreign statutes. In the international context, accordingly, foreign provisions may act as models and thus accelerate convergence.

There are, however, some pointers to suggest that there is more of an 'Americanization' than a mutual approximation.[267] Foreign legal systems today frequently take the US model as an example. By contrast, the US has recently only rarely adopted rules of foreign company or securities law, since other countries' securities law is mostly less developed (or so perceived), and for company law the regulatory competition within the US already makes a comparison of differing conceptions possible.[268] Additionally, this is strengthened by the fact that liberalization of the market, professionalization of consultants, and dispersion of shareholder ownership are typical for the US, so that with these trends in other countries convergence is also to be expected.

2. Path dependencies

The notion of 'path dependence' is often explained using the following example.[269] A long time ago, a path was trodden through a wood. Attention was paid to keeping the path far enough away from wolves' dens not to be attacked by the wolves. Later, this path was modernized into a road, even if by then the wolves were no longer threatening travellers.

This makes various degrees of path dependence clear. First-degree or weak path dependence is present where even today the way through the wood is efficient and contains no needless curves. By contrast, with second- or third-degree path dependencies, the route is inefficient from today's point of view. Second-degree or semi-strong path dependence makes it not worthwhile on a cost comparison to rip up the path, and build a new road. With third-degree or strong path dependence, it is

[263] See Part II above.
[264] Similarly Vagts (2002: 598–9); Assmann (1990: 279).
[265] Ogus (1999: 409).
[266] Cf. e.g. Berkowitz *et al.* (2003a); Schulte-Kulkmann (2003: 20–1) (for China).
[267] See also Ch. 6, section II above.
[268] Cf. Pistor *et al.* (2001: 63–4).
[269] See Roe (1997: 167); LaChance (2001: 291).

different. Here too, however, the route is not changed, since for instance the road administration has not been convinced of the need to do so, or resistance from private groups (shopkeepers etc.) stands in the way.

a) Weak path dependencies

For the present context, a weak path dependency means that in various countries shareholder law is different but nonetheless leads to comparable results. This involves primarily the cases of functional and normative convergence.[270]

This sort of path dependence cannot be doubted where, while there are dogmatic differences, the legal outcomes are identical. In other ways too, however, situations are conceivable where differing statutory protective mechanisms, market forces, ethical norms or contractual agreements can bring about a functionally comparable result. For instance, at statutory level a director's conflict of interests can be responded to by prohibition, involvement of other directors or the general meeting, or disclosure.[271] Market forces may, for example, cause information to be disclosed because of pressure from the (international) capital market and not only because of legal requirements.[272] As an example of ethical norms one might note that formerly in Japan there was a social norm against hostile takeovers, so that no statutory defence mechanisms were necessary.[273] Finally, for contractual arrangements, instead of a share market for venture capital, other company forms might make broad financing possible for start-up ventures.[274]

It is, however, problematic with these situations whether the outcomes are in fact equivalent. If, for instance, particular regulatory objectives are to be pursued through information and market forces, then, while these are more flexible regulatory mechanisms, market failure can mostly not be ruled out with complete certainty. Even in circumstances that might be weak path dependencies, the legislators' attitude that they are often sceptical to change plays an important part ('better the devil you know than the devil you don't').

b) Strong path dependencies

There may be various reasons why, despite inefficiency, the legislature continues to follow a previously trodden path. First, there may at bottom

270 See Ch. 1, section IV.1 above, and also Hansmann and Kraakman (2001: 465–6) ('harmless mutations').

271 See Ch. 5, section II.1.b above.

272 See Ch. 4, section III, preamble above.

273 See Ch. 5, section II.1.a above.

274 See Gilson (2001: 342 *et seq.*).

be an evaluation problem. Even though it is said that in the long run no legislator can legislate contrary to economic reason,[275] it is nonetheless doubtful when conduct is (objectively) economically rational. Secondly, semi-strong path dependence might entail making no change because to do so would be too burdensome and therefore not cost-effective. Here one could think, for instance, of regulatory areas such as the principle of minimum capital or the separation between supervisory and management boards, with effects that extend to broad areas of company law. This can also be underpinned theoretically: it can be argued that legislators have mostly already attained a local optimum (graphically, a 'local hill'). To be able to improve the law further in the direction of an overall optimum, they would however first have to come down from their 'local hill'. Legislators are, however, often not willing to do so.[276] Thirdly, pressure from lobbies may prevent the legislator from putting through a reform of the law.[277] Fourthly, legislators may feel emotionally tied to legal rules and institutions as expressions of a country's culture and history. Inertia may thus be justified on the ground that a country belongs to a legal family and that particular legal traditions are typical for it. Fifthly, the 'legal adaptability' of a country may be weak.[278] This would occur, for example, where law-making institutions do not consider the possibility of using the new media, and thus, for example, companies cannot correspond with their shareholders by electronic means. Sixthly and finally, political considerations may hold legislators back from an economically efficient mode of proceeding. If public interests or ideological questions are at stake, change will meet greater resistance, as can be seen for instance with the employee-codetermination issue in the EU.[279] For the political sphere, how decision-making processes come about in various countries also plays a part. According to the findings of the public choice theory, for instance, there is a difference between countries with two-party and three-party systems.[280] Moreover, China is special, since the political system on the one hand is not exposed to any pressure from voters, but on the other claims a special commitment to the common weal on the basis of the partly still-present socialist ideology.

[275] Fleischer (2001: 32).

[276] See Schmidt and Spindler (2004: 117–18).

[277] See also Coffee (1999b: 654). The reverse is the pressure that can also lead to convergence (see Ch. 9 below).

[278] See Siems (2006b).

[279] See also High Level Group of Company Law Experts (2002: 103 *et seq.*); Siems (2005a: 439–40), (2004c: 177 *et seq.*).

[280] See Ch. 7, section I.2.b above.

Despite all of this, the effect of this strong path dependence should not be over-estimated. Cultural, economic and political approximations are increasing, and may thus even be regarded as convergence forces for shareholder law.[281] While remaining differences and therefore obstacles to convergence continue to exist, they are tending to decline in intensity.

3. *Conclusion*

It is to be expected that a 'convergence through congruence' and thus also a convergence of law and reality will come about in shareholder law. The actual circumstances underlying shareholder law in the individual countries studied here are growing increasingly close, particularly for public companies. There is therefore a convergence of law, further enhanced by receptions of foreign law. To be sure, path dependencies play a role. However, resistance should be less marked than with 'convergence through pressure' (Ch. 9), because it is change in tangible circumstances and not merely pressure from individual interest groups that initiates it.

[281] See Ch. 7, section IV above.

9

Convergence through pressure

It follows from the findings of the social sciences that pressure from interest groups and other social forces can decisively influence the direction of the law.[1] In the present case, it is accordingly initially conceivable to study the possibilities of influence by company founders, management, shareholders, other stakeholders, foreign countries and international organizations (sections I to V below). Finally, it will be asked what pressure is most likely to be reflected in legislation on shareholder law and whether this will lead to convergence (section VI below).

I. Pressure from company founders

Founders may exercise pressure on legislation on the one hand through regulatory competition.[2] What this means is that someone will found a company in a particular legal system only when the law is positive for him, thus influencing legal developments (subsection 1 below). On the other hand, as with other groups, the possibility exists of asserting their interests with legislators by lobbying (subsection 2 below).

1. Regulatory competition

The phenomenon of regulatory competition for company founders has been well discussed, particularly in the US. The critical position assumes that, in conditions of competition, legislators are exposed to heavy pressure from company founders and management. There is therefore a threat

[1] See Ch. 7, section I above.

[2] See generally on regulatory competition e.g. Tiebout (1956); Heine (2003); Kieninger (2002); Esty and Geradin (2001); Müller (2000); Streit (1999); Gerken (1995).

of a 'race of laxity'[3] or a 'race to the bottom',[4] since the law is deregulated at the expense of other groups like shareholders, creditors or employees. By contrast, the counter-view stresses that there can be a 'race to the top', a spiral towards optimal protection. The pressure from company founders and management is said not to lead to one-sided law, because only competitive firms can last on the product and capital markets. As with other forms of competition, here too the market's invisible hand leads to an optimal pattern for corporate governance.[5]

This debate cannot be transferred without further ado to the international context, for it is in any case doubtful whether there can be regulatory competition at all. Several requirements would have to be met for that. First, according to the rules of private international law it must in principle be possible for company founders to be able freely to choose a particular type of company law system ('supply', subsection a below). Here considerations must also include the fact that in the US regulatory competition relates mostly not to new foundations but to reincorporations of existing firms. It thus matters particularly whether and how far this kind of change is also possible in an international context. Secondly, company founders must let themselves be 'attracted' by a legal system, given free choice ('demand', subsection b below). Thirdly, it has to be clarified whether and how legislators react to these conditions of competition, so that a convergence in shareholder law may come about (section VI.1 below).

a) Supply

Conflict of laws has been called the basic pillar for the legal treatment of the globalization of markets.[6] With respect to shareholder protection, regulatory competition is conceivable on the one hand at the level of securities law if statutory law as well as the supervisory authorities and stock exchanges enable a free choice. On the other hand, as will be

[3] Justice Brandeis in *Liggett* v. *Lee*, 288 US 517, 559 (US Supreme Court 1933) ('Companies were early formed to provide charter for corporation in states where the cost was lowest and the laws the least restrictive. The states joined in advertising their wares. The race was not one of diligency but of laxity.').

[4] Cary (1974). This terminology is now also used in Europe: see e.g. Opinion of the Advocate General La Pergola for *Centros Ltd* v. *Erhervsog Selskabsstyrelsen*, C-212/97, [1999] ECR I-1459, at 1479 note 48; Wymeersch (2000: 652), (2001a: 118–19).

[5] Romano (1993: 14 *et seq.*); see also Kieninger (2002: 100–1, 200 *et seq.*); Coffee (1999b: 650–1).

[6] Ebke (2002: 104) ('Grundpfeiler für die rechtliche Erfassung der Globalisierung der Märkte').

discussed in this section, it may be that firms can freely choose their place of incorporation and a supply market in various company-law systems thus develops.

(1) The position in the US. The US Supreme Court decided as long ago as 1868 that the interstate commerce clause of the American Constitution (Art. I s.8) must make it possible to choose the state of incorporation freely.[7] In the ensuing competition, initially New Jersey and later Delaware took the lead.[8] But not all states participated in this competition. For instance, it is evident from the success of California's company law that stricter legal systems may also play an important part.[9] Moreover, the laws of New York and California, for example, contain provisions aimed at guaranteeing the applicability of parts of domestic company law also to 'pseudo-foreign corporations'.[10]

All in all, however, the regulatory competition has had a deregulatory effect on US corporate law.[11] The most decisive point here is the market for reincorporations. A mere change in corporate domicile is not possible in the US. However, the merger of an existing company with a newly founded shell company in the target state[12] does not pose significant problems, and in particular does not lead to taxation of hidden reserves. Although the general meeting must consent, the decision to reincorporate is as a rule not affected by shareholder interests. For public companies with widely dispersed shareholdings management in any case often controls the general meeting. Otherwise, reincorporation often comes before an initial public offering, and thus before the separation of ownership and control.[13] Since here the founders wish to sell their shares, their preferences and not those of shareholders are the driving force.

(2) The position in Europe. The EU Member States take different positions. The law of the UK, Ireland and the Netherlands follows the 'incorporation doctrine' and accordingly – as in the US – regards the place of formal registration of the firm as decisive.[14] A firm properly constituted according to the law of another country is thus recognized. This has

[7] *Paul* v. *Virginia*, 75 US 168 (1868); for details see § 5.01 MBCA; Kersting (2002: 2 *et seq.*); Cheffins (1997: 422 *et seq.*); Charny (1991: 427–8); Buxbaum and Hopt (1988: 62 *et seq.*).

[8] For the reasons see Ch. 9, section VI.1 below.

[9] See Barnard (2000: 73, 75).

[10] §§ 1317 *et seq.* NYBCL; § 2115 CalGCL; see also Carney (1997: 312 *et seq.*); Drury (1998: 190); generally on 'pseudo foreign corporations' Latty (1955).

[11] See already Ch. 2, section IV.1.b above.

[12] This is possible in the US: see e.g. § 252(a) DelGCL.

[13] See Romano (1993: 33).

[14] See Clarke (1991: 161); Drury (1998: 168–9, 182).

the advantage of legal certainty, and additionally promotes mobility of international firms.[15] By contrast, for example, France, Germany, Spain and Greece used to follow the 'real-seat doctrine'.[16] The starting-point was French law, which in the mid-nineteenth century was being evaded through registration of French firms in the UK or Belgium. The French legislature accordingly provided that legally the *de facto* headquarters should be decisive. On the real-seat doctrine, accordingly, a firm founded in accordance with foreign law but having its real seat in a country either was not recognized as such, or was subjected to that country's law. This has the advantage that it is the law of the country objectively most affected that applies. A deregulation race is thus not possible. A modified approach used to be found in the Scandinavian countries ('Nordic registration doctrine').[17] Here, while the law takes the incorporation doctrine as its basis, so that it is effective foundation according to a foreign law that counts, a foreign firm must additionally register in the country of its *de facto* headquarters so that evasion of domestic law can be prevented.

Since the recent decisions of the European Court of Justice, the conflict-of-laws position in the EU has become closer to the US position. However, there are some distinctions.[18]

In the first situation, a firm is founded in accordance with one country's law but has its real seat in another country. For the country of the real seat, the ECJ decided in *Centros* that foundation or registration according to domestic law could not be required of a pseudo-foreign company.[19] It is not yet clear whether, as a corollary, a legal system is obliged to enable a pseudo-domestic company to set up in accordance with its domestic law. A counter-argument is that it is within the Member State's discretion whether and how far it allows the foundation of a specific form of company. Insofar as this is possible for domestic founders, however, the equal-treatment aspect argues in favour of not excluding founders from other EU countries.

Secondly, a (mere) transfer of registered seat may be an interesting option for firms. Its admissibility in accordance with *Centros* is supported by the fact that it may make no difference to the countries concerned whether a pseudo-foreign/pseudo-domestic company exists from the

[15] For further arguments see also Ch. 12, section II.1.a below.

[16] See Buxbaum and Hopt (1988: 226 *et seq.*); Xanthaki (2001: 2–3); Carney (1997: 316).

[17] See Anderse and Sorei (1999: 54 *et seq.*); *Centros Ltd* v. *Erhervsog Selskabsstyrelsen*, C-212/97, [1999] ECR I-1459, para. 18.

[18] See also Siems (2002c), (2007b).

[19] *Centros Ltd.* v. *Erhervsog Selskabsstyrelsen*, C-212/97, [1999] ECR I-1459.

beginning or arises at a later point in time. Since in this situation a firm's real seat does not change, social or fiscal interests are also not significantly affected. However, according to the law of most Member States, a straightforward change of registered seat is either not possible at all, or is possible only under very strict conditions.[20] Since the Commission's proposed Directive on Cross-Border Transfer of the Registered Office[21] has so far not managed to secure consensus, alternative solutions have to be found. As in the US, the possibility might therefore have arisen of being able to evade domestic law by merging the existing company with a newly founded one. Until recently, though, cross-border mergers have not been possible in the EU.[22] The Societas Europaea and the new Directive on Cross-Border Mergers[23] help only to some extent, since the national legislator can provide protection against evasion of employee co-determination. A complete move is, however, possible even today by dissolving the old company and founding a new one in the target country. Here, however, by contrast with a merger, hidden reserves must be disclosed and thus be subject to taxation.[24] Whether this can be seen as contrary to the freedom of establishment is not yet clear. The European Court of Justice has recently decided in *Hughes de Lasteyrie* that, with respect to European citizens, the transfer of their residence must not lead to the taxation of unrealized capital gain.[25] Therefore, it is possible that discrimination imposed by tax law would also be unlawful for corporations that indirectly transfer their statutory seat by transferring their assets.

Thirdly, simultaneously with or separately from a change of the registered seat, the real seat of a firm may be moved. The destination country here (the 'immigration case'), as clarified by the ECJ in *Überseering*, in principle has its hands tied because a firm that was effectively founded in accordance with foreign law and has moved its real seat abroad cannot be denied legal capacity.[26] This does not, however, as decided by the

[20] See Wymeersch (2003: 668 *et seq.*, 678); Kieninger (2002: 147 *et seq.*, 225 *et seq.*).

[21] See http://ec.europa.eu/internal_market/company/seat-transfer/index_en.htm.

[22] See Ch. 8, section III.4.a above.

[23] Directive 2005/56/EC on cross-border mergers of companies with share capital; see also Siems (2004c) and (2007b) on *SEVIC Systems AG*, C-411/03, [2005] ECR I-10805.

[24] See Werlauff (2003b: 6); Enriques (2004b: 1261); for tax law see also Directive 90/434/EEC on the common system of taxation applicable to mergers, divisions, transfers of assets and exchanges of shares concerning companies of different Member States; Directive 2005/19/EC amending Directive 90/434/EEC.

[25] *Hughes de Lasteyrie du Saillant* v. *Ministère de l'Économie, des Finances et de l'Industrie*, C-9/02, [2004] ECR I-2409.

[26] *Überseering BV* v. *Nordic Construction Company Baumanagement GmbH (NCC)*, C-275/17, [2002] ECR I-9919.

ECJ in *Daily Mail*,[27] affect the legal options of the country according to whose company law the firm was founded (the 'emigration case'). Since the country of the registered seat loses *de facto* enforcement capacity over a tax debtor, fiscal restrictions on removals in particular are permissible. Again, it is not yet clear whether the decision in *Hughes de Lasteyrie* will lead to change.

Fourthly, the Societas Europaea (SE) contributes to promoting regulatory competition. Since national legislators have considerable room for manoeuvre in the design of the SE, there will be various types of SE in Europe.[28] While a firm cannot choose among them freely, since the registered office and head office of the SE must lie in the same Member State (Art. 7 SE-Reg) and SEs can in any case only be founded for cross-border firms (Art. 2 SE-Reg), regulatory competition is still possible. First, on the merger of two companies from different Member States, a new main administrative headquarters must in any case be found. Secondly, the SE opens up the possibility of moving its seat while retaining legal capacity (Art. 8 SE-Reg).[29] For this decision, the company law of the Member States may be one of the considerations which the company will take into account.

Centros, *Überseering*, the Cross-Border Merger Directive and the Societas Europaea will therefore, on the one hand, bring enhanced competition among company legislators in the EU. On the other hand, moves of headquarters in particular have further limits set on them. Additionally, the harmonization of company law in the EU at any rate excludes regulatory competition in the harmonized areas. Finally, the ECJ has indicated in *Centros* that national legislators can restrict a change of seat for reasons of public interest and prevention of abuse.[30] Therefore, laws that may, for example, extend protection of minority shareholders, creditors or employees to pseudo-foreign companies remain at least conceivable. However, the ECJ's decision in *Inspire Art* points towards a restrictive line. In that case, the Dutch legislator had enacted a special law *inter alia*

[27] *The Queen* v. *Daily Mail and General Trust* PLC, C-81/87, [1988] ECR I-5483; confirmed in *Überseering BV* v. *Nordic Construction Company Baumanagement GmbH (NCC)*, C-275/17, [2002] ECR I-9919, paras. 61 *et seq.*; *Kamer van Koophandel en Fabrieken voor Amsterdam* v. *Inspire Art Ltd*, C-167/01, [2003] ECR I-10155, para. 103.

[28] See Ch. 1, section I above, and Siems (2005b).

[29] For tax law see e.g. Wymeersch (2003: 691 note 115, 693); Werlauff (2003b: 184 *et seq.*); Da Costa and Bilreiro (2003: 79 *et seq.*).

[30] *Centros Ltd.* v. *Erhervsog Selskabsstyrelsen*, C-212/97, [1999] ECR I-1459, para. 34; see now *Kamer van Koophandel en Fabrieken voor Amsterdam* v. *Inspire Art Ltd*, C-167/01, [2003] ECR I-10155, para. 132.

establishing provisions on minimum capital for pseudo-foreign companies. The ECJ found this inadmissible. It pointed out in particular that creditors are adequately informed by the appended indication (Ltd, NV, SA etc.) of the company's legal form that the pseudo-foreign company is subject to different legal provisions. Any further-reaching protection of creditors by additional minimum capital requirements, it said, is no more necessary than is the case for genuine foreign companies.[31]

(3) **The global position.** Still more profound differences can be found in conflicts of company laws at the global level. Alongside countries that in principle follow the incorporation doctrine,[32] many other countries, such as China, allow the establishment of foreign firms or the use of foreign legal forms only either within statutory limits, subject to governmental reservations or not at all.[33] Regulatory competition can accordingly often only develop in a weaker form ('type A regulatory competition', 'indirect competition').[34] Company founders have free choice among types of national company law only if the countries of both the registered and the real seat follow the incorporation doctrine. If that is not the case, the real-seat doctrine compels a uniform determination of the seat. In this case, the quality of company law is only one among many factors decisive for the location. Worldwide, thus, as a general rule, competition for founders is also (but not only) dependent on company law. The pressure on individual company-law systems is thus less marked than in the US and (recently) the EU. Whether one is therefore justified in seeing regulatory competition in general as a weak convergence force[35] is not yet decided by this, since it seems in any case likely that, for instance, a clearly inefficient company law may be an influencing factor against a country, albeit only one factor.

b) Demand

To the extent that businessmen can choose among company laws from various countries, it is not a matter of course that they will be attracted by

[31] *Kamer van Koophandel en Fabrieken voor Amsterdam* v. *Inspire Art Ltd*, C-167/01, [2003] ECR I-10155, in particular paras. 131 *et seq.*; see also Ch. 12, section II.1.a below.

[32] This used to be the case in Japan (see Kawamoto *et al.* (2001: paras. 128 *et seq.*)), but was changed by § 821 JapCA.

[33] §§ 192 *et seq.* ChinCA; see also Thümmel (1995: 21, 83 *et seq.*).

[34] See Heine and Kerber (2002: 51) (in contrast to 'type B-regulatory competition'); Kieninger (2002: 224 *et seq.*) (in contrast to 'institutional competition').

[35] Hansmann and Kraakman (2001: 454).

any particular legal system. While the 'Delaware effect' in the US shows that some 40 per cent of all firms listed on the NYSE deliberately opt for Delaware,[36] at European or even global level there are strong grounds militating against a comparable effect.

First, as a mirror image to the legislative possibilities (subsection a above), at global and (to a lesser extent) at European level too the company law of a particular country often cannot be chosen in isolation. Instead, the real-seat doctrine, statutory defensive measures and legal problems in moving the seat may considerably limit free choice or – especially with tax questions – *de facto* block a shift of the registered seat.

Secondly, regulatory competition does not take place if and insofar as the law is in any case identical. For the European Union, harmonization measures mean that in some areas of company law equivalent provisions apply.[37] The same is true also to the extent that, internationally, convergence forces other than regulatory competition have already led to convergence.

Thirdly, even where one can choose between differing regulations, it may not be necessary for company founders to place value on specific legal rules. Different provisions can operate in a functionally equivalent way, or the articles of association can lead to a similar legal position. Furthermore, company-law provisions may not be decisive, particularly where the company founder is at the same time the controlling shareholder and head of the firm. In this case, the legal questions affecting the relationship between the various power centres in the company retreat into the background, since the controlling shareholder can in any case largely act freely.

Fourthly, demand for the 'best legal system' may be small because it is not clear which arrangement is best for those involved. Since company founders mostly constitute the initial directors, which often has a decisive influence on a reincorporation, it might be presumed that they would prefer a lax legal system 'open to plunder', at the expense of shareholders and other stakeholders. However, on the one hand, market forces deter company founders from setting up in countries where shareholders are exploited. In order to grow, firms need fresh capital, so that shareholder interests have to be taken into account.[38] Additionally, company founders are not attracted by a system strongly deregulated in their favour if this would damage their public image. On the other hand, however, it

[36] See Bebchuk and Cohen (2003: 391).
[37] See also Enriques (2004b: 1269).
[38] See also Ch. 9, section III.1 above.

is possible for market forces to fail here. Shareholders may be poorly informed about the law, or too apathetic to perceive the dangers. In the US, the state of Delaware is an example showing that founders to some extent opt for a deregulated system with advantages in favour of management.[39] On the whole, the direction that pressure from the regulatory competition will take where additionally the influence of shareholders and other stakeholders has to be taken into account[40] is at any rate not absolutely clear.

Fifthly, founding a company abroad or moving its seat may be associated with increased logistical, linguistic and cultural costs. Decision-makers must in particular be informed about the advantages and disadvantages of the foreign law. Some voices in the literature see this as a problem particularly for small firms, since for them comprehensive information about foreign legal systems is difficult, and not worthwhile financially.[41] Other voices by contrast see it as an obstacle to large firms, since the law applicable to them is too widespread and complex for 'forum shopping'.[42] The decisive point with all of this is not just the costs for setting up a firm or moving its seat, but additionally the continuing burden associated with the applicability of a foreign legal system. Thus, particularly in the case of a legal dispute, it is necessary to be able to deal with the foreign law and have lawyers specialized in it available.

Sixthly, irrational reasons may run counter to a demand for the 'best system'. In the US, the far-reaching political, cultural and economic homogeneity means that shifting the registered seat to another state involves hardly any emotional resistance. At international level this may be different, so that it is not enough only to reckon financial advantages against costs. Firms may in particular be sceptical regarding an exotic seat and an unusual denotation of legal form. And, with respect to reincorporations, some apathy is likely if people have already become used to the current legal system.

At least at the European level, however, despite these reasons, a demand for favourable foreign company law cannot be ruled out. Current trends in the EU suggest that firms are increasingly engaging in active 'forum shopping'. Alongside the cases that have recently come before the ECJ,[43] there are on the Internet a number of intermediaries offering German firms in

[39] For examples see Ch. 5, sections I.1.a, 2.a, II.1.b above.

[40] See Ch. 9, section VI below.

[41] Forsthoff (2000: 1113); see also Gelter (2004: 180–1).

[42] Ulmer (1999b: 662); similarly Micheler (2000: 182); Grundmann (2001: 816).

[43] See Ch. 9, section I.1.a above.

particular a company foundation in the UK.[44] Since intensive use is being made of this,[45] at least for these founders language and cultural differences cannot be seen as decisive obstacles. It should however be borne in mind that the 'flight' into UK law refers particularly to the establishment of a 'Ltd' as a small company, so as thereby, for instance, to avoid the minimum capital requirement. In the US by contrast, regulatory competition typically comes about with large firms, to prepare an initial public offering, merger or takeover by moving its registered seat.[46] It therefore remains to be seen whether and how far the present trend for the EU as regards demand for companies will continue. In favour of this, for instance, is the fact that it could allow German firms to introduce the one-tier system of corporate governance and eliminate employee co-determination. However, it is also conceivable that the absence of a directive on seat transfers, laws on pseudo-foreign companies, legal harmonization through directives and the Societas Europaea as an alternative in this area may all reduce demand.

On the whole, for the EU the pressure of demand is at any rate less than in the US. The pressure is reduced still more at the international level. While agencies mediate the foundation of fiscally attractive offshore companies,[47] if two countries do not follow the incorporation doctrine, the company law remains only one factor as regards the location of the registered seat. Smaller and medium-grade differences in law will accordingly not have much effect on a firm's choice of location. Things may be different with more fundamental questions, so that in this way pressure for certain minimum standards may be exerted.

c) Conclusion

Only to a limited extent is it possible to say that competition for company founders acts as a convergence force. Legislators are sometimes not able to 'supply' a law for foreign companies. And the 'demand' from companies may also be reduced. Regulatory competition as in the US is therefore likely, despite the changes in the EU, to remain the exception, at least in the international sphere. To the extent one may talk of competitive pressure, it is doubtful in what direction the law will develop, and whether

[44] See e.g. http://www.go-limited.de; http://www.wsr-corporation.com/en/; http://www.firma-ausland.de/index.html; http://www.auslandsfirma-steuern-sparen-firmengruendung-in-england.de/uk_limited/start/index.php; http://www.ems-finanzmanagement.de/firmengruendung.htm.

[45] See the data in Becht *et al.* (2006).

[46] See Romano (1993: 33–4).

[47] See note 44 above note; generally see Murphy (2004: 72 *et seq.*).

here the situation in the US can be a model. Regarding possible responses by legislators, accordingly, it has in particular to be clarified what reasons have contributed to Delaware's supremacy in the US, what interests company founders pursue, and how counter-pressure from shareholders and other stakeholders may act (section VI below).

2. *Other forms of pressure*

Like other groups, company founders may present their interests to legislators as a lobby. This influence is not to be under-estimated. While it might be expected that company founders would be at a disadvantage in terms of economic power by comparison with representatives of existing firms, company founders are often already at the head of another firm, or the first directors of the firm being founded. With joint stock companies it should further be borne in mind that they often previously existed as a 'small company' (GmbH, Ltd etc.) or as a dependent part of a larger firm, and were thus already able to influence legislators.

Apart from lobbying activity, it is also conceivable to exert pressure on national legislators by threatening to deploy their capital elsewhere. For instance, in view of the increasing liberalization of capital markets,[48] it may be possible, instead of founding a firm domestically, to participate in foreign firms and thus ensure a capital outflow. In the interests of the domestic labour market, tax revenues and the economy in general, it is thus also in a country's own interest to promote the founding of companies at home.

II. Pressure from management

As with company founders, it is also conceivable for management (including the board of directors) to exercise pressure on legislators through regulatory competition. In the US, a reincorporation is regularly brought about by management, and is also the main instance of the 'Delaware effect'.[49] However, this cannot be generalized internationally. First of all it may be doubted whether in other legal systems the focus in deciding a move of the registered seat may not lie more with the shareholder majority than with the directors and managers. This is, however, ultimately not the point, since internationally an isolated move is often not possible for

[48] See Ch. 8, section III.1 above.

[49] See Ch. 9, section I.1.a, b above.

reasons of tax law and private international law.[50] A threatened change of the registered seat thus often becomes relevant only where the firm also moves its real seat. The potential for pressure on legislators is accordingly considerable, since a complete move by the firm would also mean losing jobs and future tax revenues domestically. However, company-law considerations play only a subordinate role in a complete change of registered and real seat, so that at most pressure for certain minimum company-law standards can be exercised in this way.

In practice what are more important are the other potential pressure points. Since a government's prospect of re-election depends to some extent on the unemployment rate, a main point here is that it is management which decides on hiring and firing employees. 'Classical lobbying' may also be influential because managers of listed and other large companies often belong to the elite of a country and maintain close ties with the administration and with politicians. This effect is enhanced through such business organizations as Keidanren in Japan or the Business Round Table in the US. And sometimes managers are (former), politicians, and politicians (former) managers. For instance, in France, the managerial elite of large firms quite commonly, consists of former politicians or high administrative officials.[51] In Germany, a number of supervisory board members come from politics.[52] In Japan, it is usual for former politicians or high officials when they retire to move into a firm with which they were previously in contact.[53] Finally, at present in the US, it can be seen that, alongside the private compaign contributions which are particularly important in the US, former company executives continue as members of the Bush administration to maintain close relations with business.[54]

Thus the free market economy, which places considerable power in the hands of enterprises, across all the countries studied here, brings with it considerable potential for pressure by managements. This pressure is not, however, uniform internationally. For instance, peculiarities in the political system (China), in party financing (US) or the enforcement of interests through social norms (Japan)[55] lead to variations in the

[50] See Ch. 9, section I.1.a, b above.

[51] See Pastre (1998: 81–2); O'Sullivan (2001: 9 *et seq.*).

[52] See the overview at http://www.miprox.de/Wirtschaft_allgemein/Herren_der_Aufsichtsraete/Aufsichtsraete.htm.

[53] See Schaede (1997: 345 *et seq.*); Kelemen and Sibbitt (2002: 292 *et seq.*).

[54] In particular, the controversial relationship between Vice President Dick Cheney and Halliburton.

[55] Cf. Milhaupt (2001: 2106).

intensity of management influence on politicians. Additionally, the direction it takes is not a matter of course. To be sure, it is clearly in the interest of managements not to have their area of competence too limited by the general meeting, to let proxy voting take the form they would like and to not be exposed to any risk of personal liability. Other regulatory areas are, however, more difficult.[56] For instance, we hear on the one hand that a developed capital market with widespread shareholder ownership is in the interest of managements, since they then have no controlling shareholders to worry about and the firm's need for capital can be met from the capital market.[57] On the other hand, it may be that a weak capital market is advantageous since board members will then be exposed to less market control and can operate through interlocking companies without necessarily any other monitoring body. Current developments, admittedly, suggest that in such countries as Germany or Japan, where to date financing from the capital market has been less important, firms' managements also value an upgrading of capital markets. It is thus not surprising that Keidanren, for instance, stresses the importance of shareholder value,[58] and in Germany business is helping to support the move towards a capital-market-oriented corporate governance.[59]

Internationalization of the economy also favours pressure for convergence. With the increasing opening up of markets, competitive pressure on firms rises. While large firms do not necessarily operate with such narrow margins that they cannot survive with a sub-optimal company law, the intensified competition means at least that, for firms with global ambitions, the idea presents itself of expanding the firm by drawing on the international capital market. The growing number of international enterprises[60] is also contributing to the fact that, through their effects on national legislators, there is increasing convergence through pressure from managements.[61] This influence is primarily aimed at removing obstacles for these firms. Alongside direct contradictions, as for instance in financial reporting, diversity in general may also be opposed. The more uniform the law, the more smoothly can multinational undertakings operate. Consequently, through both their economic power and their convergent

[56] See also Ch. 9, section I.1.b above. [57] Kübler (1998: 159).

[58] See http://www.keidanren.or.jp/english/policy/2000/061.html.

[59] For instance, by participation in drafting the GerCGK; see the list of the members of its commission available at http://www.corporate-governance-code.de/eng/mitglieder/index.html.

[60] See Ch. 8, section III.4 above.

[61] See e.g. Branson (2001: 352 *et seq.*); Brancanto and Price (2002: 59); Poe *et al.* (2002: 75).

objectives, international undertakings influence law in the direction of convergence.

III. Pressure from shareholders

As with company founders and managers, for shareholders too it is conceivable that, either through regulatory competition (subsection 1 below) or other possibilities of influence (subsection 2 below), they may exercise pressure on legislators. As in the positive law,[62] here too both 'exit' (purchase and sale of shares) and 'voice' (especially lobbying) play a part.

1. Regulatory competition

By contrast with regulatory competition for founders, the regulatory competition for shareholders is today widely recognized. In principle, domestic investors can acquire foreign shares, so that the supply of products from various countries necessary for competition is present (subsection a below). Additionally, for investors there is an incentive to demand foreign shares at least in part because of a particularly good legal system as assessed from their point of view (subsection b below).

a) Supply

In order for legislators to be able to make available to potential shareholders a variety of 'products', it must, first, be legally possible for shareholders to 'flee' into foreign shares. Secondly, there must be an adequate freedom for the legislators to shape the law. Both are in principle the case: nationals not wishing to buy domestic shares may either buy shares in foreign firms listed in the home country or buy foreign shares directly abroad.[63] To be sure, there is the limitation that for shares listed domestically the domestic securities law may overlay the foreign company law.[64] And for foreigners the purchase of domestic shares may be subject to restrictions, as is, for instance, in principle still the case in China with the separation of A-shares and B-shares.[65] On the whole, however, the trend found in international economic law is for capital movement to be liberalized.[66] Investors can accordingly, as emphasized particularly by critics of the globalization process, freely transfer their capital on a global financial market, thus deliberately bringing it under a specific legal system.

[62] See Ch. 4, section I.5 above. [63] See Ch. 8, section III.4.b, c above.
[64] See Ch. 8, section III.4.c above. [65] See Ch. 2, section III.1 above.
[66] See Ch. 8, section III.1 above.

Moreover, legislators are mostly not prevented from modelling their law in order to attract investors. While the EU through the harmonization process and the US through the mandatory requirements of securities law lay down certain minimum requirements as limitations, neither relate, at least in emphasis, to the shareholder's rights and duties to the share as a product.

b) Demand

Regulatory competition further presupposes that the law is at least one important criterion for the purchasing of particular shares. This might for various reasons not be the case.

First, for a shareholder, differences in company law might be irrelevant if as a major shareholder he in any case controls both the general meeting and management. Regulatory competition for investors that increases the pressure to reform is thus particularly to be expected with dispersed holdings. The current trend towards increasingly widespread holdings even outside the US and the UK[67] therefore implies that internationally the pressure from shareholders will increase.

Secondly, it may be doubtful which provisions are best for shareholders. Shareholders have different preferences because, for instance, some may be interested only in short-term participation with as much profit as possible, and others in longer and more active commitment to the company.[68] Moreover, even with perfect information it may often not be clear which legal model (e.g. mandatory law v. default rules, one-tier v. two-tier systems) is preferable. It might thus in principle be best for shareholders to diversify their investment over various legal systems in order to minimize the legal risk along with the factual risk. In actuality, however, investors do not so act. Instead, the pressure exerted particularly by US institutional investors[69] shows that it is mostly one's own law that is taken as a criterion for assessing foreign law.[70] That facilitates comparison and minimizes the danger of unexpected risks. It also reduces the cost of the information which would otherwise have to be secured regarding a legal system that is not only foreign but also different.

Thirdly, insofar as legal differences persist despite convergence forces, the problem of information remains present as a possible barrier to regulatory competition.[71] While the logistical, linguistic and cultural costs

[67] See Ch. 8, section IV.2.b above. [68] See Ch. 3, section II above.

[69] See Ch. 9, section III.2 below.

[70] Similar Charny (2004: 294); Komiyama and Masaoka (2002: 2); Brancanto and Price (2002: 46).

of buying foreign shares are mostly small, it may nonetheless be doubted whether it is worthwhile for an investor who has diversified into a number of shares from various countries to secure detailed information on the shareholder protection provided by the foreign legal systems concerned. Help comes, however, from intermediaries. Professional analysts and international law firms are the 'eyes and ears' of investors, and are thus able to even out the information disadvantage.[72] Additionally, for private investors, 'herd behaviour' may be rational here. Since at least the larger institutional investors are usually better informed about foreign markets, the very presence of a high proportion of foreign investors constitutes at least a pointer to a solid legal position in favour of shareholders.

Fourthly, with the information problem removed, it is still not established whether and how far legal factors and not just psychological or economic reasons are decisive for investment abroad. Alongside the high cost of information, psychological factors in particular contribute to a disproportionately high level of investment by investors in their own country, despite the liberalization of capital markets.[73] And, before an investment decision is made, shareholders concern themselves more with the economic aspects of the investment than with the details of the foreign company law.[74] For foreign investors, this suggests itself, if only because in the event of problems they are more likely to sell their shares than to become active. Additionally, US experience confirms that investors are not deterred from investing in Delaware firms merely because in that state only a few mandatory shareholder rights are provided for.

However, these reasons do not rule out regulatory competition altogether. In recent years, the proportion of foreign shareholders in domestic companies has been continuously rising.[75] In the interest of 'international pooling', the 'home bias' of investment is therefore declining. Moreover, the fact that a share purchase may often be a mere investment does not rule out the possibility for the law of a country to be reflected indirectly in an investment decision. Even if an investor primarily values the possibility of reselling, he nonetheless also profits from a shareholder-friendly company and securities law because this is positively reflected in the share price.[76] Finally, it becomes clear from demands by institutional

[71] See Rose (2001: 128 *et seq.*). [72] Cheffins (1997: 55); Grundmann (2001: 811–12).

[73] See Cornelius and Kogut (2003: 4); Doremus *et al.* (1998: 143); Baum (2000: 83).

[74] Similarly Großfeld (1998: para. 725) for national accounting laws.

[75] See Ch. 8, section III.4.b above. [76] See Ch. 9, section VI.3.b below.

investors[77] that shareholders indeed also directly value particular legal provisions.

c) Conclusion

Regulatory competition for shareholders of public companies constitutes an important convergence force. This is also confirmed by current reforms in which legislators frequently respond to the internationalization of capital markets and the legal interests of investors.[78] In detail, however, it remains to be clarified how far the law will become more uniform and how shareholder interests can be asserted *vis-à-vis* other interest groups and public interests (section VI below). Comparably with the debate over regulatory competition for company founders, here again the problem arises whether pressure for competition from shareholders may lead to a retreat of employee or creditor interests and thus a 'shareholder-friendly' variant of the 'race to the bottom'. This danger of external effects is not eliminated by the fact that shareholders, by contrast with company founders, do not determine the running of the company with effects for other stakeholders,[79] because by trading the shares of a particular firm shareholders are also exercising influence over the fate of that firm and upon third parties.

2. *Other forms of pressure*

Since regular business decisions are mostly in the hands of management, they can, for instance through hiring or firing employees, act as a lobby on the legislature. It is, by contrast, harder for shareholders to influence legislators in a similar fashion. The powers of the general meeting are today in principle limited to extraordinary decisions, and to only a few regular decisions.[80] Moreover, it is questionable who could represent shareholders as a whole, as a unitary lobby. It is therefore said that shareholders, while numerically strong, are, as an 'inchoate group' in principle not well organized and thus not in a position to influence political decisions.[81] It is different, however, where particular groups, such as shareholder associations or institutional investors, act as a powerful lobby on behalf of

[77] See Ch. 10, section I.2.a below. [78] See Ch. 9, section VI.3.a below.

[79] Contra Kieninger (2002: 271); see also Kirchner (2003: 344) ('in a globalizing world those actors who are winners are those who have better exit options').

[80] See Ch. 5, section I.1 above.

[81] Coffee (1999b: 654); see also Carney (1997: 307); Romano (1993: 59, 75) ('loosely organized, geographically dispersed group', 'asymmetric organizational advantages of managers over shareholders').

shareholder interests. For instance, the US model was marked in the past by pressure from institutional investors.[82] As the demands of in particular the largest US pension fund, CalPERS, show,[83] this influence is now extending to the global sector too. Additionally, investment and pension funds have been gaining increasing importance recently even outside the US and the UK.[84]

However, one ought not to be over-hasty in assuming this means the US shareholder model will therefore come to prevail.[85] Even the legal position in the US is by no means unambiguous, since the deregulated company law of some states, particularly the possibility of exemption from liability,[86] is also marked by manifest influence from managements. This is ultimately unsurprising because managers also act for institutional investors, and therefore the question of which managers can better assert themselves *vis-à-vis* the legislature is decisive. Furthermore, in the global context, it remains to be clarified how far the influence of foreign institutional investors can prevail over domestic managers and other stakeholders (sectionVI below).

IV. Pressure from other interest groups

As well as company founders, managers and shareholders, other interest groups may also act to shape company and securities law. Their position is, however, rather weaker, since their interests are mostly primarily protected by other areas of law. Furthermore, pressure applied by other groups as a convergence force is reduced by the fact that here more country-specific differences exist.

Any member of the public may be a creditor, employee or consumer. Since, for politicians, the prospects of re-election make it essential for them to take account of public interests, one might consequently presume that these groups would exercise considerable influence on legislators. This is, however, often not the case. In general, the public choice theory shows that large groups with diffuse member interests are hard to organize.[87] Additionally, public interest in and knowledge of the questions of company and

[82] See Hansmann and Kraakman (2001: 451 *et seq.*).

[83] See http://www.calpers-governance.org/principles/international/; see also Kissane (1997: 634 *et seq.*); André (1998: 72); West (2001a: 582–3 and note 215); Dore (2000: 91).

[84] See Ch. 8, section IV.3 above.

[85] Contra Hansmann and Kraakman (2001: 443 *et seq.*).

[86] See Ch. 5, section II.1.b above, and Ch. 4, sections I.4, II.4.a; Ch. 5, sections I.1.d, II.2.b above.

[87] See Ch. 7, section I.3 above.

securities law are mostly slight. Things are different if fundamental topics such as the competitiveness of the domestic economy or takeovers of domestic firms by foreign ones are addressed. Moreover, in the company law of some countries, employee and creditor interests play an important part. In particular, the minimum capital requirement in the EU[88] and employee co-determination on the supervisory board in Germany and China[89] bring creditor and employee protection within the regulatory scope of company law. Yet the existing differences[90] and thus also the pressure of those other stakeholders ought not to be over-emphasized. It emerges from the findings of Part II of this study – for instance on the shareholder v. stakeholder dichotomy and the current liberalizations of company law provisions on corporate finance[91] – that the division into two diametrically opposed models is unconvincing. This decreasing relevance of national differences is also fostered by two other factors. On the one hand, non-governmental organizations (NGOs) exert global influence and work particularly in favour of hitherto neglected global collective goods and consumer and employee interests. On the other hand, the protection of specific stakeholder interests is increasingly subject to the reservation of the international competitiveness of firms. Liberalization of the markets for goods, services and capital increases the pressure on legislators to subordinate protective rules for employees or creditors, in the public interest, to the desire to attract economically successful firms.

Creditors play their part too. Since they are often banks, they also, as banks, have their own interests to pursue. These interests are not confined to those as providers of outside capital. Instead, banks, as providers of financial services in IPOs and M&A transactions, also attach importance to a functional domestic capital market.

Other groups that pursue special interests due to their professional positions are lawyers, auditors and business consultants. However, it is not entirely clear how their influence might specifically affect company and securities law. On the one hand, it may be that these professions in principle oppose reforms. Lawyers, for instance, have specialized in the current law, so that re-learning would bring 'switching costs'.[92] This traditional conservatism could apply particularly where a change in the law

[88] Art. 6(1) of the Second Directive 77/91/EEC.

[89] German Co-determination Act (Mitbestimmungsgesetz) of 04.05.1976, BGBl. I 1976, 1153; § 118(2) ChinCA.

[90] See Roe (2003a). [91] See Ch. 5, section II.1.a above.

[92] Cf. Heine and Kerber (2002: 59); Luck (2001: 310); Van den Bergh (2000: 449); Bebchuk and Roe (1999: 155–6).

would be associated with simplification, clarification or harmonization, since complicated law in particular ensures, in their favour, a need for consultancy and thus lucrative employment.[93] On the other hand, it may be that lawyers press for reforms of company and securities law. Every reform initially makes renewed consultancy and perhaps the reworking of contracts, articles of association etc. necessary. Additionally, it may be in their long-term interest for the law to be further developed and to become internationally similar. If company and securities law in a legal system are attractive, the consulting professions benefit, since otherwise there might be a flight to other legal systems or forms of doing business.[94] Additionally, internationalization, convergence and harmonization may be advantageous to these groups because it enables them to extend their client base beyond the domestic market place.

In reality, in the US, Delaware lawyers in particular are an influential lobby. Since they profit from the fact that many firms are incorporated in Delaware,[95] they are interested in retaining a particularly pro-business law. Additionally, the corporate bar in the US advocates the promotion of derivative suits, because in practice such actions often primarily serve the interests of lawyers rather than the shareholders.[96] This fits in with the fact that – although there are clear differences in detail – in other countries too derivative actions are increasingly possible and made use of.[97] An additional factor in favour of some convergence of pressure is the fact that the increasingly internationalized practice in consultancy[98] tends to produce a greater harmonizing effect on national legislatures than would be the case with purely national consultants. Beyond this, however, general statements are hard to make. What influence, for instance, the legal profession has in a country also decisively depends on political factors. Thus, for example, restrictive professional licensing, and an emphasis on academic legal theories in legislation, may act negatively on lawyers' potential for pressure.[99]

V. Pressure from international organizations and foreign states

International and regional organizations usually exercise no direct pressure on company and securities law of individual countries. Instead, it

[93] Carney (1997: 306).
[94] Cf. Romano (1993: 30); see also Vagts (1972: para. 12A-64) (for auditors).
[95] See Ch. 9, section I.1.a, b above, and Ch. 9, section VI.1.a below.
[96] See Romano (1993: 22); West (2001b: 358–9, 366).
[97] See Ch. 5, section III.1 above. [98] See Ch. 8, section III.3 above.
[99] For Japan see e.g. West (2001a: 564–5, 592); Sono (2001: 55); Milhaupt and West (2003b) (regarding changes).

is particularly the WTO, the IMF, the World Bank and the OECD that promote the free movement of goods, services and capital, so that here it is convergence through congruence and not through pressure that is key.[100] Exceptions for direct provisions are, at regional level, harmonization by the EU, and, at international level, the OECD's Corporate Governance Principles.[101] Additionally, the criteria employed by the IMF and the World Bank for providing loans are aimed at orienting a country's commercial law to Western models.[102] These Structural Adjustment Programs (SAPs) are thus, alongside liberalization of foreign trade relations, privatization of state firms and currency stabilization, also directly incorporated into the pattern of company and securities law. For instance, the IMF and the World Bank demand the enhancement of management accountability and investor protection and compliance with international accounting standards,[103] so that in countries wishing to open up to world trade a Westernization of law comes about, often with the US model to the fore.[104]

This trend fits in with the fact that the US in particular also seeks, independently of international organizations, to affect the commercial law of other countries. Of the countries studied here, this influence has particularly affected Japanese company and securities law. After the Second World War, the law was initially recast according to US ideas.[105] In the post-war years, US pressure continued. Notably, the reforms in Japan in 1993 and 1994 easing the conditions for derivative actions and the shareholders' right of inspection were occasioned by the Structural Impediment Initiative Agreement (SII) between the US and Japan.[106]

VI. Legislative responses

Just like 'convergence through congruence', 'convergence through pressure' depends on communication among legislators and on path dependencies.[107] Apart from that, though, the situation here is in principle more complex, since the various factors of pressure may steer individual countries' laws in diverse directions. Things would, however, be different if the

[100] See Ch. 8, section III.1 above. [101] See Ch. 7, sections II, III above.
[102] Cf. Gilson (2001: 331); Tan (2000: 87); Roe (2002: 237); Farrar (2001: 95).
[103] See e.g. Wei (2003: 192 *et seq.*) (for the influence on China); Kim (2001: 36–7) (for the influence on South Korea).
[104] For criticism see Stiglitz (2006: 56). [105] See Ch. 1, section III.3.b above.
[106] Cf. Maruyama (1995: 290–1); Takahashi and Rudo (1998: 616); Dore (2000: 72–3).
[107] See Ch. 8, section VI above.

interplay of individual advantages and disadvantages ultimately resulted not in a multiplicity of interests but in a parallel interest of all those concerned in well-functioning enterprises. For instance, the debate on regulatory competition for the best seat has shown that firms' capital needs ensure that a system will not let shareholders be exploited.[108] Something similar can be said for other groups, since for instance the ignoring of employee interests, or too many restrictions on management, could also harm the firm's efficiency in general and thus the interests of all concerned. However, the fact that market forces do not always act to protect the interests of all concerned argues against generalizing these positions. There may, for instance, be market failure where shareholders are not informed about legal issues, or where disadvantageous aspects for one group become institutionalized in all legal systems.[109] Consequently, all groups agree only that legal rules should not be so one-sided that they would deter other groups. There is room for manoeuvre here, and many patterns are conceivable, so that, despite the interactions of individual interests, the various convergence forces can operate in different directions. Here I will on the one hand consider whether the legislators respond to pressure on them through lobbying and regulatory competition for company founders or investors. If that is so, the further question arises whether the legislators in the various countries respond in a similar fashion, so that convergence in the law is to be expected.

1. *Competition for the seat of companies*

It cannot generally be said that regulatory competition for the seat exercises pressure on legislators. While, in US states, the registered seat can be freely chosen and later moved, at the international level this is possible only to a limited extent, since either the registered and real seat must be identically located, or tax reasons militate against reincorporation. In the EU, however, recent developments indicate that, at least for incorporations, an increase in regulatory competition is to be expected.[110]

As long as competitive pressure exists, it is doubtful how legislators will respond. Apart from the direction of the competition ('race to the bottom' or 'race to the top'), it is of particular interest here whether it will lead more to convergence or divergence of legal systems. It would favour convergence if all legislators had to face the competition in a similar way,

[108] See e.g. R. Winter (1980: 91 *et seq.*); Dodd and Leftwich (1980: 100 *et seq.*).
[109] See Parkinson (1993: 187–8).
[110] See Ch. 9, section I.1.a above.

so that an approximation to the best law would be expected. Divergence might by contrast be favoured since either not all legislators have the motivation to engage in the competition, or else the competition brings a differentiation of legal systems according to differing preferences.

a) The position in the US

In the US in particular, firms incorporated in other US states have moved their seat to Delaware, or (more frequently) have reincorporated there. Various reasons have been decisive for this:[111] First, the (re-)incorporation process in Delaware is easy and quick. At the level of company law, the low degree of mandatory rules and the absence of a minimum capital requirement also help. Secondly, a specialized and qualified bar and bench guarantee a practice-oriented application of the law, so that Delaware's flexible law does not lead to any reduction in legal certainty. Network effects in particular play a decisive part in this, since, with more companies incorporated, the need for legal advice and dispute settlement and therefore also for experience and knowledge grows. Additionally, the influential bar itself exerts pressure for the continued existence of Delaware's leading position, since for instance derivative suits in Delaware can be brought only by local lawyers. Thirdly, Delaware's legislature is also dependent on the firms that have only their registered seat there. Delaware receives from them a one-off incorporation fee and a periodic franchise tax. Since these fees – by contrast with larger states – contribute a significant postion of the state budget, there is a credible commitment that the law will remain business-friendly. Fourthly, Delaware has a good reputation for (re-)incorporation. In view of this first-mover advantage, other states that have not yet gained comparable trust have difficulties competing with Delaware. Fifthly, it might be to Delaware's advantage that its law unfairly favours company founders and managements. Delaware was, for instance, the first state to introduce the possibility for articles to opt out of directors' liability for damages for breach of the duty of care.[112] This argument is not, however, free of doubt. For instance, in Delaware management has fewer possibilities for defending against hostile takeovers than in other states.[113] Again, moving the

[111] Cf. Romano (1993: 37 *et seq.*); Forstinger (2002: 44 *et seq.*); Hatzis-Schoch (1992).

[112] See Ch. 5, section II.1.b above.

[113] Although in general it has been found that stronger anti-takeover protection leads to more incorporations; Bebchuk and Cohen (2003).

domicile to Delaware often raises the share price,[114] which implies a positive evaluation of Delaware law by investors.[115]

The basic problem is therefore in which direction regulatory competition for company founders is developing. It is not at all a matter of course that all states are interested in participating in such competition. It may be the case that today Delaware's position is so dominant that other states do not really compete with it.[116] Furthermore, in most other states the influence of lawyers and the dependency on the financial advantages of (re-)incorporation are smaller than in Delaware. Also, until around 1960, lax company-law systems were uncommon in the US, without this leading to a general pressure to adapt. Finally, alongside the 'Delaware effect', there is talk also of a 'California effect'.[117] This is seen, first, in the fact that California deliberately does not have a deregulated company law, yet is not unsuccessful in the US. Secondly, California actively seeks to defend itself against evasion of its law and is also supported in this by the courts.[118]

To the extent that regulatory competition does happen, an assessment of whether developments in the US are leading to a 'race to the bottom' or a 'race to the top' depends on one's preferences.[119] The major consequence of competition is that company law is more liberal than in most other countries. This may on the one hand be seen as a failing, if one believes that market forces cannot lead to an optimum shaping of the articles of association. Shareholders would be disadvantaged since management could decisively affect the content of the articles of association. On the other hand, the flexibility of a restrained mandatory company law may also be advantageous, allowing the inefficiencies of politics to be avoided. Both the enhanced competition among legislators and the competition among drafters of the articles of association advance the innovative potential of the law, so that, as with other forms of competition, an 'optimization spiral' may arise. Disadvantage for shareholders would not be likely here since shareholder interests would also have weight, through the competition for investors (see subsection 3 below). Additionally, an

[114] But for a different result see Subramanian (2004).

[115] However, the reason for this might also be a change in strategy: cf. Romano (1993: 17–18).

[116] Bebchuk and Hamdani (2002).

[117] Vogel (1995); Barnard (2000: 73, 75).

[118] See § 2115 CalGCL; *Wilson* v. *Louisiana-Pacific Resources, Inc.*, 187 Cal. Rptr. 852, 138 Cal. App. 3d 216 (1983); *Valtz* v. *Penta Invest. Corp.*, 188 Cal. Rptr. 922, 139 Cal. App.3d 803 (1983); *North American Asbestos Corp.* v. *Superior Court*, 225 Cal. Rptr. 877, 180 Cal. App. 3d 902 (1986); *Havlicek* v. *Coast-To-Coast Analytical Services, Inc.*, 46 Cal. Rptr. 2d 696, 39 Cal. App. 4th 1844 (1995).

[119] See Ch. 9, section I, preamble above, and e.g. Bebchuk and Cohen (2003); Kelemen and Sibbitt (2002: 274–5); Coffee (1999b: 650–1); Romano (1993: 14 *et seq.*).

unfair favouring of management would even harm management itself, since otherwise, for lack of capital, the firm as a whole would be weakened and therefore exposed to a hostile takeover.

Finally, with respect to convergence, it is conceivable for regulatory competition to have led to a differentiation and a specialization of legal systems in particular types of firm.[120] Yet, this has basically not happened. Instead, studies show that in the US states company law has tended to come closer together.[121] Even if here Delaware law often has a pacemaker role, on the whole most states' laws nonetheless show more similarities with the MBCA than with the DelGCL.[122] Alongside competitive pressure, accordingly, US-specific model legislation has also contributed to a convergence of legal systems.

b) The position in the European Union

It is doubtful whether and to what extent regulatory competition in the EU for company founders will lead to changes in Member States' laws.[123] Doubts arise here, first, because competition is subject to limits on both the supply and demand sides.[124] Further, European legislators lack the financial incentives that have influenced Delaware in particular in shaping its law. In the EU, no periodic franchise tax is levied, and, when a company is founded, only administrative costs may be charged.[125] Nor do other fiscal motives exist, since in general the real seat of a firm is decisive for tax purposes.[126] For the individual Member States, accordingly, there remains, on the one hand, a possible prestige gain as a non-pecuniary advantage. On the other hand, Member States in which foreign firms choose to site their registered seat may profit from more clients for lawyers and other consultants, thus collecting more taxes and creating more jobs.[127] Here too, however, there is a necessary restriction because by comparison with Delaware no Member State's bar is comparably dependent on attracting foreign firms. Nor is anything essential likely to change, since, for instance, consultancy for German firms contemplating founding a UK company begins in Germany,[128] so that it is mainly German

[120] Cf. Daniels (1991); Rose (2001: 135–6); Kieninger (2002: 25 *et seq.*).

[121] See Romano (1993: 47); MacNeil (2000: 12); Carney (1998: 728). For a nuanced assessment of the effects of regulatory competition see also Zumbansen (2006a).

[122] Dooley and Goldman (2001: 738).

[123] Similarly Enriques (2004b); Gelter (2004), (2005).

[124] See Ch. 9, section I.1 above.

[125] See Art. 7 of Directive 69/335/EEC.

[126] See generally Werlauff (2003a: 97); Kieninger (2002: 184–5); for the UK: Omar (2000: 407–8); Cheffins (1997: 435–6); for Germany: Freitag (1999: 270); Roth (1999: 864).

[127] Armour (2005: 395).

consultants with knowledge of UK company law that benefit. Much the same presumably applies to judicial disputes among participants in companies. Even if the legal position is not yet decisively clarified here, by contrast with the US it is probably the courts of the state where those involved have their domicile and the company has its real seat that are competent.[129] Thus here again it will not be primarily lawyers in the state of incorporation but those in the state of the real seat that consult about the former's law.

Finally, it is noted in the literature that continental law-makers cannot pursue a domestic one-sided policy in favour of company founders and managements. Since in continental Europe, by contrast with the US, the focus is not simply on shareholder value but more comprehensively on all stakeholder interests, Member States would even under competitive pressure still follow different parameters.[130] A critical point to note here is that the sharp contrast between shareholder and stakeholder countries was not confirmed in this study.[131] However, it is true that, where political objectives or fundamental principles of corporate governance are raised, national legislatures often remain resolute.[132] In addition to possible counter-pressure from shareholders and other stakeholders (see subsections 2 and 3 below), accordingly, in the EU the 'multidimensionality' of company law acts as a path dependence from which legislation will not depart without further ado.

c) Divergence and convergence

At a global level, it is still more uncertain whether and to what extent legislators will compete for the seat of a company. Companies often cannot freely choose their registered seat, so that, when founding a firm or moving its seat, company law is only one criterion of decision, and one of less importance than, for instance, labour costs or tax burdens in a country. Accordingly, it is likely that competitive pressure from company founders will at best lead to minimum legal standards.

Beyond that, the fact that regulatory competition plays a dissimilar part may even cause a divergence. To the extent that regulatory competition is possible, the interests of company founders and managements will tend to be better served than in other legal systems and a deregulation of the law more often called for. Additionally, regulatory competition affects

[128] See note 44 above. [129] See Gelter (2004: 176–7).

[130] Merkt (1995: 558 *et seq.*). [131] See Ch. 5, section II.1.a above.

[132] See also High Level Group of Company Law Experts (2002: 103 *et seq.*); Regierungskommission Corporate Governance (2001: para. 7).

the openness of a legal system to reform as such. Competition speeds up innovation and imitation (Schumpeter) and acts as a discovery process (von Hayek).[133] Legislators whose company law can be evaded by domestic firms are thus more interested than others in having their law remain up-to-date and competitive. Studies agree on this, showing for instance that the company law of US states is amended more often than in other legal systems.[134] If the legislator allows no (mere) move of the registered seat, improvements will by comparison be made only in the event of a change of government, economic shocks or other one-off events. To be sure, a change is in the offing even for these 'conservative' legal systems. It is not, however, regulatory competition for company founders but regulatory competition for shareholders that is decisive here. Since pressure from shareholders for reform is increasing, even today and outside the US there is already continuous review of the competitiveness of company law. For the future, this intensification of competition will accordingly make convergence likely (subsection 3 below). By contrast, convergence through regulatory competition for the best corporate domicile for a firm represents only a weak convergence force internationally.

2. *The effect of lobbying*

It is likely that, where the same or similar groups affect legislators comparably, the law will also become more similar.

a) International lobbying

In particular, international lobbying can lead to legal convergence. The internationalization of business and politics has the consequence that managers of international enterprises, international shareholder associations, investment and pension funds, law firms, political organizations and foreign countries increasingly exert pressure on legislators across borders. This pressure does not, however, act uniformly, since both its intensity and the legislative readiness to respond differ between the individual countries. Additionally, for the national legislator the international lobbies may have reduced weight because at elections it is to domestic interest groups that they have to justify themselves. Nonetheless, in reality it appears that, for instance, the influence of international enterprises indeed affects legislation, so that critics of globalization in particular

[133] Schumpeter (1934); von Hayek (1978). [134] West (2001a: 528 *et seq.*).

criticize their excessive power, which does not have democratic legitimacy.[135] Because of the economic power of international lobbies, legislators would also harm their domestic economy if they radically opposed influential international enterprises.

It follows that international lobbying will further promote the internationalization of the economy and thereby, for instance, ease the exercise of voting rights across borders and bring together disclosure requirements. Additionally, unusual departures from international regulatory patterns are likely to be suppressed. The criterion for 'unusualness' will not, however, be some international average model. Since international lobbies are often dominated by the West and particularly the US, at least for the immediate future a (further) Westernization and Americanization is to be expected. However, it is quite conceivable for global ethical concerns also to obtain a hearing. The non-governmental organizations (NGOs) representing ethical interests are mostly locally rooted, and through their representatives in part also have influence on parties and national and international bodies.[136] Moreover, in the meantime, politics too has taken up the idea that the globalization of the economy, technology and communication must be underpinned by a globalization of ethics.[137] Economic globalization may accordingly be augmented by ethical globalization without that leading to a reduction in economic freedoms.

b) National lobbying

The situation in the national sphere is more complex still. Here the influence of persons and groups whose interests are affected by company and securities law is reflected in very diverse ways in the legislative process.

It is primarily differences in the strengths of the various groups that are responsible. A good example is the debate on the limits on hostile takeovers.[138] In some US states, anti-takeover acts were enacted so as to encourage founders and managers to establish their seat there, and to protect the employees of local firms. The interests of shareholders with dispersed holdings took second place here, since as a rule they lack

[135] See Ch. 7, section II.1 above.

[136] See Bhagwati (2004: 36 *et seq.*); Leggewie (2003: 101); for the participation of NGOs in the EU see e.g. Governance – A White Paper, COM(2001) 428, at 11 *et seq.*; Consultation document: Towards a Reinforced Culture of Consultation and Dialogue – Proposal for General Principles and Minimum Standards for Consultation of Interested Parties by the Commission, COM(2002) 277 final.

[137] See e.g. Annan (2001); Küng (2001).

[138] See Ch. 5, section II.1.a above, and Ch. 10, section II.2.a below.

organizational compactness.[139] The situation is similar in continental Europe, since managements and blockholders fearing for their power oppose the repeal of measures that can prevent takeovers.[140] Employee interests also overlap with this, and are commonly supported by influential trade unions. By contrast, the fact that in the UK and Delaware firms are more funded through the capital market than in other legal systems, and therefore dependent on investors, means that the legal framework is more friendly to takeovers. Additionally, in Delaware, employee interests of domestic firms are given little weight since many Delaware firms do not have their real seat there. Since, with hostile takeovers, lawyers are usually brought in, the strong position of the local bar is, finally, a further ground for the relatively liberal legal position in Delaware. All in all, then, there is a mixed picture of influences and this is also reflected in the law. As is the case in particular with controversial subjects, therefore, the differing weight individual groups have in various legal systems argues against strong convergence through national lobbying.

Over and above that, differences in political structures mean that the influence of national lobbies is not congruent. If political competition in a country is relatively slight, what will be decisive for regulators' conduct is not the private interests of individual lobbies but the common weal and their own interests. The general interest is served particularly by having specialized ministerial officials or other experts influence the direction of the laws. Of course, interest groups will also be heard in the law-making process. It may additionally be the case that rule-makers favour particular groups for selfish reasons, expecting specific advantages therefrom. By contrast, in fragmented systems, not only are interest groups dependent on politics but also politics is dependent on support by one or more interest groups.[141] Even diverging lobbies may thus influence politics through a variety of political representatives. Additionally, a lobby can go elsewhere if an existing interlocutor no longer can or will assert its interests.

In reality, these contrasts can be seen most clearly between China and the US. In China, for lack of political competition, legislator, government and administration can in principle act independently of lobbies. For ideological reasons, however, employee interests are taken particular account of. Additionally, forms of cooperation and mutual dependence between regulators and the regulated can be seen.[142] Since many

[139] See Ch. 9, section III.2 above.

[140] See e.g. the long history of the EU Takeover Directive narrated by Edwards (2004).

[141] Cf. Kelemen and Sibbitt (2002: 279 *et seq.*).

[142] See Heilmann (2001a), (2001b: 17).

companies are privatized state enterprises, personal relations exist between managers and politicians, so that in this way managers can bring their interests to bear. By contrast, in the US, parliamentarians and sometimes also judges are dependent on support by economic interest groups. Since most US politicians cannot finance their election campaigns themselves, they require financial support from managers of large firms and other private lobbies. Additionally, politicians must not lose sight of investor and shareholder interests, since in the US a fairly large proportion of the population holds shares or mutual funds and are thus of interest to politicians as voters.

The possibilities of influence in Germany, France and Japan lie between these extremes. Party funding often comes primarily through state funds,[143] so that the dependency of politicians on business is reduced. Similarly, by comparison with the US, investor interests play a smaller part, since fewer private individuals directly or indirectly invest in joint stock companies.[144] However, in Germany and France, for example, employee interests are given considerable weight through trade-union influence. In Germany, France and Japan, management is also favoured by the fact that, sometimes, managers are (former) politicians and politicians (former) managers.[145] Finally, in Germany and especially in Japan, reforms are being seen. The latest amendments to the German company law were largely prepared by a special commission.[146] Since business representatives, shareholder representatives and trade unionists were in the majority on the commission, it is possible to view this method of reform as 'corporatist' behaviour, delegating parts of political decision-making to private persons.[147] In Japan, since the end of seemingly invincible LDP rule in 1993, political fragmentation has increased. The government-controlled bureaucracy, and particularly the consultative body of the Ministry of Justice that hitherto drafted the laws in an academic style taking account of manifold interests, have lost their importance. Instead, the Ministry of Economics, Trade and Industry (METI), which is more open to lobbying from business, is now also involved in reforms of company and securities law. Furthermore, economic interest groups are gaining in importance because they exert influence on members of the Japanese parliament so

[143] For a general comparative overview see Ewing and Issacharoff (2006).

[144] See Ch. 8, section IV.1 above. [145] See Ch. 9, section II above.

[146] Regierungskommission Corporate Governance (2001).

[147] For criticism see Hopt (2002b: 34 *et seq.*); for corporatism see also Ch. 7, section I.3 above.

that recent reforms are based not just on government drafts but increasingly also on motions by individual parliamentarians.[148]

c) Conclusion

As a result, international lobbying leads to a certain convergence, whereas national lobbying is too diverse to make it possible to discern any clear convergence force. While in all countries the interests of individual groups play a part in shareholder law, the form and intensity in which this pressure is exerted are not at all uniform, nor is the concrete response by legislators. Accordingly, there is no clear convergence through national lobbying, so that, on that account alone, legal differences will continue to exist.

3. *Competition for shareholders*

Shareholders exert their influence on legislators not primarily as a lobby but through the possibility of buying and selling shares. Since shares today are in principle freely tradable internationally and are in demand from an international range of investors,[149] pressure on national legislators arises. It is therefore sometimes said that company and securities law will converge internationally towards the shareholder model (subsection a below). However, the limits to this convergence force must also be brought into consideration, so that ultimately a differentiated outcome is likely (subsections b and c below).

a) The evolutionary position

The international competition for shareholders is sometimes used to support the view that in future the shareholder model will prevail over alternative models (manager-oriented model, labour-oriented model, state-oriented model, stakeholder model).[150] It is seen as the only model that guarantees the competitiveness of domestic firms. Otherwise, capital would flow out to foreign firms, so that only these more efficient firms would prevail on the global market ('evolution toward efficiency' thesis;[151] 'satisfy global investors or die' argument[152]). Nor could legislators ignore these market forces. While in principle it may well be that domestic

[148] See Kelemen and Sibbitt (2002: 279 *et seq.*); Tatsuta (2004: 14); Kanda (2004: 32–3); Milhaupt and West (2003a: 322); Milhaupt (2001: 2104–5); Oda (2002: 7–8); Hayakawa (2002: 32); Aoki (2003: 17).

[149] See Ch. 9, section III.1 above.

[150] Hansmann and Kraakman (2001: 443 *et seq.*).

[151] Cf. Luck (2001: 307, 309); LaChance (2001: 279); Roe (1997: 166–7).

[152] Dore (2000: 91).

stakeholders exert more direct influence on domestic politics than a multiplicity of diversely investing national and international investors, if the weakening of domestic firms goes so far that their financial needs are not met and their products cannot be sold at competitive prices, this would have negative effects on national economic growth. Low tax revenues and high unemployment would follow, making a policy against international capital flows politically unacceptable.

This functional aspect of company and securities law is not a new phenomenon. The popularization of shares was always intended from the state's viewpoint to serve the public interest. Enterprises are not just private entities, but at the same time parts of a national economy which overall should promote the common good. Optimization of law thus concerns not just protecting shareholders or enterprises as such. Instead, the law serves to support enterprises and their functionality and productivity, so as to bring added value for the generality.[153]

Additionally, it can be seen from current reforms that legislators are in principle willing to support enhanced competitiveness. For instance, the most recent reforms in Germany are supposed to improve 'the competitiveness of German groups of companies on capital markets', to meet the 'interests of the financial markets, in particular of share owners and ultimately also of consumers and employees through transparency and control', and to bring a 'modernization of Germany as a location with the objective of creating the conditions that can take adequate account of the requirements of globalization and of the financial markets'.[154] Similar objectives can be discerned in, for example, the legislation in China, France, the UK, Australia and the EU.[155] However, these examples do not amount to absolute proof. It is also conceivable that they also contain such rhetoric in order to promote trust by voters at home and investors abroad

[153] Cf. generally Zöllner (1963: 54, 69, 78); Lutter (1973: 26 *et seq.*); Hansmann and Kraakman (2001: 4410), (2004: 18); Strine (2006: 1769) (corporate form as an instrumental means of enhancing the well-being of our society as a whole and not simply a means to enrich investors).

[154] Gesetz zur Verbesserung der Wettbewerbsfähigkeit deutscher Konzerne an Kapitalmärkten und zur Erleichterung der Aufnahme von Gesellschafterdarlehen (Kapitalaufnahmeerleichterungsgesetz, KapAEG) of 20.04.1998, BGBl. I 1998, 707; Regierungsentwurf KonTraG, BT-Drucks. 13/9712, at 2; Regierungsentwurf GerWpÜG, BT-Drucks. 14/7034, at 27–8.

[155] For China: Ong and Baxter (1999: 97); Walker (2001: 446); for France: Storp (2002: 409, 410 note 7); for the UK: Company Law Reform (2005: 8–9); for Australia: Ellett (2000: 174); Darvas (2000: 101); for the EU: Modernising Company Law and Enhancing Corporate Governance in the European Union – A Plan to Move Forward, Communication from the Commission, COM(2003) 284, at 9.

in the quality of their law. In other respects too, the view that the pressure of competition will almost automatically lead to a narrow shareholder model is open to objections.

b) Limits to convergence

One limit to convergence through competition for shareholders lies in the mere fact that, while supply and demand function well here, they do not do so perfectly.[156] Additionally, with respect to the consequences of competition, various reasons can be adduced in argument against a complete homogeneity of company and securities law.

(1) Economic efficiency as the 'prima ratio'?. The evolutionary position assumes that legislators will bow to the pressure of competition, and therefore an efficient law for investors will be created. This is, however, opposed by the fact that, in commercial law too, alongside economic interests, stakeholder protection or distributive justice may play a part. Politicians are not exposed to market pressure for economic efficiency by globalization to the same extent that firms are.[157] Since political conduct is not always economically rationalizable, it is conceivable for a legislator deliberately not to follow any purely economic notion of efficiency. It may also be that he will deliberately do without the advantages of a globalized market and instead seek, in the interest of national sovereignty, to defend his own law and prevent competition.[158] Finally, decisive importance may attach to the influence of interest groups. If, for instance, a legislator is dependent on support from a group such as the trade unions, it may be politically out of the question for him to attack particular protective institutions, such as employee co-determination.

This criticism, however, may lessen the convergence force of shareholder pressure, but does not make it invalid. A policy too detrimental to economic interests is not likely to be successful, at any rate in a democratic system. It is in the interest of all involved, not just shareholders, that markets are not restricted disproportionately. For shareholder law in particular, it is also to be borne in mind that the distinction between a pure market economy and a welfare state is not based primarily on company law but on other areas of law. The national legislator may accordingly very well yield to pressure from shareholder interests, but nonetheless uphold

[156] See Ch. 9, section III above.

[157] Milhaupt (1998: 1190–1); Roe (1998); see also Ch. 8, section I.2 above.

[158] See Baum (2000: 84–5); Romano (1993: 132).

the social nature of his market economy through, say, labour and social law.

By contrast, to the extent that the interests of existing block shareholders are involved, company law is indeed of central importance. Here it is claimed that, in countries where (to date) concentrated shareholding structures prevailed, blockholders have sought to obstruct reform. They are seen as having no interest in strengthening the rights of minority shareholders, since otherwise they would lose the gain they can derive from their power position.[159] Against this reasoning, however, is the point that, according to the findings of Part II, even in 'blockholder countries' the exploitation of minority shareholders is in principle not possible.[160] Additionally, it would not be advisable for influential shareholders to press for a law that would discriminate against other shareholders. Investors are prepared to pay a higher price for good corporate governance.[161] If there were discrimination against minority shareholders there would accordingly, at any rate in the medium and long term, be a weakening of the company in international competition. Even if blockholders might very well seek to influence the law in their direction, they will not risk *de facto* excluding other shareholders from the company.

(2) The most efficient system?. Insofar as legislators are concerned with an efficient system in the interest of the domestic economy, shareholder-centred company and securities law need not necessarily follow.

It might be pointed out that other legal or non-legal circumstances may be more important for economic success. 'It is not company law but two other things that govern the world of business: taxes and money, or personified, the Treasury and the capital market.'[162] Additionally, complementary protective factors, in particular the rule of law and effective enforcement, are decisive for growth.[163]

However, these additional requirements mean only that company and securities law codified in favour of shareholder interests does not constitute a sufficient condition for a successful national economy. A more weighty objection is that there may either be various equally

[159] See Bebchuk and Roe (1999: 143 *et seq.*); Roe (2003a: 111 *et seq.*, 116 *et seq.*); Cheffins (2003a: 17); Charny (2004: 299).

[160] See Ch. 5, section II.2 above.

[161] See McKinsey & Company (2002); Gompers *et al.* (2003).

[162] Hellwig (2001: 583) ('Nicht das Gesellschaftsrecht, sondern zwei andere Dinge regier[t]en die Welt des Wirtschaftens: Steuern and Geld, personifiziert der Fiskus and der Kapitalmarkt').

[163] Cf. Pistor *et al.* (2002).

efficient systems of company and securities law, or that at any rate no clear macroeconomic advantage of one system can be established.[164]

In support of this is, first, the fact that corporate financing through the issuing of additional shares is not the only way in which a company can seek to grow: growth through internally generated cash, the issuing of bonds, and bank loans are all possible options. The German, French and Japanese economies in particular for a long time had many successful companies which relied on bank loans. To be sure, this does not contradict the notion that today, because of the increasing opening up of finance and product markets, reliance on this form of financing alone may be disadvantageous. A shareholder-centred system benefits more than a bank-centred system from the enhanced financial power of shareholders who invest internationally. Correspondingly, a system where companies rely primarily on bank loans and where shareholdings are often interlocking is on the decline, at least for large firms.[165]

Secondly, however, it continues to be conceivable for the advantages of a legal system focused exclusively on shareholder interests to be outweighed by its drawbacks and dangers. On the one hand, the law has to balance between the interests of shareholders and management. If it were only concerned about the protection of shareholders, management would be paralyzed, the decision process retarded and economic innovation impaired. This can also be seen in the existing law.[166] On the other hand, a system entirely focused on attracting more shareholders may have the drawback that dispersed holdings could tend to increase.[167] It may follow that these shareholders, who hold only small stakes in any one particular company, are apathetic and do not effectively monitor management.[168] Nor can the selling option fully replace this. If – as is sometimes said – shareholders with dispersed holdings primarily act with a short-term focus,[169] there will be a danger that too much will be paid out in dividends and a volatile share price will result. Innovative companies in need of stable capital and companies that grow only over the long term will thus be squeezed out and a country's economy be destabilized. By contrast, a system not just focusing on the interests of investors but aiming at a balance of interests could be more stable, and in the long term more successful. If shareholders keep their shares longer and other stakeholders

164 See Bratton and McCahery (1999: 231); Jacoby (2000: 18 *et seq.*).

165 See Ch. 8, section IV.2.b above.

166 See Part II above (e.g. Ch. 5, section II.1.b).

167 For this view see Ch. 8, section IV.1.a above.

168 See Ch. 4, section II.1.b above.

169 For this debate see e.g. Berrar (2001: 31); Jacoby (2000: 21–2).

are given more weight, this may act positively upon the monitoring of management. Similarly, the inclusion of other stakeholder interests need not always be inefficient. If, for instance, employee interests are also taken into account, this evaluation of human capital may in fact be a rational business policy.

Thirdly, even where shareholder interests are pursued, legal differences are likely. Since according to the findings of Part II all the legal systems studied here already provide comprehensive mechanisms to protect shareholders, it is more the 'how' and the 'when' than the 'if' in principle of shareholder protection that is controversial. Here it is often impossible to say which solution is in general more efficient.[170] Additionally, an 'experimental divergence' may in fact correspond to regulatory competition, whereas by contrast complete convergence would rationally undermine the function of competition in promoting innovation and choice.[171]

(3) The time dependency of law. Even if in principle one can assume that legislators optimize the law in the interest of shareholders, for reasons of time dependency the law of individual countries may continue to be divergent. Differences in industrial and economic development are reflected in company and securities law.[172] This can already be seen in the historical development of the joint stock company, since industrialization raised the need for capital and led the development of elaborate company law.[173] Furthermore, it may, say, be sensible in a new market economy to guarantee the stability of young companies through blockholders or loans, and only gradually promote volatile dispersed shareholder ownership. In general, moreover, the importance of equity may be subject to change. When the economy as a whole is in trouble, public offerings fall, and the demand for shares goes down in favour of, for instance, bonds and real-estate funds. At such a time, accordingly, convergence pressure on these forms of investment increases, whereas that for a uniform pattern for shares falls.

[170] Similarly for corporate governance models Maher and Andersson (2002: 404 *et seq.*); Milhaupt (1998: 1189).

[171] For the concept of a 'competition of ideas' see Kieninger (2002: 18 *et seq.*); see also Ginsburg (2005: 323) who uses the term 'ideational convergence' when the source of convergence is ideas.

[172] See also Easterbrook (1996: 5 *et seq.*) ('no one model is best for all firms at all times'); Hansmann and Kraakman (2001: 463 *et seq.*); Van den Berghe (2002: 22 *et seq.*).

[173] See Ch. 1, sections III.2, 3.a; Ch. 7, section I above.

Moreover, as a variant of path dependence,[174] optimizations of law are often arrived at only after a time lag. Economic crises or scandals may act as catalysts against this inertia. But this need not necessarily mean convergence. Although economic scandals (such as the Enron scandal) might affect the legislators of foreign countries,[175] this is not always the case. 'Crisis-driven law' may therefore lead to divergence, because, for instance, trust and stability may in other countries still be achieved through extra-legal norms. Finally, not all legal systems amend their law primarily in cases of crises. Frequently, the difference between the US and Japan here is pointed to.[176] In the US, regulatory competition for corporate domiciles is by itself seen as making states continually develop their company law further. By contrast, the more isolated Japanese law mostly only reacts to exogenous shocks. However, even in the US, most reforms in securities law in the last 300 years came after 'bubbles' or crashes.[177] Additionally, in Japan, – as in Europe too[178] – the tendency is discernible for the continuity of the reform process to increase in the interests of competitiveness.[179] Since this reduces the intensity of path dependence, for the future an acceleration of convergence can be expected.

(4) The problem of partial receptions of foreign law. It is sometimes pointed out that a mixture of various systems does not enhance efficiency but reduces it. In any system various sub-elements complement each other, so that copying only some components of a foreign system harms institutional complementarity.[180] Exhaustive explanations are supplied by William Bratton and Joseph McCahery.[181] They point out particularly that in systems various trade-offs exist, since every advantage of intensive monitoring necessarily also has drawbacks as a consequence. Thus, a high concentration of share ownership, while enabling management to be efficiently monitored, has the drawback of lowering liquidity and raising capital costs. Similarly, while a restrictive list of management powers may help to monitor management, it brings with it the drawback of reducing

[174] See Ch. 8, section V.2 above. [175] See Davies (2004: 188–9).

[176] See West (2001a: 586 *et seq.*); Brancanto and Price (2002: 58).

[177] Banner (1997); see also Roe (1997: 182); Romano (1993: 27) ('legislators tend to function more analogously to firemen than police').

[178] See Commission Decision of 28 April 2005 establishing a group of non-governmental experts on corporate governance and company law (2005/380/EC).

[179] See Aoki (2001a: 101).

[180] See e.g. Schmidt and Spindler (2004: 121 *et seq.*); Bratton and McCahery (1999); Mann (2003); Ahlering and Deakin (2006); Baum (1998: 757–8); Gilson (2001: 335).

[181] Bratton and McCahery (1999: 213 *et seq.*, 258 *et seq.*).

managers' initiative and the firm's flexibility. However, as regards the behaviour of major shareholders, if given the chance to profit financially from their controlling position, the result will be that they may themselves act at the expense of other shareholder and stakeholder interests. Overall, according to Bratton and McCahery, the outcome is that one cannot, say, recommend either the US or continental Europe to change their systems. One cannot simultaneously claim the advantages of control by major shareholders and of market liquidity. Were one to try that, the danger would be that not the best but the worst elements of both systems would prevail.

This argument is right in saying that a rejection effect may threaten if foreign legal notions cannot be integrated into the existing system.[182] It is therefore indeed conceivable in principle for an ill-considered copying of partial elements to reduce economic efficiency. However, Bratton and McCahery are not convincing in transferring these abstract considerations to corporate governance in the US and continental Europe. This study has shown that a crude subdivision into different legal 'families' is today no longer persuasive, and that the factual circumstances too – such as shareholder structures – are also starting to come closer together.[183] Hybridisms may very well therefore work in practice. Additionally, the dialectic between 'gradualism or big bang'[184] may specifically make gradual, cautious reform rational. Since it can scarcely be established in the run-up to reforms what frictions may arise, a successful transformation of law at least temporarily requires a mixture of different systems.

c) Conclusion

Regulatory competition for shareholders acts as a convergence force. The liberalization of markets means that pressure from shareholders rises. It is therefore to be expected that legislation will pay special attention to shareholder interests. This convergence will be further enhanced by communication among legal systems. To be sure, this convergence is also subject to limitations. Since the limits extend to both the supply and demand sides and the consequences of competition, generalizations are

[182] See Ch. 8, section II.1 above; see also Rock (1995: 299) ('The great contribution of comparative corporate law, like comparative law more generally, is to help domestic lawyers ask questions they would not otherwise ask about their own law. The trap for the unwary is the temptation to believe that foreign answers tell any of us much at all about what the answers should be in our own systems.').

[183] See Part II, and Ch. 8 above.

[184] See generally Ackermann (1999: 159 *et seq.*); Bhagwati (2004: 253).

hard. Additionally, the mode of operation will vary between different legal rules, because, for instance, more uniform arrangements for the utilization of new media are more likely than for such controversial questions as the division of powers within the company (Ch. 10 below).

4. *Conclusions*

With 'convergence through pressure', it is in particular regulatory competition for shareholders that makes convergence likely. By contrast, regulatory competition for company founders and national and international lobbying are less important. Regulatory competition for the registered seat of a company is only possible in the US and to a limited extent in the EU too, but not in principle in the global context. For lobbying, national differences mean that primarily the pressure from international lobbies will lead to some convergence.

As with 'convergence through congruence' (Ch. 8 above), here too the focus of convergence lies primarily with public companies. Both competition for shareholders and international lobbying act more strongly where firms are more dependent on international capital markets and interest groups. John Coffee therefore assumes that, as in the US, a situation will develop where securities law is largely uniform but differences in company law continue to exist.[185] As a trend, this may be true.[186] But against generalization is the fact that securities law in the US contains many features that in other legal systems would belong to company law.[187] Additionally, company law is by no means neutral in capital-market terms, since it also increasingly provides investor protection.[188] For the future, in view of the demands of public companies and their shareholders, it is also likely that this trend will become still stronger.

185 Coffee (1999b: 652). 186 See also Ch. 7, section III.2 above.
187 See e.g. Ch. 2, section IV.1.b; Ch. 4, section II.3 c above.
188 See Ch. 2, section III.2 above.

10

Future convergences in shareholder law

For the *status quo* of convergence in shareholder law (Part II above) the finding was that the 'shareholder as such' (Ch. 4) could in all the countries studied be characterized by the adjectives 'profit-oriented', 'active' and 'informed'. Nonetheless, the continuing differences could also hamper the exercise of shareholder rights in foreign companies, so that, for instance, the question arises whether the law on notice periods, voting proxies etc., will continue to differ in future. In the case of provisions on the 'shareholder's position in the power structure of the company' (Ch. 5), the specific features in today's law are even more notable. Although in all the countries studied here the intrinsic decision-making powers, substantive legal protections and possibilities of legal action interpenetrate, there is greater room here for future convergence.

In this part I will investigate for both areas whether and how far the convergence forces (Chs. 8, 9) will lead to a further approximation of law. So as to avoid unreal historicism,[1] this sort of forecast can admittedly only show some trends. But even from these it becomes clear whether, and with what substantive emphases, a further convergence of shareholder law may come about, making convergence a model for the future (Part 4).

I. The 'shareholder as such'

According to the law of all the countries studied here, the shareholder can as a rule respond to a particular situation either through 'voice' or through 'exit'.[2] It is, however, questionable whether one of these options may not gain the upper hand in future. In particular, it may be possible to foresee that the decline in blockholdings and the increase in international shareholders[3] would have the consequence that voting rights would lose their importance not just *de facto* but also *de jure*. This would mean a reduction to the model of the shareholder as investor or passive spectator,[4] with only

[1] See preamble to Part III above. [2] See Ch. 4, section I.3, Ch. 5, section II above.
[3] See Ch. 8, section IV above. [4] See Ch. 3, section I.3 above.

the financial interests of the investment decision worthy of legal protection (subsection 1 below). However, it can be objected, first, that such a trend would extend only to public companies. In the future, too, there will continue to be companies with largely non-dispersed shareholder ownership, so that the decisive conflict would then rather lie in the tension between a converging investor law and (continuing) diverse provisions on membership. Additionally, for public companies, the liberalization of capital markets and the influence of the new media[5] may also lead specifically to a strengthening of shareholder power. Since shareholders can exert more pressure, the law might thereby develop in the direction of a new parliamentary or ownership model[6] in favour of increased shareholder influence (subsection 2 below).

1. *The profit-oriented shareholder*

It is generally to be expected that regulatory areas directly or indirectly concerned with the trading of shares will be optimized still further. In support of this view, in the context of 'convergence through congruence', is the fact that for companies the influence of blockholders will decline in favour of institutional investors, as well as financing through equity capital, and thus the importance of the capital markets will tend to increase.[7] Legislators will accordingly be concerned to respond to the greater *de facto* fungibility of shares. Additionally, shareholders, especially international institutional investors, exert pressure not only for international economic law to be liberalized, but also for national company and securities law to offer the best conditions for effective trade in shares. While there are criticisms on short-term trading,[8] the recent reforms show that the legislators are in principle prepared to make changes.[9] This policy is also often supported by directors and managers themselves, since they too are typically interested in improving the liquidity of their company.[10]

On the one hand, direct regulations on the processing of securities transactions ought to converge. Here it may for instance happen that the speed of processing individual transactions and the utilization of trading platforms outside the exchanges[11] will be treated legally more similarly than today. A further optimization of the 'global share programme' is also likely, so that shares that are identical on all markets can be freely traded

[5] See Ch. 8, section III; Ch. 9, section III, VI.3 above. [6] See Ch. 3, section I.1, 2 above.
[7] See Ch. 8, section IV above. [8] See Ch. 4, section I.3.a; Ch. 8, section III.1 above.
[9] See Part II above. [10] See Ch. 9, section III above. [11] See Ch. 4, section I.3.d above.

on international exchanges.[12] On the other hand, it is to be expected that the securities law provisions intended to guarantee the shareholder a sale at market value, notably through disclosure obligations and prohibitions of manipulation, will come closer together. Nevertheless, differentiations remain not just possible but also likely. It may be that some legal systems deliberately wish to address only certain companies or investors, through differences in securities law, thus bringing about a specialization of markets.[13] Additionally, developments so far have shown that even 'old securities laws', such as in the US, are subject to continual change. The dependency on factual factors such as the development of new trading platforms, the use of new media and the occurrence of scandals thus leads to convergent development patterns, though not identity of law.[14]

The increasing importance of the national and international capital market is also influencing regulations enabling profit to be realized while remaining in the company. In harmony with the present trend,[15] the provisions regarding distributions of dividends and share buybacks ought to continue to be made more flexible. Notably, the room for manoeuvre by management will be enhanced thereby. Counter-pressure from shareholders is unlikely in this respect. Increased flexibility enables internationally uniform calculations, which is also in the interests of international investors. Additionally, international competition for goods, services and capital requires companies to be able to act quickly, so that in this sphere less-strict provisions will in principle be accepted by shareholders. How any conflict between the more long-term interests of management and possible short-term investor interests will be resolved will then be decided not by statutory provisions but by market forces.

2. *The modern shareholder*

With regard to the provisions on the 'active', 'informed' and 'anonymous' shareholder, current developments indicate that a (further) harmonization of the law might come about in the EU.[16] In particular, participation and information rights in the run-up to the general meeting are to be harmonized, to facilitate the cross-border exercise of shareholder rights.

[12] See Schmitz (2002: 181 *et seq.*).

[13] See Ch. 8, section III.4.c above.

[14] See generally Ch. 9, section VI.3.b above.

[15] See Ch. 4, section I.2, 4 above.

[16] See Modernising Company Law and Enhancing Corporate Governance in the European Union – A Plan to Move Forward, Communication from the Commission, COM(2003) 284, at 13–14; Directive 2007/36/EC; see also Ch. 2, section I.2; Ch. 7, section II.3 above.

Additionally, however, there may also be a convergence of the law in the global context. The internationalization of shareholder structures raises particular problems across the countries in exercising shareholder rights, which often suggest that these rights may be delegated to proxies (subsections a and b below). Similarly, the utilization of new media is a global phenomenon.[17] Since the same legal challenges present themselves across borders, similar solutions are to be expected. Moreover, it is in the interest of both managements and shareholders that legislators enable the use of new media so as to save costs and ease communication and information (subsections c and d below).

a) The international shareholder

It is sometimes assumed that in the case of public companies the increasing shift in share ownership from blockholdings to international and/or institutional investors will intensify still further the problem of shareholders' 'rational apathy'.[18] In support of this view is the fact that, for international shareholders at any rate, personal exercise of voting rights on the spot is unprofitable, and acquiring knowledge about foreign standards, customs and firms constitutes an extra cost. Instead, the sale of shares or purely financial protective mechanisms are seen as more important for international investors. This concerns in particular international institutional investors. Since they are not the original capital providers and often invest in a diversified range of investments, their connection with individual firms and thus incentives to get involved are smaller than for individual blockholders.

It is nonetheless likely that, despite internationalization and institutionalization, shareholders will in future be even more interested in a law that enables their active conduct. Even shareholders pursuing primarily financial objectives through their participation are concerned about an effective pattern for the voting right. Otherwise, their deliberate decision to invest in shares – rather than bonds – would be left out of account. Additionally, shareholders can in this way influence profit-maximizing management of their investment.[19] This behavioural option also overlaps with actual trends. Current developments in various countries show that institutional investors are becoming more active and, for instance,

[17] See Ch. 8, section III.2 above.

[18] E.g. Strätling (2003: 79); Schneider (1990: 320); on the 'rational apathy' of shareholders see also Ch. 4, section II.1.b above.

[19] See Ch. 4, section II.1.a above.

attacking the level of executive compensation.[20] Diversification of their holdings does not stand in the way of this. Institutional investors frequently bring their interests together by forming joint organizations[21] and co-ordinating the exercise of their voting rights.[22] Both these organizations and influential individual investors additionally make demands in guidelines for good corporate governance. For instance, the Global Corporate Governance Principles of the International Corporate Governance Network (ICGN) are intended to guarantee that cost-effective proxy voting is possible, that shareholders receive information in good time and in a comprehensible form prior to the general meeting, and that at the general meeting itself all votes count.[23]

When it comes to possible legislative responses, however, a differentiated view is called for. Convergence is to be expected particularly on provisions that currently directly or indirectly disadvantage foreign shareholders by comparison with domestic ones. Pressure from international investors is strongest on these provisions. Countering resistance by managements is the fact that in public companies management too is basically interested in being able to expand the equity base through international investors.[24] Since the internationalization of investment was enabled by politics, legislators will also in principle take a positive approach to the concerns of international shareholders.[25] Additionally, the internationalization of shareholder structures is a common legal phenomenon, making similar solutions likely.[26] This argument of 'convergence through congruence' also embraces provisions that do not directly or indirectly discriminate against international shareholders, though only to a lesser degree. Such departures, for instance in the quorums for convocation, may be acceptable to participants if they are transparently informed and certain minimum standards are adhered to.

In detail, the following areas of convergence result. First, provisions for the run-up to the general meeting should tend to converge at least as far as necessary in order to allow international shareholders to participate actively. Currently, it may, for instance, be a problem that information

[20] See Ch. 4, section II.4.c above.

[21] See Bratton and McCahery (1999: 260); Tuerks (2000: 122); Cheffins (1997: 638–9) (for the UK); and e.g. the Council of Institutional Investors (http://www.cii.org).

[22] See e.g. for Germany: Noack (1994: 45–6); Schneider (1990: 323); for the UK: Van den Berghe (2002: 18–19); see http://www.calpers-governance.org/alert/proxy/.

[23] See http://www.icgn.org/organisation/documents/cgp/revised_principles_jul2005.php; Davis (1999: 386 *et seq.*); similarly André (1998: 69, 77 *et seq.*) (for CalPERS).

[24] See Ch. 9, section II above. [25] See Ch. 9, section VI.3 above.

[26] See Ch. 8, section III.4, V.1 above.

prior to the general meeting is sometimes published only in local media, and that more in-depth information can be procured only on the spot.[27] Additionally, information sent out individually by the company does not always reach the foreign investor. If shares are held by a foreign depository or a foreign financial intermediary is entered in the share register,[28] there are typically no provisions requiring the information to be sent abroad. Finally, too-short periods can act as indirect discrimination if the invitation and other information reaches foreign shareholders so late prior to the general meeting that they can no longer react either directly or through a proxy.[29]

For the future, these problems may be partly eliminated simply by legislators liberalizing the law and creating room for uniform international practice. If, for instance, legislators open up the law to the new media, then an information database on the Internet or communication by e-mail may make spatial distance irrelevant for foreign shareholders.[30] Insofar as legislators intervene actively, it is not improbable that alongside the removal of direct or indirect discriminations there may be further convergence. Among causes for this may be that international shareholders are interested in uniform provisions because, for instance, they do not wish to investigate for each of their investments whether the notice period in one legal system is four weeks or one month.[31] Additionally, unilateral pressure from one country may be decisive. It is, for example, conceivable that, following criticisms by US institutional investors, other legal systems alter the provisions regarding participation in general meetings in accordance with American record dates.[32]

Secondly, the convergence forces mean that, for voting rights, discrimination against foreign shareholders will be reduced. While the voting right itself does not differ between domestic and foreign investors,[33] the voting caps and multiple voting rights in some countries serve primarily to protect domestic shareholders.[34] Additionally, the demands of institutional investors and corporate governance guidelines suggest that the 'one share one vote' principle will increasingly prevail in public companies.[35] To be sure, a legal ban on voting caps and multiple voting rights is not absolutely

[27] Cf. Hocker (2000: 148 *et seq.*, 152–3) and Ch. 4, section II.3.b above.

[28] See Ch. 4, section IV.3.

[29] See DSW-Europastudie (1999: 95).

[30] See Ch. 10, section I.2.c below.

[31] See generally also Ch. 9, section III.1.b above.

[32] Cf. now also Art. 7(2) of Directive 2007/36/EC.

[33] In China, too, the distinction between A-shares and B-shares (see Ch. 2, section III.1 above) relates to the acquisition of shares, and not voting rights.

[34] See Ch. 4, section II.4.b above.

[35] See Ch. 3, section II above.

necessary here. Instead, listing rules or the market power of influential investors may mean that only shares with voting rights are accepted.[36]

Thirdly, it follows from the internationalization of investments that information made available to shareholders by public companies must be internationally comprehensible. This should at a factual level mean a further increase in the importance of the English language. Mandatory language rules are, however, not to be expected. Domestic information intermediaries can pass the content on to the international capital market. Additionally, for companies involved internationally, it is likely that, even without a legal obligation, they will voluntarily publish the most important company, securities and accounting law information (also) in English.

By contrast, developments to date show that, for the volume and content of disclosed information, market forces alone are not relied on.[37] Additionally, convergence of the law can already be seen. This development should continue, particularly because of the increasing pressure from international investors. International investors have an interest in more easily comparable information, through similar disclosure requirements and accounting standards, thus reducing evaluation costs. This pressure relates primarily to the high quality of collective information, in line with the mass nature of public companies, enabling monitoring from outside. Optimization of disclosure provisions, including effective enforcement of them, is not denied by the possibility of choosing a particular stock exchange. A flight into deregulated capital markets would not be advantageous for firms, since otherwise their shares would have a risk premium attached to them and be less in demand. Since, moreover, shareholders increasingly invest abroad and more readily perceive backwardness in their domestic law than hitherto, competitive pressure from abroad will be further enhanced by internal pressure.

Against convergence, however, one might object here that so far there has not been approximation but often a mere reception of the US disclosure model. For instance, American securities law influences other countries' laws without conversely US law being influenced in return. Again, in accounting law the market-oriented basis of the IAS/IFRS standard is marked more by Anglo-American than continental European principles. To date, therefore, in this area of law one can talk of 'Americanization'. Nor is this surprising for current developments, since the growing importance

36 This is sometimes already the case today: see Ch. 4, section II.4.b above.

37 See Ch. 4, section III above.

of the capital market requires more disclosure, and this was most consistently and earliest achieved in US securities law. Whether, however, in the medium and long term the leading position of the US will continue depends on a variety of economic and political reasons that cannot be predicted.[38] Figures showing that in the last twenty years the proportion of foreign investment from the US and other Anglo-Saxon countries has declined in relative terms in relation to other countries[39] might, for instance, be regarded as an indication that in future more internationally diverse investors will be exercising influence.

All in all, accordingly, an improvement in the legal position of international investors is coming about. There is at the same time an interaction with economic internationalization.[40] Increasing economic interpenetration is on the one hand a cause of the internationalization of shareholder law; on the other hand, more uniform standards are contributing to the further internationalization of the economy.

b) The delegating shareholder

Law and practice in proxy voting display clear differences in the countries studied here. However, already today, proxy voting is possible everywhere, and giving proxies to management is increasingly recognized.[41] For the future, it can be expected that, at least for public companies, the convergence will continue. Proxy voting will grow in importance, which will also lead to a shift of information and communication from the general meeting to the period prior to the meeting.

The cause of this development is, first, the approximation of shareholder structures.[42] Enhanced internationalization encourages proxies, so as to spare shareholders the costs of personal attendance at the general meeting of a foreign company. Online participation (subsection d below) is not a complete alternative, to the extent that, while it frees the shareholder from physical presence, it still requires personal involvement. Using a proxy will thus, desirably, both minimize the effort involved, yet retain the advantages of being a shareholder. This interest is also reflected in 'convergence through pressure'. International institutional investors in particular demand to be able to exercise their vote through a proxy and have the necessary information and authorizations for special instructions

[38] For the 'rise and fall of nations' see e.g. Olson (1982); P. Kennedy (1987).
[39] See Van den Berghe (2002: 63, 207–8); see also Ch. 6, section II above.
[40] See generally Ch. 8, section III above. [41] See Ch. 4, section II.3.c above.
[42] See Ch. 8, section IV above.

available.[43] Management too is in principle interested in having shareholders represented and their voting right not lapse. High participation rates reduce the risk of random majorities. Additionally, an attractively patterned voting right can be a good marketing instrument in the competition for international capital.

It follows that legislators will generally improve the possibilities of representation. Specifically, current developments already show that electronically communicated proxies are also recognized.[44] It remains to be clarified whether, for instance, this possibility requires a corresponding amendment to the articles of association, and how identification as shareholder is to be handled technically. Regarding the information that has to be supplied to shareholders in the run-up to the general meeting,[45] the gain in importance of proxies ought to lead to an improvement in the quality of information. If shareholders were not adequately informed before giving a proxy, this would neither serve shareholder interests nor banish the danger of random majorities and enhance the value of the firm.[46] To restore rationality, clearer and more detailed information is accordingly required so that shareholders can decide their vote in advance of the actual meeting by choosing different proxies or by giving special instructions.

The question of whom to appoint as a proxy also needs to be considered. The unique German system of representation through banks is on the decline.[47] Beyond this, the advantages and disadvantages of representation through management itself, through other shareholders or through independent third parties are debated. A proxy to management is today in principle possible and common in many countries.[48] In favour of this is the fact that management is in principle best able to judge business decisions, and that shareholders can in principle, while giving a proxy to management, nonetheless depart from management proposals through special instructions. A problem, though, is the danger of abuse, since for reasons of 'rational apathy' shareholders often agree with management without giving serious consideration to the question, thus making the division of powers within the company pointless. Nor is it in general a solution to authorize other shareholders. If the other shareholders

[43] See Baums (1998: 546); André (1998: 78) (for CalPERS).

[44] E.g. § 7.22 MBCA; § 212(c)(2) DelGCL; s. 333 UK-CA; § 134(3)(s.2) GerAktG; Arts. 132, 132-1 FrDécret.

[45] See Ch. 4, section II.3.b above.

[46] For the effects on 'company performance' see Strätling (2003: 77); Stapledon and Bates (2002: 605).

[47] See Ch. 4, section II.3.c above.

[48] See Ch. 4, section II.3.c above.

have their own interests in a particular decision, the problem of abuse is merely shifted. But, without interests of their own, other shareholders will, because of 'rational apathy', scarcely be willing to act as proxies.

Accordingly, it is mainly in proxies to third parties that the possibility of creating a market in voting proxies is seen. Here too, however, a number of problems are to be overcome. For instance, third parties must have an incentive to become active on behalf of shareholders and offer qualitatively valuable proposals.[49] Third parties must also be prevented from abuses of power or uncontrolled power vacuums.[50] Moreover, it must be possible for shareholders to assess the quality of the proposals. This evaluation must not be too costly for them, since otherwise individual shareholders would remain apathetic in the hope of rational conduct by other shareholders, so that here too the 'free-rider effect' would arise.[51] In view of these problems, in continental Europe legislative action is sometimes advocated. For instance, the setting up of a governmental proxy system, improvement in the position of shareholder associations or special provisions for professional voting agents are proposed.[52] Additionally, comprehensive changes, such as replacing the general meeting by a meeting of delegates to be elected for five years[53] or limiting rights of participation by attendance in favour of a meeting of agents,[54] are contemplated. In the US, by contrast, the indications are that, even without special statutory measures, private associations give voting recommendations or offer representation at domestic and foreign general meetings.[55] It should, however, be noted that these offers are directed mostly at institutional investors obliged to vote,[56] and who are accordingly prepared to pay. It is at this point that a proposal by Mark Latham operates:[57] the general meeting should decide that the firm itself will pay proxy advisory firms according to the number of shares represented by them. Since no costs arise for shareholders and

[49] Cf. Latham (2000: para. 9) ('how could a cacophony of agents make a company better managed than full-time professionals on the board?').

[50] Cf. Latham (2001: 10) ('who watches the watchers?'); cf. also Decimus Junius Juvenal (Iuvenalis), Saturae VI 347–8 ('sed quis custodiet ipsos custodes?').

[51] See also Ch. 4, section II.1 above.

[52] Cf. for Germany: Baums and von Randow (1995); Mülbert (1996b: 91 *et seq.*); Tuerks (2000: 36, 40 *et seq.*); for Switzerland: Ruffner (2000: 506 *et seq.*); for France: Becker (2001: 148); Fanto (1998: 52).

[53] Lutter (1973: 35 *et seq.*).

[54] Noack (1999: 43).

[55] Institutional Shareholder Services (ISS, http://www.issproxy.com), Investor Communication Services (ICS) of ADP's Brokerage Services Group (http://ics.adp.com), http://www.proxyvote.com; Strätling (2003: 81); Romano (2002: 539).

[56] See Ch. 4, section II.4.c above.

[57] Latham (1999a), (1999b), (2000), (2001).

they can take up the proxies' offers via the Internet without great trouble, the problem of the free-rider effect is thereby minimized.

In view of these varied proposals, it cannot at present be foreseen whether and how legislators will promote representation by third parties. Accordingly, no rapid convergence is to be expected. Instead, national reforms and market-oriented innovations are likely gradually to show how a market for voting agents can develop.

c) The information-seeking shareholder

The internationalization of shareholder structures should see provisions on collective information tend to improve and become more similar internationally (subsection a above). This does not, however, exhaust future developments, since additionally the new media will change the amount of and the impact of information.

For management, currently it is principally the cost of printing and distributing information in paper form, and the danger of abuse of individual information rights by 'disruptive shareholders', that are problematic. Since abuse by these shareholders also obstructs the other shareholders, on the shareholder side too there may be objections to too extensive individual information rights. Additionally, for internationally diversified investors, these individual rights are mostly empty, since it is often too costly to put questions at the general meeting or make use of on-the-spot rights of access to information.

Inasmuch as shareholders are sent individual information, this is in principle advantageous to them. However, if shares are held by a foreign depository or financial intermediary, it may be uncertain whether and how shareholders receive this information.[58] Furthermore, the coexistence of various information channels may raise difficulties because shareholders must give consideration to both mailed information, registries, public disclosure, press conferences etc. This problem may be exacerbated by having information and disclosure systems of various countries applied in the case of companies listed abroad. Finally, particular influential groups of investors, most notably institutional investors, will not uncommonly be favoured, producing an information gap for private investors.[59]

For management, the clear solution is the cheaper, easier distribution of information through the new media. Even today information can often be sent out through e-mail and then, for instance, be forwarded with little effort to the ultimate investor. Since firms already use their own

[58] See Ch. 4, section IV.3 above. [59] See also Ch. 4, section II.4.c above.

homepages for investor-relations purposes, the idea also suggests itself of offering on their homepages all the information they are obliged to make public. This can be further supplemented by information relating to company and securities law which is published by official or private information services.[60] Moreover, the Internet is generally increasing the density of information on company news, reducing the information deficits for private investors. For shareholders, finally, the new media offer the potential of making their shareholder rights more effective. Alongside the possibility of exercising their rights *vis-à-vis* management through e-mail, the Internet may also promote networking among shareholders. It is in particular conceivable for shareholders to communicate through chat rooms, and for the collection of votes through the homepage of shareholder associations, the firm itself or public authorities to be counted towards the quorum.

Yet, use of the new media is also associated with a number of new, and old, difficulties. First, this concerns the principles that have to be laid down to make this form of communication substantially equivalent to existing ones. For instance, it has to be clarified whether electronic signatures are necessary on e-mails, how confidential online information is to be authenticated and for how long publications must be accessible on the Internet. Secondly, the problem arises whether it should be mandatory for firms and shareholders to use the new media. While for most firms it is in any case advantageous for cost reasons to use e-mail and the Internet, in the case of smaller companies the financial costs of a professional website may exceed its utility. Additionally, online forums through which shareholders can contact each other on the firm's homepage may be disapproved of by managements. For shareholders it is at present still largely possible to avoid the new media, since, for instance, communication by e-mail requires the relevant shareholder's consent.[61] Thirdly, there may also be reservations about the practical usefulness of the new information and communication possibilities, since even they will not overcome shareholders' 'rational apathy'. Networking with other shareholders presupposes that a diversely investing shareholder sees sufficient benefit from it. Again, the new media do not make the evaluation of

[60] See e.g. already today: http://www.sec.gov/edgar.shtml; http://www.annualreportservice.com; http://www.cob.fr; http://www.euronext.fr; http://www.ebundesanzeiger.de; http://www.companieshouse.gov.uk; for private providers: http://www.euroadhoc.com; http://www.dgap.de.

[61] See e.g. § 299(3) JapCA; § 232(a) DelGCL; Goldman and Filliben (2000: 690–1) (for the SEC Rules); Siems (2002b: 203–4) (for the UK and Germany).

the information available any easier. Instead, the numerous information possibilities arising from the websites of firms, official authorities, shareholder associations, analysts, private information agencies, the financial press etc. may lead to information overload.

Despite these problems, however, positive developments, leading at least in the medium and long term to a convergence of law, are on the whole to be expected. While it is likely that legal systems will initially produce different solutions for the questions arising in connection with the use of new media, in further developments the principle of 'trial and error'[62] and international approximations in the influence of interest groups are likely gradually to lead to common standards. In the course of time, information will be better co-ordinated and processed, thus reducing the activation problem. Some assistance to cope with the information overload may, for instance, come from the bringing together of information on the company on its homepage, at a central publication unit, or at least through links to the individual information sources (registry, securities supervisors, exchanges). Additionally, information intermediaries may prevent overstrain on shareholders by processing essential information for investors. However, in any case, shareholders will in future be expected to take more individual responsibility, since in principle they will be able to inform themselves. This may also be furthered since, at least in the long term, use of the new media to access information is likely to become mandatory. Even today, it is in principle possible for anyone to access online information through free e-mail providers and Internet cafés. It is therefore likely that shareholders who want information in paper form will have to pay for that. If later only a vanishing minority wishes it, firms may be justified in no longer offering shareholders this service. No great resistance is to be expected at least in the long term, since the new media will in general improve monitoring through transparency, to the benefit of shareholders.

d) The postmodern shareholder

The discussion of influence of the new media in the study has so far referred to the fact that in some points the conventional model of the general meeting with personal attendance (including the associated information rules) will be modified. Developments may, however, go beyond this if shareholders can exercise their voting rights either through the Internet ('virtual general meeting') or even separately from a general meeting.

[62] See Ch. 8, section V.1 above.

The concept of the virtual general meeting applies, first, to the 'online general meeting'.[63] Here, a general meeting continues to be held, at a particular place. It is, however, possible for shareholders to take part online by 'e-voting'. In favour of this is, primarily, that shareholder participation in general meetings will be facilitated. Looking more closely, however, it might be doubted whether and how far online participation is necessary or sufficient for a new form of 'shareholder democracy'.[64] It may, first, be objected that shareholders can also control their voting behaviour through electronic voting proxies and special instructions while the general meeting is under way. Secondly, online participation may be too bothersome and time-consuming for them. At this point, however, one must further distinguish between different types of firms and shareholders.

While with public companies there may be some private investors interested in the new media and therefore wishing to trade shares and participate in general meetings online, for the majority of private investors the business of public companies is too complex and their own influence too small for them to be able to profit effectively from (online) participation. Things can be different for institutional investors. Since they are better able to process information, and since (despite diversification) they often hold a more than marginal number of shares, online participation can be a good compromise between activity and passivity. The prognosis for shareholders of close companies looks in any case more positive: the motivation of shareholders is typically not a problem. Additionally, the online general meeting may reduce travel costs. The same, finally, also applies to all types of company where shareholders have empowered a proxy to represent them at the general meeting. Since online participation reduces the cost of representation, shareholders can benefit from the possibilities of both giving a proxy and 'attending' the online general meeting.

From the management standpoint too, distinctions must be drawn. If shareholders and therefore also the capital market assess online general meetings positively, it makes sense for managements, for reasons of self-presentation and an optimized investor relationship, also to support them. In favour of this may also be the fact that online general meetings may reduce the costs of physically bringing shareholders together. Against this, however, is, first, a logistical burden (for instance, for a safe authentication procedure) and therefore also an increased risk of challenge from technical problems. Secondly, it may be problematic for public

[63] Terminology by Noack (2001a: 1058).

[64] On shareholder democracy see Ch. 3, section I.2 above.

companies if shareholders connected online wish to exercise not just their voting right but also their rights to speak, to ask questions and to obtain information. If this is allowed, it may lead to excessively long general meetings, or otherwise to a partial devaluation of online participation. By contrast, in view of the smaller range of shareholders, for close companies this problem generally does not arise. Additionally, here the costs of online general meetings may be smaller if and to the extent that the chair of the meeting in any case knows the shareholders involved.

In law the distinction between the different types of companies need not necessarily be reflected. Legal systems where online general meetings are already admissible or their introduction being discussed frequently confine themselves to voting rights, without considering other aspects of the general meeting. [65] This is at any rate consistent, as long as those legal systems also have no codified rights to speak, to put questions at the meeting or to obtain information for the classical general meeting.[66] Moreover, the law does not oblige firms to enable online participation. Nor is this in principle to be expected in future. It is best to make online participation dependent on the individual case (e.g. type of firm, shareholder structure). Individual shareholders are not unfairly discriminated against thereby, since they will at any rate still have the possibility of being represented at the general meeting or pressing for a change in the practice of their company. The legislator has accordingly only to lay down who is competent for this decision and what conditions may be necessary to maintain shareholder protection. Convergence in the law here is accordingly – as with the new media in other respects – to be expected more in the medium and long term, once in the course of time an internationally convincing regulatory pattern has emerged.

The same also applies in principle to the 'cyber general meeting'.[67] This means a general meeting purely on the Internet, since online participation completely replaces the physical kind. The interests and problems connected with this type of meeting in many respects resemble those of the online general meeting. However, only a few legal systems have yet introduced the possibility of a cyber general meeting.[68] This can be explained by the fact that a cyber general meeting may radically change the current understanding and culture of the general meeting. For instance, with a

[65] See § 211(a)(2) DelGCL; Art. L. 225-107(2) FrCCom; § 312 JapCA; for discussions see Modern Company Law for a Competitive Economy: Final Report (2001: paras. 7.7, 7.11); Habersack (2001: 181); Riegger (2001: 209, 213); Noack (2003: 248).

[66] See Ch. 4, section II.4.a, III.1.a above.

[67] Terminology by Noack (2002b: 878 *et seq.*).

[68] E.g. § 211(a)(2)(B) DelGCL.

cyber general meeting of a public company a debate where everyone can speak is no longer feasible. Even more than with other forms of general meeting, accordingly, information must be exchanged and communication enabled beforehand. The cyber general meeting itself could in this case be confined to briefly presenting the outcome and putting it to the vote. This may also affect the periodicity of general meetings and the structure of competences within the company. Since interim meetings will be easier to hold, so that decisions can be taken more flexibly and nearer the time, it is conceivable for shareholders (again) to be allotted more competences and thus 'take seriously' their (real or presumed) ownership position.[69]

Continuous, more intensive shareholder involvement is, however, possible not only through a cyber general meeting. Rather, it is also conceivable by separating the general meeting from the vote,[70] or questioning the general meeting as such.[71] To date in most legal systems it has been admissible only under strict conditions – if at all – to forego the general meeting in favour of a written procedure.[72] An extension to this is, however, conceivable because the functions of the general meeting (information, communication, decision) can under certain conditions be carried out just as well by other means.[73] While shareholders are supplied with special information in the run-up to the general meeting, this does not depend on the general meeting as an institution, since information can also be made available to them via e-mail or the Internet quickly and without complications before other forms of vote. Regarding these other forms of vote, in comparable fashion with the communication element of the general meeting, shareholder platforms on the Internet may serve to give answers to questions and promote discussion. Shareholders will thus be enabled to take informed, considered decisions, so that they can subsequently decide on the relevant motion in a sort of plebiscite.

Yet, at least in the medium term, neither the cyber meeting nor plebiscitary voting are likely to lead to abolition of the classical general meeting, but instead will supplement it. The annual general meeting as a gathering is thoroughly serviceable for regular objects of decision, and may also be desired by management as a PR event. Accordingly, in future, the prominent debate will be how far the law will still mandatorily prescribe

[69] See Ch. 3, section I.1; Ch. 10, section I.2.c above. [70] J. Winter (2003: 418).

[71] See Noack (2003: 249), (2002b: 874), (2002g: 15 *et seq.*).

[72] See Ch. 4, section II.2 above.

[73] For the functions of the general meeting in general see also Davies (1997b: 66); Strätling (2003: 74–5).

this classical model, and how practice will shape other possibilities. In this process, internationally diverse variants may initially develop. Since, however, the decisive causes – new media, internationalization, diversification – are international phenomena, future developments are likely to see the convergence of both the legal regimes and practical patterns.

e) Conclusions

There will be two tendencies that are at first sight contradictory. On the one hand, voting proxies will gain importance with the diversification of shareholder ownership. Even if special instructions are permissible, the decision-making process will thus be shifted into the run-up to the general meeting, so that then – putting it in a nutshell – the general meeting of the future will merely involve the minuting of votes gathered worldwide. On the other hand, the use of the new media makes it possible for shareholders themselves to become more active. Through the Internet they can access information faster and more comprehensively, and they can take part more easily and more cheaply than before in general meetings if they do so online.

But the paradox here is only an apparent one. On the one hand, the two variants have differing fields of application since proxies play a part more for small private shareholders in public companies and online participation more for institutional investors and close companies. On the other hand, the variants supplement each other in the case of online participation through a proxy, and also point in the same direction as regards the outcome: the common basic tendency is for participation of the shareholder and thus the shareholder's position as a whole to be strengthened.

As a result, it becomes clear that, contrary to some views in the literature, the future of public companies does not exclusively lie with the model of the shareholder as 'investor' and 'mere spectator'. Instead, internationalization and diversification of shareholder structures do not exclude the possibility of the shareholder acting as 'owner' or 'parliamentarian'.[74] Accordingly, in principle one ought not to advocate depriving small shareholders as 'mere investors' of voting rights and participatory rights in the run-up to the general meeting.[75] The decisive limit is instead, as it has been to date, the criterion of abuse, where it is, for instance, not possible in practice to go into all online questions from shareholders at a public company's general meeting. Additionally, for other shareholder rights it

[74] On the shareholder typology see generally Ch. 3, section I, and also Ch. 10, section I above.
[75] Contra Wymeersch (2001b: 323).

will continue to be rational to set a moderate quorum. The level of this quorum may, however, change in future according to how indirect and direct participation rates and shareholder co-ordination develop.

3. *Conclusions*

For the future too, there are limits to convergence in the law on the 'shareholder as such'. For close companies, it is conceivable that greater differences will remain than for public companies. Furthermore, it will often be only after an experimental period that the internationally best solution will become apparent. Apart from this and other path dependencies, a further convergence of law can be expected. Among the decisive convergence forces are the internationalization of firms, the approximation of shareholder structures, the new media, and shareholder pressure. For the 'profit-oriented shareholder', additionally, the influence of management means that one can assume there will be a further liberalization in profit distribution and share buybacks. In other respects, in this area it is particularly the investor-related regulatory complexes associated with trading that will be optimized for the shareholder. Furthermore, the shareholder as investor can also profit from the fact that barriers to the cross-border exercise of shareholder rights will be removed and disclosure standards brought closer together. This, as well as an improvement in the law on voting proxies, may make shareholders participate more actively in general meetings, despite internationalization and diversification of shareholder structures. Moreover, the new media will also make it possible for them to take part in general meetings indirectly, so that shareholders as a whole will in the future be able to act not just as 'investors', but also as 'owners' and 'parliamentarians'.

II. The shareholder in the power structure of the company

The law on the 'shareholder in the power structure of the company' may converge to a lesser extent than the law on the 'shareholder as such'. Provisions on company power structures do not (primarily) centre on rather technical questions such as shareholder communication or representation at the general meeting. Instead, for instance, a reform in the distribution of powers among company bodies (subsection 1 below) will bring winners and losers and may therefore meet with greater resistance. Additionally, with regard to the law governing the shareholder's relation to other participants, external factors play a greater part, so that international agreement is harder to reach:[76] some topics are politically controversial, such as for instance questions of the ranking of stakeholder interests and the law on hostile takeovers (subsection 2 below). And the enforcement of shareholder rights is dependent on the respective national procedural law (subsection 3 below), so that here evaluations from procedural law may stand in the way of convergence.

Nonetheless, in the law on the 'shareholder in the power structure of the company', some further convergence is to be expected. Where in particular sub-areas the objective is uncontroversial (for instance, avoiding abuse of power by management), enhanced communication among legislators and pressure from interest groups may lead to convergence.[77] In other respects, it is particularly the increasing importance of the international capital markets that will operate as a convergence force. Investors can exercise more pressure so that their protection will tend to improve. And the internationalization of capital markets will increase dispersed shareholder ownership, so that the associated problems of protection will become more comparable internationally.

1. *The deciding shareholder*

The stronger capital-market orientation in countries hitherto weak in this respect is associated, for instance in Germany, with shareholders being perceived more than was the case previously as 'investors', and less as 'members of an association'.[78] The conclusion often drawn is that the importance of the general meeting and thus also its powers will be reduced. For the mere investor, the competences of the general meeting are said to be irrelevant, since if unsatisfied he will in any case tend to sell his shares, leave the company in some other way or seek to obtain financial compensation.[79] Additionally, the general meeting itself is often regarded as impracticable. Because of *de facto* dependence on board recommendations, disruptive shareholders and a high absence rate, its cost often outweighs its benefit.[80]

Against this, however, it can be objected that the new media lower the costs of general meetings and make shareholder participation easier.[81]

[76] For similar distinctions see Ogus (1999: 405); Oquendo (2001: 1023).

[77] See Ch. 8, sections III, IV; Ch. 9, section III above.

[78] Drygala (2001: 299); see also Ch. 3, section I above.

[79] See Ch. 3, section I.3 above.

[80] Cf. Deutscher Notarverein eV (2001: 186); Noack (2002a: 13); see also Ch. 4, section II.1.b above.

[81] See Ch. 10, section I.2 above.

Since even shareholders pursuing primarily financial objectives through their participation are nevertheless concerned with an effective pattern for the voting right,[82] the 'shareholder as investor' has an interest in not having the voting right rendered irrelevant by too great a reduction in the competences of the general meeting. This is all the more true since the pressure and activity of (institutional) investors have been increasing lately.[83]

However, it does not follow, conversely, that the list of mandatory powers of general meetings will tend to expand. Instead, the basic division of powers between general meeting and management (including the board)[84] will be retained. There are, however, indications that this division may become more flexible in future. Particularly with close companies, it is possible to envisage a provision in the articles of association whereby shareholders would be allotted farther-reaching powers than those provided under the statutory model. If the new media enable interim meetings or interim plebiscites and shareholders are informed and motivated, it may happen here that many questions of the conduct of business will remain reserved to shareholders, so that the shareholder becomes a 'managerial partner'.[85] By contrast, for public companies the liberalization may take shape in a different direction. Both management and shareholders have a fundamental interest in ensuring their firm can succeed on the international capital market. This presupposes for instance, that the company law provisions on corporate finance are sufficiently flexible in order to meet the firm's financial needs quickly. It is accordingly in line with this trend that the provisions whereby the board may be authorized by the general meeting for a capital increase with preemption rights excluded have been eased in many countries.[86] Again, it is possible that we shall see a relaxation of the rules concerning the size of the necessary shareholder majority and the participation quorum at general meetings,[87] particularly for public companies. High majority requirements may limit companies' capacity to act, since increasingly dispersed shareholder ownership makes it harder to achieve such a majority. Moreover, in public companies shareholder protection through general meeting powers is already increasingly being replaced by other forms of protection.[88]

[82] See Ch. 3, section I.3 above. [83] See Ch. 4, section II.4.c; Ch. 9, section III above.
[84] See Ch. 5, section I.1 above. [85] Cf. J. Pound (1995), (1993).
[86] See Ch. 5, sections I.1.d, II.2.b above. [87] See Ch. 5, section II above.
[88] See Ch. 5, sections I.3, II above.

2. *The protected shareholder*

In the case of provisions on shareholder protection (in a narrow sense), convergence is favoured by the fact that the international advance of widespread share ownership[89] means that for public companies it is no longer (only) protection from blockholders that is important, even in countries hitherto weak in capital-market terms. Additionally, convergence through pressure from institutional investors[90] is likely, since (in a similar fashion internationally) such shareholders advocate, say, incentive-based remuneration for management, possibilities of control through takeovers, free trading in shares, a ban on insider dealing and provisions on directors' dealings.[91] That does not, however, mean that the convergence which is already apparent[92] will become comprehensive. For instance, differences in forms of protection, in political assessments and in regulatory competition may still stand in the way of convergence.

a) Protection against management

Protection against management covers the questions of whether managements are to be required to act primarily in the interests of shareholders and how abuse by management is to be controlled.

(1) The importance of shareholder interests. It is sometimes presumed that the 'shareholder model' of the US and the UK with its priority on shareholder interests will prevail internationally.[93] In support of such a presumption one may, first, note that the internationalization of the economy is being pushed decisively by Anglo-American-type institutions.[94] Secondly, conditions of sharpened competition might let a radically free market economy prevail, in which only a company's financial gain would count. Market liberalization and regulatory competition for company founders and capital might make it problematic for firms to take account of stakeholder interests, at the expense of economic efficiency. Furthermore, the competition for capital positively suggests that a legal system will, if it gives priority to shareholder interests, be 'rewarded' by capital inflows and thus boost the domestic economy.[95]

[89] See Ch. 8, section IV.2 above. [90] See Ch. 9, sections III, VI.3 above.

[91] Cf. Heiser (2000: 69); André (1998: 77 *et seq.*) (for CalPERS); Baums (1998: 546).

[92] See Ch. 5, section II above.

[93] See Hansmann and Kraakman (2001: 443 *et seq.*) and Ch. 8, section I.2; Ch. 9, section VI.3 above.

[94] See Ch. 8, section III above. [95] See Ch. 9, sections III, VI.3 above.

These arguments, however, call for a number of qualifications. First, it constitutes a 'double fallacy' to presume that, by contrast with the rest of the world, the Anglo-American countries have a pure 'shareholder model'. Instead, in the US and the UK, stakeholder interests also play a part. Additionally, in other countries too, considerable importance attaches to shareholder interests.[96] Secondly, while a free market economy has indeed increasingly prevailed in recent years in more and more countries, and since competition for shareholders is likely to act as a convergence force and tend to bring a strengthening of shareholder interests,[97] there are also various limits to the competition for shareholders on both the supply and demand sides and as regards the consequences.[98] Thirdly, it is also doubtful whether a radically liberal economic policy and a purely economic globalization could prevail. While managers and investors of international companies constitute influential lobbies,[99] this does not necessarily mean that government policy will focus only on business interests, if only because a large number of voters also lay value on continued account being taken of social interests. Moreover, such other institutions as non-governmental organizations (NGOs) and international organizations exercise counter-pressure, calling on international companies to adhere to social standards and codes of conduct.[100] Companies are not ignoring this, as shown by, for instance, industry's self-commitment to the UN Global Compact[101] and various sector-specific codes for multinational undertakings.[102] While the objection is conceivable that these are primarily 'PR measures' and not legally binding, the importance of soft law factors for a firm's economic success is growing, since, for instance, the increase in service functions gives human capital a stronger role in the firm's value.[103] Additionally, market forces may operate in favour of stakeholder interests. Since the range of influence of multinational companies at the same time requires increased social responsibility,[104] today both the public and, for example, rating agencies and investors themselves are placing more value on social and sustainable

[96] See Ch. 5, section II.1.a above. [97] See Ch. 8, section I.2; Ch. 9, section III above.

[98] See Ch. 9, section III.1.a, VI.3.b above. [99] See Ch. 9, section II, VI.2.a.

[100] See Leggewie (2003: 135, 144, 174); Bhagwati (2004: 36 *et seq.*); for the EU: Green Paper, Promoting a European Framework for Corporate Social Responsibility, COM(2001) 366; Corporate Social Responsibility: A Business Contribution to Sustainable Development, COM(2002) 347.

[101] See http://www.unglobalcompact.org; for an assessment see Sagafi-nejad (2005).

[102] Cf. Snyder (1999: 361 *et seq.*); Bhagwati (2004: 190–3).

[103] See Roberts and Van den Steen (2000).

[104] Similarly Van den Berghe (2002: 117 *et seq.*); Williams (2002); Dine (2005).

development.[105] Thus, despite the increase in 'faceless international investors', it should not be assumed that stakeholder interests will in future become obsolete.[106]

As a result, it continues to be a mixed picture that is presented. In spite of the increased influence of national and international investors, no absolute investor dominance at the expense of other stakeholders is to be expected. Additionally, in the mixture of shareholder and stakeholder interests, no complete convergence is likely in the future.

In sub-areas, however, convergence is conceivable. For instance, this is true of models aimed at guaranteeing conduct in the interest of shareholders through incentive-based compensation to management. Current developments are already showing that, in both law and practice, an international approximation is coming about with regard to stock options and other incentive-based remuneration models.[107] Brian Cheffins regards (further) convergence of management remuneration as rather unlikely since the factual conditions necessary for this (dispersed ownership, cross-border hiring, transnational M&As, multinational enterprises) are present only in outline, but not in general.[108] However, convergence means only approximation, not identity. It is therefore not necessary for, say, the proportion of dispersed shareholdings or the market for executives to be completely uniform internationally. Instead, it is sufficient for the economy to be internationalized so that – even according to Cheffins' criteria – the bases for internationally convergent incentive-based remuneration continue to increase.[109] The same also applies if, as argued by Amir Licht, cultural factors are regarded as decisive for patterns of remuneration, since in the cultural area too a further approximation (though not identity) is to be expected.[110]

By contrast, when it comes to defensive measures against hostile takeovers, no general convergence is to be expected. While the increase in cross-border takeovers may suggest the provision of uniform rules here,[111] the likelihood of convergence is, however, opposed, in addition

[105] See Miles (2003: 57).

[106] Contra Gordon (1999: 231) ('faceless international institutional investors may be less exposed to political and social pressure to balance shareholder interests against those of other stakeholders than inside monitors').

[107] See Ch. 5, sections I.1.c, II.1.a above.

[108] Cheffins (2003b: 12 *et seq.*); see also Ferrarini and Moloney (2004: 340) ('some convergence').

[109] See e.g. Ch. 8, sections III, IV above.

[110] See Licht (2001a: 195 *et seq.*), and Ch. 8, sections I.1, II above.

[111] Raaijmakers (2002: 224–5).

to the reasons already mentioned,[112] by the fact that it is controversial whether and to what extent defensive measures are admissible. A successful takeover may lead to a reduction in jobs, a change of management and in the cross-border context a weakening of the domestic economy. Thus, despite increased shareholder pressure, it is not inevitable that shareholders can impose their interest in a strict directors' duty of neutrality. This is confirmed by experience in both the EU and the US.[113] In the EU, the intensive and lengthy debate over uniform takeover rules has led to only minimal consensus. Similarly, the regulatory competition in the US has not led to convergence on possible defensive measures by management. Both politics and market forces thus stand in the way of international convergence.

(2) **Monitoring management.** The increasing opening up of markets in goods, services and capital[114] has already brought managements under greater control, since poorly-led undertakings will sooner or later leave the market. Additionally, shareholders in public companies are protected by the fact that in transparent and (semi-) efficient capital markets they can protect their financial interests through selling their shares. Management is also indirectly disciplined thereby, since their firms would be less successful if they failed to consider the capital market. Even if financial disclosure is improved (further) through the new media and through such private institutions as investment banks, law firms, analysts and rating agencies,[115] in future shareholder protection will nonetheless not be limited to these means. Since the possibility of market failure always exists, in both current and future law additional forms of protection are necessary.

Among these are, in particular, duties of care, loyalty and good faith. Since even now, in the legal systems studied here, the differences are more of degree than of substance,[116] and the regulatory objective is also uncontroversial,[117] it is in principle to be expected that communication and 'trial and error'[118] will lead to further convergence. The same is true of instrumental control mechanisms. Even now there is a certain approximation between 'one-tier' and 'two-tier' systems.[119] Additionally, a monitoring body or special committees can prevent those abuses that cannot be treated as infringement of specific duties. To be sure, there are also

[112] See Ch. 5, section II.1.a; Ch. 9, section VI.2.b above.

[113] See Ch. 5, section II.1.a above.

[114] See Ch. 8, section III.1 above.

[115] See Ch. 8, section III.2, 3; Ch. 10, section I.2.c above.

[116] See Ch. 5, section II.1.b above.

[117] Similarly Cunningham (1999).

[118] See Ch. 8, section V.1 above.

[119] See Ch. 5, sections I.1.c, II.1.b above.

limits to convergence. The need for change is small if one of several solutions is not compellingly superior. For instance, a director's conflicts of interests may, depending on the legal system, have the consequence of a prohibition, disclosure obligations, a fairness check in the individual case and/or collaborative powers of the other directors, a monitoring body, a committee or the general meeting.[120] In the search for functional equivalents, moreover, other areas of law have to be taken into consideration, since, for instance, procedural law generous to shareholders may constitute a substitute for weaker substantive protective provisions. Finally, differences in the influence managements are able to exert on legislators may stand in the way of convergence. For instance, in Japan, businesses are a stronger lobby than shareholders, so that they have successfully opposed mandatory independent directors and initiated the possibility of exemptions from liability.[121] In the US, pressure from managements is based particularly around regulatory competition, so that in Delaware there is less mandatory company law than in other legal systems.[122]

Over and above convergence on these general principles, it is likely that protective provisions best fitting the increasingly dispersed and internationalized shareholder structure of public companies will prevail. In harmony with the trend to date,[123] accordingly, protection through capital-market-oriented provisions will become more important even in legal systems hitherto weak in these terms. Here shareholder pressure is directed both at internationally uniform law and at effective infrastructures and enforcement of law. Finally, the internationalization of the economy will make enhanced co-operation among legislators necessary. It is accordingly to be expected in the long term that on such topics as insider dealing or disqualification of directors agreements will be reached in order to prevent the evasion of national provisions.

b) Protection against the shareholder majority

When it comes to protection against the shareholder majority, convergence is likely to be less apparent than with provisions on protection against management. However, various situations have to be distinguished. Often in close companies one or a few shareholders can control the company, bringing the structural threat of abuse of power at the

[120] See Ch. 5, section II.1.b above.
[121] See Oda (2002: 25), and Ch. 5, section II.1.b above.
[122] For the 'Delaware effect' see Ch. 9, sections I.1, VI.1.a above.
[123] See Ch. 5, section II.1.b above.

expense of the shareholder minority. Yet, for close companies the convergence forces are less marked than with public companies.

By contrast, for public companies, the situation depends on the ownership structures. If blockholders can control a public company, the abuse problem is similar to that in close companies. Since the number of such companies is falling,[124] no convergence trend in the possible legal solutions for the specific abuses can be seen, however. With respect to public companies with dispersed shareholdings, the problem of abuse is less marked, since because of the dispersed pattern of holdings, consensus at the general meeting requires support by various groups. Since in such companies shares are also easiest to sell, the market may act as a mechanism for protection. Finally, even shareholders themselves may be critical of very comprehensive minority rights, since dissatisfied shareholders can move their investment to other companies rather than disrupt the firm.

Nonetheless, it is to be expected that minority protection will develop further, simply because of the increase in the number of public companies with dispersed shareholder ownership. Here too shareholders are interested in some protection since it is always possible that a shareholder may find himself in a minority, and selling is not always a guarantee of adequate protection.[125] A majority/minority situation can also come about despite dispersed holdings where one group of shareholders pursues largely homogeneous interests. The growth in the importance of institutional investors,[126] often together holding a considerable proportion of the shares of an undertaking, may therefore present a new agency problem, necessitating protection for the other shareholders.

Moreover, there are specific forms of minority protection that suggest themselves for shareholders in public companies with dispersed holdings. In the present law, differing weights attach in the various legal systems to mandatory provisions, qualifications of the majority rule, voting provisions in cases of special interests, substantive controls on decisions and appraisal rights.[127] For public companies with dispersed holdings, however, mandatory provisions, high qualifications on the majority rule and over-strict substantive controls on decisions can be disadvantageous, since they can for example prevent necessary restructurings and capital measures. Voting prohibitions in cases of special interests also do not enter

[124] See Ch. 8, section IV.2 above.
[125] See Ch. 4, section I.3.d above.
[126] See Ch. 8, section IV.3 above.
[127] See Ch. 5, section II.2 above.

in here, since with dispersed holdings the shareholders' relationship to the company is only loose. Apart from substantive controls on abuse, the main focus will thus be on provisions guaranteeing minority shareholders financial compensation. Even in this framework, though, a variety of solutions is conceivable, as the current differences in mandatory bids, appraisal rights and compensation show.[128]

c) Conclusion

Convergence in the law relating to the protected shareholder is based particularly on the increase in investor pressure, in dispersed shareholder ownership and in reliance on the capital market. The law will thus, for example in the case of the remuneration system, provide for incentives to action by management in the interests of shareholders, and in the case of protective instruments take account of the company's ability to operate on the international capital market and of the financial interests of shareholders. To the extent that the law in books and the law in practice diverge here, these convergence forces ought additionally to improve enforcement of the law. Yet neither an exclusive focus on shareholder interests nor a comprehensive convergence is to be expected. Other stakeholders too exert influence on legislation, and legislators themselves must take more account than hitherto of various types of companies.

3. *The litigating shareholder*

To date, there has been legal convergence to the extent that, in countries where shareholders were previously unable to pursue management misconduct through the courts, or able only to a limited extent, possibilities for taking action have been extended.[129] This trend ought basically to continue. The approximations in (legal) culture[130] are promoting litigious settlement of disputes even in countries where ethics and morals previously substituted for law. One chief catalyst for this development is the increasing internationalization of lawyers.[131] Additionally, lawyers exert pressure because suits are also – or even primarily[132] – in their economic interest. Finally, increased shareholder pressure[133] is similarly contributing to an improvement in the possibilities of taking action.

[128] See Ch. 5, section II.2.c above. [129] See Ch. 5, section III.1 above.

[130] See Ch. 8, section II above.

[131] See Ch. 8, section III.3 above; see also Ch. 9, section IV above.

[132] See Ch. 5, section III.1 above. [133] See Ch. 9, section III above.

However, there are also limits to far-reaching convergence.

First, adjudication in general differs across countries. Nor is it likely in future that, say, the differences in cost provisions (for instance, on the question of contingency fees or payment of the other side's legal costs), the choice and qualification of judges (e.g. elected jury v. professional judges), the possibility of pre-trial discovery, the extent of judicial discretion and the existence of a specialized bar are likely to be levelled out.

Secondly, it is unclear how the potential for abusive suits can best be dealt with. On the one hand, a particular procedure such as payment of a security provision or internal proceedings may be provided for. On the other hand, entitlement to act may be made dependent on the person of the shareholder, and a particular minimum holding or a particular minimum period of shareholding be required.[134] This option may in particular be likely because the increasing rapidity of trade in shares and increasingly dispersed holdings mean that many shareholders only have a loose connection to 'their' company. However, the danger may then arise that for companies where a large number of shareholders has only a small and short-term participation, monitoring of management will be weakened. It cannot accordingly be foreseen at present whether the problem of abuse can be solved in a similar fashion internationally.

Thirdly, other protective and monitoring mechanisms might provide an alternative to action before national courts. For instance, the forces of the capital market and institutional protections will gain further importance.[135] Additionally, alternative dispute resolution may be advantageous because it is often faster, more discreet and cheaper for all concerned and in the international context avoids a preference for one party and the difficulties of conflict of laws. In detail, however, arbitration may raise problems of differences in national law and in the enforcement of law. For instance, in Germany, according to the prevailing opinion, arbitration agreements about shareholder rights and duties are inadmissible.[136] In view of the tendencies to the privatization of law-making[137] and to the internationalization of arbitration, however, in future a liberalization of

[134] Wymeersch (2001b: 323); see also Ch. 5, section III.1, 3 above.

[135] For the capital market see Ch. 8, section IV.2.b above; for institutional protection see Ch. 8, section III.3 (auditors, law firms, etc.), Ch. 10, sections I.2.d, II.1 (shareholder meeting), and Ch. 10, section II.2 (committees or supervisory boards), above.

[136] See BGH, BGHZ 132, 278; for a different view see e.g. K. Schmidt, in: GroßkommAktG (1995: § 246 paras. 114 *et seq.*); see also Regierungskommission Corporate Governance (2001: para. 161).

[137] See Ch. 7, section III.2, 3 above.

the law and co-operation among legislators seem not unlikely. In other respects, extrajudicial negotiations and mediation remain at any rate conceivable, so that a functional counterweight to the increase of formal company law may emerge. With all this, however, it should be borne in mind that in the future too alternative dispute settlement is no panacea.[138] A particularly problematic point is that suits against management conduct or resolutions of the general meeting are also a means of public discipline,[139] and may concern a multiplicity of persons. It may therefore be unsatisfactory (or even inadmissible) if, for instance, individual shareholders negotiate compensation with management without other shareholders being informed and deficits in the conduct of business removed. Thus, on the whole, alternative dispute resolution too is 'only' one piece of the mosaic that further supplements the combination of various protective means.

4. *Conclusions*

Although the speed of convergence on the 'shareholder in the power structure of the company' is less than that of the 'shareholder as such', here too convergence is to be expected particularly in three areas. First, protection of shareholders and its legal enforcement should become more similar, since investors can exert more pressure through the capital market and internationally the spread of share ownership will increase. This will not, however, lead to uniform law, since legislators may have different priorities, and legal rules lying outside shareholder law (e.g. conflict of laws, procedural law) differ. There will accordingly, for instance, continue to be differences in the weighting of the interests of management and other stakeholders and in suits by shareholders. Moreover, convergence operates particularly with public companies, so that for close companies more differences may continue to exist. Secondly, a certain deregulation and increased flexibility of the law is likely. This is, however, only partly based on lobbying by managements, which thereby gain room for manoeuvre. In public companies, shareholders too have an interest in, say, not having the firm's position on the capital market weakened through overly tight restrictions on the majority at the general meeting, the exclusion of pre-emption rights or restructurings. Thirdly, where the solutions in different legal systems operate in a functionally equivalent way, there may nonetheless be convergence. Communication with other countries and

[138] See Windbichler (2000: 621 *et seq.*).

[139] See Ch. 5, section III, preamble above.

reception of parts of other legal systems contribute to legislators providing for similar legal arrangements, not simply functionally 'by chance', but deliberately also in formal terms. Additionally, formal convergence may be promoted by interest groups since, for instance, similar shareholder rights reduce the costs of information that international investors have to obtain about other legal systems.

11

Conclusions to Part III

This study on developmental trends and patterns in shareholder law has highlighted the possibilities and limits of a forecast.[1] On the one hand, it has in principle been possible to show in what way the law will develop further in future (section I below), what convergence forces will be decisive thereby (section II below) and where further areas of convergence in shareholder law will be found (section III below). On the other hand, it has quite commonly been necessary to choose cautious wording ('likely', 'might' etc.) in order not to fall into false determinism. Although the predictions could be based only on present knowledge, it has also become clear how in general terms one area of commercial law is likely to develop further in the age of globalization.

I. Re-regulation

Shareholder law is 'dependent' in the sense that factual circumstances may spark off reforms of the law. The history of company and securities law shows that legal development is at least also a mirror image of economic factors.[2] This can be further confirmed by the public choice theory, according to which what counts in the political decision-making process is the decision-makers' own interests and the external influence from third parties (especially interest groups).[3] If these factors come closer together, a convergence in law is also likely.

The regulatory levels decisive for this lie basically in national acts of parliament. It is not to be expected that in shareholder law national law will become unimportant because of the possibilities of evasion and international and regional legal bases. Although it is possible that multinational enterprises may sometimes be able to evade legal rules, and internationalization and regionalization are likely to advance, a fundamental paradigm shift is not to be expected. A company is founded according to national

[1] See preamble to Part III. [2] See Ch. 7, section I. 1 above.
[3] See Ch. 7, section I. 2, 3 above.

law and is therefore bound by it.[4] For convergence developments, thus, we must in principle focus on the codified national law. While it is to be expected that the forces of the capital market and of corporate governance codes, and therefore also deregulation and self-regulation, will continue to gain importance,[5] the starting-point nonetheless remains the positive law, so that, in relation to convergence in shareholder law, the question to ask is whether the 're-regulation' of statutory law will lead to a convergence of legal systems.

II. Convergence forces

Among the causes of convergence a distinction has to be drawn between 'convergence through congruence' and 'convergence through pressure'. 'Convergence through congruence' arises where the social, political and economic bases for shareholder law become similar internationally and thus the law also becomes more similar. Convergence forces are, accordingly, the overall cultural and economic-policy approximations, the internationalization of the economy and approximations in legal culture and shareholder structures.[6] For shareholder structure in particular, it is to be expected that diversification and institutionalization will tend to increase in the case of public companies.[7] While in terms of consequences path dependencies may stand in the way of the speed and content of convergence – since here it is changes in tangible circumstances and not merely pressure from individual interest groups that lead to convergence – resistance is likely to be less marked.[8]

With 'convergence through pressure' it is particularly the regulatory competition for shareholders that makes an approximation of legal systems likely.[9] By contrast, regulatory competition for the seat of a company and national and international lobbying will have less importance. Isolated competition for seats is possible in the US, and to a limited extent in the EU, but basically not in the global context.[10] For lobbying, national differences mean that in the first place pressure from international lobbies will lead to some convergence.[11] In terms of consequences, the focal point of convergence is pressure in the case of public companies, since competition for shareholders and international lobbying are the stronger the more firms are dependent on international capital markets and interest groups.

[4] See Ch. 7, section II above. [5] See Ch. 7, section III above.
[6] See Ch. 8, sections I–IV above. [7] See Ch. 8, section IV.2, 3 above.
[8] See Ch. 8, section V above. [9] See Ch. 9, sections III, VI.3 above.
[10] See Ch. 9, sections I.1, VI.1 above. [11] See Ch. 9, section II, IV, V, VI.2 above.

Substantively, in view of the demands that public companies and their shareholders make, it is likely that the importance of investor interests will further increase.[12]

III. Changes in future law

For future convergences in shareholder law, a distinction must again be drawn between provisions on the 'shareholder as such' and provisions on the 'shareholder in the power structure of the company'. For the law on the 'shareholder as such', the internationalization of companies, approximations of shareholder structures, the new media and shareholder pressure are the decisive convergence forces. The shareholder as investor may benefit from the fact that the obstacles to cross-border exercise of shareholder rights are being removed and disclosure standards will converge.[13] These developments, and improvements in provisions on voting proxies,[14] mean that shareholders can, despite internationalization and diversification, participate actively in general meetings. Additionally, the new media will enable them to participate directly in general meetings, so that shareholders as a whole will in the future (too) be able to act not just as 'investors' but also as 'owners' and 'parliamentarians'.[15]

When it comes to provisions on the 'shareholder in the power structure of the company', the rate of convergence will be smaller.[16] However, shareholder protection ought also to become more similar because investors can exert more pressure through the capital market, and internationally dispersed shareholder ownership will increase. This will not, however, lead to uniform law, because legislators make differing evaluations, and legal norms lying outside shareholder law are too different internationally. Additionally, some deregulation and flexibilization of the law is likely. Apart from lobbying by managements, for public companies it is in the shareholder's interest too if, say, overly tight restrictions on majorities at general meetings, the exclusion of pre-emption rights or restructurings are not allowed to weaken the firm's position on the capital market.

Future convergence will also include 'convergence of law and reality'. Even in the past, positive law not uncommonly became similar. Since, however, this was sometimes an imposition or mere copying of foreign laws, their effectiveness was limited.[17] Now 'convergence through

[12] See Ch. 9, section VI.4 above.
[13] See Ch. 10, section I.1, 2.a, c above.
[14] See Ch. 10, section I.2.b above.
[15] See Ch. 10, section I.2.d, e, 3 above.
[16] See Ch. 10, section II above.
[17] See Ch. 6, section III above.

congruence' is based on a change in tangible factual circumstances, so there is no contradiction between law and facts. In 'convergence through pressure', interest groups put value on the effective enforcement of law, so that here too there will be more than formal convergence.

Although 'artificial convergence' in 'depth' will thus diminish in favour of more comprehensive convergence, overall no complete unification of law is to be expected in the future either. Differences will continue to exist as regards both facts and pressure. The convergence forces are less strongly marked particularly in the case of close companies. Even for public companies those legal differences that operate in functionally equivalent ways will not necessarily converge. To be sure, here too there may be more similarity because the communication among legal systems is increasing, and for institutional investors approximation reduces the cost of information about other legal systems.[18] Current observations indicate that US law in particular is taking on a model role.[19] Yet on the whole it is not 'Americanization' but genuine convergence that is to be expected, since the increased competitive pressure makes other countries too interested in optimizing their company and securities law.[20]

[18] See Ch. 8, section V. 1; Ch. 9, section III. 1. b above.

[19] See Ch. 6, section II, Ch. 10, section I.2.a above.

[20] See Ch. 9, section VI. 4; Ch. 10, section I. 2. a above.

PART IV

Conclusion

12

Convergence as a model for the future

At the legal-policy level, the first question arising is the proper level and form of regulation. No simple solution is to be expected here, since, for instance, when considering the variants of centralized v. decentralized or governmental v. private law-making, costs and benefits have to be weighed up in each case.[1] Thus, it has first to be clarified whether international and regional law ought to contribute even more than hitherto to a 'convergence from above' (section I below). Secondly, in cases of 'convergence from below', closer study should consider whether for instance regulatory competition, the use of self-regulation and a 'convergence principle' in case law ought to operate to bring the legal systems closer together (section II below). Finally, the issues of the substantive orientation of shareholder law will be looked at again (section III below).

I. Convergence 'from above'

International or regional organizations can act upon law 'from above' by themselves laying down uniform provisions (subsection 1. below). Since this sort of comprehensive unification of law is, however, open to objections and politically hard to achieve, it may in future be mainly other regulatory models that promise success (subsection 2. below).

1. *Reasons for unification of law*

There are a number of reasons which can be adduced for a unification of law. Furthermore, a distinction has to be drawn here between arguments for uniform law as such and unification through international and regional law.

[1] For the 'centralization debate' see e.g. Ogus (1999: 416); Grundmann (2001: 806–7); Kötz (1986: 1 *et seq.*); for the 'privatization debate' see e.g. Cheffins (1997: 126 *et seq.*, 163 *et seq.*); Milhaupt (2001: 2107–8).

Uniform law as such serves legal certainty by preventing divergent regulations leading to legal complications and economic transaction costs.[2] While in company and securities law the company's seat or place of listing in principle unambiguously determines what law applies, the increase in international undertakings means that differences in law can have negative effects for those involved. Differing legal systems may, for instance, lead to problems with stock exchange listings abroad or international mergers.[3] Additionally, international investors want their legal positions in general and the cross-border exercise of shareholder rights in particular to have a uniform pattern.[4] Without standardization of shares, a diversified commitment in various legal systems involves them in considerable information costs and uncertainties. Investors would then primarily invest in domestic firms, so as to save costs and avoid possible gaps in protection or legal disputes. The allocative advantages of an international capital market would thus not be maintained. Moreover, uniform 'rules of the game' create a 'level playing field'. If different countries cannot undercut each other and national lobbies cannot bring about over-regulated laws, all enterprises have equal opportunities, so that in the international competition for investors only their economic performance counts. For a system seeking to promote competition among firms from various countries it therefore makes sense to supplement the economic freedoms by uniform legal requirements for entrepreneurial activity.

As a means towards such uniformity, unification through international and regional law suggests itself. By contrast with regulatory competition or other possible causes of convergence, the law can in this way in principle be harmonized immediately, lastingly and reliably. Formally uniform law can additionally promote the trust of international investors. Here it is not just rational considerations that play a part, since with only functionally comparable solutions psychological market barriers may continue to operate. Furthermore, it may be advantageous in the public interest for different legal systems not to seek to attract founders or investors by means of the law. If competence is shifted to a higher level, so that only one law-maker is operating, the costs of legislation fall, and the danger of negative external effects and of a 'race to the bottom'[5] is reduced. The international or regional legislator can take the preferences of all interest groups into account in shaping the law, without any one group being able

[2] See e.g. Stephan (1999: 744 *et seq.*); Gessner (1998: 427 *et seq.*); Hopt (1998b: 99).

[3] See Ch. 8, section III.4.a, c above.

[4] See Hulle (1994: 396), and also Ch. 9, section III.1.b; Ch. 10, section I.2.a above.

[5] See Ch. 9, section I.1.a, preamble, VI.1.a above.

to escape its influence. This primacy of politics has particular importance in a globalizing economy; for otherwise it would be possible for the law of the economically stronger to prevail, through the influence of transnational undertakings. There would, then, be a threat of bias in the law, so that for instance aspects of social justice or fairness in general, as well as of protection for small shareholders and employees in particular, might be disregarded.[6] Particularly with big international companies, non-economic interests of this sort ought not to be left out of account. Their great economic power, which may exceed the influence of individual states, calls for conduct that does not neglect public and social interests.[7] For this, the law has to follow the internationalization of the economy. Since regional and international law is not tied to national territorial frontiers, it can best do justice to international interdependencies and guarantee the responsible conduct of global actors.[8]

2. *Problems and implications*

In parallel with the reasons for unification of law, however, criticisms may be made both of uniformity as such and of unification through international and regional law. For 'convergence from above', accordingly, various limitations and modifications are called for.

a) Uniform law

One widespread criticism of uniform law is that it leads to breaks with legal and extra-legal national traditions. For instance, it is said that the world should not be a 'self-service store of legal culture',[9] that differing mentalities rule out comprehensive harmonization,[10] and that various national preferences and economic, social, political and cultural differences stand in the way of uniformity.[11] While this argument is tending to lose its force, since approximations are coming about both in legal culture and in economic conditions,[12] that does not make it go away entirely. Company and securities law started from factual developments[13] and cannot ignore differences in legal culture, so that residual national

[6] See e.g. Branson (2001: 352 *et seq.*); Zuleeg (2000: 677).
[7] See also Licht (1998: 260); Teubner (1978: 120 *et seq.*).
[8] See Schnyder (2000: 515); Muchlinski (2003: 230–1).
[9] Großfeld (1996: 3) ('kein rechtskultureller Selbstbedienungsladen').
[10] Legrand (1996), (1997), (1999), (2006).
[11] Procaccia and Segal (2003: 639 *et seq.*); Pistor (2002: 121 *et seq.*); Baum (2000: 105).
[12] See Ch. 8 above. [13] See Ch. 1, section III.2, 3; Ch. 7, section I.1 above.

peculiarities indeed argue against uniformity. Moreover, company and securities law show connections with a number of other areas of law, such as procedural, banking and insolvency law, so that on those grounds too identity of law in only one sub-area could lead to frictions.

Against uniformity it may also be said that it would mean losing the special advantages that derive from a multiplicity of legal systems. If the law is uniform internationally, differentiations can no longer be made between various national preferences[14] and there will be no legal innovations at national level.[15] Additionally, it may be desirable, for both founders and shareholders, for there to be choice among different legal systems. For company founders a differentiation of company-law systems may make sense, since, say, one legal system will specialize more in large public companies and another more in close companies. Much the same applies to shareholders. According to whether a shareholder sees himself primarily as an 'owner', a 'parliamentarian' or an 'investor',[16] he may be interested in legal safeguards of differing intensities. It is, for example, entirely conceivable for an investor deliberately to invest in a company in a legal system where shareholder rights are guaranteed only restrictedly, since he regards the 'risk discount' associated with the shares as too high. The real need at international level would, then, not be for unification, but for information about opportunities, risks and peculiarities of the particular law concerned.

A first objection to this argument is that, with default instead of mandatory rules, differentiation is also possible, in this case simply through the articles of association. Furthermore, a single legal system can offer various possibilities, thus opening up choices: company law often distinguishes not just between joint stock companies and small companies, but, among joint stock companies, also between closed and open companies.[17] Additionally, stock exchange and securities law may make gradations possible within a legal system, if different exchanges, or segments in an exchange, allow firms and investors a choice. Finally, current observations also suggest that company founders and shareholders are very much interested internationally in uniform basic structures,[18] so that at least a balance must be drawn with the benefits of uniformity.

Altogether, then, one might think that, as a 'golden mean', a uniform law might be desirable only for particular regulatory complexes or only as

[14] See Kötz (1986: 12); Trachtman (1993: 65–6). [15] See also Ch. 12, section II.1.a below.
[16] See Ch. 3, section I above. [17] See Ch. 1, section II.1 above.
[18] See Ch. 9, section III.1.b; Ch. 10, section I.2.a; Ch. 12, section I.1 above.

minimum standards. Thus, uniform provisions would seem better particularly in areas involving directly cross-border aspects of law or indirectly inhibiting international businesses and shareholders. In favour of minimum standards is the fact that they allow those concerned to rely on a basis of uniform law, but still to have national distinctions and options open beyond that. However, such mixtures of international unity and national multiplicity may also be problematic or even counter-productive. With minimum harmonization, there is the danger that those involved may agree not on economically efficient minimum standards, but on the lowest common denominator politically. Mixtures may lead to contradictions, for lack of an overall international concept. Whether these drawbacks actually come about, though, depends mainly on what means are employed for convergence 'from above' and whether the regulators are able to react to any shortcomings in a rapid and balanced fashion.

b) Means towards convergence 'from above'

The direct road to uniformity is to formally unify. Problems may arise here, first, from the fact that the world community has no political constitution, no ordered structure and no legislation in the strict sense.[19] It is hardly possible to transfer mechanisms and procedures from the nation state to international and regional levels of decision-making. This is also true of the European Union. While it does display increasingly state-like features, even here codifications, at any rate comprehensive ones, are open to the objection that there is no hierarchically structured system of government or unitary cultural nation, and that the organs of the European Union are not competent for general legislation.[20] Secondly, unification through international or regional law may be associated with high transaction costs. Since the law-making structures here are often more complex and a multiplicity of differing national, regional and international interests have to be brought into harmony, procedures are sometimes slow and cumbersome.[21] Particular weight attaches to the fact that changing the law may be difficult.[22] The danger of 'petrification' may thus make the law deficient, because despite new knowledge and new facts it cannot be adjusted, or not in time. Thirdly, particular enforcement problems

[19] See Gessner and Budak (1998: 4); Leggewie (2003: 150, 155 *et seq.*).

[20] See Joerges (2003: sub III 5).

[21] Similarly McGrew (1998: 334); Behrends (2001: 95).

[22] See High Level Group of Company Law Experts (2002: 31); Wymeersch (2001a: 98); Edwards (1999: 11); Cheffins (1997: 233–4).

arise with internationalized law-making.[23] Unification of law is not yet a guarantee of uniform interpretation and application of the law, since the enforcement mechanisms are typically not internationalized in the same way. Fourthly, it may be doubted whether unification 'from above' will be balanced in content. At the international or regional level, the influence of international enterprises is considerable. By contrast, responsiveness to the interests of the common weal may be insufficiently developed, since by comparison with the national sphere the public is narrower, and as a rule represented only indirectly through national politicians.[24] Nor is it guaranteed that among the various national models the best will prevail. Since every country is basically interested in having its solution coincide with the future unitary law, legal unification may just be oriented to the country that can exercise the strongest political and economic influence.[25]

These dangers and difficulties suggest that for proper unification the law-making and enforcement processes of international and regional organizations must be made more effective. Greater involvement by non-governmental organizations (NGOs) can raise the legitimacy and transparency of international law. For the European Union, a Commission White Paper sets out 'openness, participation, accountability, effectiveness and coherence' as the guiding principles for European governance.[26] Additionally, for instance, the integration of European financial markets is to be carried out in a flexible four-stage process (the 'Lamfalussy process'). The basic political decisions are in the first stage laid down formally in framework directives or regulations. Otherwise, technical implementation measures, recommendations on questions of interpretation, guidelines and common standards are to be worked out by special committees.[27]

Making law-making processes more effective can thus also be reflected in new regulatory approaches. This is one of the main themes of the debate on future 'global governance'. Partly, this means 'good global governance', in the sense that, even in times of globalization, public goods like a stable, fair world financial system, social justice and a wholesome environment must still be ensured.[28] What is primarily in view here is, however, the

[23] See Pistor (2002: 106, 112 *et seq.*).
[24] See Leggewie (2003: 150); Van den Bergh (2000: 448).
[25] See Stiglitz (2006: 273 *et seq.*).
[26] Governance – A White Paper, COM(2001) 428; see also e.g. the special issue of *European Law Journal* 8 (2002), and, on recent developments, http://ec.europa.eu/governance/governance_eu/white_paper_en.htm.
[27] See http://ec.europa.eu/internal_market/securities/lamfalussy/index_en.htm; Ferran (2004: 58–126).
[28] See e.g. Stiglitz (2006: 269 *et seq.*).

formal aspect of governance, a term meaning, by contrast with 'government', that the control and supervision of transnational markets need to be determined by innovative regulatory philosophies.[29] Instead of mandatory, hierarchical legal norms, accordingly, it may for instance make sense to bring private persons more into law-making, or even leave it to them. Moreover, in other ways too, soft and more co-operative forms of law may promise success. Supranational and international organizations may on the one hand take on the function of co-ordinating these new regulatory networks, while on the other it may be necessary to ensure through procedural rules that all justified interests are taken into account.

These sorts of alternative means of convergence 'from above' also suggest themselves for the present context. Here, first, international organizations ought to promote co-operation and co-ordination among the various law-makers, supervisory authorities and stock exchanges. This is true especially where cross-border action is involved. For example, it would be useful, in connection with the exercise of shareholder rights, with international accounting and with combating market abuse, for international organizations like the OECD, the IASB and IOSCO, or regional organizations like the EU, to make recommendations to national law-makers.[30] To eliminate possible contradictions, conflict of laws also plays a decisive part. While harmonizations of the rules on conflict of laws may open up regulatory competition, if the economic conditions come still closer together even the competition will lead indirectly to an approximation of the substantive law.[31]

Secondly, by supporting international soft law among private persons, international organizations should also contribute to convergence. Here the use of both model laws and best-practice guidelines is to be advocated. While against this it is claimed that for instance the US model of the MBCA is not transferable to the European company-law landscape, because of different legal and sociological conditions, and that differences in national law make common statements on the governance of all (listed) companies hardly possible,[32] the law has nonetheless already come so close in all the legal systems studied here that it is no longer possible to assume differing

[29] For the term 'governance' see e.g. Rhodes (1997); for 'global governance' see e.g. Nahamowitz and Voigt (2002); Ladeur (2003: 17 *et seq.*); Leggewie (2003: 63, 187).

[30] See Ch. 2, section I; Ch. 7, section II.2, 3 above.

[31] See Ch. 12, section II.1.a below.

[32] High Level Group of Company Law Experts (2002: 32, 72); Modernising Company Law and Enhancing Corporate Governance in the European Union – A Plan to Move Forward, Communication from the Commission, COM(2003) 284, at 11–12.

basic concepts.[33] Additionally, the question of the influence of private soft law need not be dealt with abstractly. Since its success depends on whether national legislatures or firms freely take up these principles, these market forces may show whether and to what extent there is a need for this and whether effective enforcement is guaranteed. For a political assessment, what particularly matters is which private standard-setters prevail and how far state involvement or oversight is necessary. Soft law may thus, at international level above all, resolve the flexibility problem, whereas the representation problem – as also with national self-regulation[34] – may further intensify.

Thirdly, it is sensible to offer, as a special form of model provision, supranational companies. The Societas Europaea is – despite its shortcomings[35] – a step in the right direction here. While a supranational form of company initially brings an extra regulatory burden, on the whole the advantages nonetheless predominate. The supranational company is the ideal legal form for transnational undertakings, since the legal hurdles of cross-border seat-transfers and mergers can be eliminated, the economic costs of multiple subsidiaries lowered and the psychological obstacles to the choice of a particular legal system avoided. Moreover, a level playing field can be created, since firms on the international market will increasingly have the same legal form. It is admittedly a problem as to who, other than the European Union, can create a supranational legal form. This regulatory possibility is thus to be seen as more of a long-term prospect, on the premise of advancing multilateralism.

3. *Interim finding*

The arguments in favour of convergence 'from above' are only partly vitiated by the criticisms. It has, though, become clear that the procedures of international and regional law-making need to be optimized. Moreover, enhanced use should be made of alternative means of regulation, so as to avoid the problems of conventional legal unification. These statements do not yet, however, exhaust the considerations on convergence 'from above' because the evaluation of this form of convergence also depends on the possibilities and limits of convergence 'from below'. In harmony with the subsidiarity principle, accordingly, the use of international and regional law is subject to the reservation that other forms of governmental or private law-making cannot avoid or reduce the regulatory deficits.

[33] See Part II, above. [34] See Ch. 12, section II.3 below. [35] See Ch. 1, section I above.

II. Convergence 'from below'

By 'convergence from below' is meant an approximation of law not based directly on the influence of international or regional organizations. There may of course be indirect causality here too, if, say, the extension of international free trade or the enabling of regulatory competition in the European Union act as convergence forces on national legislators.[36]

In detail, with convergence 'from below', the debate on regulatory competition is often regarded as a most important aspect (subsection a below). It is, however, also conceivable for congruent factual circumstances and lobbying to lead to convergence (subsections b and c below). As well as legislation, case law may also affect the grounds for convergence and take them into account as a 'convergence principle' in applying the law (subsection 2. below). Additionally, it is possible for a deregulation of law to increase the room for manoeuvre in the articles of association and self-regulation, so that the law may approximate in this way (subsection 3. below). Here it may, however, in Walter Eucken's words, be problematic that the influence of interest groups on policy and the takeover of certain powers may threaten a 'twofold decay of the state'.[37] Accordingly, a combination of various convergence forces is to be preferred (subsection 4. below).

1. *National legislators*

Convergence through national legislators need not necessarily entail the substantive approximation of acts of parliament. Instead, the parliamentary legislator may also delegate powers, so that for instance secondary laws and rules of supervisory authorities are also to be taken into account. Differences in who is in power may also influence the content of the law. It is, for instance, not unlikely for specialized bodies drafting delegated legislation on the one hand to be more competent in economic questions than the parliamentary legislator, but on the other hand also to have a 'tunnel-vision view' and to be overconfident in their own ability to resolve problems.[38] Still more important than these demarcations, however, is the question how convergence through national legislators is to come about at all. As already mentioned with respect to forecasting the future law

[36] See Ch. 8, section III.1; Ch. 9, section I.1.a above.

[37] Eucken (1990: 328) ('zweifacher Zerfall des Staates').

[38] See Licht (1998: 279 *et seq.*); Choi (2002: 117).

(Part III above), this may be either through 'pressure', namely, regulatory competition and lobbying, or through 'congruence'.

a) Regulatory competition

Regulatory competition for investors is very possible even today.[39] By contrast, regulatory competition for founders is still often obstructed by the real-seat doctrine or comparable national protective mechanisms in company law.[40]

It is disputed whether a shift in favour of the incorporation doctrine would lead to a convergence of law. It is sometimes stressed that regulatory competition leads specifically to a divergence, it being in the nature of competition to bring specialization of legal systems and an augmentation of choices.[41] Against this is experience to date in the US, where competition for corporate domiciles has tended to bring state company laws closer together.[42] This insight can also be generalized. Regulatory competition leads more to convergence than divergence, if persons that are its target have similar preferences. This is essentially the case here. Company founders or – in the case of a seat transfer – company directors[43] have basically similar expectations of 'good company law'. For instance, incorporation should be quick and simple, the liability risk for founders and managers small and management not disproportionately cramped by over-regulation or extensive shareholder rights.

Even if regulatory competition for founders may thus act as a convergence force, this development nonetheless does not lead to an identity of law. This is partly because, even with a worldwide incorporation doctrine, the 'brakes' for regulatory competition on the demand side and the side of legal consequences would continue to exist.[44] Nor can these obstacles (for instance, language barriers) be completely removed. And it is also in the nature of competition that there will not be full convergence. Despite basically homologous preferences, there is still room for national differences in detail, so that possibilities of choice may very well make sense. Additionally, competitive pressure means that legislators are constantly concerned to improve their own legal system. There is therefore, in this respect, a 'race to the top',[45] bringing reduced regulatory errors, more

[39] See Ch. 9, section III.1 above. [40] See Ch. 9, section I.1, VI.1 above.

[41] Cf. Daniels (1991); Rose (2001: 135–6); Kieninger (2002: 25 *et seq.*).

[42] See Ch. 9, section VI.1.a above. [43] See Ch. 9, section III above.

[44] For these see Ch. 9, sections, I.1.b, VI.1 above.

[45] For the 'race to the bottom'–'race to the top' discussion see also Ch. 9, section III.1.b; Ch. 10, section I.2.a above.

innovation and faster learning effects and adaptation responses than with isolated national legislation.[46] It is also conceivable for legal systems to depart through innovations from a previous position of harmony and thus to become attractive to other legal systems as models for reception.[47]

This struggle for the best system ('regulatory Darwinism') also fits in with liberal principles. Since legal and economic systems are increasingly growing together, it is also justifiable in the international sphere to state that any restriction of freedom requires special justification ('in dubio pro libertate'). The free order of economic life is thus protected from opportunistic, arbitrary encroachments by politics, since the 'invisible hand of the market' would punish a legal system that made incorporation unattractive. In the European Union, another argument for regulatory competition is the concept of a common market. Within the EU, a company with its real seat in one Member State must, in principle, be allowed to incorporate in another Member State.[48]

From the presumption of freedom, it also follows that the mere general reference to circumvention of the company law of the state of the real seat cannot justify an exception to the incorporation doctrine. It must not in general be presumed that foreign legal systems offer less protection for shareholders, employees, creditors or public interests. Instead, it must specifically be demonstrated how far externalities bring a 'race to the bottom' at the expense of particular interest groups. This is unlikely for the interests of shareholders of public companies, if only because the internationalization of the capital market permits them to exert great competitive pressure.[49] Shareholders in close companies are by contrast already protected by the greater influence they tend to have on management. Additionally, normally the general meeting has to consent to a seat transfer, so that, to protect shareholder interests, what would be needed would be not a special link to the place of the real seat of the company but at best improved rules on voting rights.

For employees, creditors and the public, it should be borne in mind that primarily other areas of law than company law and therefore different rules of conflict of laws are relevant. If, however, employees and creditors are, in a given legal system, also protected by company law, a special link to the real seat should be possible. Since in the international context a functional approach is necessary, it cannot matter whether and to what

46 See e.g. Pistor (2002: 98); Van den Bergh (2000: 437–8); Kötz (1992: 216); Baum (2000: 104–5).

47 Trachtman (1993: 101).

48 On the ECJ case law see also Ch. 9, section I.1.a above.

49 See Ch. 9, section III.1 above.

extent a legal system technically splits up stakeholder protection among various areas of law. In departure from an across-the-board application of the company law of the place of incorporation, accordingly, a restriction of regulatory competition is justified if stakeholders cannot be equally well protected in some other way. For creditors, one might here point to possible self-protection. If creditors can recognize that a foreign company is involved, they may have the possibility of guaranteeing their legal position through contractual agreements.[50] However, market failure is not unlikely, because few people are informed of the details of foreign law, so that creditors typically cannot estimate how far contractual protection is necessary. Moreover, the law of the registered seat need not necessarily help the creditor any further. Since creditor protection is in part based on public-law powers of intervention and these powers can only operate within territorial limits, the danger exists that the creditor protection of neither the registered seat nor the real seat applies. A special linkage may accordingly be necessary in order, in the interest of the unity of the legal system,[51] to avoid a lack of norms.

Altogether, then, a modified incorporation doctrine is to be followed. This will cause further convergence, which will in principle also lead to an optimization of shareholder law. However, insofar as the law remains different, it may be justified to meet the interest in internationally uniform regulations, for instance, by harmonizing disclosure provisions. Regulatory competition, legal harmonization and national special linkages may thus supplement each other, thereby contributing to a sensible division of power between market and politics.

b) Convergence through lobbying

It is questionable whether lobbying for convergence ought to be utilized or instead prevented. Against this form of convergence it can be argued, first, that not all groups in society are equally well organizable, so that interest representation is necessarily distorted.[52] Additionally, general welfare interests, the efficiency of law and the freedom of the market may be harmed, since lobbies act only in their own interests and seek to secure profits through rent-seeking behaviour rather than performance.[53]

[50] *Kamer van Koophandel en Fabrieken voor Amsterdam* v. *Inspire Art Ltd*, C-167/01, [2003] ECR I-10155, para. 135.

[51] For the relationship between the unity of the legal system and private international law, see also Siems (2004a).

[52] See Ch. 7, section I.3 above.

[53] See Behrends (2001: 82 *et seq.*, 232).

Finally, from a democracy perspective, one might also raise objections to excessive influence of private lobbies, since non-representative group interests may impair the autonomy of parliaments.

These considerations do not, however, imply that the legislator ought to prevent all lobbying, or at least ignore it. It is basically advantageous for the quality of the law if private interest groups can point out a need for change and bring their viewpoint to bear. By contrast with corporatist modes of conduct,[54] here it is legitimate for interest groups to act purely in their own interests, since they are not integrated into the political process, so that responsibility for general interests remains with the legislative bodies. But there remains a need for action lest the legislator neglect the interest of some groups and the public because of pressure from one or more lobbies. First, the imbalanced influence of different interest groups has to be addressed by, for instance, rewards or incentives in favour of disadvantaged groups.[55] Secondly, politics must not confine its communication to a few groups. It is necessary for links with all interest groups to be strengthened, so as here too to prevent particular group interests from being ignored.[56] Thirdly, the political independence of the democratically legitimated decision-makers and the 'authenticity' of legislative decision itself must be guaranteed. For this, various concepts are being developed in both legal and political science, to structure the legislative process and ensure proper action by decision-makers.[57] Fourthly, the globalization of market forces may also prevent a national legislator from giving disproportionate weight to particular group interests. If, for instance, a legislature gives in to the rent-seeking behaviour of managements, it may be that domestic firms are unable to make headway on the international capital market. The converse position is, however, also conceivable. If, for instance, the interests of business and the market coincide, there may be deregulation at the expense of the general public. In order to prevent external effects, in this case an international solution that takes appropriate account of all interests is necessary. As with regulatory competition, thus, here too convergence 'from below' may have to be supplemented by international or regional harmonization.

[54] See Ch. 7, section I.3 above. [55] See Behrends (2001: 55–6, 69).

[56] For the EU see e.g. Consultation Document: Towards a Reinforced Culture of Consultation and Dialogue – Proposal for General Principles and Minimum Standards for Consultation of Interested Parties by the Commission, COM(2002) 277 final.

[57] See Reicherzer (2005); Behrends (2001: 232 *et seq.*); see also Ch. 7, section I.3 above.

c) Convergence through congruence

'Convergence through congruence'[58] is to be approved. If cultural, economic and factual circumstances come closer together, it also makes sense to treat increasingly equally the law of those involved. Additionally, the internationalization of the economy suggests that the law on cross-border investment and international enterprises on the one hand and on international abuses of power and enforcement problems on the other should increasingly be tackled similarly. Since national legislation will thus affect what happens in other countries, national solutions ought not to be sought in the individual countries in isolation.

2. Case law

For convergence in shareholder law, statutes are more important than courts, since codified legal rules are easier to copy from elsewhere, and statutes can tackle structural problems, and ensure legal certainty better.[59] Nonetheless, adjudication too should play its part in the convergence of law.

As a form of historical interpretation, comparative legal interpretation can be admissible, since in company and securities law national lawmakers increasingly make reference to the law of other countries.[60] This influence need not necessarily have come about directly. Instead, foreign law often has an indirect input into the legislative process, for instance, through the academic debate on 'good corporate governance'.

This effect can, moreover, be further developed into a 'convergence principle'. Alongside the genesis of legislation, another point in favour of this is that factual circumstances too are becoming increasingly similar, so that convergence of law is also justified from equal-treatment viewpoints. Since the classical ideal of the unity of the national legal system is breaking down, case law cannot escape the 'suction effect' of internationalization and globalization.[61] Moreover, the increasing foreign references in shareholder law in particular make it necessary to bring other legal systems into consideration as potential models. Legal differences may mean that investors' involvement with various legal systems is associated with

[58] See Ch. 8 above.

[59] See Ch. 2, section II; Ch. 7, section III.1 above.

[60] See Part II above.

[61] Berger (2001: 23) ('Sogeffekt'); but, regarding the US Constitution, see also *Lawrence* v. *Texas*, 123 Ct 2472, 2495 (2003) (Justice Scalia dissenting) and *Foster* v. *Florida*, 537 US 990 (2002) (Justice Thomas dissenting): 'this Court . . . should not impose foreign moods, fads, or fashions on Americans'.

considerable information costs and uncertainties. In the interests of effective shareholder protection, then, convergence of law should be included in courts' considerations, especially in relation to provisions that might directly or indirectly establish cross-border obstacles.

Neither comparative legal interpretation nor the convergence principle violate the rule that a judge must in principle only apply the law of his own country. Comparative law can be brought in as a cognitive approach in interpreting national law.[62] Its consolidation into a convergence principle is also possible. Principles are guiding criteria which because of their cogency are able to justify legal decisions.[63] They make no claim to exclusivity, but derive their actual meaning from the interaction of mutual reinforcements and limitations. It thus does not constitute inadmissible application of foreign law if the courts are enabled to steer the teleological interpretation in the direction of a convergence principle.

However, the practical implementation of convergence through case law may be problematic because the courts often lack the knowledge and the time to take comparative arguments into account.[64] Solutions are, however, conceivable. For instance, a compact comparative set of rules, created through extensive preliminary work, could make foreign law more readily accessible.[65] Moreover, the legal academia may also act as a catalyst,[66] by for instance giving more consideration in legal commentaries and textbooks to comparative lines of reasoning.

3. *Self-regulation*

In the general private law of continental Europe, the codification idea broke the legal unity of the Ius Commune.[67] Yet, for commercial law today, a mirror-image position is being debated. Deregulation of the positive law is again supposed to open up more room for those involved in economic transactions to shape the law themselves, so that in this way similar solutions can be found. In the present context, this sort of 'privatization of law' can be seen in for instance the growing freedom to contract out of statutory company law, the permitting of shareholder

62 See e.g. Zweigert (1949–50); Zweigert and Kötz (1998: 18); Kötz (2000: 832) ('Kürprogramm'); Kieninger (2002: 23).

63 Cf. Larenz and Canaris (1995: 302); Eidenmüller (1997: 122–3); Canaris (1969: 52–3).

64 See Drobnig and Van Erp (1998); Drobnig (1986); Kötz (2000); Markesinis and Fedtke (2005).

65 This is suggested by Berger (2001: 13).

66 See Kötz (2000: 841) ('Bringschuld der rechtsvergleichenden Wissenschaft').

67 See Kötz (1986: 13–14).

agreements, the influence of private associations in accounting and the advance of corporate governance codes.[68] Here, similar arguments often play a part, but the considerations below will be confined to the question of the opportunities and risks of self-regulation through corporate governance codes.

In addition to saving governmental resources, the potential advantage of corporate governance codes lies in their liberality, effectiveness and flexibility.[69] If self-regulation works, there is no need to have recourse to the harsher means of statute, so that corporate governance codes can have a deregulating effect and therefore expand freedom. There may also be particularly effective regulation because these codes are usually developed by groups that have special professionalism and expertise. Regulation 'at the coalface' that reflects the actuality of the market can thus focus effectively on the relevant conflicts of interest and find an optimum solution. This is also associated with special flexibility because codes regularly allow exceptions in justified cases and enforcement mechanisms can be more varied than with state compulsion. Additionally, codes have increased temporal flexibility, whereas amending statutes is often cumbersome and time-consuming.

However, counter-arguments can be thought of in each case. Control by private persons may be at the expense of the common good and of democracy. Where interest groups are integrated into politics, then the findings of corporatism research and of the public choice theory suggest the danger that, as with mere lobbying activity, here too they will act primarily in their own interests and not socially or for the common good.[70] Since there is no responsibility of private rule-makers to the general public, there may also be deficits in legitimation and democracy as well as a loss of sovereignty by national parliaments to be complained of. Corporate governance codes might therefore even be unlawful, since inadmissible delegation of law-making powers might lead to undermining parliaments and limiting fundamental rights of citizens with no parliamentary basis.[71] Possible adverse effects on third parties are also a price for the flexibility advantage that a small private group has over parliamentary legislative procedures.[72] If those affected by a regulation are themselves involved in

[68] See Ch. 2, section IV; Ch. 7, section III above.

[69] See e.g. MacNeil and Li (2006); Guobadia (2001: 119); for self-regulation in general see also Cheffins (1997: 364, 378 *et seq.*); Baldwin and Cave (1999: 126 *et seq.*).

[70] See Behrends (2001: 210); Ogus (2000: 587, 592); see also Ch. 7, sections I.3 above.

[71] For Germany: Wolf (2002); Kirchhof (2001: 1332–3).

[72] See Cheffins (1997: 397 *et seq.*); Zumbansen (2006b: 310).

the responsible committees, it may also happen that they end up 'making their law themselves'. Dangers of abuse are likely particularly in company and securities law, since business representatives on private decision-making bodies may exercise decisive weight. Finally, the effectiveness of corporate governance codes is not beyond doubt. For purely self-regulated law, it may be hard to do justice to the complexity of institutional realities, political decision-making processes and market mechanisms, as well as the conduct of market participants.[73] Furthermore, codified law may be superior to corporate governance codes in stability, legal certainty and enforceability.[74] Since private organizations have no public investigative or coercive means at their disposal, there is a threat of a 'pure box-ticking approach'[75] and thus of a reduction of corporate governance codes to a 'mere marketing measure'[76] and to 'tactical disinformation'[77] to attract foreign investors.

These criticisms do not, however, make corporate governance codes useless. Instead, self-regulation must be so designed as not to do harm to democracy, the common weal or third-party interests. It follows that corporate governance codes cannot replace or exclude statute law, but can act merely as an additional regulatory and protective level. Otherwise, the danger would arise of a 'quasi-legal system' which would, however, lack democratic legitimacy.

This purely supplementary nature has effects for possible ways of enforcing corporate governance codes. The consequences that corporate governance codes bring merely because of their public nature ('comply or explain')[78] are unproblematic. This influence is not to be underestimated, since accurate information on the principles for managing and monitoring the company may be decisive for whether capital providers invest in a particular firm. Since this response is a purely market-oriented one, it is something that firms themselves can very well be left responsible for. It is also conceivable for infringement of a code to be integrated into the law, for instance through principles of proper conduct of business, or commercial usage. Whether such an approach is specifically admissible will depend on the relevant national law,[79] so that here international uniformity of the codes would also presuppose a convergence of the positive law.

[73] Ebke (2002: 106); see also Cheffins (1997: 405 *et seq.*).

[74] See Coffee (2001: 67–8); Ferran (2001: 400 *et seq.*); Cheffins (1997: 383, 412 *et seq.*).

[75] Van den Berghe (2002: 166); Cheffins (1997: 650).

[76] Erhardt and Nowak (2002: 341–2) ('bloße Marketingmaßnahme').

[77] Henderson (1995: 906).

[78] See Ch. 2, section IV.3 above.

[79] See Ch. 7, section III.3 above.

By contrast, direct forms of state legal enforcement should not be used, since otherwise codes would acquire a ranking that would contradict their private origin. As examples from the past show, where self-regulation is not effective, the legislator will intervene and convert rules regarded as essential into statute law.[80] Finally, it may be doubted whether compliance with a code can or should be made a listing requirement. This depends, first, on whether stock exchanges are taken to be more in the nature of private, rather than public institutions.[81] Only if its private nature is predominant could a parallel with private trading platforms be drawn. Even in that case, though, it makes more sense for corporate governance codes merely to provide for a disclosure obligation and otherwise rely on the pressure of market forces.

Although on the view advocated here the private nature of codes should therefore be their most important aspect, it may nonetheless be necessary for the state to ensure proper conduct by private actors. Since even purely economic pressure may affect public and third-party interests, it is on the one hand conceivable to prevent market failure of codes *ex ante* by procedural rules.[82] For instance, the state may require private decision-making bodies to take shareholder, employee and consumer interests into account. Additionally, in the decision-making process, rule-of-law standards such as adequate information to those involved, minority rights and transparency of outcomes may be required. On the other hand, it is possible to put the emphasis more on *ex post* controls. Among regulatory variants here are for instance judicial or regulatory review of codes or the introduction of an ombudsman.[83] Whether the legislator ought rather to take an *ex ante* or *ex post* approach cannot be laid down *a priori*. The decision instead depends on whether and to what extent in the given legal and economic system prior trust in the given private decision-making body is justified.

On the whole, moderate utilization of corporate governance codes is to be welcomed. They cannot replace codified company and securities law. Additionally, the supplementary nature of codes means that, because of differences in national law and in the factual sphere, there are also limits to international approximation. Since, however, both the codified law and the factual circumstances are coming closer together with the internationalization of the economy, corporate governance codes can and should also act as a convergence force.

[80] See Ch. 7, section III.3 above.
[81] For the discussion see Mendiola and O'Hara (2003).
[82] See e.g. J. Black (1996: 46–7, 50), (2000), (2001).
[83] See generally Baldwin and Cave (1999: 130); for judicial review see J. Black (1996: 29 *et seq.*).

4. *Conclusion*

Convergence 'from below' can and should be used as a means to convergence. This will, however, not be comprehensive, since convergence through regulatory competition, lobbying, congruence, case law and self-regulation each affect only sub-areas of law or particular basic standards. There is accordingly still room for convergence 'from above', if and insofar as uniform regulation is also necessary. For instance, provisions on trading in securities, convocation procedures in public companies and public disclosure provisions should be approximated across the countries, since they concern cross-border questions and even small differences may impair the interests of those involved. It ought not, however, to be ignored that in many cases, such as the use of new media, it makes sense initially to permit experimental differences. The result is, then, on the one hand, at 'macro-level' a manifold pluralism of regulatory forms, with distinctions to be drawn not just between international, regional and national law but also between traditional harmonization and various forms of soft law. On the other hand, at 'micro-level' regulatory procedures have to be adjusted so that speed and efficiency on one side and balance and popular sovereignty on the other are still upheld.

III. The object of convergence in shareholder law

The guiding objective for future convergence of law ought to be the 'empowered shareholder'. The shareholder types of the 'powerless' shareholder and the 'disempowered' shareholder have to be demarcated from this. The law should neither confine the shareholder's position to that of the investor, nor accept the shareholder's 'rational apathy' as unalterable (subsections 1 and 2 below). Instead, this empowerment is intended to express, on the one hand, that it is possible and reasonable to grant the shareholder a strong position within the company (again). On the other, the shareholder is obliged himself to take the initiative and not rely exclusively on other oversight mechanisms (subsection 3 below).

1. *The powerless shareholder?*

In the debate on the shareholder's position, it has often been stressed that the shareholder in a public company is a pure investor.[84] Since he

[84] On what follows see Ch. 3, section I.3; Ch. 4, sections I, preamble, II.1.a above.

is concerned primarily with a profitable investment opportunity, he has exchanged control of the company for marketability of the shares. The possibility of selling shares on the capital market or of compensation and appraisal rights are seen as adequately guaranteeing his interests, and shareholder democracy is therefore considered as neither necessary nor sensible. A specialized and centralized management is claimed to suit the essence of the joint stock company, because shareholders lack the interest or ability to guide the firm's fortunes themselves. Shareholder voting rights could even be harmful, since managers know best what measures to take, whereas with general-meeting votes there is a danger of inconsistent, erratic decision-making. Efficient corporate governance is, then, to be ensured through market forces and other institutions such as independent directors and auditors, not through shareholder participation.

What is true in this is that the more pronounced capital-market orientation and increasing dispersion of shareholder ownership[85] also need to be reflected in the law. Given the internationalizing economy, moreover, convergence of law is to be approved.[86] Future regulatory tasks include, for instance, the international optimization of disclosure rules, provisions on share trading and compensatory rights for minority shareholders. Further, protection by good internal corporate governance structures and private institutions should be expanded. Thus, for example, the current debate on the independence of directors, auditors and rating agencies shows that indirect shareholder protection must be improved still further.

It would however be mistaken to reduce the shareholder's position to that of a mere investor on that account. The role of the shareholder as supervisor does not contradict other forms of oversight over management. Since both market and legal solutions can fail, multiple oversight and protective measures contribute to well-functioning corporate governance. Shareholder voting rights have the advantage that an efficient balancing of interests can come about within the company as an 'autonomous entity', thus reducing the need for state controls through a form of 'self-regulation'.[87] Additionally, it is justified for shareholders, by virtue of their vote, to have a prominent position in the company. By contrast with creditors and other stakeholders, shareholders cannot typically protect themselves through agreements, but rather, as 'residual claimants', they directly bear the costs and benefits of the company's economic performance.[88] Finally, the voting right does not contradict the

[85] See Ch. 8, section IV above. [86] See also Ch. 12, section I.1 above.
[87] Hill (2000b: 60); see also B. Black and Kraakman (1996).
[88] See also Ch. 4, section II.1.a above.

increasing relevance of the shareholder as investor. Shareholders can in this way influence profit-maximizing administration of their investment and thus, especially in cases where the sale of the shares is difficult or impossible,[89] have available an 'economic emergency brake'.

2. *The disempowered shareholder?*

Even if the shareholder could in principle become active, in reality shareholders' 'rational apathy' stands in the way of any lively shareholder democracy. This particularly (but not exclusively) concerns public companies with dispersed shareholder ownership, since there the shareholder can most easily respond to undesirable developments by selling shares.[90] By contrast, exercising the voting right may be unattractive because, say, the shareholder has no adequate or comprehensible information about the objects of decision, cannot contact fellow shareholders and cannot make effective use of voting proxies. Since the shareholder accordingly has a right to participate only in principle, but in practice is virtually denied it, he therefore remains 'disempowered'.

This disempowerment is, however, as can be seen from the increasing activism of institutional investors,[91] not impossible to overcome. In particular, the new media will play a decisive part in future law. They facilitate both communication and information as well as the exercise of the voting right itself (probably, mainly through online proxies in public companies and online participation in close companies).[92] However, as with the voting right as such, the law ought in principle not to distinguish between different types of company. Since use of the new media in companies is still relatively recent, it is instead better if companies can try out different ways of using them. Additionally, convergence in this area ought not to be over-hasty, in order to allow room for innovations at national legislative level too.

3. *The empowered shareholder*

For the shareholder, it is on the one hand advantageous if he is not (any longer) 'legally powerless' and 'disempowered in practice', but is granted a strong position within the company. On the other hand, this 'empowerment' also brings with it a challenge, since the shareholder must now decide for himself whether and how he wishes to become active.

[89] See Ch. 4, section I.3.d above.
[90] See generally Ch. 4, section II.1.b above.
[91] See Ch. 4, section II.4.c above.
[92] See Ch. 10, section I.2, 3 above.

This includes, first, asking shareholders, of public companies in particular, to accept more responsibility in acquiring and processing information. Since individual rights to information may be unsatisfactory here, and general disclosure may also improve the market value of the shares, public information is more important than individual rights. Furthermore, dissemination of and access to information will be faster and less complicated using the new media.[93] What may chiefly be problematic is the filtering and evaluation of this information. The law should focus here not on the professional but on the reasonable shareholder.[94] Although the involvement of institutional investors is increasing,[95] company and securities law also serve to protect the consumer, since anyone can purchase shares in public companies through the capital market. This protective function is not opposed by the fact that private investors may have recourse to the help of information intermediaries, or proxies to third parties. Even with a proxy to a third party, the ultimate responsibility remains with the shareholder, since it is only by a deliberate selection among various proxies or through instructions in the individual case that this form of exercising the voting right can serve his own interests and that of efficient corporate governance.

For the distribution of powers within the company, the list of competences ought increasingly to be made open to options in the articles of association. This will enable shareholders to provide for appropriate arrangements for the different types of company.[96] For instance, for close companies it may make sense to have a provision in the articles of association whereby shareholders are given farther-reaching powers than in the default model. In this way some questions of the conduct of business can be reserved for the shareholders, especially if the new media make interim general meetings or plebiscites possible.[97] By contrast, practice may shape the liberalization in a different direction in public companies. Both management and shareholders share a basic interest in ensuring that their firm is successful on the international capital market and thus in having, for instance, the company law provisions on corporate finance sufficiently flexible to be able to cover the firm's financial needs quickly and without undue complications.

Finally, it is in line with the emancipation of shareholders for it to be possible for shareholders to resort to litigation against management or

[93] See Ch. 10, section I.2.c above.

[94] For this debate see e.g. Merkt (2004b: 138); Cheffins (1997: 176).

[95] See Ch. 8, section IV.3 above.

[96] See also Ch. 10, section I.2.d above.

[97] See also Ch. 10, section II.1 above.

the shareholder majority. But international approximation of law here ought to be considered only with great caution. Since in procedural law national differences are considerable, at international level it is more other types of enforcement that suggest themselves. Alongside co-ordination of supervisory authorities, this concerns the various forms of alternative dispute resolution. Law-makers ought therefore to eliminate the barriers that may stand in the way of arbitration,[98] in order to enable the empowered shareholder to freely choose this particular means of enforcing his rights.

IV. Conclusion

A plurality of regulatory forms is to be welcomed. In addition to international, regional and national law, there should be further distinctions in each case between conventional harmonization and forms of soft law. Furthermore, regulatory procedures must be adjusted so as to ensure faster and more efficient procedures on the one hand, and balance and popular sovereignty on the other. Under these conditions, then, there can and should be further convergence of shareholder law. Individual differences and divergences do not stand in the way of this, since in particular the combination of different types of regulation prevents there being, say, a petrification of law or neglect of any one interest group. The substantive objective for future convergence of law ought to be the 'empowered shareholder'. It is possible and reasonable to allow the shareholder more responsibility and thus relocate him at the centre of company law.

[98] See Ch. 10, section II.3 above.

13

Summary of principal findings

As a summary, the theses set out in the introduction (in *italics* below) can be taken up again:

1. For shareholder law in the UK, the US, Germany, France, Japan and China, the division into different legal families is no longer a persuasive criterion of differentiation.[1]

Both common features and differences today often cut across the division of legal families into common law, civil law and Asian law. General statements that for instance in the US and the UK shareholders are better protected and stakeholder interests irrelevant[2] are accordingly to be rejected. Instead, in many sub-areas of shareholder law there are more differences of degree than structurally different conceptions.

2. Present shareholder law is based, internationally largely concordantly, on a basic pattern of codifications of company and securities law, supplemented by case law, articles of association, shareholder agreements and corporate governance codes.[3]

While international and regional legal bases affect national shareholder law, this happens mostly in piecemeal fashion, so that it continues to be national sources of law that mostly matter. Here, in all the legal systems studied there are similar basic patterns. Abstract conceptions focusing only or mainly on one source of law have not been reflected in the present law. Nor is control through market forces relied on exclusively.

3. Although in Germany, France, Japan and China the reception of US law has increasingly expanded the investor aspect, all the legal systems studied here show a combination of the basic models of the shareholder as 'owner', 'parliamentarian' and 'investor'.[4]

[1] See already preamble to Part II and Ch. 6, section I above.
[2] See Ch. 5, section II.1.a, b above.
[3] See Ch. 2 above.
[4] See Ch. 3, section I; Ch. 6, section I above.

For instance, in favour of the ownership analogy is the fact that shareholders can in principle freely sell their shares, and have special rights. In the sense of the democratic model, there are mechanisms enabling self-regulating organization of the company and providing for a division of powers among the individual bodies. Corporate-finance and disclosure-oriented provisions of company and securities law, finally, are aimed chiefly at the shareholder as investor.

In the hitherto weak capital-market systems of Germany, France, Japan and China, the investor-oriented provisions of US law have often been influential, for instance, in deregulating company law provisions on corporate finance, in rules on proxy voting and in disclosure through securities law.[5] Since this is not, however, the only trend, it is justifiable to speak of a combination of various models and a convergence of various legal systems.

4. Similarly, all the legal systems studied here show a combination of the 'adjectival shareholder types' ('the profit-oriented, active, informed, anonymous, deciding, protected, litigating shareholder').

Since shareholder law can concordantly be described as having various cumulative characteristics, national legislators do not follow one uniform regulatory pattern. Instead, the shareholder has, for instance, in principle the possibility both of exercising the right to vote and also of selling his shares ('voice' and 'exit').[6] Moreover, in the area of corporate governance too, various protective and regulatory mechanisms operate together.[7]

5. In detail, the provisions referring to the typical original shareholder rights (the 'shareholder as such')[8] *show a greater degree of convergence than the provisions on the 'shareholder in the power structure of the company'.*[9]

The legal specificities are more marked in relation to the shareholder's position in the power structure of the company, because functionally a number of regulatory variants often exist, and evaluations or legal rules outside shareholder law may be relevant. For instance, for shareholder protection various measures may oppose misconduct by managements,[10] and in the event of shareholder litigation differences in procedural law may stand in the way of convergence.[11]

[5] For corporate finance see Ch. 4, sections I.4, II.4.a; Ch. 5, sections I.1.d, II.2.b, above; for proxy voting see Ch. 4, section II.3.c above; for disclosure see Ch. 2, section III.1; Ch. 4, section III.2; Ch. 5, section II.1.b above.

[6] See Ch. 4, sections I.3, 5, II above.

[7] See Ch. 5, section II above.

[8] See Ch. 4 above.

[9] See Ch. 5 above.

[10] See Ch. 5, section II.1.b above.

[11] See Ch. 5, section III above.

With the more technical provisions on the 'shareholder as such', the remaining differences are based mainly on details. These differences in convocation notice periods, forms of voting proxies, multiple voting rights, vote capping, rights of inspection etc. may, however, also hamper the exercise of shareholder rights in foreign companies.

6. It follows from historical precedents, the findings of the public choice theory and studies on the influence of interest groups that changes in factual circumstances can exert decisive influence on future shareholder law and thus act as 'convergence forces'.[12]

The development of the law does not follow purely deterministically from factual factors. Instead, the law may also, conversely, influence reality, and political decision-makers may feel themselves committed to the common good and not to particular interests. Nonetheless, in the present context, it is precisely the 'dependency' of shareholder law that is interesting. For, to the extent that extralegal circumstances come closer together, it is likely that these developments will also be reflected in a convergence of law.

7. Although international and informal regulation will grow in importance, for future development of convergence it is still codified national law that will count most.[13]

What has particularly to be asked is whether 're-regulation'[14] of statutory law will lead to convergence of legal systems. In the study of future developmental trends and patterns, accordingly, it is not convergence 'from above'[15] (i.e. through international or regional law) but 'from below' that is the more important.

8. As the social, political and economic conditions that form the background to shareholder law come closer together internationally, the law itself will also grow more similar ('convergence through congruence').[16]

In relation to the convergence forces acting on national legislators, it is often primarily regulatory competition that is mentioned, and here cultural and economic differences are seen as obstacles to convergence. It follows, however, from the present study that, particularly for public companies, 'convergence through congruence' acts as a strong convergence force. For example, the increased use of modern forms of communication,

[12] See Ch. 7, section I above.
[13] See Ch. 7, sections II, III above.
[14] See Ch. 11, section I above.
[15] See Ch. 7, section IV above.
[16] See Ch. 8 above.

approximations in economic policy, company and shareholder structures, increasing cross-border investment and mergers, the liberalization of capital markets and reforms in pension provisions are also reflected in shareholder law. Additionally, a retreat of existing path dependencies is contributing to a convergence of law.

9. In situations where individual interest groups press for an approximation of laws ('convergence through pressure'), 'regulatory competition for shareholders' will take on increasing importance compared with 'regulatory competition for company founders' and 'lobbying'.[17]

The liberalization of markets increases the pressure shareholders can exert. This means that the trend to be expected is for legislation to give particular weight to shareholder interests especially in public companies although no unitary model is to be expected. Much the same is true of other forms of convergence through pressure. While (isolated) regulatory competition for corporate domiciles is possible in the US and to a limited extent in the EU, in the global context it plays a lesser role. For lobbying, national differences mean that in the main the pressure from international lobbies should lead to some convergence.

10. It will above all be the internationalization of enterprises, the approximation of shareholder structures, the new media and shareholder pressure that will contribute to a convergence of law and of its implementation.[18]

For the law on the 'shareholder as such',[19] obstacles to the cross-border exercise of shareholder rights ought to be removed, and disclosure standards ought to converge. Additionally, the new media will facilitate shareholder participation in general meetings or plebiscitary decision-making procedures. Regarding the law on the 'shareholder in the power structure of the company',[20] the pace of convergence ought instead to be slower. Here too, however, convergence may come about in the interests of international competitiveness, for instance in investor protection and in more flexible law.

Future convergence will also involve a 'convergence of law and reality'.[21] Even in the past, the positive law was commonly approximated. Since, however, this sometimes involved the imposition of or a simple copying of foreign laws, their actual effectiveness was limited. Nowadays 'convergence through congruence' is based on a change in the factual circumstances,

[17] See Ch. 9 above. [18] See Ch. 10 above. [19] See Ch. 10, section I above.
[20] See Ch. 10, section II above. [21] See Ch. 6, sections III; Ch. 11, section III above.

so that fewer contradictions between law and facts arise. In 'convergence through pressure', interest groups lay weight on effective enforcement of the law, so that here too it will not only be formal convergence that will come about.

11. At legal-policy level, for a convergence in shareholder law the various modes of regulation must be coordinated and their procedures optimized.[22]

Alongside international, regional and national law, a further distinction is to be drawn in each case between conventional harmonization and various forms of soft law. Furthermore, regulatory procedures must be adapted so that, on the one hand, speed and efficiency and, on the other hand, balance and popular sovereignty are maintained. On these preconditions, accordingly, further convergence of shareholder law can and should in principle come about. Individual differences and divergences do not stand in the way of this, since the very combination of different regulatory types prevents a petrification of law or the neglect of particular interest groups from occurring.

12. For the converging law, the shareholder as 'empowered shareholder' should return to the centre of company law.[23]

The 'empowered shareholder' has to be distinguished from the 'powerless' and the 'disempowered' shareholder. The law should neither restrict the shareholder's position to that of investor, nor treat the shareholder's 'rational apathy' as unalterable. Instead, 'empowerment' should, on the one hand, bring out the point that it is possible and sensible to give the shareholder (back) a stronger position. On the other hand, the empowered shareholder is also obliged to take the initiative and not rely exclusively on other control mechanisms.

[22] See Ch. 12, sections I, II above.

[23] See Ch. 12, section III above.

REFERENCES

Abeltshauser, Thomas E. (1998), *Leitungshaftung im Kapitalgesellschaftsrecht*, Cologne: Heymanns.

Ackermann, Rolf (1999), *Pfadabhängigkeit, Institutionen und Regelreform*, PhD Thesis, Freiburg.

Adams, Michael (1994), Die Usurpation von Aktionärsbefugnissen mittels Ringverflechtung in der 'Deutschland AG', *AG* 148.

Ahlering, Beth, and Deakin, Simon (2006), Labour Regulation, Corporate Governance and Legal Origin: A Case of Institutional Complementarity?, Working Paper, available at http://ssrn.com/abstract = 898184/ (and forthcoming in *Law and Society Review*).

Albert, Michel (1991), *Capitalism contre Capitalism*, Paris: Editions du Seuil.

Alemann, Ulrich von (2000), Lobbyismus heute – Neue Herausforderungen durch Globalisierung, Europäisierung und Berlinisierung, *Wirtschaftsdienst* 139.

Allen, William (1998), The Corporate Director's Fiduciary Duty of Care and the Business Judgment Rule Under US Corporate Law, in: Hopt, Klaus J., Kanda, Hideki, Roe, Mark J., Wymeersch, Eddy, and Prigge, Stefan (eds.), *Comparative Corporate Governance: The State of Art and Emerging Research*, Oxford: Clarendon, p. 307.

Anderse, Paul Krüger, and Sorei, Karsten Engsig (1999), Free Movement of Companies from a Nordic Perspective, 6 *MJ* 47.

Anderson, Kent (2001), Kent's World: A Personal Approach to the Various Worlds of Japanese Law, 12 *ZJapanR* 36.

André, Thomas J. (1998), Cultural Hegemony: The Exportation of Anglo-Saxon Corporate Governance Ideologies to Germany, 73 *Tul. L. Rev.* 69.

Annan, Kofi (2001), *Dialogue Among Civilizations*, Paris: Unesco.

ANSA (Association National de Sociétés par Actions) (2003), Proxy Voting Reform in France: A Guide to Non-Resident Shareholders, 2nd edition, available at www.ansa.asso.fr/site/acv_index_uk.asp.

Aoki, Hiroko (2001a), Revisions of Corporate Law, 11 *ZJapanR* 97.

(2001b), The New Regulatory and Supervisory Architecture of Japan's Financial Market, 12 *ZJapanR* 101.

(2003), Neuregelungen von Aufsicht, Rechtsdurchsetzung und Finanzdienstleistungen in Japan, 16 *ZJapanR* 13.

Arlt, Marie-Agnes (2005), Frankreich, in: Kalss, Susanne (ed.), *Vorstandshaftung in 15 europäischen Ländern*, Vienna: Linde, p. 467.

Armour John (2005), Who Should Make Corporate Law? EC Legislation versus Regulatory Competition, 58 *Current Legal Problems* 369.

Armour, John, Deakin, Simon, and Konzelmann, Sue (2003), Shareholder Primacy and the Trajectory of UK Corporate Governance, 41 *BJIR* 531.

Armour, John, and Skeel, David A. (2007), Who Writes the Rules for Hostile Takeovers, and Why? The Peculiar Divergences of US and UK Takeover Regulation, 95 *Geo. L.J.* (forthcoming).

Arnim, Hans Herbert von (1977), *Gemeinwohl und Gruppeninteressen*, Frankfurt (Main): Metzner.

Aronson, Bruce E. (2003a), Reconsidering the Importance of Law in Japanese Corporate Governance: Evidence from the Daiwa Bank Shareholder Derivative Case, 36 *Cornell Int'l L.J.* 11.

(2003b), Learning from Comparative Law in Teaching US Corporate Law: Director's Liability in Japan and the US, 22 *Penn St. Int'l L. Rev.* 213.

Assmann, Heinz-Dieter (1990), Einführung und Verformung westlichen Rechts im Finanz- und Kapitalmarktrecht Japans, in: Coing, Helmut, Hirano, Ryuichi, Kitagawa, Zentaro, Murakami, Junichi, Nörr, Knut Wolfgang, Oppermann, Thomas, and Shiono, Hiroshi (eds.), *Die Japanisierung des westlichen Rechts*, Tübingen: Mohr Siebeck, p. 275.

(2003), Corporate Governance im Schnittfeld von Gesellschaftsrecht und Kapitalmarktrecht, *Festschrift Kümpel* 1.

Bachmann, Gregor (2001), Verwaltungsvollmacht und 'Aktionärsdemokratie': Selbstregulative Ansätze für die Hauptversammlung, *AG* 635.

Bagel, Friderike (1999), *Der Ausschluß des Bezugsrechts in Europa*, Cologne: Heymanns.

Baldwin, Robert, and Cave, Martin (1999), *Understanding Regulation: Theory, Strategy, and Practice*, Oxford: Oxford University Press.

Bälz, Moritz (2002), Appraisal Rights in Japanese Corporate Law, 13 *ZJapanR* 129.

(2006), Liberalized Rules for the Restructuring of Japanese Companies: Mergers, Demergers, and Share Exchanges under the New Company Law, 21 *ZJapanR* 19.

Banner, Stuart (1997), What Causes New Securities Regulation?: 300 Years of Evidence, 75 *Wash. U.L.Q.* 849.

Barca, Fabrizio, and Becht, Marco (eds.) (2001), *The Control of Corporate Europe*, Oxford: Oxford University Press.

Barnard, Catherine (2000), Social Dumping and the Race to the Bottom: Some Lessons for the European Union from Delaware, 25 *E.L. Rev.* 57.

Bastian, Daniel, and Germain Michel (1972), *Frankreich, Jura Europae, Droit des societés, Gesellschaftsrecht*, Munich: Beck.

Baum, Harald (1996), Der Markt für Unternehmen und die Regelung von öffenltichen Übernahmenangeboten in Japan, *AG* 399.

(1997), Börsen- und Kapitalmarktrecht in Japan, in: Hopt, Klaus J., Rudolph, Bernd, and Baum, Harald (eds.), *Börsenreform – Eine ökonomische, rechtsvergleichende und rechtspolitische Untersuchung*, Stuttgart: Schäffer-Poeschel, p. 1265.

(1998), Zur Diskussion über vergleichende Corporate Governance mit Japan, 62 *RabelsZ* 739.

(2000), Globalization, Capital Markets and Possible Regulatory Responses, in: Basedow, Jürgen, and Kono, Toshiyuki (eds.), *Legal Aspects of Globalization*, The Hague: Kluwer Law International, p. 77.

Baum, Harald and Hayakawa, Masaru (1994), Die rechtliche Gestaltung des japanischen Finanzmarktes, in: Baum, Harald, and Drobnig, Ulrich, *Japanisches Handels- und Wirtschaftsrecht*, New York: de Gruyter, p. 495.

Baums, Theodor (1998), Shareholder Representation and Proxy Voting in the European Union: A Comparative Study, in: Hopt, Klaus J., Kanda, Hideki, Roe, Mark J., Wymeersch, Eddy, and Prigge, Stefan (eds.), *Comparative Corporate Governance: The State of Art and Emerging Research*, Oxford: Clarendon, p. 545.

(1999), Globalisierung und deutsches Gesellschaftsrecht: Der Fall Daimler-Chrysler, in: Künzel, Rainer (ed.), *Profile der Wissenschaft. 25 Jahre Universität Osnabrück*, Osnabrück: Rasch, p. 235.

(2000), Empfiehlt sich eine Neuregelung des aktienrechtlichen Anfechtungs- und Organhaftungsrechts, insbesondere der Klagemöglichkeit von Aktionären?, *Gutachten des 63. Deutschen Juristentages*, Munich: Beck.

Baums, Theodor, and Möller, Matthias (2000), Venture Capital: US-amerikanisches Modell und deutsches Aktienrecht, in: Baums, Theodor; Hopt, Klaus J., and Horn, Norbert (eds.), *Corporations, Capital Markets and Business in the Law (Liber Amicorum Buxbaum)*, London: Kluwer, p. 33.

Baums, Theodor, and Randow, Philipp von (1995), Der Markt für Stimmrechtsvertreter, *AG* 145.

Baums, Theodor, and Wymeersch, Eddy (eds.) (1999), *Shareholder Voting Rights and Practices in Europe and the United States*, London: Kluwer Law International.

Bebchuk, Lucian Arye (1994), Efficient and Inefficient Sales of Corporate Control, 109 *Q.J. Econ.* 957.

(2002), The Case Against Board Veto in Corporate Takeovers, 69 *U. Chi. L. Rev.* 973.

(2005), The Case for Increasing Shareholder Power, 118 *Harv. L. Rev.* 833.

(2006), Letting Shareholders Set the Rules, 119 *Harvard Law Review* 1784.

Bebchuk, Lucian Arye, and Cohen, Alma (2003), Firm's Decision Where to Incorporate, 46 *J. L. & Econ.* 383.

Bebchuk Lucian Arye, Cohen, Alma, and Ferrell, Allen (2002), Does the Evidence Favor State Competition in Corporate Law?, 90 *Cal. L. Rev.* 1775.

Bebchuk Lucian Arye, and Ferrell, Allen (2001), The Race to Protect Managers from Takeovers, in: Esty, Daniel C., and Geradin, Damien (eds.), *Regulatory Competition and Economic Integration*, Oxford: Oxford University Press, p. 68 (also published in: (1999) 99 *Colum. L. Rev.* 1168).

Bebchuk Lucian Arye, and Fried, Jesse M. (2004), *Pay Without Performance: The Unfulfilled Promise of Executive Compensation*, Cambridge, MA: Harvard University Press.

Bebchuk Lucian Arye, and Hamdani, Assaf (2002), Vigorous Race or Leisurely Walk: Reconsidering the Competition over Corporate Charters, 112 *Yale L.J.* 553.

Bebchuk Lucian Arye, and Roe, Mark J. (1999), A Theory of Path Dependence in Corporate Ownership and Governance, 52 *Stan. L. Rev.* 127 (also published in: Gordon, Jeffrey N., and Roe, Mark J. (eds.), *Convergence and Persistence in Corporate Governance*, Cambridge: Cambridge University Press, 2004, p. 69).

Becht Marco, Mayer, Colin, and Wagner, Hannes F. (2006), Where Do Firms Incorporate?, Working Paper, available at http://ssrn.com/abstract=906066.

Becker, Bernd Christian (2001), *Die institutionelle Stimmrechtsvertretung der Aktionäre in Europa*, Frankfurt (Main): Lang.

Becker, Michael (1997a), *Verwaltungskontrolle durch Gesellschafterrechte*, Tübingen: Mohr Siebeck.

(1997b), Börsen- und Kapitalmarktrecht der Vereinigten Staaten, in: Hopt, Klaus J., Rudolph, Bernd, and Baum, Harald (eds.), *Börsenreform – Eine ökonomische, rechtsvergleichende und rechtspolitische Untersuchung*, Stuttgart: Schäffer-Poeschel, p. 755.

Behrends, Sylke (2001), *Neue Politische Ökonomie*, Munich: Vahlen.

Benes, Nicholas (2005), Japan Needs Real Merger Reform and Disclosure, December 2005 *IFLR* 25.

Berg, Stefan, and Stöcker, Mathias (2002), Anwendungs- und Haftungsfragen zum Deutschen Corporate Governance-Kodex, *WM* 1569.

Berger, Klaus Peter (2001), Auf dem Weg zu einem europäischen Gemeinrecht der Methode, *ZEuP* 4.

Berkowitz, Daniel, Pistor, Katharina, and Richard, Jean-Francois (2003a), Economic Development, Legality, and the Transplant Effect, 47 *Europ. Econ. Rev.* 165.

(2003b), The Transplant Effect, 51 *Am. J. Comp. L.* 163.

Berle, Adolf A. (1993), For Whom Corporate Managers Are Trustees: A Note, 45 *Harv. L. Rev.* 1365.

Berle, Adolf A., and Means, Gardiner C. (1932), *The Modern Corporation and Private Property*, revised edition, New York: Legal Classics Library, 1993.

Berndt, Markus (2002), *Global Differences in Corporate Governance-Systems*, Wiesbaden: Deutscher-Universitäts-Verlag.

Bernholz, Peter (1969), Einige Bemerkungen zur Theorie des Einflusses der Verbände auf die politische Willensbildung in der Demokratie, 22 *Kyklos* 276.

Berrar, Carsten (2001), *Die Entwicklung der Corporate Governance in Deutschland im internationalen Vergleich*, Baden-Baden: Nomos.

Berrisch, Georg M. (2004), Cancún – was nun?, *RIW* 69.

Beyme, Klaus von (1980), *Interessengruppen in der Demokratie*, Munich: Piper, 5th edition.

Bhagwati, Jagdish (2004), In Defense of Globalization, Oxford: Oxford University Press.

Black, Bernard S. (1990a), Shareholder Passivity Reexamined, 89 *Mich. L. Rev*. 520.

(1990b), Is Corporate Law Trivial?: A Political and Economic Analysis, 84 *Nw. U. L. Rev.* 542.

(1997), Shareholder Activism and Corporate Governance in the United States, in: Newman, Peter (ed.), *The New Palgrave Dictionary of Economics and the Law*, New York: Grove's Dictionaries, p. 459.

Black, Bernard S., and Kraakman, Reinier (1996), A Self Enforcing Model of Corporate Law, 109 *Harv. L. Rev*. 1911.

(2002), Delaware's Takeover Law: The Uncertain Search for Hidden Value, 96 *Nw. U. L. Rev*. 521.

Black, Julia (1996), Constitutionalising Self-Regulation, 59 *MLR* 24.

(2000) and (2001), Proceduralizing Self-Regulation (Part I and Part II), 20 *O. J. L. S.* 597 and 21 *O. J. L. S.* 33.

Blair, Margaret M. (2004), Reforming Corporate Governance: What History Can Teach Us, *Berkeley Bus. L.J.* 1.

Blair, Margaret M., and Stout, Lynn A. (1999), A Team Production Theory of Corporate Law, 85 *Va. L. Rev*. 247.

Blumental, David (1998), 'Reform' or 'Opening'? Reform of China's State-Owned Enterprises and WTO Accession – The Dilemma of Applying GATT to Marketizing Economies, 16 *UCLA Pac. Basin L.J.* 198.

Bogdandy, Arnim von (2000), *Gubernative Rechtssetzung*, Tübingen: Mohr.

Borgmann, Christopher (1996), *Der Organstreit in der Kapitalgesellschaft: eine rechtsvergleichende Untersuchung zum deutschen, französischen und englischen Recht*, Heidelberg: C. F. Müller.

Bottomley, Stephan (1999), Company Law in Japan, in: Tomasic, Roman (ed.), *Company Law in East Asia*, Aldershot: Ashgate, p. 39.

Boyle, Anthony James (2003), *Minority Shareholders' Remedies*, Cambridge: Cambridge University Press.

Braendle, Udo (2006), Shareholder Protection in the USA and Germany – 'Law and Finance' Revisited, 7 *German Law Journal* 257.

Brancanto, Carolyn, and Price, Michael (2002), The Institutional Investor's Goals for Corporate Law in the Twenty-First Century, 25 *Del. J. Corp. L.* 35.

Branson, Douglas M. (2000), Teaching Comparative Corporate Governance: The Significance of 'Soft Law' and International Institutions, 34 *Ga. L. Rev.* 669.

(2001), The Very Uncertain Prospect of 'Global' Convergence in Corporate Governance, 34 *Cornell Int'l L.J.* 321.

(2002), The Social Responsibility of Large Multinational Corporations, 16 *Transnational Law* 121.

Bratton, William W., and McCahery, Joseph A. (1999), Comparative Corporate Governance and the Theory of the Firm: The Case Against Global Cross Reference, 38 *Colum. J. Transnat'l L.* 213 (also published in: McCahery, Joseph A., Moerland, Piet, Raaijmakers, Theo, and Renneboog, Luc (eds.), *Corporate Governance Regimes – Convergence and Diversity*, Oxford: Oxford University Press, 2002, p. 23).

Buxbaum, Richard M., and Hopt, Klaus J. (1988), *Legal Harmonization and the Business Enterprise*, Berlin, New York: de Gruyter.

Cadbury Report (1992), Committee on the Financial Aspects of Corporate Governance, *Report of the Committee on the Financial Aspects of Corporate Governance*.

Campbell, David (1999), What Is Meant by 'the Rule of Law' in Asian Company Law Reform?, in: Tomasic, Roman (ed.), *Company Law in East Asia*, Aldershot: Ashgate, p. 11.

Canaris, Claus-Wilhelm (1969), *Systemdenken und Systembegriff in der Jurisprudenz*, Berlin: Duncker & Humblot.

Canner, Stephen J. (1998), The Multilateral Agreement on Investment, 31 *Cornell Int'l L.J.* 657.

Cardilli, Maria Camilla (2004), Regulation without Borders: The Impact of Sarbanes–Oxley on European Companies, 27 *Ford. Int'l L. J.* 785.

Carney, William J. (1997), The Political Economy of Competition for Corporate Charters, 26 *J. Legal Stud.* 303.

(1998), The Production of Corporate Law, 71 *S. Cal. L. Rev.* 715.

Cary, William L. (1974), Federalism and Corporate Law: Reflections Upon Delaware, 83 *Yale L.J.* 663.

Chan, Kay-Wah (2005), Foreign Law Firms: Implications for Professional Legal Education in Japan, 20 *ZJapanR* 55.

Chandler, Alfred D. (1990), *Scale and Scope: The Dynamics of Industrial Capitalism*, Cambridge, MA: Harvard University Press.

Chantayan, Franck (2002), An Examination of American and German Corporate Law Norms, 16 *St John's J. Legal Comment.* 431.

Charny, David (1991), Competition Among Jurisdictions in Formulating Corporate Law Rules: An American Perspective on the 'Race to the Bottom' in the European Communities, 32 *Harv. Int'l L.J.* 423.

(1998), The German Corporate Governance-System, *Colum. Bus. L. Rev.* 145.

(2004), The Politics of Corporate Convergence, in: Gordon, Jeffrey N., and Roe, Mark J. (eds.), *Convergence and Persistence in Corporate Governance*, Cambridge: Cambridge University Press, p. 293.

Cheffins, Brian R. (1997), *Company Law: Theory, Structure, and Operation*, Oxford: Oxford University Press.

(2000), Minority Shareholders and Corporate Governance, 21 *Comp. Law.* 41.

(2001a), Does Law Matter? The Separation of Ownership and Control in the United Kingdom, 30 *J. Legal Stud.* 459.

(2001b), The Metamorphosis of 'Germany Inc.': The Case of Executive Pay', 49 *Am. J. Comp. L.* 497.

(2001c), History and the Global Corporate Governance Revolution: The UK Perspective, 43/4 *Bus. Hist.* 87.

(2002), Putting Britain on the Roe Map: The Emergence of the Berle–Means Corporation in the United Kingdom, in: McCahery, Joseph A., Moerland, Piet, Raaijmakers, Theo, and Renneboog, Luc (eds.), *Corporate Governance Regimes – Convergence and Diversity*, Oxford: Oxford University Press, p. 147.

(2003a), Law as Bedrock: The Foundations of an Economy Dominated by Widely Held Public Companies, 23 *O. J. L. S.* 1.

(2003b), Will Executive Pay Globalise Along American Lines, 11 *Corporate Governance* 8 (similar version published as: Cheffins, Brian R., and Thomas, Randall S., Regulation and the Globalization (Americanization) of Executive Pay, in: Milhaupt, Curtis J. (ed.), *Global Markets, Domestic Institutions*, New York: Columbia University Press, 2003, p. 155).

(2003c), Mergers and Corporate Ownership Structure: The United States and Germany at the Turn of the 20th Century, 51 *Am. J. Comp. L.* 473.

(2006), Dividends as a Substitute for Corporate Law: The Separation of Ownership and Control in the United Kingdom, 63 *Washington and Lee Law Review* 1273.

Chen, Albert H. Y. (1999), Towards a Legal Enlightenment: Discussions in Contemporary China on the Rule of Law, 17 *UCLA Pac. Basin L.J.* 125.

Choi, Stephen J. (2002), Channeling Competition in Global Securities Markets, 16 *Transnat'l Law.* 111.

Clark, Gordon L. (2002), European Pensions and Global Finance: Continuity or Convergence?, 7 *New Political Economy* 67.

Clarke, Donald (2006a), The Independent Director in Chinese Corporate Governance, 36 *Del. J. Corp. L.* 125.

(2006b), Lost in Translation? Corporate Legal Transplants in China, Working Paper, available at http://ssrn.com/abstract=913784.

Clarke, Donald, Murrell, Peter, and Whiting, Susan (2006), The Role of Law in China's Economic Development, Working Paper, available at http://ssrn.com/abstract=878672.

Clarke, Michael G. (1991), The Conflicts of Law Dimension, in: Trenton, Celia A. (ed.), *Corporate Law: The European Dimension*, London: Butterworths, p. 161.

Claussen, Carsten Peter, and Bröcker, Norbert (2000), Corporate-Governance-Grundsätze in Deutschland – Nützliche Orientierungshilfe oder regulatorisches Übermaß?, *AG* 481.

Coase, Ronald H. (1937), The Nature of the Firm, 4 *Economica* 386.

Coffee, John C. (1991), Liquidity versus Control: The Institutional Investor as Corporate Monitor, 91 *Colum. L. Rev.* 1277.

(1996), Organhaftung im amerikanischen Recht, in: Feddersen, Dieter, Hommelhoff, Peter, and Schneider, Uwe H. (eds.), *Corporate Governance*, Cologne: Otto Schmidt, p. 165.

(1999a), Privatization and Corporate Governance: The Lessons from Securities Market Failure, 25 *J. Corp. L.* 1.

(1999b), The Future as History: The Prospects for Global Convergence in Corporate Governance and Its Implications, 93 *Nw. U. L. Rev.* 641.

(2001), The Rise of Dispersed Ownership: The Roles of Law and the State in the Separation of Ownership and Control, 111 *Yale L.J.* 1 (also published in: Hopt, Klaus J., and Wymeersch, Eddy (eds.), *Capital Markets and Company Law*, Oxford: Oxford University Press, 2003, p. 663).

(2002a), Convergence and Its Critics: What Are the Preconditions to the Separation of Ownership and Control?, in: McCahery, Joseph A., Moerland, Piet, Raaijmakers, Theo, and Renneboog, Luc (eds.), *Corporate Governance Regimes – Convergence and Diversity*, Oxford: Oxford University Press, p. 83.

(2002b), Racing Towards the Top?: The Impact of Cross-Listings and Stock Market Competition on International Corporate Governance, 102 *Colum. L. Rev.* 1757 (shorter version also published in: Milhaupt, Curtis J. (ed.), *Global Markets, Domestic Institutions*, New York: Columbia University Press, 2003, p. 437).

(2003), What Caused Enron?, in: Cornelius, Peter, and Kogut, Bruce Mitchel, *Corporate Governance and Capital Flows in a Global Economy*, Oxford: Oxford University Press, p. 29.

Comberg, Philip (2000), *Die Organisationsverfassung der Aktiengesellschaft in China*, Hamburg: Institut für Asienkunde.

Company Law Reform (2005), Presented to Parliament by the Secretary of State for Trade and Industry by Command of Her Majesty, Cm 6456, available at www.dti.gov.uk/cld/WhitePaper.pdf.

Conard, Alfred (1969), Fundamental Changes in Marketable Share Companies, in: Conard, Alfred (ed.), *International Encyclopedia of Comparative Law*, Tübingen: Mohr Siebeck, Ch. 6.

Conrad, Harald (2003), Sustaining Old Age Security in Japan: Towards a New Public–Private Mix, 15 *ZJapanR* 199.

Cook, Jennifer and Deakin, Simon (1999), Stakeholding and Corporate Governance: Theory and Evidence on Economic Performance, Resesarch Paper, available at www.cbr.cam.ac.uk/publications/index.htm.

Cools, Sofie (2005), The Real Difference in Corporate Law Between the United States and Continental Europe: Distribution of Powers, 30 *Del. J. Corp. L.* 697.

Cornelius, Peter, and Kogut, Bruce Mitchel (2003), Introduction, in: Cornelius, Peter, and Kogut, Bruce Mitchel (eds.), *Corporate Governance and Capital Flows in a Global Economy*, Oxford: Oxford University Press, p. 1.

Cornette de Saint-Cyr, Anne Sophie (2002), Cross-Border Mergers, *ICCLR* 343.

Cox, James D., and Hazen, Thomas Lee (2003), *Corporations*, 2nd edition, New York: Aspen.

Crabb, Kelly (1987), The Reality of Extralegal Barriers to Mergers and Acquisitions in Japan, 21 *Int. L.* 97 (also published in: Milhaupt, Curtis J. (ed.), *Japanese Law in Context: Readings in Society, the Economy, and Politics*, Cambridge, MA: Harvard University Asia Center, 2001, p. 490).

Crook, Kimberley (2004), Accounting for Share-Based Remuneration, in: Ferrarini, Guido, Hopt, Klaus J., Winter, Jaap, and Wymeersch, Eddy (eds.), *Reforming Company and Takeover Law in Europe*, Oxford: Oxford University Press, p. 347.

Cruz, Peter de (1999), *Comparative Law in a Changing World*, 2nd edition, London: Cavendish.

Cunningham, Lawrence A. (1999), Commonalities and Prescriptions in the Vertical Dimension of Global Corporate Governance, 84 *Cornell L. Rev.* 1133.

Da Costa, Carla Tavares, and Bilreiro, Alexandra de Meester (2003), *The European Company Statute*, The Hague: Kluwer Law International.

Dahrendorf, Ralf (2002), *Die Krisen der Demokratie*, Munich: Beck.

Dalloz (2005), *Code des sociétés et des marchés financiers*, 21st edition, Paris: Dalloz.

Dam, Kenneth W. (2006), China As a Test Case: Is the Rule of Law Essential for Economic Growth, Working Paper, available at http://ssrn.com/abstract_id=880125.

Daniels, Ronald J. (1991), Should Provinces Compete? The Case for a Competitive Corporate Law Market, 36 *McGill Law Journal* 138.

Darvas, Paula (2000), Australia: Corporate Law: Into the Next Millennium, 21 *Comp. Law.* 101.

Davies, Paul L. (1997a), Institutional Investors as Corporate Monitors in the UK, in: Hopt, Klaus J., and Wymeersch, Eddy (eds.), *Comparative Corporate Governance – Essays and Materials*, Berlin: de Gruyter, p. 47.

(1997b), *Gower's Principles of Modern Company Law*, London: Sweet & Maxwell, 6th edition.

(1999), United Kingdom, in: Baums, Theodor, and Wymeersch, Eddy (eds.), *Shareholder Voting Rights and Practices in Europe and the United States*, London: Kluwer Law International, p. 331.

(2001), Struktur der Unternehmensführung in Großbritannien und Deutschland – Konvergenz oder fortbestehende Divergenz?, *ZGR* 268 (English version in (2002) 2 *ICCLJ* 435).

(2003), *Gower and Davies' Principles of Modern Company Law* 7th edition, London: Sweet & Maxwell.

(2004), Post-Enron Developments in the United Kingdom, in: Ferrarini, Guido, Hopt, Klaus J., Winter, Jaap, and Wymeersch, Eddy (eds.), *Reforming Company and Takeover Law in Europe*, Oxford: Oxford University Press, p. 185.

Davies, Paul L., and Hopt, Klaus J. (2004), Control Transactions, in: Kraakman, Reinier, Davies, Paul, Hansmann, Henry, Hertig, Gérard, Hopt, Klaus J., Kanda, Hideki, and Rock, Edward, *The Anatomy of Corporate Law*, Oxford: Oxford University Press, p. 157.

Davis, Stephen M. (1999), Bridging the Accountability Gap: An Agenda for Global Share Voting Reform, in: Baums, Theodor, and Wymeersch, Eddy (eds.), *Shareholder Voting Rights and Practices in Europe and the United States*, London: Kluwer Law International, p. 383.

De Kluiver, Harm-Jan, and Van Gerven, Walter (eds.), *The European Private Company?*, Antwerp: Maklu, p. 21.

Deakin, Simon (2001), Regulatory Competition versus Harmonization in European Company Law, in: Esty, Daniel C., and Geradin, Damien (eds.), *Regulatory Competition and Economic Integration*, Oxford: Oxford University Press, p. 190.

Dean, Meryll (2002), *Japanese Legal System*, 2nd edition, London: Cavendish.

Deminor (2005), Application of the One Share–One Vote Principle in Europe, available at www.abi.org.uk/BookShop/ResearchReports/DEMINOR_REPORT.pdf.

Deng, Jiong (2005), Building an Investor-Friendly Shareholder Derivative Lawsuit System in China, 46 *Harv. Int'l L.J.* 347.

Dernauer, Marc (2005), Die japanische Gesellschaftsrechtsreform 2005/2006, 20 *ZJapanR* 123.

Deutscher Notarverein e.V. (2001), Stellungnahme zum Fragenkatalog der Regierungskommission 'Corporate Governance – Unternehmensführung, Unternehmenskontrolle, Modernisierung des Aktienrechts' v. 20.09.2000, *NZG* 185.

Dine, Janet (1995), Private Property and Corporate Governance, Part II, Content of Directors' Duties and Remedies, in: Macmillan (Patfield), Fiona (ed.), *Perspectives on Company Law*, Volume 1, The Hague: Kluwer Law International, p. 115.

(2005), *Companies, International Trade and Human Rights*, Cambridge: Cambridge University Press.

(2006), Drafting Company Law in Transition Economies, 1 *JCL* 338.

Dodd, Peter (1932), For Whom Are Corporate Managers Trustees?, 45 *Harv. L. Rev.* 1145.

Dodd, Peter, and Leftwich, Richard (1980), The Market for Corporate Charters: Unhealthy Competition vs. Federal Regulation, in: Posner, Richard A., and Scott, Kenneth E., *Economics of Corporation Law and Securities Regulation*, Boston and Toronto: Little, Brown and Company, p. 100.

Donald, David C. (2005), Shareholder Voice and Its Opponents, 5 *JCLS* 305.

Dooley, Michael P., and Goldman, Michael D. (2001), Some Comparisons Between the Model Business Corporation Act and the Delaware General Corporation Law, 56 *Bus. Law.* 737.

Dore, Ronald (2000), *Stock Market Capitalism: Welfare Capitalism, Japan and German versus the Anglo-Saxon*, Oxford: Oxford University Press.

Doremus, Paul N., Keller, William W., Pauly, Louis W., and Reich, Simon (1998), *The Myth of the Global Corporation*, Princeton: Princeton University Press.

Downs, Anthony (1968), *Ökonomische Theorie der Demokratie*, Tübingen: Mohr (original version: *An Economic Theory of Democracy*, 1957).

Dreher, Meinrad (1999), Wettbewerb oder Vereinheitlichung der Rechtsordnungen in Europa?, *JZ* 105.

Drobnig, Ulrich (1986), Rechtsvergleichung in der deutschen Rechtssprechung, 50 *RabelsZ* 610.

Drobnig, Ulrich, and Van Erp, Sjef (eds.) (1998), *The Use of Comparative Law by Courts*, The Hague: Kluwer Law International.

Druey, Jean Nicholas (1999), General Report, in: Baums, Theodor, and Wymeersch, Eddy (eds.), *Shareholder Voting Rights and Practices in Europe and the United States*, London: Kluwer Law International, p. 367.

Drury, Robert R. (1998), The Regulation and Recognition of Foreign Corporations: Responses to the Delaware Syndrome, 57 *CLJ* 165.

Drygala, Tim (2001), Die Vorschläge der SLIM-Arbeitsgruppe zur Vereinfachung des Europäischen Gesellschaftsrechts, *AG* 291.

DSW-Europastudie (1999), *Eine rechtsvergleichende Studie über Minderheitenrechte der Aktionäre sowie Stimmrechtsausübung und -vertretung in Europa*, Deutsche Schutzvereinigung für Wertpapierbesitz eV.

Ducouloux-Favard, Claude (1992), L'histoire des grandes sociétés en Allemagne, en France et en Italie, *Rev.int.dr.comp.* 849.

Dunlavy, Colleen A. (1998), Corporate Governance in the Late 19th Century Europe and the US – The Case of Shareholder Voting Rights, in: Hopt, Klaus J., Kanda, Hideki, Roe, Mark J., Wymeersch, Eddy, and Prigge, Stefan (eds.), *Comparative Corporate Governance: The State of Art and Emerging Research*, Oxford: Clarendon, p. 5.

Dyck, Alexander, and Zingales, Luigi (2004), Private Benefits of Control: An International Comparison, 49 *J. Finance* 537.

Easterbrook, Frank H. (1996), Federalism and European Business Law, in: Buxbaum, Richard M., Hertig, Gerard, Hirsch, Alain, and Hopt, Klaus J. (eds.), *European Economic and Business Law*, Berlin: de Gruyter, p. 1.

Easterbrook, Frank H., and Fischel, Daniel R. (1991), *The Economic Structure of Corporate Law*, Cambridge, MA: Harvard University Press.

Ebke, Werner F. (1999a), Das Schicksal der Sitztheorie nach dem Centros-Urteil des EuGH, *JZ* 656.

(1999b), Unternehmensrechtsangleichung in der Europäischen Union: Brauchen wir ein European Law Institute?, *Festschrift Großfeld* 189.

(2000), Accounting, Auditing and Global Capital Market, in: Baums, Theodor, Hopt, Klaus J., and Horn, Norbert (eds.), *Corporations, Capital Markets and Business in the Law (Liber Amicorum Buxbaum)*, London: Kluwer, p. 113.

(2002), Wirtschaft und Recht im Zeichen der Globalisierung, *Festschrift Druey* 99.

Edwards, Vanessa (1999), *EC Company Law*, Oxford: Clarendon.

(2004), The Directive on Takeover Bids – Not Worth the Paper It's Written On?, 1 *ECFR* 416.

Eidenmüller, Horst (1997), Rechtsanwendung, Gesetzgebung und ökonomische Analyse, 197 *AcP* 80.

Eisele, Ursula Shibumi (2001), Die neuen Vorschriften des Aktientauschs und der Aktienübertragung: Einführung und Gesetzesübersetzung, 11 *ZJapanR* 223.

(2004a), *Holdinggesellschaften in Japan: Entwicklung, Verbot, Wiederzulassung und aktueller Rechtsrahmen*, Tübingen: Mohr Siebeck.

(2004b), Konzerneigenschaft horizontaler japanischer Unternehmensgruppen?, 17 *ZJapanR* 115.

Eisenberg, Melvin A. (1989), The Structure of Corporate Law, 89 *Colum. L. Rev.* 1461.

(1999), The Conception that the Corporation Is a Nexus of Contracts, and the Dual Nature of the Firm, 24 *J. Corp. L.* 819.

Ekkenga, Jens (1998), *Anlegerschutz, Rechnungslegung und Kapitalmarkt*, Tübingen: Mohr Siebeck.

Ellett, Fiona (2000), Australia and the UK on the Quest for the Best Corporate Practice, in: Macmillan, Fiona (ed.), *International Corporate Law*, Volume 1, Oxford: Hart, p. 173.

Elsing, Siegfried H., and Van Alstine, Michael P. (1999), *US-amerikanisches Handels- und Wirtschaftsrecht*, 2nd edition, Heidelberg: Recht und Wirtschaft.

Enriques, Luca (2000), The Law on Corporate Directors' Self-Dealing: A Comparative Analysis, 2 *ICCLJ* 297.

(2002), Do Corporate Law Judges Matter? Some Evidence from Milan, 3 *EBOR* 765 (shorter version also published as: Off the Books, But on the Record:

Evidence from Italy on the Relevance of Judges to Quality of Corporate Law, in: Milhaupt, Curtis J. (ed.), *Global Markets, Domestic Institutions*, New York: Columbia University Press, 2003, p. 257).

(2004a), Silence Is Golden: The European Company as a Catalyst for Company Law Arbitrage, 4 *JCLS* 77.

(2004b), EC Company Law and the Fears of a European Delaware, *EBLR* 1259.

Erhardt, Olaf, and Nowak, Eric (2002), Die Durchsetzung von Corporate-Governance-Regeln, *AG* 336.

Escher-Weingart, Christina (2001), *Reform durch Deregulierung im Kapitalgesellschaftsrecht*, Tübingen: Mohr Siebeck.

Esty, Daniel C., and Geradin, Damien (eds.) (2001), *Regulatory Competition and Economic Integration*, Oxford: Oxford University Press.

Eucken, Walter (1990), *Grundsätze der Wirtschaftspolitik*, 6th edition, Tübingen: Mohr.

Euroshareholders Corporate Governance Guidelines (2000), available at www.ecgi.org/codes/documents/european_shareholders.pdf.

Ewing, Keith, and Issacharoff, Samuel (eds.) (2006), *Party Funding and Campaign Financing in International Perspective*, Oxford: Hart.

Expert Group on Cross-Border Voting (2002), *Consultative Document on Cross-Border Voting in Europe and Final Report*.

Fabritius, Andreas (2004), Aktuelle Fragen des Übernahmerechts, Erfahrungen aus der Praxis, in: Gesellschaftsrechtliche Vereinigung (ed.), *Gesellschaftsrecht in der Diskussion 2003*, Cologne: Otto Schmidt, p. 45.

Fama, Eugene (1970), Efficient Capital Markets: A Review of Theory and Empirical Work, 25 *J. Finance* 383.

(1980), Agency Problems and the Theory of the Firm, 88 *J. Polit. Economy* 288.

Fama, Eugene, and Jensen, Michael (1983), Separation of Ownership and Control, 26 *J. L. & Econ.* 301.

Fanto, James A. (1998), The Role of Corporate Law in French Corporate Governance, 31 *Cornell Int'l L.J.* 31.

Farrar, John H. (2001), Developing Appropriate Corporate Governance in China, 22 *Comp. Law.* 92.

Farrar, John H., Furey, Nigel E., Hannigan, Brenda M., and Wylie, Philip (1998), *Company Law*, 4th edition, London, Dublin, Edinburgh: Butterworths.

Faugérolas, Laurent (2003), Impact of the Takeovers and Their Regulation on French Company Law and Practice in: Hopt, Klaus J., and Wymeersch, Eddy (eds.), *Capital Markets and Company Law*, Oxford: Oxford University Press, p. 327.

Ferran, Eílis (1999), *Company Law and Corporate Finance*, Oxford: Oxford University Press.

(2001), Corporate Law, Codes and Social Norms – Finding the Right Regulatory Combination and Institutional Structure, 1 *JCLS* 381.

(2003a), Legal Capital Rules and Modern Securities Markets – The Case for Reform, as Illustrated by the UK Equity Markets, in: Hopt, Klaus J., and Wymeersch, Eddy (eds.), *Capital Markets and Company Law*, Oxford: Oxford University Press, p. 115.

(2003b), The Role of the Shareholder in Internal Corporate Governance: Enabling Shareholders to Make Better-Informed Decisions, 4 *EBOR* 491 (also published in: Ferrarini, Guido, Hopt, Klaus J., Winter, Jaap, and Wymeersch, Eddy (eds.), *Reforming Company and Takeover Law in Europe*, Oxford: Oxford University Press, 2004, p. 417).

(2004), *Building an EU Securities Market*, Cambridge: Cambridge University Press.

Ferrarini, Guido (2003), Shareholder Value and the Modernisation of European Corporate Law, in: Hopt, Klaus J., and Wymeersch, Eddy (eds.), *Capital Markets and Company Law*, Oxford: Oxford University Press, p. 223.

Ferrarini Guido, and Moloney, Niamh (2004), Executive Remuneration and Corporate Governance in the EU: Convergence, Divergence, and Reform Perspectives in: Ferrarini, Guido, Hopt, Klaus J., Winter, Jaap, and Wymeersch, Eddy (eds.), *Reforming Company and Takeover Law in Europe*, Oxford: Oxford University Press, p. 267.

Fleischer, Holger (2001), Grundfragen der ökonomischen Theorie im Gesellschafts- und Kapitalmarktrecht, *ZGR* 1.

(2002), Das neue Recht des Squeeze out, *ZGR* 757.

(2004), The Responsibility of the Management and Its Enforcement, in: Ferrarini, Guido, Hopt, Klaus J., Winter, Jaap, and Wymeersch, Eddy (eds.), *Reforming Company and Takeover Law in Europe*, Oxford: Oxford University Press, p. 373.

Fleischer, Holger, and Jänig, Ronny (2002), Verantwortlichkeit für falsche Kapitalmarktinformationen in Frankreich – das droit des marchés financiers, *RIW* 729.

Fleischhauer, Jens (2001), Hauptversammlung und Neue Medien, *ZIP* 1133.

Flume, Werner (1960), *Grundfragen der Aktienrechtsreform*, Düsseldorf: Handelsblatt.

Förster, Christian (2002), Die Bedeutung der Unternehmensgröße in Japan am Beispiel der Mindestkapital- und Publizitätsregelungen, 14 *ZJapanR* 91.

Forsthoff, Ulrich (2000), Rechts- und Parteifähigkeit ausländischer Gesellschaften mit Verwaltungssitz in Deutschland? – Die Sitztheorie vor dem EuGH, *DB* 1109.

Forstinger, Christin M. (2002), Delawares komparative Vorteile, *ZfRV* 41.

Foster, Nicholas H. D. (2000), Company Law Theory in Comparative Perspective: England and France, 48 *Am. J. Comp. L.* 573.

(2006), Perception, Language and Reality in Corporate Law Theory, 17 *King's College Law Journal* 299.

Franke, Siegried F. (1996), *(Ir) rationale Politik?*, Marburg: Metropolis.

Fraune, Christian (1996), *Der Einfluss institutioneller Anleger in der Hauptversammlung*, Cologne: Heymanns.

Freitag, Robert (1999), Der Wettbewerb der Rechtsordnungen im Internationalen Gesellschaftsrecht, *EuZW* 267.

Frentrop, Paul (2002), *A History of Corporate Governance*, Brussels: Deminor.

Frey, Bruno S. (1980), Ökonomische Theorie der Politik, in: Albers, Willi *et al.* (eds.), *Handwörterbuch der Wirtschaftswissenschaft*, Stuttgart: Fischer, Volume 5, p. 658.

Friedl, Markus J. (2002), Ein Plädoyer für Tracking Stocks, *BB* 157.

Friedman, Lawrence (1990), Some Thoughts on Comparative Legal Culture, in: Clark, David S. (ed.), *Comparative Law and Private International Law: Essays in Honour of John Henry Merryman*, Berlin: Duncker & Humblot, p. 49.

Fu, Peggy H. (2001), Developing Venture Capital Laws in China: Lessons Learned from the United States, Germany and Japan, 23 *Loy. L.A. Int'l & Comp. L.J.* 487.

Fu-Tomlinson, Yingxi (2005), Red Tape Casts Shadow on Cross-Border M&A, in *IFLR Guide to China.*

Fukushima, Glen S. (1988), The Liberalization of Legal Services in Japan: A US Government Negotiator's Perspective, 21 *Law in Japan* 5 (also published in: Milhaupt, Curtis J. (ed.), *Japanese Law in Context: Readings in Society, the Economy, and Politics*, Cambridge, MA: Harvard University Asia Center, 2001, p. 61).

Fukuyama, Francis (1992), *The End of History and the Last Man*, New York: Free Press.

Gebhardt, Immanuel (1999), Der chinesische Kapitalmarkt auf dem Weg zu neuen Regelungen, *Newsletter der Deutsch-Chinesischen Juristenvereinigung*, 1999/2.

Geiger, Rainer (1998), Towards a Multilateral Agreement on Investment, 31 *Cornell Int'l L.J.* 467.

Gelter, Martin (2004), Wettbewerbsbedingungen im europäischen Gesellschaftsrecht, *ZfRV* 170.

(2005), The Structure of Regulatory Competition in European Corporate Law, 5 *JCLS* 247.

Gerke, Wolfgang, Bank, Matthias, and Steiger, Max (2003), The Changing Role of Institutional Investors – A German Perspective in: Hopt, Klaus J., and Wymeersch, Eddy (eds.), *Capital Markets and Company Law*, Oxford: Oxford University Press, p. 357.

Gerken, Lüder (ed.) (1995), *Competition among Institutions*, London: Macmillan.

Gessner, Volkmar (1998), Globalization and Legal Certainty, in: Gessner, Volkmar, and Buda, Ali Cem (eds.), *Emerging Legal Certainty: Empirical Studies on the Globalization of Law*, Aldershot: Ashgate, p. 427.

Gessner, Volkmar and Budak, Ali Cem (1998), Introduction, in Gessner, Volkmar and Buda, Ali Cem (eds.), *Emerging Legal Certainty: Empirical Studies on the Globalization of Law*, Aldershot: Ashgate, p. 3.

Gierke, Otto von (1954), *Das deutsche Genossenschaftsrecht*, Volume I, Darmstadt: Wissenschaftliche Buchgemeinschaft (first published in 1868).

Gilson, Ronald J. (2001), Globalizing Corporate Governance: Convergence of Form or Function, 49 *Am. J. Comp. L.* 329 (also published in: Gordon, Jeffrey N., and Roe, Mark J. (eds.), *Convergence and Persistence in Corporate Governance*, Cambridge: Cambridge University Press, 2004, p. 128).

Gilson, Ronald J., and Gordon, Jeffrey N. (2003), Controlling Controlling Shareholders, 152 *U. Penn. L. Rev*. 785.

Ginsburg Thomas B. (2001), In Defense of 'Japanese Law', 12 *ZJapanR* 27.

(2005), The Regulation of Regulation: Judicialization, Convergence, and Divergence in Administrative Law, in: Hopt, Klaus J., Wymeersch, Eddy, Kanda, Hideki, and Baum, Harald (eds.), *Corporate Governance in Context*, Oxford: Oxford University Press, 321.

Glanzmann, Lukas (2002), Das Proporzwahlverfahren (cumulative voting) als Instrument der Corporate Governance, *Festschrift Druey* 401.

Glenn, H. Patrick (1993), La civilisation de la common law, *Rev.int.dr.comp*. 559.

(2004), *Legal Traditions of the World*, 2nd edition, Oxford: Oxford University Press.

Goddard, Robert (2003), 'Modernising Company Law': The Government's White Paper, 66 *MLR* 402.

Goergen, Marc, and Renneboog, Luc (2001), Strong Managers and Passive Institutional Investors in the UK, in: Barca, Fabrizio, and Becht, Marco (eds.), *The Control of Corporate Europe*, Oxford: Oxford University Press, p. 259.

Goldman, Michael D., and Filliben, Eileen M. (2000), Corporate Governance: Current Trends and Likely Developments for the Twenty-First Century, 25 *Del. J. Corp. L.* 683.

Gompers, Paul A., Ishii, Joy L., and Metrick, Andrew (2003), Corporate Governance and Equity Prices, 118 *Q.J. Econ*. 107.

Gordley, James (1993), Common law und civil law: Eine überholte Unterscheidung, *ZEuP* 493.

(2001), Legal Reasoning: Some Parallels in Common Law and Civil Law, in: Assmann, Heinz-Dieter, Brüggemann, Gert, and Sethe, Rolf (eds.), *Unterschiedliche Rechtskulturen – Konvergenz des Rechtsdenkens/Different Legal Cultures – Convergence of Legal Reasoning*, Baden-Baden: Nomos, p. 63.

Gordon, Jeffrey N. (1989), The Mandatory Structure of Corporate Law, 89 *Colum. L. Rev*. 1549.

(1991), Shareholder Initiative: A Social Choice and Game Theoretic Approach to Corporate Law, 60 *U. Cin. L. Rev*. 347.

(1994), Relational Investors: A New Look at Cumulative Voting, 94 *Colum. L. Rev.* 124.

(1999), Pathways to Corporate Convergence? Two Steps on the Road to Shareholder Capitalism in Germany: Deutsche Telekom and Daimler Chrysler, 5 *Colum. J. Eur. L.* 219.

(2003), Convergence on Shareholder Capitalism: An Internationalist Perspective, in: Milhaupt, Curtis J. (ed.), *Global Markets, Domestic Institutions*, New York: Columbia University Press, p. 214.

(2004), The International Relations Wedge in the Corporate Convergence Debate, in Gordon, Jeffrey N., and Roe, Mark J. (eds.), *Convergence and Persistence in Corporate Governance*, Cambridge: Cambridge University Press, p. 161.

Goshen Zohar (2003), Controlling Corporate Self-Dealing: Convergence or Path-Dependency, in: Milhaupt, Curtis J. (ed.), *Global Markets, Domestic Institutions*, New York: Columbia University Press, p. 15.

Goulding, Simon (1995), The Private Company in the United Kingdom, in: De Kluiver, Harm-Jan, and Van Gerven, Walter (eds.), *The European Private Company?*, Antwerp: Maklu, p. 55.

Grant, Wyn (2000), Globalisation, Big Business and the Blair Government, CSGR Working Paper No. 58/00, available at www2.warwick.ac.uk/fac/soc/csgr/research/abstracts/abwp5800/.

Grantham, Ross (1998), The Doctrinal Basis of the Rights of Company Shareholders, 57 *CLJ* 554.

Green, Nick (2001), *Corporate Finance Guideline*, Institute of Chartered Accountants.

Grier, Nicholas (1998), *UK Company Law*, Chichester: Wiley.

Griffin, Stephen (2000), *Company Law*, Harlow: Pearson, 3rd edition.

Großfeld, Bernhard (1971), Management and Control of Marketable Share Companies, in: Conard, Alfred (ed.), *International Encyclopedia of Comparative Law*, Tübingen: Mohr Siebeck, Ch. 4.

(1995), *Internationales und Europäisches Unternehmensrecht. Das Organisationsrecht transnationaler Unternehmen*, 2nd edition, Heidelberg: C. F. Müller.

(1996), *Kernfragen der Rechtsvergleichung*, Tübingen: Mohr.

(1998), *Bilanzrecht*, 3rd edition, Heidelberg: C. F. Müller.

(2001), *Rechtsvergleichung*, Wiesbaden, Westdeutscher Verlag.

(2002), Cross-Border Mergers: Corporate Accounting/Corporate Valuation, 101 *ZVglRWiss* 1.

Großfeld, Bernhard, and Deilmann, Barbara (1990), Historische und gegenwärtige Entwicklungen im deutschen Aktienrecht, in: Coing, Helmut, Hirano, Ryuichi, Kitagawa, Zentaro, Murakami, Junichi, Nörr, Knut Wolfgang, Oppermann, Thomas, and Shiono, Hiroshi (eds.), *Die Japanisierung des westlichen Rechts*, Tübingen: Mohr Siebeck, p. 255.

Großkommentar zum AktG (1992–) (eds. Hopt, Klaus J., and Wiedemann, Herbert), 4th edition, Berlin: de Gruyter.

Group of German Experts on Corporate Law (2002), *Stellungnahme zum Konsultationsdokument der High Level Group on Corporate Law*, available at www.jura.uni-duesseldorf.de/dozenten/noack/texte/sonstige/hlg.pdf.

Grumann, Marc-Olaf, and Soehlke, Raphael (2001), Namensaktie und Hauptversammlung, *DB* 576.

Grundmann, Stefan (2001), Wettbewerb der Regelgeber im Europäischen Gesellschaftsrecht – jedes Marktsegment hat seine Struktur, *ZGR* 783 (English version: Regulatory Competition in European Company Law – Some Different Genius?, in: Ferrarini, Guido, Hopt, Klaus J., and Wymeersch, Eddy (eds.), *Capital Markets in the Age of the Euro*, The Hague: Kluwer Law International, 2002, p. 561).

Grundmann, Stefan, and Möslein, Florian (2003), Die Goldene Aktie und der Markt für Unternehmenskontrolle im Rechtsvergleich – insbesondere Staatskontrolle, Höchst- und Mehrfachstimmrechte sowie Übernahmemaßnahmen, 102 *ZVglRWiss* 289.

Grunewald, Barbara (1997), Das Recht zum Austritt aus der Aktiengesellschaft, *Festschrift Claussen* 103.

Gesellschaftsrecht (2002), 5th edition, Tübingen: Mohr Siebeck.

Gruson, Michael (2001), Global Shares of German Corporations and Their Dual Listings on the Frankfurt and New York Stock Exchanges, 22 *U. Pa. J. Int'l Econ. L.* 185.

Guo, Richard (2006), Foreign Buyers Get First Bite at G-share Market, February 2006 *IFLR* 41.

Guobadia, D. A. (2001), The Rules of Good Corporate Governance and the Methods of Efficient Implementation: A Nigerian Perspective, 22 *Comp. Law.* 119.

Guntz, Peter (1997), *Treuebindungen von Minderheitsaktionären*, Berlin: Duncker & Humblot.

Guyon, Yves (1995), Wandelschuldverschreibungen und Optionsanleihen im französischen Recht, *ZGR* 208.

(1998), Zur Gestaltungsfreiheit im französischen Gesellschaftsrecht, in: Lutter, Marcus, and Wiedemann, Herbert, *Gestaltungsfreiheit und Gesellschaftsrecht*, Berlin: de Gruyter, p. 297.

(1999), France, in: Baums, Theodor, and Wymeersch, Eddy (eds.), *Shareholder Voting Rights and Practices in Europe and the United States*, London: Kluwer Law International, p. 95.

Habersack, Mathias (1996), *Die Mitgliedschaft – subjektives und 'sonstiges' Recht*, Tübingen: Mohr.

(2001), Aktienrecht und Internet, 165 *ZHR* 172.

Haley, John O. (1978), The Myth of the Reluctant Litigant, 4 *JJS* 359.

(1988), Redefining the Scope of Practice under Japan's New Regime for Regulating Foreign Lawyers, 21 *Law in Japan* 18 (also published in: Milhaupt, Curtis J. (ed.), *Japanese Law in Context: Readings in Society, the Economy, and Politics*, Cambridge, MA: Harvard University Asia Center, 2001, p. 58).

Hall, Art Alcausin (2001), International Banking Regulation into the 21st Century: Flirting with Revolution, 21 *N.Y.L. Sch. J. Int'l & Comp. L.* 41.

Hall, Peter A., and Soskice, David (eds.) (2001), *Varieties of Capitalism*, Oxford: Oxford University Press.

Hamermesh, Lawrence A. (1998), Corporate Democracy and Stockholder-Adopted By-Laws: Taking Back the Street?, 73 *Tul. L. Rev.* 409.

Hamilton, Robert W. (1992), *Corporations*, 3rd edition, St Paul, MN: West.

Hanloser, Stefan (2001), Proxy-Voting, Remote-Voting und Online-HV – § 134 III 3 AktG nach dem NaStraG, *NZG* 355.

Hansmann, Henry, and Kraakman, Reinier (2001), The End of History for Corporate Law, 88 *Geo. L.J.* 439 (also published in: Gordon, Jeffrey N., and Roe, Mark J. (eds.), *Convergence and Persistence in Corporate Governance*, Cambridge: Cambridge University Press, 2004, p. 33, also published as: Towards a Single Model of Corporate Law? in: McCahery, Joseph A., Moerland, Piet, Raaijmakers, Theo, and Renneboog, Luc (eds.), *Corporate Governance Regimes – Convergence and Diversity*, Oxford: Oxford University Press, 2002, p. 56).

(2004), What Is Corporate Law?; Agency Problems and Legal Strategies; The Basic Governance Structure, all in: Kraakman, Reinier, Davies, Paul, Hansmann, Henry, Hertig, Gérard, Hopt, Klaus J., Kanda, Hideki, and Rock, Edward, *The Anatomy of Corporate Law*, Oxford: Oxford University Press, pp. 1, 21 and 33.

Hantke-Domas, Michael (2003), The Public Interest Theory of Regulation: Non-Existence or Misinterpretation?, 15 *Europ. J. Law & Econ.* 165.

Harbarth, Stephan (2001), Abwehr feindlicher Übernahmen in den USA, 100 *ZVglRWiss* 275.

Hardt, Michael, and Negri, Antonio (2000), *Empire*, Cambridge, MA: Harvard University Press.

Hartmann, Lutz (2000), Die französischen Société par Actions Simplifiée – eine zukunftsweisende Gesellschaftsform, *WM* 1530.

Hashimoto, Motomi (2002), Commercial Code Revisions: Promoting the Evolution of Japanese Companies, Nomura Research Institute Paper No. 48, available at www.nri.co.jp/english/opinion/papers/index.html.

Hatzis-Schoch, Brent (1992), Die Bedeutung von Delaware für das US-amerikanische Gesellschaftsrecht, *RIW* 539.

Hay, Colin (2004), Common Trajectories, Variable Paces, Divergent Outcomes? Models of European Capitalism under Conditions of Complex Economic Interdependence, 11 *Rev. Int. Polit. Economy* 231.

Hayakawa, Masara (1996), Die Aktionärsklage im japanischen Gesellschaftsrecht, *Festschrift Mestmäcker* 891.

(1997), Shareholders in Japan: Attitudes, Conduct, Legal Rights, and Their Enforcement, in: Baum, Harald (ed.), *Japan: Economic Success and Legal System*, Berlin: de Gruyter, p. 235.

(2002), Die Reform des Gesellschaftsrecht vom Mai 2002 und Corporate Governance in Japan, 14 *ZJapanR* 31.

(2003), Die Neuregelung von Verschmelzung, Spaltung und Gründung von Holding-Gesellschaften, 16 *ZJapanR* 59.

Hayakawa, Masaru, and Raidl-Marcure, Elisabeth (1992), Japanische Gesellschaftsrechtsreform: Teilnovelle 1991 zum Aktien- und GmbH-Recht, *RIW* 282.

Hayek, Friedrich August von (1978), Competition as a Discovery Procedure, in: Hayek, Friedrich August von (ed.), *New Studies in Philosophy, Politics, Economics and the History of Ideas*, Chicago: Chicago University Press, p. 179.

Heilmann, Sebastian (2001a), Der chinesische Aktienmarkt (I). Staatliche Regulierung und institutioneller Wandel, Working Paper China Analysis No. 3, available at www.chinapolitik.de/studien/index.htm.

(2001b), Der chinesische Aktienmarkt (II). Schlüsselakteure und inoffizielle Spielregeln, Working Paper China Analysis No. 4, available at www.chinapolitik.de/studien/index.htm.

Heine, Klaus (2003), *Regulierungswettbewerb im Gesellschaftsrecht*, Berlin: Duncker & Humblot.

Heine, Klaus, and Kerber, Wolfgang (2002), European Corporate Laws, Regulatory Competition and Path Dependence, 13 *Europ. J. Law & Econ.* 47.

Heiser, Kristian (2000), Can Securities Law Approaches Be Harmonised with Essential Principles of Company Law?, *EBLR* 60.

Hellwig, Hans-Jürgen (2001), Angleichung des Gesellschaftsrechts in Europa – Notwendigkeit, Schwerpunkte und Wege aus der Sicht des Kapitalmarkts, *EWS* 580.

(2005), The Transatlantic Financial Markets Regulatory Dialogue, in: Hopt, Klaus J., Wymeersch, Eddy, Kanda, Hideki, and Baum, Harald (eds.), *Corporate Governance in Context*, Oxford: Oxford University Press, p. 363.

Henderson, Dan F. (1995), Foreign Acquisitions and Takeovers in Japan, 40 *St Louis U.L.J.* 897.

Henle, Walter (1999), Neue gesetzliche Grundlagen für das Shareholder-Value-Denken in Deutschland, in: Kübler, Friedrich (ed.), *The International Lawyer, Freundesgabe für Wulf H. Döser*, Baden-Baden: Nomos, p. 161.

Henn, Günter (1994), *Die Rechte des Aktionärs*, Cologne: Schmidt.

(2002), *Handbuch des Aktienrechts*, 7th edition, Heidelberg: C. F. Müller.

Herdegen, Matthias (2002), *Internationales Wirtschaftsrecht*, 3rd edition, Munich: Beck.

Hertig, Gérard (2000), Western Europe's Corporate Governance Dilemma, in: Baums, Theodor, Hopt, Klaus J., and Horn, Norbert (eds.), *Corporations, Capital Markets and Business in the Law (Liber Amicorum Buxbaum)*, London: Kluwer, p. 265.

(2004), Convergence of Substantive Law and Convergence of Enforcement: A Comparison, in: Gordon, Jeffrey N., and Roe, Mark J. (eds.), *Convergence and Persistence in Corporate Governance*, Cambridge: Cambridge University Press, p. 328.

Hertig, Gérard, and Kanda, Hideki (2004), Creditor Protection; Related Party Transactions, both in: Kraakman, Reinier, Davies, Paul, Hansmann, Henry, Hertig, Gérard, Hopt, Klaus J., Kanda, Hideki, and Rock, Edward, *The Anatomy of Corporate Law*, Oxford: Oxford University Press, pp. 71 and 101.

Hertig, Gérard, Kraakman, Reinier, and Rock, Edward (2004), Issuers and Investor Protection, in: Kraakman, Reinier, Davies, Paul, Hansmann, Henry, Hertig, Gérard, Hopt, Klaus J., Kanda, Hideki, and Rock, Edward, *The Anatomy of Corporate Law*, Oxford: Oxford University Press, p. 193.

Hicks, Andrew (2000), Millennial Law: Philosophy, Politics and Economics, 21 *Comp. Law*. 92.

Higgott, Richard, and Reich, Simon (1998), Globalisation and Sites of Conflict: Towards Definition and Taxonomy, CSGR Working Paper, available at www2.warwick.ac.uk/fac/soc/csgr/research/abstracts/1/.

High Level Group of Company Law Experts (2002), *A Modern Regulatory Framework for Company Law in Europe*, available at http://ec.europa.eu/internal_market/company/docs/modern/report_en.pdf.

Hill, Jennifer (2000a), Public Beginnings, Private Ends – Should Corporate Law Privilege the Interest of Shareholders, in: Macmillan, Fiona (ed.), *International Corporate Law*, Volume 1, Oxford: Hart, p. 17.

(2000b), Visions and Revisions of the Shareholder, 48 *Am. J. Comp. L.* 39.

Hirschman, Albert O. (1974), *Abwanderung und Widerspruch*, Tübingen: Mohr Siebeck (English version: *Exit, Voice and Loyalty*, Cambridge, MA: Harvard University Press, 1970).

Hirte, Heribert (1998), Die aktienrechtliche Satzungsstrenge: Kapitalmarkt und sonstige Legitimation versus Gestaltungsfreiheit, in: Lutter, Marcus, and Wiedemann, Herbert, *Gestaltungsfreiheit und Gesellschaftsrecht*, Berlin: de Gruyter, p. 61.

(2000), Der Einfluss neuer Informationstechniken auf das Gesellschaftsrecht und die corporate-governance-Debatte, in: Baums, Theodor, Hopt, Klaus J., and Horn, Norbert (eds.), *Corporations, Capital Markets and Business in the Law (Liber Amicorum Buxbaum)*, London: Kluwer, p. 283.

(2003), Kapitalgesellschaftsrecht, 4th edition, Cologne: RWS Kommunikationsforum.

Hocker, Ulrich (2000), Minderheitenschutz und Recht der Aktionäre in Europa, *Festschrift Bezzenberger* 147.

Hodgson, Stephen, Kellenter, Wolfgang, Müller, Georg, and Triebel, Volker (1995), *Englisches Handels- und Wirtschaftsrecht*, 2nd edition, Heidelberg: Recht und Wirtschaft.

Hofstede, Geert H. (1980), *Culture's Consequences: International Differences in Work-Related Values*, Beverly Hills: Sage (2nd edition: *Consequences: Comparing Values, Behaviors, Institutions and Organizations Across Nations*, 2003).

Hommelhoff, Peter (1985), Eigenkontrolle statt Staatskontrolle, in: Schubert, Werner, and Hommelhoff, Peter (eds.), *Hundert Jahre modernes Aktienrecht*, Berlin: de Gruyter, p. 53.

(2000a), Anlegerinformationen im Aktien-, Bilanz- und Kapitalmarktrecht, *ZGR* 748.

(2000b), Das Unternehmensrecht vor den Herausforderungen der Globalisierung, *Festschrift Lutter* 95.

Hopt, Klaus J. (1975), *Der Kapitalanlegerschutz im Recht der Banken*, Munich: Beck.

(1976), Vom Aktien- und Börsenrecht zum Kapitalmarktrecht? – Teil 1, 140 *ZHR* 201.

(1980), Ideelle und wirtschaftliche Grundlagen der Aktien-, Bank- und Börsenrechtsentwicklung im 19. Jahrhundert, in: Coing, Helmut, and Wilhelm, Walter (eds.), *Wissenschaft und Kodifiation des Privatrechts im 19. Jahrhundert*, Frankfurt (Main): Klostermann, p. 128.

(1985), Self-Dealing and Use of Corporate Opportunity and Information: Regulating Directors' Conflicts of Interest, in: Hopt, Klaus J., and Teubner, Gunther, *Corporate Governance and Directors' Liabilities*, Berlin: de Gruyter, p. 285.

(1992), Directors' Duties to Shareholders, Employees, and Other Creditors: A View from the Continent, in: McKendrick, Ewan, *Commercial Aspects of Trust and Fiduciary Obligations*, Oxford: Oxford University Press, p. 115.

(1998a), Gestaltungsfreiheit im Gesellschaftsrecht in Europa. Generalbericht, in: Lutter, Marcus, and Wiedemann, Herbert, *Gestaltungsfreiheit und Gesellschaftsrecht*, Berlin: de Gruyter, p. 123.

(1998b), Europäisches Gesellschaftsrecht – Krise und neue Anläufe, *ZIP* 96.

(2000), Common Principles of Corporate Governance in Europe?, in: Markesinis, Basil L. (ed.), *Millennium Lectures*, Oxford: Hart, p. 105 (also published in: McCahery, Joseph A., Moerland, Piet, Raaijmakers, Theo, and Renneboog, Luc (eds.), *Corporate Governance Regimes – Convergence and Diversity*, Oxford: Oxford University Press, 2002, p. 175; and in German in (2000) *ZGR* 779).

(2002a), Gesellschaftsrecht im Wandel, *Festschrift Wiedemann* 1013.

(2002b), Unternehmensführung, Unternehmenskontrolle, Modernisierung des Aktienrechts – Zum Bericht der Regierungskommission Corporate Governance, in: Hommelhoff, Peter, Lutter, Marcus, Schmidt, Karsten, Schön, Wolfgang, and Ulmer, Peter (eds.), *Aktienrecht für globale Kapitalmärkte*, Heidelberg: Recht und Wirtschaft, p. 27.

(2004), Trusteeship and Conflicts of Interest in Corporate, Banking and Agency Law: Towards Common Legal Principles for Intermediaries in the Modern

Service-Oriented Society, in: Ferrarini, Guido, Hopt, Klaus J., Winter, Jaap, and Wymeersch, Eddy (eds.), *Reforming Company and Takeover Law in Europe*, Oxford: Oxford University Press, p. 51.

Hopt, Klaus J., and Wymeersch, Eddy (2003), Preface, in: Hopt, Klaus J., and Wymeersch, Eddy (eds.), *Capital Markets and Company Law*, Oxford: Oxford University Press.

Hopt, Klaus J., Wymeersch, Eddy, Kanda, Hideki, and Baum, Harald (eds.) (2005), *Corporate Governance in Context*, Oxford: Oxford University Press.

Horioka, Charles Yuji (2001), Japan's Public Pension System in the Twenty First Century, in: Blomström, Magnus, Gangnes, Byron, and La Croix, Sumner, *Japan's New Economy: Continuity and Change in the Twenty-First Century*, Oxford: Oxford University Press, p. 99.

Horn, Norbert (1979), Aktienrechtliche Unternehmensorganisation in der Hochindustrialisierung, in: Horn, Norbert, and Kocka, Jürgen, *Recht und Entwicklung der Großunternehmen im neunzehnten und frühen zwanzigsten Jahrhundert*, Göttingen: Vandenhoeck & Ruprecht, p. 123.

Howson, Nicholas C. (2005), Regulation of Companies with Publicly Listed Share Capital in the People's Republic of China, 38 *Cornell Int'l L.J.* 237.

Huang, Hui (2005), China's Takeover Law: A Comparative Analysis and Proposals for Reform, 30 *Del. J. Corp. L.* 145.

Hüffer, Uwe (2006), *Aktiengesetz*, 7th edition, Munich: Beck.

Hulle, Karel van (1994), Gesellschaftsrecht, in: Lenz, Carl Otto (ed.), *EG-Handbuch Recht im Binnenmarkt*, 2nd edition, Herne: Neue Wirtschafts-Briefe, p. 395.

Huntington, Samuel P. (1993), The Clash of Civilizations, 72 *Foreign Affairs* 22.

(1996), *The Clash of Civilizations and the Remaking of World Order*, New York: Simon and Schuster, 1996.

(1999), Keynote Address, in: The Colorado College (ed.), Cultures in the 21st Century: Conflicts and Convergences, 32 *Colorado College Studies* 1.

Husa, Jaako (2004), Classification of Legal Families Today: Is It Time for a Memorial Hymn, *Rev.int.dr.comp.* 11.

Hüther, Mario (2001), Namensaktien, Internet und die Zukunft der Stimmrechtsvertretung, *AG* 68.

(2002), *Aktionärsbeteiligung und Internet*, Cologne: Heymanns.

Igarashi, Toshiko (2001), Where Are We Going?: The Process of Change in Japanese Corporate Governance, 12 *ZJapanR* 69.

Immenga, Ulrich (1985), Company Systems and Affiliation, in: Conard, Alfred (ed.), *International Encyclopedia of Comparative Law*, Tübingen: Mohr Siebeck, Ch. 7.

Inaniwa, Kouchi, and Brondics, Klaus (1987), Aktionär und Aktiengesellschaft in Japan, *RIW* 13.

Ireland, Paddy (1999), Company Law and the Myth of Shareholder Ownership, 62 *MLR* 32.

Ishikawa, Akira (2005), Über die Stellung der ausländischen Rechtsanwälte in Japan, 19 *ZJapanR* 19.

Jacobs, Geert, and Macours, Kristof (2001), Tracking Stock: A European Perspective, 8 *Journal of International Banking and Financial Law* 372.

Jacoby, Sanford M. (2000), Corporate Governance in Comparative Perspective: Prospects of Convergence, 22 *Comp. L. L. & Pol'y J.* 5.

James, Harold (2002), *The End of Globalization: Lessons from the Great Depression*, Cambridge, MA: Harvard University Press.

Janssen, Markus (2001), Verarbschiedete Gesetzes: Berichte über die 151. und 152. Sitzungsperiode des Japanischen Parlaments, 12 *ZJapanR* 249.

Janssen, Markus, Koma, Fumio, Kuroda, Shintaro, and Schimmann, Peter (2002), New Rules for Share Structure and Governance of Japanese Corporations, 13 *ZJapanR* 253.

Jayme, Erik (2003), Die kulturelle Dimension des Rechts – ihre Bedeutung für das Internationale Privatrecht und die Rechtsvergleichung, 67 *RabelsZ* 211.

Jensen, Michael C. (1986), Agency Costs of Free Cash Flow, Corporate Finance, and Takeover, 76 *Am. Econ. Rev.* 323.

Jensen, Michael C., and Meckling, William H. (1976), Theory of the Firm: Managerial Behavior, Agency Costs and Ownership Structure, 3 *J. Finan. Econ.* 305.

Jhering, Rudolph von (1915), *The Struggle for Law*, Chicago: Callaghan and Company.

Joerges, Christian (2003), On the Legitimacy of European Private Law, *Electronic Journal of Comparative Law* 7.3, available at www.ejcl.org/73/art73-3.html.

Johnson, Benjamin W. (2002), German Corporate Culture in the Twenty-First Century: The Interrelation between the End of Germany Inc. and Germany's Corporate Capital Gains Tax Reform, 11 *Minn. J. Global Trade* 69.

Johnson, Simon, La Porta, Rafael, Lopez-de-Silanes, Florencio, and Shleifer, Andrei (2000), Tunneling, 90 *Amer. Econ. Rev.* 22.

Jordan, Cally (2005), The Conundrum of Corporate Governance, 30 *Brook. J. Int'l L.* 983.

Joussen, Peter (2000), Der Auskunftsanspruch des Aktionärs, *AG* 241.

Kahn-Freund, Otto (1974), Uses and Misuses of Comparative Law, 37 *MLR* 1.

Kalss, Susanne (2001), *Anlegerinteressen*, Vienna: Springer.

Kamar, Ehud (1998), A Regulatory Competition Theory of Indeterminacy in Corporate Law, 98 *Colum. L. Rev.* 1908.

Kanda, Hideki (1997), Trends in Japanese Corporate Governance, in: Hopt, Klaus J., and Wymeersch, Eddy (eds.), *Comparative Corporate Governance – Essays and Materials*, Berlin: de Gruyter, p. 185.

(2000), Globalization of Capital Markets: A Perspective from Japan, in: Basedow, Jürgen, and Kono, Toshiyuki (eds.), *Legal Aspects of Globalization*, The Hague: Kluwer Law International, p. 69.

(2004), Understanding Recent Trends Regarding the Liability of Managers and Directors in Japanese Corporate Law, 17 *ZJapanR* 29.

Kawamoto, Ichiro (1994), Handels- und Gesellschaftsrecht, in: Baum, Harald, and Drobnig, Ulrich, *Japanisches Handels- und Wirtschaftsrecht*, New York: de Gruyter, p. 47.

(1999), Die Praxis der Aktionärsklage in Japan, *Festschrift Großfeld* 529.

Kawamoto, Ichiro, Kishida, Masao, Morita, Akira, Kawaguchi, Yasuhiro, and Iga, Yoshiko (2001), *Japan, Corporations and Partnerships*, The Hague: Kluwer Law International.

Keidanren (2001), A Proposal for Better Corporate Accounting, available at www.keidanren.or.jp/english/policy/2001/013.html.

Kelemen, Daniel R., and Sibbitt, Eric C. (2002), The Americanization of Japanese Law, 23 *U. Pa. J. Int'l Econ. L.* 269.

Kennedy, Paul (1987), *The Rise and Fall of Great Powers: Economic Change and Military Conflict from 1500 to 2000*, New York: Random House.

Kersting, Christian (2002), Corporate Choice of Law – A Comparison of the United States and European Systems and a Proposal for a European Directive, 28 *Brook. J. Int'l L.* 1.

Kessler, Jürgen (1998), Leitungskompetenz und Leitungsverantwortung im deutschen, US-amerikanischen und japanischen Aktienrecht, *RIW* 602.

Keynes, John Maynard (1993), in: Moggridge, Donald (ed.), *The Collected Writings of John Maynard Keynes*, Toronto: University of Toronto.

Kieninger, Eva M. (2002), *Wettbewerb der Privatrechtsordnungen im Europäischen Binnenmarkt*, Tübingen: Mohr Siebeck.

Kim, Hwa-Jin (2001), Taking International Soft Law Seriously: Its Implications for Global Convergence in Corporate Governance, *Journal of Korean Law* 1.

Kinoshita, Tsuyoshi (2001), Legal System and Legal Culture in Japan, 11 *ZJapanR* 7.

Kirchhof, Paul (2001), Demokratie ohne parlamentarische Gesetzgebung?, *NJW* 1332.

Kirchner, Christian (2003), Shareholder Value: A New Standard for Company Conduct in: Hopt, Klaus J., and Wymeersch, Eddy (eds.), *Capital Markets and Company Law*, Oxford: Oxford University Press, p. 341.

Kishida, Masao (1999), Japanese Legal Accounting System, *Festschrift Großfeld* 569.

Kissane, Mary E. (1997), Global Gadflies: Applications and Implications of US-Style Corporate Governance Abroad, 17 *N.Y.L. Sch. J. Int'l & Comp. L.* 621

Kissinger, Henry A. (1994), *Diplomacy*, New York: Simon & Schuster.

Klauer, Irene (1998), *Die Europäisierung des Privatrechts: Der EuGH als Zivilrichter*, Baden-Baden: Nomos.

Klein, William A., and Coffee, John C. (2002), *Business Organization and Finance*, New York: Foundation Press.

Kleindiek, Detlef (2003), Die Zukunft der Rechnungslegung in kleinen und mittleren Unternehmen, in: Gesellschaftsrechtliche Vereinigung (ed.), *Gesellschaftsrecht in der Diskussion 2002*, Cologne: Otto Schmidt, p. 3.

Kliesow, Olaf (2001), *Aktionärsrechte und Aktionärsklage in Japan*, Tübingen: Mohr Siebeck.

Knieper, Rolf (2002), Die Bedeutung des Zivil- und Wirtschaftsrechts – Rechtssystem für Direktinvestionen in der VR China, 101 *ZVglRWiss* 220.

Ködderitzsch, Lorenz (2001a), Rechtsvergleichende Anmerkungen zum japanischen Verschmelzungs- und Spaltungsrecht, 11 *ZJapanR* 65.

(2001b), Änderungen des Handelsgesetzes mit Wirkung zum 1. Oktober 2001, 12 *ZJapanR* 139.

Kolk, Ans (1999), International Codes of Conduct and Corporate Social Responsibility, 8 *Transnational Corporation* 143.

Kölner Kommentar zum Aktiengesetz (1986–) (ed. Zöllner, Wolfgang), 2nd edition, Köln: Heymanns.

Komiyama, Makoto, and Masaoka, Yukinobu (2002), Corporate Governance: A New Phase for Japanese Companies, Nomura Research Institute Paper No. 47, available at www.nri.co.jp/english/opinion/papers/index.html.

Korch, Rainer (2002), *Ringbeteiligungen von Aktiengesellschaften: Gesellschafts- und kartellrechtliche Aspekte*, Cologne: Heymanns.

Kötz, Hein (1986), Rechtsvereinheitlichung – Nutzen, Kosten, Methoden, Ziele, 50 *RabelsZ* 1.

(1992), Alternativen zur legislatorischen Rechtsvereinheitlichung, 56 *RabelsZ* 215.

(1998), Abschied von der Rechtskreislehre?, *ZEuP* 493.

(2000), Der Bundesgerichtshof und die Rechtsvergleichung, *Festgabe 50 Jahre Bundesgerichtshof*, Volume II, p. 825.

Kozuka, Sôichirô (2001), The Reformation of Corporate Law in Japan and the Use of Information and Communication Technology, *EBLR* 318.

(2003), The Use of Stock Options as Defensive Measures: The Impact of the 2001 Amendments to the Corporate Law on Corporate Controls in Japan, 15 *ZJapanR* 135.

(2006), Recent Developments in Takeover Law: Changes in Business Practices Meet Decade-Old Rule, 21 *ZJapanR* 5.

Kraakman, Reinier (2004), Disclosure and Corporate Governance: An Overview Essay, in: Ferrarini, Guido, Hopt, Klaus J., Winter, Jaap, and Wymeersch, Eddy (eds.), *Reforming Company and Takeover Law in Europe*, Oxford: Oxford University Press, p. 95.

Kramer, Ernst A. (2001), Konvergenz und Internationalisierung der juristischen Methode, in: Assmann, Heinz-Dieter, Brüggemann, Gert, and Sethe, Rolf (eds.), *Unterschiedliche Rechtskulturen – Konvergenz des*

Rechtsdenkens/Different Legal Cultures – Convergence of Legal Reasoning, Baden-Baden: Nomos, p. 31.

Krämer, Hans-Jörg (2002), *Das Unternehmensinteresse als Verhaltensmaxime der Leitungsorgane der Aktiengesellschaft im Rahmen der Organhaftung*, Berlin: Tenea.

Krause, Hartmut (2002), Prophylaxe gegen feindliche Übernahmeangebote, *AG* 133.

Krauss, Reinhard (1980), *Intersystemare Kooperationen und Anpassungsprozesse zwischen westlichen und östlichen Wirtschaftssystemen*, Frankfurt: R. G. Fischer.

Kropff, Bruno (1965), *Aktiengesetz mit Begründung des Regierungsentwurfes*, Düsseldorf: IDW.

Kübler, Friedrich (1998), *Gesellschaftsrecht: die privatrechtlichen Ordnungsstrukturen und Regelungsprobleme von Verbänden und Unternehmen*, 5th edition, Heidelberg: C. F. Müller.

Küng, Hans (ed.) (2001), *Globale Unternehmen – globales Ethos*, Frankfurt (Main): FAZ-Verlag.

Kurtz, Jürgen (2003), NGOs, the Internet and International Economic Policy Making – The Failure of the OECD Multilateral Agreement on Investment, 3 *Melbourne Journal of International Law* 213.

La Porta, Rafael, Lopez-de-Silanes, Florencio, and Shleifer, Andrei (1999), Corporate Ownership around the World, 54 *J. Finance* 471.

(2006), What Works in Securities Law?, 61 *J. Finance* 1.

La Porta, Rafael, Lopez-de-Silanes, Florencio, Shleifer, Andrei, and Vishny, Robert W. (1998), Law and Finance, 106 *J. Polit. Economy* 1113.

(2000a), Agency Problems and Dividend Policies Around the World, 55 *J. Finance* 1.

(2000b), Investor Protection and Corporate Governance, 58 *J. Finan. Econ.* 3.

LaChance, Craig (2001), Nature v. Nurture: Evolution, Path Dependence and Corporate Governance, 18 *Ariz. J. Int'l & Comp. L.* 279.

Ladeur, Karl-Heinz (2003), Globalisation and the Conversion of Democracy to Polycentric Networks, EUI Working Paper, available at http://cadmus.iue.it/dspace/bitstream/1814/199/1/law03-4.pdf.

Lang, Jeffrey (1998), Keynote Address, 31 *Cornell Int'l L.J.* 455.

Larenz, Karl, and Canaris, Claus-Wilhelm (1995), *Methodenlehre der Rechtswissenschaft*, 3rd edition, Berlin: Springer.

Larsson, Tomas (2001), *The Race to the Top: The Real Story of Globalization*, Lanham: National Book Network.

Latham, Mark (1999a), Corporate Governance in Japan: A Future Scenario, available at www.corpmon.com/publications.htm.

(1999b), The Road to Shareholder Power, available at www.corpmon.com/publications.htm.

(2000), The Internet Will Drive Corporate Monitoring, available at www.corpmon.com/publications.htm.

(2001), Democracy and Infomediaries, available at www.corpmon.com/publications.htm.

Latty, Elvin R. (1955), Pseudo Foreign Corporations, 65 *Yale L.J.* 137.

Lau, Kun Luen Alex (1999), People's Republic of China: The New Shanghai Stock Exchange Listing Rules: An Egg Hatched or an Egg within an Egg, 20 *Comp. Law*. 243.

Leader, Sheldon (1995), Private Property and Corporate Governance, Part I: Defining the Interests, in: Macmillan (Patfield), Fiona (ed.), *Perspectives on Company Law*: Volume 1, London: Kluwer Law International, p. 85.

Learmount, Simon (2002), *Corporate Governance: What Can Be Learned from Japan?*, Oxford: Oxford University Press.

Lebrun, Laurie N. (2001), Recent Amendments to the Commercial Code of Japan: Impact on Mergers & Acquisitions, 32 *Law & Pol'y Int'l Bus.* 811.

Leggewie, Claus (2003), *Die Globalisierung und ihre Gegner*, Munich: Beck.

Legrand, Pierre (1996), European Legal Systems Are Not Converging, 45 *ICLQ* 53.

(1997), The Impossibility of Legal Transplants, 4 *MJ* 112.

(1999), *Fragments on Law-As-Culture*, Deventer: W. E. J. Tjeenk Willink.

(2005), Paradoxically, Derrida: For a Comparative Legal Studies, 27 *Cardozo L. Rev.* 631.

(2006), *Le droit compare*, 2nd edition, Paris: Presses Universitaires de France.

Lehmann, Jürgen (1990), Missbrauch des Auskunfts-, Frage- und Rederechts, in: Timm, Wolframm (ed.), *Missbräuchliches Aktionärsverhalten*, Cologne: RWS-Forum, p. 51.

Lele, Priya P., and Siems, Mathias M. (2007), Shareholder Protection: A Leximetric Approach, 17 *JCLS* 17.

Leube, Hans Peter (2003), Corporate Governance the American way?, *RIW* 98

Leung, Erika, Liu, Lily, Shen, Lu, Taback, Kevin, and Wang, Leo (2002), Financial Reform and Corporate Governance in China, Working Paper, available at http://mitsloan.mit.edu/50th/pdf/corpgovchinapaper.pdf.

Licht, Amir N. (1998), International Diversity in Securities Regulation: Roadblocks on the Way to Convergence, 20 *Cardozo L. Rev.* 227.

(2001a), The Mother of All Path Dependencies: Towards a Cross-Cultural Theory of Corporate Governance-Systems, 26 *Del. J. Corp. L.* 147.

(2001b), David's Dilemma: A Case Study of Securities Regulation in a Small Open Market, 2/2 *Theoretical Inquiries in Law* 5.

(2004a), Legal Plug-Ins: Cultural Distance, Cross-Listing, and Corporate Governance Reform, 22 *Berkeley J. Int'l L.* 195.

(2004b), The Maximands of Corporate Governance: A Theory of Values and Cognitive Style, 29 *Del. J. Corp. L.* 649.

Licht, Amir N., Goldschmidt, Chanan, and Schwartz, Shalom H. (2001), Culture, Law, and Finance: Cultural Dimensions of Corporate Governance Laws, Working Paper, available at http://ssrn.com/abstract = 277613.

(2005), Culture, Law, and Corporate Governance, 25 *Int'l Rev. L. & Econ.* 229.

Lipton Martin, and Rosenblum, Steven (2003), Election Contest in the Company's Proxy: An Idea Whose Time Has Not Come, 59 *Bus. Law.* 67.

Liu, Lawrence S. (2001), Chinese Characteristics Compared: A Legal and Policy Perspective of Corporate Finance and Governance in Taiwan and China, available at http://ssrn.com/abstract = 273174.

Lombardo, Davide, and Pagano, Marco (2000), Legal Determinants of the Return on Equity, Working Paper, available at http://ssrn.com/abstract = 209310.

Lowenstein, Louis (1999), Corporate Governance and the Voice of the Paparazzi, Working Paper No. 132, Center for Law and Economic Studies, Columbia University School of Law, available http://ssrn.com/abstract = 163386.

Luck, Kwek Mean (2001), The End of History for Corporate Governance or Just Another Moment in Time, 19 *C&SLJ* 305.

Luhmann, Niklas (1997), Ethik in internationalen Beziehungen, in: Lütterfelds, Wilhelm, and Mohrs, Thomas (eds.), *Eine Welt – eine Moral?*, Darmstadt: Wissenschaftliche Buchgesellschaft, p. 156.

Lutter, Marcus (1973), *Der Aktionär in der Marktwirtschaft*, Berlin: de Gruyter.

(1980), Theorie der Mitgliedschaft, 180 *AcP* 84.

(1991), Anteilseigner und Unternehmen, in: Lutter, Marcus, and Semler, Johannes (eds.), *Rechtsgrundlagen freiheitlicher Unternehmenswirtschaft*, Cologne: Otto Schmidt, p. 15.

(1998a), Limited Liability Companies and Private Companies, in: Conard, Alfred (ed.), *International Encyclopedia of Comparative Law*, Tübingen: Mohr Siebeck, Ch. 2.

(1998b), Gesellschaftsrecht und Kapitalmarkt, *Festschrift Zöllner* 363.

Luttermann, Claus (1999), Dialog der Kulturen, *Festschrift Großfeld* 771

Lynch Fannon, Irene (2003), *Working within Two Kinds of Capitalism*, Oxford: Hart.

Mace, Dan (2000), The Purpose of Company Law and Company Lawyers in a Global Arena, 21 *Comp. Law.* 56.

MacNeil, Iain G. (2000), Competition and Convergence in Corporate Regulation: The Case of Overseas Listed Companies, Working Paper, available at http://ssrn.com/abstract = 278508.

(2002), Shareholders' Pre-emptive Rights, *Journal of Banking Law* 78.

(2005), *An Introduction to the Law on Financial Investment*, Oxford: Hart.

MacNeil, Iain G., and Lau, Alex (2001), International Corporate Regulation: Listing Rules and Overseas Companies, 50 *ICLQ* 787.

MacNeil, Iain G., and Li, Xiao (2006), 'Comply or Explain': Market Discipline and Non-Compliance with the Combined Code, 14 *Corporate Governance* 486.

Maher, Maria, and Andersson, Thomas (2002), Corporate Governance: Effects on Firm Performance and Economic Growth, in: McCahery, Joseph A., Moerland, Piet, Raaijmakers, Theo, and Renneboog, Luc (eds.), *Corporate Governance Regimes – Convergence and Diversity*, Oxford: Oxford University Press, p. 386.

Mahoney, Paul G. (1997), The Exchange as Regulator, 83 *Va. L. Rev.* 1453.

Mann, Alexander (2003), *Corporate Governance-Systeme, Funktionen und Entwicklung am Beispiel von Deutschland und Großbritannien*, Berlin: Duncker & Humblot.

Manne, Henry (1965), Mergers and the Market for Corporate Control, 73 *J. Polit. Economy* 110.

Marini, Philippe (1996), *La modernisation du droit des sociétés. Rapport au premier ministre* ('Marini Report').

Markesinis, Sir Basil (1994), *The Gradual Convergence: Foreign Ideas, Foreign Influences, and English Law on the Eve of the 21st Century*, Oxford: Clarendon Press.

Markesinis, Sir Basil, and Fedtke, Jörg (2005), The Judge as Comparatist, 80 *Tul. L. Rev.* 11.

Markowitz, Harry M. (1971), *Portfolio Selection: Efficient Diversification of Investments*, Yale: Yale University Press.

Marutschke, Hans Peter (1999), *Einführung in das japanische Recht*, Munich: Beck.

Maruyama, Shuhei (1995), Historischer Überblick über das Aktienrecht Japans, 94 *ZVglRWiss* 283.

Maslen, Susan (1998), Japan and the Rule of Law, 16 *UCLA Pac. Basin L.J.* 281.

Matsudo, Jiro (1959), Das neue japanische Aktienrecht, 24 *RabelsZ* 115.

McCormack, Gerard (1998), Institutional Shareholders and the Promotion of Good Governance, in: Rider, Barry A. K. (ed.), *The Realm of Company Law*, London: Kluwer Law, p. 131.

(2000) Company Law and the New Millennium: Some Cautionary Tales from the Past, 21 *Comp. Law.* 57.

McDonnell, Brett H. (2002), Convergence in Corporate Governance – Possible, But Not Desirable, 47 *Vill. L. Rev.* 341.

McGrew, Anthony G. (1998), Global Legal Internationalization and Present-Day Patterns of Globalization, in: Gessner, Volkmar, and Buda, Ali Cem (eds.), *Emerging Legal Certainty: Empirical Studies on the Globalization of Law*, Aldershot: Ashgate, p. 325.

McKinsey & Company (2002), *Global Investor Opinion Survey on Corporate Governance*.

Meier-Schatz, Christian (1991), American Legal Harmonization from a European Perspective, in: Buxbaum, Richard M. (ed.), *European Business Law: Legal and Economic Analyses on Integration and harmonization*, Berlin, New York: de Gruyter, p. 61.

Menden, Björn (1999), *Corporate Governance in Japan*, Marburg: Förderverein Marburger-Japan-Reihe.

Mendiola, Alfredo, and O'Hara, Maureen (2003), Taking Stock in Stock Markets: The Changing Governance of Exchanges, Working Paper, available at http://ssrn.com/abstract = 431580.

Merkt, Hanno (1991), *US-amerikanisches Gesellschaftsrecht*, Heidelberg: Recht und Wirtschaft (2nd edition, 2006, together with Stephan R. Göthel).

(1995), Das Europäische Gesellschaftsrecht und die Idee des 'Wettbewerbs der Gesetzgeber', 59 *RabelsZ* 545.

(2000), Die Geschichte der Namensaktie, in: Rosen, Rüdiger von, and Seifert, Werner G. (eds.), *Die Namensaktie*, Eschborn: DAI, p. 63.

(2001a), Liberalisierung des europäischen Binnenmarktes durch Angleichung des Gesellschaftsrechts, in: Kitagawa, Zentaro, Murakami, Junichi, Nörr, Knut Wolfgang, Oppermann, Thomas, and Shiono, Hiroshi (eds.), *Regulierung – Deregulierung – Liberalisierung*, Tübingen: Mohr Siebeck, p. 321.

(2001b), *Unternehmenspublizität*, Tübingen: Mohr Siebeck.

(2004a), Die Pluralisierung des europäischen Gesellschaftsrechts, *RIW* 1.

(2004b), Disclosing Disclosure: Europe's Winding Road to Competitive Standards of Publication of Company-Related Information, in: Ferrarini, Guido, Hopt, Klaus J., Winter, Jaap, and Wymeersch, Eddy (eds.), *Reforming Company and Takeover Law in Europe*, Oxford: Oxford University Press, p. 115.

(2004c), European Company Law Reform: Struggling for a More Liberal Approach 1 *ECFR* 3.

Merle, Philippe (2005), *Droit commercial, Sociétés commerciales*, 10th edition, Paris: Dalloz.

Merryman, John Henry (1999), *The Loneliness of the Comparative Lawyer*, The Hague: Kluwer Law International.

Mestmäcker, Ernst-Joachim (1958), *Verwaltung, Konzerngewalt und Rechte der Aktionäre*, Karlsruhe: Müller.

Michalsky, Udo (1991), Vergleichender Überblick über das Recht der Kapitalgesellschaften in Frankreich, *DStR* 1563.

Micheler, Eva (2000), The Impact of the Centros Case on Europe's Company Laws, 21 *Comp. Law.* 179.

Michelman, Frank (1988), Law's Republic, 97 *Yale L. Rev.* 1493.

Miles, Lilian (2000), Unresponsive Shareholders in Public Companies, Dial 'M' for Motivate, 21 *Comp. Law.* 142.

(2003), Company Stakeholders: Their Position under the New Framework, 24 *Comp. Law.* 56.

Milhaupt, Curtis J. (1996), A Relational Theory of Japanese Corporate Governance: Contract, Culture, and the Rule of Law, 37 *Harv. Int'l L.J.* 3.

(1998), Property Rights in Firms, 84 *Va. L. Rev.* 1145 (also published in: Gordon, Jeffrey N., and Roe, Mark J. (eds.), *Convergence and Persistence in Corporate Governance*, Cambridge: Cambridge University Press, 2004, p. 210).

(2001), Creative Norm Destruction: The Evolution of Nonlegal Rules in Japanese Corporate Governance, 149 *U. Pa. L. Rev*. 2083.

(2002), On the (Fleeting) Existence of the Main Bank System and Other Japanese Economic Institutions, 27 *Law & Soc. Inquiry* 425.

(2005), In the Shadow of Delaware? The Rise of Hostile Takeovers in Japan, 105 *Colum. L. Rev.* 2171.

Milhaupt, Curtis J., and West, Mark D. (2003a), Institutional Change and M&A in Japan: Diversity Through Deals, Center for Law and Economic Studies, in: Milhaupt, Curtis J. (ed.), *Global Markets, Domestic Institutions*, New York: Columbia University Press, p. 295.

(2003b), Is the Japanese Bureaucracy Hollowing Out? Evidence from the Market for Legal Talent, 15 *ZJapanR* 5.

Miller, Geoffrey (1998), Political Structure and Corporate Governance: Some Points of Contrast Between the United States and England, *Colum. Bus. L. Rev.* 51.

Milman, David (1999), *Company Law in Europa: Recent Developments*, London: DTI.

Mitnick, Scott (2001), Cross-Border Mergers and Acquisitions in Europe: Reforming Barriers to Takeovers, *Colum. Bus. L. Rev.* 683.

Miwa, Yoshiro, and Ramseyer, Mark (2002a), The Fable of the Keiretsu, 11 *J. Econ. Manage. Strategy* 169.

(2002b), The Myth of the Main Bank: Japan and Comparative Corporate Governance, 27 *Law & Soc. Inquiry* 401.

(2005a), Does Relationship Banking Matter? The Myth of the Japanese Main Bank, 2 *J. Empirical Legal Stud*. 261.

(2005b), The Multiple Roles of Banks? Convenient Tales from Modern Japan, in: Hopt, Klaus J., Wymeersch, Eddy, Kanda, Hideki, and Baum, Harald (eds.), *Corporate Governance in Context*, Oxford: Oxford University Press, p. 527.

Modern Company Law for a Competitive Economy (1999), Developing the Framework, Presented by the Company Law Steering Group (UK), available at www.dti.gov.uk/cld/modcolaw.htm.

Modern Company Law for a Competitive Economy: Final Report (2001), Presented by the Company Law Steering Group (UK), available at www.dti.gov.uk/cld/final_report/index.htm.

Modernising Company Law (2002), Presented to Parliament by the Secretary of State for Trade and Industry by Command of Her Majesty, Cm 5553, available at www.dti.gov.uk/companiesbill/whitepaper.htm.

Moerke, Andreas (2003), Rumble in the Boardroom? The Change of Japanese Corporate Governance Schemes, 15 *ZJapanR* 142.

Mojuyé, Benjamin (2000), French Corporate Governance in the New Millennium: Who Watches the Board in Corporate France?, 6 *Colum. J. Eur. L.* 73.

Möllers, Thomas M. J. (1997), Anlegerschutz durch Aktien- und Kapitalmarktrecht, *ZGR* 334.

Muchlinski, Peter Thomas (2003), Globalisation and Legal Research, 37 *Int. L.* 221.

Mülbert, Peter O. (1996a), *Aktiengesellschaft, Unternehmensgruppe und Kapitalmarkt*, 2nd edition, Munich: Beck.

(1996b), *Empfehlen sich gesetzliche Regelungen zur Einschränkung des Einflusses der Kreditinstitute auf Aktiengesellschaften? Gutachten E für den 61. Deutschen Juristentag*, Munich: Beck.

(1997), Shareholder Value aus rechtlicher Sicht, *ZGR* 129.

(2003), Die Abschwächungen des mitgliedschaftlichen Bestandsschutzes im Aktienrecht, *Festschrift Ulmer* 433.

Müller, Markus (2000), *Systemwettbewerb, Harmonisierung und Wettbewerbsverzerrung*, Baden-Baden: Nomos.

Müller-Erzbach, Rudolf (1929), *Umgestaltung der Aktiengesellschaft zur Kerngesellschaft verantwortungsvoller Großaktionäre*, Berlin: Heymann.

Münchener Kommentar zum Aktiengesetz (2000–), 2nd edition, Munich: Beck.

Murphy, Dale D. (2004), *The Structure of Regulatory Competition*, Oxford: Oxford University Press.

Myners, Paul (2001), Institutional Investment in the UK: A Review, available at www.hm-treasury.gov.uk./Documents/Financial_Services/Securities_and_Investments/fin_sec_mynfinal.cfm.

(2005) Pre-emption Rights: Final Report, available at www.dti.gov.uk/files/file28436.pdf.

Nahamowitz, Peter, and Voigt, Rüdiger (eds.) (2002), *Globalisierung des Rechts II: Internationale Organisationen und Regelungsbereiche*, Baden-Baden: Nomos.

Nahr, J. Christian (2003), Publizitätspflicht in den USA, *RIW* 115.

Narusawa, Takashi, Emori, Masafumi, and Ohmori, Satoshi (2001), Rebirth of Japanese Companies Through Governance Reforms, Nomura Research Institute Paper No. 25, available at www.nri.co.jp/english/opinion/papers/index.html.

Nelken, David (ed.) (1997), *Comparing Legal Cultures*, Aldershot: Dartmouth.

Neumann, Peter A. (2003), Private Acquisitions by Foreign Investors in China: Is the Party Finally Over?, *China Law & Practice*, April 2003, 13.

Neyer, Jürgen (1998), Binding Territoriality and Functionality? Globalization Meets the Law, in: Gessner, Volkmar, and Buda, Ali Cem (eds.), *Emerging Legal Certainty: Empirical Studies on the Globalization of Law*, Aldershot: Ashgate, p. 401.

Noack, Ulrich (1994), *Gesellschaftervereinbarungen bei Kapitalgesellschaften*, Tübingen: Mohr.

(1999), *Entwicklungen im Aktienrecht 1999/2000*, Frankfurt (Main): Deutsches Aktieninstitut.

(2000a), Die Umstellung von Inhaber- auf Namensaktien, *Festschrift Bezzenberger* 291.

(2000b), Die organisierte Stimmrechtsvertretung auf Hauptversammlungen – insbesondere durch die Gesellschaft, *Festschrift Lutter* 1463.

(2001a), Online-Hauptversammlung, *NZG* 1057.

(2001b), Stimmrechtsvertretung in der Hauptversammlung nach NaStraG, *ZIP* 57.

(2002a), Zukunft der Hauptversammlung – Hauptversammlung der Zukunft, in: Zetzsche, Dirk, *Die virtuelle Hauptversammlung*, Berlin: Erich Schmidt Verlag, p. 13.

(2002b), Gesellschaftsrecht und Informationstechnik, *Festschrift Druey* 870.

(2002c), Neuerungen im Recht der Hauptversammlung durch das Transparenz- und Publizitätsgesetz und den Deutschen Corporate Governance-Kodex, *DB* 620.

(2002d), Grenzüberschreitende Stimmrechtsausübung – Ein Abenteuer im Binnenmarkt, *WM* 68.

(2003), Hauptversammlung der Aktiengesellschaft und moderne Kommunikationstechnik – aktuelle Bestandsaufnahme und Ausblick, *NZG* 241.

Noack, Ulrich, and Zetzsche, Dirk (2002), Die Legitimation der Aktionäre bei Globalaktien und Depotverbuchung, *AG* 651.

Norberg, Johan (2003), *Das kapitalistische Manifest*, Frankfurt (Main): Eichborn.

Norton, Joseph J., and Olive, Christopher D. (2001), A By-product of the Globalization Process: The Rise of Cross Border Bank Mergers and Acquisitions – The US Framework, 56 *Bus. Law*. 591.

Nottage, Luke (2001), Japanese Corporate Governance at a Crossroads: Variation in Varieties of Capitalism?, 27 *N.C. J. Int'l & Com. Reg*. 255.

Nunnenkamp, Peter (2006), Liberalisation and Regulation of International Capital Flows: Where the Opposites Meet, in Grote, Rainer, and Marauhn, Thilo (eds.), *The Regulation of International Financial Markets*, Cambridge: Cambridge University Press, p. 259.

O'Kelley, Charles R., and Thompson, Robert B. (1996), *Corporation and Other Business Associations*, 2nd edition, Boston: Little, Brown and Company (3rd edition, 1999).

Oda, Hiroshi (1999), *Japanese Law*, 2nd edition, Oxford: Oxford University Press.

(2002), Corporate Law Reform in Japan 2001/2002: Deregulation of Company Law?, 14 *ZJapanR* 5.

(2005), Comprehensive Overhaul of the Securities and Exchange Law: The Draft on the Trading of Financial Products of 2006, 21 *ZJapanR* 225.

Ogus, Anthony (1999), Competition between National Legal Systems: A Contribution to Economic Analysis to Comparative Law, 48 *ICLQ* 405.

(2000), Self-Regulation, in: Bouckaert, Boudewijn, and De Geest, Gerrit (eds.), *Encyclopedia of Law and Economics*, Volume V, Cheltenham: Edward Elgar, p. 587.

(2002), Comparing Regulatory Systems, Working Paper, available at www.competition-regulation.org.uk/publications/working_papers/wp35.pdf, now also published in: Parker, David, and Saal, David (eds.), *International Handbook on Privatization*, Cheltenham: Edward Elgar, 2003, Ch. 23.

Olson, Mancur (1965), *The Logic of Collective Action: Public Goods and the Theory of Groups*, Cambridge, MA: Harvard University Press.

(1982), *The Rise and Decline of Nations: Economic Growth, Stagflation and Social Rigidities*, New Haven: Yale University Press.

Omar, Paul J. (2000), Centros Revisited: Assessing the Impact on Corporate Organisation in Europe, *ICCLR* 407.

(2001), Company Law Review in France, *EBLR* 76.

Ommeslaghe, Pierre Van (1990), Capital and Securities of Marketable Share Companies, in: Conard, Alfred (ed.), *International Encyclopedia of Comparative Law*, Tübingen: Mohr Siebeck, Ch. 5 I.

Ong, Kingsley T. W., and Baxter, Colin R. (1999), A Comparative Study of the Fundamental Elements of Chinese and English Company Law, 48 *ICLQ* 88.

Oquendo, Ángel R. (2001), Breaking on Through to the Other Side: Understanding Continental European Corporate Governance, 22 *U. Pa. J. Int'l Econ. L.* 975.

Osugi, Kenichi (2002), Americanization of Stock Corporation Laws Around the World and Shareholders' Derivative Suits as a Forgotten Element Therein, 13 *ZJapanR* 29.

O'Sullivan, Mary (2001), Change and Continuity in the French System of Corporate Governance, Working Paper, available at www.insead.fr/projects/cgep/Research/NationalSystems/NSCGFR0101without.pdf.

Pagano, Marco (2002), The Performance of European Stock Exchanges: Evidence from Listing Decisions, in: Ferrarini, Guido, Hopt, Klaus J., and Wymeersch, Eddy (eds.), *Capital Markets in the Age of the Euro*, The Hague: Kluwer Law International, p. 297.

Pagano, Marco, and Volpin, Paolo (2005), The Political Economy of Corporate Governance, 95 *Amer. Econ. Rev.* 1005.

Papmehl, Markus A. (2002), Delaware Corporate Law: Entstehungsgeschichte und Gründe für den Führungsanspruch im US-Gesellschaftsrecht, 101 *ZVglRWiss* 200.

Pappenheim, Rainer (2001), *Neue Institionenökonomik und politische Institutionen*, Frankfurt (Main): Lang.

Parkinson, John E. (1993), *Corporate Power and Responsibility*, Oxford: Oxford University Press.

Pastre, Oliver (1998), Corporate Governance: The End of 'L'exception Francaise'?, *Colum. Bus. L. Rev.* 79.

Peerenboom, Randall (2002), The New Foreign Investment Guidelines and Market Reform in China, *China Law & Practice*, April 2002, 19.

Pellens, Bernhard, and Hillebrandt, Franca (2001), Vorzugsaktien vor dem Hintergrund der Corporate Governance-Diskussion, *AG* 57.

Peltzman, Sam (1976), Towards a More General Theory of Regulation, 19 *J. L. & Econ.* 211.

Pennington, Robert R. (1994), Vereinigtes Königreich, in: *Jura Europae, Droit des societés*, Munich: Gesellschaftsrecht, Beck.

Perino, Michael A. (2003), American Corporate Reform Abroad: Sarbanes–Oxley and the Foreign Private Issuer, 4 *EBOR* 213.

Peters, Hans-Rudolf (1981), *Grundlagen der Mesoökonomie und Strukturpolitik*, Stuttgart: Uni-TB.

Pißler, Benjamin (2001), Zur Rolle der Rechtsprechung im chinesischen Aktienmarkt. Erste Welle von Schadensersatzklagen chinesischer Anleger, Working Paper China Analysis No. 10, available at www.chinapolitik.de/studien/index.htm.

(2002a), Zur Rolle der Rechtsprechung im chinesischen Aktienmarkt: ein UpdateWorking Paper China Analysis No. 12, available at www.chinapolitik.de/studien/index.htm.

(2002b), Corporate Governance in der VR China: Neue Vorschriften für börsenzugelassene Gesellschaften-, Zur Rolle der Rechtsprechung im chinesischen Aktienmarkt: ein Update, Working Paper China Analysis No. 17, available at www.chinapolitik.de/studien/index.htm.

(2002c), Schritte zur Öffnung des chinesischen Kapitalmarkts für ausländische Anleger: Übertragung von staatseigenen Aktien und QFII-Methode, Working Paper China Analysis No. 19, available at www.chinapolitik.de/studien/index.htm.

(2002d), Übersetzung mit Anmerkungen zu den Mitteilungen über den Erlass des 'Standards der Corporate Governance börsenzugelassener Gesellschaften', available at www.jura.uni-goettingen.de/chinarecht/020107.htm.

Pistor, Katharina (2002), The Standardization of Law and Its Effect on Developing Economies, 50 *Am. J. Comp. L.* 97.

Pistor, Katharina, Keinan, Yoram, Kleinheisterkamp, Jan, and West, Mark D. (2001), The Evolution of Corporate Law, Working Paper, available at www.worldbank.org/wdr/2001/bkgroundpapers/pistor.pdf.

(2002), The Evolution of Corporate Law, *U. Pa. J. Int'l Econ. L.* 751 (shorter version of the 2001 Working Papers).

Pistor, Katharina, Raiser, Martin, and Gelfer, Stanislaw (2000), Law and Finance in Transition Economies, 8 *Economics of Transition* 325.

Planck, Marina (1995), *Aktionärsklagen im französischen und deutschen Recht unter Einbeziehung der neueren Rechtsentwicklung in Belgien*, Frankfurt (Main): Lang.

Png, Cheong Ann (1996), Some Concerns about Chinese Company Law, 17 *Comp. Law.* 199.

Poe, Mark, Shimizu, Kay, and Simpson, Jeannie (2002), Revising the Japanese Commercial Code: A Summary and Evaluation of the Reform Effort, *Stanford Journal of East Asian Affairs* 71.

Popper, Karl (1994), *Logik der Forschung*, 10th edition, Tübingen: Mohr Siebeck (1st edition: 1934).

(1987), *Das Elend des Historizismus*, 6th edition, Tübingen: Mohr Siebeck (English: *The Poverty of Historicism*, 1947).

(1992), *Die offene Gesellschaft und ihre Feinde* (2 Volumes), Tübingen: Mohr Siebeck, 7th edition (English: *The Open Society and Its Enemies*, 1958).

(1973), *Objektive Erkenntnis*, Hamburg: Hoffmann und Campe (English: *Objective Knowledge*, 1972).

Pound, John (1993), The Rise of the Political Model of Corporate Governance and Corporate Control, 68 *N.Y.U. L. Rev.* 1003.

(1995), The Promise of the Governed Corporation: The Limits of Economic Solutions, 73 *Harv. Bus. Rev.* 89.

Poutianen, Annika (2001), Shareholders and Corporate Governance: The Principle of One Share–One Vote, *EBLR* 67.

Procaccia, Uriel, and Segal, Uzi (2003), Thou Shalt Not Sow Thy Vineyard with Divers Seeds? The Case Against the Harmonisation of Private Law, in: Hopt, Klaus J., and Wymeersch, Eddy (eds.), *Capital Markets and Company Law*, Oxford: Oxford University Press, p. 639.

Raaijmakers, Theo (2002), Takeover Regulation in Europe and America: The Needs for Functional Convergence, in: McCahery, Joseph A., Moerland, Piet, Raaijmakers, Theo, and Renneboog, Luc (eds.), *Corporate Governance Regimes – Convergence and Diversity*, Oxford: Oxford University Press, p. 205.

Rahn, Gunther (1994), Recht und Rechtsmentalität in Japan, in: Baum, Harald, and Drobnig, Ulrich, *Japanisches Handels- und Wirtschaftsrecht*, New York: de Gruyter, p. 1.

Raiser, Thomas (2001), *Recht der Kapitalgesellschaften*, 3rd edition, Munich: Vahlen.

Rajan, Raghuram, and Zingales, Luigi (2003), The Great Reversals: The Politics of Financial Development in the Twentieth Century, 69 *J. Finan. Econ.* 5.

Ranft, M. Florian (1999), *Handbuch Wirtschaft und Recht in Asien, Länderteil China*, Munich: Beck.

Rappaport, Alfred (1986), *Creating Shareholder Value*, New York: Free Press.

Rebérioux, Antoine (2002), European Style of Corporate Governance at the Crossroads: The Role of Worker Involvement, 40 *JCMS* 111.

Rechenberg, Wolf-Georg Frhr. von (1986), *Die Hauptversammlung als oberstes Organ der Aktiengesellschaft*, Heidelberg: Recht und Wirtschaft.

Regierungskommission Corporate Governance (2001), *Unternehmensführung – Unternehmenskontrolle – Modernisierung des Aktienrechts*.

Reicherzer, Max (2005), *Die Authentizität des Gesetzgebungsverfahrens*, Berlin: Duncker & Humblot.

Reimann, Helga (2002), *Globalisierung. Die universelle Herausforderung*, Konstanz: UVK Verlagsgesellschaft.

Reisberg, Arad (2006), Derivative Actions and the Funding Problem: The Way Forward, *JBL* 445.

Renner, Wolfgang (2002), Holzmüller-Kompetenz der Hauptversammlung beim Erwerb einer Unternehmensbeteiligung?, *NZG* 1091.

Rhodes, Rod (1997), *Understanding Governance*, Buckingham: Open University Press.

Ricardo, David (1817), *On the Principles of Political Economy and Taxation*, Prometheus Books (cited version: London: Dent, 1973).

Riegger, Bodo (2001), Hauptversammlung und Internet, 165 *ZHR* 204.

Roberts, John, and Van den Steen, Eric (2000), Shareholder Interests, Human Capital Investment and Corporate Governance, Working Paper, available at http://ssrn.com/abstract=230019.

Rock, Edward B. (1995), America's Fascination with German Corporate Governance, *AG* 291.

Rock, Edward, Kanda, Hideki, and Kraakman, Reinier (2004), Significant Corporate Actions, in: Kraakman, Reinier, Davies, Paul, Hansmann, Henry, Hertig, Gérard, Hopt, Klaus J., Kanda, Hideki, and Rock, Edward, *The Anatomy of Corporate Law*, Oxford: Oxford University Press, p. 131.

Rodatz, Peter (1995), Einige Bemerkungen zu den Besonderheiten im japanischen Gesellschaftsrecht, in: Menkhaus, Heinrich (ed.), *Das Japanische im japanischen Recht*, Munich: Iudicum, p. 247.

(2002), Rezension: Olaf Kliesow, Aktionärsrechte und Aktionärsklage in Japan, 13 *ZJapanR* 299.

Rodemann, Carsten (1998), *Stimmbindungsvereinbarungen in den Aktien- und GmbH-Rechten Deutschlands, Englands, Frankreichts und Belgiens: Eine rechtsvergleichende Untersuchung*, Cologne: Heymanns.

Rodrik, Dani (1999), Modernization and the Confucian World, in: The Colorado College (ed.), *Cultures in the 21st Century: Conflicts and Convergences*, Colorado College Studies Number 32, p. 83.

Roe, Mark J. (1991), A Political Theory of American Corporate Finance, 91 *Colum. L. Rev.* 10.

(1994), *Strong Managers, Weak Owners: The Political Roots of American Corporate Finance*, Princeton: Princeton University Press.

(1996a), Some Differences in Corporate Structure in Germany, Japan, and the United States, in: Port, Kenneth L. (ed.), *Comparative Law – Law and the Legal Process in Japan*, Durham, NC: Carolina Academic Press, p. 320 (also published in: (1993) 102 *Yale L. J.* 1927).

(1996b), German 'Populism' and the Large Public Corporation, in: Buxbaum, Richard M., Hertig, Gerard, Hirsch, Alain, and Hopt, Klaus J. (eds.), *European Economic and Business Law*, Berlin: de Gruyter, p. 241.

(1997), Path Dependence, Political Options, and Governance Systems, in: Hopt, Klaus J., and Wymeersch, Eddy (eds.), *Comparative Corporate Governance – Essays and Materials*, Berlin: de Gruyter, p. 165.

(1998), Backlash, 98 *Colum. L. Rev.* 217.

(2000), Political Preconditions to Separating Ownership from Corporate Control, 53 *Stan. L. Rev.* 539 (shorter version also published in: McCahery, Joseph A., Moerland, Piet, Raaijmakers, Theo, and Renneboog, Luc (eds.), *Corporate Governance Regimes – Convergence and Diversity*, Oxford: Oxford University Press, 2002, p. 113).

(2002), Corporate Law's Limits, 31 *J. Legal Stud.* 233 (also published as: What Corporate Law Cannot Do, in: Milhaupt, Curtis J. (ed.), *Global Markets, Domestic Institutions*, New York: Columbia University Press, 2003, p. 107).

(2003a), *Political Determinants of Corporate Governance*, Oxford: Oxford University Press.

(2003b), Delaware's Competition, 117 *Harv. L. Rev.* 588.

Romano, Roberta (1993), *The Genius of American Corporate Law*, Washington: AEI Press.

(2002), Less Is More: Making Institutional Investor Activism a Valuable Mechanism of Corporate Governance, in: McCahery, Joseph A., Moerland, Piet, Raaijmakers, Theo, and Renneboog, Luc (eds.), *Corporate Governance Regimes – Convergence and Diversity*, Oxford: Oxford University Press, p. 507 (also published in: (2001) 18 *Yale J. on Reg.* 174).

(2005), The Sarbanes–Oxley Act and the Making of Quack Corporate Governance, 114 *Yale L. J.* 1521.

Rose, Paul (2001), EU Company Law Convergence Possibilities after Centros, 11 *Transnat'l L. & Contemp. Probs.* 121.

Rossi, Guido (2003), Do Good Governance Recommendations Change the Rules for the Board of Directors? in: Hopt, Klaus J., and Wymeersch, Eddy (eds.), *Capital Markets and Company Law*, Oxford: Oxford University Press, p. 493.

Roth, Günther H. (1972), *Das Treuhandmodell des Investmentrechts*, Frankfurt (Main): Athenäum.

(1999), Gründungstheorie: Ist der Damm gebrochen?, *ZIP* 861.

(2003), Die (Ohn-)Macht der Hauptversammlung, *ZIP* 369.

Ruffner, Markus (2000), *Die ökonomischen Grundlagen eines Rechts der Publikumsgesellschaft*, Zürich: Schulthess.

Rugman, Alan M. (2001), *The End of Globalization: Why Global Strategy Is a Myth and How to Profit from the Realities of Regional Markets*, New York: Amacon.

Ryn, Jean van (1990), Capital and Securities of Marketable Share Companies, in: Conard, Alfred (ed.), *International Encyclopedia of Comparative Law*, Tübingen: Mohr Siebeck, Ch. 5 II.

Sagafi-nejad, Tagi (2005), Should Global Rules Have Legal Teeth? Policing (WHO Framework Convention on Tobacco Control) vs. Good Citizenship (UN Global Compact), 10 *Int. J. Bus.* 363.

Saito, Maki (2004), Zur anstehenden Novellierung des japanischen Gesellschaftsrechts, 18 *ZJapanR* 210.

Salacuse, Jeswald W. (2003), Corporations American Style or with a European Touch? Corporate Governance, Culture and Convergence, *EBLR* 471.

Salwin, Lester N. (1962), The New Commercial Code of Japan: Symbol of Gradual Progress Toward Democratic Goals, 50 *Geo. L. J.* 478.

Schaede, Ulrike (1997), The 'Old Boy' Network and Government–Business Relationships in Japan, in: Baum, Harald (ed.), *Japan: Economic Success and Legal System*, Berlin: de Gruyter, p. 345.

Schaefer, Franz, and Eichner, Christian (2003), Abwehrmöglichkeiten des Vorstands von börsennotierten Aktiengesellschaften bei feindlichen Übernahmeversuchen – ein Rechtsvergleich zwischen Deutschland und den USA, *NZG* 150.

Schäfer, Hans-Bernd, and Ott, Claus (2000), *Lehrbuch der ökonomischen Analyse des Zivilrechts*, 3rd edition, Berlin: Springer (English version: *Economic Analysis of Civil Law*, Northampton, MA: Edward Elgar, 2004).

Schemann, Andreas (1998), Konvergenztheorem oder Kulturkreisparadigma?, 29 *Rechtstheorie* 565.

Schenck, Paul-Christian (1997), *Der deutsche Anteil an der Gestaltung des modernen japanischen Rechts- und Verfassungswesens: Deutsche Rechtsberater im Japan der Meiji-Zeit*, Stuttgart: Steiner.

Schick, Rainer (2002), Neue Perspektiven für Banken in China nach dem WTO-Beitritt, *Die Bank* 295.

Schimmann, Peter, and Janssen, Markus (2004), Verabschiedete Gesetze: Bericht über die Gesetzgebungstätigkeit des japanischen Parlaments von der 156. bis zur 159. Sitzungsperiode, 17 *ZJapanR* 195.

Schindler, Darius Oliver, and Witzel, David (2001), Bedarf es einer neuen gesetzlichen Regelung des Anfechtungsrechts zur Bekämpfung räuberischer Aktionäre?, *NZG* 577.

Schindler, Hendrik (1999), *Das Austrittsrecht in Kapitalgesellschaften*, Munich: Beck.

Schipani, Cindy A., and Liu, Junhai (2002), Corporate Governance in China: Then and Now, *Colum. Bus. L. Rev.* 1.

Schlitt, Michael (2003), Die neuen Marktsegmente der Frankfurter Wertpapierbörse, *AG* 57.

Schmidt, Dominique (1998), Gestaltungsfreiheit im französischen Gesellschaftsrecht, in: Lutter, Marcus, and Wiedemann, Herbert, *Gestaltungsfreiheit und Gesellschaftsrecht*, Berlin: de Gruyter, p. 291.

Schmidt, Karsten (2002), *Gesellschaftsrecht*, 4th edition, Cologne: Heymanns.

Schmidt, Reinhard H., and Spindler, Gerald (2004), Path Dependence and Complementary in Corporate Governance, in: Gordon, Jeffrey N., and Roe, Mark J. (eds.), *Convergence and Persistence in Corporate Governance*, Cambridge: Cambridge University Press, p. 114.

Schmitz, Franz W. (2002), *Die Umstellung von Inhaber- auf Namensaktien durch deutsche Aktiengesellschaften*, Berlin: Tenea.

Schneider, Uwe H. (1990), Auf dem Weg in den Pensionskassenkorporatismus?, *AG* 317.

(2000), Kapitalmarktorientierte Corporate Governance-Grundsätze, *DB* 2413.

Schnyder, Anton K. (2000), Internationales Wirtschaftsrecht – zu Begriff und Phänomenologie, in: Baums, Theodor, Hopt, Klaus J., and Horn, Norbert (eds.), *Corporations, Capital Markets and Business in the Law (Liber Amicorum Buxbaum)*, London: Kluwer, p. 515.

Scholler, Heinrich (2000), Die Bedeutung der Lehre vom Rechtskreis und der Rechtskultur, 99 *ZVglRWiss* 373.

Schruff, Wienand (1996), Accounting Standards in Practice, in: Buxbaum, Richard M., Hertig, Gerard, Hirsch, Alain, and Hopt, Klaus J. (eds.), *European Economic and Business Law*, Berlin: de Gruyter, p. 163.

Schulte-Kulkmann, Nicole (2003), Rechtszusammenarbeit im Kontext der europäisch-chinesischen Beziehungen, Working Paper China Analysis No. 24, available at www.chinapolitik.de/studien/index.htm.

Schulze-Osterloh, Joachim (2001), Das deutsche Gesellschaftsrecht im Banne der Globalisierung, *ZIP* 1433.

(2003), Internationale Rechnungslegung für den Einzelabschluss und für Unternehmen, die den öffentlichen Kapitalmarkt nicht in Anspruch nehmen, *ZIP* 93.

Schumpeter, Joseph Alois A. (1934), *The Theory of Economic Development: An Inquiry into Profits, Capital, Credit Interest and Business Cycle*, Cambridge, MA: Harvard University.

(1987), *Kapitalismus, Sozialismus und Demokratie*, 6th edition, Tübingen: Mohr Siebeck.

Seibert, Ulrich (1999), OECD Principles of Corporate Governance – Grundsätze der Unternehmensführung und -kontrolle für die Welt, *AG* 337.

Seidel, Wolfgang (2004), Der Deutsche Corporate Governance-Kodex – eine private oder doch eine staatliche Regelung?, *ZIP* 285.

Seita, Alex Y. (1997), Globalization and the Convergence of Values, 30 *Cornell Int'l L.J.* 429.

Senger, Harro von (1994), *Einführung in das chinesisches Recht*, Munich: Beck.

Senghaas, Dieter (1998), *Zivilisierung wider Willen. Der Konflikt der Kulturen mit sich selbst*, Frankfurt (Main): Suhrkamp (English version: *The Clash within Civilisations: Coming to Terms with Cultural Conflicts*, London: Routledge, 2001).

Sharma, Rajesh (1999), Company Law, in: Guiguo, Wang, and Mo, John (eds.), *Chinese Law*, The Hague: Kluwer Law International, p. 369.

Sherman, Howard (2004), Corporate Governance Ratings, 12 *Corporate Governance* 5.

Shishido, Zenichi (1997), Legal Monitoring Systems in Japan: Legal Possibilities and Current Practice, in: Macmillan (Patfield), Fiona (ed.), *Perspectives on Company Law*, Volume 2, London: Kluwer Law International, p. 149.

(2000), Japanese Corporate Governance: The Hidden Problems of Corporate Law and Their Solutions, 25 *Del. J. Corp. L.* 189.

Shleifer, Andrei, and Vishny, Robert W. (1997), A Survey of Corporate Governance, 52 *J. Fin.* 737.

Shumo, Cai, and Yingxia, Deng (2001), Corporate Governance in China – Obstacles and New Development, 29 *IBL* 455.

Siebel, Ulf R. (1997), Vorzugsaktien als 'Hybride' Finanzierungsform und ihre Grenzen, 161 *ZHR* 628.

Siegel, Mary (1995), Back to the Future: Appraisal Rights in the Twenty-First Century, 32 *Harv. J. on Legis.* 79.

Siems, Mathias M. (2000), Der Regierungsentwurf für ein Gesetz zur Namensaktie und zur Erleichterung der Stimmrechtsausübung (NaStraG), *NZG* 626.

(2002a), Der Neoliberalismus als Modell für die Gesetzgebung?, *ZRP* 170.

(2002b), Neue Medien im UK Company Law, *RIW* 202.

(2002c), Convergence, Competition, Centros and Conflicts of Law: European Company Law in the 21st Century, 27 *E.L. Rev.* 47.

(2002d), Shareholders, Stakeholders and the 'Ordoliberalism', 13 *EBLR* 139.

(2003), Der anonyme Aktionär – The anonymous shareholder – L'actionnaire anonyme, *ZGR* 218.

(2004a), Die Harmonisierung des Internationalen Deliktsrechts und die Einheit der Rechtsordnung, *RIW* 662.

(2004b), Die Idee des Neoliberalen im deutschen Recht, 35 *Rechtstheorie* 1.

(2004c), The European Directive on Cross-Border Mergers: An International Model?, 11 *Colum. J. Eur. L.* 167.

(2005a), The Impact of the European Company (SE) on Legal Culture, 30 *E.L. Rev.* 431.

(2005b), What Does Not Work in Comparing Securities Laws: A Critique on La Porta et al.'s Methodology, *ICCLR* 300.

(2005c), Anspruchsziele bei betrügerischen Täuschungen des Kapitalmarktes, *ZfRV* 184.

(2005d), Welche Auswirkung hat das neue Verfolgungsrecht der Aktionärsminderheit? – Eine rechtsvergleichende Folgenanalyse des § 148 AktG-E, 104 *ZVglRWiss* 376.

(2005e), Numerical Comparative Law – Do We Need Statistical Evidence in Order to Reduce Complexity?, 13 *Cardozo J. Int'l & Comp. L.* 521.

(2005f), The Case Against Harmonisation of Shareholder Rights, 6 *EBOR* 539.

(2006), Legal Adaptability in Elbonia, 2 *International Journal of Law in Context* 393.

(2007a), Legal Origins: Reconciling Law and Finance and Comparative Law, 52 *McGill Law Journal* 55.

(2007b), SEVIC: Beyond Cross-Border Mergers, *EBOR* 307.

Siems, Mathias M., and Gelter, Martin (2005), Judicial Federalism in the ECJ's Berlusconi Case: Towards More Credible Corporate Governance and Financial Reporting?, 46 *Harv. Int'l L.J.* 487.

Siepelt, Stefan (1992), *Das Rederecht des Aktionärs in der Hauptversammlung*, Frankfurt (Main): Lang.

Simmonds, Ralph (2001), Why Must We Meet? Thinking about Why Shareholders Meetings Are Required, 19 *C&SLJ* 506.

Smith, Adam (1776), *An Inquiry into the Nature and Causes of the Wealth of Nations* (cited version: Oxford: Clarendon Press, 1976).

Smith, Douglas Gordon (1996), A Comparative Analysis of the Proxy Machinery in Germany, Japan and the United States: Implications for the Political Theory of American Corporate Finance, 58 *U. Pitt. L. Rev.* 145.

(1998), The Shareholder Primacy Norm, 23 *J. Corp. L.* 277.

Snyder, Francis (1999), Governing Economic Globalisation: Global Legal Pluralism and European Law, 5 *ELJ* 331.

Sonnenberger, Hans Jürgen (1991), *Französisches Handels- und Wirtschaftsrecht*, 2nd edition, Heidelberg: Recht und Wirtschaft.

Sonnenberger, Hans Jürgen, and Autexier, Christian (2000), *Einführung in das französische Recht*, 3rd edition, Heidelberg: Recht und Wirtschaft.

Sono, Hiroo (2001), The Multiple Worlds of 'Nihon-hô', 12 *ZJapanR* 50.

Soros, George (1998), *The Crisis of Global Capitalism*, New York: Public Affairs.

Spamann, Holger (2006), On the Insignificance and/or Endogeneity of La Porta et al.'s 'Anti-Director Rights Index' under Consistent Coding, Working Paper, available at http://ssrn.com/abstract=894301.

Spindler, Gerald (1998), Deregulierung des Aktienrechts, *AG* 53.

(2000), Internet und Corporate Governance – ein neuer virtueller (T)Raum?, *ZGR* 420.

(2006), Stimmrecht und Teilnahme an der Hauptversammlung, in: Gesellschaftsrechtliche Vereinigung (ed.), *Gesellschaftsrecht in der Diskussion 2005*, Cologne: Dr Otto Schmidt, p. 31.

Stapledon, Geoff P., and Bates, Jonathan J. (2002), Reducing the Costs of Proxy Voting, in: McCahery, Joseph A., Moerland, Piet, Raaijmakers, Theo, and Renneboog, Luc (eds.), *Corporate Governance Regimes – Convergence and Diversity*, Oxford: Oxford University Press, p. 567.

Stedman, Graham, and Jones, Janet (1998), *Shareholders' Agreements*, 3rd edition, London: Sweet & Maxwell.

Steinberg, Marc I. (2003), Insider Regulation – A Comparative Analysis, 37 *Int. L.* 153.

Stephan, Paul B. (1999), The Futility of Unification and Harmonization in International Commercial Law, 39 *Va. J. Int'l L.* 743.

Stigler, George J. (1971), The Theory of Economic Regulation, 2 *Bell. J. Econ.* 3.

Stiglitz, Joseph E. (2006), *Making Globalization Work*, London: Penguin.

Stober, Rolf (1999), Globalisierung der Wirtschaft und Rechtsprinzipien des Weltwirtschaftssystems, *Festschrift Großfeld* 1173.

Storp, Roger (2002), Reform des französischen Unternehmensrecht im Rahmen des Gesetzes über 'Neue Wirtschaftliche Regulierungen' vom 15.05.2001, *RIW* 409.

Stout, Lynn A. (2003), On the Export of US-Style Corporate Fiduciary Duties to Other Cultures: Can a Transplant Take?, in: Milhaupt, Curtis J. (ed.), *Global Markets, Domestic Institutions*, New York: Columbia University Press, p. 46.

Strätling, Rebecca (2003), General Meetings: A Dispensable Tool for Corporate Governance of Listed Companies?, 11 *Corporate Governance* 74.

Streit, Manfred E. (1999), *Systemwettbewerb als Herausforderung an Politik und Theorie*, Baden-Baden: Nomos.

Strine, Leo E. (2006), Towards a True Corporate Republic: A Traditionalist Response to Lucian's Solution for Improving Corporate America, 119 *Harr. L. Rev.* 1759.

Subramanian, Guhan (2004), The Disappearing Delaware Effect, 20 *J. L. Econ. & Org.* 32.

Sunstein, Cass R. (1985), Interest Groups in American Public Law, 38 *Stan. L. Rev.* 29.

Takahashi, Eiji (1997), Changes in the Japanese Enterprise Groups?, in: Baum, Harald (ed.), *Japan: Economic Success and Legal System*, Berlin: de Gruyter, p. 227.

(2003), Corporate Governance und die Reform des Gesellschaftsrechts in Deutschland und Europa, 16 *ZJapanR* 121.

Takahashi, Eiji, and Kirchwehm, Oliver (2003), Liberalisierung des Erwerbs eigener Aktien in Japan, *RIW* 757.

Takahashi, Eiji, and Rudo, Joachim (1998), Bestandsaufnahme: Die japanische Aktienrechtsreform des Jahres 1997, *RIW* 615.

(2000), Missbrauch von Aktionärsrechten in Japan und Deutschland, in Müller-Freienfels, Wolfram, and Stoll, Hans (eds.), *Recht in Japan*, Volume 12, Baden-Baden: Nomos, p. 71.

Takahashi, Eiji, and Sakamoto, Tatsuya (2004), Japanese Corporate Law: Important Cases in 2002 and 2003, 17 *ZJapanR* 241.

(2005), Japanese Corporate Law: Important Cases in 2003 and 2004, 20 *ZJapanR* 241.

(2006), Japanese Corporate Law: Two Important Cases Concerning Takeovers in 2005, 21 *ZJapanR* 231.

Takahashi, Eiji, and Shimizu, Madoka (2005), The Future of Japanese Corporate Governance: The 2005 Reform, 19 *ZJapanR* 35.

Tan, Lay Hong (2000), Corporate Governance Issues in PRC Companies, 21 *Comp. Law.* 87.

Tanabe, Mitsumasa (2000), Changing Climate in Japanese Business Circles, 21 *Comp. Law.* 66.

Taniguchi, Yoichiro (1988), Japan's Company Law and the Promotion of Corporate Democracy: A Futile Attempt?, 27 *Colum. J. Transnat'l L.* 195.

Tatsuta, Misao (2004), Fundamental Issues of Corporate Governance in Japan, 17 *ZJapanR* 5.

Teichmann, Christoph (2001), Corporate Governance in Europa, *ZGR* 645.

Teubner, Gunther (1978), *Organisationsdemokratie und Verbandsverfassung*, Tübingen: Mohr.

Thompson, Robert B. (1999), Accounting in a Global Market and in an Electronic Age, *Festschrift Großfeld* 1243.

Thümmel, Martin (1995), Einführung, in: Steinemann, Matthias, Thümmel, Martin, and Zhang, Xuan, *Kapitalgesellschaften in China*, Hamburg: Institut für Asienkunde, p. 5.

Tiebout, Charles M. (1956), A Pure Theory of Local Expenditures, 64 *J. Polit. Economy* 416.

Tomasic, Roman, and Fu, Jian (1999), Company Law in China, in: Tomasic, Roman (ed.), *Company Law in East Asia*, Aldershot: Ashgate, p. 135.

Tonner, Martin (2002), *Tracking Stocks*, Cologne: Heymanns.

Trachtman, Joel P. (1993), International Regulatory Competition, Externalization, and Jurisdiction, 34 *Harv. Int'l L.J.* 48.

Trendelenburg, Hortense (2002), Cross-Border Mergers: Problems and Solutions, 30 *IBL* 69.

Tuerks, Robin A. (2000), *Depotstimmrechtspraxis versus US-proxy-system*, Munich: Beck.

Tunc, André (1991), Corporate Law, in: Buxbaum, Richard M. (ed.), *European Business Law: Legal and Economic Analyses on Integration and Harmonization*, Berlin: de Gruyter, p. 199.

Ueda, Junko (2000), Japan's Current Move Towards Statutory Reform: Is It a Breakthrough to a New Era?, in: Macmillan, Fiona (ed.), *International Corporate Law*, Volume 1, Oxford: Hart, p. 179.

(2005) A Comparative View of the Two Corporate Statutory Reforms: The UK and Japan, *ICCLR* 421.

Ulmer, Michael J. (1998), *Harmonisierungsschranken des Aktienrechts*, Heidelberg: Winter.

Ulmer, Peter (1999a), Die Aktionärsklage als Instrument zur Kontrolle des Vorstands- und Aufsichtsratshandelns, 163 *ZHR* 290.

(1999b), Schutzinstrumente gegen die Gefahren aus der Geschäftstätigkeit inländischer Zweigniederlassungen von Kapitalgesellschaften mit fiktivem Auslandssitz, *JZ* 662.

(2002), Aktienrecht im Wandel, 202 *AcP* 143.

Utsumi, Kenji (2001), The Business Judgment Rule and Shareholder Derivative Suits in Japan: A Comparison with Those in the United States, 14 *N.Y. Int'l L. Rev.* 129.

Vagts, Detlev F. (1972), Law and Accounting in Business Associations, in: Conard, Alfred (ed.), *International Encyclopedia of Comparative Law*, Tübingen: Mohr Siebeck, Ch. 12A.

(1998), Gestaltungsfreiheit im amerikanischen Aktienrecht, in: Lutter, Marcus, and Wiedemann, Herbert, *Gestaltungsfreiheit und Gesellschaftsrecht*, Berlin: de Gruyter, p. 283.

(2000), Securities Regulation – An Introduction, in: Conard, Alfred (ed.), *International Encyclopedia of Comparative Law*, Tübingen: Mohr Siebeck, Ch. 10.

(2002), Comparative Company Law – The New Wave, *Festschrift Druey* 596.

Van den Bergh, Roger (2000), Towards an Institutional Legal Framework for Regulatory Competition in Europe, 53 *Kyklos* 435.

Van den Berghe, Lutgart (2002), *Corporate Governance in a Globalising World: Convergence or Divergence? A European Perspective*, Boston: Kluwer Academic Publishers.

Van der Elst, Christoph (2003), The Equity Markets, Ownership Structures and Control: Towards an International Harmonisation?, in: Hopt, Klaus J., and Wymeersch, Eddy (eds.), *Capital Markets and Company Law*, Oxford: Oxford University Press, p. 3.

Van Hoecke, Mark, and Warrington, Mark (1998), Legal Cultures and Legal Paradigms: Towards a New Model for Comparative Law, 47 *ICLQ* 495.

Vogel, David (1995), *Trading Up: Consumer and Environmental Regulation in a Global Economy*, Cambridge, MA: Harvard University Press.

Vogenauer, Stefan (2001), *Die Auslegung von Gesetzen in England und auf dem Kontinent*, Tübingen: Mohr Siebeck.

Walker, Jordon (2001), Corporate Governance in East Asia: Evidence and Justifications, 19 *C&SLJ* 437.

Wallace, Perry E. (2002), The Globalization of Corporate Governance: Shareholder Protection, Hostile Takeovers and the Evolving Corporate Environment in France, 18 *Conn. J. Int'l L.* 1.

Wang, Jiang-yu (2000), China's Securities Experiment: The Challenge of Globalisation, available at www.geocities.com/pennwang/research/ressec/ressecindex.htm.

Watson, Alan (1974), *Legal Transplants*, Edinburgh: Scottish Academic Press (2nd edition, 1993).

Wedderburn of Charlton, Lord (1985), The Legal Development of Corporate Responsibility: For Whom Will Corporate Managers Be Trustees? in: Hopt, Klaus J., and Teubner, Gunther, *Corporate Governance and Directors' Liabilities*, Berlin: de Gruyter, p. 3.

Wei, Yuwa (1998), A Chinese Perspective on Corporate Governance, 10 *Bond L. Rev*. 363.

(2002), Corporatization and Privatization: A Chinese Perspective, 22 *Nw. J. Int'l L. & Bus*. 219.

(2003), *Comparative Corporate Governance: A Chinese Perspective*, The Hague: Kluwer Law International.

Weisbrot, Mark (1998), Globalization for Whom?, 31 *Cornell Int'l L.J.* 631.

Weller, Michael, and Zahn, Andreas (2000), Die Namensaktie in anderen Europäischen Ländern, in: Rosen, Rüdiger von, and Seifert, Werner G. (eds.), *Die Namensaktie*, Eschborn: DAI, p. 177.

Werder, Axel von, Talaulicar, Till, and Kolat, Georg L. (2005), Compliance with the German Corporate Governance Code: An Empirical Analysis of the Compliance Statement by German Listed Companies, 13 *Corporate Governance* 178.

Werlauff, Erik (1993), *EC Company Law*, Copenhagen: Jurist- og økonomforbundets.

(2003a), The SE Company – A New Common European Company from 8 October 2003, *EBLR* 85.

(2003b), *The Law of the European Company*, Copenhagen: DJOF.

West, Mark D. (1999), Information, Institutions, and Extortion in Japan and the United States: Making Sense of Sokaiya Racketeers, 93 *Nw. U. L. Rev*. 767.

(2001a), The Puzzling Divergence of Corporate Law: Evidence and Explanations from Japan and the United States, 149 *U. Pa. L. Rev*. 528.

(2001b), Why Shareholders Sue: The Evidence from Japan, 30 *J. Legal Stud*. 351.

Wheeler, Sally (2002), *Corporations and the Third Way*. Oxford: Hart.

Whincop, Michael J. (2001), The Role of the Shareholder in Corporate Governance: A Theoretical Approach, 25 *Melbourne U. L. Rev*. 418.

Whitley, Richard (1999), *Divergent Capitalisms*, Oxford: Oxford University Press.

Whittington, Richard, and Mayer, Michael (2000), *The European Corporation*, Oxford: Oxford University Press.

Wiebe, Andreas (2002), Vorstandsmacht statt Bankenmacht?, 166 *ZHR* 182.

Wiedemann, Herbert (1980), *Gesellschaftsrecht*, Munich: Beck.

(1989), *Organverantwortung und Gesellschafterklagen in der Aktiengesellschaft*, Opladen: Westdeutscher Verlag.

Wiegand, Wolfgang (2000), Die Amerikanisierung des Rechts, insbesondere des Bank- und Wirtschaftsrechts, in: Baums, Theodor, Hopt, Klaus J., and Horn, Norbert (eds.), *Corporations, Capital Markets and Business in the Law (Liber Amicorum Buxbaum)*, London: Kluwer, p. 601.

Wiener, Jarrod (1999), *Globalization and the Harmonization of Law*, London: Pinter.

Wiethölter, Rudolf (1961), *Interessen und Organisation der Aktiengesellschaft im amerikanischen und deutschen Recht*, Karlsruhe: Müller.

Wilhelm, Jan (1998), *Kapitalgesellschaftsrecht*, Berlin: de Gruyter.

Williams, Cynthia (2002), Corporate Social Responsibility in an Era of Economic Globalization, 35 *U.C. Davis L. Rev*. 705.

Williams, Cynthia, and Conley, John M. (2005), An Emerging Third Way? The Erosion of the Anglo-American Shareholder Value Construct, 38 *Cornell Int'l L.J.* 493

Windbichler, Christine (2000), Alternative Dispute Resolution v. Shareholders' Suits?, in: Baums, Theodor, Hopt, Klaus J., and Horn, Norbert (eds.), *Corporations, Capital Markets and Business in the Law (Liber Amicorum Buxbaum)*, London: Kluwer, p. 617.

Winter, Jaap (2003), Cross-Border Voting in Europe, in: Hopt, Klaus J., and Wymeersch, Eddy (eds.), *Capital Markets and Company Law*, Oxford: Oxford University Press, p. 387.

Winter, Ralph K. (1980), State Law, Shareholder Protection, and Theory of the Corporation, in: Posner, Richard A., and Scott, Kenneth E., *Economics of Corporation Law and Securities Regulation*, Boston and Toronto: Little, Brown and Company, p. 91.

Wirth, Gerhard, and Arnold, Michael (2002), Anfechtungsklagen gegen Squeeze-out-Hauptversammlungsbeschlüsse wegen angeblicher Verfassungswidrigkeit, *AG* 503.

Wohlwend, Corrado (2001), *Die Hauptversammlung im Wandel der Kommunikationsformen*, Frankfurt (Main): Lang.

Wolf, Martin (2002), Corporate Governance. Der Import angelsächsicher 'Self-Regulation' im Widerstreit zum deutschen Parlamentsvorbehalt, *ZRP* 59.

(2004), *Why Globalization Works*, New Haven: Yale University Press.

Wollschläger, Christian (1997), Historical Trends in Civil Litigation in Japan, Arizona, Sweden, and Germany: Japanese Legal Culture in the Light of Judicial Statistics, in: Baum, Harald (ed.), *Japan: Economic Success and Legal System*, Berlin: de Gruyter, p. 89.

Wong, Huen, and Cox, Owen (2002), Foreign Law Firms Set to Expand in China, *China Law & Practice*, March 2002, 54.

Worthington, Sarah (2000), Corporate Governance: Remedying and Ratifying Directors' Breaches, 116 *LQR* 638.

(2001a), Reforming Directors' Duties, 64 *MLR* 439.

(2001b), Shares and Shareholders: Property, Power and Entitlement, 22 *Comp. Law*. 258 and 307.

Wunderlich, Michael, and Labermeier, Alexander (2000), Rechtliche Behandlung, Übertragung und Börsenhandel von Namensaktien in den USA, in: Rosen, Rüdiger von, and Seifert, Werner G. (eds.), *Die Namensaktie*, Eschborn: DAI, p. 143.

Wymeersch, Eddy (1995), Unternehmensführung in Westeuropa, *AG* 299.

(2000), Centros: A Landmark Decision in European Company Law, in: Baums, Theodor, Hopt, Klaus J., and Horn, Norbert (eds.), *Corporations, Capital*

Markets and Business in the Law (Liber Amicorum Buxbaum), London: Kluwer, p. 629.

(2001a), Company Law in Europe and European Company Law, in: *1st European Jurists Forum*, Baden-Baden: Nomos, p. 85.

(2001b), Gesellschaftsrecht im Wandel: Ursachen und Entwicklungslinien, *ZGR* 294.

(2001c), Current Company Law Reform Initiatives in the OECD Countries: Challenges and Opportunities, available at www.law.rug.ac.be/fli/WP/WPindex.html.

(2002), Convergence or Divergence in Corporate Governance Patterns in Western Europe?, in: McCahery, Joseph A., Moerland, Piet, Raaijmakers, Theo, and Renneboog, Luc (eds.), *Corporate Governance Regimes – Convergence and Diversity*, Oxford: Oxford University Press, p. 230.

(2003), The Transfer of the Company's Seat in European Company Law, 40 *Common Market Law Review* 661.

(2005), Implementation of Corporate Governance Codes, in: Hopt, Klaus J., Wymeersch, Eddy, Kanda, Hideki, and Baum, Harald (eds.), *Corporate Governance in Context*, Oxford: Oxford University Press, 403.

(2006), Enforcement of Corporate Governance Codes, 6 *JCLS* 113.

Xanthaki, Helen (2001), Centros: Is This Really the End for the Theory of the Siege Reel, 22 *Comp. Law*. 2.

Xi, Chao (2006), Institutional Shareholder Activism in China: Law and Practice, 17 *ICCLR* 251 and 287.

Xuereb, Peter G. (1989), *The Rights of Shareholders*, Oxford: BSP Professional Books.

Yanaga, Masao (2001), New Regulations for E-Commerce in Japan, 12 *ZJapanR* 145.

(2003), Neue Entwicklungen im Japanischen Bilanzrecht: Die Reform des Jahres 2003, 15 *ZJapanR* 111.

Yavasi, Mahmut (2001), Shareholding and Board Structures of German und UK Companies, 22 *Comp. Law*. 47.

Yuan, Anyuan (2001), China's Entry into the WTO: Impact on China's Regulating Regime of Foreign Direct Investment, 35 *Int. L.* 195.

Zehou, Li (1999), Modernization and the Confucian World, in: The Colorado College (ed.), *Cultures in the 21st Century: Conflicts and Convergences*, Colorado College Studies Number 32, p. 37.

Zetzsche, Dirk (2004), Explicit and Implicit System of Corporate Control – A Convergence Theory of Shareholder Rights, Working Paper, available at http://ssrn.com/abstract = 600722.

Zhang, Jim Jinpeng, and Lowe, Jung Y. (2001), Foreign Investment Companies Limited by shares: The Latest Chinese Organization for Major International Ventures, 21 *Nw. J. Int'l L. & Bus*. 409.

Zimmer, Daniel (1996), *Internationales Gesellschaftsrecht*, Heidelberg: Recht und Wirtschaft.

Zinser, Alexander (2002), Der Beitritt der Volksrepublik China zur WTO: rechtliche Rahmenbedingungen und Auswirkungen, *EuZW* 208.

Zöllner, Wolfgang (1963), *Die Schranken mitgliedschaftlicher Stimmrechtsmacht bei den privatrechtlichen Personenverbänden*, Munich: Beck.

(1994), Aktienrechtsreform in Permanenz, *AG* 336.

(2000), Zur Problematik der aktienrechtlichen Anfechtungsklage, *AG* 145.

Zuleeg, Manfred (2000), Federalization Through Law – An Evergreen, in: Baums, Theodor, Hopt, Klaus J., and Horn, Norbert (eds.), *Corporations, Capital Markets and Business in the Law (Liber Amicorum Buxbaum)*, London: Kluwer, p. 669.

Zumbansen, Peer (2006a), Spaces and Places: A Systems Theory Approach to Regulatory Competition in European Company Law, 12 *European Law Journal* 534.

(2006b), The Parallel Worlds of Corporate Governance and Labor Law, 13 *Indiana Journal of Global Legal Studies* 261.

Zweigert, Konrad (1949–50), Rechtsvergleichung als universale Interpretationsmethode, 15 *RabelsZ* 5.

Zweigert, Konrad, and Kötz, Hein (1998), *Introduction to Comparative Law*, 3rd edition, Oxford: Clarendon.

INDEX

For EU product safety concerns, contact us at Calle de José Abascal, 56–1°, 28003 Madrid, Spain or eugpsr@cambridge.org.

www.ingramcontent.com/pod-product-compliance
Lightning Source LLC
LaVergne TN
LVHW050300210926
848481LV00014BA/89